Preservation and Conservation: Principles and Practices

Preservation and Conservation: Principles and Practices

Proceedings of the
North American International Regional Conference

Conducted under the auspices of the
International Centre for Conservation, Rome, Italy
and the
International Centre Committee of the
Advisory Council on Historic Preservation

The Preservation Press

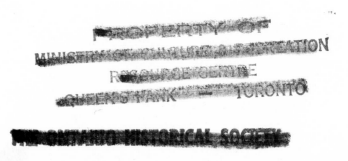

The Preservation Press
National Trust for Historic Preservation
1785 Massachusetts Avenue, N.W.
Washington, D.C. 20036

Conference sponsored by:
International Centre for Conservation, Rome, Italy
International Centre Committee of the Advisory Council on Historic Preservation

Williamsburg, Va., and Philadelphia, Pa.
September 10-16, 1972

The conference, administered by the National Trust for Historic Preservation,
was made possible by grants from Colonial Williamsburg Foundation; International Centre for Conservation; National Endowment for the Humanities;
National Park Service, U.S. Department of the Interior; National Trust for
Historic Preservation; and Pennsylvania Historical and Museum Commission.

Designed by Hubert W. Leckie. Printed in the United States of America.

Library of Congress Cataloging in Publication Data

North American International Regional Conference (1972:
   Williamsburg, Va., and Philadelphia, Pa.)
   Preservation and conservation.

   1. Historic sites—Conservation and restoration—Congresses. 2. Monuments—
Preservation—Congresses. 3. Architecture—Conservation and restoration—
Congresses. I. International Centre for the Study of the Preservation and the
Restoration of Cultural Property. II. United States. Advisory Council on
Historic Preservation. International Centre Committee. III. Title.
CC135.N67 1972   363.6'9   82-399
ISBN 0-89133-029-1   AACR2

Cover: Detail of a door from Engine Company No. 5, the former Bank of
Columbia (1796), Washington, D.C. (Photo: John J. G. Blumenson)

Foreword

For five days in September 1972, 140 of the leading professional practitioners in the conservation and preservation fields met for the first time as a group in Williamsburg, Va., and Philadelphia, Pa. Their goal was to learn more about one another's practices and problems and to explore areas where one group might be able to assist the other. The contents of this volume are an account of those proceedings.

Sponsors of the conference were the International Centre for the Study of the Preservation and the Restoration of Cultural Property, Rome, Italy, and the Rome Centre Committee of the Advisory Council on Historic Preservation.* The conference proposal was developed in early 1971 at meetings of the Rome Centre Committee. The committee's concept and plans were initially approved by the Advisory Council on Historic Preservation, and at the Sixth General Assembly of the Rome Centre, held in April 1971, attending nations approved the centre's budget for 1971–72, which committed the centre to an expenditure of $30,000 "for the organization of three meetings, to be held in . . . Mexico, New Delhi, and the United States, respectively, in order to examine the problems particular to each region thus benefitting from the experience of international experts." The authority for the conference derives from Article I, section b, of the Rome Centre

---

* Since this conference, the centre has expressed the desire to be known as the International Centre for Conservation rather than the Rome Centre. The committee has changed its name to the International Centre Committee of the Advisory Council on Historic Preservation.

statutes, which permit the convening of international meetings for coordinating, stimulating or instituting research in the preservation and restoration of cultural property.

In proposing the conference, the Rome Centre Committee agreed that one of the greatest immediate needs in the United States was the establishment of closer relations between architect–restorers (those concerned with the restoration and rehabilitation of historic structures) and conservators (those concerned with the preservation of materials and objects) and that a formal exchange of information between the two general disciplines would be profitable.

The definition of the need for closer relations rested upon several basic presuppositions:

1. that many architects are called upon to perform restoration work, although few possess competency in this specialty;

2. that in order to be a competent restorationist, the practitioner should have special knowledge beyond that normally required of an architect, specifically, an intimate knowledge of the history of architecture and a knowledge of the history of building technology, of research techniques and of the composition, deteriorating factors and treatment of historic building materials;

3. that conservators are specially equipped to provide useful information concerning the composition, deteriorating factors and treatment of historic building materials;

4. that conservators will be better equipped to provide necessary information after they become more fully acquainted with problems confronting architects and with techniques employed in restoration. Conservators especially need to explore ways of adapting their small-scale preservation techniques for objects to the large-scale problems of buildings; and

5. that mutual benefit would result from the integration of elements in the formal subject matter of both disciplines into certain special and general training courses. Basic to the integration would be a knowledge of what courses are now available in both fields.

Members of the Rome Centre Committee also agreed that conservators and restorationists participating in a conference would benefit from hearing about experiences of Europeans in dealing with similar problems in techniques and training.

The conference program was planned and participants invited by the North American International Regional Conference Program Steering Committee, which consisted of John D. McDermott of the Advisory Council on Historic Preservation; James R. Short,

Colonial Williamsburg; William J. Murtagh, National Park Service, U.S. Department of the Interior; Russell V. Keune, AIA, and Anne E. Grimmer, National Trust for Historic Preservation in the United States; and Robert M. Organ and Peter G. Powers, Smithsonian Institution. Administrative services and coordination for the conference were provided by the National Trust.

In addition to support from the Rome Centre, generous grants for the meeting and the preparation of this publication were awarded by the National Endowment for the Humanities; Colonial Williamsburg; the National Park Service, U.S. Department of the Interior; and the Pennsylvania Historical and Museum Commission. A complete transcript of the meeting was prepared by the staff of Colonial Williamsburg, while the National Trust assumed editorial responsibility for the proceedings. Sharon W. Timmons, assistant editor for special projects, The Preservation Press, edited the papers, commentaries and discussion under the direction of Vice President/Editor Terry B. Morton and Assistant Director/Managing Editor Lee Ann Kinzer. Editorial assistance was provided by Deborah Holmes. The Smithsonian Institution Press offered its services in designing and producing the proceedings. The Rome Centre Committee is grateful for the assistance of all these organizations.

Arrangements made by staff members of Colonial Williamsburg, Independence National Historical Park, the Athenaeum of Philadelphia, the Philadelphia Historical Commission and the Philadelphia Museum of Art contributed much to the conduct of the conference, as did the hospitality extended by these organizations and others. Mrs. Charles J. Biddle and National Trust President and Mrs. James Biddle graciously entertained paper writers and commentators at a concluding luncheon in their family home, Andalusia.

This volume includes edited texts of the essays and commentaries prepared for the conference. All program participants were asked to review their remarks prior to publication. The discussions that followed each of the sessions have been summarized for the convenience of readers.

RUSSELL V. KEUNE, AIA
Program Coordinator for the Conference

Contents

Preservation and Conservation: Introductory Statement

HAROLD J. PLENDERLEITH

The experimental nature of the present meeting is perhaps its most outstanding feature, for this is the first time that architectural preservationists have been confronted (in the best sense of the term) by museum conservators. The two groups have many interests in common: Both are concerned with materials, their characteristics and permanence, and both are interested in the environment.

The training of conservators and preservationists is, to a degree, similar; courses required for would-be conservators often parallel closely those required for potential preservationists. It seemed likely, therefore, from the outset that each group could learn a good deal from the other, and on reading through the preprint of the papers to be presented at this conference, it became clear that this would prove to be a very profitable week for all in terms of discussing questions of mutual interest.

Most of my personal experience has been in the museum field. For many years, I was an active museum scientist and, therefore, concerned mostly with the conservation of art objects in museums and galleries. I can, however, recall many interesting occasions when conservators were called upon to work with architects, notably in restoration work in English cathedrals. I believe the many problems that arose in London during and immediately after World War II led me to the first realization that it is not enough

Harold J. Plenderleith is director emeritus of the International Centre for the Study of the Preservation and the Restoration of Cultural Property, Rome, Italy.

to be a specialist in the conservation of works of art located indoors. This idea became a conviction after carrying out one or two missions for the United Nations Educational, Scientific and Cultural Organization (UNESCO), visiting foreign countries where one was so often brought face to face with problems that required a thorough knowledge of external environments and climates, architectural appreciation and some slight knowledge of engineering, other professional help usually being unavailable.

Fate, coupled with the determination of an obstinate appointments board, brought me in 1959 from my position with the British Museum in London to Rome to serve as director of the International Centre for the Study of the Preservation and the Restoration of Cultural Property. At the Rome Centre (as it came to be called), I found that there were not two separate worlds of conservation and preservation, however convenient this might be for purposes of classification. There is only one world. Conservators and preservationists are all under one umbrella, so to speak. For example, the Rome Centre staff, which consists primarily of conservators like myself, has been called on to assist in salvage operations of Nubian temples in Egypt and Sudan; cleaning and consolidation of cave murals in Ajanta, India; preservation work in the prehistoric city of Mohenjo-Daro, Pakistan; consolidation of church frescoes in Göreme, Turkey; and all sorts of work in South Korea and elsewhere. Many of these assignments required novel initiatives that were only remotely related to museum conservation. This is why I believe this conference is particularly appropriate, for it embraces both architectural preservation and conservation, two complementary activities having the same ultimate goal, namely, the protection of man's cultural heritage. At last, conservators and preservationists are meeting to talk about mutual interests.

The Rome Centre actually does not recognize a difference between preservation and conservation. While staff members are not architects, nor have they ever been claimed to be such, the centre does have the potential to assist architectural preservation projects. It recognizes, for example, the importance of interdisciplinary services and is in a position to supply these services. Also, it is small enough and young enough as an institution to be able to take action at the slightest notice. Let me give two examples to illustrate this point.

One Thursday, the Rome Centre received a telephone call from the Smithsonian Institution reporting that the famous Sigiriya frescoes in Ceylon had been gravely damaged by a madman who had splashed them with bright paint. If the paint was allowed to become too dry, it would be impossible to remove without irreparable damage. Two days later, a technician-restorer from the Rome Centre was on an airplane heading for Ceylon, fully equipped to investigate and, we hoped, deal with the matter. He was able to cable success within a fortnight. This action saved some ten unique wall paintings, although two others were unfortunately slashed all over and permanently disfigured. This emergency action of saving the paintings was carried out by a museum conservator, but it was considerably more than museum conservation work.

On another occasion, I set off for Seoul, South Korea, on an extensive UNESCO program. I began by visiting the famous circular temple of Sokkulam, a very inaccessible place located on a mountaintop in the southern part of the country. Here, there were magnificent granite bodhisattvas built into the circular wall of the temple, but they were dripping with water, stained by iron deposits and covered with mud. Realizing the danger to the structure from frost action and so forth, I scrapped the UNESCO program and assembled a digging force to locate the source of the water, which was eventually traced to a holy well at the back of the carvings that had become filled with silt. My initial crew of nine men grew as requests for assistance were sent down the mountain, and the labor force reached a total of more than 100 coolies sent up by a grateful government to help with the work. The water now runs harmlessly around the temple in an open channel. Anyone could have done this, but if I, as a museum conservator, had been content only to remove the iron stains and clean the mud off these indoor sculptures, the problem would not really have been solved. One cannot erect an artificial boundary between the conservation of works of art located indoors and those that are exposed to the elements.

I could give many other similar examples but it would be more useful, I believe, to enunciate the major traits that are essential in the makeup of a conservator. Architectural preservationists may wish to consider if these have application in their own field. Apart from the necessary disciplinary training, a good conservator must have three things: confidence, caution and a sense of responsibility.

Confidence, which is acquired by the accumulation of knowledge and practical experience, is as essential for the conservator as it is for the surgeon performing a delicate operation. The museum conservator must have the self-confidence that comes from being able to think imaginatively, not only with his mind but also with his hands. Also, as Robert M. Organ says in his paper, conservators should envisage clearly the ultimate goal before beginning any treatment. This is often very difficult, Richard D. Buck points out, but we at least must try to have a clear view of the goal.

In conservation work, there is a dictum that nothing should be done that cannot, if necessary, be undone easily in the future. This dictum of caution has been found to be essential in conservation work, for experience has taught us that one cannot always rely on nature to provide a second chance if something goes wrong. Experience also has taught us that of all possible solutions to a problem, there is only one best solution and it is often elusive. It must be searched for, with great patience if need be, and found; then comes the decision whether, with a minimum concession to chance and accident, it can ever be realized in practice.

An ever-present sense of responsibility is the conservator's over-riding and guiding principle. His responsibility is, first of all, to the object and to all it represents historically and aesthetically. Everything that is done to an object must be justified, for at this stage the writing on the wall is clearly legible. It says that all actions can and must be expressed ultimately as a "profit and loss account." What is gained in stability may be offset by some undesirable change in aesthetic quality, the veiling of a characteristic feature or the accentuation of something that is undesirable. Even the loss of some part seemingly immaterial to the present generation may become a cause of deep concern to later generations. So in all decisions that relate to cultural property, one has a special responsibility to posterity. The conservator's duty is to study the whole object in depth and to make final decisions only after scrutinizing the "profit and loss account" with a full sense of responsibility. The modern conservator realizes, too, as was never realized in the early days of the profession, the lasting value of a complete documentation of decisions and actions. Such documentation is useful not only in a historical way, but also in justifying actions taken and in training successive generations of conservators. In short, in dealing with a conservation problem, the aim is to search out and apply the best solution involving the minimum of loss and to meticulously document failures as well as successes.

As I have admitted, I speak from the limited viewpoint of the art conservator. Conditions are subject to some variation where antiquities or natural history objects are concerned, and I am sure they vary also in the case of monuments. I believe it would be instructive if these variations emerge in the discussions planned. It is good to have principles, but we all should welcome the opportunity to test their validity in the course of these deliberations. All of us share similar aims and aspirations to preserve and conserve cultural property. We believe that a formal confrontation between our two fields will likely be a good and profitable thing. We conservators know that we have a great deal to learn from preservationists, much of which will be of value in helping us work together. We hope that we will be able to offer preservationists something in return that will be equally stimulating.

The great variety of the conference program and the limited time available makes it obvious that this conference can be little more than a superficial survey, and since it is the first meeting of conservators and preservationists, it may be that this is as far as the discussion can go. Even so, the conference will have proved its value if we eventually part company having extended our circle of professional friends and our knowledge of their particular aptitudes and achievements. One would like to think that there is at least a chance that we may find a lasting mutual interest that will tempt us to meet again for the purpose of pursuing such studies in more detail. I would hope so.

I believe the stage is now set for what I confidently expect will be a memorable and rewarding meeting.

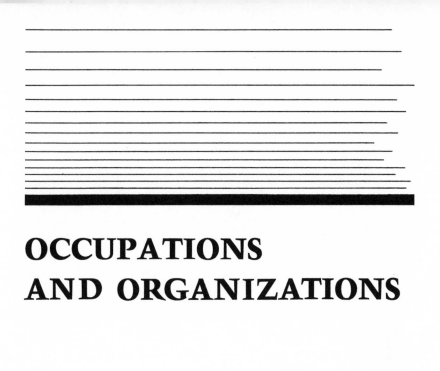

OCCUPATIONS
AND ORGANIZATIONS

Occupations

THE ROLE OF THE ARCHITECT IN HISTORICAL RESTORATIONS

CHARLES E. PETERSON, FAIA

This being a meeting of professionals, I assume that I can go directly to the architect's main problems. I will not waste any time with optimistic generalities—let us save them to comfort our clients in the difficult and expensive business of historical restoration.

First, I ask you to consider the general practice of architecture as we know it today. It was a long time in developing and sometimes—even yet—seems to live only from crisis to crisis. Our first American cities were planted well before the profession was firmly established even in Great Britain.[1] On this side of the Atlantic, an architect had to be a jack of many trades.

DEVELOPMENT OF THE PROFESSION IN THE UNITED STATES

Robert Smith of Philadelphia, who probably designed more buildings in colonial America than anyone else, was called "architect" only part of the time.[2] Although Benjamin Henry Latrobe is considered the first modern practitioner of architecture in the United States, he was forced to do many other kinds of work, such as designing steam engines, to make a precarious living for his family.[3] His pupils, Robert Mills and William Strickland, planned canals and located railroads, as well as designing buildings. Thomas U. Walter, one of Strickland's pupils, did several types of

---

Charles E. Peterson, FAIA, is an architectural historian, restorationist and planner in Philadelphia, Pa.

1

work successfully before he became the Architect of the U.S. Capitol in conflict with Capt. Montgomery C. Meigs of the U.S. Corps of Engineers. Since that colossal struggle of professional prerogatives, architects and civil engineers have increasingly limited their work to their own specialized fields. Architects pretty much gave up designing steam engines, canals and railroads—even before they went out of style.[4] This retrenchment was inevitable, because the fast development of new materials and techniques made construction methods increasingly complicated. In the field of buildings alone, architects are even now kept busy trying to stay abreast of new fads in design and mechanical innovations.[5]

Today, it has even been demanded that architects provide leadership in such important concerns as social justice and the quality of the environment. One must wonder if they can reasonably be expected to design good buildings, as well as to do so many other things. Expecting the impossible can only result in disappointment. When the results of an architect's work are poor, his reputation (and that of his colleagues) is likely to suffer. This happens all too often in the field of historical restoration.

SOME RESTORATION FAILURES

The shortcomings of architects in the field of historical restoration began long ago. It became clear, even in the days of Latrobe, that the most talented designers could not always be trusted around important landmarks. In the summer of 1796, the owner of Green Spring, a great plantation house built by Virginia's Gov. Francis Berkeley a few miles from Williamsburg, asked Latrobe to make plans to improve the old mansion, then about a century and a half old. Latrobe, a facile watercolorist, made a record of its appearance before drawing up plans for the "improvements."[6]

What Mills and Strickland did later to the Pennsylvania State-House, which is now called Independence Hall and is perhaps America's most important building, is also revealing. Similar misadventures have continued right up to the present time. Some of our most stylish architects have proposed—and have carried out—gruesome butcheries on historic buildings.

Something certainly must be done about the situation but, as far as I am aware, little is now contemplated at the highest levels to insure quality in restoration work. The architectural profession should police its own ranks, if for no other reason than that many laymen have done their homework in history (as a hobby) and are today well ahead of architects.[7]

2

PROTECTION AGAINST INCOMPETENCE

During the Middle Ages, builders' guilds understood how to discipline the performance of their trainees, and they obtained quality work in exchange for exclusionary rights. Today, there is a need to consider what measures could be taken along these lines to protect historic architecture from incompetent professionals.

Building has always been an expensive art, and qualification for formal licensing by examination is universally required for architects today. Architects must fulfill specific educational and apprenticeship requirements and must pass rigorous written tests to demonstrate their knowledge of the requirements for structural safety in buildings and their capability in general design. However, the training and experience that can produce handsome modern schoolhouses and efficient hospitals do not guarantee good results in historical restoration. The question is: What measures could induce good results?

First, it should be made clear what a restoration architect is and what he does. Basically, a restoration architect needs the same abilities as other architects, but since the buildings he works on already exist, his problem is first to understand thoroughly the work done by others before him. This requires a detailed study of the structure's fabric and an intensive search for—and analysis of—written, printed and drawn documents. In other words, the restoration architect must be a historian, too.

To diagnose failures of structure and finish, the restoration architect must understand the technology of early American buildings—just as a doctor must understand physiology and anatomy before he practices therapy or performs surgery. The restoration architect must identify incongruous elements for removal and then arrange for reinforcements and repairs to be made. He must design missing parts, specify the type and quality of materials (including the old, the used and the reproduced) and determine the correct finish. Like other architects, he makes estimates, calls for bids, selects contractors, educates constructors, inspects the work, shuts down the job when necessary and recommends payments. In addition, he adds modern features as needed, which may require, for example, a knowledge of plumbing codes. The restoration architect must educate his client as to what is best and tactfully resist the client's worst ideas. He will probably have to write out carefully reasoned justifications so that the client can raise money. Later, the restoration architect may have to defend the final result in the public press. In addition to these tasks, he should prepare records so that future restoration architects will

3

be intelligently informed and so that guides can explain the structure to tourists.[8]

In the early 1930s, I was fortunate to view closely the work of William Graves Perry, Thomas Mott Shaw and Andrew Hepburn in the development of Colonial Williamsburg. This experience made a deep and lasting impression. I never observed a more hard-working or inspired staff; they gave me a sense of quality for which I am ever grateful.

Not long afterward, when I decided that I would never become a match for McKim, Mead and White (for today, substitute Skidmore, Owings and Merrill)—at least not while in the National Park Service—I undertook a long-term study of historic structures —"taking the veil" as one of my colleagues has called it. The restoration field was not crowded then, but there were still quite a few general practitioners who could design an acceptable Georgian mansion for a well-to-do client.[9] Today, nearly all the large drafting rooms that could handily do such work on a paying basis are gone. The competent professionals who remain are hardly known to administrators who handle public monies. As a result, things happen to historic buildings that should not happen to a doghouse. I believe that the architectural profession should either address this matter in a serious way or publicly abandon the field.

It may be too much to expect today's general practitioner of architecture to produce accurate restorations. After 40 years of study old buildings across this country, I find every new restoration project I undertake full of surprises. Such projects demand all the resources one can muster to solve their problems—even in small structures that superficially appear to be simple ones. How, then, can an architect who has never taken the time to study an old building suddenly assume the public responsibility of restoring one?

As a registered architect, I am legally competent to design a skyscraper in Pennsylvania. But, for obvious reasons, I would reject such a job if it were offered to me. Obversely, the general practitioner should decline historical restoration work. But he seldom does, especially if money and prestige are involved, and he attempts to get by, one way or another. Pretending to a competence in historical restoration that one does not possess is an insult to the historical community, and it usually damages the public's confidence in architects.

In the face of such hazards, how can the character of old architecture be protected? Can anyone propose anything less drastic than special licensing?

4

RELATIONSHIPS OF RESTORATION ARCHITECTS TO OTHER PROFESSIONALS

The following brief comments are personal observations on the relationships of restoration architects to other professionals.

Planners

There should be a good working relationship between restoration architects and planners, but few planners seem to care for old buildings, and hardly any have paid much attention to the historical arrangement of man-made structures on the land. It has been my experience that city planners as a group have been the worst enemies of historic preservation.[10]

Landscape Architects

Although landscape architects have generally worked reasonably well with restoration architects, few, if any, of them have a thorough knowledge of early plant materials and arrangements.

Building Mechanics

The men who actually assemble a building on its site—by hand or with machines—work closely with the architect. In practice, it is just about impossible to define the boundaries between the two vocations. Architects must still rely on traditional practices and standards of the trades, for no building can be built with all of its details fully covered by drawings and written specifications. There is a great deal of give-and-take on the job, especially in restoration work. To me, working directly with good mechanics in solving problems is one of the great pleasures of building.

Suppliers

It is difficult today to procure many building materials that were once commonplace, and the economics of building make it difficult to obtain anything that is not emitted from a machine, cut off in standard lengths and screwed together by workers of doubtful skill.[11] Clearly, there is a need to encourage and organize suppliers of such items as authentic hardware, lighting fixtures and wallpaper. People who do good work should be patronized, or they will eventually be starved out of business.

Archaeologists

By origin, the term *archaeologist* refers to a specialist concerned with a broad range of material objects recovered from both above and under the ground. In recent times, sites have been excavated by archaeologists who claim a special knowledge and understanding of anything that can be dug up, but who often seem not to understand buildings at all and sometimes do not even have the intuition to look in the right places for the remains of structures.

On the other hand, most architects have neither the time nor the patience to solve problems of stratigraphy, which require a considerable knowledge of small artifacts. Well-meaning architects and archaeologists often find themselves in conflict. A modus vivendi certainly needs to be established in the form of guidelines for cooperation between these two fields.

Museum Professionals

In the days when many art museums were snatching rooms from early American houses, curators were often accused of grand larceny. Hopefully, such practices have ceased. Museum conservators who, like preservationists, work with stone, wood and paint (if not brick) may be able to help in some restoration projects.

In my opinion, though, preservationists most need museums of architecture where collections can be assembled, knowledge developed and reference works published. Such museums should be operated on national, state and local levels.[12] Each restored building should have its own exhibit showing how the building was originally constructed, what changes it has suffered and how it was restored, as well as a secure storage area for specimens removed from the original fabric.

AVAILABLE TRAINING

Apprenticeship to a qualified practitioner has always been required for architectural licensing, and there is no doubt in my mind that it is the most necessary part of preparation for practice. The time-honored British institution of pupilage was used by Latrobe, who served as master of Mills and Strickland, with obviously good results. This system has been the normal American procedure ever since. However, most prospective architects are now required to spend at least four or five years in university classrooms before entering the office of a qualified architect to learn how to be useful and how to make a living.

Today's standard undergraduate school does not have much to offer the aspiring restoration architect that will be useful to him. Many schools do not even provide a quick survey of the history of American architecture. And none, to my knowledge, offers a history of building materials and construction methods, which is so relevant to the understanding of old structures. This is doubly unfortunate, because there are no reference books on the subject either. A survey made by the Whitehill Committee of the National Trust for Historic Preservation, with the assistance of the Ford Foundation, confirmed the inadequacy of architectural schools in the United States.[13]

6

In 1964, the Columbia University School of Architecture inaugurated a one-year graduate course of studies leading to a master's degree in architecture; the program is under the leadership of James Marston Fitch.[14] While the program's development has been hampered by a lack of funds, it has grown steadily, and its graduates have found useful places in the professional world. In 1970, the University of Florida School of Architecture made a small but definite beginning with a master's program under the direction of F. Blair Reeves.[15] I do not mean to disparage the accomplishments of these two institutions by insisting that they need help.

As an American, I am deeply concerned that while the United States is now officially committed to historic preservation on a grand scale, it is poorly equipped to produce high quality and authenticity in the vast number of architectural restoration projects that lie ahead.

Before concluding this discussion on training, tribute should be paid to the Historic American Buildings Survey (HABS) for its long-term, widespread contributions. When organized in 1933, the HABS called for advice from such acknowledged leaders of the restoration profession as William Graves Perry of Boston, Mass.; Albert Simons of Charleston, S. C.; and Richard Koch of New Orleans, La.[16] The careers of such scholars as Frederick D. Nichols of Charlottesville, Va.; Richard W. E. Perrin of Milwaukee, Wis.; and Samuel Wilson, Jr., of New Orleans, La., were launched at that time. The HABS summer program for architectural students, inaugurated in 1951, brought into the historical restoration community such now highly placed professional men as Ernest Allen Connally from Harvard, F. Blair Reeves from the University of Florida, Russell V. Keune and Lee H. Nelson from the University of Illinois and E. Blaine Cliver from the Carnegie Institute of Technology, to name some of those present at this conference.[17] The HABS is where many architects got acquainted with *buildings* (as opposed to books and talk about buildings).

ORGANIZATIONS INVOLVED IN HISTORIC PRESERVATION

The following organizations have been involved in the problems described. The list includes both those that began as pioneers and newer ones that show promise.

1. *The Carpenters' Company of the City and County of Philadelphia* (founded 1724) organized and conducted a pioneering architectural school from 1833 to 1842, restored its own hall in 1857 as an American Revolution landmark open free to the public and is currently planning a 1974 symposium on the history of the

American building industry, a vitally important subject for restoration architects.

2. *The Mount Vernon Ladies' Association* (1856) carefully restored over the years—and now preserves—a great Virginia plantation. The permanent staff includes an architect for restoration. The association has developed a small but valuable architectural museum at Mount Vernon that is open to visitors.

3. *The American Institute of Architects* (1857) has had a committee on historic preservation for years, but seems to prefer a weak one. Much less than one percent of the annual budget is allocated to this committee, which generally is not consulted on the most crucial preservation issues.[18] Editors of AIA publications have generally been friendly to historical writers, although they have published relatively little on the subject.

4. *The U.S. National Park Service* (1916) holds the stewardship of most of the historic structures owned by the nation. It developed two major corps of restoration architects (beginning in 1931 and again in 1951), but it currently employs few restoration specialists. Today, the Park Service's projects are generally planned by outside firms, some with little experience in this type of work. To correct this situation, a historic building preservation center was proposed several years ago for Philadelphia, but it has not been developed.[19]

5. *The Society of Architectural Historians* (1941) is now dominated by academic art historians and publishes relatively little of use to restoration architects.

6. *The National Trust for Historic Preservation* (1949) has never proved itself much concerned about quality in restoration work, possibly because it did not have an architect on its staff until 1969. It now has three and things are looking up. The Trust has published almost nothing of technical assistance to restoration architects, but there are rumors that this situation is going to change.

7. *The Association for Preservation Technology* (1968), formed through Canadian initiative, has a large membership of architects and related professionals. It sponsors an annual conference of specialists and publishes a quarterly *Bulletin* that includes useful source material.

8. *The Society for Industrial Archeology,* formed within the last year, intends to publish material of interest to the restoration architect, although it has many other concerns that must be accommodated also.

8

CRAFTSMEN OF THE BUILDING TRADES

There has been a considerable wailing and wringing of hands by those who appreciate quality craftsmanship in buildings and have seen its decline as the machine becomes increasingly dominant. It is my opinion, however, that the old crafts can be revived. What is needed for such a revival is encouragement, not necessarily the expenditure of large sums of money. The two basic ingredients of such encouragement are continuous employment and plenty of appreciation when quality results are achieved by individuals. The feasibility of this concept has already been demonstrated.

The longer the delay in establishing a substantial program for the revival of old crafts, the more difficult it will be to accomplish. One of the most obvious dangers is the loss of the old builder's vocabulary. Many of the terms used to describe building parts and processes were transmitted orally and do not appear in written records.[20] Fortunately, mechanical aptitude survives in the human genes, and a gifted craftsman can usually teach himself to reproduce most early types of handiwork.[21] Given an opportunity to work continuously over a period of years, he can become a master craftsman in the old-fashioned sense.

To become proficient, a craftsman needs to be monitored in his progress and accomplishments and promoted whenever possible. In 1956, architect Henry A. Judd of the National Park Service and I worked out specifications for a new position entailing this type of work and successfully promoted its approval by the U.S. Civil Service Commission. The position was called buildings restoration specialist, a tag designed to make the man wearing it feel a little more important than an ordinary carpenter—which he was.[22]

THE LANDSCAPE ARCHITECT

Today, the responsibilities of the landscape architect may range from choosing plant materials for a backyard garden to organizing a save-the-environment corporation that worries publicly and publishes brochures. Education for historical work by the landscape architect should comprehend detailed subjects ranging from horticultural stock [23] and pebble pavements to layouts of historic farms and great battlefields.

Landscape architects capable of doing this kind of work competently were never numerous and are now (as far as I know) almost nonexistent. This subject deserves lengthier treatment; Ralph Griswold, FASLA, of Pittsburgh, Pa., and Williamsburg, Va., for instance, could provide valuable information about what is needed and how it can be accomplished.

CONCLUSION

Although the propositions presented in this paper have not been adequately discussed, it is hoped that some doors have been opened that will not be closed until the most urgent needs are publicly recognized and suitable measures to meet them are under way.

NOTES

1. An interesting work on the establishment of architecture as a profession is Barington Kaye, *The Development of the Architectural Profession in Britain, A Sociological Study* (London: George Allen & Unwin, 1960).

2. For a list of the work of Robert Smith (c. 1722–77), see Charles E. Peterson, "Carpenters' Hall, Historic Philadelphia," *Transactions of the American Philosophical Society* (Philadelphia, 1953), vol. 43, pt. I, pp. 119-23. Philadelphia builders froze out the English emigré Benjamin Henry Latrobe who tried to set up an architectural practice there. Talented amateurs like John Dorsey who gave their plans away also posed a threat.

3. Talbot Hamlin, winner of a Pulitzer Prize, gives a splendid account of the architect in *Benjamin Henry Latrobe* (New York: Oxford University Press, 1955).

4. Engineering has been divided into many categories without fatal damage to that profession; for example, today it is not likely that an acoustical engineer would attempt to design a highway.

5. In the superaffluent period after the Civil War, a high-level set of ethics was promulgated by the American Institute of Architects, then quite new. Although under attack from one direction or another ever since, the AIA still sets the general tone on such matters.

6. Thomas Tileston Waterman and John A. Barrows, *Domestic Colonial Architecture of Tidewater Virginia* (1932; reprint ed., New York: Da Capo Press, 1968), pp. 12–13.

7. What can the historically informed public do when a prestigious architect develops a bad restoration program, duly endorsed by high officials and promoted in a full-scale publicity campaign including seductive watercolor renderings? If the threat is not recognized soon enough and no indignant citizens are available to spring to the defense, another historic landmark either disappears or is degraded to live ever after in shame.

8. Historic buildings, no matter in what type of ownership, are all more or less in the public domain. They have a prickly public to please, not one to be underestimated.

9. Designing a Georgian mansion well required a genuine competence, even though many details could be copied from old buildings. For architectural offices in distant cities, such as Denver or San Francisco, there were books that provided authentic full-size molding profiles. At the same time, there were few practitioners who could have undertaken quality restoration work according to the best standards of today.

10. Fifty-nine certified historic buildings within two blocks of my house in Philadelphia have been torn down in the last 10 years in accordance with planners' concepts of redevelopment.

11. Certain sizes and species of lumber—and even such staples as linseed oil (from which all house paints were made not long ago)—are now nearly impossible to procure. The available supply of antique lighting fixtures and hardware is inadequate also. Old carriage lamps look ridiculous on old houses. Antique window glass is hard to procure and difficult to use.

12. A proposal partially carried out in Saint Louis, Mo., 30 years ago is discussed in Charles E. Peterson, "A Museum of American Architecture, A Proposed Institution of Research and Public Education," *The Octagon, A Journal of the American Institute of Architects* 8, no. 11 (November 1936): 3-7.

13. This once promising attempt at reform seems to have died of inertia.

14. A master's program is also available for nonarchitects.

15. At the University of Florida, it is possible to obtain a master's degree in history and preservation at the end of six years. None of these degrees have as yet been awarded. Mr. Reeves to author, May 23, 1972. The Whitehill Report recognized the potentials of the University of Virginia in the preservation field, as it did Cornell University for planning studies.

16. The purpose and scope of the HABS was first outlined in a Park Service memorandum dated November 13, 1933. It may be found complete in the *Journal of the Society of Architectural Historians* 16, no. 3 (October 1957): 27–31. An early recognition of the need for special training of architects may be found in Grant C. Manson, "Training Architects for Restoration," *Journal of the Society of Architectural Historians* 14, no. 2 (May 1955): 28–29.

17. For a clear statement on the educational impact of HABS work, see Ernest Allen Connally, "Preserving the American Tradition," *Journal of the American Institute of Architects* 34, no. 5 (May 1961): 56–60.

18. A century ago, AIA President Richard Upjohn, an eminent New York architect, counseled the members assembled at the national convention to study and appreciate early American buildings. Today, such advice from the institute's president would be almost unimaginable.

19. A major collection of artifacts was assembled by the National Park Service in Saint Louis, Mo., before World War II for an architectural museum, but it was subsequently disposed of. See Peterson, "A Museum of American Architecture," and Charles E. Peterson, "The Museum of American Architecture: A Progress Report," *Journal of the Society of Architectural Historians* 1, nos. 3–4 (July–October 1941): 24–26. A great deal of valuable material from the reports of Park Service architects could be published, but thus far little has been.

20. This situation is discussed briefly in the introduction to *The Rules of Work of the Carpenters' Company of the City and County of Philadelphia, 1786* by Charles E. Peterson (Princeton, N.J.: Pyne Press, 1971), p. xxii.

21. A good example is the work of Park Service Buildings Restoration Specialist Gordie Whittington. Architect Lee H. Nelson reported on Whittington's work in "Simplified Method for Reproducing Wood Mouldings," *Bulletin of the Association for Preservation Technology* 3, no. 4 (1971): 48–51.

22. Not every applicant made the grade, but on one memorable day in 1962 guests from all over the East were invited to see some of them at work in Philadelphia, and the morale was high indeed.

23. Certain old-fashioned plant varieties to complete a garden may be quite difficult, if not impossible, to find. Landscape architects and others must encourage and patronize knowledgeable growers.

CLIO AND THE SHIP OF THESEUS: THE ROLES OF HISTORIANS, ARCHITECTURAL HISTORIANS, CURATORS AND EDUCATIONAL INTERPRETERS IN PRESERVATION *

RICHARD M. CANDEE

The influence of the history museum—a term used throughout this paper to include only those institutions operating one or more historic structures—on the development of the historic preservation movement in the United States and Canada is in many ways unique. Critics and apologists alike agree that these museums, consisting of one or more restored buildings, have contributed to the way in which North Americans perceive their past.[1] Indeed, the link between historic preservation and the interpretation of history has been so strong that by the mid-1950s Kenneth Chorley, president of Colonial Williamsburg, contended that: "The purpose of any historic preservation—the one and only purpose—is to communicate the lessons of history, in order that the present and the future may learn from the past."[2]

There is abundant evidence that for many years the terms *preservation, restoration, historic house museum* and *outdoor history museum* were considered nearly synonymous. Two weeks after the 1963 Williamsburg, Va., Seminar on Preservation and Restoration, Ada Louise Huxtable, *New York Times* architectural writer, published an important challenge to this notion, condemn-

---

* For the philosophical question of the "restoration" of the ship of Theseus as told in *Plutarch's Lives* and its modern analogy in American preservation, see Walter Muir Whitehill, *Independent Historical Societies* (Boston: Boston Athenaeum, 1962), pp. 461-79.

Richard M. Candee is a researcher in architecture at Old Sturbridge Village, Sturbridge, Mass.

ing it for encouraging "the present widespread corruption of preservation practices." She wrote:

The fault and the danger are in the preservation philosophy that Williamsburg represents, which is less a philosophy than a disease that might be called galloping restorationitis. It has infected innumerable cities and towns and antiquarian societies, and has turned the preservation movement upside down when its first aim should be—and originally was—to save fine old buildings of any period as a living part of the community.[3]

Although Ms. Huxtable's thesis that the original aim of the preservation movement was to preserve "fine old buildings of any period" may be open to challenge, she deftly identified the confusion that exists when the term *preservation* is used to mean restoration employed for the purpose of historical interpretation.

One reaction to this criticism has been a movement back to the antirestoration philosophical position of the British architectural theorist William Morris.[4] For example, the Society for the Preservation of New England Antiquities has decided to conserve recently acquired buildings and family collections exactly as they were left by the last owners, without restoration, as records of the cumulative histories of the buildings, collections and their owners. While such a moratorium on restoration as the major activity of a history museum must undoubtedly be limited in its application, this action suggests that total preservation is an archival function as much as a technique for teaching history.[5]

INTERDISCIPLINARY CONTRIBUTIONS TO PRESERVATION PRACTICES

Rather than debate the assumption that the purpose of historic preservation is the teaching of history, I would like to investigate the ways in which this belief has affected the definition of the roles of historians, architectural historians, curators and interpreters engaged in preservation work. To do this, it is necessary to trace the institutionalization of their roles in the preservation process. It will become apparent that this institutionalization is a by-product of the intense and unique relationship existing between history museums and the historic preservation movement as it evolved in the United States.[6]

By the time the preservation community had become involved in the internal debate over the goals of preservation, as reflected in Ms. Huxtable's remarks and in the papers presented at the 1963 Williamsburg seminar, it was generally accepted that research was needed for "proper" restoration and that both research and education were the responsibility of the history museum. Furthermore,

14

it was recognized that the development of criteria for the evaluation of buildings to be preserved for nonmuseum use demanded both historical and architectural research.[7] These principles reflect one of the major contributions of the close relationship between history museums and the historic preservation movement. It was within these museums that an interdisciplinary task-force approach to the joint aims of research and education was developed —an approach that eventually brought together historians, architectural historians, curators and educators, as well as restoration architects (the original architectural historians) and archaeologists.

This type of task force on research and education, which existed in embryonic form during the years when Colonial Williamsburg was being restored, was institutionalized in the National Park Service (NPS). In the Park Service, research historians assembled documentary evidence on NPS historic properties, and architects (acting in their traditional preservation role of architectural historian) provided physical analyses of buildings and the alterations made to them. These analyses, combined with archaeological evidence, became the key documents used by architects to guide restoration programs, by curators to furnish the buildings and by educational interpreters to explain the results to the visiting public. Although the research and educational task forces developed by many other history museums interpreting historic buildings was organized each in its own way, the institutionalization of the roles of the varied professions in the preservation process resulted. This institutionalization was a significant development in the history of the preservation movement, and one that has yet to be described in detail. Its importance derives from the fact that because of the symbiotic tie between history museums and the historic preservation movement, the concept of an interdisciplinary approach to the preservation of buildings for the teaching of history is now broadly applied in other areas of preservation.[8]

While the interdisciplinary task forces associated with history museums were developing their own methods of selection and restoration, new legal and governmental techniques for preservation were being developed through the establishment of historic districts in Charleston, S.C.; Savannah, Ga.; and other cities in the East. In these instances, preservation was not directed toward teaching history, but toward general protection of the man-made environment.

The founding of the National Trust for Historic Preservation in 1949 places it symbolically in the midst of these two developing trends. In 1956, the National Trust adopted a second, revised edition of its statement "Criteria for Evaluating Historic Sites and

Buildings." These criteria, which emphasize the historical and cultural significance of structures, contrast with the criteria used in the College Hill Study, conducted in Providence, R.I., in 1959. This study attempted to go beyond the criteria of the National Park Service and the National Trust by evaluating individual buildings as part of a continuous architectural development and as part of a neighborhood, in order to plan for the preservation of large groups of related buildings in situ and to encourage a visual integration of architectural styles from the past to the present.[9]

THE ROLE OF THE ARCHITECTURAL HISTORIAN

The attitudes of professional historians toward historic preservation are also relevant. One of my colleagues noted in another context that, despite the lip service American historians pay to the value of artifacts in the study of history, most of them do not consider objects (buildings, for example) as sources of historical evidence.[17] This opinion is confirmed by Walter Rundell's recent study of the profession [18] and by an impressionistic survey I made of three leading professional journals—*The William and Mary Quarterly, The American Historical Review* and *The Journal of American History.* I observed that the only references in these journals to historic preservation between 1965 and 1972 were the book reviews of Charles B. Hosmer's *Presence of the Past* and Clifton L. Lord's *Keepers of the Past* and a notice of the 1968 annual meeting of the Organization of American Historians at which the American Association of State and Local History cosponsored a session that included a discussion of National Park Service programs.[19]

The academic historian does not view his own role in the selection and preservation of historic sites or buildings in the same light as does the architectural historian. Rather, as Yale professor R. W. Winks suggested in a paper given at the 1972 Organization of American Historians' annual meeting in a session entitled "Comparative Aspects of Historical Preservations," historians view preservation as a continuing public process in which the professional historian apparently takes no active part.[20]

This view totally ignores historians who received their training in undergraduate and graduate academic programs in American history and who are employed by national or state park services, state historical societies and large museums. Until recently, contributions of these historians were largely programmatic, that is, designed to meet the research and educational needs of their organizations. Because their work was generally local or focused on a specific site, their audience popular and their publications limited, these historians have always been assigned a lower status within the profession of history, a status on a par with a high school history teacher.

This lower status within the profession, however, has not been exclusively confined to nonacademic historians. American historians with specific interests in the role of the arts, literature or anthropology in history or with other methodological ideas outside the mainstream of the profession, have viewed themselves as being at the lower end of the academic pecking order. The formation of special programs and academic departments in American studies or American civilization may have been as much a response to this self-view as it was an attempt to provide a more broadly based interdisciplinary approach to the study of American history and the arts. The publication of *American Quarterly*, the professional journal of the American Studies Association, marks the success of these developments in an institutional sense. *American Quarterly* annually offers a selective bibliography of journal literature relevant to American studies. These listings show that there is a general lack of interest among the strictly academic journals in the publication of preservation-related research. This situation has resulted in the extensive use of museum, historical society and preservation agency publications as outlets for the research findings of cultural historians.[21]

Directly related to this academic movement is the more recent burgeoning of cooperative museum-university graduate programs based largely on the American studies model. American history-related museums offer graduate training for academic or museum careers, thus providing a new source of historians, curators and educators for history museums. The traditional tie between the museum and preservation fields makes such training appropriate for both traditional and newly developing careers in preservation.[22]

THE NATIONAL REGISTER OF HISTORIC PLACES

In 1965, a special committee on historic preservation, working under a Ford Foundation grant to the United States Conference of Mayors, recommended legislation that included the creation of a national register of historic places under the Park Service. This recommendation was implemented by the National Historic Preservation Act of 1966. A look at the backgrounds of the staff members employed in 1972 by the National Register of Historic Places, which operates under the Park Service's Office of Archeology and Historic Preservation, shows that a majority of its members were trained as historians and that it currently employs only two architectural historians, in contrast to the Historic American Buildings

Survey and the National Historical Landmarks Program (both also within the Office of Archeology and Historic Preservation), which employ architectural historians with backgrounds in art history as well as architectural historians who are trained architects. The result of this imbalance in the National Register's staff is evident in the method it adopted to achieve a balanced inventory of historical, architectural and archaeological resources within each state. The National Register's guidelines for state agencies charged with surveying state resources and preservation planning call for a thematic approach to the historical resources of each state.[23] This method for encouraging a broad selection of sites and buildings worthy of preservation has much in common with the type of historical interpretation offered by many history museums and national historical parks. In contrast to the criteria developed by architectural historians and city planners, which are based primarily on visual or architectural relationships, National Register guidelines emphasize historical relationships.

The belief that the purpose of preservation is indeed the teaching of history is evident in the guidelines' recommendations for state governments. Each state is requested to form a review board consisting of at least one historian, one architect (a reflection of the continuing belief in the architect's role as an architectural historian or aesthetician) and an archaeologist. This body reviews and passes on the merits of each nomination to the National Register. Nationally, the review boards include 74 architects, 70 archaeologists, 131 historians, 17 architectural historians and 16 "preservationists" of unspecified training (table 1).[24]

While the composition of review boards differs widely from

Table 1 OCCUPATIONS OF MEMBERS OF STATE REVIEW BOARDS

Occupation	Number
Historian	131[a]
Architect	74[b]
Civil engineer	4
Anthropologist/archaeologist	70
Architectural historian	17
Preservationist	16
State employee not in any of the previous categories	57
Other	95

SOURCE: *A Guide to State Programs* (Washington, D.C.: National Trust for Historis Preservation, 1972); also included are data on the members of the New York and Maine state review boards, which were not listed in the guide.

a Includes 36 academic, 65 nonacademic and 30 unspecified historians.

b Includes landscape architects.

18

state to state (for example, the Rhode Island board includes three architectural historians and one nonacademic historian), there is a preponderance of historians on review boards, a fact that deserves some attention. Thirty of the historians are merely listed as "historians" with no affiliation, 36 hold academic positions and there is a generational difference between staff members of state agencies and members of state review boards. Not only do staff members of state agencies tend to be younger than state review board members, but they come to their jobs with more varied educational backgrounds. The latter also seems to be characteristic 65 hold nonacademic positions, generally with historical societies and museums. It is not surprising, therefore, that many states are making use of the National Register grant-in-aid program to fund state-owned historic sites and history museums, rather than supporting sites and structures selected on the basis of visual or architectural criteria stressing the broader aims of environmental protection.

One case that illustrates this point is the Payne House (known as the Prudence Crandall House, c. 1805) in Canterbury, Conn. A survey identified the house as having national importance, as it was the site of a short-lived school for young Negro girls organized by Prudence Crandall in 1833. The house was acquired in 1969 by the Connecticut Historical Commission (in this case, a body distinct from the review board). Although five separate areas in the town, including the community in which the Payne House is located, were deemed worthy of listing as historic districts by the initial survey, only the house was placed in the National Register. The state's acquisition of the building, now under development as a black history museum, may include plans for blacktopping the wooded areas near the house for visitor parking. Subsequent to the initial survey, a modern store with its own blacktop parking lot was opened on the corner opposite the Payne House, effectively destroying the district potential of the community. If the state compounds this sad mistake by adding its own visitor parking lot, it will be proof of the priority of history over environmental protection, a story that could be repeated in every part of the country.

Elsewhere, the prospect for continued "museumization" at the expense of traditional landscape or townscape patterns is not so imbalanced. Individuals who are employed by state agencies administering National Register programs and who are charged with the daily operation of surveying, planning, nomination processing and overseeing grants-in-aid tend to represent a wider range of occupations than exists on review boards (table 2). Nationally, 43 historians, 22 archaeologists and 21 architectural historians are

**Table 2   OCCUPATIONS OF STATE STAFF PERSONNEL
ADMINISTERING NATIONAL REGISTER PROGRAMS**

Occupation	Number
Historian	43
Archaeologist	22
State parks employee	23
Architectural historian	21
Educational interpreter	21
Planner	11
Preservationist	10
Architect/draftsman	5
Engineer	1

SOURCE: *A Guide to State Programs* (Washington, D.C.: National Trust for Historic Preservation, 1972); also included are data on the state staff personnel for New York and Maine, which were not listed in the guide.

employed on the staffs of state agencies charged with the administration of National Register programs. Only 5 architects or draftsmen are listed on these staffs, although 11 planners and 10 unspecified "preservationists" are included. Although this classification of job titles does not provide evidence, my experience suggests that there is a generational difference between staff members of state agencies and members of state review boards. Not only do staff members of state agencies tend to be younger than state review board members, but they come to their jobs with more varied educational backgrounds. The latter also seems to be characteristic of the headquarters staff of the National Trust. Within the three departments dealing most directly with preservation and the public, there are two architects and a doctor of education directing the activities of two art historians, an architectural historian, a planner, a lawyer and graduates of two university-museum programs, among others.

This broadening of professional staffs is a hopeful sign, especially the inclusion of those taught to view the elements of the environment as primary sources. It remains to be seen whether, with the enlarged scope of the research and education task force, such institutions as the National Trust will develop new criteria for the preservation of the "average structures in the total environment" that William J. Murtagh called for in 1967 to meet the needs of preservation's real constituency, the people who are "concerned over the appearance of their communities." [25]

NEW DIRECTIONS

Those engaged in environmental conservation must differentiate more clearly the various approaches to preservation. Institutions need to clarify their own priorities and public roles. Museums and environmental protection may be too incompatible for any single agency to handle. If so, the National Trust, for example, might do itself a service by divesting itself of museum properties and concentrating its full efforts on assisting national, state and local efforts in identifying and appropriately preserving the man-made environment.

Certain buildings or sites may call for total preservation, without restoration, of the complete physical environment as it has evolved to the present day. This form of archival conservation might include not only domestic buildings evidencing changing social and aesthetic tastes, but also craft and industrial complexes that continue traditional processes in their original contexts. A museum may be the solution in the former case, but not necessarily in the latter. The preservation of craft and industrial complexes, like that of archaeological sites, is justified as a means of insuring their continued survival for study.

In other cases, where a structure and its contents have been permanently separated, nonmuseum solutions abound, including continued use, rehabilitation, adaptive use and architectural alteration. Public, semipublic or private preservation agencies should assist the preservation effort by separating themselves from museum activities and devoting their staffs and funds to fostering the nonmuseum aspects of preservation. This nonmuseum approach would undoubtedly require a reconsideration of traditional rationales for public assistance to preservation and a consideration of new policies, such as assistance to private owners or developers for building conservation without restoration and without public access requirements.

Finally, restoration ought to be limited to museums and used as a technique of education, and museums should be relegated to a minor role in the preservation movement. Clearly, such use of old buildings may be justified by a demonstrable need for total (archival) preservation; for the prevention of on-site destruction, where no other legal or financial recourse may be found; or for the adaptive use of a structure as a museum in combination with, or as a catalyst to, widespread nonmuseum preservation in a locale. However, the same criteria for appropriateness should be applied to the establishment of a museum as would be applied to alteration or demolition. Ripping interiors out of otherwise well-preserved structures or tearing whole buildings out of their original contexts should be considered as destructive to the local environment as is demolition. The 20-year average life-span of local historical societies also suggests that their in-situ history museums ought not be considered as permanent preservation solutions and should certainly not serve as models for local preservation.

This nonmuseum approach to preservation demands a reevaluation by both the professions and organizations discussed in this paper. Only if some of the ideas derived from this approach are accepted by those engaged in preservation careers will wider public support be generated. If they are accepted, we may find that there are more purposes to which historic preservation could address itself than simply the teaching of history.

NOTES

1. For a criticism of the "museumization" of preservation and history, see David Lowenthal, "The American Way of History," *The Columbia University Forum* 9, no. 3 (summer 1966): 27–32; David Lowenthal, "The American Scene," *Geographical Review* (April 1968): 61–88; Ada Louise Huxtable, *Will They Ever Finish Bruckner Boulevard?* (New York: Macmillan Co., 1970), pp. 210–12, 221–24; and Kenneth Chorley and Louis C. Jones, "Primer for Preservation: Preservation: What's Wrong? A Look at Historic Preservation," *History News* 19, no. 6 (April 1964): 95–98 (also issued as American Association for State and Local History Technical Leaflet 19).

2. Chorley and Jones, "Primer for Preservation," p. 1.

3. Ada Louise Huxtable, "Dissent at Colonial Williamsburg," *New York Times,* September 22, 1963. See also the public response, "About Williamsburg," *New York Times,* October 13, 1963.

4. John Summerson, "Ruskin, Morris, and the 'Anti-Scrape' Philosophy," in *Historic Preservation Today: Essays Presented to the Seminar on Preservation and Restoration,* ed. James R. Short (Charlottesville: University of Virginia Press, 1966), pp. 23–32.

5. George L. Wrenn, III, "What Is a Historic House Museum?" *Historic Preservation* 23, no. 1 (January–March 1971): 55–58.

6. For a discussion of the parallel experience of the Canadian preservation movement, see Frederick L. Rath, Jr., and Merrilyn Rogers O'Connell, comps., *Guide to Historic Preservation, Historical Agencies, and Museum Practices: A Selective Bibliography* (Cooperstown: New York State Historical Association, 1970), pp. 11–12; and Georges-E. Gauther, "Museum Development in Canada's Centennial Year," *Museum News* 45, no. 7 (March 1967): 11–16.

7. Louis C. Jones, "The Trapper's Cabin and the Ivory Tower," *Museum News* 40, no. 7 (March 1962): 11–16; Freeman Tilden, *Interpreting Our Heritage: Principles and Practices for Visitor Services in Parks, Museums, and Historic Places,* rev. ed. (Chapel Hill: University of North Carolina Press, 1957), pp. 5–6, 18–25; and James R. Short, ed., *Historic Preservation Today: Essays Presented to the Seminar on Preservation and Restoration* (Charlottesville: University of Virginia Press, 1966). For a discussion of the status of research in restoration before the advent of the task-force approach at Colonial Williamsburg, see Charles B. Hosmer, Jr., *Presence of the Past: A History of the Preservation Movement in the United States Before Williamsburg* (New York: G. P. Putnam's Sons, 1965), pp. 273–87; for research standards of a later date, see Orin M. Bullock, *The Restoration Manual* (Norwalk, Conn.: The Silvermine Press, Inc., 1966), pp. 13–77.

8. This is not to imply that the museum field has found a means of setting standards for either research or educational practices in history or in other disciplines related to museums. The procedure for accreditation of museums by the American Association of Museums does not include any evaluation of research or educational practices nor have there been any guidelines established for such evaluation. (See *Museum Accreditation: A Report to the Profession* [Washington, D.C.: American Association of Museums, 1970].) For information on the embryonic task-force approach to research and education used at Colonial Williamsburg, see W. A. R. Goodwin, "The Restoration of Colonial Williamsburg," *National Geographic Magazine* 71, no. 4 (April 1937): 432–43; and the citations and bibliographies in Marcus Whiffen's two studies, *The Eighteenth-Century Houses of Williamsburg*, Williamsburg Architectural Studies Series (Williamsburg, Va.: Colonial Williamsburg, 1969) and *The Public Buildings of Williamsburg*, Williamsburg Architectural Studies Series (Williamsburg, Va.: Colonial Williamsburg, 1958).

9. For a review of the development of legal techniques for preservation, see Jacob H. Morrison, *Historic Preservation Law*, 2d ed. (Washington, D.C.: National Trust for Historic Preservation, 1965); Stephen W. Jacobs, "Architectural Preservation in the United States: The Government's Role," *Curator* 9, no. 4 (December 1966): 307–30; and Carl Feiss, "Historic Town Keeping," *Journal of the Society of Architectural Historians* 15, no. 4 (December 1956): 2–6. For a classification of other criteria and methods for area preservation before the College Hill Study, see David E. Finley, *History of the National Trust for Historic Preservation, 1947-1963* (Washington, D.C.: National Trust for Historic Preservation, 1965). The contrasting sets of preservation criteria of the National Trust and the College Hill Study are published together in "A Report on Principles and Guidelines for Historic Preservation in the United States," *Preservation Leaflet Series*, no. 115 (Washington, D.C.: National Trust for Historic Preservation, 1964).

10. Nicholaus Pevsner, "The Return of Historicism," *Journal of the Royal Institute of British Architects* 68, 3d ser. (1961): 3. Bruce Allsopp, *The Study of Architectural History* (London: Studio Vista, 1970), pp. 71–75.

11. See the results of the AIA Committee on Historic Resources' questionnaire to schools of architecture on education in American architectural history and preservation, presented to the committee September 16–17, 1971; Turpin C. Bannister, "The Contribution of Architectural History to the Development of the Modern Student-Architect," *Journal of the Society of Architectural Historians* 2, no. 2 (April 1942): 5–7; and "Architectural History and the Student Architect: A Symposium," *Journal of the Society of Architectural Historians* 26, no. 3 (October 1967): 178–98.

12. John Maass, "Where Architectural Historians Fear to Tread," *Journal of the Society of Architectural Historians* 28, no. 1 (March 1969): 3–8.

13. Ibid., p. 6.

14. Ibid., pp. 3–6.

15. Alan Gowans, "Preservation," *Journal of the Society of Architectural Historians* 24, no. 3 (October 1965): 252–53.

16. Allsopp, *Study of Architectural History*, pp. 92–119. Some architectural historians have shown increasing interest in the vernacular architecture of Great Britain, according to R. W. Brunskill in *The Illustrated Handbook of Vernacular Architecture* (New York: Universe Books, 1971), pp. 18–19; the same could be said of the United States since Maass' criticism was published.

17. Darwin P. Kelsey, "Outdoor Museums and Historical Agriculture," *Agricultural History* 46, no. 1 (January 1972): 108–9.

18. Walter Rundell, Jr., *In Pursuit of American History: Research and Training in the United States* (Norman: University of Oklahoma Press, 1970), pp. 155–58.

19. See *The Journal of American History* 55, no. 2 (September 1968): 359–60; 53, no. 1 (June 1966): 155–56; and 52, no. 3 (December 1965): 659–60.

20. R. W. Winks, "Visible Symbols of an Invisible Past: The United States, Canada, and Australia" (paper delivered at the annual meeting of the Organization of American Historians, Washington, D.C., April 5, 1972).

21. See, for example, "Articles in American Studies, 1970," *American Quarterly* 23, no. 3 (August 1971): 357–446. *Museum News* and *History News* provide regular publication outlets for articles related to the preservation of history museums, and *Historic Preservation* and the *Bulletin of the Association for Preservation Technology* provide outlets for many types of preservation-related research.

22. Five graduate programs in American culture, two in American history and two museum programs, in addition to other programs related to architecture, conservation and photography, are recommended in *Historic Preservation: Careers for Archaeologists, Architects, Curators, Historians, Landscape Architects, Lawyers, Planners* (Washington, D.C.: National Trust for Historic Preservation, n.d.).

23. *Historic Preservation Grants-in-Aid Policies and Procedures: National Register of Historic Places* (Washington, D.C.: National Park Service, 1972), pp. 1–33.

24. All figures are drawn from *A Guide to State Programs* (Washington, D.C.: National Trust for Historic Preservation, 1972), with the addition of the unlisted review boards of New York and Maine. In the guide, the category of architecture, for convenience, encompasses all architectural disciplines, including planning and landscape architecture, without differentiation.

25. William J. Murtagh, "Commentary on Landmark Preservation in the United States," *Curator* 10, no. 2 (June 1967): 158.

THE ROLE OF THE CONSERVATOR

CAROLINE K. KECK

All of us joined in this conference share a commendable objective, the preservation of cultural heritage. This is an uneasy world. For any society to look backward with a sense of pride gives comfort that it may likewise look forward with hope. Evidences of man's creative genius serve to separate him from the insensitive destroyers whom we discredit as barbarians. In all periods, contemporary artists have found encouragement to refine their personal efforts by studying earlier masterpieces. As ordinary people, we are subconsciously moved by the expectation that if we show respect for the accomplishments of those now dead, the future might accord our era the same flattery. Weigh as we may these and other motives for our urge to prolong what we value in the present and the past, let us accept for our activities the burden of responsibility they entail. For however we may strive to avoid hypocrisy and shun exploitation in our preservation zeal, we who are gathered here are partners in the manufacture of illusions.

This is unavoidable. Anything we do or do not do in our preservation efforts expresses a decision on our part made in the light of our time. The dilemma that confronts us is that fabrications of man have a dual nature. They are constructed of matter and, as such, deteriorate according to the laws that govern all matter.

Caroline K. Keck is a professor in the Conservation of Historic and Artistic Works Program, Cooperstown Graduate Programs (a joint project of the State University College at Oneonta and the New York State Historical Association), Cooperstown, N.Y.

They are also imbued with an immaterial content, the fusion of an artist with his environment. The impact of any created form, a quality variously described as aesthetic, emotional, intellectual or spiritual, cannot be divorced from the form's physical components. No matter which specialist among us is expert in the identification of the form's original structure and the analysis of the subsequent changes it may have experienced, each generation and each separate individual will interpret the work of the past in subjective terms. While we may find that determining how to restrain or reverse the changes inflicted by deterioration is far from cut and dried, there is greater unanimity regarding these procedures than there will be in specifying the correct quality of an original impact. It would be senseless to deny that the forms that result from our activities will not color the face of history.

Reverence for the past has seldom been based on an inviolate image. Our ancestors considered the casual altering of an earlier form both practical and permissible. Like a remodeled building, the palimpsest, the recut ivory, the regilded statue and the repainted picture merely continued what was functional or beloved or wonderous. Instances of almost total transformation were not uncommon. Sometimes these were due to hostility toward the immediate past, but more often were due to a preference for modernization. Authenticity as a serious aim was neither philosophically evaluated nor lucrative. The restorer was the person employed to make an old item last longer. He concealed damages in tune with the tastes of his time without regard to original style, and often without regard to original composition. Until the late 19th century, few people disapproved of such an approach so long as the work complied with current interpretations.

The primary demand in restorations was a return to completeness. Except in periods of romanticism, which, after all, had their own methods for transformation, this held true throughout the centuries. No other fabrications appear to have suffered more from this prejudice for completeness than architecture and paintings. It is the special nature of a painting to be exposed to view. Exposure made paintings, like buildings, vulnerable to ravages from the environment and from the hands of man. Whereas sculpture is a three-dimensional actuality that retains its actuality even when a part is lost, buildings and paintings are two-dimensional compositions of three-dimensional structure that lose their impact as entities when voids occur. Why this is can be argued, but not dismissed. The *Venus di Milo* is acceptable without arms; the *Mona Lisa* with a great hole would not be tenable nor would the Lincoln Memorial. In certain forms of creative art, disruptions are too disturbing to viewers. If we combine this characteristic of human response with the long-term complacency toward surface alterations as the legitimate method for concealing damage, we can understand why restoration was deemed the art of disguise.

Semantics add to our difficulties. For many of us, the word *restoration* is synonymous with alteration and is a term that has acquired a derogatory flavor. It is foolhardy to take offense to a word that we happily claim for our personal state after the benefits of a fine vacation. Discredit associated with the title of restorer stems from our 20th-century concept that what is preserved should serve as a historical witness. It is as unfair for us to refute the labors of our predecessors in restorations as it will be for our descendants to damn ours for prolonging images that they may interpret offensively. As Sir Kenneth Clark points out in his television series on civilization, historical judgments are tricky. The truth is still circumscribed. We may not presume to establish absolutes.

The painter Eugène Delacroix is credited with saying that each pretended restoration is a hundred times more regrettable than the ravages of time because it gives us not a restored original, but *another* painting. Unless it be placed in a permanently static atmosphere, no painting—nor for that matter any other created form—whether recent or ancient, escapes constant change from the moment it leaves the hands of its creator. What we may claim today are facilities that enable us to approximate more closel· the birth images compatible with the thinking of our time. We can scientifically record degradation and remains; we can photographically document for the future what we inherited and how we presume to alter it for survival. Call us *conservators* if the word suggests the improvement in our capabilities, as well as the broadening of our field's scope, to confront the weighty problems of maintenance. Hazards of survival for all matter now assume mountainous proportions. Our world has added to the forces of uncivilized nature mechanical vibrations on, above and below the earth's surface, artificial light and heat and deadly pollutants. To restore anything is no mean task.

We think of ourselves as the medical end of the art world. The analogy is valid. When medicine emerged from its cloaks of secrecy and myth to become a profession, it commenced to amass a body of shared knowledge founded on experience, experiments and observations. With persistent research came innovations that honed the application of skills. The rise of universities devoted to the training of doctors assured that the hoard of information became part of a requisite background for succeeding generations of practitioners. This has provided society with a reliable standard for optimum medical performance. To a far lesser degree, both in length of time and in quantity of personnel, conservators have paralleled and are paralleling this development.

Most restorers in past centuries were artists who were otherwise incompetent to earn a living. Here and there, a few great masters would touch up their own and the works of others with the inevitable embellishments that creative genius is never able to suppress. As a rule, though, it remained for those not gifted enough to execute acceptable work to be paid pittances for abusing and embalming the productions of their betters. Case histories of famous art, extant and lost within memory, are replete with horror stories of the criminally destructive treatments inflicted on them in the name of preservation. Many a great work that we have inherited is sadly no more than a corpse decked by the ghostly mockery of its assassin's hand. We may take pride in our revulsion to these blatant malpractices. They were condoned partly because they did not offend majority opinion and partly because they were the only performances possible from the indifferent efforts of an untutored and unhonored category of worker.

The idea of training is to profit from the lessons learned by others. The idea that training is necessary to perform restoration is not unique to our time, but general consensus that it should be required for competent practice is a recent innovation. Only a little more than a decade ago, there was no formal academic schooling available in the United States where a student could acquire an education in the conservation of historic and artistic works. Today there are only three such institutions: New York University's Conservation Center, a five-year course accepting four to five students annually; the program of the Intermuseum Conservation Association at Oberlin, Ohio, which accepts three students a year for its three-year course; and the conservation training school of the Cooperstown Graduate Programs, where ten students are admitted yearly to a three-year course. All these are postgraduate curriculums with prerequisites in science, art history and manual dexterity. From their instructions, we may anticipate a limited number of professionally competent conservators, a hard-won, valuable change in attitude toward the status of the restorer.

Before we unduly inflate our egos for the wisdom of our time, let us note that almost 200 years ago a group of specially trained practitioners existed who for 20 years performed comprehensive restorations on the pictorial treasures of Venice until the end of that republic. In the forthcoming publication of the Edwards manuscripts,[1] four points of consideration are outlined for the establishment of a public school of restoration (in this case, within the Academy of Fine Arts in Venice) which could constitute a sound basis for any of our current funding appeals. These are (1) the need for such a school, (2) the theoretical and practical instructions to be offered, (3) the formal structure of the new institution and (4) the cost of this institution.

Freely transcribed from the almost illegible Italian script are precise statements that we could employ verbatim. Edwards held that a painting restorer need not possess the genius of a great artist nor his creative imagination, but before a youth passed into the workshop, he must have mastered the study of fabrication techniques and acquired skill in these techniques. Once admitted, the trainee should, with the instruction, supervision and example of an experienced professor of this art, begin to practice various restoration tasks, know the variety of solvents and their required degrees of concentration and learn that great diligence is essential for the decisive success of a restoration! Edwards' attitude of mind, his concern for optimum execution stands forth as dedicated as our own. He made preliminary examinations, studied deterioration, identified materials and kept voluminous records (fig. 1). One of his most endearing comments on the subject of paintings was to the effect that their natural substances consist of complex heterogenous elements artificially held together contrary to their natural affinities, a deduction on the behavior of artistic works in almost any field continually frustrating to his contemporary colleagues. Although Edwards could hardly foresee the nightmares we face in problems of maintenance, it was his emphasis on the excessive deterioration suffered by paintings within the atmosphere of Venice, so humid and filled with salts, that impelled the old Venetian Senate to issue its Decree of September 3, 1778, ordering their great public undertaking in preservation.

We could use more like him today.

No, we cannot pride ourselves on unique superiority. We may boast the wealth of advantages supplied us by the Industrial Revolution and the progress of science. We may be justified in feeling there is a wider persuasion, spotty but spreading to the corners of our planet, that the preservation of cultural heritage is vital to social welfare. We had best think of ourselves as Edwards thought of himself, as temporary custodians of what is consigned to our care for its survival. If there are more of us on his side after 200 years, we have greater need of each other to cope with our increased problems.

Sommario di tutti li pagamenti fatti dalla sud.ª Cassa in anni undici all'Ispettore dei ristauro generale delle più d'Itture, giusto a Decr. dell'Eccmo Senato 3 Settembre 1778.

La prima Colonna nota le Date delle Fedi consegnate dal Eccmo Senº 1º del Gº dietro le quali vengono corrisposte li pagamenti.

2ª 3ª 4ª Colonna, dimostrano il numero di Piedi gº di lavoro corrispondente alle tre Classi diverse, nelle quali dev'esser diviso il lavoro medesimo

5ª Colonna dimostra i rilasci fatti alla sud.ª Cassa in sconto delle prestanze

6ª Colonna dimostra li pagamenti netti dai sud.i rilasci

In fine si trovano dichiarate le partite di denaro compreso nelle Fedi segnate con asterisco * in margine della prima Colonna, il qual denaro non appartiene al Contratto del suo ristauro ma riguarda oggetti separati da esso

N.B. Essendosi creduto che fosse meglio indicare li rotti di piede quadro col numero delle oncie quadre che risultano in ogni moltiplicazione, invece di segnarle nel solito modo che rappresentagli stessi rotti con qualche improprietà d'espressione, si avverte che le somme dei rotti va divisa per 144 perchè oncie 144 quadre fanno un Piede quadrato

Data delle Fedi	Lavori di 1ª Classe		Lavori della 2ª Classe		Lavori della 3ª Classe		Rilasci alla Cassa pub.ª		Contanti netti dai rilasci	
	Piedi	oncie	Piedi	oncie	Piedi	oncie	Effettivi	grossi	Effettivi	grossi
22 Xbre 1778	76	72	137	—	76	48			651	22
23 Mar 1779	133	58	58	70	119	6			709	22
7 Giug	318				279				1372	18
27 Agos	202	113	102	13	29	108			451	11
4 Ott	149	120	118	104	53	72			832	20
19 Xbre 15 Mar 1780	158	75	89	—	51	72			1653	1
24 Ag	53	97	235	139	38	22			747	
8 Giug	119	24	101	23	111	69			752	7
28 Ag	142	19	41	14	99	65			755	12
23 7bre	134	4	97	12	75	70			733	18
22 9bre	247	129	39	39					832	1
29 Xbre	74	120	99	6	29	36			491	6
17 Feb	152	8							456	4
10 Ap 1781	178	49	102	72	11	129			802	5
12 Giug	251	80	93	16	11	120			981	22
26 7bre	375	48	64	102	45	124			1349	9
20 Xbre	25	104	346	88	44	100			924	1
23 Feon			338	110					762	5
26 Mar 1782			255	2					573	18
6 Giug	330	8							990	5
14 7bre	191	125	255	132	129	56			1343	20
18 8bre	203	117	230	125	147	97			1412	9
20 Feb	47	81	126	27	170	28			647	21
10 Ap 1783	203	92	47	74					807	18
11 Giug	99	60	84	89	265	125			887	2
2 Ott	239	34	297	41	330	132			1912	23
19 Xbre	203	2			98	73			756	16
14 Feb	362	1	102	13					1315	15
7 Giug 1784	306	110	90	137					1135	1
28 Ag	181	69			204	123			669	17
12 Gen	354	33	155	62	39	9			1471	
10 Mar 1785	275	101							827	1
2 Giug	360	3	90	17	93				1598	8
	6458	126	3874	72	2532	77			32281	2

Segue

Few classifications of historic and artistic works present the same contexts, purposes, preservation requirements or have identical responses to the environments in which we expect them to last. Not everyone may feel convinced that prolonging the existence of an image is requisite for his special use of it. Archaeologists are not always concerned with what happens to the materials they extricate, once they have rung from the bones every scrap of relevant information. Neither the resultant rubble at some digs nor the preservation of the uncovered finds are necessarily important to archaeological research. Historians and collectors would be better served if every archaeological expedition included in its membership at least one well-trained conservator. The change from an enveloping subsurface to an atmospheric exposure can be violent and its effects on vulnerable materials disastrous. Repeatedly, the uncontrolled methods employed to permit immediate viewing of encrusted finishes and designs have inflicted tragic loss; impatient haste has destroyed many retrieved objects. Admittedly, postponing detailed examination until such can be arranged within an often-distant laboratory to provide minimum degrading reaction for delicate treasures would cost time and money. However, such a procedure would permit initial observations to be enjoyed by other scholars and would take into account the fact that the impact of actual remains is not separable from physical components. If the archaeologist could curtail his personal drive for instant knowledge, this generosity would allow his colleagues in other professions to study his discoveries at optimum state. We do need each other.

Artifacts housed in collections are seldom destined for use. The rare procelains, furniture, even rugs and costumes in museums are not intended to function as they once may have any more than the altarpieces that are displayed in dank surroundings lighted by smoking tapers. Discussions continue as to whether any museum rarities should even be touched by the public. The concept of pres-

FIGURE 1. *Summary of all payments made during 11 years by the Public Treasury to the director of the General Restoration of Public Paintings Program, which was established by the Senatorial Decree of September 3, 1778. The first column gives the dates on which the accounts were submitted to the treasurer for payment. The second, third and fourth columns give the number of square feet of paintings treated, divided into three categories (determined by the condition of the works and the need for restoration). (The fractions of square feet are designated in square inches, 144 square inches = 1 square foot.) The fifth column indicates the amount of discount allowed the Public Treasury for its services. The sixth column shows the net cost. Those entries designated by an asterisk were not included in the program of restoration established by the decree but were treated anyway. (From the Edwards Papers, Accademi di Belle Arti, Venice)*

31

ervation consistently applied to museum materials, which are kept in varying ranges of miniclimates, is to do nothing in your efforts to preserve that may not easily be undone or redone. The dictum of reversibility for treatments is viable and justified under the given circumstances. Nothing lasts forever, not even repairs; they wear out, too. The philosophy in this approach guarantees the ease with which future conservators may repeat or alter our preservation work with minimal hazard to the remains of the original. It also bows to the art historian to whom the museum conservator remains subservient. Scientific facilities may dictate what can be adjudged as superfluous and may advisedly be removed from an original artifact, but scholarly opinion will determine the eventual appearance to be exhibited. Scholars have been known to change their views. The conservator may produce and interpret evidence of physical alterations, but the final decision on the desired impact of an image in a museum collection rests with the art historian.

The museum conservator can often diminish the speed of material deterioration by planning the control of destructive agents within a building environment. Light, relative humidity, air pollution and vandalism have feasible, if expensive, systems for their regulation. With the assistance of engineers, administrators and lawyers, these may be effectively applied. However, this is not so with outdoor displays, whether totem poles or obelisks, industrial equipment or vehicles, log cabins or the residences of Presidents. Here, the cherished principle of reversibility plays second fiddle to the need to defend against attacks from a belligerent environment and population. Methods for preservation of this category of artifact are forced to compromise with even our concept of proper impact. The integrity of the created image, so righteously governing the museum practitioner, cannot be accorded the same importance in the face of uncontrollable conditions for exhibition. Adjustments are necessary.

Nothing we attempt to preserve is hampered by more stringent regulations than old buildings. A building, ancient or contemporary, selected for long-term survival must either house some appropriate activity of a local group or function as a museum itself. However alien to its original impact within our crowded quarters, traffic and encompassing pressures, the form this prolongation will assume will be determined by the legal restrictions for human security. Originally, a building may have been surrounded by lawns and trees; warmed by fireplaces; illuminated with candles; its timbers, walls and roof fashioned in combustible wood; and accommodated with no more than an adjacent outhouse. Unavoidable for our society are the established standards of building codes, zoning, fire prevention, sanitation and provisions for bodily comfort. Area laws can be neither ignored nor bypassed. The consolidation of structure; the installation of plumbing, heating and artificial illumination; and provisions for occupancy will impose alterations inevitably influencing the appearance, inside and out, of any preserved edifice. Compromise between the original image and the preserved form it is forced to assume is an obvious necessity.

The ways in which we elect to preserve our separate specialties of interest are peculiar to their unique differences. If we can admit the diversity of demands we face and agree to disagree on applications of theory and practice, we can profit from sharing many portions of our expertise. Limited as we are, museum conservators can offer four main services: We are competent to determine the physical condition of collected items and what is involved for their remedial care and upkeep; we are knowledgeable to advise on whether an artifact is what it purports to be; we are useful consultants on the security for interior displays; the answers we supply on estimates of damage, cost and feasibility of repair for the items in our field are apt to be accurate. Our interpretation of the behavior of materials tends to be limited to the climatic confines in which we operate and inappropriate for those in which we have little experience. There are unknown factors everywhere. The exchange of information, however seemingly slight in its importance, might save colleagues in preservation the expense and time of exploring byways already mapped. To fail to invite help from one another is too costly for our common aim.

Giorgio Cavaglieri holds that "old buildings need a lot of new love."[2] So do all old forms, whether animate or inanimate. Our concern for what has lasted and for what we hope to have last longer is the same as that expressed by Edwards toward the paintings in 18th-century Venice and as that expressed today by the Rome Centre's vast embrace of universally valued inheritance. Only the adjective *new* differentiates the efforts of our generations. For us, *new* comprises our increased proficiencies to battle with our added difficulties. Accepting the good with the bad, if we can cooperate each with the other, we may be able to execute the best preservation possible within the confines of our human potential and the concepts of our period in time.

NOTES

1. Bettina Raphael, "Edwards Manuscripts," unpublished research done on Smithsonian-Rome Centre grant, Cooperstown Graduate Programs, Cooperstown, N. Y., 1971.

2. Giorgio Cavaglieri, president of the New York Chapter of AIA, in an address to technical personnel of the Port of New York Authority and the South Street Seaport Planning Conference, July 1970.

THE ROLE OF THE ARCHAEOLOGIST IN THE CONSERVATION-PRESERVATION PROCESS

STANLEY SOUTH

As interest in the conservation, preservation and interpretation of historic sites and structures continues to increase, there is a growing awareness of the need for archaeological research in addition to traditional historical documentation. Preservationists, in their efforts to perpetuate historical heritage through physical remains that have survived, are looking to the documentation lying beneath the earth's surface to provide evidence not obtainable from written documents. Historians and architects now look to the archaeological record for specific architectural and historical clues in the form of structural and artifactual details. Anthropologists examine archaeological data for cultural patterns and reconstruct the cultural processes represented by artifacts in a more rigorously scientific manner than ever before. As a result of this heightened awareness of the importance of archaeology, there is an increasing emphasis on the complete examination of the total architectural, historical and archaeological documentation of historic properties, which is necessary to insure proper execution of the conservation-preservation process.

EDUCATION OF THE ARCHAEOLOGIST

With this growing demand for archaeological services has come the need for increased educational opportunities in the field of archaeology. Traditionally, classical archaeology has been taught

Stanley South is an archaeologist in the Division of Advanced Studies and Research of the Institute of Archeology and Anthropology at the University of South Carolina, Columbia, S.C.

by classics departments and the archaeology of early man by anthropology departments. Most American archaeologists have received their training in anthropology departments, but more recently, an interest in historical archaeology has been one factor in the establishment of American studies programs, and many history departments now offer courses in historical archaeology. Summer field schools and workshops are being offered with greater frequency to answer the increasing demand for archaeologists competent to deal with sites on both prehistoric and historic levels.

There are also several organizations that offer archaeologists the opportunity for professional association with colleagues and valuable publications. The Society for American Archaeology, which publishes *American Antiquity*, is the primary American professional organization devoted to American archaeology of the prehistoric period. The Archaeological Institute of America publishes articles on the antiquity of the world in its journal, *Archaeology*. In 1960, the Conference on Historic Site Archaeology was founded to publish papers by archaeologists dealing with historic sites. Papers from the conferences of this organization are published annually as *The Conference on Historical Site Archaeology Papers*. In 1967, the Society for Historic Archaeology was founded, and this organization publishes the journal *Historical Archaeology*.

WHAT ARCHAEOLOGICAL INVESTIGATION CAN REVEAL

Although the contribution of archaeology to nontechnological areas of historic preservation is limited, archaeological investigation can yield certain types of specific information concerning particular sites, such as details of architectural features, the exact locations of and temporal relationships among these features and an idea of their uses.

Archaeological excavation of shops and industrial waste sites can greatly increase understanding of the technology of particular crafts at various periods. The waste-casting sprues and fragments of castings from a brass foundry or a silversmith's shop or the kiln waster dump of a potter's shop are valuable repositories of information concerning the evolution of these technologies. Such sites containing valuable data gain attention because of their value to the archaeologist. These are sites that an archaeologist can "get his teeth into," as well as his trowel, because the artifacts they contain lend themselves to quantification and stratigraphic analysis, in addition to being important "time capsules" containing artifacts from specific time periods.

Other sites do not yield positive results in such a dramatic way. For instance, maps and records relating to Bethabara, an 18th-century Moravian settlement in North Carolina, revealed the location of the gunsmith's shop, brothers' house, blacksmith's shop, millwright's house, tailor shop, *Gemein Haus* (church), apothecary shop, doctor's laboratory and pottery shop. With the exception of the pottery shop's ruins, the excavation of this entire site did not yield a single clue that was sufficient to allow the archaeologist to arrive at a proper interpretation of the uses of these structures. This would be a somewhat dismal record for archaeological recovery, were there not other questions of interest in addition to the limited one involving the specific function a particular structure served within its community.

The total excavation of a site is not always necessary to obtain important information. Architectural details, such as walkways, doorways, outbuildings and drainage systems, and landscaping can be determined by excavating around standing structures, as well as by examining subsurface remains of ruins. The work done at the Paca House in Annapolis, Md., is an example of what an integrated team of research specialists in history, landscaping, architecture and archaeology can contribute to the conservation–preservation–restoration–interpretation process. Here, under the direction of Historic Annapolis, Inc., these specialists worked together to achieve mutual goals of restoring and interpreting the house and gardens of William Paca, a signer of the Declaration of Independence.

One of the primary questions archaeological research can answer for preservationists concerns the temporal relationships among the various occupations of a historic site. Some studies made of artifacts recovered from archaeological sites emphasize the association of certain artifact types with particular individuals or structures. This emphasis frequently occurs in research conducted for restoration purposes, which often focuses on a historic figure associated with a site. Another, broader type of study reflects the archaeologist's interest in establishing general temporal and spatial relationships among artifacts. This latter approach is valuable for interpretations of archaeological excavations that are primarily concerned with a broad level of interpretation, rather than with information concerning specific individuals or sites. The first type of analysis, in its concern with specifics, tends to be historical in its focus, whereas the second is more closely related to science.

The scientific approach was taken in a recent study of ceramics recovered from 18th-century British-American sites in which a mathematical formula was used to determine a mean date for the samples. The data were compared with the known period of occupation of the site, and in many cases, they corresponded remarkably well with the known median occupation date.[1] The success of the application of a mathematical formula to archaeological data is explained in this case in terms of the horizon concept, which postulates a broad and rapid spread of ceramics from British sources during the 18th century.[2] Similar studies involving a statistical treatment of archaeological data are being undertaken with increasing frequency to expand and test data recovery from historic sites and to construct hypotheses for use in examining cultural processes.

NEW CHALLENGES AND EXPANDING RESPONSIBILITIES

Bones, seeds, pollen and cysts caused by human and animal parasites, all of which may be recovered from garbage dumps, privies and cesspools, have just begun to reveal data through archaeological recovery and analysis. Social scientists have a growing interest in questions concerning past social and health conditions, disease, human parasites, diet, and sources and availablity of food in relation to the ecology of an area, as revealed through archaeological investigation and correlated with historical references. By meeting this challenge, archaeologists are making possible a more penetrating view of past patterns of human behavior than has previously been possible through the use of traditional archaeological materials and techniques.

The archaeologist has an expanding responsibility to go beyond limited inquiries that seek merely to validate a historic site through the correlation of archaeological findings with documentary evidence, to list the presence or absence of artifact types for the purpose of establishing the temporal position of a site, to reveal architectural features for the purpose of reconstruction and restoration, to exhibit ruins for the entertainment of visitors to historic sites or to recover and preserve relics from the past for the purpose of hoarding them in repositories and museums. His view must be as broad as the questions being asked by archaeologists, sociologists, anthropologists, ecologists, biologists, archaeoparasitologists and other scientists, who are turning to archaeology for help with special problems in their spheres of interest. However, although the scope of archaeology is broadening, its primary emphasis will continue to be on material culture, because much basic research in typology and stratigraphy is still needed to determine the temporal positions of artifacts found on historic sites and to arrive at a better definition and understanding of these artifacts.

This discussion has emphasized the broad role and goals of archaeology in the conservation-preservation process. These goals prevail regardless of the limited objectives often motivating the sponsors of archaeological research, who are usually interested in:

1. the validation of a historic site in relation to documents
2. the discovery of architectural features
3. the determination of the occupation sequence of the site
4. the determination of the temporal occupation of the site
5. the recovery and preservation of artifacts associated with the occupation of the site
6. the development of the site as a historical exhibit

These limited objectives are oriented toward restoration, reconstruction, exhibition of ruins for public viewing or acquisition of relics for exhibit purposes. The archaeologist must play a major role in these activities if he is to fulfill his responsibility to the historic site he has researched. His report and suggestions, in the form of site development guidelines, combined with the historical and architectural documentation form the foundation for the development and interpretation of the historic site.

PROMOTING ACCURACY IN PRESERVATION PROJECTS

An important function of the archaeologist is to make the public aware of the importance of historic preservation.[3] An archaeologist who finds that an archaeological document he has prepared to describe a historic property does not coincide with the preconceived plans of sponsors of the research may come into conflict with the sponsoring group. For example, to remain true to archaeological data revealing foundations for brick structures, he may have to fight to keep "typical" log cabins from being moved onto a site. If he disdains such involvement and limits his contribution strictly to an archaeological report, he is not completely fulfilling his role in the conservation-preservation process.

Preservationists should strive to achieve the greatest possible degree of accuracy in historical, architectural and archaeological research in order to insure the closest possible correlation between the reality of the past and contemporary explanatory exhibits. Historic structures and sites can create a greater appreciation of one's heritage. Those who have the responsibility for shaping attitudes of and providing an understanding of the past to present and future generations should be aware that it is only through what is done today—in the planning, development and interpretation of historic sites—that the future can know the past. If researchers and developers of historic sites, in their enthusiasm or in the name of "history" and "restoration," damage, destroy or distort surviving clues, rather than interpret them competently, they will have destroyed the truth, and future interpretations of history will be based not on the true evidence, but on their misleading interpretations. These researchers and developers are the only people who have the opportunity to observe the complete historical, architectural and archaeological evidence. This latter type of evidence can be recovered from the earth only once, because the archaeological process is destructive, erasing as it reveals. There is no second chance.

Preservationists should guard against the kind of impulsive planning and development represented by the "log-cabin syndrome," that is, the removal of log cabins from the countryside to quickly constructed pseudohistorical towns, regardless of the historical focus or the archaeological merit that the sites might otherwise possess. The minds of children and unsuspecting adults are shaped by such distortions, which emerge as full-blown creations of the current age, with little relation to the past as it is revealed through research and archaeology.

Preservationists should also guard against the pitfalls of creating "instant history," that is, historical reconstructions insufficiently related to the heritage of people, their possessions and the historic sites associated with them. Those who construct explanatory exhibits in the form of parapets and palisades, ruins and cabins and who erect restorations and reconstructions of historic sites should be constantly aware that they are creating historical images that will leave lasting impressions in many minds. If the buildings reconstructed today are not based on careful research, they will eventually have to be replaced by more accurate representations, and in the meantime, they will have given a false image to all who have viewed them.

THE ARCHAEOLOGIST AS A CONSERVATOR

In addition to the responsibility for discovering and interpreting archaeological data and for insisting upon accuracy in preservation projects, the archaeologist must often also be a scientist-conservator. While in the field, he may have to face the same conservation-preservation problems regarding archaeologically recovered artifacts as does the conservator working in the laboratory. And, when the archaeological program does not include the services of a staff conservator, the field archaeologist is required to perform necessary treatment or to stabilize the object so that is can be examined and treated later. The following discussion relates some of the unique conservation challenges that face the archaeologist working in the field and the new techniques being used to meet these challenges.

The field archaeologist can ruin data of value to the conservator through careless or uninformed handling of archaeological materials. For instance, the entire pattern on an overglazed, enameled porcelain fragment taken from wet earth can be removed in an instant by an uninformed worker who "cleans" the soil from the sherd with his thumb. Similarly, when a delft-bowl fragment is removed from damp soil, the entire tin-enameled glaze sometimes separates from the sherd body as the sherd is lifted. In such cases, steps must be taken immediately to bond the glaze to the body of the sherd to allow the piece to be removed intact for later restoration. Some tinned sheet iron is so delicate and has so decayed in the earth that steps must be taken immediately to bond the object's piecrust-type flakes to strengthen it for removal to the laboratory for further treatment and preservation.[4] There are many similar examples of the need for care in the field.

The value of such care is obvious. The architect working on a preservation project is aided in restoration studies by the archaeological recovery of plaster and paint from ruins and by the recovery of iron hardware. From archaeological fragments, the restorationist concerned with furnishings can derive a wealth of information regarding the ceramic and glassware furnishings of a structure.

Some archaeological data, such as posthole, postmold and pit outlines, are of such a delicate nature that previously they could only be recorded, photographed and excavated. Today, however, the use of polyurethane and fiber-glass resin has made it possible to lift the profiles of archaeological features directly from the earth and carry them to a museum for exhibit purposes or to a classroom for use as teaching aids, permitting students to practice drawing true soil profiles before going into the field.[5]

Delicate burned features, such as pits full of corncobs, can be successfully removed intact from the field by excavating around the pit and placing it on a supporting framework after impregnating the carefully cleaned cobs with polyurethane resin and also soaking the soil matrix with resin. Similar techniques, using various impregnating-solidifying solutions, have long been used by archaeologists to remove delicate objects from a field matrix, particularly to remove skeletal material. However, the archaeologist must decide in advance whether he desires to obtain a radiocarbon date, since use of such solutions will render items useless for obtaining radiocarbon dates. This caution also applies to laboratory conservators, who can easily contaminate samples by careless or uninformed cleaning, treatment or storage of archaeological materials that may eventually need to be dated through radiocarbon or other analysis.

If a well or a feature below water is excavated, artifacts made of wood, leather and cloth and other usually perishable objects will often be recovered intact. In such situations, the archaeologist and the conservator are confronted with many preservation problems, both in the field and in the laboratory. Underwater archaeology presents an entire complex of preservation problems that must be solved before recovered items can become part of an interpretive exhibit. It is especially important in programs dealing with underwater sites that sufficient funding be arranged before the work begins to provide for the proper recovery and preservation of important objects.

CONCLUSION

The role of the archaeologist in the conservation-preservation process is a broad one, involving, in addition to the preparation of the archaeological document, active participation in master planning; basic historical, architectural and artifact research; scientific analysis; artifact preservation; and development and interpretation of the historic site. It is no longer expected, however, that a single individual will handle all of these aspects. Rather, the archaeologist, architect, restoration specialist, administrator, historian and conservator, as well as the contractor, now work together on many projects to achieve the same goal: "To preserve the physical remains of our past and to employ them in perpetuating our historical heritage."[6]

NOTES

1. Stanley South, "Evolution and Horizon as Revealed in Ceramic Analysis in Historical Archeology," in *The Conference on Historic Site Archaeology Papers, 1971*, ed. Stanley South, vol. 6 (Columbia: University of South Carolina, Institute of Archeology and Anthropology, 1972), pp. 71–116.

2. Gordon R. Willey and Philip Phillips, *Method and Theory in American Archaeology* (Chicago: University of Chicago Press, 1958), pp. 31–34.

3. J. C. Harrington, *Archeology and the Historical Society* (Nashville, Tenn.: American Association for State and Local History, 1965), p. 8.

4. Stanley South, "Excavating the Fortified Area of the 1670 Site of Charles Towne, South Carolina," in *The Conference on Historic Site Archaeology Papers, 1969*, ed. Stanley South, vol. 4 (Columbia: University of South Carolina, Institute of Archeology and Anthropology, 1971), pp. 37–60.

5. Stanley South," "A Method of Removing Soil Profiles," in *Notebook 2* (Columbia: University of South Carolina, Institute of Archeology and Anthropology, 1970), pp. 3–7.

6. Harrington, *Archeology*, p. 8.

42

BIBLIOGRAPHY

Harrington, J. C. *Archeology and the Historical Society*. Nashville, Tenn.: American Association for State and Local History, 1965.

South, Stanley. "Excavating the 18th Century Moravian Town of Bethabara, North Carolina." *The Florida Anthropologist* 18, no. 3, pt. 2 (1965): 45–60.

——————. *The Paca House, Annapolis, Maryland*. Alexandria, Va.: Contract Archaeology, Inc., 1967.

——————. "Wanted! An Historical Archaeologist." *Historical Archaeology* 3 (1969): 75–84.

——————. "Restoration Archeology at the Paca House, Annapolis, Maryland." Paper read at the 6th Annual Pennsbury Manor Americana Forum, September 25, 1970, in Morrisville, Pa.

——————. "A Method of Removing Soil Profiles." In *Notebook 2*, pp. 3–7. Columbia: University of South Carolina, Institute of Archeology and Anthropology, 1970.

——————. "What Archeology Can Do To Expand Historical Research." In *The Conference on Historic Site Archaeology Papers, 1968*, edited by Stanley South, vol. 3, pp. 50–57. Columbia: University of South Carolina, Institute of Archeology and Anthropology, 1970.

——————. "Excavating the Fortified Area of the 1670 Site of Charles Towne, South Carolina." In *The Conference on Historic Site Archaeology Papers, 1969*, edited by Stanley South, vol. 4, pp. 37–60. Columbia: University of South Carolina, Institute of Archeology and Anthropology, 1971.

——————. "The Historical Archeologist and Historic Site Development." In *The Conference on Historic Site Archaeology Papers, 1970*, edited by Stanley South, vol. 5, pp. 90–113. Columbia: University of South Carolina, Institute of Archeology and Anthropology, 1971.

——————. "Evolution and Horizon as Revealed in Ceramic Analysis in Historical Archeology." In *The Conference on Historic Site Archaeology Papers, 1971*, edited by Stanley South, vol. 6, pp. 71–116. Columbia: University of South Carolina, Institute of Archeology and Anthropology, 1972.

Willey, Gordon R., and Phillips, Philip. *Method and Theory in American Archaeology*. Chicago: University of Chicago Press, 1958.

ADMINISTRATIVE, LEGAL AND CITY PLANNING ASPECTS OF HISTORIC PRESERVATION PROGRAMS

HARMON H. GOLDSTONE, FAIA

Many different disciplines are involved in the conservation and restoration of old buildings. Skills required for this work are varied, ranging through the arts and sciences and including both professions and crafts. Most of these skills are highly specialized and require academic training.

It was originally proposed that this paper discuss the roles of three types of specialist involved in the conservation–preservation process — the administrator, the lawyer and the city planner — and explain the relationship of their roles to those of the other professionals to be discussed at this conference. I would like to change the emphasis, however, and describe instead the administrative, legal and city planning needs of a conservation–preservation program. Whether these needs are met by one or more individuals, who may or may not be specially trained in administration, law or city planning, will depend on circumstances. Moreover, the responsibilities of administrators, lawyers and city planners often overlap. The needs are there; how and by whom the needs are met is of secondary importance.

THE VALUE OF "NONPRESERVATION" PROFESSIONALS

It is my firm conviction that individuals with some combination of general legal, planning and administrative skills have an impor-

Harmon H. Goldstone, FAIA, is chairman of the New York City Landmarks Preservation Commission.

tant role in conservation–preservation programs. These individuals' participation is crucial if the special skills of preservation professionals are to be truly effective. The inclusion of such individuals is especially important in urban preservation programs, where the truly decisive factors in saving old buildings are more apt to lie in the political, legal and economic arena rather than in the field of specialized preservation technologies.

Individuals who can meet administrative, legal or city planning needs of a conservation–preservation program are best equipped to coordinate the efforts of the program's preservation professionals. In addition, they can bridge the gap between the world of the scholar–scientist and the hard, cruel world outside. Without such a bridge, even the most capable staff of preservation professionals is apt to fail.

WHY LANDMARKS ARE LOST

The question of why landmarks are lost should be asked at the outset. Why are fine old buildings torn down? Why are they allowed to decay so that they have to be torn down? Or why, as often happens, are they "modernized" in such a fashion that one wishes they had been torn down?

These are hard questions that cannot be dismissed lightly. It may be comforting to imagine that some malign fate, some diabolical plot, is working against efforts to preserve our architectural heritage. But such comforting fancies do not save buildings. The facts are real and, if buildings are to be saved, the facts must be squarely faced.

First, preservationists must accept certain inexorable realities. Buildings, like people, grow old. The repair or deferred maintenance of an old building is usually expensive. The uses for which a structure was originally designed can become obsolete. The people who originally used a building may die or move away. Fashions change. Urgent new needs compete for limited amounts of land. And most people like to make money; in particular, they expect a fair return on their investments. There is nothing inherently evil about any of these facts. They are simply the inescapable elements of a very real problem. No amount of hopeful thinking can wish them away.

In addition, there are the factors of ignorance, indifference and inertia to be faced. Many people know little about architecture or history; of those who do know something, most are preoccupied with other concerns. Of the few who both know and are concerned, a great number, unfortunately, feel that circumstances are so unfavorable for preservation that the loss of old buildings is inevitable.

The primary responsibility of those who deal with a preservation project's administrative, legal and city planning needs is to deal with these realities. In discussing this responsibility, I am limited to my own experience in New York City, because that is the only place where I have worked and its problems are the only ones I know on a first-hand basis; however, it would be surprising if the same problems, although perhaps in differing degrees, do not also exist in other cities. New York is, after all, a composite of five boroughs. The Bronx, Brooklyn, Manhattan, Queens and Staten Island probably vary as much in geography, history, culture and economics as any five cities picked at random. And New York City, as a whole, has a long-established and unenviable record of tearing itself apart. Years ago, Walt Whitman referred to the "pull-down-and-build-over-again spirit" of the city. If landmarks preservation can succeed in New York, it ought to be successful anywhere.

CREATING A LANDMARKS PRESERVATION COMMISSION

Since landmarks are lost by forces at work in the public domain, it follows that the battle to save them must be fought in the public arena. To be truly effective, a landmarks preservation commission must be a public body. It must be an integral part of the government within which it has to work.

Private organizations can and do perform an invaluable service in educating the public, in political lobbying, in training technicians and in building a constituency. They are, in fact, the most effective of all voices in attempting to reverse the forces of ignorance, indifference and inertia. They are much freer in what they can do and say than any public body, supported by public funds, can afford to be. They are also effective in keeping official representatives on their toes; however, in the day-to-day battles of landmarks designation and enforcement of a landmarks law, of attack and defense, no private body can compete with the effectiveness of an officially constituted component of government. No private body — except one organized on an ad hoc basis, working from crisis to crisis — can marshal the various government agencies whose combined efforts are often needed to save a landmark.

There are times when a vociferous private protest can be valuable, even essential, in developing the sense of crisis that may be needed to force public action. At other times, a shrill and persistent clamor can defeat its own ends. A public body must remain balanced and fair, responsive but also responsible. It must try to reconcile the just claims not only of preservationists, but also of bankers, real estate operators, traffic engineers and the humble and usually silent taxpayer. It must never promise more than it can deliver. And it must do all this in a goldfish bowl of publicity, usually with an underpaid and overworked staff. As Fidel Castro recently remarked, in a rather wistful manner, "It is easier to wage guerilla warfare than to govern."

As soon as a public body, such as a landmarks preservation commission, is created, an administration is needed to operate it. It is necessary to organize an office in which the diverse talents of specialists can be effectively coordinated. Budgets must be prepared and fought for. Civil service requirements and union regulations must be coped with, but first they must be understood and accepted. The jealously guarded jurisdictions of other agencies must be learned and respected in order to win their respect and cooperation. Volunteer workers, who can provide invaluable assistance, must be recruited, trained, guided and kept interested in their assignments.

Meetings must be conducted and endless conferences attended. Above all, letters must be promptly answered and complaints promptly investigated. Press, radio and television representatives must be provided, on an impartial basis, with information of public interest. Media representatives are sophisticated and should be treated accordingly; no one is quicker than a good reporter to detect when questions are being evaded or to resent any attempt at exploitation.

To fulfill these responsibilities obviously requires administrative experience, and governmental experience is an added advantage. Operating a city agency is not the same as operating a business. Successful businessmen seldom care whether they are liked or not; politicians are not reelected if they are not liked.

The internal organization of a landmarks preservation office necessarily will vary from place to place, and it also will vary over time. If the experience of New York City's landmarks preservation office is any guide, the initial phase of the workload will be concentrated on archival research and documentation. During this period, a commission must decide what is worth saving and why. Then, as the inventory of designated landmarks grows, attention gradually will shift to enforcement procedures and the search for effective conservation and restoration techniques. Basic research, of course, never actually stops, but it becomes increasingly directed toward the case-by-case problems of particular buildings. In addition, the research staff must be ready to answer the wide variety of historical and architectural questions that come in from the general public.

Once established, a preservation commission has a continuing

48

need for legal services. Circumstances dictate whether these services should be provided by the chairman of the commission, a specially appointed member of the commission, a member of the staff, a member of the city's legal department or some combination of these. Landmarks legislation is a relatively new field, and, inevitably, landmark laws will be attacked in the courts. In making difficult decisions, a commission may also be well advised to seek legal advice. Furthermore, there is a need for meticulous compliance with all requirements of the law—that is, a need to publish notices of public hearings, to notify owners of proposed actions and to keep records and transcripts of official meetings and decisions.

Landmarks preservation laws are, in a broad sense, an extension of the powers that most American cities have enjoyed since 1916: to control their growth and development through zoning and planning legislation. In this sense, the preservation of urban landmarks and historic districts can be considered as an extension of the city planning process. Both types of law impose, in the public interest, certain restraints on the use of private property. In many cases, landmarks preservation commissions have, in fact, been set up as adjuncts to existing city planning commissions or even been completely integrated into them. The organizational advantages and disadvantages will doubtless vary from place to place. Whether administratively separate—as in New York City—or administratively united, however, the work of a landmarks preservation commission must be closely coordinated with the planning and zoning process if it is to be truly effective. Following are specific examples of how this interlocking action has worked in New York City.

THE NEW YORK CITY LANDMARKS PRESERVATION COMMISSION

The New York City Landmarks Preservation Commission was established in 1965 by an amendment to the New York City Charter[1] and it operates with the limitations and powers given it by chapter 8-A of the Administrative Code of the City of New York.[2] It took more than two years to draft what is familiarly known as the New York City Landmarks Preservation Law and to coordinate it with other local laws.

The city statute was, in turn, based on a piece of state enabling legislation commonly known as the Bard Act of 1956.[3] Because of this tie to the state law, the commission recently won an injunctive action against a state agency that was acting in conflict with the city statute.[4]

The New York City landmarks law has proved to be effective primarily because it is fair. It contains an equitable balance between public and private interests. No commission action is taken without a full public hearing in which those opposed and those in favor of the action may be heard. The law provides various rights and forms of relief to insure that a private property owner does not carry an unfair burden. It also specifies the steps and the time limitations for each move in the procedure specified for trying to reconcile the private interests of a property owner with the public interest which the commission was established to defend.

The law is also realistic. It recognizes that there are, and there probably always will be, cases in which no viable solution for the preservation of a landmark can be found, even with the best will on everybody's part. In such cases, the law permits the demolition of a landmark, but only after every possible alternative has been exhaustively explored.

This provision for demolition was initially attacked by preservationists on the grounds that it would weaken the whole law. Experience has shown, on the contrary, that this flexibility—this recognition that some cases present insuperable difficulties— actually strengthens the law. It is significant that, in the course of preserving some 360 individual landmarks, only one has been lost as a result of this provision.

Legal Strategy

It is important in establishing the validity of new laws and rulings that each favorable decision be used as a stepping stone to the next case.[5] The New York City Landmarks Preservation Commission has, on occasion, become involved in passionate disputes as to whether a door on a particular Federal-style house should have six or eight panels. Although such matters are quite rightly of critical importance to the architectural historian, it would be a strategic mistake for a commission to become involved in a lawsuit over them. Such involvement might succeed in preserving one door, but it equally well might mean the loss of the entire landmarks preservation law. On the other hand, the commission has been able to take a unanimous stand against powerful interests on matters of fundamental principle. The commission was fully aware of the long legal fight that might ensue when it denied Penn Central Railroad and a speculative developer the right to demolish the south facade of Grand Central Terminal or, alternatively, to build a 60–story skyscraper above the terminal, giving it the appearance of an elephant doing a handstand on a barrel. The issue is still before the courts; the ultimate outcome will affect landmarks legislation throughout the country.

City Planning Functions

Quite unexpectedly, New York City's landmarks law has proved to be a most effective device for the stabilization of residential neighborhoods, a surprise that has been recognized by the city administration. What began as the hobby of a handful of architectural antiquarians has turned into a potent tool that city planners envy.

When the landmarks law was first being drafted about 10 years ago, landmarks were thought of as beautiful or historic buildings. Almost as an afterthought, it was suggested that certain areas of the city, while not having the architectural or historical importance required for designation of an individual landmark, did, nevertheless, have a certain character that set them apart from their surroundings and that this character might well be worth preserving. At the time, it was thought that Greenwich Village, Brooklyn Heights and possibly one or two other areas might be designated as historic districts, and a provision for doing so was written into the statute. No one could have remotely foreseen that New York City would now have 18 officially designated historic districts, with a total of more than 6,000 individual properties under the jurisdiction of the Landmarks Preservation Commission.

The designation of an area as a historic district seems to give people living there a new pride in their neighborhood. They suddenly take an intense interest in seeing their surroundings preserved and improved. All sorts of cooperative community activities spring up. Young families—often headed by professionals and businessmen—give up their plans of moving to the suburbs and use their energies instead to renovate old row houses in the central city. These people are just the sort of active, productive citizens that the city is most anxious to retain.

The designation of individual landmarks has also had a social impact far wider than the architectural historians would ever have imagined. The man in the street has discovered that history and beauty are all around him—in all sorts of neighborhoods and right on the sidewalk. Appreciating architecture does not require a trip to a museum.

The preservation of certain individual landmarks, in the face of forces working toward their destruction, has presented the commission with some fascinating challenges. Each case is a story unto itself. Each solution has pointed the way to new techniques that often have wider applications.

In a broad sense, landmarks survive, can be made to survive or are lost in one of the following six ways:

1. Preservation is most firmly assured when a building continues to serve the function for which it was built. An example of this is New York City's famed City Hall (fig. 1), which was built as the city's third center of local government in 1802–11 and continues admirably to fill the same function today.

FIGURE 1. *City Hall in City Hall Park, New York City. (New York City Landmarks Preservation Commission)*

2. Sometimes, with no effort on the part of preservationists, an unexpected new use is spontaneously found for an old building. For instance, the Metropolitan Savings Bank in New York City has been adapted to serve as the First Ukrainian Church (fig. 2).

3. In other cases, after serving several functions, a building may seem to have no viable future in the open marketplace. If the building is an extraordinarily fine example of architecture or if it has great historical importance or other unique and irreplaceable qualities, its retention for educational purposes may be justified on the basis of these qualities. For example, New York City's Federal Hall National Memorial (fig. 3), which was originally the Customs House and later served as a subtreasury, is now operated

FIGURE 2. *First Ukrainian Assembly of God building on East 7th Street, New York City, formerly the Metropolitan Savings Bank. (John B. Bayley, courtesy of New York City Landmarks Preservation Commission)*

FIGURE 3. *Federal Hall National Memorial on Wall Street, New York City. The building originally was the Customs House and later a subtreasury. (New York City Landmarks Preservation Commission)*

as a museum by the National Park Service. Other examples include some of the historic house museums that are scattered through the city's five boroughs. In addition, on Staten Island, the whole village of Richmondtown has been preserved to illustrate changing ways of small-town life over two and a half centuries.

4. To conceive and carry out the transformation of an old building to serve new uses can be a real challenge to an architect's ingenuity. In contrast to the type of spontaneous transformation described in paragraph 2, the conscious effort to discover a viable new function for an old structure usually takes place under pressure of a crisis. Unless a new use or a new user can be found in a matter of weeks or even days, the landmark, no matter how widely loved, may soon be a parking lot. One of the strengths of New York City's landmarks law is that it provides a breathing space, a moratorium from the wrecking crew, in which to develop a solution. The conversion of the Astor Library into the successful Public Theatre is one example of this kind of transformation in which the commission played a crucial role. The transformation of the Jefferson Market Courthouse (fig. 4) in Greenwich Village into a branch of the New York City Public Library was accomplished before the commission was fully established; it was achieved through well-organized private pressure and the cooperation of a number of city agencies.

5. Occasionally, no way can be found to save a landmark except to move it. This was an unusually appropriate solution in the case of the Edgar Laing Stores building in New York City (fig. 5), which lay in the path of the Washington Street urban renewal project. One of the earliest examples of James Bogardus' cast-iron technique, the building was taken apart, just as Bogardus claimed it could be, and is scheduled for reerection on a nearby site.

6. The Leonard Jerome House (fig. 6) in New York City, the girlhood home of Winston Churchill's mother, is the one designated landmark that has been lost under the demolition provision of the New York City landmarks law. While the loss is deeply regretted, it illustrated once and for all that the New York City landmarks law is both realistic and fair. With the best will on the part of everyone concerned, and after extensive exploration of numerous alternatives, it simply proved impossible to devise a viable future for this building.

In addition to giving new life to designated landmarks and historic districts, New York City has evolved a very close interlocking of landmarks and zoning legislation. Just as landmarks preservation has proved to be a valuable tool in city planning, the

FIGURE 4. *Greenwich Village branch of the New York City Public Library, formerly the Jefferson Market Court House. (New York City Landmarks Preservation Commission)*

55

FIGURE 5. *Edward Laing Stores building in downtown Manhattan as it looked at the corner of Washington and Murray streets before disassembly and proposed reerection on a nearby site. (New York City Landmarks Preservation Commission)*

FIGURE 6. *Leonard Jerome House at Madison Avenue and 26th Street, New York City, before its demolition in 1968. (New York City Landmarks Preservation Commission)*

City Planning Commission has proved to be a valuable ally of the Landmarks Preservation Commission.

The following descriptions of sections of the Zoning Resolution that have been added by amendment illustrate how important such support can be.[6]

1. In section 22-13, an exception is made, particularly in densely built-up residential districts, to allow philanthropic and nonprofit institutions to use, under appropriate restrictions, former private residences as their offices or headquarters. This has permitted preservation of some of the great mansions on the upper east side of Manhattan.

2. Sections 11-121, 12-10 and 23-69 provide for the control of the height of new structures in certain historic districts. The height of any new structure can be a matter of vital importance in a neighborhood with an essentially uniform cornice line.

3. Section 74-79 provides for the transfer of development rights. This highly original idea permits the owner of a designated landmark, which is generally a low building, to sell or lease his valuable unused potential floor area to neighboring property owners. Such transfers are effected under special permits that provide for design controls on the adjoining new structures to be erected and require that appropriate provisions be made for the permanent maintenance of the landmark.

4. Sections 74-71 permits a modification, with appropriate safeguards, of zoning restrictions pertaining to the use of designated landmarks. This provision recognizes that needs change and that frequently the only way to save a landmark is to find some new use for it—a use that a rigid application of the zoning laws might not permit.

5. Section 74-72 allows, through special permit, the relaxation of height and setback restrictions for buildings adjoining designated landmarks. This gives the City Planning and the Landmarks Preservation commissions the opportunity to impose design controls requiring that certain new buildings be compatible with the landmarks they adjoin.

6. Sections 89-00 through 89-07, recently approved by the City Planning Commission and the Board of Estimate, provide for the creation of a special South Street Seaport District within the broader boundaries of the Brooklyn Bridge Southeast Extension, known as Manhattan Landing. The new district extends along the East River shorefront between the Brooklyn Bridge and the Battery and includes at least 21 designated landmarks. The planning

for this special district is, in many ways, designed for the effective perpetuation and use of the valuable concentration of landmarks it contains.

CONCLUSION

This paper has pictured the challenges and opportunities open to the administrator–lawyer–city planner in the historic preservation process. The extent to which an individual is trained as an administrator, a lawyer or a city planner is less important than his appreciation of the crucial role he can play.

NOTES

1. Local Law No. 46 of 1965, passed by the New York City Council on April 6, 1965, and signed into law by Mayor Robert F. Wagner on April 19, amended the Charter of the City of New York by the addition of the following language as section 2004 of chapter 63, which established the Parks, Recreation and Cultural Affairs Administration.

Landmarks Preservation Commission

1. There shall be in the administration a landmarks preservation commission consisting of eleven members. The membership of such commission shall include at least three architects, one historian qualified in the field, one city planner or landscape architect, and one realtor. The membership shall include at least one resident of each of the five boroughs.

2. (a) The members of the commission shall be appointed by the mayor for terms of three years, provided that of those members first taking office, three shall be appointed for one year, four for two years and four for three years. Each member shall serve until the appointment and qualification of his successor. The terms of members taking office shall commence on the date of their appointment.

(b) Before making any appointment of a member who is required to be an architect, historian or city planner or landscape architect, the mayor may consult with the fine arts federation of New York and any other similar organization. In the event of a vacancy occurring during the term of a member of the commission, the mayor shall make an interim appointment to fill out the unexpired term of such member, and where such member is herein required to have specified qualifications, such vacancy shall be filled by interim appointment, in the manner herein prescribed, of a person having such qualifications.

3. The members of the commission, other than the chairman, shall serve without compensation, but shall be reimbursed for expenses necessarily incurred in the performance of their duties. (As amended by Local Law No. 64 of 1968.)

4. The mayor shall designate one of the members of the commission to be chairman and one to be vice-chairman. The chairman and vice-chairman shall serve as such, until a successor or successors are designated. The commission shall appoint an executive director who shall devote full time to his duties. The commission shall submit an annual report on its activities to the mayor.

5. The commission may employ technical experts and such other employees as may be required to perform its duties, within the appropriations therefor.

6. The commission shall have powers and duties as shall be prescribed by law with respect to the establishment and regulation of landmarks, portions of landmarks, landmark sites and historic districts.

2. Chapter 8-A of the Administrative Code of the City of New York is too long to quote in its entirety, but the following index of its sections will give an indication of the scope of its provisions: section 205–1.0, Purpose and declaration of public policy. 207–1.0, Definitions. 207–2.0, Establishment of landmarks, landmark sites and historic districts. 207–3.0, Scope of commission's powers. 207–4.0, Regulation of construction, reconstruction, alterations and demolition. 207–5.0, Determination of request for certificate of no exterior effect. 207–6.0, Factors governing issuance of certificate of appropriateness. 207–7.0, Procedure for determination of request for certificate of appropriateness. 207–8.0, Request for certificate of appropriateness authorizing demolition, alterations or reconstruction on ground of insufficient return. 207–9.0, Regulation of minor work. 207–10.0, Maintenance and repair of improvements. 207–11.0, Remedying of dangerous conditions. 207–12.0, Public hearings; conferences. 207–13.0, Extension of time for action by commission. 207–14.0, Determinations of the commission; notice thereof. 207–15.0, Transmission of certificates and applications to proper agency. 207–16.0, Penalties for violations; enforcement. 207–17.0. Reports by commission on plans for proposed projects. 207–18.0, Regulations. 207–19.0, Investigations and reports. 207–20.0, Applicability. 207–21.0, Separability.

3. Subdivision 25–a of section 20 of the General City Law was enacted April 2, 1956; it was amended January 30, 1968, and is now incorporated in the General Municipal Law as section 96–a, which reads:

Protection of historical places, buildings and works of art. In addition to any power or authority of a municipal corporation to regulate by planning or zoning laws and regulations or by local laws and regulations, the governing board or local legislative body of any county, city, town or village is empowered to provide by regulations, special conditions and restrictions for the protection, enhancement, perpetuation and use of places, districts, sites, buildings, structures, works of art, and other objects having a special character or special historical or aesthetic interest or value. Such regulations, special conditions and restrictions may include appropriate and reasonable control of the use or appearance of neighboring private property within public view, or both. In any such instance such measures, if adopted in the exercise of the police power, shall be reasonable and appropriate to the purpose, or if constituting a taking of private property shall provide for due compenstion, which may include the limitation or remission of taxes.

4. Justice Edward J. Greenfield of the New York State Supreme Court, in granting a temporary injunction against the Health and Mental Hygiene Facilities Improvement Corporation prohibiting their demolition of structures in Mount Morris Park Historic District without prior approval of the Landmarks Preservation Commission, stated, inter alia:

Section 96–a of the General Municipal Law, which was enacted at the same legislative session which passed the Health and Mental Facilities Improvement Act, empowered municipal corporations, counties, towns and villages to provide "for the protection, enhancement, perpetuation and use of places, districts, buildings, structures, works of art, and other objects having a special character or special historical or aesthetic interest or value." . . . Thus we are confronted with the unlikely anomaly that the Legislature, on one hand, has created in municipalities the power over and beyond the zoning laws to preserve designated landmark areas, and on the other hand granting extraordinary powers to a state public benefit corporation to construct a mental hygiene facility, even if it means the tearing down of historic or esthetic buildings singled out as landmarks. . . . How vain and foolish it is [on the part of the Health and Mental Hygiene Facilities Improvement Corporation] to proceed headlong on a course once embarked upon, giving no heed to other voices, refusing all alternatives

and all consultation—ironically insisting on the demolition of sound and beautiful buildings which are historic landmarks from a less hectic era.
Montgomery v. State,
328 N.Y.S. 2d 189 (1972)

5. The following citations are legal landmarks themselves:

There is no merit to petitioner's contention that the determination is unsupported by substantial evidence. A hearing was held and the issues thoroughly aired. The architectural, historical and aesthetic value of the improvement was fully established, and the court may not substitute its judgment for that of the administrative agency (Matter of Kilgus v. Board of Estimate of City of New York, 308 N.Y. 620; Matter of Wiener v. Gabel, 18 App. Div.2d 1025 [2d Dept., 1963]). Such values are a "valid subject of legislative concern" and "reasonable legislation designed to promote that end is a valid and permissible exercise of the police power" (People v. Stover, 12 N.Y.2d 462, 467 [1963]).
Manhattan Club v. Landmarks Preservation Commission,
51 Misc.2d 556, 273 N.Y.S. 2d 848 (1966)

We deem certain of the basic questions raised to be no longer arguable. In this category is the right, within proper limitations, of the state to place restrictions on the use to be made by an owner of his own property for the cultural and aesthetic benefit of the community. . . . It is unnecessary to trace the course of judicial thinking in this field. It is now the prerogative of the state, if not its province, to so act where the conditions exist and where constitutionally guaranteed rights are not infringed.
Trustees of the Sailors' Snug Harbor v. Platt,
29 App. Div.2d 376, 288 N.Y.S. 2d 314, (1st Dept., 1968)

6. All references are to sections of the Zoning Resolution of the City of New York, adopted by the Board of Estimate on December 15, 1960, effective December 15, 1961, and as subsequently amended.

COMMENTARY

CHARLES B. HOSMER, JR.

In my research on professional groups that carry out preservation and restoration projects, I have encountered some architects and archaeologists who consider themselves second-class citizens in their professional fields. Several of the speakers at this conference, particularly Charles E. Peterson, have mentioned this. I would like to speak to this problem that faces those who choose to work in the field of historic preservation.

It is true that professionals who work in the preservation field sometimes seem to be left out of the mainstream of their professions. One historian who has devoted his career to historic preservation told me that year after year when he attended American Historical Association meetings, his fellow historians would ask, "What are you doing now?" in a tone of voice that conveyed the hope that he would reply, "I am no longer with the National Park Service." An archaeologist told me that when he attended the Oriental Institute at the University of Chicago in the 1930s, his colleagues expressed similar attitudes on hearing that he was going to Jamestown, Va., to dig for artifacts that were 300 years old or less. His colleagues, of course, were heading for the Valley of the Kings in Egypt or some other exotic place, and his work was

Charles B. Hosmer, Jr., is associate professor of history at Principia College, Elsah, Ill. He is author of *Presence of the Past—A History of the Preservation Movement in the United States Before Williamsburg* (New York: G. P. Putnam's Sons, 1965).

considered of minor significance. It seems to me, however, that a greater problem than the prestige accorded to professionals in preservation is the question of whether or not there is a "preservation fraternity."

The participants in this conference have all been trained as professionals. How do they view the other professions involved in preservation, and how do the professions mesh in a restoration project? The restoration of buildings in Colonial Williamsburg and the development of the Colonial National Historical Park illustrate what happens in nearly every project in which several professions are involved, that is, one profession becomes dominant and the others become secondary to it, with the result that most of the decisions made reflect the viewpoint and values of the dominant profession. Maybe this phenomenon is simply human nature. I am not even certain whether it is undesirable or desirable; it simply happens.

For the first 15 years of the project, the restoration of Colonial Williamsburg was approached from a purely architectural viewpoint. That may not necessarily be bad. I was surprised to discover that during these formative years, the restoration was not handled by the staff of Colonial Williamsburg. The architectural firm of Perry, Shaw and Hepburn of Boston, Mass., worked under contract. There were no school-trained historians on Colonial Williamsburg's staff until 1938, when one was retained as an editor to produce reports for the architectural department. The first archaeologists hired by Colonial Williamsburg were assigned to excavate the Wren Building. None of them knew anything about historic site archaeology, but their assignment was to excavate building foundations, determine what kind of building had been there and recover just enough artifacts to reveal what each building's function had been. Proof that the restoration of Colonial Williamsburg was an architectural project from start to finish was provided in 1932 when the Raleigh Tavern was opened to the eager public as an exhibition building. At the last minute, it was realized that hostesses had to be trained—and trained quickly! What were these hostesses supposed to do and say? Nobody had even thought about the problem.

The decision to reconstruct Williamsburg's first capitol was an architectural decision. A decision to reconstruct the second capitol would have been a historical decision, because it was in the second building that important events leading to the birth of this nation occurred. (These historic events are obviously a factor in Colonial Williamsburg's attraction for visitors, and it is unfortunate that the orientation film shown to visitors depicts Patrick Henry giving his famous speeches in a building that burned some 20 years before he came to Williamsburg as a colonial burgess!) However, the justification for reconstruction of the first capitol was based on excellent architectural grounds; researchers knew much more about it than the second capitol. Architecturally, the first building had more appeal to the restorationists.

The National Park Service developed the Colonial National Historical Park, which is just a few miles from Williamsburg, along different lines. At the time the park was being developed, the real power behind the decision making in the Park Service was its director, Horace Marden Albright, who was, and is, interested in history. He hired the first chief historian of the National Park Service, Verne Chatelain. Mr. Chatelain in turn hired at least two historians for every architect, engineer and landscape architect in the Park Service. By the mid-1930s, he had hired about 500 historians associated with different emergency programs of the New Deal; Mr. Chatelain told me recently that he would have hired more if he had been able to.

The criteria used by the Park Service to decide what to save and how to treat what was saved reflected the thinking of these historians. They thought in terms of battlefields and buildings associated with specific historic events. Architects, engineers and professionals in the Department of Plans and Designs often performed tasks based on decisions made by Park Service historians. Monuments possessing only architectural significance were rarely considered by the Park Service. The first purely architectural monument to become part of the Park Service system was probably Hampton, the late Georgian mansion built in 1790 in Towson, Md., by Charles Ridgely, a member of the Maryland House of Burgesses; actually, the Mellon family and the National Gallery of Art were responsible for the Park Service's consideration of the property.

Another point about the "preservation fraternity" that concerns me is the amount of respect that exists among the professions. Does one profession become dominant in a particular restoration project as a result of a lack of respect for the work of the other professions involved? Have one or more professions been left out of this meeting? There is, in fact, one group of professionals that, I believe, is conspicuously missing from this conference—administrators. Harmon H. Goldstone comes closest to representing them and describing their role in preservation. These administrators are not necessarily trained in restoration or historical research techniques, but they exercise great influence over preservation projects. They make decisions, contact boards of trustees and spend money; however, some of them fail to recognize the importance of providing restoration architects and other professionals in preservation with sustained employment.

In studying the history of Colonial Williamsburg, I was stunned to learn that in 1933 John D. Rockefeller, Jr., the project's patron, decided that the restoration was finished and dismissed the Perry, Shaw and Hepburn team, which consisted of 25 or 30 young men who had become extremely knowledgeable about problems associated with the restoration of 18th-century buildings in Virginia. Similarly, the Park Service started its Mission 66 program in the middle 1950s, and by the middle 1960s it was over. The 10-year program was established to hire and train construction specialists to work on various projects designed to ready national parks for the 50th anniversary of the park system. What good is it to train individuals to do sophisticated work and then to tell them that the projects they are working on are going to end? Administrators must recognize their responsibility to provide permanent employment for these professionals if they expect to continue to call on their services.

The importance of obtaining the cooperation of another group, the general public, can be illustrated with an example from the Park Service's past. The Civil War ended at the village of Appomattox Court House, Va., and surrender terms were worked out in the Wilmer McLean House. In the 1890s, plans were made to move the house to the World's Columbian Exposition in Chicago, Ill. The promoters ordered measured drawings and photographs to be made before the building was dismantled. They stacked bricks and wood from the house in the village, but the house never left the town.

In the early 1930s, the Park Service acquired some land in the center of the village and sponsored a national architectural competition to design a monument commemorating the end of the Civil War. A young architect won the competition, and his design was published. However, village residents were not interested in this plan; they held unswervingly to the idea that the village of Appomattox Court House should be restored to its original appearance and that the McLean House should be reconstructed.

In 1935, Joel W. Flood, an active local lawyer and former member of the United States House of Representatives, pushed a bill through Congress appropriating $100,000 to reconstruct both the McLean House and the courthouse, the latter of which by then had partially burned. The National Park Service, which was going through an antireconstruction phase, made every effort to prevent the reconstructions. In 1940, Chief Historian Ronald F. Lee, now deceased, went to Appomattox Court House to propose using the site of the McLean House as an archaeological exhibit. His plan included exposing the basement and constructing an interpretive shelter to display photographs and a model of the house. What actually happened was what Park Service historians refer to as "Lee's second surrender at Appomattox."

Mr. Lee discovered that Mr. Flood and the local citizens had not changed their ideas in the slightest in five years. The McLean House would rise again from its ashes, so to speak. Acceding to the wishes of the local citizens, the Park Service began to make preparations for the reconstruction of the house. When vines were cleared away, it was found that 80 percent of the original bricks were still there. For the project, the Park Service organized a team, a remarkable idea, I think, for 1940. A historian, an archaeologist and an architect were sent to Appomattox Court House, and they wrote a report, "The Collaborative Justification for the Reconstruction of the Wilmer McLean House," which showed that reconstruction was possible. They even had the Federal Bureau of Investigation test the contractor's plans that were discovered to be sure they were on genuine paper of the 1890s. Finally, in 1950, the reconstructed McLean House, with reproduction furniture, was opened to the public.

This experience illustrates the necessity for communication among professionals in the field, administrators and the general public. Professionals must be able to communicate to administrators and the public the significance and soundness of their proposals and decisions.

What hope is there for doing this? Perhaps one of the things that needs to be done is for preservationists to stop talking to each other and start talking to administrators and to the public. Professionals in preservation usually find it difficult to communicate with these groups, partly because preservationists lack a clearly defined philosophy. The problem is caused by a lack of time; preservationists do not generally have time to formulate an honest and realistic rationale for their work. Few projects are like the restoration of Colonial Williamsburg, which continued for such a long period that the ideas behind it evolved as the project progressed, with the result that what began as an architectural project eventually became an interpretive program. Today, most preservation efforts are undertaken in haste, under emergency conditions. When a historic building or an architecturally significant district is in danger of destruction, crucial decisions must be made quickly concerning such things as whether it is worth fighting for, what should be done with it, where money can be obtained for the project.

Another reason that preservationists are misunderstood and never seem to acquire any professional or public standing is that preservation is an irrational activity. The whole idea of arresting the forces of change does not seem logical. The public is amused at preservation activities, and professionals in preservation make matters worse by being so serious. A sense of humor about restoration work is needed. Preservationists should talk about their mistakes and not be so deadly serious about them.

This communication gap could be bridged if there were a professional organization (or organizations) devoted to historic preservation that would try to establish legitimacy for the field. As Stanley South indicates, a conference of historic site archaeologists has been established at the University of South Carolina. These historic site archaeologists should not worry about convincing Egyptologists or archaeologists in other specialities of the value of their work; it is more important that they make the public and administrators of preservation projects aware of the need for archaeological investigation at historic sites and of the legitimacy of their profession.

I am not confident that there is, as yet, a professional organization of restoration architects. The organizations Mr. Peterson mentions appear to be developing in that direction. At one time, it looked as if the Society of Architectural Historians would develop into such a group; it did not. Richard M. Candee describes them, accurately I believe, as a group of academics who are interested in describing buildings in Italy and other parts of Europe but have little interest in barns or other vernacular architecture in this country. There is truthfully no professional organization of restoration architects at this time.

Professional historians in preservation face a similar situation. Most of their colleagues do not even admit that restoration exists as a legitimate field, and historians who work for the Park Service, for example, have really "taken the veil," to use Mr. Peterson's words.

To summarize, there is a need, first, for organizations and professionals engaged in historic preservation activities to take a new pride in their work, despite the lack of prestige usually accorded them by their own fields, and to begin to earn suitable professional and public standing for their work. Second, professionals must communicate their needs to administrators more effectively, particularly the need for continuing employment, which is, I believe, an even greater problem than the lack of training programs. Training programs are meaningless unless jobs are available. Third, preservation professionals need to develop a much greater sense of the worth of their associates, that is, the other professionals they work with. Finally, preservationists need to be more catholic about approaches to restoration projects that they are not working on. I have heard several critical remarks about Colonial Williamsburg at this conference. I must say, however, that the more I have studied the project's history and tried to understand what was intended, the more I respect what was accomplished. Each restoration project should be treated as unique and judged in terms of what it was intended to be. I am tired of the terms *good* and *bad*. What was done at Colonial Williamsburg was as fully justified in its context at the time as the recent decision of the Society for the Preservation of New England Antiquities to not do any restoration work on properties it acquires. There is room in the preservation field for many types of approach to projects, and there is no reason for preservationists to condemn approaches that are different from theirs. It should be possible to have some sense of professional unity combined with a diversity of approaches.

DISCUSSION

Comments made by the panelists and audience during the discussion on occupations involved in preservation are summarized in the following paragraphs.

Preservation is a field with a future, but it presently faces some serious job problems. For example, beginning architects employed by public preservation agencies may find their work experience overlooked when they apply for licensure. An architect must have a certain number of years of practical experience to qualify for the licensing examination. Unfortunately, some licensing boards in the past have not given an applicant full credit for experience gained outside the office of a practicing architect. Thus, the beginning, preservation-interested architect who wishes to become licensed and also wants a full range of preservation experience, including work on public projects, may face a real career dilemma. Also, in today's tight economy, beginning professionals must consider the financial outlook. A private-practice salary is often higher than the salary that a public preservation agency can offer.

Some job difficulties may be attributed to administrators' misunderstanding of the role of various professions in a project or program. To efficiently and properly manage a project or program, administrators, that is, those people who make major decisions on how money is to be spent, must have a thorough understanding of the work of the various professions involved. Such understanding is often lacking and administrators need to be made more aware of what and how each profession can contribute. Perhaps administrators of preservation projects and programs should be selected from the ranks of those professions involved in the field so that they will have a technical background on which to base their decisions.

It is questionable whether all of the occupations reviewed can truthfully be called "professions." Some are still developing and, therefore, cannot now fully justify the establishment of extensive training programs. Why train generalists or specialists in preservation when there are no jobs for graduates? On the other hand, is it necessary that jobs be assured them? In this modern age, too many people believe they must be assured of a job before they become involved in a field. Dedication to an ideal is just as important as a job in the field. People who believe in their work, do it well and communicate the value of their activities to their colleagues and communities often can create their own jobs. Then, too, the federal government, with its expanding involvement in preservation, should be a source for many preservation-related jobs in the future.

Although it is true that professionals in preservation are, as Dr. Hosmer said in his commentary, often considered "second-class citizens" by their professional colleagues in their special field, such as history or architecture, there is a prospect that this image will change now that preservation interests are broadening and more professions are being drawn into the field. Modern preservation activities require an orchestration of effort among many disciplines.

Organizations

COMMENTS ON 21 LEADING CONSERVATION-PRESERVATION ORGANIZATIONS

ROBERT E. STIPE

My assignment is to comment on the work of 21 selected "lead" organizations in the fields of historic preservation, museum operations and conservation and several professional groups related to these fields, in addition to commenting on the work of American, Canadian and national and international governmental organizations in preservation and conservation. This particular task has been a most stimulating, yet also frustrating and frightening, experience. The only comfort I find in my situation is the dictionary definition of *comment,* which tells me that I am free to make critical notes, reflections and observations.

Normally, I do not apologize in advance for what I have to say, but in the present situation there are a number of limitations that should be noted. First, it was understood that the organizations would submit statements on their goals, programs and so forth by the beginning of June. As of late August, 10 of the 21 organizations had submitted the requested materials. Twelve days before this meeting, I received, through the courtesy of Russell V. Keune at the National Trust for Historic Preservation, materials concerning some of the remaining organizations. These materials are of unknown origin and uncertain authorship or date. Finally, I gathered from secondary sources the barest bits and pieces of

Robert E. Stipe is professor of public law and government and assistant director of the Institute of Government, University of North Carolina at Chapel Hill, N.C.

information on two of the organizations—wholly insufficient for the purpose. On one group, I still have no information. The statements submitted range from one or two–page letters to well-thought-out 15 to 20–page essays. Some enclosed 40 pages or more of annual reports, minutes and other types of material. Altogether, the information on organizations now consists of several hundred pages and fills a thick notebook.

There are other limitations of an internal sort for which the organizations asked to submit statements should not here be held responsible. These are the limitations of any one individual to comprehend fully the vast organizational world of preservation and conservation. To make matters worse, the commentator on this organizational world is not a historian, architect, restorationist, conservator or archaeologist—nor am I really professionally qualified in any of the fields on which I have been asked to comment. My undergraduate training was in theoretical economics and my professional training in the fields of law and urban planning. Thus, I am an "outsider" commenting on a subject that perhaps could be treated better by one who is privy to the inner workings of these vast, complex fields and the organizations that exist to serve them.

Finally, there are some built-in biases and prejudices. I should announce that I am a member of several of the organizations on which I have been asked to comment: the National Trust for Historic Preservation, American Association for State and Local History, International Council of Monuments and Sites and Society of Architectural Historians. Any partiality shown to these groups must be taken with a grain of salt.

It was hoped by the sponsors of this conference that the papers submitted by the 21 organizations would constitute a definitive, detailed "who's who" of preservation. There were, of course, other organizations that might reasonably have been included, but were not. Requests for statements were addressed primarily to leaders of the Western world's preservation-conservation movement: the

American Association of Museums (AAM),

American Association for State and Local History (AASLH),

American Institute of Architects (AIA),

American Society of Landscape Architects (ASLA),

Association for Preservation Technology (APT),

Canadian Association of Museums,

    National Historic Sites Service of the Canadian Department of Indian Affairs and Northern Development,

International Council of Monuments and Sites (ICOMOS),

International Council of Museums (ICOM),

International Centre for the Study of the Preservation and the Restoration of Cultural Property (Rome Centre),

American Group of the International Institute for Conservation of Historic and Artistic Works (IIC-AG),

National Park Service (NPS),

National Trust for Historic Preservation (National Trust),

Royal Architectural Institute of Canada (RAIC),

Smithsonian Institution, Society of Architectural Historians (SAH),

Society for Historical Archaeology (SHA),

Library of Congress,

Intermuseum Conservation Association (ICA),

American Society of Civil Engineers (ASCE)

and Society for American Archaeology (SAA).

What do these organizations do? Without any attempt to categorize activities, I have compiled a list of about 15 separate but related types of activity these organizations are engaged in, and an outsider such as myself can only be amazed at how much they do or purport to do. One's principal reaction upon looking at the voluminous summary mentioned previously is a rather euphoric one: "All is well in the preservation world."

While the organizations' emphases vary, one is immediately struck by the frequent, almost universal use of such words as *promote, encourage, support* and *coordinate* in their individual statements of corporate purpose. The range of activities is broad. Some organizations are involved in accrediting and standard-setting; this is especially true of those representing museum and conservation interests and those of the design professions. All of the organizations claim to provide services to their members. Most produce publications. Some are essentially research oriented. Others provide opportunities for training; almost all sponsor meetings and conferences on national, regional and/or local levels. Some lobby in Congress and in state legislatures. Some maintain lists of consultants and specialists. A few conduct tours. A few, especially those representing the design professions, spend a good deal of effort attempting to motivate their members to take an interest in preservation and conservation. The government agencies surveyed are involved in preservation through ownership of historic properties, documentation, regulation, grant-in-aid programs, the maintenance of artifact collections and documentary source materials, surveying and listing and so forth. A few of the groups fulfill a public relations function. All appear to coordinate with all the

73

others; every group seems to liaise with every other group.

One marvels at the number of man-hours probably involved in setting up and attending the numerous conferences sponsored by these organizations and the total number of pages printed in their journals, abstracts, book reviews, laboratory analyses, articles and minutes in one year. There appear to be hundreds of thousands of individual members and thousands of member institutions that belong to these groups. There is considerable evidence that preservation and conservation are ideas whose day has finally arrived: Membership rolls of those organizations that maintain individual memberships appear to have more than doubled in the last six to eight years. Foundation support is evident and consistent, and government funding for the whole range of preservation-conservation activities represented by the United States and Canadian governmental organizations has increased dramatically in recent years. Conservation technology is expanding rapidly. Preservation technology is coming into its own.

The picture appears rosy, but there are clouds on the horizon. From reading the statements submitted, one could get the impression that everything is fine. But one wonders: Can it really be this cozy?

Note these items for example. The SHA states that one of its purposes is to "foster appreciation of the rules of evidence common to the archeological profession *but notably lacking in certain other areas of restoration endeavors.*" The outsider wonders what motivated the group to tack on such a qualification. Then, one hears a restoration architect assert at this conference that few archaeologists understand buildings and that some of them do not even have the intuition to look in the right places for the remains of structures. A conservator also grumbles that archaeologists destroy valuable remains in their haste to excavate and through their inability to properly protect artifacts in the field. "Impatient haste has destroyed many retrieved objects," notes Caroline K. Keck. In another conference paper, Charles E. Peterson asserts that "city planners as a group have been the worst enemies of historic preservation."

Differing philosophies also confuse the picture. The policy of one major government agency states that the prime purpose of national historical parks is to promote an appreciation of history. Picnicking is permitted only if eating facilities are so far away that visitors would otherwise go hungry, and camping is not allowed in any event, because it is potentially harmful to the historical atmosphere. The policy of another government agency, while not downgrading the importance of history, requires that statewide plans for historic preservation "reflect the impact of *contemporary* events or developments," therefore establishing "a basis for a lively program by recognizing . . . the environmental struggle, racial and ethnic developments . . . urban and rural movements. . . ." The same policy suggests a new emphasis on historic districts and the downgrading of reconstructions.

The National Historic Preservation Act of 1966 made some mention of buildings of local significance; however, relatively few buildings of local significance have been entered in the National Register of Historic Places. Also, it was presumed by supporters and sponsors of the legislation that it would give preference in matters of financial aid to privately owned buildings that would remain in nonmuseum uses, that is, those serving everyday purposes, rather than to state historic sites or historic house museums. Now there is growing evidence that these good intentions have been forgotten.

There are other clouds in the preservation picture. We find one restoration architect wondering in his paper whether restorationists should really be concerned with the quality of the whole environment, lest they take on too much and do everything badly. To the contrary, a member of the staff of an outstanding outdoor museum implicitly expresses pleasure at the thought that the preservation movement is finally beginning to take serious account of planning, townscape and landscape values. Concerning this, we find the National Trust for Historic Preservation cohosting a one-week workshop in England for a group of Loudoun County, Va., commissioners and planning board members, during which trip the entire focus was on the planning and development process and other environmental matters. Scarcely a word was said about historic buildings. Six months later, during a planning conference held at one of the Trust's 12 historic properties, the principal subjects of discussion concerned such matters as townscape, landscape, open space, parks, recreation, taxation and zoning. Again, there was no mention of historic buildings. Coincidentally, it might be noted that the Advisory Council on Historic Preservation is looking for an urban planner to add to its staff.

Things are not always what they seem! Preservation and conservation are taking on new meanings.

These areas of difference and disagreement are the basis for my earlier comment that this assignment has been frustrating as well as stimulating. One knows very well that written statements summarizing organizational programs and policies do not tell the whole story. There are currents and crosscurrents within the preservation field that must be reckoned with, and there are outside forces at work that will shortly change the traditional scene in any event. Organizational policies and structures are typically a reflection of what groups *have* been doing; they say little about what the groups *ought* to be doing. I am, therefore, much more concerned about what the summaries submitted do not express, especially in terms of a coherent preservation-conservation philosophy. The structures and programs that have been created are not going to be the same five or ten years from now. While we preservationists can congratulate ourselves generally for past achievements, some questions must be raised about the kinds of structures and objectives that are needed for the future.

Questions relating to organizational structure bother me little. The structures of existing organizations (i.e., the 21 organizations under discussion) seem to serve reasonably well the programs and, in turn, the preservation-conservation philosophies that exist today, in spite of a general underfunding of programs and the lack of certain types of skills among the staffs of these organizations. For example, current preservation philosophy says basically that it is better to maintain than to repair, better to repair than restore, better to restore than reconstruct and so forth. It is a philosophy that, I believe, tends ultimately to emphasize history at the expense of architecture, one that has not broken as far away from the historic house-museum–historic-site philosophy as leaders of the preservation movement hoped it might when the 1966 act was passed and one that is essentially inward-looking and ingrown— of great relevance only to those with much more training, more sophisticated tastes and greater aesthetic sensibilities than the average citizen.

Thus, strengthening the institutional-organizational effectiveness of preservation implies that we preservationists are going to have to do a number of things, included in which is the creation of a radical and rapid change in our total preservation philosophy. I believe the organizational and philosophical considerations are greatly intermingled.

The first problem is to improve the preservationist's image in the outside world. Perhaps one productive approach to this problem would be to look to the consumers of what preservation has to offer. Here, the museum field has a somewhat easier time, if for no other reason than that museums can (if they wish) respond more quickly to changes in consumer demands. Today's children are, for the most part, avid consumers of museum services, much more so than my generation. They are especially interested in museums of science and technology, nature museums and museums that deal with the environmental crisis and ecological issues that are so uppermost in the minds of the younger generation. History museums among most of the youth of my acquaintance are a dead issue and so are many historic sites. I am inclined to believe that their preference for nature and science museums exists because the historic house museum or historic site has been regarded as the end product of an effort, a result in itself, rather than a beginning point with continuing importance and reference in the daily lives of people. "I've been there; why go again?" is the reaction heard so often when suggesting a visit to a historic site to a young person or a Scout troop. Museums, in other words, can keep up with changing interests and fashions; historic buildings find it difficult to do so. It is harder to make the general public aware of the continuing usefulness of a historic building or site unless the building or site can become a focal point for daily events that are important in the life of the community. As Sir John Summerson delightfully put it in 1947 in one of the essays in his book *Heavenly Mansions:*

. . . old buildings are different. Like divorced wives they cost money to maintain. They are often dreadfully in the way. And the protection of one may exact as much sacrifice from the community as the preservation of a thousand pictures, books or musical scores.

Part of the present predicament of the preservation movement, I believe, is that most preservationists and, hence, the institutions representing them have turned inward. I have been told, for example, of one state that produced a magnificent and expensive booklet explaining the statewide plan for historic preservation. The publication made an excellent case for the conservation of historic buildings and areas and did so at considerable expense. Who got the book? It was distributed free of charge and in limited quantity to members of the state historical society and to the antiquarian community, but not to others in any great quantity. An argument can be made that the preservation story could have been told just as effectively on a single sheet of newsprint that could have been stuffed into the grocery bags of 500,000 supermarket shoppers. Another state maintains a first-rate mobile history museum. For several days a month, it makes scheduled visits to schools. The remainder of the time it sits in its garage—when it might well be sitting in the parking lot of a local shopping center.

How long will we preservationists wait for the public to come to us? Where is the prime-time television show that can effectively sell the importance of historic buildings, show the interesting collections of the many great and small museums or explain the fascinating work of the conservator, the restoration architect or the archaeologist? If the preservation-conservation fight is an underfunded, unsupported and often lost cause, it is largely because we preservationists have not made our case in terms of today's market. Richard D. Buck, director of the ICA, makes the point that cooperation requires more than sympathetic inclinations; there must be activists among administrators, too. Simply stated, preservation-conservation organizations still place too much emphasis on service to their members. They should also be effectively presenting the preservation story to the public.

A second major problem, not unrelated to the withdrawal symptoms of the first, is to acknowledge the need for greater involvement on the part of related interests and professions, not only those represented at this conference. At the national level, much credit should go to the AIA. It has a long and distinguished record of activism in the preservation field: fighting for the retention of important buildings, pressing for legislation and demonstrating its institutional commitment to preservation through the acquisition of the Octagon House (1800), in Washington, D.C. There are even some state and local AIA chapters that have demonstrated a commitment to historic preservation. Offices of the North Carolina chapter, for instance, are in an old water tower in Raleigh; the tower was specifically adapted for such use. But how does preservation reach architectural practitioners with its message? Last week, I read a speech given by an officer of an AIA region at one of the regional AIA conferences. In his message, there was impassioned discussion about the population explosion, the urban crisis and the important role of the architect in influencing public policy for better planning and design, the elimination of visual pollution and so forth. But then the speaker got down to the specifics—such things as the need for new methods and procedures in office practice embracing a team approach, the need for architects to provide services faster and more efficiently by obtaining a better understanding of management science, the architect's responsibility for cost control and new techniques for speeding up architectural production by computers. But not one word was said about historic architecture.

Preservationists simply have not sold the importance of old buildings to those who should understand it most readily—architects. If, as some assert, the architectural historian has come of age as a separate professional, it is in part a consequence of the abdication of the average architectural practitioner of one of his traditional roles. For in spite of the excellent work of the national ASLA, ASCE and AIA committees on historic preservation, the average practitioners of my acquaintance in these professions—a representative sample, I believe—still have not got the preservation message.

Like it or not, this is a new day, the day of the interdisciplinary approach. Last fall, I spent a grueling two weeks as a student at the Institute of Advanced Architectural Studies at the University of York in England. Conservation area studies were undertaken as studio projects. Planners did the architectural work, architects did the planning and administrative work and, of course, the quantity surveyors tore up the work of both. This was the most useful experience I have yet had in years of preservation-planning work, because suddenly I understood what the restoration architect has to contend with.

How have the 21 lead organizations in the preservation-conservation field adapted to this new interdisciplinary approach? What have they done to encourage other professional organizations to become supporters of preservation? Have they used an imaginative approach to educate and bring onto the preservation-conservation team such groups as the American Bar Association, National Association of Real Estate Boards, National Association of Housing and Redevelopment Officials and American Institute of Planners? (I should note parenthetically that the National Trust has indeed made some headway with lawyers and that some planners have made notable contributions. I disagree with Mr. Peterson's comment on planners. As a class, they are not insidious; they are merely uninformed and generally disinterested.) Should we preservationists wait for them to "see the light" or should we help them see it? To this list of professionals that should be included on the preservation-conservation team, add bankers and officials of insurance companies, lending institutions and, most important, the officials of local and state governments. If preservation-conservation remains low on the totem pole of public priorities, this suggests that there is a big job that just is not being done.

A third organizational problem facing groups in the preservation-conservation field is the old one of getting more value for the dollar, making better use of existing funds. Organizations could, if they wished, modernize the flow of information. Training programs for conservators, restorationists and others could be standardized to some extent. AASLH cassette lectures are one new approach to education; the National Trust lecture-and-slide shows are another. Consider the possibilities in the "telelecture" conferences conducted by Dr. John Austin, who teaches environmental engineering at Clemson University, using telephoned television appearances by guest lecturers. These conferences are described in some detail in the May 1, 1972, issue of *Chemical and Engineering News*. Could we not at least call a moratorium on the publication of conference proceedings (maybe even on conferences) for a year and catch up on our reading?

Another means of making existing dollars go further would be a central, computerized, cooperative abstracting and bibliographical reference service covering a wide range of preservation-conservation subjects. Last year, both Paul E. Wilson, professor of law at the University of Kansas, and I, unknown to one another, compiled almost identical bibliographies on the legal aspects of historic preservation. One of us could have done something else useful to the cause had we known what the other was doing. I would note in passing that several of the 21 organizations under discussion maintain rosters of experts and consultants in various preservation-conservation fields. It seems at least plausible that what works for the ICA on a cooperative basis in providing technical services might work in other areas as well, if preservation organizations have the imagination and willingness to make these things work.

Executive and leadership retreats seem to work for the church, business and industry. What arrangements have been made for presidents and directors of preservation-conservation associations to get together to explore opportunities for minimizing overlapping and duplicating services, to coordinate conference calendars and programs or to see how several organizations might put their combined influence behind good legislation and mount unified opposition to the bad? What can national organizations do to promote coordination among professional groups at the state level? I do not know of any state where the state historic preservation officer, the AIA preservation coordinator, the ASCE preservation officer, National Trust Advisors and members of other professional organizations have ever even sat down in the same room together.

The "Preservation Mafia" of Washington, D.C., that is, preservation leaders from such diverse agencies as the U.S. Department of Housing and Urban Development, Department of Transportation, Council on Environmental Quality, National Park Service, Smithsonian Institution and the National Trust, are in a position where they can keep in touch on a regular, but informal, basis. This opportunity for discussion is quite useful. In this connection, it should be noted that there are already pressures in some organizations, such as the National Trust, for regional offices. Granted there are difficulties and complexities of locating a number of preservation-conservation regional offices in the same city or building (perhaps even in the same cities in which related federal agencies maintain field offices), but couldn't we preservationists at least discuss the possibility? Perhaps these are crackpot ideas, but the preservation movement is not so affluent that it can afford to overlook any possibility.

My remarks thus far have been aimed primarily at institutional-organizational considerations; however, as I mentioned earlier, institutions merely reflect the current interests, moods, needs and programs of the constituencies, whether individuals or institutions, that make up their memberships. Programs of organizations active in the preservation-conservation field reflect existing preservation-conservation philosophy. This philosophy is always subject to change—in fact, it is changing now—and if we attempt to foresee the institutional requirements of tomorrow, we must also try to divine some of the emerging changes in preservation-conservation philosophy. What is the outlook?

As I have suggested, we preservationists and conservationists tend to talk too much to ourselves—in conferences such as this one, through our publications, through our shared interests. We must come to accept that there is a big world out there, and if we are honest, we have to admit that preservation-conservation is not high on the list of priorities, given today's total spectrum of societal desires and needs. The public is generally indifferent to our efforts. Preservation and conservation are typically regarded as the special province of the wealth; the elite; and the white, educated, middle and upper classes. In spite of the recent growth of preservation-conservation organizations and increased government and private support, in terms of the real job to be done, we have a long way to go to convince the public that preservation is worthwhile. Why is this so?

I believe the basic disinterest of the American public-at-large in preservation-conservation matters is rooted in several traditions. It should be acknowledged that most of the population still believe that change is inevitable, that "you can't stop progress." Such words as *bigger, faster* and *more modern* are usually equated with *better*. As a nation, our attitudes toward the past are ambivalent. For one thing, the preferred link to the past is, in my opinion, not architecture, but decorative arts. This attitude is reflected in the fact that more people would probably read *Antiques,* to cite an example, than the *SAH Journal* if a more popular version of the latter existed. I also happen to believe the American public prefers a romanticized version of the past rather than the real thing; this preference has resulted in a proliferation of imitative architecture from earlier periods while the old buildings of real integrity are destroyed. Third, the American life-style has become so containerized that people are much more conscious of interior spaces than exterior ones. Most people have simply become hardened to the exterior appearance of a community—its architecture, spaces and relationships, that is, its total visual form. As a nation, America does not care much for art, and I see little evidence that the rich are more interested in preservation and conservation than the middle class or the poor.

It is important to recognize that the nation's life-style has changed drastically in the last 20 years. We are now mobile and rootless. We have less willingness to invest in historic properties as dwellings because for the most part we know we will soon leave, even if for another job with the same company. It is a standing joke that the familiar acronym IBM stands not only for International Business Machines Corporation but also means "I've been moved!" In any event, this new life-style puts less emphasis on the amenities provided in earlier buildings: space, privacy, character, individuality and a sense of place. The emphasis now is on suburbs with their new houses, which in turn generates a taste for more of the same. The city's commercial life follows families to the suburbs, and the inner city (and its best buildings) goes to ruin.

Younger families, which I have always regarded as prime candidates for inner-city housing, just are not interested in investing there. The lack of money for rehabilitation and the uncertain future of most inner-city neighborhoods from social, racial and economic viewpoints militate against the recycling of older properties in the city. Repairs cost more, loans are harder to get and more equity is required.

Perhaps the biggest problem in this area is the contemporary social upheaval the country is experiencing—a problem easy for us, from our elitist intellectual vantage point, to ignore—but the real root of most preservation problems.

First, there is racial discord. There is an unwillingness by both blacks and whites to allow neighborhoods where significant numbers of blacks live to be integrated. This intransigence creates many problems: the alleged equation "historic preservation= Negro removal" (probably true), finding the proper level of property maintenance or rehabilitation and deciding which properties must be preserved at all costs.

Second, there is a growing articulate public rejection of preservation programs in inner-city areas and elsewhere. Not only do inner-city black residents oppose preservation, but so do others, such as farmers, working-class people and many intellectuals, who quite sincerely believe preservation is not really an important issue. Blacks and other ethnic groups have withdrawn into a life where the emphasis is on cultural separatism. A limited contact with diversity of any kind is preferred. Black nationalism is the most extreme expression of this movement. Moreover, there is a total rejection of the concept of a common or shared heritage or a "common good." Viewed from this perspective, *With Heritage So Rich* was absolutely the wrong title for that book.

The point is, and this is fundamental, that the new emphasis is on many heritages—such as the black, chicano, Polish—and growing numbers of people have either apathy or positive antipathy toward the preservation of a "common" past, particularly when that past glorifies a tradition they now find repugnant. For an excellent discussion of this problem, read Grady Clay's article, "Townscape and Landscape: The Coming Battleground," in the January–March 1972 issue of *Historic Preservation*.

All of this poses difficult problems for the preservation-conservation movement. For example, the great plantation homes of the South are well preserved and showpieces of their kind. Consider the difficulties in showing the southern plantation in its entirety: The slave cabins are gone, the slave furniture and clothes are gone (worn out and not handed down), there are no paintings of slave families, there are few diaries and genealogies are very difficult to research. Public records are skimpy, and major documentary sources are likely to be criminal court records and property records, hardly an aspect of the past in which present-day blacks would be interested; however, if one pursues the idea that in the interest of intellectual completeness the story of the people who built the great houses and plantations should be told, then there is a challenge in this situation for the archaeologist and the oral history specialist.

In the counterpart urban situation, there is a challenge to the museologist and the conservator. Perhaps some old slums should be saved and listed, as is, in the National Register. Perhaps storefront museums based on themes and activities of current and daily interest to present neighborhood inhabitants would be a step in the right direction.

The implications of these impending changes for preservation, particularly for organizations that represent professions involved in the field, are fairly obvious. Organizations not only reflect their members' desires; they also serve as cultural "tastemakers." They therefore share much of the responsibility for the ultimate direction, content and philosophy of the preservation-conservation movement. Whether and to what extent preservation-conservation organizations will rise to new opportunities in what for most of us will be strange, sometimes unpleasant, foreign intellectual territory remains to be seen.

At the very least, I believe a reexamination is needed of some aspects of the preservation philosophy that was hammered out at Williamsburg some 10 years ago. The purpose of preservation to begin with and, indeed, its relevance to the whole of society is at stake.

FOR FURTHER INFORMATION: ADDRESSES OF THE 21 LEADING CONSERVATION-PRESERVATION ORGANIZATIONS

*If you are interested in obtaining specific information on the philosophy, goals, programs and activities of any of the 21 organizations mentioned by Mr. Stripe, you may write the organization directly. Current addresses are listed below.**

American Association for State and Local History
1315 8th Avenue, South
Nashville, Tenn. 37203

American Association of Museums
2233 Wisconsin Avenue, N.W.
Washington, D.C. 20007

American Institute of Architects
1735 New York Avenue, N.W.
Washington, D.C. 20006

American Society of Civil Engineers
345 East 47th Street
New York, N.Y. 10017

American Society of Landscape Architects
1750 Old Meadow Road
McLean, Va. 22101

Association for Preservation Technology
Box 2487, Station D
Ottawa, Ontario, Canada K1P 5W6

Canadian Museums Association
Box 1328, Station B
Ottawa, Ontario, Canada K1P 5R4

Canadian Department of Indian Affairs and Northern Development
National Historic Sites Service
400 Laurier Avenue
Ottawa, Ontario, Canada K1A 0H4

Intermuseum Conservation Association
Allen Art Building
Oberlin, Ohio 44074

International Centre for the Study of the Preservation and the Restoration of Cultural Property
Via di San Michele, 13
00153 Rome, Italy

International Institute for Conservation of Historic and Artistic Works
Headquarters
608 Grand Buildings
Trafalgar Square
London, WC 2N 5HN, England
American Group
c/o C.T. Corporation System
918 16th Street, N.W.
Washington, D.C. 20006

International Council of Monuments and Sites
Headquarters
Hôtel Saint Aignan
75, rue du Temple
75003 Paris, France
U.S. ICOMOS
1522 K Street, N.W.
Suite 430
Washington, D.C. 20005

International Council of Museums
Headquarters
Maison de l'UNESCO
1, rue Miollis
75015 Paris, France
U.S. National Committee
2233 Wisconsin Avenue, N.W.
Washington, D.C. 20007

Library of Congress
1st Street, and Independence Avenue, S.E.
Washington, D.C. 20540

---

* Statements submitted by the 21 conservation-preservation organizations are on file in the National Trust archives and are available to researchers.

National Trust for Historic
Preservation
740-748 Jackson Place, N.W.
Washington, D.C. 20006

Royal Architectural Institute of
Canada
151 Slater Street
Suite 1104
Ottawa, Ontario, Canada K1P 5H3

Smithsonian Institution
1000 Jefferson Drive, S.W.
Washington, D.C. 20560

Society for American Archaeology
c/o R.E.W. Adams
College of Humanities and Social
Science
University of Texas at San Antonio
4242 Piedras Drive East
San Antonio, Tex.

Society for Historical Archaeology
c/o Roderick Sprague
Department of Anthropology
University of Idaho
Moscow, Idaho 83843

Society of Architectural Historians
1700 Walnut Street
Room 716
Philadelphia, Pa. 19103

U.S. Department of the Interior
National Park Service
18th and C Streets, N.W.
Washington, D.C. 20240

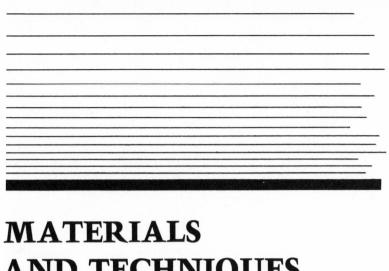

MATERIALS
AND TECHNIQUES

Wood

QUESTIONS OF PRESERVATION AND
A NEW X-RAY INVESTIGATIVE TECHNIQUE

GEORGE L. WRENN III

This paper is divided into two parts, the first discussing my experiences as a preservation administrator, the second describing an X-ray technique being developed by David McLaren Hart of Topsfield, Mass., a consultant to the Properties Department of the Society for the Preservation of New England Antiquities. Mr. Hart's technique is being presented at this conference for the purpose of determining whether such a technique has been considered or developed elsewhere for use on wood structures and for eliciting suggestions concerning its practicability, use and further development.

SOME PROBLEMS OF THE PRESERVATIONIST

The subject of this paper, the preservation of wood, is broad and has many possible facets. In presenting the principal problems of a harried preservation administrator, I hope to be helpful to preservationists in the field, whose problems are numerous. From an overall view, these problems are twofold: time and money. There is not enough of either for any preservationist, but for the private preservation organization without a dependable source of public or private support, the problems are particularly acute. Since my own experience as a preservation administrator and those of the organization for which I work are the basis of this discussion, let me briefly describe that organization, its history, its holdings and, most important, its approach to historic preservation.

George L. Wrenn III is associate director of the Society for the Preservation of New England Antiquities, Boston, Mass.

What Is the SPNEA?

The Society for the Preservation of New England Antiquities (SPNEA) was founded in 1910 and is the largest regional preservation organization in the United States. It now owns more than 60 historic properties, as well as numerous collections of architectural and other artifacts. Although the majority of the society's historic structures are houses, it also owns a cooperage, a gristmill and a meetinghouse. In addition, there are a great number of outbuildings (barns and other structures, some of which are quite large) connected with some of the properties.

Wood was in plentiful supply in New England, and all but three of the houses owned by the SPNEA are of wood-frame construction; the others, which are of brick, have wooden interior structural members and roof framing. Of course, wood is used in innumerable other ways throughout all of the structures—for sheathing, clapboarding, shingling on roofs and walls, flooring and paneling. Each area where wood is used in a structure is subject to a variety of vicissitudes, such as weather, rot, insect activity and just plain wear, not to mention man's efforts to be helpful.

The original construction dates of SPNEA properties range from the middle of the 17th century to the third quarter of the 19th century, and, of course, almost all of the structures include additions, remodelings and repairs made at later times. These raise the issue of how historic structures should be approached. The SPNEA believes that the approach is of paramount importance and must be determined before beginning work on any structural or other type of problem. The society's position is that any material dating from the "historic period" of a structure is precious and is to be preserved in place if at all possible, consistent with the safety and well-being of the rest of the structure. The historic period of a structure is the entire period from the time of construction to the time when it enters preservation status, that is, when it is acquired by a preservation organization.

This approach, to which there are exceptions that are beyond the scope of this paper, presents certain problems that are not the same as those associated with a "total" restoration, that is, a restoration of the house to its appearance when originally built. The increased difficulty of investigation is one such problem. In a total restoration, later surface material is removed, so that original structural members may be revealed. For instance, 17th-century structural members that were originally exposed on the interior of a house were often plastered over at a later time. Complete restoration would require removing the plaster, and the condition of the original structural members would be clearly seen. Preservation, as practiced by the SPNEA, calls for retaining the plaster. The problem, therefore, is to determine the configuration and condition of structural members in terms of both scholarship and safety. (The second section of this paper is devoted, in part, to this problem.)

The Need To Know
The next obvious and difficult problem inherent in this approach to preservation is how to treat a given situation once it is known to exist. Preservationists need to know what techniques exist (and what new techniques are under development) that will enable them to preserve structures without disturbing elements that they would prefer to leave in place.

Since one of the purposes, if not the primary purpose, of this conference is to bring together practitioners of preservation (such as the SPNEA), conservators from the museum world and scientists from different disciplines who have the knowledge to help preservationists solve their problems, it is appropriate to state that the present situation is not a particularly satisfactory one to preservationists.

Often, preservationists lack the necessary knowledge; in many cases, they are unaware of information sources on wood, masonry, paint, paper, leather, metals and other materials. Poor communications in the field and lack of time prevent them from using the entire range of potentially helpful publications available. They do not know how to locate consultants on specific or general problems, how to determine the cost (if any) of consultant services or if and where the money for such services can be obtained.

What is needed is some sort of information clearinghouse, national or international in scope. This function could be served by a new organization set up for that purpose, such as the National Building Research Institute that was proposed a few years ago, or by an existing organization, such as the Association for Preservation Technology, the National Trust for Historic Preservation, the Smithsonian Institution or the Rome Centre.

The advancement of SPNEA's knowledge would not only help the society in dealing with problems associated with its own buildings, but would also have wide-reaching benefits throughout New England. In New England, private preservation efforts far outweigh public ones. Small, local historical societies which, typically, own and maintain one historic house proliferate in the area. There are also innumerable houses of architectural and historical value owned by individuals. Many of these organizations and

91

individuals seek help from the SPNEA, because it is the regional preservation organization and because its level of professionalism and knowledge is generally more advanced than that of the small society or of the individual. Sometimes, however, the society feels inadequate or, to put it more accurately, is inadequate to the task. The SPNEA would like to provide more and better help to these organizations and individuals and to deal more adequately with its own structures. In fact, the society is studying the need for proper conservation facilities in New England and the feasibility of cooperating with other institutions in setting up such facilities. In the meantime, the SPNEA must continue to develop knowledge and techniques to cope with problems encountered in its own buildings.

Specific Problems

What, then, are some of the specific problems the SPNEA faces in dealing with wooden elements in its own houses? The principal ones are the most obvious—how to deal with deterioration conditions caused by the depredating effects of rot and insects.

INSECTS. The damage that can be caused by insect activity is extensive. Powder-post beetles, carpenter ants and termites may have been at work, and each requires its own treatment. Beetles are perhaps the hardest with which to cope.

One particular fumigation program, developed by the SPNEA for a group of houses and outbuildings, illustrates several practical and philosophical aspects of the dilemma. The buildings were afflicted with evident beetle activity and consequent deterioration of wooden structural members and other wooden elements. The proper procedure, it seems to me, would have been to investigate the entire subject of insect control before doing anything; however, there was not enough time to locate sources of technical information and to conduct the research necessary for a thorough investigation.

One consultant in the field said that, where there is no ready access to a structure's infected areas, elements should be taken apart and the infected areas sprayed or injected with the proper poison. This advice went "against the grain" because preservationists generally agree that, if at all possible, elements should not be removed but rather treated in place. Furthermore, the procedure is enormously expensive and was far beyond the available, limited resources of the properties in question. Thus, the time problem was compounded by the money problem.

As preservation administrator, I rejected the injection method and sought the services of a professional firm specializing in the eradication of insects and other animals or diseases harmful to wood. I was at a disadvantage in this situation, because I was forced to rely on individuals who stood to gain from the assignment and who knew more about the subject than I did. My only defense was to seek a firm of good reputation by asking for recommendations from former clients, who were able to confirm only that their troubles had not recurred in the last two, three or five years. A firm was contacted, a program agreed upon and a survey of the various houses and outbuildings taken. Estimates were submitted and accepted, and the program was implemented. It involved fumigation with cyanogen chloride gas. Human and animal residents of each house moved out, and each house was sealed as well as possible by chinking and blocking (not by an envelope). The gas was released and allowed to operate for a period of time, after which the house was opened and aired; the residents then returned. There were complaints about the tarnishing of objects that had been left behind despite warnings to remove them. Also, a smell remained—as does the question of whether the residue is dangerous.

The real question is whether this approach was the proper one. The answer can only be "no." The program worked as desired, and the techniques used may well have been good ones, at least for the short run. (Of course, the long run counts far more than the short run.) It is clear, however, that a better approach is possible, one that involves disinterested advice on the latest techniques and their implementation.

What is needed is a central organization—either a foundation or a government agency—that could be called on to provide reasonably priced assistance. It is hoped that conferences such as this one, attended by scientists and preservation practitioners from many different areas and institutions, will contribute helpful answers to some of these problems. In the meantime, problems accumulate, and rapid, on-the-spot pragmatic solutions must be found for them.

DRY ROT FUNGUS. Of the other problems affecting wood, those caused by dry rot fungus are perhaps the worst. Operating independently or in conjunction with beetles, dry rot fungus causes wood to deteriorate under certain environmental conditions. Sills, framing members and other wooden elements rot. The structure may in time become dangerously weak.

One necessary step in solving the problem is, of course, to correct conditions that permit dry rot fungus. Damp basements must be kept dry through proper ventilation. To provide such ventilation, a dehumidifier may have to be installed and connected into the house's drainage system. As historic houses are often only partially heated (that is, heated only in the apartment occupied by the caretaker), another possible solution would be the installation of a complete heating system for the entire house. Such a system would help alleviate dampness in the basement and would reduce temperature and humidity fluctuations in the rest of the house. The proper design of such heating systems for maximum control of temperature and humidity and for minimum disturbance of structural elements, surfaces and furnishings is yet another problem.

Once the conditions that allowed dry rot fungi to exist are corrected, affected members themselves must be treated. Here, there are a number of problems, some that are caused by SPNEA's philosophical approach to preservation and some that are practical. For instance, the SPNEA believes in trying to preserve as much wood of the historic period as possible, even to the still sound portions of a rotted sill. Can the fungus be satisfactorily treated in situ? If so, can treated areas be "filled" so that they can be preserved and have the necessary strength? If new wood must be introduced, there is the problem of how it should be treated prior to its introduction to prevent it from becoming infected.

The preservation of a structural member that has lost strength or that perhaps was never sufficiently strong is another problem. Rather than replace such a member, the SPNEA attempts to find ways to introduce a new member (or members) to do the job. Generally, these are of wood, but the use of steel or other metals may seem to be appropriate. Yet, there is disagreement as to whether or not the introduction of steel framing members in a wood-frame structure is a correct technique to use in all circumstances. This method was used recently by the SPNEA, when a concealed L-shaped steel piece was introduced along the outer surfaces of a partially rotted corner post in an effort to preserve it. Were we solving the problem or making future trouble because of the differing coefficients of expansion or other factors? Where does one turn for a definitive answer without having to take an inordinate amount of time?

WEATHER AND WEAR. Other problems involving wood that face the preservationist in the day-to-day handling of historic buildings are the effects of weather and wear. Sometimes, the problem is to preserve old and worn surface materials that have been exposed to weather. For example, shingles or clapboards in a somewhat deteriorated condition and with a natural rather than painted finish may need to be stabilized and protected from further deterioration, if this is possible. Or, in the case of a door that has retained remnants of its original paint, the objective may be to preserve the paint. The preservationist needs to know if there is a tested and proved transparent coating that will permanently protect both the wood and the paint without causing discoloration.

At some historic house museums, visitation is so heavy that flooring has to be replaced periodically. The SPNEA does not allow such heavy visitation at its houses, but the society nevertheless must face the problem, albeit over a longer period of time. One easy way to solve the dilemma, of course, is to use a covering that protects the floor, but it will also alter the historical appearance. What is needed is a treatment for wood that would not alter its appearance but would increase its life-span significantly. It is important to know if such a treatment exists.

X-RAY ANALYSIS: A NEW TECHNIQUE

A new technique has been developed that offers the possibility of help with a major problem, namely, the investigation of wooden elements with minimum disturbance. The following discussion, written by David McLaren Hart, concerns the use of an X-ray technique to analyze structural and other elements hidden from view in order to determine both their condition and their configuration. If it proves viable for these purposes, this technique will be a valuable tool for preservationists, particularly with regard to historic buildings, where it is desirable not to disturb the structure by dismantling it. Initial investigation of the process has begun, with the assistance of the SPNEA staff and James Ballou, a Salem, Mass., architect. Investigation under laboratory and field conditions has established basic parameters of the system's capabilities and limitations.

The X-ray system employed for the investigation uses a portable generating source, the only requirement for operation being an outlet with a 110-volt alternating current. Polaroid sheet film with the necessary processing equipment is used for the actual recording. The Polaroid process is, of course, advantageous in that any errors in exposure, distance or alignment can be easily corrected after the short development time. A permanent record can be created by photographing the finished Polaroid product.

X rays are high-energy radiation, capable of penetrating most materials. They are absorbed to varying degrees by building materials, and the resulting patterns appear on exposed film, thus giving a "picture" of internal composition. In use, the X-ray source is set up approximately 3 feet from one side of the wall, and the film, in its holder, is placed against the opposite side of the wall. After exposure, the film packet is processed for 45 seconds.

The examples of X-ray investigations in figures 1–9 illustrate the advantages and limitations of this method encountered so far. One example is a 4-by-10-inch portion of a partially deteriorated summer beam recently removed from the House of Seven Gables (1668)—also known as the John Turner House—in Salem, Mass., and investigated under laboratory conditions. The X ray (fig. 1), compared with a photograph (fig. 2) of the same section of the beam, shows the deteriorated area as light, as opposed to the sound wood in the darker, lower part of the X ray.

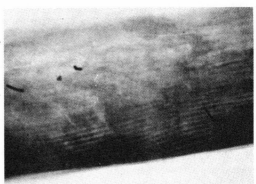

FIGURE 1. *X ray of a summer beam in the House of Seven Gables, Salem, Mass. A portion of the beam was removed from the first-floor south parlor during renovations in 1972. (David McLaren Hart)*

FIGURE 2. *Carpenter Ed Storey reveals the extent of insect damage in a summer beam from the House of Seven Gables. (David McLaren Hart)*

Another example, also investigated under laboratory conditions, is a common post-brace joint (fig. 3). In the X ray (included in the photograph), the mortise-tenon shape is clearly defined, and the soundness of the wood is evidenced by the uniform appearance, complete with wood grain.

The next example, taken in situ, illustrates the external and internal conditions of a ceiling in the House of Seven Gables, where a crack (fig. 4) made investigation desirable. The X ray (fig. 5) shows the existence of uniform-size lathing on one side of the joist and nonuniform-size lathing on the other. From this, it was clear that the ceiling on one side of the room had been repaired.

FIGURE 3. *Photograph and X ray of a common post-brace joint. This chestnut beam (c. 1790) was removed from a house in Bethlehem, Conn., in 1971. (David McLaren Hart)*

FIGURE 4. *Crack in the first-floor dining-room ceiling of the House of Seven Gables. (David McLaren Hart)*

Another example is of the chair rail in the Withdrawing Room in the First Harrison Gray Otis House (1795–96), SPNEA's headquarters in Boston, Mass. Figure 6 shows the rail with its incised decorations somewhat obscured by many layers of paint. The X ray (fig. 7) shows clearly the outline of the decorative elements. Darker areas in the incisions were caused by the heavy accumulation of lead paint.

The SPNEA's Codman House (c. 1740) in Lincoln, Mass., provided another interesting field example of the apparent failure of a cross-member supporting a stair landing. The deflection was noticeable, being approximately 2 inches in the 9-foot span (fig. 8).

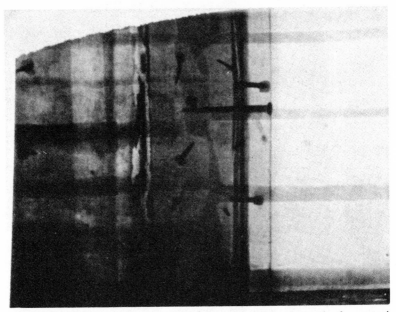

FIGURE 5. X ray of the ceiling crack shown in figure 4 reveals the use of uniform-size lathing on one side of the joist, nonuniform-size on the other. (David McLaren Hart)

FIGURE 6. Chair rail located in the first-floor parlor of the First Harrison Gray Otis House, Boston, Mass. (David McLaren Hart)

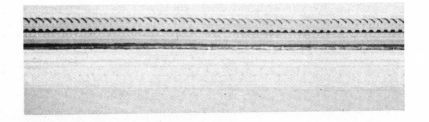

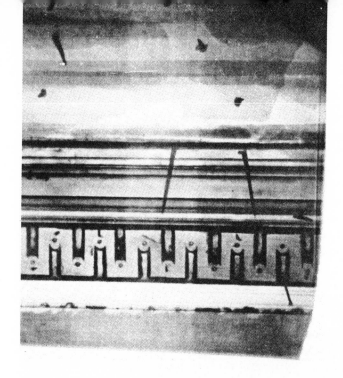

FIGURE 7. *X ray of the chair rail in figure 6 clearly shows the outline of decorative elements that have been hidden by paint. (David McLaren Hart)*

FIGURE 8. *Deflection due to presumed failure of a cross-member supporting a stair landing in the Codman House, Lincoln, Mass. (David McLaren Hart)*

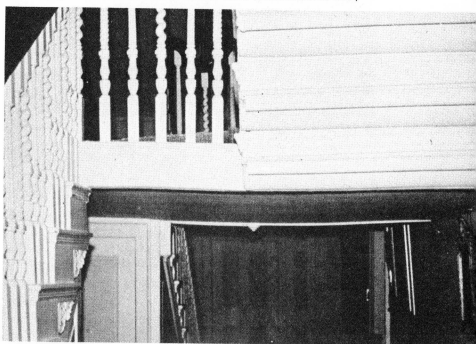

An X ray revealed the unexpected; the area had already been worked on, as wire lathing was evident (fig. 9). The dark area on the left side of the X ray is probably a steel reinforcing member, as the rate of X-ray penetration of steel is extremely slow. The stair landing had been reinforced without jacking up the sagging portion. Thus, it is now unnecessary to remove surface materials to determine the condition of the stair, because the existence of the steel member can be checked by drilling a small hole.

The advantages of field examination by X ray are evident; limitations so far seem to stem from the desirability of taking the X ray straight-on to achieve clarity and the lack of depth in the usually be overcome by a careful study of the X ray, using established standards and observations.

In summary, this X-ray process has definite advantages in the investigation of structural conditions in historic buildings. The cost of X-ray analysis is certainly far less than that involved in removing material. In a scholarly sense, this technique permits investigation of areas that the preservationist would rather not expose, and thus, it can contribute significantly to the cause of preservation.

FIGURE 9. *X ray of the cross-member shown in figure 8 reveals previous repairs. (David McLaren Hart)*

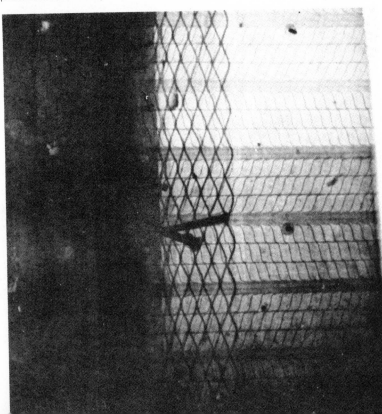

THE CHARACTERIZATION AND
PRESERVATION OF WOOD

HAROLD TARKOW

Nothing is more remindful of mortality than the Biblical phrase "dust to dust." The professional environmentalist speaks of "closing the circle." The traditional biologist refers to "the carbon cycle"—that process by which carbon dioxide is consumed and returned to the atmosphere at equal rates. The consumption occurs through the photosynthesis process, that is, the synthesis of vegetative tissues from carbon dioxide, water and inorganic salts, using sunlight as the source of energy and chlorophyll as the catalyst. These plant tissues, in the form of such things as flowers, sugarcane, poison ivy, trees and crabgrass, are storehouses of useful energy. Animals consume considerable quantities of this vegetation, transform it into energy for their own needs and release carbon dioxide into the atmosphere. Microorganisms also use these plant tissues for their energy and carbon needs, eventually returning the carbon to the atmosphere as carbon dioxide. One need only recall the musty odor in wet forests to appreciate the extent to which wood is involved in the carbon cycle. Wood can also be burned to recover its heat energy. This stored energy is released as heat and light in a dramatic way during a forest fire. Thus, wood has a propensity to deteriorate; however, this deterioration occurs only when conditions favor it. In the absence of favorable conditions, the deterioration rate of wood is so sub-

Harold Tarkow is assistant director of chemical utilization and protection research at the U.S. Forest Products Laboratory, Madison, Wis.

stantially reduced that the wood remains essentially inert and unchanged. Some knowledge of the characteristics of wood and the various deterioration processes that affect it is necessary to understand the procedures recommended for preserving and prolonging the useful life of wooden and wood-based objects of historical significance.

CHARACTERISTICS OF WOOD

To the touch, wood is a substantially solid material. Yet only 20 to 40 percent of the total volume of air-dried wood (that is, of most commercial species) is composed of actual wood substance. The remaining 60 to 80 percent consists of air-filled spaces or cells, which can be seen under a microscope (fig. 1). Wood is, therefore, a porous material, possessing excellent insulating and working qualities. However, because of the highly variable communication capabilities between cells, the permeability of wood varies greatly.

Wood substance is essentially a mixture of carbohydratelike materials (60 percent or more) and lignin (30 percent or more), with an average elementary composition of 50 percent carbon, 44 percent oxygen and 6 percent hydrogen and a density of about 1.45 grams per milliliter. During the growth of a tree, wood substance is laid down as the wall material of highly elongated arrays

FIGURE 1. *Air-filled spaces or cells in a section of softwood. (U.S. Forest Products Laboratory)*

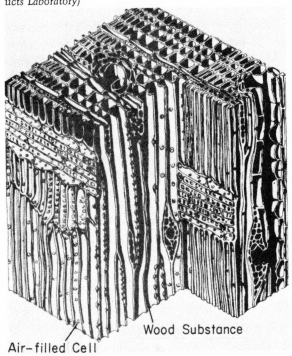

Wood Substance

Air-filled Cell

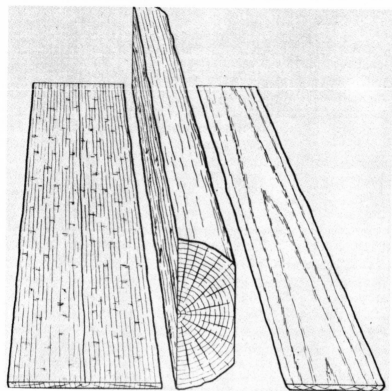

FIGURE 2. *Left, quarter-sawn board. Notice that annual growth rings form angles of approximately 90 degrees to faces of the board. Right, plain-sawn board. Annual growth rings form smaller angles with faces of the board than those on a quarter-sawn board. (U.S. Forest Products Laboratory)*

of cells. The characteristic grain of wood derives from the longitudinal orientation of these millimeter-long cells, which is predominantly parallel to the direction of growth. Each year, a growth layer is laid down, producing annual rings whose appearance in different wood surfaces produces the wood's characteristic and aesthetically pleasing features. The arrangement of cells in the radial direction (perpendicular to the rings) is different from that in the tangential direction (parallel to the rings). These different arrays of cells are responsible for directional properties of wood. Strength, elastic and swelling properties are different in the three directions. Depending on how the wood is cut, boards with different properties are obtained (fig. 2).

An important physical difference among various species is the relative amount of wood substance, that is, the wood's bulk density. The variation in relative amounts of wood substance and air-filled cells produces balsa, with a density of approximately 0.1 gram per milliliter; Douglas fir, with 0.5 gram per milliliter; and maple, with 0.7 gram per milliliter. These types of wood have approximately the same chemical composition, yet, because of the

103

variation in their bulk densities, balsa is excellent for rafts, Douglas fir for construction and maple for flooring. Table 1 gives the bulk densities of some common species.

Species also differ in the kind and amount of extractives associated with their wood substance. Generally consisting of less than 10 percent of the wood substance, extractives account for such properties as resistance to decay or susceptibility to attack by insects.

Table 1 AVERAGE DENSITY OF COMMON U.S. WOOD SPECIES

Species	Density (g/ml)
Aspen	0.38
Yellow birch	0.62
Cottonwood	0.40
Douglas fir	0.48
Hemlock	0.42
White oak	0.68
Black walnut	0.55

NOTE: Data are based on samples with a 12-percent moisture content.

Wood absorbs and releases moisture in response to changes in relative humidity. The average moisture content of wood used in interiors shows seasonal variations (table 2). As a consequence, the volume of wood changes with atmospheric conditions. This change produces significant directional effects, which can produce adverse weathering problems. Little change in dimension occurs in the longitudinal direction. Swelling or shrinking occurs mainly in the tangential and radial directions, with the swelling or shrinking in the tangential direction being about twice that in the radial direction. (Table 3 gives data on the swelling of Sitka spruce for

Table 2 AVERAGE MOISTURE CONTENT IN WOOD IN INTERIOR USE IN 10 U.S. CITIES

City	Moisture Content (%)	
	July	January
Albuquerque, N.M.	6.0	7.0
Atlanta, Ga.	11.5	8.5
Boston, Mass.	13.0	7.0
Dallas, Tex.	9.0	9.0
Duluth, Minn.	10.5	5.0
Madison, Wis.	16.0	6.0
New Orleans, La.	13.5	12.5
New York, N.Y.	12.5	7.0
Seattle, Wash.	11.0	8.0
Washington, D.C.	11.0	8.0

Table 3 SWELLING OF SITKA SPRUCE WITH CHANGES
IN RELATIVE HUMIDITY

Relative Humidity Interval (%)	Swelling (%)		Ratio of Tangential to Radial Swelling
	Tangential	Radial	
30-65	1.62	0.77	2.1
30-80	2.75	1.31	2.1
30-90	4.15	1.91	2.1
65-90	2.64	1.18	2.2
80-90	1.43	0.59	2.4

various changes in relative humidity.) The swelling of wood during a relative humidity interval is a function of the wood's bulk density. Thus, when the relative humidity is between 30 and 90 percent, the tangential swelling of high-density maple is about 5½ percent, and the radial swelling is about 2½ percent. Such anisotropic (that is, directional) behavior causes changes in the wood's shape, following the wood's swelling or shrinking (fig. 3).

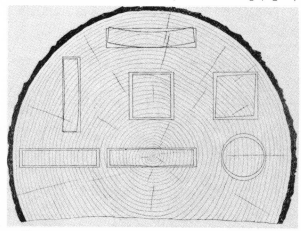

FIGURE 3. *Effect of anisotropy following shrinkage on the shape of wood sections with moisture contents of less than 30 percent. (U.S. Forest Products Laboratory)*

AGENTS RESPONSIBLE FOR THE DETERIORATION OF WOOD

Certain external agents promote the deterioration of wood under varying environmental conditions.

Liquid Water

The time required for swelling to attain equilibrium in wood depends on a moisture property of wood known as the *diffusion constant,* which describes the rate at which moisture moves through the wood under standard conditions. This rate is a directional property and is considerably higher in the longitudinal direction. Diffusion occurs when there are differences in moisture content within a piece of wood. A difference in moisture content creates a difference in the degree of swelling in different regions. If the tendency to swell is opposed, a stress is created, which can be harmful.

Moisture absorption in wood can be prevented by applying a force that opposes the volume change. If the force exceeds some relevant strength property, "something has to give." For example, ancient Egyptians split rocks by wedging dry plant tissues into cracks of the rocks and adding water. A rock split when the plant tissues' swelling stresses exceeded the rock's cleavage strength. As moisture diffuses into wood, the swelling tendency of a small volume of wood is opposed by the small volume immediately ahead of it. If the moisture gradient is small, as when the diffusion constant is small or the driving force is weak, swelling stresses are small and harmless. Where the moisture gradient is large, for example, if the driving force is strong (as when a surface is suddenly wetted with liquid water), swelling stresses often exceed the strength of the wood and failure occurs.

The penetration of liquid water into wood is facilitated by capillarity or *wicking*. Wicking is the spontaneous movement of a liquid through a structure containing small capillaries (cells, in the case of wood). In wood, this phenomenon occurs within a few fiber diameters in the transverse directions or within a few fiber lengths in the longitudinal direction. Such rapid (and shallow) penetration is instantly followed by the rapid diffusion of the water into cell walls. (Stresses as high as 12,000 pounds per square inch have been recorded when the maximum instantaneous swelling pressure of wood wetted under such conditions was measured.) On subsequent rapid drying, surface areas dry first. Shrinkage in these areas is opposed by water-swollen tissues located deeper in the wood. These rapid interchanges of moisture on surface areas contribute to the type of deterioration known as *weathering*. Figure 4 shows an unprotected panel of Douglas fir after several years of weathering. Destructive action is especially prominent at end-grain surfaces (not shown). Such destructive actions accelerate further deterioration by other agents, such as decay fungi.

Ultraviolet Radiation
The lignin component of wood is extremely absorptive in the ultraviolet region of solar radiation. Although the penetration of such light is shallow, surface absorption leads to severe embrittlement and loss of wood substance. Obviously, such action occurs

FIGURE 4. *Weathered, unprotected Douglas fir panel. (U.S. Forest Products Laboratory)*

only outdoors. In the absence of surface protection, the combined action of rapid moisture exchange, decay and ultraviolet radiation (that is, weathering) causes wood to erode at a rate of about ¼ inch per century.

Decay Fungi

Decay fungi are serious wood-destroying agents. They enter wood as spores and develop long strands, or *hyphae,* that penetrate to great depths. These fungi, which use cellulose and some lignin for food, destroy cell walls and change the physical characteristics of wood, resulting in decay. Under conditions favorable to them, decay fungi are very destructive, especially to the sapwood. There are three requirements for the growth of fungi: a temperature range of 50° to 100°F, air and a moisture content in excess of 30 percent (that is, the presence of some free water). At equilibrium, a moisture content as high as 30 percent is reached only when the relative humidity is 100 percent. Decay, therefore, does not generally occur indoors. However, a moisture content of 30 percent or higher is possible even though the ambient humidity is less than 100 percent, for example, in wooden structures that are in contact with moist soil or that are above wet soil but are poorly ventilated; in wood joints, which can trap liquid water; and in weathered wood with cracks or checks, which can also trap water.

Wood-staining Fungi

Unlike decay fungi that derive their carbon and energy from the wood substance in cell walls, wood-staining fungi get their principal support from readily available and accessible materials (that is, extractives) in special cells. These fungi have no serious effect on wood, but they produce blue or other colored stains on wooden surfaces. They, too, can survive only when the wood they attack has a high moisture content.

Insects

Damage caused by insects to wood in use is more erratic than that caused by fungi. Under damp conditions, the decay of wood is unavoidable. Infestation with insects, however, occurs only if female insects can deposit their eggs in the wood. Larvae, which tunnel through the wood in search of food and shelter, can cause serious damage. Some insects, such as termites, utilize wood substance (that is, cell walls) as a source of energy and carbon. Other insects feed on certain extractives, such as starch in the sapwood. Still others require fungi in addition to wood substance.

Normally, subterranean termites live in moist soil and enter wood only to seek food and shelter. They can cause considerable damage to wood in warm or moderate climates. Dry-wood termites, on the other hand, are entirely wood-inhabiting. After flights, pairs of them enter cracks in wood to start new colonies. A high moisture content in the wood is not necessary; in fact, dry-wood termites can readily thrive at moisture contents as low as 10 to 12 percent. Although subterranean and dry-wood termites are restricted to certain areas of the United States, few wood species are immune to attack by either type of termite if conditions are favorable.

Powder-post beetles (*Lyctus*) lay their eggs in certain hardwoods, such as oak and ash, whose vessels are large enough to accommodate the eggs. Emerging larvae tunnel through the wood, seeking starch granules in the sapwood. Undigested wood passes through their guts. Wood is susceptible to attack by these insects only during seasoning and storage, prior to conversion to lumber. Thus, the problem is generally not a recurring one.

Other common wood-destroying insects are the furniture beetle (commonly known as the woodworm) and the death-watch beetle. These insects are less discriminating than powder-post beetles about the species they attack. They lay their eggs in surface cracks or crevices in exposed wood surfaces. On emerging, larvae burrow through the wood, seeking out fungi as a food supplement. These insects can attack relatively dry wood that has been previously invaded by fungi.

Knowing the conditions under which the deteriorating agents of wood function, one can understand the recommendations for preventing their actions and thereby preserving wooden objects and structures.

PROTECTION AGAINST WOOD-DETERIORATING AGENTS

Weathering

The weathering of wood is caused in part by rapid wetting and drying, which are accompanied by destructive stresses. Rapid wetting of wood can be prevented by applying coatings or finishes, which also protect the wood against ultraviolet radiation. Coatings slow the penetration of water vapor and liquid water (that is, rain) into wood. The retarding influence of different coatings on the rate of water-vapor movement in wood is shown in figure 5. As moisture enters wood that has been coated, swelling occurs slowly, and stresses are easily accommodated by plastic adjustments. However, if the coating weathers badly, it may cease to protect the wood against penetration by liquid water, making the wood susceptible to fungal attack. The importance of proper selection and maintenance of coatings cannot be overstated.

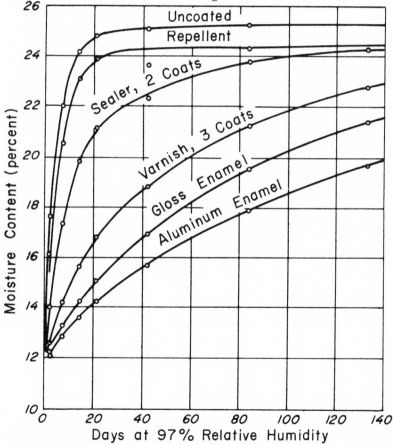

FIGURE 5. *Rate of water-vapor movement in wood protected by different coatings. (U.S. Forest Products Laboratory)*

FIGURE 6. *Back of untreated wood panel, the front of which was exposed to liquid water. (U.S. Forest Products Laboratory)*

FIGURE 7. *Back of protected wood panel, the front of which was exposed to liquid water. A water repellent provided protection against penetration by the liquid water. (U.S. Forest Products Laboratory)*

Water repellents are another means of protecting wood against penetration by liquid water (figs. 6 and 7). Joints where wooden elements meet are extremely vulnerable because they readily trap liquid water, which, of course, leads to the development of the stresses previously mentioned and the creation of conditions conducive to decay. Ideally, vulnerable areas of wooden elements should be dipped in a solution of a water-repellent preservative before a joint is assembled. Such solutions contain a preservative against fungal attack, such as penta (for example, pentachlorophenol), and a water repellent, such as wax (for example, paraffin

110

oil), which prevents liquid water from penetrating the joint. Capillarity carries the treatment solution to surface areas. The solvent should be allowed to evaporate from the wood before the joint is assembled to provide a good base for a coating of paint. Alternatively, a solution can be applied to assembled joints by liberal brushing. Surfaces with exposed end-grain, such as those of posts, telephone arms, laminated beams, rafters or porch steps, are especially vulnerable to weathering and deterioration and should be treated with a water-repellent preservative before being painted.

Decay Fungi

Wood in contact with the ground is subject to decay. Telephone poles and fence posts can be protected by pressure treatments with creosote or other preservatives of proved efficiency—both oilborne and waterborne solutions. Green posts can be treated by prolonged immersion in aqueous solutions of certain inorganic salts.

The adverse effects of moisture and decay do not occur in wood used in interiors. Relative humidities indoors are below saturation, and moisture contents of wood are generally below 15 percent (table 2). Under such conditions, fungal attack will assuredly not occur. In fact, it cannot be overstated that, in the absence of insects, wood kept indoors—away from fire and accumulations of liquid water—is indestructible. In damp places, such as improperly ventilated basements, where the relative humidity may reach 100 percent, decay is a serious threat. The remedy, obviously, is to provide ventilation and to remove the cause of water accumulation.

Insects

Where subterranean termites are a problem, the preferred protective treatment for a wooden building is to poison the soil around the foundation and beneath the building. Chemical poisons include chlordane and related materials; however, because of their residual effects, these chemicals are under scrutiny by the U.S. Environmental Protection Agency for possible environmental impact. Dry-wood termites are tropical and semitropical insects. They do little damage to wood in temperate regions compared to that done by subterranean termites.

Wood can be protected from attack by beetles by providing proper sanitation and avoiding the introduction of infested wood. Infested wood can be sterilized by fumigation with toxic vapors, such as methyl bromide. Permanent protection can be provided by coating all surfaces of uninfested finished products with film-forming finishes that prevent insects from laying eggs on bare wood. Wood can also be protected, of course, by impregnation (or

111

brushing) with suitable wood preservatives, such as lindane or penta.

PROVIDING PROTECTION TO DETERIORATING WOOD IN USE

Preservationists are generally concerned with arresting destructive action under way in historically interesting and important structures rather than with protecting newly assembled structures. Damage to historic structures may be caused by continuous outdoor exposure with inadequate protection or by insect damage. On-site treatments are necessary in these situations. Still another source of destructive action is the drying of waterlogged wooden objects after they have been submerged under water for centuries.

Dry Objects (Indoors)

If seemingly sound wood shows evidence of exit or bore holes, insect damage must be suspected. Further damage can be prevented by fumigation with poisonous gases, such as methyl bromide, in sealed chambers or by brushing the wood with liberal amounts of solutions containing toxic materials, such as penta or lindane, in nonstaining solvents. The insecticide solution should be injected into all exit holes and brushed freely and repeatedly over rough surfaces where unpainted wood is exposed. After the solvent has evaporated, exit holes should be filled with soft wax. Precautions should be taken to avoid inhalation or contact with the skin.

Wooden Objects (Outdoors)

Common causes of deterioration in wooden objects located outdoors are weathering and decay, especially in damp areas of objects or in such "water traps" as joints. Ventilation is helpful. The involved area should be brushed with a 5 percent penta solution, which is available commercially (again, to be used with caution). Greases containing 10 percent penta are available for application on relatively dry areas and are quite efficient, for example, when applied on joints. Penta penetrates both by diffusion and by capillarity.

Consolidation of Weakened Wood

Following the satisfactory arrest of deterioration caused by a biological agent, wood may be seriously weakened because of eroded pockets, etc. Plastic wood, judiciously applied, can be helpful in this case. Waxes may also be used. Synthetic resins, such as polyvinyl acetate dissolved in nine parts toluene and one part acetone, have also been used successfully. In addition, many proprietary consolidants are available.

Waterlogged Wood

When wood is submerged in water for many years, its cell cavities become filled with water (that is, waterlogged). In addition, a slow chemical reaction known as *hydrolosis* (chemical action involving water) weakens cell walls. If walls are weakened severely enough, when the wooden object is dried, the surface tension force may be sufficient to draw in, or collapse, the walls. Severe checking usually follows. Under such circumstances, the object's historical value can be considerably impaired. Treatments using the water-soluble chemical polyethylene glycol–1000 (PEG–1000) permit waterlogged wooden objects to be dried without serious distortion. When a waterlogged objected is treated with a PEG–1000 solution, the chemical diffuses into swollen cell walls and displaces the water there. Figure 8 shows a waterlogged 5/8-inch board removed from a *bateaux* in New York after about 250 years of submersion. Figure 9 shows a section of the board after it was treated with PEG–1000 and air-dried; it is obvious that little damage occurred on drying. Figure 10 shows an adjacent untreated section that was air-dried from its waterlogged condition. Considerable distortion and checking are evident.

FIGURE 8. *Section of waterlogged yellow-pine board after 250 years of submersion. (U.S. Forest Products Laboratory)*

FIGURE 9. *Section of waterlogged yellow-pine board submerged for 250 years after treatment with PEG–1000 for four hours and air drying. (U.S. Forest Products Laboratory)*

113

FIGURE 10. *Section of waterlogged yellow-pine board submerged for 250 years, untreated and air-dried from its waterlogged condition. (U.S. Forest Products Laboratory)*

SUMMARY

Wood is a biodegradable material. From an environmental viewpoint, this is an advantage possessed by few raw materials. Under certain conditions, wood deteriorates through a sequence of events and finally reverts to its elements—carbon dioxide, water and energy. The environmentalist would say when this reversion occurs that the circle has closed.

Agents and processes destructive to wood include weathering, decay fungi (in wet wood) and certain insects; however, the action of these destructive forces can be completely arrested by proper treatment and maintenance. Generally, treatments must be performed by skilled specialists, especially when unique problems relating to the preservation of historically valuable objects are involved.

There is abundant evidence for the claim that wood has a long life when it is properly treated or maintained. The siding of many houses built during Revolutionary War times and properly maintained through periodic painting is still in excellent condition. Many Stradivarius violins are sound and play as sweetly as they did when they were made by the master more than 400 years ago. Wooden objects removed from Egyptian tombs, where the key preservatives were dryness and isolation from insects, are in good physical condition. Structural members in well-designed Japanese temples that are hundreds of years old are still in sound condition.

Although the ability of wood to maintain its integrity and aesthetic quality has long been known, these attributes are not sufficiently appreciated. It is hoped that this discussion will be useful to preservationists in their endeavors to preserve some of the valuable and irreplaceable wooden objects and structures of the past.

114

COMMENTARY

JOHN I. REMPEL, MRAIC

I am always amazed and impressed by the complexity and sophistication of present-day preservation techniques used to combat such problems as those mentioned by George L. Wrenn and Harold Tarkow.

The following paragraph from Bulletin 111 of the Building Division of the National Research Council, Ottawa, Canada, emphasizes one of the problems Mr. Tarkow discusses—fungi:

The reproductive power of fungi is fantastic when it is considered that one square foot of dry rot fungus fruit body can produce five million spores per minute over a period of several days. These microscopic dust-like particles are shed in clouds from mature fruit bodies and being very light can be carried over great distances. Therefore, there is every likelihood that spores of wood-rotting fungi will be present wherever wood is used.

In other words, every piece of 2-by-4 should be considered potentially infected. As I picture these clouds of myriads of little creatures flying about looking for mischief, I am amazed that we preservationists have done as well as we have in controlling them. Five million spores per minute adds up to 300 million per hour or 7.2 billion per day!

There are several points with regard to all types of restoration projects, not just those involving wooden structures, that I believe

John I. Rempel, MRAIC, is a restoration architect in private practice in Toronto, Canada.

are relevant for discussion at this conference. These include responsibilities of preservationists toward small preservation projects, the need to educate laymen to the potentials of historic preservation and specific technical needs, the establishment of a central preservation information exchange and an emphasis on the value of thorough structural research of all buildings being preserved.

All the participants at this conference are specialists in one area or another. I really do not like the term *specialist,* because it generally designates a narrow field of knowledge, although it is knowledge in great depth. Specialized knowledge is, of course, a prerequisite for becoming a scientist, but it is more important for those who are actively engaged in various areas of historic preservation and research to have a general awareness of all the specialties represented at this conference and their applications. Our work as preservationists is too broad and too general to do otherwise, but I do not advocate the jack-of-all-trades approach. Preservationists working on the North American continent will probably never have the problem of a Venice, a Florence after the flood or the prodigious task of reconstruction like that undertaken in Warsaw. Our problems are unique to this continent and require their own solutions.

When preservation projects are mentioned, many of us perhaps unconsciously think of a type of project that falls into what may be called the "elite class." These are either government-supported or privately funded projects that have the resources required to undertake archaeological studies and to make thorough scientific and structural analyses and that employ the latest and most sophisticated preservation techniques. However, there are many projects that do not belong to this elite class, that is, small projects of purely local historical value (and often little of that) that are undertaken by enthusiastic laymen without any training, who work with limited funds and often without any government assistance. This situation may not exist in foreign countries but it certainly exists in the United States and Canada.

I want to put in a good word for small, local preservation projects. Preservationists should feel a sense of responsibility toward these projects and the people who undertake them, and they should offer all the assistance possible. These small projects demand great ingenuity since, for financial reasons, groups sponsoring these projects usually cannot call on specialists for assistance. This is one reason why "general practitioners" in preservation should be aware of the latest preservation techniques and special problems involved in their use on small projects. We preserva-

116

tionists need to develop a sixth sense to assist us in making pragmatic decisions. We should develop an instinct for a reasonably correct guess. This approach is not scientific, but there will always be problems associated with preservation projects and they will always have to be solved in some way.

I have two hobbies: One is historic preservation and restoration and the other is historical research, especially in the history of technology. From experience, I have found that attempts to solve minor problems of small, local projects frequently lead to the discovery of important historical information. For example, last fall the president of a small, local historical society in Monroe County, Mich., which is about 60 to 70 miles south of Detroit, wrote to me concerning the construction of a small building that the society wanted to move and use as a museum. When workers began to dismantle the building, some peculiar construction was found. The society asked for my help. I had no problem identifying the construction, which was typical early French-Canadian; and I was delighted to assist on this project, because it provided me with some valuable historical information. Detroit was originally a French settlement, and some of the settlement was known to have spilled across the river into Canada. There are examples of early French-Canadian construction around the Windsor area in Canada. I did not know, however, how far this type of construction had penetrated into the United States, and this project provided me with photographs and documentation proving that it was used at least 60 or 70 miles south of Detroit. Thus, a small preservation project led to a discovery that was important to me as a historian.

The next point I would like to discuss is education. By education, I do not mean public relations or graduate-level training, but rather the education of the layman. My concern is twofold. In the first place, it is desirable to have an educated public because the only way to foster a sense of civic pride is to develop public judgment and discrimination. The sense of civic pride in national monuments is much more developed in Europe than it is in North America. It is, however, true that in Europe this pride is frequently mixed with a generous amount of nationalism; nevertheless, the pride is real, and I believe that a certain amount of nationalism is harmless. A few years ago, a Greek immigrant from Athens, who worked as a cook in a restaurant around the corner from the school where I was teaching architecture, attended my course. He was potentially a good draftsman, although too old to start as a junior draftsman, and he was keen on architecture. Once when we were discussing design, he said, "You know, when you walk past the Acropolis and look at the Parthenon it makes you feel good inside." That statement came from a short-order cook in a restaurant! I wish that North Americans felt the same way about their national monuments.

The second aspect of my concern with education may sound devious, but sometimes it is necessary to be devious. Most politicians are cautious about approving funds for a project that may have a doubtful reception by their constituents. If, however, a politician's constituents have a sense of history and civic pride, they will appreciate historic preservation projects and encourage their representative to obtain funds for them. The representative will be pleased to help his constituents because it will provide him with a "cause" and will justify him in the eyes of the voters, and projects may receive much needed money.

Mr. Wrenn discusses the great need for a preservation center, a repository that would contain information on every conceivable aspect of preservation and could provide names of specialists to preservationists seeking advice. This center should be a place where both amateurs and professionals could receive suggestions for solutions to problems and appropriate procedures to use. A knowledge of desirable preservation methods and procedures would assist preservationists in making pragmatic decisions in situations where resources are limited and it is necessary to make the best of the situation but retain an easy conscience. Charles E. Peterson has developed detailed plans for this type of institution, and I hope that someday the idea will be implemented. Currently, the Association for Preservation Technology comes close to being such an institution in many respects.

Another important need is an emphasis on the value of thorough structural research of all buildings involved in preservation projects. Again, there is usually no problem in obtaining structural analyses for the elite types of project mentioned previously, but it is sometimes a great problem with small projects. There are cases where "surgery" is the only solution, even at the risk of leaving scars. The X-ray technique discussed in Mr. Wrenn's paper would help in many cases, but there probably will still be situations when personal inspection of the structure will be desirable or necessary. I have seen too many small projects where structural analysis has been badly neglected with disastrous results. The reason for this neglect is that most preservation activities are concerned with a project's visual aspects, such as the correctness of the paint color and furnishings. Since a building's structure is generally hidden from view, this aspect is often neglected, especially if a compromise is necessary.

In Europe, structural frames made of timber have passed through a definite and traceable development, a development that may encompass 600 or 700 years. In North America, of course, the time scale is considerably compressed, but even here there is evidence of a definite progression of structural change. For example, in old timber frames, principal structural members were always much stronger than necessary, probably because sizes were arrived at by empirical methods. Another important point to consider in dating a frame is the type of joint used, that is, the method by which stress is transferred between any two members. It is in the joints that a definite development can be traced, both in European and in North American structures. To my knowledge, Cecil A. Hewett, author of *The Development of Carpentry, 1200–1700* (Newton Abbot, England: David & Charles, 1969), was the first person to make a thorough study of the development of joints in structural frames. His research shows a logical sequence from dated buildings—beginning about 1200—and he has concluded that, at least in England, a timber frame can be dated with reasonable accuracy by its joints. I believe Mr. Hewett was also the first person to suggest possible early structural assembly procedures, a topic about which there exists practically no literature. Since assembly procedures were one aspect of the building trade that an apprentice had to learn on the job, there was no reason to write them down. In trying to reconstruct these procedures, there is a danger of interpolating our own ideas, that is, of thinking in terms of tractors, derricks and bulldozers instead of in terms of pike poles and gin poles as early builders did. The study of past construction principles and methods has been neglected, and we have all seen examples of the use of inappropriate structural procedures in restoration.

An experience I had with the preservation of a gristmill illustrates the importance of a thorough understanding of historical construction principles and methods. The mill had to be removed from its site to allow for the construction of a road. Fortunately, local preservationists had made a thorough documentary study of the structure. Pertinent dates and the sequence of owners were known. It was assumed that the mill as it stood was the original structure; however, as the siding was being removed from the east end during the dismantling, I saw a kind of joint in several places that was never used as an end joint. It was used only as an intermediate joint. Therefore, I knew that the structure being dismantled was not the total original building. A part was missing, although there was no outward evidence of it. Then, I had what was perhaps my greatest luck in research. I found the name of the woman who had been the last inhabitant of the mill. She was a widow and had remarried and moved several hundred miles north. I succeeded in learning her new name and address. I wrote to her, explaining the problem, and she sent me two old, crumpled snapshots, one showing the complete original structure and the other showing three bays in the process of being dismantled. If this information had not been obtained and the mill had been preserved on the basis of the assumption that the structure being dismantled was the complete original building, there would not have been room for all of the machinery.

In conclusion, I would emphasize the need for general practitioners to keep fully informed of the latest preservation techniques so that they will know what options there are in any given situation and be able to choose the best solution according to the circumstances.

I would also strongly suggest that general practitioners make every effort to assist in educating the public about preservation and that preservationists assist even the smallest local projects, gratuitously if necessary. As Harold J. Plenderleith has said, preservationists must develop a sense of duty and responsibility. Perhaps there should be a preservationist oath similar to the medical profession's Hippocratic oath. Even greater needs, however, are the establishment of a central preservation information exchange and an emphasis on the value of thorough structural research, which often yields more positive and definitive information than documents.

COMMENTARY

BRUNO MÜHLETHALER

On reading the papers presented at this conference, I was impressed by the fact that many preservationists believe they lack access to important technical information necessary to properly preserve buildings. In addition to being asked for information on supply sources, specifications and technical data relating to materials, institutions and professionals with expertise in preservation are often consulted with the expectation that they will provide official sanction for the use of unconventional methods. Those asking for assistance frequently fail to recognize that their problem may be quite complex and that the attention of specialists may be required to find a solution. (George L. Wrenn illustrates this situation very well in his paper.) Although there is a great deal of scientific information that could be brought to bear on these problems, it is, unfortunately, not always available to those who need it. How can preservationists obtain the information science can offer them?

This question concerns me greatly, since, as a conservation researcher for the Landesmuseum (the Swiss national museum) and other Swiss museums, I sometimes serve as a technical consultant to groups involved in safeguarding monuments and sites. Participants in this conference have suggested various ways of bridging this information gap, for example, through the publication of

Bruno Mühlethaler is chief of the Research Laboratory, Landesmuseum, Zürich, Switzerland.

glossaries, specifications and leaflets and the establishment of a preservation information clearinghouse. My experience in Switzerland has convinced me that the most effective way to make relevant information available to preservationists is to organize an institution consisting of individuals who know how to relate scientific facts to practical problems and who have a broad understanding of the economic, technical and scientific aspects of historic preservation. These individuals should be able to provide diagnostic services to preservationists in the field, recommend appropriate actions and assist and supervise the application of the methods and procedures recommended.

One situation will illustrate the importance of having trained laboratory assistants work in the field: The Research Laboratory of the Landesmuseum developed specifications for a one-layer plaster based on a simple formula. Precise instructions were given on the materials to use (including such details as the grain size, distribution and percentage of the sand to use and the percentage of clay material to be incorporated into the mixture) and on the method of application. Nevertheless, when the formula was used, failure was reported in some instances. Investigations in the field generally revealed that the sand had not been stored properly or the wrong sand had been selected and that the plaster had not been applied properly.

An institution of the kind suggested should be able to solve problems submitted to it either by using its own facilities or by assigning problems (or parts of problems) to outside specialists. In addition, such an institution would also have a teaching function, perhaps based on courses developed in conjunction with other educational institutions.

It might be useful to describe where and how Swiss preservationists obtain assistance. Unlike most other European countries, Switzerland has no federal law for the protection of the artistic patrimony. However, certain agencies that can provide assistance have been established within the government. Under the Federal Department of the Interior is the Federal Commission for Historic Monuments, which was founded in 1917 by an order of the Federal Council. The commission consists of 13 architects, archaeologists and art historians, all of whom serve without pay. They are elected for a four-year period and can serve two terms. In addition to maintaining an inventory of national monuments and sites, the commission supervises the activities of cantonal and communal authorities charged with the care of historical monuments and determines the historical value of objects and sites to be preserved. It also makes recommendations to the federal government for grants to cantonal or communal authorities or to private owners to support the care of historic sites and objects. For the works being undertaken at present, about 13 million Swiss francs are available; approximately 7 million Swiss francs are reserved each year in the federal budget for such financial support.

A few years ago, the commission pointed out to the Federal Council that the preservation and conservation of monuments required an interdisciplinary approach, and the Federal Department of the Interior assembled a group of consultants who agreed to contribute their professional skills, without pay, to preservation work. This group included a music conductor, who worked with problems in the preservation of organs; a glass painter, who specialized in windows and stained glass; a stonecutter, who was an expert on stonework; a petrographer from the Federal Institute of Technology, who dealt with geological problems, historical sources of stone and so forth; a private petrographer, who conducted analyses of old mortars and plasters; archaeologists, who conducted archaeological research; specialists from the Federal Institute of Testing Materials, who worked with problems involving the preservation of wood, heating of restored buildings and physics of stone, mortar, plaster and wood; and researchers from the Research Laboratory of the Landesmuseum, who conducted analyses and investigations of historical polychromy and paint and dealt with other chemical and technical problems.

In 1972, it was decided to institutionalize the activities of these experts, and the Institute for the Care of Monuments was created within the Faculty of Architecture at the Federal Institute of Technology. In addition to having the skills of consultants at its disposal, the institute has a research budget and currently employs a historian, who is responsible for archival research and for inventory work. There are plans to hire a chemist, a mineralogist and some technical assistants in the future; however, there are no plans to build special facilities for the institute. Research will be done in existing facilities, such as the Research Laboratory of the Landesmuseum.

The initiation of professional training programs for preservationists as well as for craftsmen is one goal of the institute. Educational programs related to historic preservation are, however, now offered by the Federal Institute of Technology. Two seminars have been organized there, one dealing with technical aspects of preservation and the other dealing with its nontechnical aspects. Although these seminars do not provide formal professional training for preservationists, they do offer valuable information on the possibilities and limitations involved in the application of conservation science to the preservation of historical monuments and sites.

DISCUSSION

Comments made by the panelists and audience during the discussion on wood are summarized in the following paragraphs.

Specialists are not always aware of organizations in existence that share with them an interest and expertise in areas of mutual concern. This is true with regard to those interested in the preservation of materials used in art and architecture, as many of these materials are also used in commercial or industrial applications. For example, probably few preservationists are aware of the Building Research Institute, with headquarters in Washington, D.C. Although the institute deals primarily with contemporary building problems, it has at least once in the past sponsored a discussion of problems associated with historic buildings at its annual meeting. The Association for Preservation Technology (APT), a young, joint Canadian–American organization, has attracted a respectable membership in its first years of operation, but it is not widely known either.

There are other special-interest organizations that share conservators' and preservationists' concerns, including several that deal with wood and its protection from destructive agents. For example, the American Wood-Preservers' Association is located in Washington, D.C. Admittedly, this organization's main concern is the preservation of wood in industrial use, but it may be able to offer some information and assistance to conservators and preservationists. The International Council on Monuments and Sites has sponsored several conferences on the preservation of wooden monuments and structures, and more technical meetings on the subject are planned. Several participants at this conference were unaware of the U.S. Forest Products Laboratory until this meeting afforded them the opportunity to meet and hear Mr. Tarkow, the laboratory's assistant director for chemical utilization and protection research. It would be worthwhile for both conservators and preservationists to become aware of such organizations with similar interests and to learn more about these organizations' activities.

The abundance of organizations that may be able to help solve technical problems in conservation and preservation, combined with the general lack of knowledge about such groups, proves that a preservation center, such as that discussed at this conference, is urgently needed—if only to provide the names of organizations or individuals that may be able to be of assistance. To simply say that such a center is needed is not enough. If some organization or group of organizations does not accept the challenge of planning and implementing this suggestion, the preservation center may remain only an idea to be discussed again year after year.

In addition to knowing what organizations may be able to help, it would be useful if there were more publications on technical aspects of preservation. At present, the APT publishes a quarterly bulletin devoted to topics in preservation technology, but there are few other technical publications in the preservation field. There are, however, plans to make available information on specific problems. The National Park Service, in its role as administrator of funds allocated under the National Historic Preservation Act of 1966, learns a great deal about problems encountered in preservation projects and the ways in which they are handled. The Park Service currently plans to group the information and reports it has received into categories and to publish lists of the type of information available. If information on a specific problem is not available from these records, the Park Service will attempt to direct inquiries to a professional who is knowledgeable in the problem area. Perhaps some consideration should be given to compiling this information for eventual publication.

The Park Service also has established a technical press that will, among other projects, publish findings from the historic structures reports on buildings administered by the Park Service. In addition, the publication of a handbook of preservation is planned; it will be primarily for federal agency use but will be available to the public, too. Such publications undoubtedly can help preservationists, and perhaps conservators, solve some of the difficult problems they face.

Among these problems is the control of insects, as both Mr. Wrenn and Mr. Tarkow mentioned in their papers. At Colonial Williamsburg, the furniture beetle is a considerable problem. It has

125

been found that the beetles generally attack only 75-year-old or older wood, but recently the insects have been noticed attacking 35-year-old pine. To combat the problem, three coats of a chemical solution known as Rentokil was sprayed on the wood. Brushing was not used because once an attack has started, this method of application usually does not penetrate deeply enough into the wood to be effective. Even spraying can be ineffective because the solution may simply stay on the surface of the infested wood. The recommended procedure in cases of prolonged attack is fumigation, which can be easily used for antique furniture but is awkward for use on buildings. There is a question, too, about whether some fumigants cause an objectionable discoloration. Preservationists who have used fumigants report that in their limited experience (primarily with methobromide and hydrasonic acid), the only bad effect has been the tarnishing of some metals.

Another insect that causes much damage is the subterranean termite, which, as Mr. Tarkow pointed out in his paper, enters wood from warm, moist soil seeking food and shelter. One way to eradicate these termites or to hold them in check is to poison the soil around a structure. This procedure must be carried out by professionals, as some of the chemicals that are commonly used for this purpose are under careful scrutiny by the U.S. Environmental Protection Agency. Before hiring someone to do this kind of work, it may be useful to check with the local or state department of agriculture, department of health or both.

Liquid water poses the most serious threat to wood. Paint gives some protection by preventing rapid entry of liquid water into the wood, but there are some buildings that should not be painted (e.g., in preservation projects involving barns or shacks in an early settlement or in a historic mining area). For these buildings, water repellent can take the place of paint. The repellent can be composed simply of wax dissolved in a neutral solvent, or it may also contain pentachlorophenol, a fungicide that will slow down the weathering process. The wax prevents the rapid movement of liquid water into the wood, but it is degradable, thus making periodic reapplication of the water repellent necessary. The solvent to be used should be tested first to make sure that it does not produce an objectionable discoloration. One important point is that special protection, perhaps immersion in the water repellent, should be provided when the end-grain of wood is exposed, because water is readily absorbed by this part of wood.

Unbarked wood that must remain unbarked for historical reasons may be treated in a similar manner as unpainted wood, using a pentachlorophenol solution where decay hazards are not great. However, wood to be treated in this manner must be thoroughly dry and not in contact with the ground. If it is in contact with the ground, more drastic treatment, such as creosoting, is required.

Perhaps the best protection against water damage is good design, which may not be applicable for preservationists, and regular maintenance. Overhangs are quite effective in keeping liquid water away from wood; thus, they minimize the sharp swelling stresses that develop when water hits wood. On the other hand, clogged or deteriorated rain gutters may force water to run down the side of a building or result in the development of destructive ice stands where water alternately freezes and thaws, sometimes seeping through the roof when the rain gutters cannot accommodate the runoff.

Proper installation of wooden elements will also provide some protection. This is especially true for wooden shingles, which are now rotting out in 5 years whereas they used to last from 25-30 years. There is a myth that this is happening because of air pollution, but pollution primarily affects growing trees. Once a log has been converted to lumber, the effect of pollution is negligible, although there may be some change in the surface condition. The impregnation of shingles, which is done primarily to reduce the fire hazard, has no effect on the wood's susceptibility to decay. Perhaps the real reasons that modern shingles do not last are that there is not as much growth-type grain wood being produced from which to manufacture shingles and the method of installation is faulty. Shingles should be made from large trees with resinous and fine-grained wood, and they should be installed with room to "breathe." Today, shingles are generally placed directly on a solid deck with pegboard beneath. This can result in the creation of dangerous water pockets. It is important to provide breathing room not only to eliminate these water pockets, but also, because shingles are vulnerable to the full impact of rain, snow and solar radiation.

Solar radiation can damage shingles and other wooden elements, because wood contains chemicals that absorb ultraviolet light and, in so doing, make the wood brittle. The wood can then be "sandblasted" by sand or dust blowing in the air; this action is known as sand erosion. In Switzerland, where ultraviolet light is intense (because the higher altitude, the more intense the radiation), it has been observed that ultraviolet light can deteriorate wooden boards or beams almost completely. Some people have attempted to solve the problem by incorporating ultraviolet absorbers into the wood, but since the radiation process continues and does not stabilize, these absorbers have a short life expectancy and must be replaced often.

X rays, on the other hand, may prove to be of great value to preservationists in ways such as that described in Mr. Wrenn's paper. Perhaps the use of stereoscopic X rays would make interpretation of photographers easier. Conservators have used this technique for some time and have found that stereoscopic X-ray photographs not only show the various paint layers but also can be made to magnify the separation between layers. Infrared photography possibly could be useful in discovering framework that is hidden by plaster. However, to date no infrared-photography experiments known to conference participants have been successful.

Actually, the responsibility for much damage to objects and buildings rests with man, who has not always maintained the objects and buildings entrusted to his care. Often, man does not make a thorough structural analysis when trying to preserve a building, and problems may arise when this occurs.

All too often architects are anxious to remove wood that has been damaged. Why not instead impregnate the wood with supportive material? This can, of course, be done, but several difficulties may result. For one thing, there is probably no consolidant that, after solidification, has characteristics similar to those of wood. The result of impregnation would be a composite, and perhaps rigid, material. Impregnation might also cause a chemical reaction that would produce an objectionable surface condition.

There are several products on the market designed for such use, however. One, a liquid called Gammapar, is essentially Lucite or Plexiglas. After impregnation with Gammapar, old wood doubles its weight and generally the surface of the wood changes. After sanding, the impregnated wood may be used for various purposes. The Kansas City Air Terminal has selected Gammapar-impregnated wood for use as flooring. Because Gammapar is essentially Lucite or Plexiglas and, therefore, should scratch rather easily, it will be interesting to note how the flooring wears under the feet of thousands of air travelers. Another product, called Calignam, is supposed to be useful in restoring ship timbers that are deteriorating because of water. Epoxy resin, which has a variety of uses, is helpful in consolidating small wooden elements.

Masonry and Masonry Products: Brick, Adobe, Stone and Architectural Ceramics

PROBLEMS AND TECHNIQUES OF PRESERVATION

ORIN M. BULLOCK, JR., FAIA

It is a challenge to the current generation of architects to keep informed about the tremendous number of technological developments that have occurred during the past several decades. Familiarity with building methods, materials and equipment in common use as recently as the turn of the century contributes little to an architect's practice today. As a result, the profession has failed to provide training in historic building practices or to encourage interest, study or understanding of the subject. Meanwhile, rapid growth and renewal have resulted in tragic losses of old buildings, creating an increasing demand to conserve significant examples of our architectural heritage. Growing numbers of technicians in the field, office and laboratory are belatedly dedicating themselves to the task of understanding the design, materials and building techniques of the past so that they can direct the preservation of older buildings without sacrificing their character.

GENERAL PRESERVATION PROBLEMS

Brick, adobe, stone and architectural ceramics are all subject to deterioration caused by (1) water, dampness and chemical action; (2) settlement, failure of lintels or arches, inadequate structural design, corrosion or failure of metal inserts, leaching of mortar

---

Orin M. Bullock, Jr., FAIA, is a restoration architect in private practice in Baltimore, Md.

jointing and inadequate fabrication or manufacture; and (3) poor workmanship in bonding, incorporation of wooden members within the fabric, penetration of the fabric by roots and tendrils of vines and neglect.

With the exception of the bulldozer, the most fatal hazard to all structures is abandonment, which accelerates deterioration. The process of deterioration following abandonment is well described by Roland Richert and Gordon Vivian.

First, there is the deposition on the floor of wind and water-borne material. This deposition continues until it is covered by collapse of the roofing and dislodged sections of wall. Once the roofing is gone, stability of walls is markedly weakened and the generally poor materials and faulty construction are particularly vulnerable to the elements. Moisture from snow and rain melt out the mud mortar; thin unbonded facing is separated by frost action; rotting of wood parts (beams, lintels, or ceiling inclusions) leaves overlying masonry unsupported; pressure from fallen material dislocates remaining walls, and the accumulation of debris ponds surface water leaving basal areas subject to moisture penetration and erosion.[1]

BRICK

Brick, a modular, man-made building material used since ancient times for both structural and ornamental purposes, is classified as soft-mud, stiff-mud or pressed brick. Preservation and restoration problems most frequently involve soft-mud or pressed brick.

Characteristics of Brick

STRUCTURAL USE. The structural uses of brick include foundations, walls, floors and all forms of arch in every organic system of construction. Brick is used entirely concealed by stucco, plaster or other finishes and in exposed locations, both inside and outside. Brick is fireproof when hard burned. If placed on a substrate of an adequate bearing capacity, properly bonded, well laid in cement mortar and protected from dampness, it has a long life and requires minimum maintenance.

DECORATIVE USE. Brick is available in many colors and textures and may be further varied by selection from the run of the kiln for uniform color, rubbing or grinding. It may be cast before burning to form moldings or decorative devices, or it may be carved after being laid. The variety of brick bonds is limited only by the imagination of the architect, master builder or artisan.

Preservation Problems

In addition to the general problems previously mentioned, brickwork is subject to efflorescence, spalling and dusting (or disintegration). Also, Hugh Braun describes a fungus, spread by spores, whose long tendrils creep considerable distances to find wood, penetrating mortar joints of brick walls with such determination that a whole wall may become filled with a mass of threadlike tendrils.[2] Donald W. Insall warns that a capillary rise of moisture, called *rising damp,* causes deterioration of mortar and encourages infestation by wood-feeding insects.[3]

Preservation Techniques

EFFLORESCENCE. Efflorescence usually originates in the mortar, but it may occur in the brick itself. Soluble salts, principally sodium carbonate, potash and magnesia, in the brick or the mortar are dissolved by water absorbed by the mortar and later precipitated to the surface, leaving a white deposit as the water evaporates. When dry, the deposit can usually be brushed off, but the brick may have to be washed and rewashed until the offending salts have been leached out. To eliminate efflorescence permanently, the brick must be protected from water and dampness.

SPALLING AND DUSTING. Deterioration caused by spalling and dusting can be stopped only by replacing any unsound brick. There seems to be no way to stop disintegration of soft brick once it has started.

CRACKING CAUSED BY SETTLEMENT. The failure of lintels or other structural deficiencies may be corrected following normal building practices, such as underpinning, replacement or resetting of lintels and arches and replacement of cracked brick.[4]

REPOINTING OF JOINTS. Repointing usually involves an entire wall, in order to keep the repair inconspicuous. All loose or deteriorated mortar must be removed to a depth of about three-quarters of an inch before repointing, to insure watertight integrity. Great care must be taken to avoid enlarging the width of the joints by cutting or chipping the brick. The use of a Carborundum blade in a Skill-Saw is a fatal mistake; even expert mechanics, using every precaution, find it difficult to keep the blade from cutting into the brick. The use of properly sized chisels to rake the joints is slower but somewhat less hazardous to the brick.[5] A lime mortar matching the original work in color and texture, with an admixture of portland cement to improve its resistance to water, should be used.

REMOVAL OF PAINT. Before attempting to remove paint from brick, experimentation should be done to find the chemical that will be most effective yet will not damage the brick.[6] Wire brushing or sandblasting old brickwork results in permanent damage;

these practices destroy the surface of the brick and enlarge the joints, completely altering the brick's color and character. The removal of casein paint is a problem for which no universally effective solution has been found.[7]

WATERPROOFING BRICK WALLS. A coat of at least a 4 percent solution of naphtha-based silicone material gives good protection against damage by moisture if carefully applied to a brick wall, but to be effective it must be reapplied every few years.[8] A penetrating water-repellent coating sold under the trade name Hydrozo has a claimed life of 35 years and has given apparent satisfaction in many applications.

ADOBE

Adobe was one of the earliest permanent building materials used in the United States.[9] Perhaps the country's earliest continuously occupied settlement is Acoma Pueblo in New Mexico, which dates from about 1200. This now sparsely inhabitated pueblo of adobe and stone, parts of which have been reconstructed, still survives. Many early examples of 18th and 19th-century adobe missions, churches and domestic buildings exist intact in Texas, Arizona, New Mexico and California.[10]

Adobe buildings, which are cool in summer and relatively warm in winter, are admirably suited to the climate of the Southwest. The ready availability of the material for their construction in the region insured their popularity.

Characteristics of Adobe

STRUCTURAL USE. Adobe is suitable for most of the uses that have beeen found for brick, including roof decks on which the adobe is laid over wooden framing while in its plastic condition.

DECORATIVE USE. Adobe buildings are usually simple statements deriving their interest and charm more from their form and mass than from applied decoration. Exceptions are the California houses with porches and galleries and the great churches, some of which have utilized burned adobe brick to achieve lavish baroque ornamentation rivaling that found in Latin America.[11]

Preservation Problems

The problems encountered in the preservation of adobe structures stem not only from a lack of maintenance and the nature of the material, but also from numerous inherent structural faults. The preservationist must identify obvious or impending deterioration and its causes and contrive means to correct the faults. Because of the nature of the material, the problems of restoring adobe structures call for unique applications of normal engineering procedures.[12]

In brief, preservation problems of adobe are all caused by water and dampness, aided by structural faults and vandals; solutions range from protection and preventive maintenance to stabilization or restoration.

Preservation Techniques

The major factor in the disintegration of adobe structures is moisture that enters the walls, by either capillary or gravitational action. This penetration by moisture is one of the most troublesome conditions to control.[13]

All subsurface stabilization treatment should be applied at one time, rather than over a period of years, as moisture can work its way around a patch that is too small. Defective structural work, which includes walls and footings, must, of course, be replaced before waterproofing. Buildings to be erected in a location subject to rising damp should be protected by placing membrane waterproofing under the footing or on top of a concrete footing.

Walls above grade may be made moisture resistant after cracks, small breaks and other wall failures have been repaired by applying stucco reproducing the wet clay and gypsum mixture or the lime clay with which many walls were originally coated. Since this stucco does not repel water, a silicone treatment is also needed. The danger of a bond failure between the original walls and the stucco can be reduced by applying galvanized chicken wire to the walls to reinforce the stucco and to provide a mechanical bond with the walls.[14] Holes and badly eroded areas should be filled with plastic adobe that closely resembles the original, and the surface of the stucco should follow the original surface as nearly as possible and be of uniform thickness. A wide variation in thickness will produce shrinkage cracks that reduce the effectiveness of the waterproofing.

Adobe walls intended to retain their adobe brick character (and not be stuccoed) may be made water resistant by applications of hydrocarbon-base silicones.

STONE

Characteristics of Stone

The stone commonly used in building construction includes granite, greenstone and basalt (igneous); sandstone, limestone and marl (sedimentary); and marble and slate (metamorphic).

STRUCTURAL USE. Granite, limestone and sandstone are the stones most commonly used for structural elements.

135

DECORATIVE USE. For decorative purposes, marble is competitive with all other types of stone, except that the extensive use of marble for exterior decoration is seldom found in structures other than monuments or mausoleums.

Preservation Problems

Problems are caused by the differential settlement of foundations initiated by the ordinary operation of soil mechanics, sometimes aggravated by such changing conditions as the drying of formerly wet areas.[15]

The trial-and-error nature of early structural design and contemporary neglect of subsurface testing have resulted in buildings with unequal bearing on their foundations. This hazard, combined with alterations or additions to the structure, may change the distribution of loads, causing failures in the superstructure.

Vibrations from heavy traffic, reverberations from large organs, the motion of heavy bells, sonic booms or even the pounding of dancing feet may cause movement and damage to a structure. The introduction of temperature control is partly responsible for the damage done to the United States Capitol, as it alters the temperature differential between the inside and outside.

Masonry failure is caused by the improper selection and use of materials, such as a combination of materials of different hardness; placement of large units adjacent to small ones; or timber members that shrink or deteriorate.

Preservation Techniques

Cracked and leaning walls do not in themselves mean that a building is in imminent danger of falling down. It must first be determined whether the cracks and the variations from proper alignment are recent or of long standing. The activity of a crack may be seen on an old dirty surface where the relative brightness of cracks can be compared. Continuing movement traceable to foundation settlement may be checked by placing, and later checking, plaster "telltales" over the cracks.

Inclination of walls may be checked with a plumb bob, and continuing movement, if any, can be detected by periodic readings. It should be remembered that many old walls were built out of plumb and are still perfectly stable.[16]

Footings may be underpinned, but care must be taken to insure that when the new foundation is loaded it does not change the action of the forces and initiate a new movement. In cases where underpinning directly under the original foundation has questionable stability or endangers an old wall, cast-in-place concrete beams may be poured in the wall and carried on girders supported on steel cribbage foundations on either side of the line of the wall. Such a system, stabilizing but not supporting the old walls, was used in the reconstructed Wren Building in Williamsburg.[17]

The deterioration of the surface of stone buildings is caused by the nature of the stone, the manner of its fabrication and setting and the chemical action of the elements. The latter may be controlled to a degree by frequent cleaning and periodic treatment with water repellents.[18] Such maintenance will slow the process of decay, but the only cure will be removal and replacement of the decomposed stone.

Plastic repair of stonework has been done effectively in recent years, but the permanency of such "dentistry" has not been fully proved by time. This technique involves cutting out the damaged parts and replacing them with a plastic material, reinforced and keyed to the original work.[19]

TERRA-COTTA

Terra-cotta is a hard-burned cast clay product used since ancient times. Many specimens of terra-cotta bas-reliefs and other ornaments have been found in perfect condition in Herculaneum and Pompeii. Terra-cotta was apparently "rediscovered" and developed as a structural and fireproofing material after the Chicago Fire in 1871 and, in the form of architectural terra-cotta, was widely used during the first quarter of the 20th century.

In 1875, the first cast-iron columns (there were two of them), in the Chicago Club later called the DeJonge Restaurant, were fireproofed with burned clay, finished in painted plaster and topped with an ornamented architectural terra-cotta capital.[20] The Studio Building on West 55th Street in New York City, designed by R. H. Robertson in 1883, included a band of architectural terra-cotta ornaments with areas of faience tile.[21] Both the rapid development of the steel-frame office building, which seemed to call for lightweight curtain walls, and the eclectic taste of the time contributed to the widespread use of architectural terra-cotta.

Characteristics of Terra-Cotta

Architectural terra-cotta emits a metallic sound when struck and has a close, uniform color and texture when fractured, a surface hard enough to resist a knife scratch and glazing that will not chip off. It is usually cast hollow and is generally formed by being pressed into a mold of plaster of paris that is cast from a clay mold, as sculptures often are modeled. Terra-cotta clay, which induces crisper, more vigorous modeling, is used for making the matrix. When designs are not to be repeated, as for cartouches or other individual sculptures, the subject is modeled in terra-cotta clay

137

and fired directly, thus preventing loss of refinement or sharpness of detail and texture and allowing deep undercutting not possible when a mold is used.[22]

The variety of surface textures and finishes that can be achieved in terra-cotta is almost unlimited. A range of color and glazes is obtainable by applying a slip of creamy consistency before firing. The coloring, which may be varied on an individual block, permits the widest range in design.

The glaze on architectural terra-cotta, like that on chinaware and some pottery, is vitreous, that is, in the nature of glass, burned on, firmly united with the body, hard and durable.[23] It is one of the few materials of permanent character that permits architects to use color outdoors, while also maintaining control over the texture.[24]

Preservation Problems and Techniques

The preservation of architectural terra-cotta elements depends largely on the recognition and appreciation of their cultural and architectural value by architectural critics and the public. Like all elements of building design and construction, terra-cotta goes out of fashion from time to time, and this seems to be its current fate. It is to be hoped that before it is too late, some of the better examples of its many uses may be preserved.

The preservation of architectural terra-cotta calls for treatment identical to that for other masonry; namely, maintenance or restoration of the structural stability of the building. Terra-cotta itself is not in serious danger of failing unless the building it embellishes is destroyed. Failures, other than those noted for stone, are related to securing the terra-cotta units to the structure. To resecure these units to a structure, ties and bonding methods that follow normal good construction practices should be used.

NOTES

1. Roland Richert and Gordon Vivian, comps., *Handbook for Ruins Stabilization*, Part 2, Field Methods, revised version of *Ruins Stabilization* (formerly issued as vol. 23 of the 1962 Administrative Manual of the U.S. Department of the Interior, National Park Service), mimeographed (Washington, D.C.: U.S. Department of the Interior, National Park Service, 1962), chap. 1, p. 2.

2. "The way to cope with this situation is to cut horizontal chases every two or three feet in the wall, each chase penetrating nearly to the centre of its thickness, make a temporary dam of clay at the edge of each chase, and completely fill the trough thus created with fungacide, allowing it to seep down through the wall by gravity. Care must be taken to employ a solution which will not subsequently stain the plaster." Hugh Braun, *The Restoration of Old Houses* (London: Faber & Faber, Ltd., 1954), p. 100. See also Donald W. Insall, *The Care of Old Buildings: A Practical Guide for Architects and Owners* (reprint ed., London: Harrison & Sons, Ltd., 1958), p. 55 for a discussion of fungal poisons, etc.

3. Insall, *Care of Old Buildings*, p. 35.

4. Ibid., pp. 28–33.

5. Penelope Hartshorne, "Repointing of Brick Mortar Joints in Historic Buildings," in *Early American Brick Masonry and Restoration of Exterior Brick Walls*, proceedings of the 3d Annual Historic Structures Training Conference, August 9, 1963, ed. Lee H. Nelson (Philadelphia: National Park Service), pp. 1–5.

6. Gary Dysert, "A Report on the Use of Fluoride Brick and Stone Cleaners," in *Early American Brick Masonry*, pp. 6–9.

7. Frank A. Smith III, "Restoration of Masonry," *Building Research Journal of Building Research Institute* 1, no. 5 (September–October 1964): 40–43.

8. Ibid., chap. 2, p. 42; see also Richert and Vivian, *Ruins Stabilization*, p. 23; and Insall, *Care of Old Buildings*, pp. 37–38.

9. W. Ellis Groben, *Adobe Architecture: Its Design and Construction* (Washington, D.C.: U.S. Government Printing Office, 1941).

10. Robert G. Ferris, ed., *Explorers and Settlers* (Washington, D.C.: U.S. Government Printing Office, 1968). This book traces the history of adobe buildings in the United States and includes many illustrations.

11. Ibid., pp. 143, 148.

12. "In brief, the structural faults most commonly encountered, aside from the fact that only mud and stone and wood which was difficult to process, were used are:
1. No foundations.
2. Foundations narrower than the walls they support.
3. Construction over loose and unconsolidated fill.
4. Long spans over openings often supported by extremely small lintels.
5. Lack of bond at wall junctures.
6. Lack of headers or ties through walls, where there is more than one width of stone.
7. The incorporation of large horizontal wood beams in masonry walls.
8. The inclusion in walls, at ceiling height, of horizontal areas of bark, splints, rods, and other ceiling materials." Richert and Vivian, *Ruins Stabilization*, chap. 1, p. 2.

13. "Methods employed in the past to prevent moisture from reaching and being absorbed into walls have included (1) surface drainage, (2) subsurface drainage by means of tile and gravel backfills, (3) construction of concrete curtain walls to cut off the movement of water, (4) sealing the backs or subsurface portions of walls with impervious coatings." Ibid., chap. 3, p. 2. [*Author:* To which should

be added, flashing and counter-flashing at parapets and other penetrations through the roof and the coating of exterior walls with water-resistant materials.]

14. Groben, *Adobe Architecture*, p. 10.

15. "The Cabildo at New Orleans, constructed between 1794 and 1797 [was built on a foundation which was laid in] shallow trenches which were dug around the perimeter, a clay blanket spread over the base of the cutting, and cypress planks laid over the clay up to about six inches below grade level. Spread footings of brick for the piers and walls were built up directly on the planks. Subsequent lowering of the water table by drainage exposed the wood to rot, with the result that the walls and piers settled irregularly, cracking the stone flooring in places and causing the St. Ann Street wall of the Presbytère to lean 11 inches out of plumb." Carl W. Condit, *American Building: Materials and Techniques from the Beginning of the Colonial Settlements to the Present* (Chicago: University of Chicago Press, 1968), p. 37.

16. Insall, *Care of Old Buildings*, p. 30.

17. Orin M. Bullock, Jr., *The Restoration Manual* (Norwalk, Conn.: Silvermine Publishers, Inc., 1966), p. 88.

18. Insall, *Care of Old Buildings*, p. 62.

19. Ibid., pp. 64–65.

20. "Early Attempts at Fireproofing," *Architectural Record* 25, no. 5 (May 1909): 375–80.

21. Montgomery Schuyler, "The Works of R. H. Robertson," *Architectural Record* 6, no. 2 (October–December 1896): 198.

22. Eugene Clute, "Using Terra Cotta as Terra Cotta," *Architecture* 63, no. 4 (April 1931) 193–98.

23. William Luther Mowll, "Profiles and Materials," *Architectural Record* 45, no. 2 (February 1919): 146.

24. Leon V. Solon, "The Artistic Expansion of Architectural Clay Products," *The Architectural Forum* 27, no. 3 (September 1917): 77–80.

BIBLIOGRAPHY

Baker, Ira O. *A Treatise on Masonry Construction.* 9th ed. New York: John Wiley & Sons, 1905.

Braun, Hugh. *The Restoration of Old Houses.* London: Faber & Faber, Ltd., 1954. Illustrated with drawings and photographs. Deals with problems of restoration in England, many of which have application in the United States.

Bullock, Orin M., Jr. *The Restoration Manual.* Norwalk, Conn.: Silvermine Publishers, Inc., 1966. Deals with the methodology of restoration.

Condit, Carl W. *American Building: Materials and Techniques from the Beginning of the Colonial Settlements to the Present.* Chicago: University of Chicago Press, 1968. An excellent coverage of the work of the colonial period, as well as more recent developments. Bibliography includes sources often overlooked.

Groben, W. Ellis. *Adobe Architecture: Its Design and Construction.* Washington, D.C.: U.S. Government Printing Office, 1941. An excellent outline of the history of adobe construction, its preservation and restoration and modern methods of construction in the manner of the ancient craft.

Insall, Donald W. *The Care of Old Buildings: A Practical Guide for Architects and Owners.* Paperback reprint by *The Architect's Journal* for the Society for the Protection of Ancient Buildings. London: Harrison & Sons, Ltd., 1958. An exceptionally important and detailed guide providing solutions for many of the problems confronted by restorationists. It is regrettable that it has apparently been printed only in paperback and may not be widely available in the United States.

Insall, Donald W. *The Care of Old Buildings Today, A Practical Guide.* London: The Architectural Press, 1972. A greatly enlarged treatment of the same material contained in the previous book. This hardcover, beautifully designed book includes much that applies directly to conservation in the United States.

Nelson, Lee H., ed. *Early American Brick Masonry and Restoration of Exterior Brick Walls.* Proceedings of the 3d Annual Historic Structures Training Conference, Philadelphia, Pa., 1963. Mimeographed. An exceptional collection of technical papers that warrants publication and wide distribution.

Nelson, Lee H., and Dalibard, Jacques, eds. *Bulletin of the Association for Preservation Technology* 3, no. 4 (1971). Articles from the bulletin particularly recommended for reading in connection wtih the subject of this paper are: Donavan Purcell, "Stone Preservation in Europe and the British Isles," pp. 65–67; George L. Wrenn III, "The Bricklayers Company of the City and County of Philadelphia," pp. 73–75; and Hugh C. Miller, "Philosophies and Techniques for the Restoration of the Antiquities," pp. 54–64.

Powys, A. R. *The Repair of Ancient Buildings.* London: J. M. Dent & Sons, Ltd., 1929. While giving particular reference to preservation in England, this book includes many helpful suggestions.

Richert, Roland, and Vivian, Gordon, comps. *Handbook for Ruins Stabilization,* Part 2, Field Methods, revised version of *Ruins Stabilization* (formerly issued as vol. 23 of the 1962 Administrative Manual of the U.S. Department of the Interior, National Park Service). Washington, D.C.: U.S. Department of the Interior, National Park Service. Mimeographed. While written for the preservation of ruins in the southwestern part of the United States, the handbook is a valuable contribution to the literature on the technology of masonry preservation.

BRICK, ADOBE, STONE AND ARCHITECTURAL CERAMICS: DETERIORATION PROCESSES AND CONSERVATION PRACTICES

GIORGIO TORRACA

Masonry materials form a heterogenous class that may be divided into two main groups for the purpose of describing deterioration processes and, up to a point, conservation practices. One group includes hard, brittle, porous materials exhibiting good cohesive strength and limited plasticity. Mortar, plaster, stone, brick and all ceramics fall within this category, regardless of chemical composition. Soft materials with poor cohesive strength and some plasticity belong to the second group, which includes all materials made primarily of unbaked clay (adobe, mud, soil, sod, etc.) and exhibiting the properties of such clay. The chemical and physical properties of this second group are far more homogeneous than those of the first.

HARD MASONRY MATERIALS: DETERIORATION PROCESSES

Porosity and Water

Porosity is one of the main characteristics of hard masonry materials. The total porosity is the empty volume contained in a solid; it is usually expressed as a percentage and can be measured in different ways, each yielding different results.

A porous material can be viewed as a solid mass containing a network of galleries so irregular in its scheme and in the size and

---

Giorgio Torraca is deputy director of the International Centre for the Study of the Preservation and the Restoration of Cultural Property, Rome, Italy.

shape of the tubes that it is almost impossible to describe in a simple way.

Pores differ in dimension and profile from point to point within themselves and also differ from each other; they may or may not be accessible from the exterior of the mass. They vary in size from the molecular order of magnitude (that is, a thousandth of a micron) up to the millimeter range. The approximate size distribution of pores in a given mass can be determined by laboratory methods based on the calculation of distribution curves. Unfortunately, results vary according to the method used, and a sample measured twice by the same method will yield two different results.

Porosity, the main structural property of porous solids, can be measured only approximately. In addition to its external surface, a porous solid has a large internal surface, comprising the surfaces of all its internal tubes. The surface of any solid material is a special region where not all the electrical forces keeping it together are evenly distributed; some of these forces are free to attract extraneous atoms in the atmosphere by a process known as *adsorption*. Because a surface collects many intruding atoms, some of which are in an excited state and react chemically with other intruders or with the solid material of the surface, a porous material is far more reactive than a compact one.

At room temperature, most chemical reactions are initiated by the presence of water; thus, if water gains access to the network of pores, chemical reactions caused by atoms adsorbed on the surface or carried along by the water can be expected. The water may also freeze, forming crystals of ice and causing mechanical stresses. Furthermore, the water may evaporate, leaving behind materials that were dissolved in it; these materials often form crystals. Crystals of soluble salts in a material's pores endanger its structure, especially if their hydration states and volumes change according to atmospheric conditions. Although the cause is not understood in detail, the catastrophic effect of crystal growth on the cohesion of porous materials is a well-proved fact.

Small pores are often called *capillaries;* capillaries suck water into them if the material in their walls attracts water and is easily wetted. Since all constituents of masonry materials are polar in nature and are easily wetted by water, hard masonry materials exert a definite suction and the smaller the capillary the stronger its suction.

Thus, if a masonry material comes in contact with water, there is a good possibility that it will be injured. The likelihood is greater if soluble salts are carried along by the water, if reactive gases are present in the atmosphere or if the temperature frequently drops below the freezing point.

It can be concluded from this discussion that an ideal masonry material with no pores would deteriorate at a very slow rate, because only its external surface would be available for adsorption and the access of water. However, a material with small pores does not deteriorate more slowly than one with large pores. As the pore size is reduced, the suction increases, and mechanical stresses resulting from the crystallization of soluble salts or the formation of frost may be more likely to break pore walls. Actually, experience shows that materials containing pores of 1 micron diameter (or a fraction thereof) are prone to failure more than materials containing larger pores.

Further information on the behavior of porous materials has been published.[1]

Chemical Processes

The structure of porous masonry materials can be described as an aggregate of crystalline particles of various sizes and characteristics held together by thin layers of a cement that often is cryptocrystalline or noncrystalline. Although the cement represents a small percentage of the solid, the chemical behavior of the material in deterioration processes depends more on the nature of its cement than on that of its crystalline particles. There are basically four kinds of cement in traditional masonry materials: calcium carbonate, silicates, silica and calcium sulfate, which is the binding agent in plaster of paris. Calcium carbonate and most silicates are easily decomposed by acidic solutions, while calcium sulfate is somewhat soluble even in pure water. Silica cements are impervious to most reagents, but unfortunately they are found only in igneous rocks and silex, which are highly resistant to chemical deterioration.

All masonry materials, except those having a silica cement, are sensitive to an acidic environment, while plaster of paris is vulnerable even to water.

Atmospheric water (that is, rain or condensation) is slightly acidic, even in the absence of air pollution, because of the carbon dioxide dissolved in it. The chemical action of water on most masonry materials, therefore, occurs in any atmosphere, but often it proceeds slowly. This action can increase if the temperature rises, so that direct chemical action of relatively pure rainwater can become a significant factor in the deterioration process in hot and damp climates (that is, in tropical regions). In polluted atmospheres, rain and condensation water (particularly the latter) are

145

more acidic due to the presence of sulfuric acid formed by the combustion of sulfur-containing fuels; consequently, the rate of deterioration is sharply increased.

There is much basic information available on the chemical behavior of masonry materials, especially stone.[2]

Access of Water
The access of water to porous masonry materials may be caused by rain. Water reaches a masonry surface when the rain hits the surface directly; it may also reach the surface indirectly, falling somewhere else on the building and gaining access through a more complicated path. The latter case often produces the worst damage, because the rainwater picks up soluble materials along its path, and destructive crystallization processes occur when the water evaporates. Faulty disposal of rainwater is the most frequent cause of deterioration in ancient masonry.[3]

Water also penetrates porous masonry materials through capillary action. The suction is exerted by capillaries, as mentioned previously. The height of the capillary rise of water in porous masonry materials depends mainly on the pore size (the smaller the size, the higher the rise) and the rate of evaporation from the external surface (as evaporation increases, the rise is reduced). The capillary rise increases with time, as soluble salts are carried by water into the masonry and become concentrated there when the water that carries them evaporates from the side surfaces of the wall. The increased concentration of soluble salts causes in turn another force of attraction for water since it must diffuse from low salinity to high salinity regions. The result is that an equilibrium is never reached, and the capillary rise of water increases with the structure's age. Old thick masonry sometimes shows capillary rises as high as 8 to 10 meters (4 to 5 meters is common). Sometimes the water drawn up by capillary action into the masonry is rainwater that has been discharged near the base of a wall by a faulty gutter system.

Finally, water can gain access to masonry materials directly through the air, either by condensation or by the deposition of aerosols, such as mist, fog or salt spray. Condensation occurs when the air is damp and the masonry surface is colder than the dew point of the air. Condensation occurs on the coldest surface available; therefore, "cold" materials, that is, materials with high density and high thermal conductivity, are most affected by it. Metals and compact types of stone are examples of such cold materials; concrete is colder than brick and lime mortars.

Condensation water is far more dangerous than rainwater because it sweeps a large volume of air in front of the cold surface (the *Stefan effect*), cleaning it completely of all suspended dirt or gaseous pollutants. Liquid solutions containing free sulfuric acid then form on masonry surfaces in polluted atmospheres, and particles of carbon black, iron oxides, calcium sulfate and other substances are deposited.

Aerosols are liquid or solid particles suspended in gases—in this case, air. Liquid droplets formed around sodium chloride crystals, spread in the air by sea spray, can travel long distances over land, becoming progressively more acidic as they meet city atmospheres or gases originating in swampy areas.[4] Aerosols hit surfaces that are particularly exposed to air currents and discharge their particles on them. They are also attracted by cold surfaces, where they produce effects similar to those of condensation, even if the temperature of the surface does not drop below the dew point. Seaside buildings are obviously most exposed to aerosols.

It is often not easy to decide by which mechanisms water has gained access to a masonry material. Condensation, in particular, is often not sufficiently considered, the humidity it produces being attributed to rising damp when it appears in the lower register of walls or to the penetration of rain when it appears in ceilings and vaults. The consequences of misjudgment are often ruinous. As a general rule, in the case of cold, compact, low–porosity materials, it would be wise to suspect condensation first, while the reverse attitude might be taken for more porous materials. Accurate temperature–humidity surveys should be made as often as possible.

A characteristic feature of water distribution inside hard porous masonry materials is the existence of a critical water content that depends on the type of porosity and the nature of the material.[5] Above the critical content, water can move freely in the liquid state inside the porous body, whereas below the critical value, water is held inside pores and can be removed only by evaporation. It is often difficult to dry a masonry structure because the critical water content may be quite high. For instance, in walls containing hygroscopic soluble salts, as in Venice, the critical water content can be as high as 18 percent.

The existence of a critical water content causes also the characteristic distribution of rising damp in masonry; walls appear wet up to a certain height in a structure where the water content is at the critical value. Above this point, walls appear dry, and the water content drops sharply to a low level.

Wind, Mechanical Stresses, Thermal Cycles

Often, in cases involving extensive damage to masonry, the deterioration attributed to wind erosion is actually caused by a combination of salt crystallization (due to rising damp) and high air speed near the masonry surface. At high air speeds, evaporation of the liquid emerging through pores occurs so rapidly that there is no liquid film on the surface, and evaporation takes place inside the pores themselves, producing greater deterioration of the material.[6]

Wind, therefore, should not be considered as an independent deteriorating agent, but should be thought of mainly as an **aggravating** factor in rising damp and salt crystallization. However, one instance of pure wind deterioration occurred in Abu Simbel, Nubia, Egypt, after the reconstruction of the rock temple there, when a violent windstorm seriously damaged the face of one of the large figures on the facade of the Nefertari temple. The damage occurred in just one night, and it was probably caused by little stones collected by the wind in the flat area in front of the temple.

Whether mechanical stresses originating from thermal shock can cause deterioration of masonry materials without the concurrence of other causes is problematical. On large blocks, stresses produced by thermal expansion and contraction can reach high values and cause cracking of the material, but in small blocks, such as those normally used in masonry construction, this is not likely to happen; however, thermal stresses can become an important factor if the blocks are so tightly mounted as to aggregate expansion. D. T. Griggs appears to deny that thermal cycles alone can induce cracking of hard masonry surfaces. Nevertheless, he indicates that, under high humidity, microscopic surface cracks soon appear in samples exposed to thermal cycles.[7] Some experts believe that such microcracks represent the beginning of the deterioration process, because they encourage the access of water to the internal structure of the porous material.[8]

From the mechanical viewpoint, the main characteristics of hard porous masonry materials are hardness and brittleness. These materials exhibit good resistance to compressive stresses but weak and unpredictable behavior toward tensile stresses. The formation of frost and salt crystallization are destructive processes because they cause tensile stresses in a material's pores.

According to recent Russian studies, the mechanical properties of brittle porous materials are strongly affected by the adsorption of extraneous substances on the surfaces of the porous materials.[9] In general, adsorption of substances similar in structure to the porous one (in this case, ionic or high-polarity materials) tends to increase brittleness, as the microcracks formed under tensile stresses are stabilized. However, some plastic behavior can be induced by contact with substances completely different in structure from the porous, brittle one (in this case, nonionic, covalent molecules), as adsorption of polar materials inside the cracks is hindered; as a consequence, cracks are not stabilized and may close again.

Because an improvement of the mechanical characteristics of masonry materials is the main purpose of consolidation processes, these theories may be important to future research.

Biological Action

Geologists and petrologists have long debated whether biological action is an important cause of rock deterioration and soil formation or only a consequence of previous disintegration caused by chemical and physical factors.

Biological action includes implantation of living organisms, such as lichens, algae, mosses, molds, fungi and bacteria, on the surface of a masonry material. This action produces visible color effects. Black, gray, white or yellow lichens; green algae and mosses; colonies of variously colored molds; and fungi and bacteria of every conceivable color can be seen on deteriorating masonry surfaces, producing the "picturesque" aspect so pleasing to the eye during the romantic era.

The best known effects of biological action are rather superficial, however. Extensive deterioration of stone, and of masonry in general, has recently been attributed to colonies of bacteria of the sulfur cycle [10] and of the nitrogen cycle; [11] these colonies are capable of synthesizing sulfuric and nitric acid, respectively, starting from gaseous materials in the atmosphere. Oxalic acid and more complex organic acids produced by other living organisms may be responsible for other deterioration processes in which the sulfur and nitrogen cycles cannot be involved (that is, where there are neither nitrates nor sulfates in the deteriorated material). [12]

Biological studies of masonry deterioration are complicated by the fact that biological activity probably follows seasonal cycles and is erratically distributed over surfaces. Furthermore, the complexity of laboratory techniques used to examine masonry surfaces makes extensive studies long and costly. These factors hinder the progress toward a clear assessment of biological deterioration processes, and the identification of these processes often remains hypothetical.

A basic characteristic of biological activity is that it is always associated with the presence of water. This simplifies the search for causes of deterioration, as access of water is also the basic cause of most physical and chemical deterioration processes. From the viewpoint of essential diagnosis and conservation, a strict distinction between biological and physicochemical processes may not be necessary.

Study and Diagnosis of Deterioration Processes
The importance and complexity of deterioration processes make it absolutely necessary that these processes be identified before conservation measures are taken. The most important diagnostic aids now available to conservationists are the following.

1. Analysis of the chemical composition and structure (that is, porosity) of a masonry material.

2. Analysis of deterioration products. In addition to the usual chemical analysis of sulfates, nitrates and chlorides, X-ray diffraction and thermogravimetric analyses can give important indications. Average samples taken over reasonably large but homogeneous surfaces should be used whenever possible.

3. Temperature and humidity surveys of the whole structure in which the affected masonry is located. To be really effective, such surveys should include daily and seasonal cycles and should be carried out at a large number of points.

4. Identification of active vegetation and microorganisms.

5. Careful inspection of the rainwater distribution in the structure.

It might be argued that often such diagnostic research does not support any conclusions, as the great number of possibilities and theories of masonry deterioration preclude a clear interpretation of results. Obviously, some simplifying assumptions must be introduced to make possible the reduction of diagnostic data to a simple model on which conservation techniques can be based. The form in table 1 is proposed in the hope that it may allow such simplification.

Table 1. PROPOSED FORM FOR EVALUATING CAUSES OF DETERIORATION

	Process Inducing Stress				
Method of Access of Water	*Evaporation and Frost Crystallization of Soluble Salts*	*Solution or Chemical Reaction*	*Thermal Shock*	*Wind*	*Biological Activity*
Rain—direct					
Rain—indirect					
Rising damp					
Condensation (or aerosol)					

This method attributes any alteration of masonry materials to a combination of two causes: the way in which water gains access and some special process inducing mechanical or chemical stress. Twenty-four combinations are possible, each one causing a specific problem. The conservationist should first try to eliminate the causes of the problem and then to palliate its effects.

Not all combinations have the same probability of appearance; furthermore, some types of climate obviously favor some combinations and reduce the probability of others. As an example, in cold to temperate climates, condensation is a likely source of trouble (particularly on cold materials), and it can combine with frost, evaporation and solutions to produce serious problems. In my experience, rising damp combined with evaporation and thermal shock is the main offender in hot, dry climates. In tropical climates, direct solution by rain and biological activity based on all four sources of humidity are principal causes of damage.

HARD MASONRY MATERIALS: CONSERVATION PRACTICES

Aims and Means

Deterioration of masonry surfaces is as natural as the weathering of rocks, and it is not likely that a way will soon be found to arrest it completely. However, many cases of decay are accelerated by accidental factors; this acceleration may be called "pathological" because it progresses at rates far greater than rates of natural erosion. Although accelerated decay also occurs in nature (for instance, when sudden catastrophic events accelerate geological erosion), it is now known that pathological developments occur frequently in environments modified by human activities. Conservation measures should eliminate any pathological components of deterioration in order to return the deterioration rate to a constant level.

Since the access of water to porous masonry materials is frequently associated with the creation of pathological conditions, control of all forms of water is perhaps the most important method of eliminating masonry problems. The treatment of damage to masonry caused by rising damp, condensation and ineffective rainwater disposal, while not within the scope of this paper, is covered in specialized literature on the subject.[13]

Conservators should be aware that the problem of humidity control in masonry is not as straightforward as might be expected. The identification of humidity sources may involve serious difficulties. Furthermore, some drying processes that have gained widespread acceptance, such as electroosmosis or syphons, have insufficient scientific bases or have even been demonstrated by impartial scientific tests not to work at all.[14]

Other conservation practices aim at restoring a deteriorated material by imparting to it a satisfactory appearance (that is, cleaning treatments) or sufficient mechanical strength (that is, consolidation treatments). These practices will be analyzed in detail later and are discussed according to the materials on which they can be applied.

Another group of conservation practices included for discussion are those designed for the protection of masonry materials; these practices may be regarded as particularly important where walls, or parts of them, have particular historical or artistic value. The need for protection arises because some causes of deterioration (for instance, condensation on external surfaces) cannot be eliminated by conventional humidity-control techniques. Furthermore, most consolidation techniques do not guarantee that deterioration will not recur as soon as exposure to damaging conditions is resumed.

One method of protection is the application of a surface coating of a weather-resistant material. This is acceptable only if the coating can be firmly anchored on a sound material, that is, if the masonry beneath the coating is in good condition or has been suitably consolidated. Such surface coatings must always be considered as temporary, as their life is limited to a number of years (5 to 10 years for most materials presently in use), after which removal and application of the same (or an improved) coating is necessary.

The use of movable screens may be suitable for the protection of some external surfaces. In cold or temperate regions, several causes of deterioration, including frost, condensation and air pollution, are most active in winter, and it has been suggested that external surfaces of artistic value (for example, reliefs and stuccos) might be protected by simple plastic screens that could be removed during the warm season to allow viewing.[15] This method of protection is similar to one adopted in some regions for the protection of fruit trees in winter; it may be equally effective for monuments.

In cold or temperate climates, thermal protection should also be considered. Since deterioration processes often attack cold surfaces, valuable surfaces could be protected by an automatic system that switches on a heater when adverse climatic conditions develop.[16]

The last practice to be dealt with, in terms of conservation techniques in general, is the removal and substitution of deteriorated materials. To a conservator of materials, a substitution is the equivalent of destruction. It should be allowed only when absolutely necessary for structural reasons or to prevent water from entering a structure. In ancient masonry, every substitution entails a loss of authenticity and value; if the substitution goes beyond a certain point, the whole structure looks as if it were a copy of the old one. Therefore, the conservationist should always be willing to fight as long as possible for the most battered piece of material, the aim being to preserve it in its original location and not to destroy it on the pretext of "restoration," a respectable word that covers a great deal of abuse.

The removal of objects of artistic value from weather-exposed structures for placement in protective museum situations is a different issue. It may be imperative to remove such objects in many cases; however, before disassembling complex decorative structures, the damage caused the building as a whole should be seriously considered. This is a problem that concerns the art historian and the architect far more than the conservator of materials.

Conservation of Stone

CLEANING. A large number of methods are used for the cleaning of stone masonry. Mechanical action alone may be used, as in dry-grit blasting or cleaning with rotating Carborundum tools. Water, in the liquid state or as steam, is often used as a cleaning agent, and it is also used in conjunction with mechanical cleaning techniques, in wet-grit blasting, for instance. Chemical methods are frequently used to remove hard crusts from stone; hydrofluoric acid or acid ammonium fluoride are preferred reagents, as they are believed to form calcium fluoride, a stable compound, on stones containing calcium carbonate.

An experiment comparing merits and drawbacks of various industrial cleaning procedures was carried out by the British Building Research Station, Garston, England.[17] Results of other important experiments were published by the ITBTP.[18] The conclusion to be drawn from such studies is that fast, low-cost industrial cleaning processes may endanger such surfaces as those that are carved, as such processes can cause heavy losses of the weathered material whose preservation is necessary to retain the stonework's original appearance. Furthermore, several industrial procedures produce an irregular surface that weathers faster than a smooth, compact surface. Protective treatment should be undertaken after cleaning when these procedures are used.

More delicate cleaning techniques, suited to objects of artistic importance, have been developed at the Victoria and Albert Museum, London. These techniques include the use of a fine spray of distilled water; the application of packs of absorbing clays and

153

distilled water; and microblasting, a technique which employs an airbrasive unit and microscopic glass beads.[19] The Istituto Centrale del Restauro, Rome, recently developed a slightly basic synthetic jelly that is capable of removing tough crusts in a few hours.[20] Finally, experiments conducted in Venice, involving the cleaning of art works with laser beams, show considerable promise.[21] This technique, however, has not yet advanced past the laboratory scale.

STONE CONSOLIDATION. Practical attempts to consolidate stone and scientific inquiries concerning stone consolidation began during the first half of the 19th century. Contrary to the widespread belief that stone consolidants are inefficient or even noxious to stone, several processes available now appear to perform rather well in controlled experiments.

Two types of error contribute to the bad reputation of stone consolidants. First, some of the treatments carried out in the past did not penetrate the surface sufficiently, and consequently there was the formation of a hard crust that was not anchored to a sound base material. The final result was usually the exfoliation of the whole treated crust. Most modern consolidation methods avoid this pitfall through the use of adequate techniques for deep impregnation; these methods can be applied directly to buildings.

The second frequently made error is the assumption that a stone consolidant also provides protection and will keep stone in good condition indefinitely, without need of further intervention. Most consolidants have a rather limited protective capability; they are not intended to arrest deterioration in an aggressive environment, although such an environment must always be assumed to exist where stone masonry undergoes serious deterioration. Generally, either a protective treatment should be applied to the consolidated stone or environmental conditions modified to inhibit the deterioration process.

The existing literature on stone preservation processes is numerous; fortunately, it has been reviewed recently.[22] The following paragraphs discuss contemporary techniques.

Consolidation techniques can be divided into inorganic and organic methods, according to the type of chemical process used to cement together the loosely bound material formed by the deterioration process. Supporters of inorganic consolidation methods claim that cements similar in structure to original materials can be formed through suitable inorganic reactions. These cements should have long lives and exhibit coefficients of expansion similar to that of the original stone. Fluosilicates of zinc and magne-

154

sium or silicates of sodium and potassium are examples of cementing materials that were used in the past and are still in use today. They induce consolidation through the precipitation of silica inside a material's pores. The recent use of ethyl silicate appears to have eliminated a serious drawback of such techniques, namely the formation of soluble salts as by-products of the consolidating reaction. Ethyl silicate (alone or combined with methyl-tri-ethoxy-silane) is the starting point of a consolidation method that is also based on precipitation of silica but does not form permanent by-products.[23] In the baryta technique,[24] suitable mainly for limestone, consolidation is based on the formation of barium carbonate, an insoluble salt that exhibits some protective action against pollutant acids.

Because inorganic methods act mainly through the formation of precipitates inside a material's pores or at the edges of crystal grains, these methods cannot fill cracks or reattach loose pieces of stone when there are large gaps in the material. In such cases, it is necessary to use a cement possessing filling power, such as one of the structural adhesives or stuccos suitable for use on stone that are now formulated with polyester or epoxy resins. These cements have gained widespread acceptance.

Organic consolidation methods are based mainly on synthetic resins. Although their life expectancy appears to be shorter than that of inorganic consolidants, organic polymers have the advantage of improving mechanical properties of porous materials by reducing their brittleness.

Epoxy resins and silicone resins are currently the most promising organic consolidants.[25] Epoxy resins have excellent adhesive properties and good weather resistance, although they tend to discolor with time. Silicone resins have good aging properties due to their partially inorganic structure.

On the whole, advantages and drawbacks of organic and inorganic consolidation methods appear to be well balanced. There are some recent indications that it may be possible to combine the advantages of both types of consolidation method by using mixed treatments. The previously mentioned modified ethyl silicate treatment can be considered halfway between silicates (inorganic) and silicones (mostly classified as organic). A new stone consolidant based on a mixture of ethyl silicate (inorganic) and a low-viscosity epoxy resin (organic) was recently announced.[26]

Another recent development that appears promising, although limited in application to single objects of dimensions up to the life-sized statue and complex structures that can be dismantled, is a process based on monomer impregnation and successive polymerization by irradiation with gamma rays obtained from special radioactive sources. Since any kind of monomer can be used, the plastic material created inside the stone exhibits properties that can be adjusted to produce the best mechanical or chemical properties.[27] Concrete treated with a similar process at the Brookhaven National Laboratory, Upton, N.Y., withstood numerous freeze-thaw and acid corrosion tests.

Stones consolidated by several of these new treatments are performing well throughout the world, some having been exposed since 1965. Apart from the problem of cost, these treatments seem to have few disadvantages, even if their useful life proves to be relatively short, because there appears to be no obstacle to repeating the treatment.

PROTECTION OF STONE. General considerations concerning the protection of masonry materials also apply to stone. The practice of applying protective coatings to stone is ancient; it was mentioned by Vitruvius and frequent references have been made to it in the literature ever since.[28] Beeswax, linseed oil, tallow and other materials, including even cheese, are mentioned in the formulas. The foregoing materials have often performed well but, with the exception of beeswax, they age rather rapidly and require frequent reapplication.

Paraffin waxes and salts of stearic acid are modern substitutes for traditional protective coatings, and new possibilities are offered by such materials as synthetic resins, silicones, acrylics and polyvinyl acetate. The relative merits of these various types of coating have not yet been fully assessed. Although their life expectancy is certainly longer than that of traditional materials, these modern coatings must always be considered as temporary maintenance expedients, requiring periodic renewal.

In a class by itself is a new method of protection based on the application of hygroscopic materials to stone surfaces. These materials stabilize humidity on a stone surface to prevent such destructive processes as salt crystallization and freezing. Hygroscopic coatings can be based on hygroscopic salts or hydrophilic resins. It is too early, however, to determine their actual performance.

Conservation of Brick Masonry

Due to the high porosity of bricks, brick masonry is subject to penetration by water, either in the form of rising damp or rain, and to evaporation followed by the crystallization of soluble salts. On the other hand, being a warm material, brick masonry is generally less subject to condensation than is compact stone. However, condensation does occasionally occur in colder parts of a brick building, such as wet walls, interior surfaces of roofs and vaults and floors where the masonry rests on a heavy base or directly on the ground.

Conservation of brick masonry mainly requires methods to inhibit the access of water; the use of damp proof courses and control of rain disposal are the most important conservation measures.

In old, damp masonry, interrupting the access of water does not usually result in the immediate elimination of dampness and efflorescence. Because old bricks and mortars are loaded with hygroscopic salts, they have a tendency to dry at a very slow rate or even to absorb humidity from the air in very damp climates. Furthermore, when a wall starts to dry, the rate of crystallization on its surface accelerates and deterioration increases rapidly. Although this condition is usually only temporary and is followed by a stable condition, it can produce much damage.

Since deterioration occurs on the surface on which evaporation takes place, the main defense against the crystallization of salts is the creation of a new sacrificial surface by the application of a temporary porous layer over the surface to be protected. This layer can consist of a temporary plaster; an absorbing clay, such as attapulgite; or a paper paste. Once the dangerous phase is past, the temporary protection can be removed, along with all the salts that have crystallized into it.

Techniques for the consolidation and protection of stone masonry also apply to brick masonry, although they are not frequently used.

Conservation of Plaster
Being normally porous materials of relatively low density, plasters are mainly affected by deterioration caused by the evaporation of water in masonry. Condensation is possible in cold parts of buildings, however, particularly in interiors of buildings that are warmly heated in winter. Damp proof courses and provisions against condensation are obviously important as preventive measures against plaster deterioration.

Salt extraction can be performed with clays, such as sepiolite or attapulgite, or with a paper paste. Similar procedures can also be useful in removing water-soluble spots. Plasters can also be cleaned by applying jellies made of starch, or methyl cellulose, and water. The jelly is spread on the plaster surface and removed mechanically after drying; contaminating materials are often removed with it, as they are transported onto the surface layer during evaporation.

Plaster is often soiled by biological activity; diluted ammonia can be used to remove growths of molds, algae and similar agents. However, it is advisable to request expert advice to identify the deteriorating agent (algae, molds, mosses, etc.) and to formulate the best plan to check infection and avoid its recurrence. Biological deterioration of plaster surfaces can be extremely complicated.

Like stone, deteriorated plaster can be consolidated by inorganic consolidation methods. Calcium bicarbonate or baryta techniques have been proposed for this purpose;[29] however, when the plaster includes a surface decoration, there is a danger that inorganic methods may cause a change in the surface color.

Consolidation is often realized by means of solutions of thermoplastic resins, such as acrylics or polyvinyl acetate; these resins also act as protective coatings for the surface. The use of emulsions is not advisable, because an emulsified resin does not readily penetrate plaster, but tends to form a skin on the plaster's surface.

Deterioration sometimes causes a loss of adhesion between the plaster and the core of the wall; this may be attributed either to the crystallization of salts or to bacterial action at the interface of the plaster and the core of the wall.[30] In order to reinstate adhesion between an ancient plaster and the wall core, an adhesive composition should be injected into the gap and pressure applied to the surface until the adhesive sets. For this purpose, restorers of murals employ a mixture of casein, lime and polyvinyl acetate emulsion. It requires some experience to prepare this mixture satisfactorily; polyvinyl acetate emulsions brought to proper consistency with calcium carbonate and water probably perform as well or better.

Conservation of Architectural Ceramics

General properties of architectural ceramics are quite similar to those of bricks; therefore, deterioration processes and conservation techniques are the same for both.

Causes of deterioration of architectural terra-cotta and faience were examined in detail in a report published by the British Building Research Station in 1929.[31] I am not aware that anything of importance has been published on this subject since then.

According to the report, terra-cotta generally possesses excellent weathering properties. Some instances of failure may be attributed to defects caused by improper manufacturing techniques, either in the molding stage, resulting in delamination, or in the firing process (that is, underburning). Underburning is a frequent defect when narrow dimensional tolerances are specified, because the manufacturer tries to avoid the warping that can be caused by firing at a high temperature. Underfired ceramics are light in color and show poor resistance to weathering. The report also states that the weathering behavior of terra-cotta is directly related to its mechanical strength and that the strongest ceramic materials exhibit the best aging properties.

The most important cause of deterioration of architectural ceramics appears to be salt crystallization. In London, efflorescence on architectural terra-cotta was found to be composed mainly of sodium sulfate and calcium sulfate. The report attributed the formation of these sulfates mainly to action on the ceramics of acidic gases present in the atmosphere. It is important, therefore, to remove soluble salts when deterioration is detected.

Architectural terra-cotta can be consolidated by using one of several techniques developed for the treatment of stone. Because of the chemical nature of the most common ceramics, ethyl silicate, silicones or silicate-silicone mixtures appear to be the best choices for consolidation, although epoxy-silicate mixtures may also be effective. A description of the use of silicone resin to consolidate the terra-cotta decoration on the facade of a church in Chivasso, Italy, was published recently.[32]

The color of decorative ceramics is obviously important when deciding which consolidation treatment to use. Because some consolidation treatments can cause discoloration, all proposed treatments should be carefully tested on similar, but unimportant, materials before application to the objects to be preserved.

Ceramics used in architectural decoration may or may not be glazed. When glazes are employed, serious conservation problems are created. Being almost nonporous, these glazes tend to arrest evaporation, but they can crack under strong pressures caused by the formation of frost or salt crystallization in pores of the porous ceramic body under the glaze. This cracking results in a flaking of the glassy surface material.

In addition, the types of colored glaze that contain considerable amounts of alkaline material can be damaged in acidic environments if condensation occurs on the glazed object's surface. Conservation of colored glazes exposed to the atmosphere or to damp internal environments can be difficult. In addition to the usual treatment of the ceramic body, special measures are necessary to consolidate and protect the glaze layers. Although I lack direct experience with glazed tiles and little information has been published on the restoration of these ceramics, it is suggested that a solution of thermoplastic synthetic resins, such as acrylics or polyvinyl acetate, should prove useful for fixing loose flakes on glazes. This solution also will give some degree of protection to the tiles' surfaces. Since mechanical requirements for glazed tiles are not stringent, thermoplastic resins appear sufficiently strong for the consolidation of the glaze layer. These resins have the advantage of producing little or no color change and are easily removed.

SOFT INCOHESIVE MASONRY MATERIALS: DETERIORATION PROCESSES AND CONSERVATION PRACTICES

Clay Structure and Clay Masonry Materials

Clays are widely distributed minerals created by the weathering of several types of rock. They have a platelike structure in which individual plates (or *packs*) are held together by secondary forces (that is, dipole attractions) that are weaker than normal valence bonds between atoms. Because these packs are loosely held together by electrical attraction forces, water can force its way between the packs, exploiting its attraction force (that is, its hydrogen bond) toward hydroxyl groups present on the surface of the packs. The water can remain between packs, increasing the distance between them, reducing the force of attraction that holds them together and causing overall swelling of the clay.

Swollen clay is plastic, greasy and sticky. If given a shape (and little strength is required to shape swollen clay), it will maintain the shape; if applied to another material, even on a vertical surface, it will adhere. Swollen clay is, therefore, a versatile material, but unfortunately, on exposure to air, it loses most of the water between its packs and most of its plasticity. Dry clay retains its original shape, although there is some contraction, but it is weak and brittle because it is held together only by secondary electrical forces. Dry clay is easily eroded by mechanical action and washes away when water runs on its surface. If immersed in water, it crumbles into a fine dust.

Wet clay is used as a binder of clay masonry materials, but it cannot be used alone because on drying it contracts and cracks.

Inert materials, such as silt and sand of various compositions, can be used as fillers; some soils naturally contain the proportion of fillers to clay necessary for making mud bricks or mortars.

The properties of clay materials improve if the materials are reinforced with organic fibrous materials (straw and camel hair have often been used), and the addition of low-cost organic materials with adhesive properties, such as camel dung or vegetal extracts, can improve weather resistance considerably.

In clay materials, capillary forces are counteracted by a swelling process that occurs when water gains access to the masonry; pores are squeezed and blocked, and for this reason, clay is often used as a barrier against humidity. The rise of humidity in mud-brick walls is extremely slow, and the sharp boundary between wet and dry regions that occurs in normal brick masonry is not found in mud-brick and clay mortar masonry.[33] Thus, evaporation and salt crystallization processes are limited to a restricted band (the width of which is in the range of 1 foot) immediately above the soil level.

Deterioration Processes

If clay masonry materials were not susceptible to being washed away by rain, they might be considered among the best construction materials available because of their favorable properties (that is, humidity control and thermal insulation). However, where water is allowed to run on such materials' surfaces, it produces deep furrows rapidly; if water has direct access to the top of a clay masonry wall, it can progressively enlarge any surface crack and eventually split the wall open. If a pool of water forms at the foot of a mud-brick wall, it can erode the wall's base and cause a rapid collapse.[34]

Other deterioration processes, such as evaporation and salt crystallization, may occur on vertical surfaces of mud-brick masonry, but the intensity of these processes cannot compare with the destruction rate caused by the direct action of water.[35]

Conservation Practices

An analysis of deterioration processes in clay masonry has established that the conservation of structures made of this material requires the prevention of direct action by rainwater on unprotected horizontal surfaces, runs of rainwater on vertical surfaces and the formation of pools of water at the foot of walls. These main requirements should be met before applying any surface treatment to the material. They can be fulfilled in one of three ways:

1. The easiest method, which is the most objectionable from an architectural viewpoint, is to cover the whole structure with a suitable roof and to control the discharge of rainwater in such a way that no pool can form near clay masonry parts of the structure.
2. In the case of an archaeological excavation of structures that do not appear to have major significance, reburial of the structures in sterile sand or soil, after they have been thoroughly documented, is the soundest and most economical policy.
3. A stout capping of a rain-resistant material can be applied over all of the structure's horizontal surfaces, in conjunction with measures to prevent rainwater and other forms of water from running over wall surfaces and forming pools at the foot of walls.

161

After these measures are taken, a surface treatment can be applied to all of the structure's vertical surfaces. These provisions may be even more expensive than the building of a complete protective structure, but they are more respectful to the structure's character.

Of the several types of capping material that have been tested, soil-cement appears to be the most promising in terms of cost, appearance and performance.[36] In Iraq, a soil-cement composed of clay-rich soil, sand, straw and 10 percent portland cement has been used. Soil-cement bricks, made in steel molds, or mortars are used for capping and repairing walls.

The problem of the surface treatment of structures constructed of soft masonry materials is complicated by the low cohesive strength of these materials. In practice, only total penetration of the structure by the preservative agent can insure a good anchorage for the weather-resistant layer. Because the cost of total penetration is prohibitive (without even considering the technical difficulties), treatment reinforces only the surface layer, and this layer is held to the untreated core only by the cohesive force of the material itself, that is, the force that binds the last treated particle to the first untreated one. Good anchorage can be achieved by creating an irregular interface between the treated and the untreated layers, increasing the adhesion of the surface layer and discouraging detachment. Another possible course is to lock the treated layer to the core through injections of a suitable adhesive.

In any case, it is most important to prevent water from gaining access to the interface behind the treated crust; the capping should protect the all-important edge of the wall and protrude slightly over it if possible. Ethyl silicate showed considerable promise as a surface protective agent in a large-scale experiment carried out in Iraq by an international team organized by the Rome Centre;[37] however, since only two years have passed, it is too early to determine its effectiveness.

NOTES

1. B. H. Vos and E. Tammes, *Moisture and Moisture Transfer in Porous Materials* (Delft, Holland: Instituut TNO voor Bouwmaterialen en Bouwconstructies, 1969); id., "Suction of Groundwater," *Studies in Conservation* 16, no. 4 (1971): 129. D. B. Honeyborne and P. B. Harris, "The Structure of Porous Building Stone and Its Relation to Weathering Behaviour," in *Proceedings of the 10th Symposium of the Colston Research Society*, ed. D. H. Everette and F. S. Stone (London: Butterworths, 1958), pp. 343–65. R. J. Schaffer, *The Weathering of*

Natural Building Stone (London: Her Majesty's Stationery Office, 1950). J. R. J. Van Asperen De Boer and T. Stambolov, The Deterioration and Conservation of Porous Building Materials in Monuments: A Literature Review (Rome: International Centre for the Study of the Preservation and the Restoration of Cultural Property, 1972). E. M. Winkler, "Decay of Stone," in 1970 New York Conference on Conservation of Stone and Wooden Objects, ed. G. Thompson, 2 vols. (London: International Institute for Conservation of Historic and Artistic Works, 1971), 1:1–14.

2. Schaffer, Weathering of Natural Building Stone, pp. 26–40. De Boer and Stambolov, Deterioration and Conservation of Porous Building Materials, pp. 11–15. C. Camerman, "Les pierres de taille calcaires, leur comportement sous l'action des fumées," Annales des Travaux Publics de Belgique 104, no. 1 (1951): 9–42; ibid., no. 2 (1951): 243–63; ibid., no. 3 (1951): 509–32; ibid., no. 4 (1951): 601–34; ibid., no. 5 (1951): 829–56; ibid., no. 6 (1951): 1019–41; ibid., 105, no. 1 (1952): 57–77. A. Kieslinger, Zerstörungen an Steinbauten (Leipzig and Vienna: Deuticke, 1932); id., "Les principaux facteurs d'altération des pierres à batir," in Colloques sur l'altération des pierres: Bruxelles 1966-1967, (Paris: International Council on Monuments and Sites, 1968), pp. 1–37.

3. G. Massari, Batiments Humides et Insalubres (Paris: Eyrolles, 1971).

4. E. Eriksson, "The Yearly Circulation of Chlorides and Sulfur in Nature; Meteorological, Geochemical and Pedological Implications," Tellus 11, no. 4 (1959): 375–403; ibid., 12, no. 1 (1960): 63–109.

5. Vos and Tammes, "Suction of Groundwater," pp. 135–6.

6. Schaffer, Weathering of Natural Building Stone, pp. 51–52.

7. D. T. Griggs, "The Factor of Fatigue in Rock Exfoliation," Journal of Geology 44 (1936): 783–96.

8. G. Biscontin, L. Marchesini and S. Frascati, "L'alteration dans les marbres saccharoides," in First International Symposium on the Deterioration of Building Stone, La Rochelle, 1972, ed. V. Romanowsky (Chambery: Les Imprimeries Réunies de Chambery, 1973), pp. 189–99.

9. E. Shchukin, "The Rebinder Effect," Soviet Science Review 3, no. 3 (1972): 157–67.

10. J. Pochon, "Facteurs biologiques de l'altération des pierres," in Colloques sur l'altération des pierres, pp. 99–117.

11. J. Kauffmann, "Corrosion et protection des pierres calcaires des monuments," Corrosion-Anticorrosion 8, no. 3 (1960): 87–95.

12. M. E. K. Henderson and R. B. Duff, "The Release of Metallic and Silicate Ions from Minerals, Rocks and Soils by Fungal Activity," Journal of Soil Science 14, no. 2 (1963): 236–46.

13. Vos and Tammes, "Suction of Groundwater," pp. 140–1. Massari, Batiments Humides, pp. 158–498. E. B. Grunau, La lutte contre l'humidité dans les façades, trans. R. Lucron (Paris: Eyrolles, 1970). R. T. Gratwick, Dampness in Buildings (London: Crosby, Lockwood & Sons, Ltd., 1966). R. W. Castle, Damp Walls (London: The Technical Press, Ltd., 1964).

14. Massari, Batiments Humides, pp. 354–64. A. Watson, "Measurement of Moisture Content in Some Structures and Materials by Microwave Absorption," Building Research Station Current Papers, Research Series no. 63 (Garston, England, 1965).

15. Giorgio Torraca, "Importance of Climatic Factors in Stone Deterioration: Possibilities of Seasonal Protection of Stones" (in Italian), in La Conservazione delle Sculture all'Aperto, ed. R. Rossi-Manaresi and E. Riccomini (Bologna: Centro Conservazione Sculture all'Aperto, 1971), pp. 157–59.

16. G. Massari, "Lutte contre l'Alteration du Marbre à l'Interieur des Eglises Venitiennes," (UNESCO Document SHC/CONF. 44/7 (Paris, 1970). (Also in "Stage d'Etudes sur le Conservation des Monuments en Pierre, Venice 22–27 June 1970," mimeographed).

17. "Cleaning External Surfaces of Buildings," *Building Research Station Digest*, no. 113 (January 1970): 1–4.

18. M. Mamillan, "Recherches recentes sur le nettoyage des façades en pierre calcaire," supplement to *Annales de l'Institut Technique du Batiment et des Travaux Publics* 17, no. 199–200 (1964): 858–88.

19. K. Hempel, "The Restoration of Two Marble Statues by Antonio Corradini," *Studies in Conservation* 14, no. 3 (1969): 126–31. K. Hempel and A. Moncrieff, "Summary of Work on Marble Conservation at the Victoria and Albert Museum Conservation Department up to August 1971," in *The Treatment of Stone*, ed. R. Rossi-Manaresi and Giorgio Torraca (Bologna: Centro Conservazione Sculture all'Aperto, 1971), pp. 165–81.

20. P. Mora and L. Mora, "Removal of Weathering Crusts from Limestone" (in Italian), paper no. 12 of the Consiglio Nazionale della Ricerene. Centro Cause Deperimento e Metodi di Conservazione delle Opere d'Arte (Rome, 1972).

21. J. L. Asmus, L. Lazzarini and L. Marchesini, "Laser for the Cleaning of Statuary; Initial Results and Potentialities" in *First International Symposium on the Deterioration of Building Stone, La Rochelle 1972*, pp. 89–94.

22. Seymour Z. Lewin, "The Preservation of Natural Stone, 1893–1965: An Annotated Bibliography," *Art and Archaeology Technical Abstracts* 6, no. 1 (1966): 185–272. J. Riederer, "The Conservation of German Stone Monuments," in *The Treatment of Stone*, pp. 105–36.

23. J. Riederer, "Stone Conservation with Silicate Esters," mimeographed (Rome: International Centre for the Study of the Preservation and the Restoration of Cultural Property, 1972).

24. Seymour Z. Lewin, untitled contribution to the discussion in "Stage d'Etudes sur la Conservation de la Pierre," UNESCO Document SHC/MD/14 (Paris, 1970), p. 12.

25. W. Domaslowski, "L'affermissement structurel des pierres avec des solutions à base de résines époxides," in *Conservation of Stone and Wooden Objects*, 1: 85–101. K. Hempel, "Experiments of Consolidation with Epoxy Resin Maraglas A 665" (in Italian), in *Conservazione delle Sculture all'Aperto*, pp. 212–16. K. Lal Gauri, "Cleaning and Impregnation of Marble," in *The Treatment of Stone*, pp. 231–37. L. Marchesini and F. Valcanover, "A Consolidation Process for Marble Sculptures" (in Italian), *Bollettino Istituto Centrale del Restauro* (1966): 121–35.

26. R. A. Munnikendam, "The Combination of Low Viscosity Epoxy Resins and Siliconesters for the Consolidation of Stone," in *The Treatment of Stone*, pp. 197–200.

27. L. de Nadaillhac, "Utilisation du rayonnement gamma dans la conservation des biens culturels," ibid., pp. 73–79.

28. R. Rossi-Manaresi, "On the Treatment of Stone Sculptures in the Past," ibid., pp. 81–104.

29. E. Denninger, "Die chemischen Vorgänge bei der Festigung von Wandmalereien mit sogenannten Kalksinterwasser," *Maltechnik* 64 (1958): 67–69.

30. Riederer, "Conservation of German Stone Monuments," pp. 110–11.

31. W. A. McIntyre, *Investigation into the Durability of Architectural Terracotta and Faience*, Building Research Station Special Report no. 12 (London: His Majesty's Stationery Office, 1929).

32. L. Marchesini and G. Biscontin, "Essai de consolidation sur la façade en terre cuite d'une église," in *The Treatment of Stone*, pp. 45–64.

33. A. Bruno et al, "Contribution to the Study of the Preservation of Mud-Brick Structures," *Mesopotamia* 3 and 4 (1968, 1969): 443–73.

34. C. R. Steen, "Some Recent Experiments in Stabilizing Adobe and Stone," in *Conservation of Stone and Wooden Objects*, 1: 59–64.

35. Giorgio Torraca, "An International Project for the Study of Mud-Brick Preservation," ibid., pp. 47–57.

36. C. R. Steen, "Experiments in Processes of Preserving Unfired Earth Bricks— 1970," mimeographed (Santa Fe, N.M.: C. R. Steen, 1970). G. Gullini et al., "Preservation of Mud Brick Structures," *Mesopotamia* 7 (1972): 259–87.

37. Torraca, "Mud-Brick Preservation," pp. 51–52. Gullini et al., "Mud Brick Structures," pp. 278–86.

COMMENTARY

LEE H. NELSON

Unfortunately, there has been a tendency for restoration architects to regard conservation scientists as being unsympathetic to their problems. However, after talking to the conservators at this conference and reading their papers, I have concluded that they *are* sympathetic to preservationists' problems and that both groups share many of the same frustrations. Because of this conference, historic preservation in the United States will never be the same.

Before commenting specifically on the papers by Orin M. Bullock and Giorgio Torraca, I have a few general comments. First, in general I agree with what Mr. Bullock states. He has faced the same physical problems that we in the National Park Service have dealt with over the years, with about the same base of knowledge. With regard to Dr. Torraca's paper, I can only say that preservationists have a lot of studying to do before they are as knowledgeable about masonry materials as conservation scientists. Finally, the wide divergence in the professional disciplines represented by these papers makes apparent the need for a glossary—that is, a dictionary of terms used to describe materials, problems and techniques associated with historic preservation—so that architects and scientists can speak to each other without an interpreter. Although our interests are similar, our vocabularies are quite different.

As for specific comments, I heartily concur with Mr. Bullock's

Lee H. Nelson is a restoration architect with the National Park Service, working at Independence National Historical Park, Philadelphia, Pa.

remarks about hazards of removing paint from brick walls, especially about the hazards of sandblasting, which seems to be the most commonly used method in the United States. I have seen far too many buildings damaged by sandblasting, despite claims of so-called skilled blasters. As Mr. Bullock notes, the damage caused by sandblasting is permanent, both visually and structurally. Yet, despite cautions from every quarter, many architects and building owners still specify sandblasting, even for buildings of particular significance. Perhaps a special publication is needed to graphically demonstrate the dangers of this practice. It should be widely disseminated, not only to the architectural profession but to all those who must make decisions about cleaning masonry buildings. Mr. Bullock's section on paint removal from brick also includes a footnote reference to a report by Gary Dysert on the use of fluoride brick and stone cleaners, which was presented at the 3d Annual Historic Structures Training Conference, sponsored by the Park Service. In fact, such cleaners are not intended to be used as paint removers.

Mr. Bullock's discussion of specific problems related to stone-masonry mentions the differential settlement of foundations and other structural problems, but it should also mention the damage caused by simple erosion or wear, pollution, the freeze-thaw cycle and faulty rainwater disposal, as well as problems caused by porosity of the stone. The author does allude to damage caused by temperature differentials between interiors and exteriors of structures, a subject about which I am concerned. I am especially interested in atmospheric control systems that maintain high humidity levels in order to preserve artifacts or antique furnishings, but that may do so at the expense of the integrity of building fabric, especially if the building is a historic structure rather than a specially designed museum. Such systems can create a winter-time dew point within a masonry wall which may aggravate the deterioration of brick or stone, as well as dry rot in wooden structural members embedded in the wall. In my opinion, this potentially serious problem, caused by well-intentioned curators, makes us victims of our own technology, and the problem certainly deserves attention. Perhaps this topic should be reserved for a conference similar to this one that would also include mechanical engineers (who may be the second worst enemies of historic preservation, after the city planners as mentioned by Charles E. Peterson).

Dr. Torraca's discussion of the deterioration processes that affect hard masonry materials seems remarkably clear. I must confess that some of us "chemical illiterates" tend to regard people who profess to cure stone diseases with some suspicion. Admittedly, this suspicion derives from experiences with salesmen or advocates of particular proprietary products, rather than with scientists. It is refreshing, therefore, to read a discussion on the problems we restoration architects face presented in an objective, scientific fashion; however, I have some questions.

In the section on porosity and water, the author states, "Crystals of soluble salts in a material's pores endanger its structure, especially if their hydration states and volumes change according to atmospheric conditions." Does an increase in volume produce a chemical or a mechanical stress, or both? Dr. Torraca also states that "the catastrophic effect of crystal growth on the cohesion of porous materials is a well-proved fact." This is another instance of the need for a glossary of definitions and certainly of the need for architects to be more knowledgeable about chemical processes that affect building materials. To most architects, the catastrophic effect of crystal growth on porous materials is a little-known "well-proved fact." It is not clear whether Dr. Torraca's discussion of chemical processes and the cements that hold crystalline particles together refers primarily to stone or also includes brick. I do not understand any part of Dr. Torraca's allusion to the Rebinder effect.

The section entitled "Study and Diagnosis of Deterioration Processes" should be helpful to archtiects, and further descriptions of the diagnostic aids available to conservation scientists would be valuable. Such detailed descriptions would, of course, require another paper, but it would indeed be a welcome sequel.

Dr. Torraca's discussion of the cleaning of stone is not particularly helpful. The National Park Service has not had good results using acid ammonium fluoride, which he describes as a preferred reagent. The author also states that the use of epoxy and silicone resins to consolidate stone offers the brightest outlook so far, but the Park Service used an epoxy for this purpose and found that rapid discoloration resulted.

Dr. Torraca's comprehensive list of references is especially valuable, since there is a desperate need for how-to-do-it literature. Unfortunately, some of this literature has not been translated into English and, thus, for practical purposes, it is unavailable to architects in the United States. In any case, as Dr. Torraca points out, the existing literature on stone preservation is extensive, and it behooves architects to become cognizant of that literature and generally to become better informed about information sources.

Although a considerable amount of practical experience has been gained during the last 30 years or more in the United States and Canada, it has not been recorded and, therefore, remains almost as remote as publications written in foreign languages. Preservationists working for the Park Service and on private projects have used many different methods to solve specific problems of masonry deterioration, cleaning, paint removal, consolidation, waterproofing and structural stabilization, with widely varying results. For example, some years ago, the Park Service briefly tested and then applied a type of acid ammonium fluoride to several historic buildings in Philadelphia and in 1963, the Park Service prepared a free leaflet about this product and its application. Unfortunately, discoloration of the brickwork has occurred in every instance of the product's use. This experience should be made known to other preservationists. Similarly, the Park Service has used a number of proprietary processes for waterproofing; the effectiveness and possible side effects of these processes should be evaluated and reported.

I am sure that, given the opportunity, most preservationists would be eager to share their experiences, however modest or unscientific. I propose that, as an outgrowth of this conference, several concerned organizations cosponsor and invite a number of preservationists and scientists to submit case histories related to their successes and failures, so that others engaged in preservation can benefit from these frequently isolated experiences. These accounts could be compiled and used as the bases for how-to-do-it or how-not-to-do-it recommendations, which could then be evaluated by conservation scientists. I believe the availability of this type of information would be well received and would contribute to a more scientific approach to historic preservation.

COMMENTARY

SEYMOUR Z. LEWIN

I have spent a good deal of time during the past 10 years seeking literature on the deterioration and conservation of masonry and masonry products, and I know of no publications that give as comprehensive, intelligible and objectively well balanced an overview of this subject as the papers presented at this conference by Orin M. Bullock and Giorgio Torraca. If this meeting has accomplished nothing more than stimulating them to prepare and offer these papers, it will have accomplished more than the majority of meetings I have attended in the last 10 years.

As has been repeatedly stated and made excessively clear, the principal culprit in the deterioration of masonry, masonry-type products, stone and ceramics is water. There is an observation in Dr. Torraca's paper that ought to be memorized by every architect and every person concerned with preservation and restoration. He writes:

Thus, if a masonry material comes in contact with water, there is a good possibility that it will be injured. The likelihood is greater if soluble salts are carried along by the water, if reactive gases are present in the atmosphere or if the temperature frequently drops below the freezing point.

This quotation emphasizes that the culprit is not merely water, but liquid water that comes and goes. For example, in one series of experiments in my laboratory, the base of a test wall was kept

Seymour Z. Lewin is professor of chemistry at New York University, New York, N. Y.

continually wet and the top of the wall kept continually dry, so that there was a variation from wet to dry from the base to the top. There was, of course, an interface where the wall ceased to be wet and started to be dry. Soluble salts in the water were transported up the wall and deposited at the point where the wall began to dry out. It was found that where steady conditions were maintained—so that the base of the wall was always wet, the top was always dry and the gradient between wet and dry was constant— there was no deterioration in the perpetually wet and perpetually dry areas. The only parts that deteriorated were those that alternated between wet and dry conditions. I believe this finding is borne out by experience in the field. It is the alternation between wet and dry conditions that leads to the kinds of microscopic decay that are described in Dr. Torraca's paper.

There is, of course, another type of deterioration, namely, that which involves structural, engineering and mechanical problems or problems associated with poor construction, the shifting of foundations and other phenomena as discussed by Mr. Bullock.

Mr. Bullock mentions that he has had problems with the removal of casein paint from brick; I am sure that many other people have also encountered this problem. For whatever worth it may have for this situation, I have found that the application of a combination of the enzyme trypsin (which is available from biochemical supply houses and is relatively inexpensive) and monosodium dihydrogen phosphate, dissolved in water, softens casein paints and allows them to be brushed away, no matter how old the paints may be.

I would like to draw an analogy between human deterioration and preservation and architectural deterioration and preservation. There are certain kinds of decay in human beings about which little can be done because the decay mechanism is not understood in sufficient detail. Cancer is an example. Once cancer has taken hold, there is usually little that can be done, because the biological mechanisms that cause noncancerous cells to change into cancerous ones are not completely understood. On the other hand, there are kidney diseases that can be treated, because the ways these diseases cause decay and damage are understood and because a method has been developed that permits the blood to bypass a person's kidney and pass through an artificial kidney machine that purifies it while the kidney rests or is operated on. This process, however, is expensive. To maintain a patient on an artificial kidney machine for a year costs upward of $30,000. In this case, the problem can be solved, but the difficulty is that the solution is expensive.

The preservation of artifacts, buildings and monuments presents a similar situation. As Dr. Torraca's paper indicates, enough is known at the present time to preserve any structure, but in most cases the cost of preservation is so great that it is unfeasible in a practical sense. For example, where the culprit is water, which is the case in all instances of masonry deterioration except those involving structural weakness, all that is necessary to preserve the physical integrity of a structure is to arrange for good water runoff and to avoid condensation by keeping walls and other parts of the structure at a temperature above that of the surrounding environment. With heaters arranged around the walls, good drains, gutters along the roof and so forth, any structure can be preserved, including one made of adobe. However, the cost of these measures may not be justified. What is needed in this case, as in the treatment of kidney disease, is not new methods of treatment but more economical ways to achieve the goal. Many of the chemical treatments of masonry and stone are designed for that purpose; they cannot do anything that cannot be done in other ways, but they are more economical to use.

Nevertheless, the axiom that you get what you pay for, although not a hard and fast rule, is often borne out in restoration work and should be kept in mind when one is considering possible treatments.

DISCUSSION

Comments made by the panelists and audience during the discussion on brick, adobe, stone and architectural ceramics are summarized in the following paragraphs.

How should brick, adobe, stone and architectural ceramics be cleaned and repaired? This question is perhaps one of the most difficult ones for the restoration architect to answer. There are, of course, products that are used for cleaning and repair work, but some can create complicated long-range problems.

As Mr. Bullock and Mr. Lewin mentioned in their discussions, casein paint poses special problems for the restoration architect, but it can be removed with a solution of phosphate, the enzyme trypsin and water. Since casein is a polymer that contains both calcium and protein, this solution essentially "digests" the old paint. The phosphate draws out the calcium, while the trypsin breaks the protein into small units that may be washed or brushed away. However, applying this solution can be difficult, especially with vertical walls, because the surface being treated must be kept wet with solution for a sufficient time to allow the "digestion" to occur. The older the casein paint, the longer it takes for the paint to soften.

If there is doubt about whether the paint in question is a casein paint, a simple flame test may be made. To perform the test, first scrape off a small sample of the paint and add concentrated hydrochloric acid to the sample. If it is a casein paint, some of the calcium in the paint will solubilize. The solution should then be heated in a flame, like that of a Bunsen burner, and a platinum or Nichrome wire dipped into the heated solution. If a fleeting red flame appears, calcium is present and the sample is a casein paint.

173

When performing this test, be careful that there is no mortar included in the sample, since mortar also contains calcium.

Alkalies or acids used in cleaning masonry buildings can cause much damage. Alkalies, even sodium carbonate (plain washing soda), can cause minor damage to brick or stone and major damage to mortar, as alkalies attack all silicic materials, including concrete; however, the attack takes place slowly, and the changes that occur may not be noticed until months or years later. The same is true when acids attack silicic materials, and this delay in noticing damage has resulted in some bad construction practices. For example, it has long been a standard technique to wash down old and new masonry buildings with muriatic, or hydrochloric, acid. The acid then attacks any calcareous material, first forming calcium chloride, which leads to the development of disfiguring efflorescence, and eventually weakening the strength of the masonry. The calcium chloride, or other solubilized calcium compounds, produced by the use of muriatic acid is held within the masonry by capillary forces and comes out only slowly over several years as water migrates through the masonry.

Another major problem in restoring a masonry wall is repointing. Often, mortar joints have badly deteriorated, and replacing the mortar is tedious. Could a gun filled with a commercial sealant, such as a plastic, be used to fill the joints? This question is worth investigation, but several points should be taken into consideration initially. First, the sealant's composition and characteristics must be determined. It should have a reasonably long life expectancy and should not present any aesthetic problems. Cement has been used for repointing but, like the use of muriatic acid for cleaning, this is not a good practice. Cement produces substances, primarily calcium carbonate from excess lime in the cement, that migrate into the masonry and produce efflorescence.

As for stone repair products, there are many proprietary materials on the market for this purpose. Some perform rather well; others contain cement and should be regarded with suspicion for the same reason cement should not be used for repointing. There is also a question of aesthetics and philosophy. Certainly, no cracks or other avenues of entry for water should be left open, but should not some consideration be given to allowing the building to "show its age," so to speak?

Adobe is an especially difficult material to preserve. In national parks in the southwestern United States, various petroleum sealants have been tried, but in general these do not sufficiently penetrate into in situ materials to be effective. It was suggested that a hydrocarbon-base silicone be used for waterproofing;

however, experience has shown that this process, along with other waterproofing techniques, is not always completely successful. Adobe walls in parks of the Southwest have been recapped with soil cement, simply because this was the best solution available. Its use is not entirely satisfactory, though. Soil cement and adobe weather differently, and in a few years, the soil cement does not match the original adobe in either color or texture. Perhaps the best way to preserve adobe buildings is to continue the historic maintenance process. From the day these buildings were constructed, they were continually subject to erosion, cracking and so forth and were continually patched by their owners.

Since water is a major threat to adobe, as well as to other masonry materials, it would be worthwhile for architects to become more knowledgeable about the fundamental nature of water. They should know about the molecular structure of water and understand fully the phenomenon of surface tension, which results in capillary action, and the effects that voids in masonry have on the migration of water. In fact, architects are usually dismally ignorant of the fundamental nature of the materials they use. This fact is particularly frightening when one realizes that architects write specifications for new buildings and for the preservation of old ones.

It might be useful to plan another meeting where scientists could explain about the chemical nature of the materials architects use and implications for the problems encountered by architects. Perhaps the Rome Centre or some other group should offer professional analysis services to aid the architect in making decisions. Several years ago, a bill to create a National Building Research Institute was submitted to the United States Congress, but no action has yet been taken on the legislation.*

This discussion highlights the difference between a technician and a professional. A technician employs certain techniques and skills to accomplish a task; a professional uses the same techniques and skills but does so with greater understanding and the ability to change techniques or approaches to suit the situation. It is especially important for the professional to tailor techniques to each situation because each kind of masonry, each kind of stone, each kind of problem is unique.

---

* Authorization for the creation of the institute was among the provisions of the Housing and Community Development Act that was signed into law in August 1974.

Masonry and Masonry Products: Mortar, Plaster/Stucco and Concrete

THE USE AND PRESERVATION OF MORTAR, PLASTER/STUCCO AND CONCRETE

JOHN D. MILNER, AIA

This paper examines mortar, plaster/stucco and concrete in terms of their individual characteristics in structural and decorative use, the problems relating to their conservation and preservation and techniques employed for their restoration. Edward V. Sayre thoroughly explores the chemical composition of these materials and the approach to their conservation in his paper, "Deterioration and Restoration of Plaster, Concrete and Mortar." This paper addresses the architectural aspects of the problem and is based on both documentation and personal experience.

MORTAR

In its broadest sense, mortar may be defined as a plastic building material produced by mixing a cementing agent, an aggregate, water and possibly a binder. Technically, the term *mortar* includes plaster/stucco and concrete, but in this paper, concrete is discussed separately and mortar is considered a binding substance for masonry construction units.

Characteristics of Mortar

Until the introduction of cements in the late 18th century, mortar, consisting of a mixture of sand or clay, lime and water, was the material used to lay and set masonry units such as stone, brick, tile and adobe. The early mortar did not join masonry units to-

John D. Milner, AIA, is a restoration architect and president of the National Heritage Corporation, West Chester, Pa.

gether by adhesion, but rather served as a complementary material that, when set, filled the voids between the individual units and provided a firm bed for the masonry above it. With mortar packed solidly around all pieces, uniform compression in the wall could be achieved and undue stress avoided.

The texture and color of early mortars varied greatly, depending on the locality; the types of clay, sand and lime available; and the preferred mix of the builder. The clay may have been red, yellow or brown; the sand fine or coarse, brown, white or yellow; and the lime fine or lumpy. Clay and lime mortars can be categorized as soft mortars because when firmly set they remain somewhat flexible and porous, and for this reason, they were generally laid in heavier quantities and thicker joints than harder mortars which were developed later.

The use of cement greatly altered the character of mortars. The addition of cement to the mixture of sand and lime produced a much harder and more durable material, which possessed adhesive qualities for bonding masonry units together. The texture and color of cement mortars also varied, depending on the type of sand and cement used. These mortars can be categorized as hard mortars, because when set, they become quite strong and are less porous than previous mortars—in fact, they are almost structural in themselves. Because of their strength and adhesive properties, they were generally laid in lesser quantities and thinner joints than earlier mortars had been.

Preservation Problems

My experience with mortar preservation and restoration has been limited to the Middle Atlantic region of the United States, but within that relatively small area, I have encountered a variety of situations, several of which help to illustrate the scope of the problems.

The John Chad House (1724) in Chadds Ford, Pa., is a small two and a half story stone-bank structure constructed of native gneiss granite fieldstone. The walls are approximately 20 inches thick and were laid up with a soft clay and lime mortar and pointed with lime-sand mortar, using flat flush joints. While about 50 percent of the original pointing had survived in relatively good condition, much of the interior clay and lime mortar had deteriorated into a dry powder with no structural quality. Due to poor subsurface soil conditions, settlement in the building had caused serious cracks and bulges throughout three of the exterior walls. This problem was intensified by the lack of any sound interior mortar to cushion the settlement.

The remedy involved first the underpinning of all affected walls with broad reinforced concrete footings. Then the pointing was removed from the walls in the vicinity of the failures and a liquid cement mortar was worked into the voids between the stones in the interior of the wall. The seriously bulged sections were removed and relaid in mortar with new steel reinforcing bars. The wall surface was then repointed to a depth of about 3 inches, with the joints matching the original ones in color, texture and tooling.

The Tannery Building (1762) in Bethlehem, Pa., is a three and a half story industrial building constructed of native limestone. The walls are approximately 24 inches thick and were laid up with a strong lime mortar. The same mortar was used for the pointing, which was executed on the first floor in the form of a flattened ridge joint and in the upper floors in the form of a pointed ridge joint. The interior walls, in areas not plastered, were pointed with a broad flat joint, almost approaching parging. There were no major structural failures in the walls, and the mortar in the interior of the walls had remained firm and sound. About 50 percent of the original pointing had deteriorated to the extent that repointing of these areas was required. Since in many areas new pointing would abut existing pointing, a close match in both color and texture was a primary concern. A mixture of white cement, lime, yellow sand and brown sand (1:2:3:3) was used, and the new pointing was brushed, when nearly set, with a stiff bristle to expose the lime and aggregate. A clear silicone sealer was then applied to the entire wall surface to reduce penetration by moisture.

The Thomas Massey House (1696–1735) in Broomall, Pa., a two and a half story farm residence, was constructed in several sections, the earlier of red clay brick burned on the site and the later of native gneiss granite fieldstone. The walls were laid up and pointed with a lime-sand mortar, which has survived in remarkably good condition. The interior mortar is sound, and the pointing will require only minor patching when restoration work begins. The new mortar texture and color, as well as the tooling (grapevine on the brickwork, ridge V on the stonework), must be matched in order to assure an overall homogeneous appearance of the restored wall surfaces. The lime used in the original pointing was coarse, consisting of chunks as large as 1/8 inch in diameter. This lumpy lime can be duplicated by exposing bags of standard builders lime to prolonged dampness for a period of about six months. The lime congeals in lumps and, when mixed with the new mortar, provides the desired final appearance.

Restoration Techniques: Points to Remember

In undertaking the restoration or patching of original mortar in masonry buildings, several points must be considered. The formula of the new mortar must match, as closely as possible, that of the original mortar. If the original mortar was of soft lime or clay, mortar, the new mortar must approximate that and not be a hard cement substance, since differences in the coefficient of expansion, absorptive qualities and flexibility are likely to cause problems in the future. The reverse is also true: A soft mortar should not be used for repairs on a building originally constructed with hard mortar.

In matching the color and texture of original mortars, it is important to use natural materials, not artificial dyes or stains. Although an immediate color match may be achieved with dyes or stains, the effect is not likely to be lasting, and the natural aging process of the original and new materials will differ, destroying that initial similarity of appearance.

Although in situ preservation of original fabric, such as mortar, is important to the building conservator, its long–range effect on other elements of the building, such as the interior features, must be considered. For example, defective pointing, although original, may permit moisture penetration which will eventually cause deterioration eleswhere in the building. Exterior sealers are a possible solution to this problem, but they are ineffective without constant renewal. Removal and replacement of the original pointing may be the best and most logical answer.

PLASTER AND STUCCO

The terms *plaster* and *stucco* have always been used interchangeably. For example, the craftsman who applies both plaster and stucco has been known as a "plasterer," a word derived from a Greek word meaning "to daub on." However, a fine distinction does exist between the compositions of these materials, and it should be recognized. As used in this paper, the terms refer to two separate and distinct building components.

In historical writings, plaster is generally defined as a material used to cover, for decorative purposes, an independent structural surface (either horizontal or vertical). It is composed of a mixture of burnt and powdered lime or gypsum, sand and water. The application of plaster is usually confined to interior surfaces where weathering is not a serious consideration.

Stucco, although often referred to as plaster, usually implies a material applied, for both decorative and protective purposes, to a structural surface on the exterior of a building where strength, durability and weather resistance are desired characteristics. Like plaster, it is a mixture of lime and water, but the aggregate, either in lieu of or in addition to sand, is often a crushed masonry material such as marble, travertine or brick. When set, stucco forms a hard coating which is more impervious to penetration by moisture than plaster and which can be molded and polished to simulate stone or clay tile. Stucco has been used since Grecian and Egyptian times both as an interior and as an exterior coating for monumental as well as more modest buildings where sculptural decoration was desired or where a solid, durable base was required for painted decoration.

The following paragraphs examine the variations in the use and application of plaster and stucco and the problems encountered in the preservation and restoration of these materials.

Plaster

Plaster has been a popular and widely used architectural medium since early recorded history. Until the introduction in the 18th century of various cements as additives to improve strength, hardness and setting time, the basic ingredients of plaster remained unchanged. The mixing of crushed and powdered limestone or gypsum with fine sand and water produced a plastic substance that could be spread evenly over an infinite variety of building configurations to give a tight, finished and smooth surface to otherwise rough masonry or wooden walls and ceilings. Intended either as a flat, molded or incised finish in itself or as a base for other finishes such as paint, paper or canvas, plaster not only was decorative but also offered protection against wind, cold, dust and fire.

Plaster is applied directly to the surface of a masonry wall or to a secondary support framework, known as *lathing*, fastened to the surface of the wall. The components of plaster are a cementing agent, an aggregate and a binder, combined in various proportions depending on the use. The aggregates and binders are inert materials, while the cementing agent, in the form of a paste, is responsible for setting and hardening the mixture. Binders such as straw, animal hair (ox, horse, pig, goat, etc.) or jute fiber were commonly used in the past.

Plaster is generally applied in a series of coats, from one to three, again depending on its use and the desired effect. The "scratch coat" (or first coat) is applied directly to the supporting wall or lathing and provides a base on which to apply succeeding coats. The "brown coat" or "floating coat" is then applied over the scratch coat to form a base for the final "white coat" or "putty coat." In addition to providing a flat, smooth and clean finished surface, plaster is capable of being shaped, either in place or in molds, to create an almost infinite variety of architectural decoration.

The most common problem encountered in the preservation and restoration of plaster surfaces is the weakening of the material's bond with its supporting structure. In the case of plaster applied directly to the interior surface of exterior masonry walls, moisture penetration through the walls causes gradual deterioration of the plaster and, hence, a breakdown of its bond with the wall. The most effective method for alleviating this problem is to introduce a dead air space between the masonry and the plaster, but this approach is prohibitively expensive and, therefore, impractical in most situations. Since preservation of the original plaster in situ is usually of paramount importance, steps must be taken to prevent moisture from penetrating the exterior surface of the wall. The most direct and practical method for accomplishing this is the application of an exterior sealer. A number of sealers designed for this purpose are available, and each should be evaluated in terms of its suitability for the specific project in question. No single application will permanently solve this problem; applications must be repeated systematically as part of a continuing preservation–maintenance program.

Once the problem of penetrating moisture has been dealt with, restoration repairs to defective plaster can be undertaken. In circumstances where small sections of a plaster wall have pulled away from the masonry supporting wall, it may be possible to cut a series of holes in the plaster, force an epoxy or similar adhesive into the void between the two materials and then press the plaster back against the wall, in effect gluing it in place. This method, although time–consuming and therefore expensive, is particularly appropriate where original surface decoration in the form of painted designs, paper, applied plaster ornament or other such treatment is in place and must be preserved. In situations where this approach is not warranted, the defective areas should be cut out and replaced with new material.

In the case of plaster that has been applied over wooden lathing on walls and ceilings, the loss of bond or key with the lathing may have resulted from settlement in the structure, deterioration of the lathing or plaster due to prolonged moisture, deterioration of the nails securing the lathing to its supporting studs or joists or deflection of the ceiling joists. If the key with the lathing is relatively sound but the lathing has pulled away from its supporting framing, it is usually possible to press the surface back into place and secure it with screws, refastening the lathing to the studs or joists. Where the key has been broken, it may be necessary to remove and replace the defective section, unless access can be gained to the back surface of the plaster to permit the installation of new bonding and support material. J.F.S. Jack has written a comprehensive explanation of this procedure.[1]

The plaster surfaces of early houses have often been whitewashed or painted numerous times, resulting in a heavy buildup of material as much as $1/8$ inch thick. Invariably, sections of this paint have flaked away, leaving a pockmarked and generally uneven surface. It is impractical and often impossible to remove the remaining paint, which is firmly bonded in place, without damaging the original plaster surface. It is, therefore, advisable to remove all loose paint with a wide, flat wall scraper; sand the rough edges; thoroughly wash the wall with a detergent to remove the dust and grease film; rinse with clean water; and then apply a plaster sealer and finish paint coat.

Plaster surfaces occasionally develop a network of hairline cracks that are not indicative of any serious defect but do pose a cosmetic problem in terms of restoration. A specific example of this situation can be found in the Lockwood–Mathews Mansion in Norwalk, Conn. The mansion, built in 1865, is a massive stone structure with highly decorated and elaborate interior plasterwork. The wall plaster was applied directly to the masonry bearing walls and, although sound, is now laced with thousands of random hairline cracks, which are quite visible on close inspection. The wall surfaces are decorated with painted and goldleafed floral designs in the form of panels and borders, most of which are in good condition. Covering the walls with canvas to restore a smooth homogeneous appearance to the surface has been done in similar projects, but for this project was rejected because preservation of the original paint was considered of the utmost importance. Cutting out each crack and filling it with plaster was rejected on the basis of its prohibitive expense. It was ultimately decided to attempt to spackle the cracks where possible, clean the walls thoroughly and retouch the existing paint where necessary. The hairline cracks will still be visible, but this was considered to be the best approach under the circumstances.

Stucco

In its earliest form, stucco was similar to plaster, as crushed marble, travertine or other masonry aggregate was used either in place of or in addition to sand. The resulting material was of a consistency similar to that of plaster when mixed and applied, but when set, it became harder than plaster and was, therefore, more durable and resistant to penetration by water. In addition, it could be polished to simulate fine stonework.

The Egyptians used stucco extensively as a thin coating or wash over rough masonry walls to conceal the stone joints and to provide a sound base for wall paintings. The Greeks and Romans made almost universal use of stucco and began to develop the technique of modeling the material to create sculptural effects in their architectural ornaments. This type of fine, hard stucco was often referred to as stucco–duro, and it enjoyed a revival during the Renaissance. However, its use declined thereafter because of the unavailability of proper materials and the desire of builders to find a surface coating that would be less complex and easier to produce.

Until the end of the 18th century, common stucco was usually identical to plaster, being composed of a mixture of lime, sand and animal hair. It had little resistance to water, and its survival depended on periodic applications of lime wash or a similar protective surface coating. About the turn of the 19th century, various Roman (or natural) cements came on the market, and because they set quicker and harder, they were particularly suitable for use in stucco. Portland cement became popular during the 19th century and gradually replaced the earlier Roman cements because it provided an even harder and more durable surface.

Stucco, unlike plaster, is seldom applied over lathing, but is generally applied directly to the exterior surface of a masonry wall. Bond with the wall is achieved by the natural adhesive quality of stucco to masonry and also by the keying effect achieved by forcing the stucco into the joints between the masonry units. Depending on its use, stucco is applied, like plaster, in a series of coats.

From its first use, stucco has often been molded or incised to produce a variety of architectural effects. A common treatment was scoring the material with a narrow flat tool in a consistent pattern of horizontal and vertical lines to simulate the mortar joints of a cut stone masonry wall. This practice was used in the United States during the 18th century and more frequently during the 19th century. One interesting example of this application is the Sebastian Goundie House in Bethlehem, Pa. Built in 1812, the Goundie House is a two and a half story brick townhouse elevated on a rubblestone foundation. There is an 8-inch belt course, executed in stucco to simulate stone, on the main facade at both the first and second-floor levels. In addition, the rubblestone foundation is covered with a coat of stucco which was scored with a mason's pointing tool in a pattern that matches the brick coursing above. The stucco has been painted dark red to match the brick, giving the overall impression of a completely brick building. While the simulated stone facade is rather common, the use of scored stucco to imitate brickwork is, in my experience, unusual.

The problems involved with the preservation and restoration of original stucco surfaces are similar to those encountered with plaster, with the additional requirement of direct protection from penetration by moisture. There are no single answers to problems created by the deterioration of stucco surfaces due to simple erosion, chemical effects of air pollution, freezing and thawing of absorbed water or loss of bond with the supporting wall. Each situation must be approached individually and all options considered, with primary importance assigned to the preservation of the original fabric in situ. Replacement of defective sections or the building up of eroded areas is preferable to complete replacement of the wall surface. The techniques employed are similar to those used for the preservation of plaster. When patching defective areas, it is extremely important that the new material match the original material as closely as possible in proportion of mix, texture, density and appearance. For instance, a hard portland–cement stucco is unsatisfactory for patching a lime–sand stucco because the difference in their physical properties makes it impossible to achieve a homogeneous surface that will react equally to all external conditions. In patch work, feather edges between new and old fabric should be avoided since these are likely to crack with any movement in the stucco. G. E. Bessey has written an informative article on this subject.[2]

Parging or Dashing

The terms *parging* or *dashing* generally refer to the application of a crude mortar, plaster or stucco coating to a rough stone masonry wall, usually as a sealer. Such treatment is commonly found on the walls of foundations, basements, barns, minor utility buildings, outbuildings or houses built of small and uneven stone where an aesthetically acceptable appearance is not deemed necessary or cannot be achieved by standard pointing. The stone walls of a building were often parged years after construction to seal the wall against penetrating moisture and drafts.

The material used for parging was often a simple lime–sand mortar identical to that used in constructing the wall or a simple stucco composed of lime, sand and animal hair. It was usually applied in a rather crude manner without any attempt to achieve a smooth or finished surface.

An example of the use of parging is the Hans Herr House near Lancaster, Pa. Built in 1719 by Mennonite immigrants from the

Palatinate region of Germany, the one and a half story house is one of the earliest known examples of pure Swiss–Germanic architecture in the United States. The building was constructed of sandy limestone excavated from the site in relatively small units. The texture of the masonry wall with its small random stones did not lend itself to customary pointing techniques, and for this or other cultural or philosophical reasons, the builders chose to coat the surface with a thin layer of the same mortar with which they were constructing the wall. The parging is not of uniform thickness and does not cover all of the stonework; however, it renders a rather homogeneous, if crude, appearance to the exterior walls and protects the porous stone from the elements. A similar treatment was applied to the interior masonry walls in the attic and loft, while the walls of the main floor were coated with heavy finish plaster.

The preservation and restoration of the original parged walls in the Herr House is complicated, not by the deterioration of the original parging, which is remarkably sound, but by the numerous repairs and alterations that were made to the walls using mortars that did not even approximate the original either in composition or in appearance. The problem, therefore, is to remove those areas of mortar and parging that tend to destroy the overall appearance of the building and replace them with new material that matches the original. Again, it is important to achieve this match by using natural lime and sand, not artificial coloring agents.

Plaster on Paling
Characteristic of early Germanic building construction is the use of floor and roof insulation known as *paling.* Paling consists of wooden slats, approximately 1½ by 3 inches, mortised into continuous rebates in floor joists or wall studs and wrapped with ryegrass or straw soaked in a paste of clay and water. The slats and their grass wrapping fill the spaces between the joists, studs and rafters and, once the plaster ceiling below and the wooden floor (or plaster wall surfaces) above have been installed, provide effective insulation between the adjacent spaces. This method was used primarily between heated and unheated spaces, such as a parlor and a loft. In early Germanic structures, the plaster was applied directly to the straw and clay wrapping, and its structural support depended on creating an adequate bond or key with the strands of straw. The problem of preserving this type of original system depends largely on the maintenance of satisfactory bond. If the bond is secure, the plaster surface can be treated as discussed previously. If the bond has deteriorated, it will probably be neces-

sary to remove the plaster surface and replace it with new lathing and plaster.

Wattle and Daub

The term *wattle and daub* generally defines a method used to fill the voids in the framework of timber buildings and is similar to paling except that 1-inch-diameter sticks are often used in lieu of the 1½-by-3-inch slats. The sticks are woven together to form a webbing upon which the clay and straw mixture is applied. Plaster is then generally applied over the wattle and daub to seal the wall. The preservation problems with this system are similar to those encountered with paling.

Rough Casting

Rough casting is a form of stucco treatment that was popular in the United States during the 19th and early 20th centuries. It is defined in *The Modern Builders Guide* by Minard Lefever as follows:

Rough–casting is an outside finishing cheaper than stucco. It consists in giving the wall to be rough–casted a pricking-up coat of lime and hair; and when this is tolerably dry, a second coat of the same material, which is laid on the first, as smooth and even as can be. As fast as this coat is finished, a second workman follows the other with a pail of rough–cast, which he throws on the new plastering. The materials for rough–casting are composed of fine gravel, with the earth washed cleanly out of it, and afterwards mixed with pure lime and water, till the entire together is of the consistence of a semi–fluid; it is then spread or rather splashed, upon the wall by a float made of wood. This float is five or six inches long, and as many wide, made of half–inch deal, to which is fitted a rounded deal handle. The plasterer holds this in his right hand, and in his left a common white–wash brush; with the former he lays on the rough–cast, and with the latter, which he dips in the rough–cast, he brushes and colours the mortar and rough–cast that he has spread, to make them, when finished and dry, appear of the same colour throughout.[3]

The preservation and restoration techniques for rough casting are similar to those used for stucco, with the additional requirement to match the size and texture of the gravel aggregate when replacement is required.

CONCRETE

Concrete, although technically considered a type of mortar, can be considered separately because, unlike other varieties of mortar, it is generally formed in masses that act as independent structural elements. Concrete is composed of a mixture of cement, sand, gravel (or other aggregate) and sufficient water to cause the cement to harden and bind the entire mass.

The Romans have been credited with the first use of construction material resembling modern concrete. They discovered that it was possible to build massive but inexpensive walls by mixing together sand, small stones and a hydraulic cement, composed largely of volcanic deposits, and then pouring this substance into wooden forms to harden.

Concrete made with portland cement came into use in the United States during the latter part of the 19th century, but did not gain wide acceptance until the 20th century.

As I am not personally familiar with the problems of preserving and restoring concrete structures, discussion of these matters is best left to others.

NOTES

1. J. F. S. Jack, "Notes on the Repair and Preservation of Decorated Plaster Ceilings," *Royal Institute of British Architects Journal* 57, 3d ser. (September 1950): 416–19.

2. G. E. Bessey, "The Maintenance and Repair of Regency Painted Stucco Finishes," *Royal Institute of British Architects Journal* 57, 3d ser. (February 1950): 143–45.

3. Minard Lefever, *The Modern Builders Guide* (1833; reprint ed., New York: Dover Publications, 1969), p. 131.

BIBLIOGRAPHY

Anderson, William James. *The Architecture of Ancient Rome*. London: B. T. Batsford, 1927.

Atkinson, Robert. *Theory and Elements of Architecture*. Vol. 1, pt. 1. New York: Robert M. McBride, 1926.

Bankart, George Percy. *The Art of the Plasterer*. London: B. T. Batsford, 1908.

Bessey, G. E. "The Maintenance and Repair of Regency Painted Stucco Finishes." *Royal Institute of British Architects Journal* 57, 3d ser. (February 1950): 143–45.

Bullock, Orin M., Jr. *The Restoration Manual*. Norwalk, Conn.: Silvermine Publishers, Inc., 1966.

Burns, Robert Scott. *The Colonist's and Emigrant's Handbook of the Mechanical Arts*. Edinburgh: Blackwood, 1854.

Curran, C. P. *Dublin Decorative Plasterwork of the Seventeenth and Eighteenth Centuries*. London: Tiranti, 1967.

Downing, Andrew Jackson. *The Architecture of Country Houses*. 1850. Reprint. New York: Da Capo Press, 1968.

Encyclopaedia Britannica. Vol. 18. Chicago: Encyclopaedia Britannica, 1960.

Encyclopaedia Britannica. Vol. 18. Chicago: Encyclopaedia Britannica, 1964.

Encyclopedia of World Art. Vol. 13. London: McGraw-Hill, 1967.

Fyfe, Theodore. *Hellenistic Architecture.* Rome: L'Erma (Erminia and Giorgio Bretschneider), 1965.

Granquist, Charles. "Ornamental Plastering." *Historic Preservation* 22, no. 3 (April–June 1970): 11–16.

Gwilt, Joseph. Preface to *An Encyclopaedia of Architecture.* Rev. ed. London: Longmans Green, 1888.

Jack, J. F. S. "Notes on the Repair and Preservation of Decorated Plaster Ceilings." *Royal Institute of British Architects Journal* 57, 3d ser. (September 1950): 416–19.

Kimball, Sidney Fiske. *Domestic Architecture of the American Colonies and of the Early Republic.* New York: Dover Publications, 1966.

Lefever, Minard. *The Modern Builders Guide.* 1833. Reprint. New York: Dover Publications, 1969.

Merrifield, Mary Philadelphia. *The Art of Fresco Painting.* London: C. Gilpin, 1846.

Morrison, Hugh Sinclair. *Early American Architecture: From the First Colonial Settlement to the National Period.* New York: Oxford University Press, 1952.

Ritchie, T. *Canada Builds, 1867-1967.* Toronto: University of Toronto Press, 1967.

Van Den Branden, Felicien, and Hartsell, Thomas L. *Plastering Skill and Practice.* Chicago: American Technical Society, 1953.

Vitruvius, Pollio. *Vitruvius, On Architecture.* Edited from Harleian manuscript 2767. London: W. Heinemann, 1931–34.

DETERIORATION AND RESTORATION OF PLASTER, CONCRETE AND MORTAR

EDWARD V. SAYRE

This paper discusses plaster, concrete and mortar in terms of their chemical composition, reviews the deterioration of these materials and suggests possible conservation treatments for them.

In terms of chemical components, plaster is considered in this paper as being formed primarily of calcium carbonate or calcium sulfate dihydrate (or a mixture of the two); concrete as primarily a mixture of calcium silicates and aluminates; and most mortar as a mixture of calcium carbonate and concrete. It should be remembered that minor constituents and impurities, whether introduced in the original preparation of a material or added in some later treatment, can significantly affect the deterioration process. In addition, the physical structure of a material significantly influences its resistance to deterioration. A notable example of this type of influence is the effect of air-filled voids in concrete, which can either increase or decrease the concrete's resistance to frost damage, depending on their nature and distribution.

PLASTER

Plaster is used not only as a general wall covering, but also as a support for frescoes. Often, it is molded into decorative stuccowork. Both lime plaster and gypsum plaster have been used extensively from the time of the earliest civilizations. Often, as in the

Edward V. Sayre is adjunct professor of fine arts at the Conservation Center of the Institute of Fine Arts at New York University, New York, N.Y., and senior chemist at Brookhaven National Laboratory, Upton, N.Y.

case of some types of New Kingdom Egyptian plaster, analysis shows them to be mixtures containing major proportions of calcium carbonate and sulfate.[1] Such natural organic polymeric binding materials as egg albumin, keratin, casein or glue have occasionally been added to, or painted on, these plasters. In recent years, different types of plaster have been experimentally combined with various synthetic polymers (e.g., methacrylate, vinyl acetate, urea melamine and epoxy ester resins). In contrast to concrete and mortar, air is seldom deliberately entrained into plaster; however, such solid aggregates as sand, volcanic ash, loess and other soils and clays are often added. In principle, a mud or clay wall coating can be considered as plaster, but in this paper only man-made construction materials that become firm through chemical actions will be so considered.

Lime Plaster

A predominant constituent of lime plaster is calcium carbonate. From early historical periods, this type of plaster has been made by roasting limestone until it has largely decomposed into lime. The lime is then mixed with water and an aggregate to achieve a proper state of plasticity. It is then molded or applied in position and allowed to harden. The cementing of the mixture is achieved by the slow regeneration of calcium carbonate through reaction of the mixture with carbon dioxide in the air. The solid thus formed is similar to a fine-grained and relatively nonporous limestone, and the problems of its deterioration and treatment are analogous to those of limestone and marble.

Almost every type of deterioration experienced by lime plaster, and for that matter by all of the materials discussed here, is strongly affected and accelerated by the presence of water. Pure liquid water alone should have relatively little effect on "pure" lime plaster. However, when water reaches plaster, it almost always contains some dissolved acidic gases, such as carbon, sulfur or nitrogen oxides, that cause chemical alteration and dissolution of the plaster. Also, water usually contains some dissolved salts that contribute to the development of destructive efflorescence.

Plaster itself frequently contains relatively water-soluble constituents, the solution of which weakens its structure and the redeposition of which leads to the development of destructive mechanical stresses. Hence, water percolating through plaster-coated walls leads to a breakdown of the plaster. Therefore, a frequently encountered problem in the conservation of plaster-coated walls and wall paintings done on plaster is the elimination of sources of water that are affecting the wall and its plaster. This is often accomplished by (1) installing an impervious barrier between the source of the water and the plaster to be protected, (2) interposing a void between the source and the inner wall or (3) waterproofing the outer surface of the building. Lead dykes are sometimes placed horizontally across walls near ground level to block the upward migration of groundwater through capillary action, and vertical impervious layers are often placed in walls to prevent water from migrating inward. Such measures can be effective, although they are relatively expensive to carry out. In underground structures, where it would be necessary to excavate around the structure to insert any isolating layer, it is often more practical to leave the structure so exposed standing free of the surrounding stone or soil. Waterproofing exterior walls with sealing coatings may produce some protection for a period of time, but such coatings have a limited lifetime. They may also have undesirable effects on the appearance and durability of the walls.

Possibly the most elaborate installation for isolating a lime plaster structure and protecting it from moisture is that supporting Leonardo da Vinci's *Last Supper* in the convent church of Santa Maria delle Grazie at Milan. The painting, along with its plaster support, was detached from the wall on which it was originally placed to prevent the moisture that percolates through the wall from reaching it, and it is also gently heated electrically to prevent moisture from condensing on its surface.

Corrosive acidic gases present in sizable concentrations in today's polluted atmospheres and in solution in water exposed to these atmospheres can deteriorate lime plaster in several ways. These include (1) direct solubilization of the carbonate structure, causing leaching of the binding material and the formation of destructive efflorescent salt deposits; (2) pulverization of the carbonate structure through chemical alteration, which includes among changes in crystal structure instances of expansions in molecular size that generate internal stresses; and (3) formation of hydrated crystals that undergo volume changes with changing humidity and, hence, also generate internal stresses.

Carbon dioxide and water produce a temporary solubilization of calcium carbonate by converting it to bicarbonate. Although the bicarbonate usually reverts to calcium carbonate, the process results in a breakdown in structure and the development of efflorescence. In relatively unpolluted rural areas in Italy, fresco paintings have been found covered with an efflorescent layer of nearly pure calcium carbonate. The surfaces of such paintings are often covered with small pitlike cavities. Both effects were probably produced by the reaction of the plaster support with carbon dioxide and moisture.

Sulfur dioxide and water can undergo a series of distinctive reactions with calcite. One reaction of sulfurous acid with calcium carbonate is the formation of calcium bicarbonate and bisulfite, both of which are relatively water soluble. Hence, rainwater in which some sulfur dioxide is dissolved can wash away a carbonate surface on which it falls. Also, of course, the calcium bicarbonate and bisulfite can be carried in solution through the plaster and deposited beneath or on the surface. Oxidation and hydration eventually convert the bisulfite to calcium sulfate dihydrate; that is, mineral gypsum. The complete conversion of the calcium carbonate into gypsum nearly doubles the volume. The efflorescence found on the surfaces of Italian frescoes in urban and industrial atmospheres is usually pure gypsum. Frescoes so exposed also tend to develop swollen bulges beneath their outer pigmented layers; these bulges contain unconsolidated, powdery material rich in gypsum. The bulges eventually swell to the extent that the surface containing them breaks open, and a bare area of plaster, which increases rapidly in size as more and more of the surrounding surface falls off, is exposed. This swelling can result from the conversion of gypsum of (1) calcite in situ beneath the surface or (2) calcium bicarbonate and bisulfite deposits near the surface. The gypsum itself is slightly water soluble, and the action of water might cause it to migrate to some extent.

Another aspect of the generation of sulfates within plasters is that they often contain magnesium carbonate that, in turn, is transformed into a hydrated sulfate. The hydrated magnesium sulfates are all water-soluble and, therefore, migrate readily and change their states of hydration when humidity and temperature fluctuate greatly. The stress forces created by such changes of hydration can be extremely great. These forces are capable of literally pushing apart the structure enclosing the hydrate.

On reaction with calcite, nitrogen oxides form water-soluble nitrates and nitrites. Other water-soluble calcium compounds sometimes formed through the action of air pollutants include chlorides and salts of organic acids. Of course, a variety of water-soluble salts may also have been included in the original plaster and its support. An outstanding example of the destructive effect of migration and deposition of a simple soluble salt exists in the tomb of the New Kingdom Egyptian Queen Nefertari at Luxor. Sodium chloride has been deposited beneath the surface of the painted walls of this tomb, causing the outer painted surfaces to be compeltely pushed off the wall. In some parts of the wall, the sodium chloride layer has built up to a thickness as great as 2 centimeters. This deposition occurs beneath the surface rather than on it because evaporation of the water carrying the salt occurs at that depth.

As with stone, it is possible for plaster to be attacked by molds and microorganisms. Because plaster is usually used indoors, it is not likely to be subjected to penetration by roots and tendrils of larger plants. However, molds and bacteria can be found on plaster and are thought by some conservators to contribute significantly to deterioration on occasion.

Plaster is not often subjected to freeze–thaw cycles with their attendant trapped moisture which so often damages materials exposed to the weather. This type of attack is discussed in more detail in the section on concrete.

Treatment of damaged lime plaster usually requires both (a) consolidation and repair of the existing damage and (b) protection against continued attack. A large number of organic binding materials are used to fasten down plaster that has become loose and friable. Polyvinyl alcohol, polymethyl methacrylates and soluble nylon are among those most frequently employed by art conservators. These materials function reasonably well and, if the treated material is well protected, should last for some years. However, organic materials tend to have much shorter lifetimes than inorganic ones. They eventually break down, discolor and oxidize into acidic compounds. Such oxidation of organic material within lime plaster can result in a slow internal corrosion of the plaster.

All of the inorganic materials used to consolidate and protect limestone can be used on lime plaster. Such methods include treatment with magnesium or zinc fluosilicate, fluosilicic acid, hydrofluoric acid or fluorides to create inert calcium fluoride and silica within the plaster. Reasonably small objects may be exposed to gaseous silicon tetrafluoride. Silica may also be generated within deteriorated plaster by treatment with various silicate esters. Solutions of sodium silicate have even been used, but they should be considered for treatment only if it is certain that the treated objects will be well protected from water.

Because of the chemical similarity of calcium, barium and strontium and because of the insolubility and inertness of many barium and strontium salts, there is a long history of treating calcium carbonate structures with solutions of barium or strontium compounds. Such treatment immediately converts any water-soluble sulfates present into inert barium or strontium sulfate. In the 19th century, it was observed that treatment with barium hydroxide tended to consolidate damaged calcium carbonate structures. In general, barium hydroxide treatments result in the eventual formation of barium carbonate within the treated structure. Arthur H. Church treated stone surfaces repeatedly with barium hydroxide, allowing the hydroxide to react with carbon dioxide in the air between treatments.[2] Maxmilian Dennstedt increased the rate of carbonate formation by exposing the hydroxide-treated surface to an atmosphere of carbon dioxide.[3] Seymour Z. Lewin promoted the conversion to carbonate more effectively by adding urea to the barium hydroxide solution.[4] The urea produces a slow, controlled precipitation of barium carbonate from the homogeneous solution, according to the reaction

$$Ba(OH)_2 + (NH_2)_2CO \rightarrow BaCO_3 \rightarrow +2NH_3$$

The slow growth of carbonate crystals from the homogeneous solution results in a particularly well crystallized cohesive structure. Although the barium carbonate formed this way is essentially as chemically reactive as calcite, the sulfur oxides in the air slowly convert it to barium sulfate, which is extremely insoluble and chemically inert. The barium sulfate tends to protect the carbonate over which it is formed from acidic attack. This type of treatment may be extended by providing for direct precipitation of the protective barium sulfate in a slow, controlled manner from the homogeneous solution.[5] This is accomplished by adding the water-soluble salt barium ethyl sulfate to the barium hydroxide solution. The deposition occurs through the reaction

$$Ba(OH)_2 + Ba(C_2H_5SO_4)_2 \rightarrow BaSO_4 + 2C_2H_5OH$$

$$\rightarrow$$

The second product of this reaction, ethyl alcohol, evaporates harmlessly.

Barium treatments deposit the protective material as deeply within the treated structure as the aqueous solutions will carry the reactants. Also, if carried out correctly, none of the treatments will completely seal the surface and cut off the normal flow of water vapor into and out of the plaster. Instead, they tend to cover the reactive carbonates within the structure. In applying such deposition treatments to a structure whose surface must remain totally free of deposits, such as a fresco, the surface can be protected by first placing a layer of Japanese mulberry paper on it and then placing a thick layer of cellulose pulp thoroughly wetted with the treatment solution on the mulberry paper. Keeping the outer pulp layer wet with the solution during the period required for proper reaction will guarantee completion of the treatment. Deposition occurring exterior to the treated structure will occur within the paper and pulp layers, and the deposits will come off when the paper and pulp layers are removed. Frescoes in Florence have been successfully treated in this manner with barium hydroxide solutions.[6] In this instance, treatment was preceded by careful wetting of the walls with an aqueous ammonium carbonate solution. Specimens taken from Florentine frescoes have also been successfully treated with a barium hydroxide-barium ethyl sulfate solution, and it was found that the deteriorated support structure was consolidated and that the appearance of the pigment layers was not appreciably altered in color or appearance.[7]

Gypsum Plaster

Gypsum plasters are those whose principal binding component after setting is calcium sulfate dihydrate, or mineral gypsum. For many centuries, these plasters have been formed by heating gypsum to various high temperatures, causing a partial or complete dehydration of the heated mineral. On the addition of water, the reaction of rehydration regenerates a crystalline gypsum that is firmly consolidated. A number of types of gypsum plaster, with greatly differing setting characteristics, are available. Plaster of paris, the most common of them, is prepared by heating gypsum to about 150°C. in open vessels. Its composition is largely calcium sulfate hemihydrate (that is, $CaSO_4 \cdot \frac{1}{2}H2O$), and it sets rapidly. The rate of setting can be retarded by adding 0.1 percent keratin or by forming the hemihydrate through an autoclave treatment. More slowly setting plasters are formed by heating gypsum to temperatures sufficiently high to dehydrate the calcium sulfate completely. Of these, anhydrous gypsum plaster is formed by heating gypsum to about 200°C, and Keene's cement and parian cement by heating to 600°C and adding slightly less than 1 percent potassium alum or potassium sulfate as an accelerator. Estrich Gips, an extremely slow-setting plaster, can be formed by heating gypsum to 1,100°–1,200°C. It is composed of anhydrous calcium sulfate and lime. The conservation problems associated with all of these types of gypsum plaster are basically the same, once the plaster is set. Moreover, with a few exceptions, the deterioration problems are similar to those encountered with lime plaster.

Gypsum plaster is inherently more water soluble than lime plaster and, hence, is more susceptible to damage by water; however, it is considerably more inert toward acidic substances and is correspondingly less sensitive to air pollutants. Another characteristic way in which gypsum plaster differs from lime plaster is that at sufficiently high temperature and low humidity, it will spontaneously decompose through dehydration. At temperatures of 75°–100°F. (24°–38°C), relative humidity in excess of 35 to 45 percent must be maintained to prevent such spontaneous dehydration. Fortunately, the rate of such dehydration is slow, and occasional departures from stable ambient conditions do not result in immediate extensive damage.

Virtually all of the conservation treatments outlined for lime plaster can be applied to gypsum plaster, with the possible exception of those involving soluble barium or strontium salts. When barium or strontium solutions are applied to gypsum, they convert it to barium and strontium sulfates, which are considerably more insoluble than gypsum. In some circumstances, a light treatment of this type might help bring about some consolidation of a broken–down structure and protect any calcium carbonate present in the plaster. Heavy treatments of this type, however, might cause deterioration through excessive conversion of the sulfate.

CONCRETE

The invention of hydraulic cement is attributed to Roman builders who discovered that if they mixed lime with pozzolana (pulvis puteolanus), a volcanic earth occurring in large deposits near Rome and Naples, the two formed a mixture that set strongly under water and was fire resistant. The quality of this early concrete is well demonstrated in the many sound Roman concrete structures still standing. Modern types of cement, such as portland cement, are more often manufactured by grinding, firing and regrinding together roughly two parts limestone or other calcareous material and one part clay, shale or other argillaceous material. Ground gypsum and other additives are added after firing. The resultant product is a complex mixture of calcium aluminosilicates that, in the case of portland cement, is roughly equivalent to a combination of 60 to 67 percent lime, 17 to 25 percent silica, 3 to 8 percent alumina, 0.5 to 6 percent iron oxide, 0.1 to 4 percent magnesia, 1 to 3 percent sulfur trioxide and 0.5 to 1.3 percent soda or potash.

A great variety of cement is manufactured today, including a number of variations of portland cement and modern equivalents of pozzolana cement in which burnt clays and pulverized fuel ash are substituted for volcanic material. Rather different in their basic composition are two types of modern cement developed to produce concrete that is highly resistant to sulfate and other chemical attack. These are the high-alumina and supersulfate cements. In high-alumina cement, aluminates with an alumina content as high as 45 percent replace silicates. Such cement is usually manufactured from bauxite and limestone. These raw materials tend to fuse completely during firing; hence, the resulting cement is frequently sold under such names as Ciment Fondu, Cemento Fuso or Schmelzzement. High-alumina cement is also desirable because of its rapid hardening and excellent refractory qualities. Supersulfate cement is manufactured from blast furnace slag and gypsum, with the addition of a small amount of portland cement. Also available are special types of cement that expand rather than contract on setting and are useful for producing sharply defined castings. The choice of the right cement for the job is obviously a primary consideration in using cement for conservation purposes.

There is also great variety in the proportions in which cement, water, the aggregate, air, air-entraining agents and other additives are mixed to form the final concrete mixture. The chemical reactions of setting are extremely complex, as they form a variety of colloidal and crystalline products of a hydrated silicate and aluminate nature. Frequently cited as a typical reaction product is the mineral tobermorite, which is a long-chain inorganic polymer with the formula $[Ca_5(Si_3O_9H)_2 \cdot 4H_2O]_x$. Also, some free calcium hydroxide or carbonate is usually formed and significantly affects the susceptibility of the finished concrete to acidic attack.

Although most types of concrete are usually less affected by hydrolytic and acidic action than is lime plaster, they are not immune to such attack. When exposed to an aqueous solution with pH as low as 3.5 to 4, concrete often deteriorates rapidly. Concrete is also badly damaged by efflorescent and subsurface salt deposits. Because it is often used outdoors, it is frequently damaged by frost and by the growth of plants and microorganisms on it.

Many types of concrete deteriorate rapidly if exposed to solutions containing soluble sulfates. If mildly attacked by sulfates, the concrete will develop a whitish appearance. At a more advanced stage, it expands, cracks and spalls. It eventually becomes friable throughout and is finally reduced to a powder. The sulfate ions react with concrete components to form the mineral ettringite (that is, $3CaO \cdot Al_2O_3 \cdot 3CaSO_4 \cdot 32H_2O$). Other products, which produce a considerable expansion in crystalline volume, are formed also. The susceptibility to attack seems to depend on the concentration of tricalcium aluminate (that is, $3CaO \cdot Al_2O_3$) in the original cement. Protection against sulfate attack is best provided by blocking the source of sulfate ions or by using sulfate-resistant cement, such as high-alumina or supersulfate cement.

The freezing of water within pores of concrete can be destructive in two ways: (1) through the direct expansion that occurs on freezing and (2) through the growth of ice crystals previously formed by processes involving migration of moisture through the concrete to the frozen layer. This latter process can result in the

199

breakdown of the concrete in layers parallel to the outer surface. The presence, in the cement structure, of open pores leading to the suface promotes such frost attack; however, the presence of trapped air bubbles within the concrete structure tends to protect the concrete from frost damage, provided that the bubbles do not form continuous channels. Accordingly, in current practice up to 10 percent air or other gas is deliberately entrained within the concrete at the time of formation. This is accomplished by (1) adding materials such as hydrogen peroxide or powdered aluminum or zinc that react with the moist cement to generate gases, (2) reducing surface tension through the introduction of surface-active agents and (3) using dispersing agents that prevent coagulation without appreciably lowering surface tension.

Surface treatment by any of the impregnating agents discussed under lime plaster can be applied to concrete. Because of concrete's silicic nature, inorganic impregnants depositing silica would seem to be particularly appropriate. When concrete is exposed on external surfaces, organic treatments should be avoided unless only relatively temporary protection is desired. Also, if external exposure is involved, the concrete should not be given a treatment that attempts to seal the surface. Experience has shown that all such "impermeable" layers are eventually broken. When this occurs, water and other destructive agents tend to accumulate beneath the "protective" surface, resulting in decay beneath it and eventually spalling off of the surface. Attempts to seal off a surface have frequently resulted in more damage than if the concrete had been left untreated.

MORTAR

Mortar ranges in composition from straight lime plaster to concrete, but most modern types of mortar are mixtures of cement, lime and sand. The lime content of mortar tends to be from one to three times that of cement so that mortar can be expected to have many properties similar to lime plaster. When mortar is intended for external use, air is usually deliberately entrained within it. For example, the American Society for Testing and Materials Standard 91–60 specifies that there should be not less than 12 percent air in mortar.

The deterioration and conservation problems of mortar are similar to those of plaster and concrete. Because of the high concentration of calcium carbonate in mortar, a barium inorganic impregnation treatment would be more appropriate than a silicon one.

NOTES

1. A. Lucas and J. R. Harris, *Ancient Egyptian Materials and Industries*, 4th ed. (New York: St. Martins Press, Inc., 1962).

2. Arthur H. Church, "Treatment of Decayed Stonework in the Chapter House, Westminster Abbey," *Journal of the Society of Chemical Industry* 23, no. 824 (1904).

3. Maxmilian Dennstedt, stone colouring and preserving cements. British Patent 13,761 (1884).

4. Seymour Z. Lewin, composition for preserving limestone structures. U.S. Patent 3,577,244 (1971).

5. Edward V. Sayre, "Direct Deposition of Barium Sulfate from Homogenous Solution within Porous Stone," in *1970 New York Conference on Conservation of Stone and Wooden Objects*, ed. G. Thomson, 2 vols. (London: International Institute for Conservation of Historic and Artistic Works, 1971), 1:115-17

6. E. Ferroni, V. Malaguzzi–Valeri and G. Rovida, "Experimental Study by Diffraction of Heterogeneous Systems as a Preliminary to the Proposal of a Technique for the Restoration of Gypsum Polluted Murals" (Paper delivered at the International Council of Museums Conference, Amsterdam, September 1969).

7. Edward V. Sayre, "Investigation of Italian Frescos, Their Materials, Deterioration and Treatment," in *Application of Science in Examination of Works of Art*, ed. William J. Young (Boston: Museum of Fine Arts, 1973), pp. 176–81.

COMMENTARY

HARLEY J. McKEE, FAIA

Although the fields of architecture and chemistry are clearly separate, architects and chemists do have one thing in common. Like chemists, architects depend on observations to determine what has happened to materials. Chemists, of course, have developed theoretical knowledge concerning the behavior of materials and their interaction with other substances in the universe and are, therefore, more scientific in their approach than are architects, who rely on random observations. Both professionals, however, depend to a great extent on actual experience.

I was particularly pleased by the comment made during the discussion on brick, adobe, stone and architectural ceramics about the value of a professional viewpoint in preservation efforts. The restoration of historic buildings certainly needs a professional approach.

As Giorgio Torraca points out, professional scientific analysis is important. Some architects have understood this. In about 1846, before choosing Seneca sandstone for the first Smithsonian building in Washington, D.C., architect James Renwick had about 15 kinds of stone analyzed by a chemist. The choice has proved to be a good one. Many architects, however, have neglected chemical analysis. I believe this is so because architects are generally more interested in the function of a material—that is, the ability to

---

Harley J. McKee, FAIA, is professor emeritus of architecture at Syracuse University, Syracuse, N.Y.

provide support and shelter and to withstand wear—than they are in the material itself. Also, the architect considers materials as elements of a system, and he looks for a material that will serve a certain purpose in the system. These attitudes, I believe, result in the architect's lack of respect for materials, as opposed to the respect shown by other professionals, such as conservators and chemists, who work with the same materials. For example, there is a definite difference between the conservator's and the architect's attitudes toward materials that are hidden within a building, such as mortar, which is hidden except at surface joints; and plaster, which is often covered with paper or some other material. Exterior stucco is a little more visible, but it also is often painted or covered.

In addition, most surfaces that architects deal with are unornamented and, as with materials hidden in a building, they respect that kind of surface less than an ornamental one. Certainly architects value relief ornamental plaster or painting on walls that reveals the artist's touch more than plain surfaces, and they realize that these artistic surfaces need and deserve to be treated by the conservator's methods. I do not believe that architects can add anything to these methods. They can only recognize that ornamental surfaces often require this important, expensive and delicate treatment and see that it is provided.

I will state briefly some of the problems facing restoration architects for the benefit of those who do not belong to this profession. My personal experience is limited to the United States, and since I deal primarily with small and relatively plain buildings, most of which are houses, this discussion will consider problems most common to that type of building. Of course, restoration architects also deal with monumental buildings, each of which has its own character and preservation problems, but one cannot generalize about them as easily as about small, relatively plain architecture.

Masonry buildings were relatively uncommon in the early days of this country, although they became popular later and today constitute a significant portion of the buildings being preserved. The walls of these masonry buildings were usually made redundantly strong, so that the problem of support does not occur often. Weak mortar was perfectly adequate in these buildings' walls. More commonly, problems arise from damage caused by alterations and, perhaps the most common cause of problems, improper repointing of joints.

A number of speakers at this conference have stressed the need for continuous maintenance, which is obviously the best way to preserve a building. However, restoration architects are often hired to work on buildings whose maintenance has been neglected, and most of the buildings' preservation problems are associated with this neglect. The restoration architect's job is to restore a building to its original condition. After that, proper maintenance measures can be initiated.

All of the masonry materials John D. Milner and Edward V. Sayre discuss—mortar, plaster/stucco and concrete—were used in the past in varying degrees.

Plastered interior walls and ceilings are, of course, common in historic buildings. From the mid-19th century on, molded plaster cornices were used, in addition to conventional ornaments of plaster. Exterior stucco is less common, although in some areas it presents considerable problems. Concrete was rarely used as a building material before the late 19th century. Even then, it was largely confined to publicly financed engineering projects.

Natural cement, not portland cement, was the material commonly used for these early engineering works. The loose way in which the term *portland cement* is used by people writing about historic architecture has caused great confusion. There were a number of so-called gravel wall houses constructed during the mid-19th century. Several can be found in central New York state, among other places. Little is known about these buildings. Some of them have poured walls, which were made by pouring a lime or cement and gravel mixture into 14 or 15-inch-deep courses. When one course was sufficiently hard, the forms were moved up and another one poured. Some buildings made of concrete blocks also appear to date from the mid-19th century. It is not known whether lime cement or natural cement concrete was used in these buildings. None, however, is considered historically important, and they have not been carefully studied or proposed as subjects for restoration.

Lime is a basic ingredient of mortar, plaster and stucco. The kind of lime used today has a controlled uniformity, but this was certainly not true in the past. The lime used in the past was variable, as Mr. Milner mentions. It contained shells or stones of varying composition, with impurities in them. The method of calcining the lime also differed from that used today, that is, the fuel used for calcining, temperature, time requirements, etc., were different. The handling and slaking of lime were also different, as were the proportions of lime and other ingredients used in making mortar and the methods by which the lime and other ingredients were mixed together to form mortar. In addition, there was the old custom of keeping lime for a year or two in a pit in the ground before it was used. Although experiments conducted by Bryan Higgins, a noted English scientist, in the late 18th century proved that this was an undesirable practice, it continued to be recommended in handbooks on the subject until the middle of the 19th century. There were many myths about mortar and mortar materials. One was that the hardness of the stone from which lime was obtained corresponded to the hardness of the mortar. This, too, continued to be believed long after it was disproved by chemical and physical analyses and tests.

In the early 19th century, government specifications for public buildings began to call for natural cement as an ingredient in mortar, along with the traditional lime and sand. Since about 1880 or 1885, rigid nonabsorbing masonry has been favored. Hard masonry units, with hard cement mortar between them, are now used, and modern builders try to avoid pinholes and hair cracks and attempt to keep moisture out of the mortar or, at least, drain out the moisture that gets into it. Walls in historic buildings, however, were laid upon a plasic mortar cushion. The mortar hardened slowly, and the whole wall relied on its mass rather than on cohesive mortar for its stability. The mortar adjusted to the load and allowed the wall to breathe. I believe it is a mistake to try to mix the two systems, that is, to add hard cement to a mortar that is to be used for restoration work. How much portland cement can be safely mixed into a lime-sand mortar that is to be used with soft, old brick? The Ministry of Public Buildings and Works in London recommends matching the absorbency of the mortar used in restoration to that of soft brick, since early brick was soft and since using a hard mortar with it accelerates deterioration of the brick. This also applies to soft, porous stone. I was interested in a comment made during the discussion on brick, adobe, stone and architectural ceramics that the Rome Centre also has found that cement should not be added to mortar destined for use in restoring old buildings. In England, the addition of hydraulic lime to the mortar, rather than cement, has proved preferable.

Until the late 19th century, plaster in the United States was made of lime, sand and hair, and its hardness varied. Some plasters were soft; others were moderately hard, although certainly not as hard as the plasters that came into use near the end of the 19th century and that were made largely by proprietary processes and sold under trade names. In some old buildings, there were ornamental surfaces made largely of plaster of paris.

Today, when a plain wall, which architects are accustomed to dealing with, is replaced, hard plaster is usually used because it is the material that modern masons know how to use. However, when dealing with ornamental plaster surfaces, most architects recognize that special problems are presented and that the advice of conservators and chemists is required. Mr. Milner gives an interesting summary of the problems involved in dealing with ornamental surfaces, determining their value and avoiding unnecessary damage to them.

The question of moisture in exterior walls has been mentioned frequently at this conference. I believe that we may have to learn to live with the situation just as original residents of historic buildings did, but this increases preservation problems. I am not certain which is worse in this matter, the disease or the cure. People persist in heating buildings in winter more than their predecessors did and in air-conditioning them in summer, so condensation is bound to occur. If waterproof coatings are applied on the outside or inside of a building, moisture will be trapped in the walls and this invites trouble. I do not believe there is any way to keep water vapor, and eventually condensed water vapor, out of a wall. Yet if the water remains in the wall, problems are certainly going to occur and these problems can become quite complex. If an interior surface is being replaced, a vapor barrier can be installed to provide some help. But if a frescoed wall or other ornamental feature is involved, the entire wall may have to be detached and moved out a few inches to allow air circulation behind it, or it may be necessary to install a special circulating system of the types mentioned by Dr. Torraca and Dr. Lewin.

Concrete is not often found in structures that are being preserved in the United States at the present time, but preservationists will undoubtedly face problems concerning the preservation of such structures in the near future. When these problems do arise, the advice of chemists will be essential in establishing whether architects are dealing with lime concrete, natural cement or, during later periods, portland cement concrete. I believe that anyone who claims to have found portland cement used in a building constructed before about 1870 should be required to prove the claim. I do not say that instances of such use never occurred, but I think that we should be skeptical about the claims. Also, portland cement is incompatible with lime stucco and natural cement stucco. I have seen examples of stucco that have ben patched with portland cement stucco, and the patches have come off. The stabilization of old masonry walls with portland cement grout is another questionable practice, in my opinion. Rigid lumps, which are likely to break off from untreated portions of the wall, are formed.

COMMENTARY

GIORGIO TORRACA

While reading John D. Milner's paper, I find myself experiencing a kind of inferiority complex similar to the feelings Lee H. Nelson alluded to when commenting on my paper, "Brick, Adobe, Stone and Architectural Ceramics: Deterioration Processes and Conservation Practices." I do not understand every point Mr. Milner mentions, but I have learned a lot. This leads me to believe that preservationists should not feel any inferiority to conservation scientists, because the situation can be reversed! We scientists do not know exactly what preservationists face in the field; only by working together can each group learn about the other's problems, and this learning process is slow. Furthermore, if preservationists do not understand what a chemist is saying, it is the chemist's fault, usually because he has used some unfamiliar terms or has failed to explain terms properly. If this situation occurs, ask for an explanation immediately and start again.

Both Mr. Milner's paper and the paper by Edward V. Sayre stimulate a consideration of what accomplishments architects and conservation scientists, working together, might expect to achieve in the restoration of buildings.

One point that comes out quite clearly in Mr. Milner's paper is that each case must be treated individually. It should be emphasized that thorough study of a case is difficult and complicated.

Giorgio Torraca is deputy director of the International Centre for the Study of the Preservation and the Restoration of Cultural Property, Rome, Italy.

Not only must there be chemical analyses of materials that are deteriorating but also a study of the building's environment and a determination of the causes of deterioration.

A second point is that architects should not design for maximum stability, since materials, by their nature, do not last forever. The ideal is to design for a given type of maintenance. Designs should include a consideration of the type of maintenance that can and will be given to the buildings involved, so that interventions, when necessary, can be accommodated. The principle behind this point is that the less the original structure is disturbed the better it is.

The third point I would like to emphasize is the importance of feedback. Information must come back from the field to the scientific laboratory so that it can be determined whether actions suggested by the laboratory were useful and appropriate. Answers to important questions must be provided: Did the suggested treatment work or did it not? What state was the deteriorated material in before treatment and after? Answers to the latter question can be extremely revealing and can open the way for progress toward better solutions to problems. Unfortunately, there is little feedback from practicing architects to conservation scientists. Perhaps the importance of feedback needs special emphasis by both those in the field and those in the laboratory.

I admire Dr. Sayre's work, and there are many points I would like to discuss with him. For now, however, I will limit my comments to the current debate, which he mentions, over impregnation versus consolidation, that is, the use of organic or inorganic materials for the repair of deteriorated masonry. Dr. Sayre is predisposed to the use of inorganic treatments, but, as an organic chemist, I would point out that there are some advantages for organic treatments also. One of these advantages is that once a masonry material has been treated with an organic product, the result is a new composite material; it is not simply an inorganic material plus a nearby organic material. This new composite material will have its own characteristics, and while the effects of aging on the new material cannot be completely determined or understood at first, there have been some composite materials containing organic substances that have lasted quite well. For example, there are some well-preserved sandstones that were originally colored by organic dyes—dyes so fugitive that they normally would not stand exposure, but when they are absorbed inside pores of the inorganic sandstone, they are quite resistant to fading. Organic treatments also offer an advantage from the mechanical viewpoint inasmuch as they usually induce a more plastic behavior in masonry than do inorganic treatments, which tend to increase brittleness or, at best, not to affect plasticity at all.

The argument over which type of treatment method is best will probably go on and on. However, in my opinion, there are points both for and against the use of organic and inorganic methods, and the person responsible for overseeing the treatment of a masonry building should be aware of the advantages and disadvantages of each method.

DISCUSSION

Comments made by the panelists and audience during the discussion on mortar, plaster/stucco and concrete are summarized in the following paragraphs.

From the points made in the paper and commentaries, it is obvious that maintenance is an important aspect of the preservation of masonry materials. The idea expressed by Dr. Torraca of designing for a specific type of maintenance is thought provoking and should be considered carefully by all architects. This aspect of building is often overlooked, intentionally or unintentionally, during the design phase.

It might also be useful for restoration architects to know about early maintenance practices used on masonry buildings, but there are difficulties in documenting these early techniques. For one thing, there has been little written about masonry in North America as compared to wood or other architectural materials. The few reference sources that exist on the subject are mostly 19th-century books that vary greatly in quality. This variation is due in part to the practice, common at that time, of pirating information from other, often older books, with the result that information in the reference book was sometimes outdated and many of the practices described in it had been abandoned. Geology books of the period may offer the most useful information, especially if they include a chapter on economic geology. Some states issued excellent geologic reports quite early, but most of those available today are from the late 1800s and early 1900s.

The *Journal of the Society of Architectural Historians* has published bibliographies of handbooks and other publications available to colonial architects and builders, including Helen Park's

"A List of Architectural Books Available in America before the Revolution" [20, no. 3 (October 1961): 115-130] and Charles E. Peterson's "Architectural Books, 1760" [12, no. 3 (October 1953): 28]. Today, a comprehensive bibliography of architectural, engineering and other publications that include descriptions of early maintenance practices would be a welcome addition to preservation literature.

Of course, if a building has not been maintained properly, the restoration architect faces many varied problems. Two buildings in Saint Paul, Minn.—the State Capitol and the Old Federal Courts Building—illustrate three common problems. For example, the marble moldings, projections, corner pieces and carvings on the exterior of the less-than-70-year-old State Capitol are now almost crystalline and are eroding rapidly. This situation is not really unusual, for protuberances generally begin to weather before flat surfaces. Probably the best approach to this problem is to perform a thorough scientific analysis to determine exactly what is happening and why. Then an appropriate procedure for repair or consolidation may be formulated and suitable maintenance practices instituted.

The granite exterior of the Old Federal Courts Building is also suffering some deterioration. There is serious spallation of the granite in the base course, which over the years has become covered with a black deposit of city grime. Such spallation is not uncommon. Perhaps one of the most dramatic examples is Luxor, Egypt, where granite ruins have been buried in the earth for centuries. Upon excavation, the granite appears to be in good condition but soon layers suddenly begin to peel off. It has been assumed that this spallation is caused by the hydrolysis of certain minerals within the stone, but this assumption has not been proved. In the case of the Old Federal Courts Building, the spallation may well be due to some type of hydrolytic attack.

Another problem that architects will encounter in the restoration of the Old Federal Courts Building is the removal of paint, a subject scheduled for more extensive discussion later in this conference. In this case, green paint was applied over portions of the marble interior; the major question is how it may be removed without damaging or disfiguring the marble. Finding the answer to this question may be difficult, because the correct paint removal technique will depend on both the nature of the paint and the nature of the surface to which it has been applied.

The National Trust for Historic Preservation might be of help in situations such as these. The establishment of a roster of experts who could consult with restoration architects would be a worthwhile project, as would the organization of traveling teams that could bring expertise and information to architects in the field.

The American Concrete Institute, through its Committee on the History of Concrete, is willing to offer its expertise and to assist in developing standards for restoration work. The committee, which is just now developing its goals, asks for help in return: Committee members wish to talk with technologists, architects and others who can provide information on early concrete structures, and they are interested in seeing or learning about the technology of both concrete structures under restoration and those about to be demolished.

Metals: Tin, Copper, Iron, Lead, Steel and Aluminum

ARCHITECTURAL METALS: THEIR DETERIORATION AND STABILIZATION

JOHN G. WAITE

Metals are, in general, those substances that have a peculiar luster and hardness, can conduct heat and electricity, are opaque and possess certain mechanical properties, the most remarkable of which is their power to resist deformation. Furthermore, all metals have a crystalline structure; are malleable and ductile (that is, they can be hammered or rolled into thin sheets or be drawn into wire); possess tenacity (that is, they resist being pulled apart into individual particles); are fusible (that is, they become liquid when heated at high temperatures); have a high specific gravity or density; form positive ions when in solution; and lose electrons during chemical reactions.

In chemistry, a metal is defined as an element that yields positively charged ions in aqueous solutions of its salts. Another definition is that a metal is a lender of electrons. During electrolysis, metals are set free at the negative pole (that is, the cathode) and nonmetals are set free at the positive pole (that is, the anode). However, recent advances in physics and chemistry indicate that traditional distinctions between metals and nonmetals do not always hold true, because some elements act as metals under certain conditions and as nonmetals under others.

In this paper, only those metals, often in the form of alloys, that have been traditionally used for architectural purposes are con-

John G. Waite is senior historical architect for the Division for Historic Preservation, New York State Office of Parks and Recreation, Albany, N.Y.

sidered. These metals are aluminum, copper, lead, tin, iron and steel. (See table 1 for basic information on these metals.)

Table 1   BASIC INFORMATION ON VARIOUS METALS

	Aluminum	Copper	Lead	Tin	Iron
Symbol	Al	Cu	Pb	Sn	Fe
Atomic weight	27	63.5	207.1	118.7	55.8
Atomic number	13	29	82	50	26
Density (specific gravity)	2.702	8.97	11.34	7.28	7.86
Melting point, °C	660	1,083	327.5	231.8	1,535
Boiling point, °C	2,467	2,595	1,744	2,260	3,000

ARCHITECTURAL USES OF METALS

Because of their inherent physical and mechanical properties, as well as their relative availability, some metals have been successfully used as building materials, usually as parts of structural systems or as sheathing for weather protection. Often, such metal architectural members also have a secondary function as large-scale decorative elements.

This paper deals only with large, nonremovable metal architectural elements that must be treated in situ because of the impracticability of treating them in a laboratory. Although metals have been widely used in other architectural applications, such as fastenings and small decorative elements, only those applications relating to structural systems and weather protection will be reviewed. The preservation and conservation of small, removable metal architectural elements fall within the realm of more conventional museum conservation processes; they can, therefore, be treated under closely controlled laboratory conditions in the same way that other artifacts are handled.

THE FAILURE AND DETERIORATION OF ARCHITECTURAL METALS

Deterioration is generally defined as a material's loss in value or a decrease in the material's ability to fulfill the function for which it was intended.[1] Deterioration usually refers to the breakdown of a material due to natural causes, although deterioration can also be either directly or indirectly caused by man. Deterioration may also be defined as a transition process whereby a material goes from a higher to a lower energy state. Although deterioration usually infers a chemical change, under some conditions, the change can be physical rather than chemical.

Corrosion

The major form of deterioration of architectural metals is corrosion. Often called oxidation, corrosion is the chemical reaction of a pure metal with oxygen or other substances. In nature, there is no stability or permanence because decay and reconstruction are continuously occurring. Architectural metals are constantly undergoing changes of state because of their exposure to the atmosphere, heat, moisture and other agents.

Almost all metals become coated with a thin metallic oxide film shortly after exposure to the air. This film is caused by the metal's reaction with oxygen and/or sulfides or other ions and may render the metal more noble and, hence, less susceptible to corrosion. As the film accumulates, it may insulate the metal from the surrounding oxygen. The nature of the metal and the quality of the film determine to what degree corrosion of the metal is controlled. With some metals, the oxide coat forms a tough membrane that restricts the passage of metal ions out of it or oxygen in through it. In other cases, such as the rusting of iron, the oxide does not form a tough protective coating, but rather permits continued oxidation until the metal deteriorates to the point where it loses those particular engineering properties that originally made it useful.

The following are forms of corrosion:

Uniform attack. In this type of corrosion, a metal corrodes evenly in areas where it is exposed to corrosive agents.

Pitting. Pitting occurs when a corrosive attack is localized on a metal.

Selective attack. This type of attack occurs when a metal was never actually homogeneous; only certain phases are attacked.

Corrosion cracking. Cyclic stresses set up in the metal may cause corrosion fatigue which, in turn, results in corrosion cracking; this cracking breaks open the protective oxide coating and exposes the metal to corrosive agents.

Erosion. Erosion occurs when the corrosion-resistant oxide film or layers of the protective corrosion product on a metal are removed by abrasion, exposing the metal to corrosive agents.

Galvanic action. Two dissimilar metals usually differ in their electrode potential. If they are immersed in the same electrolyte, electrons will flow from the less noble (or more active) metal through the solution to the more noble (or less active) metal. In some cases, the electrolyte may be moisture or condensation on surfaces of the metals.

Concentration cell. Corrosion is caused by a concentration cell when an electrolytic cell is set up by the trapping of oxygen adjacent to a metal.

High-temperature corrosion. A kind of dry oxidation occurs at high temperatures, leaving corrosion products on the surface of the metal. If the film of these corrosion products is porous, the corrosion can continue unabated. If it is nonporous, the film can be highly protective.[2]

The corrosion rate is affected by primary and secondary factors.[3] Primary factors include the electrode potential of dissimilar metals in an electrolytic situation, hydrogen overvoltage, the metal surface's physical nature and the surface's ability to form a protective film. Secondary factors include the rate of hydrogen-ion activity, the influence of oxygen in solution when it is adjacent to the metal (that is, the existence of an oxygen concentration cell), other ions present in the solution, the rate of flow, the temperature, static stresses present in the metal, cyclic stresses present (which cause corrosion fatigue that may lead to corrosion cracking) and effects of dissimilar metals.

Atmospheric corrosion is the most common form of corrosion to which architectural metals are exposed. This type of corrosion is an electrochemical reaction that results when a film of moisture on a metal surface serves as an electrolytic film, containing gases and vapors absorbed by the moisture. The atmospheric corrosion rate generally increases with humidity. Once a critical humidity level is reached, corrosion proceeds rapidly. Generally, an increase in temperature also causes an increase in the corrosion rate.

Industrial atmospheres contain, along with oxygen, water and carbon dioxide, such corrosive agents as soot, fly ash and sulfur compounds that are ordinarily in reduced states, for example, as hydrogen sulfide (H_2S), sulfur dioxide (SO_2) and sulfur trioxide (SO_3). These compounds are produced by the combustion of sulfur–containing fuels, especially coal.[4]

Marine atmospheres also contain corrosive agents, such as chlorides in the air and salt particles from the sea, that are deposited on metal surfaces. These corrosive agents in marine atmospheres may affect architectural metals as far as 60 or 70 miles from the sea.

Indoor corrosion is caused by the burning of coal, which releases sulfur compounds that combine with condensed moisture on unprotected metal surfaces to form corrosive acids.

Architectural metals in contact with soils are subject to corrosion caused by acids, alkalies, dissolved salts, sulfides, water, oxygen and anaerobic sulfate-reducing bacteria.

216

Metals in contact with water are also subject to corrosion because of dissolved solids and gases, including oxygen, present in the water. Seawater is especially corrosive.

Corrosive agents, other than oxygen and sulfur compounds, that attack architectural metals include acids, alkalies, salts, organic compounds and such halogens as fluorine, chlorine, bromine and iodine. These agents are found in many forms—scum, mud and marine plants, as well as seawater and fresh water.

Metal architectural elements fail from causes other than corrosion. These causes can be either from physical actions, such as abrasion, or from combinations of physical and chemical actions, such as weathering.

Abrasion

Abrasion is the erosion of a metal caused by dirt, dust, sand, grit, sleet or hail. Such abrasives also encourage corrosion by the removal of a metal's protective oxide coating. This form of deterioration is especially critical on metal flashings and valleys on slate roofs. As the slate deteriorates, particles of the slate break off and are washed down valleys, causing erosion of the metal elements.

Creep

Creep is the slow, continuous flow of roofing metals under sustained stressing and sometimes under relatively high temperatures.[5] The stressing may be related to thermal expansion and contraction. Creep is an especially critical problem with sheet–lead roofs.

Fatigue

The repeated application of cyclic stresses to a point where fracturing occurs is termed fatigue. It has been estimated that approximately 90 percent of the structural failures of railroad bridges are fatigue failures that developed late in the structure's life.[6]

Fire

Unprotected metal framing members become plastic and fail rapidly with the sudden application of high temperatures.

Overaging

Properties of a metal change because of metallurgical changes in the metal's structure. This condition, referred to as overaging, is relatively rare in architectural metals.

Overloading

Overloading is the stressing of a metal member beyond its capacity, resulting in the metal's fracturing or failure. This may occur through the application of static loads, dynamic loads, thermal stresses or settlement stresses, either singly or in combination.

Weathering

A metal subjected to the weather is exposed to various chemical and physical agents, singly and in combination. This often results in a kind of synergism, that is, action in which the total effect is greater than the sum of individual effects.

GENERAL PRESERVATION AND STABILIZATION METHODS

Unfortunately, much of the technology developed for the treatment of small metal artifacts by museum conservators in carefully controlled laboratory environments has not been used to any great extent in the preservation of architectural metals. The architect often deals with metal elements that are used either as structure or for weather protection, such as siding, roof covering or flashing. When these elements fail or become deteriorated, it is usually not practical to treat them as museum objects under laboratory conditions, because of their size or because they are parts of the building's integral construction and, therefore, cannot be removed easily and replaced. If a roof fails, for example, it is not only the roofing material that is affected; the structure and fabric of the entire building, as well as its contents, are also endangered. It is not surprising, then, to find that the usual treatment for architectural metals that have failed is the removal and replacement of the deteriorated elements with new materials.

A practical reason for this replacement is cost. The architect usually deals with construction tradesmen, who, although skilled in conventional building techniques, have neither the training or experience nor the facility with scientific techniques for the conservation of such materials in place. It is, therefore, often less expensive to replace a deteriorated metal than to experiment with its preservation, which, even if successful, may add only a few years to the material's life expectancy.

Maintenance, therefore, becomes a key factor in the preservation of metal architectural elements. Because, for obvious cultural reasons, it is far more desirable to retain genuine old fabric and workmanship than to replace it with even the highest-quality modern reproduction fabric, it is essential that sound maintenance and protective procedures be carried out on a regular basis. Professional advice should be sought concerning the most effective preservation techniques, especially those relating to the application of paints. In the case of metal structural systems, periodic inspections should be made.

Along with maintenance, there are a number of other methods for metal preservation through the prevention and control of corrosion. They include proper initial design for the installation of metals; environmental control through the use of inhibitors and passivators, dehumidification, deactivation, deaeration and cathodic and galvanic protection; the use of metallic and surface conversion coatings; the use of ceramic coatings; and the selection and application of organic coatings to protect metals.[7]

Proper Design

Among factors to be considered when using metal components are the selection of suitable corrosion-resisting materials, avoidance of contact between dissimilar metals, provisions for the removal of trapped water and avoidance of areas where water could accumulate and stagnate and control of metallurgical factors, such as heat treatment and stress relief. Proper design should also provide for avoiding internal stresses caused by sun and shade. Usually, as much shop fabrication of metal components as possible is desirable to help avoid pockets that may trap water.

Environmental Control

Although not often used for protecting architectural metals, environmental control techniques can be useful Such techniques include the use of inhibitors and passivators, dehumidification, deactivation, deaeration and cathodic and galvanic protection.[8]

Metallic Coatings

Protective metallic coatings, designed to isolate metals from corrosive agents, are applied in several ways, including electrode positioning, metal spraying, deposition of the metallic coating from a vapor phase, dipping the metal to be protected into the molten metal to be used as the coating, adhesive–metal powder techniques and metallurgical bonding through rolling.[9] For architectural metals, hot–dip coating processes are widely used. These processes produce various types of coating, including galvanized, sherardized, terne and hot–dip tin coatings.

Ceramic Coatings

Ceramic coatings consist of inorganic glasses loaded with refractory or other materials to aid adhesion, to decrease the ceramic material's brittleness and its tendency to break off because of thermal differences and often to achieve decorative colors and textures.[10] The use of this kind of corrosion protection for in situ architectural metals is not common.

Organic Coatings

The use of organic coatings (or paints) to protect metals from corrosion is widespread. Generally, the success of a coating depends on the methods used to prepare the metal surface for painting and the type and method of application of the primer and finish coats. Paints can be used to inhibit corrosion by causing a sluggish movement of ions between the metal and the corrosive agent.

The treatment of metal surfaces in preparation for painting can be divided into three categories: mechanical, thermal and chemical methods. Chemical methods include acid pickling and phosphate dipping. Thermal methods include the heating of a corroded surface with oxyacetylene burners to remove corrosion products. Mechanical methods include scraping, wire brushing, grit blasting and sandblasting (both wet and dry).

Once a metal surface has been cleaned of all corrosion products, a primer coat containing a liquid vehicle and a corrosion–resisting pigment is applied. When the primer is thoroughly dry, finish coats are applied. These coats generally consist of lacquers, varnishes, enamels or special coatings.

Other organic coatings include catalyzed or conversion coatings that consist of an epon, which may be modified with such other resins as vinyls, alkyls, polyesters, etc.; polyfluorinated ethylenes (for example, Teflon); synthetic rubber; neoprene; rubber based on organic polysulfides (for example, Thiokol); bituminous materials; and high-temperature organic paints formulated from silicone resins, ceramic-type pigments and inert fillers.[11]

Other Forms of Protection
The following forms of deterioration of metal architectural members are controlled using the techniques listed.

Abrasion. Painting the metal surface slows down the deterioration rate. Ultimately, replacement of the damaged member is necessary.

Creep. Removing the damaged fabric, melting it and recasting it in its original form is often the only cure for failure caused by creep.

Fatigue. Often the only solution for metal members damaged by fatigue is additional bracing or replacement of the damaged member.

Fire. Metal structural elements may be protected to some degree from fire damage by the installation of insulative masonry cladding, such as concrete or clay tile.

Overloading. A metal structural member that has failed because of overloading must be either replaced or supplemented by additional bracing.

Overaging. A metal element, especially a structural one, that has failed because of overaging usually must be replaced.

Weathering. Because of the complexity and variety of deterioration caused by weathering, individual chemical and physical corrosive agents must be identified and dealt with accordingly, usually on an individual basis.

ALUMINUM

Architectural Uses

Aluminum is a relatively new architectural metal. However, since World War II, it has been usely widely for a variety of purposes, including sheet roofing, roofing shingles, flashings, gutters and downspouts, copings, skylights, crestings and cornices, siding, corrugated siding, spandrels, mullions, windows, storefronts and marquees, facades, doors, hardware, fences, gates, lighting fixtures, grilles and railings, structural members, ventilators and ducts and mesh and wire cloth.

Deterioration and Stabilization

CORROSION. Aluminum combines readily with oxygen and resists further corrosion by the formation of a transparent, tightly adherent oxide film, which forms quickly and is relatively inert to further chemical action. Aluminum also resists attack by sulfur compounds, including hydrogen sulfide and sulfur dioxide; other atmospheric gases; seawater; moisture; and many kinds of soil.

Agents that actively attack aluminum include alkalies, hydrochloric acid, lead–based paints, green or damp wood, certain wood preservatives, lime mortar, portland cement, plaster, concrete and chlorides.[12]

Aluminum should be coated where it comes in contact with corrosive agents. Where aluminum touches masonry, a protective coating is necessary; this coating can consist of a heavy–bodied bituminous paint that is covered with two coats of aluminum metal and masonry paint. Other methods for providing protective coatings for aluminum include anodizing (an electrochemical method); electroplating; covering the metal with a porcelain or a vitreous enamel (an inorganic method); and painting (an organic method).[13] If any of these methods are used, the aluminum surface must be carefully prepared so that the coating formed will adhere. This surface preparation and coating application usually must be done only in a shop under controlled conditions.

Many aluminum architectural elements are manufactured with an anodized coating, which is often decorative. This kind of coating should be protected by applying a coat of varnish or protective wax, because there is no practical way to restore a damaged anodized coating other than factory refinishing.[14]

Decorative aluminum architectural elements are available with a variety of tooled finishes, including an embossed finish, a sand-blasted finish, a wire-brushed (or satin) finish and a buffed (or polished) finish. Although the best method of preserving a finish is by applying a protective coat of varnish or lacquer and then preventing dirt and grime from accumulating on the surface, it is sometimes necessary to restore surfaces. A sandblasted surface can be restored by sandblasting again. A wire-brushed surface can be restored by hand brushing with German silver wires using a finishing compound of ground pumice stone and water. Hand rubbing with pumice is used to restore a buffed surface.

GALVANIC ACTION. When aluminum is in contact with metals other than zinc, cadmium, magnesium and nonmagnetic stainless steel, it is subject to various types of galvanic action. Because of this reaction with dissimilar metals, aluminum should be insulated from them by paints, mastics or other nonconductive materials. Only aluminum nails and rivets should be used with aluminum sheet roofing and flashings.

MECHANICAL BREAKDOWN. Aluminum roofing can be broken down by fatigue caused by thermal expansion and contraction. Adequate expansion joints must be provided in an aluminum roof.

Aluminum can also be eroded by abrasives because of its softness. This problem is especially critical in roof valleys and flashings. Depending on the extent of the damage, the metal element must either be coated with paint or be replaced by a new, heavier-gauge aluminum element.

Aluminum elements can be joined together by oxygas or acetylene welding, brazing, resistance welding, inert-gas shielded arc processes, soldering, adhesive bonding, bolting and riveting.[15]

Because welding and soldering processes are difficult to undertake under field conditions, replacement is usually the most practical solution to the problem of a damaged aluminum architectural element, either structural or sheathing. Soldering should never be used for repairing a damaged aluminum roof, because of the potential galvanic action between the solder and the aluminum. Aluminum roofing is applied with riveted or other mechanical, nonsoldered and nonwelded joints.

COPPER

Architectural Uses

The principal architectural use of copper is as a roof covering. Sheet copper has long been used for roofing, and some English churches have copper roofs that are now more than 300 years old. Christ Church, Philadelphia, Pa., had a copper roof that was 130

222

years old when it was removed in the mid-1960s.

Copper, along with its alloys bronze and brass, is also used for roofing shingles, decorative roofing details, spandrels, roof ridges, crestings, cornices, flashings, gutters and downspouts, dormers, plumbing pipes, decorative exterior sheathing, hardware, weather stripping, screening, louvers, vents, wall ties, anchors, screws, nuts, bolts, protective barriers, mesh and wire cloth and lighting fixtures.

Deterioration and Stabilization

CORROSION. Copper is highly resistant to corrosion by air and sea-water. On exposure to an atmosphere that contains such impurities as sulfur compounds, a natural patina, which retards further corrosion, is formed. The color of the patina turns from brown to black to green and takes 8 to 10 years to develop fully. Although this protective patina is often called copper carbonate, it consists mostly of copper sulfate. The most common sulfur compounds that react with copper to form this patina are hydrogen sulfide and sulfur dioxide. However, sulfur trioxide in the atmosphere can unite with water to form sulfuric acid, which is very destructive to copper.[16] Copper is also attacked by alkalies, ammonia (which causes corrosion cracking), carbon monoxide at high pressure, combustion gases, illuminating gas and sulfate-reducing bacteria (which can act as corrosion catalysts). Effects of radiation and light on copper have not been studied extensively and, consequently, little is known of them.[17]

For additional protection against corrosion and tarnishing, the International Copper Research Association recommends the application of an inorganic undercoating followed by a clear, protective polyvinyl fluoride coating. This application will give up to 25 years of protection. A common protective treatment of architectural copper sheets is the application of a lead coating, which gives long-term protection to the copper, provided the coating is not broken by abrasives or internal stress workings. The coating does, however, change the color of copper sheets to that of lead. The lead coating must be applied to new copper sheets at the mill; it cannot be applied to old copper in place.

A new, clear acrylic lacquer coating called Incralac has been developed by the International Copper Research Association to protect copper sheeting. The system consists of an acrylic resin, a chelating agent (that is, benzotriazole) and a leveling agent in toluene or butyl acetate. Three separate coatings build up a protective coating more than 0.001 inch on a copper surface.[18]

GALVANIC ACTION. Copper is low in the galvanic series and,

therefore, is usually not subject to galvanic action. However, if an electrolyte is present, the copper will act as a cathode and will corrode other metals near the contact area. When copper is used for roofing or flashings, it should be separated from other metals by insulating materials and it should be fastened only with copper or bronze nails and clips.

MECHANICAL BREAKDOWN. Because copper is a soft metal, its erosion by abrasives is a serious problem, especially when it is used for roof flashings and valleys. The copper can be worn until it is so thin that it fails. If the erosion is detected in time, the copper can be protected by the application of paint. However, if the erosion is too extensive, the copper element must be replaced by a new copper element, preferably of a heavier gauge with a lead coating.

Because copper has a high expansion coefficient, the greatest danger to a copper roof is excess working, caused either by the original installation or through drumming caused by inadequate support.[19] It is important that the initial design of the copper element provide for adequate expansion joints, as well as for smooth and continuous wood sheathing to provide proper support. If these are not provided, fatigue and, eventually, cracking will occur. Once a sheet of copper has failed because of fatigue cracking, it must be replaced by new sheeting.

The wood sheathing for a copper roof should be covered with a rosin building paper before the copper is installed. The rosin paper usually makes the soldering of joints easier. An asphalt or bituminous building paper should not be used with copper because of the danger of corrosion.

If it is desirable to remove the patina on a copper element and restore its surface appearance to that of virgin copper, this can be done with a mixture of chemical and abrasive methods. Such chemical compounds as rottenstone and oil, whiting and ammonia and precipitated chalk and ammonia can be used with mild abrasive techniques, such as rubbing with a clean, soft cloth.[20] Steel wool and harsh abrasives should never be used. Once corrosion products have been removed, the copper surface can be protected by applying a coat of lacquer after the surface has been thoroughly cleaned.

LEAD

Architectural Uses

Lead is one of the oldest and most long–lasting roofing metals. A number of lead roofs dating from the 15th and 16th centuries still exist in Europe. In addition to sheet roofing, lead is used for decorative spandrels, gutters (often ornate), leader heads, downspouts, cast decorative elements, cupolas, spires, mullions, vibration-insulation pads in foundations, radiation insulation and plumbing pipes. It is also used as a protective coating on sheet iron; such coated sheet iron is known as *terneplate* (see the discussion on tin).

Deterioration and Stabilization

CORROSION. Lead is one of the most durable metals used in architecture. It resists corrosion by not reacting with many compounds and solutions. With certain others, it reacts by forming a protective coating. Lead resists corrosion by most acids, including chromic, sulfuric, sulfurous and phosphoric acids. It is corroded by hydrochloric, hydrofluoric, acetic, formic and nitric acids.[21]

Lead is highly resistant to atmospheric corrosion. Sulfur fumes react with lead to form a protective sulfate layer. Lead also resists corrosion by seawater, salt solutions, neutral solutions and many types of soil. However, it is attacked by alkalies and, therefore, should not be laid in contact with lime mortar, portland cement or uncured concrete. Lower fatty acids given off by wood and many types of varnish and plastic also attack lead. Special care should be taken to protect lead from contact with oak, because tannic acid in the wood will attack the metal. With lead roofing, this precaution can be taken by installing building paper between in lead and the wooden sheating.

Lead flashings and gutters are attacked by acid-charged washings from lichens growing on roofing slate. It may be possible to control this situation by the installation of a copper strip on the roof, because it has been noted that stone roofs under copper telephone wires are lichen free.[22]

GALVANIC ACTION. Galvanic action is usually not a problem with lead, because the protective coating that usually forms over the lead acts as an electrical insulator.

RADIATION. Radiation can cause lead to corrode severely. The radiation ionizes the nitrogen in the air to form nitrogen oxides which, in turn, combine with water in the air to form nitric acid, which attacks lead.[23]

MECHANICAL BREAKDOWN. Lead, like copper, is subject to damage by erosion and abrasion because of its softness. Lead roof flashings and valleys are especially vulnerable to abrasion caused by dirt particles, sleet, hail and rain. If the erosion is detected before excessive damage is done, the lead can be protected by an application of paint. Otherwise, if the damage is localized, it can be repaired by lead burning. If the damage is extensive, the sheet must be removed and replaced by a new sheet of heavier weight. Damaged lead roofs should not be patched by soldering or with asphalt or bituminous compounds.

Because lead has a relatively high expansion coefficient (three times that of steel), it is subject to creep and fatigue cracking caused by cyclical temperature changes. When this occurs, the damaged sheet often must be removed and replaced by a heavier sheet. If the sheet has not actually cracked, it is sometimes possible to drive it back into place. However, once the sheet has cracked, it must be either replaced or repaired by lead burning.

On historic buildings, the deteriorated lead roof sheeting is often removed, melted down and recast into new sheeting of the same dimensions.

It is important that adequate expansion joints be provided in sheet-lead roofs to allow for thermal expansion and contraction. The underlaying of a rosin building paper facilitates the lead sheeting's thermal movement. The wooden roof sheathing must provide adequate support for the lead sheeting or it will accelerate failure caused by creep.

TIN

Architectural Uses

By far, the most common architectural use of tin is as a protective coating for iron or steel sheets. If the coating is of pure tin, the material is called *tinplate* or *bright tin*, and if the coating is a mixture of lead (75 to 90 percent) and tin (usually 10 to 25 percent), it is called *terneplate* or *leaded tin*. Both types of plated tin were widely used in the United States beginning in the late 18th century. Tinplate was usually used in sheets of 10 by 14 inches, 14 by 20 inches or 20 by 28 inches as roofing pans, flashings, gutters, downspouts and leader heads. Occasionally, tinplate was also used for interior wall and ceiling sheathing.

Deterioration and Stabilization

When pure tin is exposed to low temperatures for long time periods, it disintegrates and crumbles to a gray powder.[24] This deterioration is called *tin pest* or *tin plague* and is usually not a problem with the tinplate or terneplate used in architecture.

Tin by itself is mechanically weak and is, therefore, used primarily for coating stronger materials. The tin (and lead and tin) plating on iron sheets is a stable coating that resists atmospheric corrosion. Tin is normally covered by a thin stannic oxide film, which resists corrosion by oxygen, moisture, sulfur dioxide and hydrogen sulfide. However, tin is attacked by acids and acid salts in the presence of oxygen, marine atmospheres and certain alkalies.[25]

It is important that the tin (or lead and tin) coating on sheet iron maintain its integrity. Once the plating has been broken and the iron exposed to oxygen, deterioration is accelerated because of the galvanic action between the tin and the iron. The tin (or the lead and tin) acts as a cathode to the iron and increases the corrosion in areas where the iron is exposed.

To protect tin-plated iron roofing, both sides of the tinplate should be shop coated before it is installed with a priming coat of linseed-oil base, iron oxide paint and finish coats or a lacquer containing silicone or acrylic resin.[26] The external paint coating should be renewed every few years to keep the metal from corroding.

A nonacidic vapor barrier should be installed under the metal roofing to prevent condensation from forming on the bottom of the metal plate. Often tinplate and terneplate roofs rust out from the bottom because, although it is relatively easy to protect the roof's exterior by painting, it is impossible to renew protection on the bottom without removing the roof.

Tinplate and terneplate roofs should be laid over a rosin building paper. Building papers containing acids, bitumen, asphalt or aluminum should never be used in conjunction with tinplate or terneplate. Tar or bituminous roofing compounds should never be used to coat or patch a tinplate or terneplate roof. Instead, only paints compatible with the metal should be used.

If a joint in a tinplate or terneplate roof opens up, it should be repaired by cleaning and resoldering. If a roofing pan fails, it should be removed and replaced with a new pan compatible with the rest of the roofing. It is possible to remove and replace a whole section of roofing if needed.

It does not appear to be practical to recoat a damaged roofing pan with new tin under field conditions. If much of the roofing is deteriorated to the point where pans are corroded through and it is not possible to preserve the roof in place, often the most practical solution is to remove the existing roof and replace it with a new one that has components identical in size and jointing to the original. If protection from atmospheric corrosion, longevity and freedom from maintenance are important considerations, it is often desirable to use lead-coated copper for the new roof, rather than installing new tinplate or terneplate. However, the entire roof must be replaced, or galvanic problems will develop between the new lead-coated copper and the remaining tinplate or terneplate.

IRON AND STEEL

Architectural Uses

CAST IRON. Cast iron is an iron-carbon alloy with a high carbon content (more than 1.7 percent) and varying amounts of silicon, sulfur, manganese and phosphorus. It is easily poured while molten into molds; however, it is too hard and brittle to be shaped by hammering, rolling or pressing.

Characteristics of various types of cast iron are determined by their composition and techniques used in melting, casting and heat treating the metal. Constituents that affect the iron's ductility, brittleness, toughness and strength include ferrite, cementite, pearlite and graphite carbon.

Cast iron is one of the most useful architectural metals. It is used for such structural members as columns, beams, built-up girders, trusses and dome framing; entire facades; roofing slabs; decorative roofing details and crestings; roof ridges; gutters and downspouts; doors; window and door shutters; cornices, grilles and railings; balustrades; stairways; brackets; plumbing pipes, fittings and fixtures; fences and gates; benches; hardware; and ornamental ironwork.

WROUGHT IRON. Wrought iron is a commercial iron consisting of slag (iron silicate) fibers entrained in a ferrite matrix.[27] It is almost pure iron with less than 1 percent carbon. The slag content, usually about 2.5 percent, is in a purely physical association (that is, it is not alloyed). Wrought iron is soft, malleable, tough, fatigue resistant and easily worked by forging, bending, rolling and drawing. Architecturally, it is used for structural members, sheathing, roof sheeting, roofing plates (either tinplate or terneplate), pipes, chains, grilles, railings, fences, screens, balustrades and other decorative objects.

STEEL. Steel is an iron–carbon alloy containing not more than 2 percent carbon; it is malleable in block or ingot form. Steel may also contain phosphorus, sulfur, oxygen, manganese, silicon, aluminum, copper, titanium, molybdenum and nickel. Properties of different types of steel vary greatly in relation to their chemical composition and the type of heat treatment and mechanical working used during manufacture. Properties affected include strength, hardness, ductility, abrasion resistance, weldability, machinability and corrosion resistance.

The type of steel used for most structural applications is a grade of plain carbon steel. High-strength alloy steels are available for specialized installations. In addition to structural applications, steel is used in architecture as sheets and plates; corrugated sheets; ornamental and hollow metalwork; grilles and railings; doors; windows; shutters; sheet roofing, flashings, gutters and downspouts (either galvanized, tinplate or terneplate); stairways; brackets; mesh and wire cloth; chains; cables; screening; and miscellaneous hardware.

GALVANIZED STEEL. Galvanized steel consists of a zinc coating on steel sheets. It is used for roofing, siding, decking, cladding, ductwork and calamein work (that is, the cladding of wooden windows and doors to make them fire resistant).

STAINLESS STEEL. Stainless steel is an alloy of iron (more than 50 percent) and chromium (more than 11.5 percent).[28] Other additives may include nickel, columbium, molybdenum, phosphorus, selenium, silicon, sulfur, titanium and zirconium. Stainless steel is hardened by cold working and is resistant to corrosion and heat. It has characteristics of high thermal expansion and low heat conductivity.

Stainless steel is used for sheet roofing, flashings, gutters, leaders, windows, doors, storefronts, wall sheathing, louvers, screens, railings, fascias, cables and fastening devices.

Deterioration and Stabilization

GENERAL CORROSION OF IRON AND STEEL. Except for some corrosion-resistant alloy steels and stainless steels, all types of unprotected iron and steel oxidize rapidly when exposed to an atmosphere in the presence of moisture. The oxidation of iron and steel is a highly destructive process. The product of this oxidation is rust, which at first consists of a mixture of ferrous and ferric hydroxides and later becomes a hydrated ferric oxide with some traces of a carbonate.[29] When salts that can act as electrolytes are present, the corrosion of iron and steel is accelerated and made more complicated. If oxidation is not arrested, the corrosion rate will accelerate until the metal is destroyed.

Iron and steel are also corroded by seawater, salt air, acids, soils and some sulfur compounds.

Although architectural metals are most often protected from oxidation by painting, other methods, including the electroplating of other metals and humidity control, are also used. The U.S. Navy has had success in preventing rust on ships in its mothball fleet by using a "sealed-zone" technique where the relative humidity in a sealed zone is maintained below 30 percent.[30] Similar techniques may be used temporarily for architectural applications.

In the restoration of historic iron and steel structures, the retention of details that provide crevices or pockets to catch and hold water should be avoided wherever possible. If it is necessary to maintain such details for historical reasons, they should be carefully cleaned and protected against oxidation.

As mentioned previously, painting is the most common method of controlling the oxidation of iron and steel. In order for a paint to successfully protect the iron or steel, the metal surface must be thoroughly cleaned and prepared for painting. There are a number of different methods for cleaning iron and steel, ranging from flame cleaning and chemical methods to physical techniques, such as wire brushing and grit blasting as indicated in table 2. The type of preparation for painting that is used depends on the degree to which the surface has deteriorated, the amount and fineness of the architectural detail on the surface and the type of paint to be used. It is critical that all iron and steel surfaces be free of oil, grease and moisture before painting. All mill scale and rust also must be removed. Once the metal has been cleaned, it should be painted as soon as possible.

When dealing with architectural iron or steel elements in place, it is often difficult to clean the metal properly. Acid pickling is not possible and sandblasting, flame cleaning and scraping are dif-

Table 2 METHODS FOR SURFACE PREPARATION OF IRON AND STEEL FOR PAINTING

Types of Cleaning	How Done	Characteristics of Cleaned Surface	Type of Paints Used With This Cleaning
Flame cleaning	Oxyacetylene flame consisting of a series of small, closely spaced flames that are very hot and projected at high velocity	Reduces ordinary rust to iron oxide and pops off loose mill scale; after flame cleaning the surface should be wire-brushed	Alkyd and phenolic vehicle paints, baked enamels
Iron phosphate	Metal is immersed in an alkali pre-cleaner and then immersed in a patented solution containing ferric phosphate	Surface provides excellent adhesion for paint and retards rusting	Baked enamels
Pickling (phosphoric acid)	Metal is immersed in warmed dilute phosphoric acid with added rust inhibitors; does not need finishing	Removes all dirt, rust, and mill scale and gives the surface a protective film which retards rusting and is a good base for painting	Natural-drying-oil and resin vehicle paints

Types of Cleaning	How Done	Characteristics of Cleaned Surface	Type of Paints Used With This Cleaning
Pickling (sulfuric acid)	Metal is immersed in warmed dilute sulfuric acid with other chemicals which confine the action largely to rust and scale and is then rinsed	Removes all dirt, rust and mill scale and gives the surface a slight etching which helps adhesion of the paint	Vinyl, alkyd and phenolic vehicle paints, baked enamels
Rust removers	Applied by brush or spraying, the phosphate type forms a film and retards rusting	Generally used in maintenance painting and with on-site painting where slight rusting has occurred	All types of paint used for maintenance and on-site painting
Sand blasting and grit blasting	Sand or steel grit (crushed shot) in a range of No. 10 to No. 45 screen sizes and dry compressed air at 80 to 100 lb. per sq. in.	Removes all dirt, rust, tight mill scale and all other surface impurities; also roughens the surface, thus providing the best condition for adhesion of the paint	Coal-tar enamels and vinyl vehicle paints; baked enamels; also used for alkyd and phenolic vehicle paints
Solvent cleaning	Wiped with turpentine or mineral spirits	Removal of dirt, oil and grease	Oil-base paints
Wire brushing	Wire brushes operated either by hand or mechanically	Removes rust and loose mill scale but will not remove tight scale or rust. Too much wire-brushing gives a polished surface which has poor paint adhesion properties	Natural-drying-oil and resin vehicle paints

NOTE: From *Materials for Architecture: An Encyclopedic Guide* by C. Hornbostel © 1961 by Litton Educational Publishing, Inc. Reprinted by permission of Van Nostrand Reinhold Company. Page 357.

ficult and expensive.[31] When dealing with delicate detailing, mild abrasive methods, such as cleaning with aluminum oxide paper, must be used rather than wire brushing or other harsh abrasive methods. Chemical rust removers based on ammonium citrate, oxalic acid, phosphoric acid or hydrochloric acid are also effective.[32] However, these must be used carefully and patiently.

The cleaning and painting of iron or steel should be carefully supervised and inspected. No painting should be done when the temperature is below 50°F or when there is a high degree of humidity. The surface of the metal must be absolutely dry and free of moisture. It is a good practice to consult the paint manufacturer concerning the compatibility of the proposed cleaning technique and the types of paint to be used for the priming and finish coats.

There are a number of anticorrosive pigments for use in paints available for use as priming coats for iron and steel, including red lead, white lead, zinc chromate, basic lead–silico–chromate and zinc dust.[33] Fast-drying priming coats require better surface preparation. Old and corroded surfaces require a slow–drying, oil–based primer.

Red lead is one of the most widely used primers for iron and steel. It has a strong affinity for linseed oil and forms lead soaps that become tough elastic films impervious to water.

Zinc chromate, when diluted with iron oxide, possesses corrosion-inhibitive qualities similar to red lead. Lead chromate also provides protection against corrosion but opinions differ as to its merits.

A number of paint types used on iron and steel and their recommended uses are indicated in table 3. In addition to these types of paint, flaky or micaceous iron ore and aluminum paints, using an oil vehicle, provide a satisfactory coating without a priming coat.[34] Tar and bituminous paints are also used for protecting iron and steel. However, they break down when exposed to light and run in the summer and crack in the winter. Synthetic resin paints provide a thinner film and dry faster than oil–base paints. However, they do not protect the metal as long. Epoxy–resin paints, although difficult to use, provide a highly watertight surface. Lacquers, often including silicone or acrylic resins, are also used to provide tough, hard coatings for iron and steel.

Oils, greases and waxes have been widely used for the preservation of iron and steel in museum situations. In some architectural cases, certain waxes may be used to protect iron or steel elements.

CORROSION OF CAST IRON. Cast iron develops a protective scale on its surface and is, therefore, more corrosion resistant than steel. Cast iron has generally good resistance to corrosion caused by atmospheres and soils.

With cast iron, however, there are problems with mechanical defects, such as air holes, cold shuts, cracks and cinders, all of which can greatly reduce the strength of the cast–iron member. The cast iron must be carefully manufactured and its composition closely controlled. A number of new, nondestructive tests, using, for example, fluorescent materials and ultraviolet lamps, have been developed to detect these potential defects in cast–iron structural elements.

Several cast-iron-fronted buildings in New York City have been carefully dismantled and stored for reerection.[35] Because connect-

Table 3   TYPES OF PAINT USED FOR PAINTING METAL

Type of Paint	Surface Preparation and Pretreatment	Priming Coat	Intermediate Coat* (Undercoat)	Finish Coat	Major Use on Iron and Steel
Alkyd vehicle	"Commercial" blast cleaning, pickling, flame cleaning, no pretreatment required	Red-lead alkyd varnish primer	Same as priming coat except tinted with carbon black or lamp black to a contrasting color (in relation to priming coat)	Aluminum alkyd, black alkyd, white or tinted alkyd paint	For the exterior exposed to severe weather conditions; for the interior where mild chemical exposure, high humidity and infrequent condensation exist
Coal-tar	Blast cleaning to white metal; surface to be cleaned and prime coat immediately applied	Coal-tar enamel primer applied hot	None	Coal-tar enamel applied hot	For the exterior where iron and steel are to be installed underground or in and under water
		Coal-tar enamel	Coal-tar paint	Coal-tar paint	Same as coal-tar enamel except not as good for foundations in and under water
Oil-base vehicle	Solvent cleaning, wire brushing; no pretreatment necessary	Red-lead oil-base primer	Same as priming coat except tinted with carbon black or lamp black to a contrasting color (in relation to coat)	Aluminum varnish or black, white or tinted oil-base paint	For the exterior exposed to normal weather conditions; for the interior where moderately corrosive conditions exist

233

Type of Paint	Surface Preparation and Pretreatment	Priming Coat	Intermediate Coat* (Undercoat)	Finish Coat	Major Use on Iron and Steel
Phenolic vehicle	"Commercial" blast cleaning, pickling, flame cleaning; no pretreatment necessary	Red-lead mixed-pigment phenolic varnish primer		Aluminum phenolic, black phenolic, white or tinted phenolic paint	For the exterior where iron or steel is immersed in fresh water or exposed to high humidity and condensation; for the interior only where conditions are the same as the exterior
Vinyl vehicle	"Commercial" blast cleaning, pickling; after cleaning surface to be pretreated with basic zinc chromate vinyl butyral washcoat	Vinyl red-lead primer	Same as priming coat except tinted with lamp black to a contrasting color	Aluminum vinyl, black vinyl, or vinyl-alkyd paint in white, black, red, yellow or orange	For the exterior where iron or steel is immersed in salt or fresh water or exposed to high humidity and condensation; for the interior where flame resistance, mildew resistance, corrosion resistance and easy maintenance are necessary

*The intermediate coat can be the same as the finish coat but tinted to a contrasting color.

NOTE: From *Materials for Architecture: An Encyclopedic Guide* by Hornbostel © 1961 by Litton Educational Publishing, Inc. Reprinted by permission of Van Nostrand Reinhold Company. Page 356.

ing nuts and bolts on such buildings generally have corroded and must be burned off with a torch, it is mandatory that workmen be extremely careful so as to avoid fracturing cast–iron structural elements by uneven heating. This is especially critical if the work is done in cold weather, as cast iron, although normally brittle, is especially susceptible to fracturing when cold.

CORROSION OF WROUGHT IRON. Although wrought iron rusts more quickly than cast iron, the corrosion of wrought iron can be

234

more readily measured and the degree of deterioration more easily ascertained. Wrought iron is resistant to progressive corrosion.

In the case of local corrosion occurring on a wrought-iron structural element, the damaged element may be repaired by the welding of new metal sections to the corroded area to strengthen it.

CORROSION OF GALVANIZED STEEL. The durability of galvanized steel is dependent on the thickness of its protective zinc coating, the type of additional protective coatings and the kind of corrosive environment to which the steel is exposed. Galvanized steel can be used in direct contact with wood, concrete, mortar, lead, tin, zinc and aluminum.[36] Galvanic action occurs when galvanized steel is in contact with other types of metal.

When used with redwood or cedar, galvanized steel should be protected from acids in these types of wood with a bituminous paint. The zinc coating on the steel is also attacked by other acids and chemical fumes.

Although galvanized steel can be painted, special surface treatments may be necessary. The metal surface should be weathered before painting. However, it should not be allowed to weather until rust appears. If an old galvanized steel roof has begun to rust, it should be treated with zinc oxide and flake aluminum priming coats followed by a finish coat containing flaky aluminum and flaky micaceous iron ore pigments. Rust may also be arrested by the application of a zinc–rich paint.[37]

CORROSION OF STAINLESS STEEL. Stainless steel has a high resistance to heat and corrosion. Chromium and chromium-nickel stainless steel are among the few metals that remain substantially unaltered in appearance after being exposed to the atmosphere. Stainless steel resists corrosion by hydrogen sulfide and sulfur dioxide. It also has good resistance to corrosion caused by water and some soils. Consequently, stainless steel is often left with a natural finish.

Stainless steel is corroded by mortar, and galvanic action occurs when it is in contact with aluminum.[38] However, a rubber-base asphalt, applied where the steel is in contact with these materials, can prevent corrosion.

FIGURE 1. *Corrosion of corrugated aluminum siding on a commercial building in Green Island, N.Y., caused by salts used for melting snow. (John G. Waite)*

FIGURE 2. *Corrosion of a copper roof ridge on the Dakota (1884), New York City, caused by the use of an asphalt roofing compound for temporary patches over nailheads and joints between ridge sections. (John G. Waite)*

236

FIGURE 3. Damage to the 18th-century Statue of Neptune on the Place Stanislas, Nancy, France, caused by creep of the lead. (John G. Waite)

FIGURE 4. Underside of a section of terneplate roofing from Hyde Hall (1817-33), a New York State historic site administered by the Division for Historic Preservation, New York State Office of Parks and Recreation, near Cooperstown, N.Y. The section corroded from the underside because there was no vapor barrier, and condensation was free to form on the metal roofing. (John G. Waite)

FIGURE 5. Workman replaces the deteriorated tinplate roof at Olana (1870-74), a New York State historic site administered by the Division for Historic Preservation, New York State Office of Parks and Recreation, near Hudson, N.Y. Pan dimensions and flashing details of the new lead-coated copper roof duplicate those of the original. (John G. Waite)

FIGURE 6. Detail of cast-iron lintel in the brick blast furnace constructed by Abraham Darby I in 1658 at Coalbrookdale, England. The blast furnace was recently excavated and stabilized. However, it was not made weathertight, and water penetrating the upper part of the furnace percolated through the masonry, picking up soluble salts from the mortar and brick. This combination of water and dissolved salts has seriously corroded the cast-iron lintel. (John G. Waite)

FIGURE 7. *Detail of the framing and muntins of the Palm House at Kew Gardens, London, showing the corrosion caused by the condensation of moisture on iron structural members and glass. (John G. Waite)*

FIGURE 8. *Cast-iron elements from the facade of the Edgar Laing Stores, New York City. The Laing Stores building was erected by James Bogardus in 1849 and had one of the earliest cast-iron fronts. The building was demolished in 1971 for an urban renewal project, but its cast-iron facade was carefully dismantled so that it could be reerected at a later date. (Jack E. Boucher, Historic American Buildings Survey)*

239

NOTES

1. Glenn A. Greathouse and Carl J. Wessel, eds., *Deterioration of Materials: Causes and Preventive Techniques* (New York: Reinhold Publishing Corp., 1954), p. 4.

2. F. L. LaQue and H. R. Copson, eds., *Corrosion Resistance of Metals and Alloys*, 2d ed. (New York: Reinhold Publishing Corp., 1963), pp. 7–37.

3. Greathouse and Wessel, *Deterioration of Materials*, pp. 241–54.

4. LaQue and Copson, *Corrosion Resistance*, p. 46.

5. Greathouse and Wessel, *Deterioration of Materials*, p. 238.

6. W. H. Munse, J. E. Stallmeyer and F. P. Drew, *Structural Fatigue and Steel Railroad Bridges* (Chicago: American Railway Engineering Association, 1968), p. 2.

7. Greathouse and Wessel, *Deterioration of Materials*, p. 301.

8. Ibid., pp. 264–74.

9. Ibid., p. 275.

10. Ibid., p. 286.

11. Ibid., pp. 291–93.

12. Caleb Hornbostel, *Materials for Architecture: An Encyclopedic Guide* (New York: Reinhold Publishing Corp., 1961), pp. 19, 28.

13. Ibid., pp. 29, 34–36.

14. *Aluminum in Architecture* (Pittsburgh, Pa.: Aluminum Company of America, 1932), p. 160.

15. Hornbostel, *Materials for Architecture*, pp. 26–27.

16. Ulick R. Evans, *The Corrosion and Oxidation of Metals: Scientific Principles and Practical Applications* (London: Edward Arnold, Ltd., 1960), p. 486.

17. Henry Leidheiser, Jr., *The Corrosion of Copper, Tin, and Their Alloys* (New York: John Wiley and Sons, Inc., 1971), pp. 51, 52, 54, 63, 193, 230.

18. Joseph B. Long, manager, Tin Research Institute, Inc., Columbus, Ohio, to author, June 23, 1972.

19. Donald W. Insall, *The Care of Old Buildings: A Practical Guide for Architects and Owners* (London: Architectural Press, 1972), p. 101.

20. Harold L. Peterson, "Conservation of Metals," *History News* 23, no. 2 (February 1968): 25–32. Also available as American Association for State and Local History Technical Leaflet 10, rev. ed.

21. *Lead in Modern Industry* (New York: Lead Industries Association, 1952), p. 51.

22. Insall, *Care of Old Buildings*, p. 100.

23. LaQue and Copson, *Corrosion Resistance*, p. 289.

24. Leidheiser, *Corrosion of Copper, Tin*, p. 326.

25. Ibid., p. 262. LaQue and Copson, *Corrosion Resistance*, pp. 260, 263, 264.

26. Long to author, June 23, 1972.

27. LaQue and Copson, *Corrosion Resistance*, p. 305.

28. Ibid., p. 375.

29. Harold J. Plenderleith and A. E. A. Werner, *The Conservation of Antiquities and Works of Art*, 2d ed. (London, New York: Oxford University Press, 1971), p. 281.

30. Evans, *Corrosion and Oxidation of Metals*, p. 531.

31. F. Fancutt and J. C. Hudson, *Protective Painting of Structural Steel* (New York: MacMillan Co., 1957), p. 64.

32. Peterson, "Conservation of Metals," p. 26.

33. *Paints and Protective Coatings* (Washington, D. C.: Departments of the Army, Navy and Air Force, 1969), p. 8-3.

34. Evans, *Corrosion and Oxidation of Metals*, p. 571.

35. Michael W. Gold, "Bogardus Cast Iron: Designed to be Dismantled and Rebuilt," *Historic Preservation* 23, no. 3 (July-September 1971), pp. 12-19. John G. Waite, ed., *Iron Architecture in New York City: Two Studies in Industrial Archeology* (Albany: New York State Historic Trust, 1972).

36. Hornbostel, *Materials for Architecture*, p. 461.

37. Evans, *Corrosion and Oxidation of Metals*, pp. 586–87.

38. Hornbostel, *Materials for Architecture*, p. 444.

BIBLIOGRAPHY

BOOKS

Aluminum in Architecture. Pittsburgh, Pa.: Aluminum Company of America, 1932.

Bakhalov, G. T., and Turkovskaya, A. V. *Corrosion and Protection of Metals*. Elmsford, N.Y.: Pergamon Press, 1965.

Bloxam, Charles Loudon. *Metals: Their Properties and Treatment*. New York: D. Appleton and Co., 1872.

Condit, Carl W. *American Building: Materials and Techniques from the Beginning of the First Colonial Settlements to the Present*. Chicago History of American Civilization. Chicago: University of Chicago Press, 1968.

Cushman, Allerton S., and Gardner, Henry A. *The Corrosion and Preservation of Iron and Steel*. New York: McGraw-Hill Book Co., 1910.

Evans, Ulick R. *The Corrosion and Oxidation of Metals: Scientific Principles and Practical Applications*. London: Edward Arnold, Ltd., 1960.

Fairbairn, William. *On the Application of Cast and Wrought Iron for Building Purposes*. London: John Weale, 1857–58.

Fancutt, F., and Hudson, J. C. *Protective Painting of Structural Steel*. New York: MacMillan Co., 1957.

Fitch, James Marston. *American Building: 1: The Historical Forces That Shaped It*. 2d ed. rev. and enl. Boston: Houghton Mifflin Co., 1966.

Greathouse, Glenn A., and Wessel, Carl J., eds. *Deterioration of Materials: Causes and Preventive Techniques*. New York: Reinhold Publishing Corp., 1954.

Grover, H. J., Gordon, S. A., and Jackson, L. R. *Fatigue of Metals and Structures*. Washington, D. C.: Department of the Navy, 1954.

Hornbostel, Caleb. *Materials for Architecture: An Encyclopedic Guide*. New York: Reinhold Publishing Corp., 1961.

Illustrations of Iron Architecture, made by The Architectural Iron Works of the City of New York. New York: Baker & Godwin, 1865.

Insall, Donald W. *The Care of Old Buildings: A Practical Guide for Architects and Owners*. London: Architectural Press, 1972.

LaQue, F. L., and Copson, H. R., eds. *Corrosion Resistance of Metals and Alloys*. 2d ed. New York: Reinhold Publishing Corp., 1963.

Lead in Modern Industry: Manufacture, Applications and Properties of Lead, Lead Alloys, and Lead Compounds. New York: Lead Industries Association, 1952.

Leidheiser, Henry, Jr. *The Corrosion of Copper, Tin, and Their Alloys*. New York: John Wiley and Sons, Inc., 1971.

Munse, W. H., Stallmeyer, J. E., and Drew, F. P. *Structural Fatigue and Steel Railroad Bridges*. Chicago: American Railway Engineering Association, 1968.

Newman, John. *Metallic Structures: Corrosion and Fouling, and their Prevention*. London: E. & F. N. Spon, 1896.

Nield, B. J. *Problems in Service—Metallurgical Considerations, Avoidance of Failure*. New York: American Elsevier Publishing Co., 1970.

Paints and Protective Coatings. Washington, D. C.: Departments of the Army, Navy and Air Force, 1969.

Plenderleith, Harold J., and Werner, A. E. A. *The Conservation of Antiquities and Works of Art*. 2d ed. London, New York: Oxford University Press, 1971.

Salvadori, Mario G., and Heller, Robert. *Structure in Architecture*. Englewood Cliffs, N.J.: Prentice-Hall, Inc., 1963.

Waite, Diana S. *Nineteenth Century Tin Roofing and Its Use at Hyde Hall*. Albany: New York State Historic Trust, 1971.

Waite, John G., ed. *Iron Architecture in New York City: Two Studies in Industrial Archeology*. Albany: New York State Historic Trust, 1972.

ARTICLES AND PERIODICALS

Degan, Eugene B. "Building with Bronze." *Buildings: The Construction and Building Management Journal* (January 1966).

Gold, Michael W. "Bogardus Cast Iron: Designed to be Dismantled and Rebuilt." *Historic Preservation* 23, no. 3 (July–September 1971): 12–19.

Jack, J. F. S. "The Cleaning and Preservation of Bronze Statues." *The Museum Journal* 50, no. 10 (January 1961): 231–36.

Osburn, Donald H., and Foehl, John M. "Coloring and Finishing of Copper Metals." *Construction Specifier* (October 1963): 50–55.

Peterson, Charles E. "Iron in Early American Roofs." *The Smithsonian Journal of History* 3, no. 3 (fall 1968): 41–76.

Peterson, Harold L. "Conservation of Metals." *History News* 23, no. 2 (February 1968): 25–32. (Also available as American Association for State and Local History Technical Leaflet 10, rev. ed.)

242

THE CORROSION OF TIN, COPPER, IRON AND STEEL AND LEAD

ROBERT M. ORGAN

Certain characteristics of corrosion are common to all metals, and these characteristics deserve consideration prior to the discussion of corrosion of specific metals.

COMMON CHARACTERISTICS OF CORROSION

Most simple metals are unstable, tending to react with chemical elements in the environment to re-form minerals similar to those from which they were extracted. Therefore, they do not remain unchanged under atmospheric conditions.

Within a fraction of a second after a laboratory-clean metal is exposed to the atmosphere, a thin, invisible skin of oxide, or sometimes of sulfide, forms. This skin continues to thicken, sometimes with diminishing speed, forming a protective film which may be said to *passivate* the metal. At other times, this thickening may be at a constant or an accelerating speed, resulting in the formation of an unprotective film that allows the metal to corrode steadily into a mineral.

Modern metallic hardware is often deliberately passivated (described as *chromated, anodized,* etc.) by methods that yield epitaxial films whose crystal structure continues that of the underlying metal, free from atomic "dislocations" and voids that facilitate breakdown. Such protective films of oxide form naturally if

Robert M. Organ is chief of the Conservation-Analytical Laboratory at the Smithsonian Institution, Washington, D.C.

the air to which the freshly cleaned metal is exposed is free of such contaminants as sulfides, sulfur dioxide, volatile organic acids or dust. The passivated object can then resist attack by large concentrations of these same corrosive contaminants. On the other hand, a cleaned metal exposed immediately to an unsuitable atmosphere will not acquire a protective film and will corrode progressively.

If two different metals in electrical contact are exposed to even a slight film of moisture, one will corrode and the other will not. The metal that corrodes is commonly described as the *baser metal* and the one that does not corrode is known as the *nobler metal.* All metals can be arranged in a series of decreasing nobility. Several such series exist, as the sequence of metals changes with conditions. One of these, the electromotive series, is measured with pure, clean metals. A series more representative of practical conditions would include the passivated metals. An example of this kind of reaction is the corrosion of galvanized iron. In this instance, the zinc (the base metal) coating the iron (the nobler metal) will corrode rather than the iron as long as any zinc remains; thus the baser metal protects the nobler one.

Adjacent areas of an item made of one alloy may act differently. One area may be corroding (base), while another may be protected (noble). The corroding area is called the *anodic area,* and the protected one is known as the *cathodic area.* This situation occurs because one area (1) has a slightly different alloy composition from the other, (2) contains inclusions that encourage chemical attack or (3) is shielded locally from atmospheric oxidation (also known as *differential aeration)* by finger grease (resulting in corroded-in fingerprints); contact with wood, vegetation, etc.; or unremoved soil or oxides.

The corrosion products that develop on metals take several physical forms that have acquired names descriptive of the human reaction to them. For example, the overall atmospheric darkening of silver is known as *tarnish.* It is never called the "patina of time." Pewter objects (made of tin alloys) may have a dull smooth surface coating described as patina, but the same coating, if it is cracked because the object has been dropped or is not smooth because the object has not been kept polished, is a crust. An object made of tin may also acquire a so-called warty patina, nodules of oxide that are slightly raised above the surrounding surface; these warts are actually rooted deep in the unchanged metal and if extracted, leave pits. The surface of an object made of copper alloys may grow into an irregular multicolored corrosion crust, but such a crust often contains hidden within it a smooth, similarly multicolored or black surface that is valued as a patina on some art objects. The valued patina contains minerals identical to those in the overlying unsightly crust.

So-called diseases of metal museum objects usually appear suddenly as spots on an object's surface. These then either grow in size or increase in number. These spots consist of minerals identical to those found in patinas on other objects. The spotting is a disease only because it indicates chemical instability incompatible with preservation of the object's appearance and material as it existed at the time of accession.

TIN

This warm–white, soft metal is seldom seen in its pure form in historic houses. However, it is a major constituent of the several alloys known as pewter. In early times, these pewter alloys contained lead and tin, but later the poisonous lead was replaced by copper, especially in artifacts that had to be mechanically strong, such as flatware. Modern types of pewter contain more than 90 percent tin, with varying percentages of copper and antimony. The metal colloquially described as tin is actually tinplate: a sheet of iron or mild steel coated with a layer of tin 0.03 inch or less thick. A related material known as terneplate is coated with an alloy of three parts lead to one part tin.

Pure tin is one of the least corrodible of metals, less so than copper in the usual environments, because in moist air, the metal acquires a thin film of stannous oxide, which is protective until it becomes relatively thick.[1] The presence of the usual alloying elements (i.e., lead or antimony and copper) increases the corrosion rate.

The continued growth of a surface oxide film results in a loss of protection to the underlying tin, because the film becomes porous. Ions such as chloride, sulfate and nitrate (but not sulfide) lodging in the film can prevent the metal from regaining its passivity. Over prolonged periods, layering develops, and part of the stannous oxide changes into stannic oxide. The mixed oxide is a gray white material somewhat similar in appearance to metallic tin but hard and brittle. Ancient tin and pewter objects, therefore, acquire surface cracks easily, and frequently, the cracking is followed by a loss of flakes of the crust. The tendency to flake is increased if soft stannous chloride is present in the crust. A surface film of stannous oxide grows less rapidly in dry conditions, the drier the better, but a relative humidity of less than 50 percent will probably serve to prevent rapid loss of protection.

A protective film more effective than that which forms naturally in air on freshly cleaned tin can be formed by cathodically reducing the tin in an aqueous solution of 0.1N Na_2CO_3 (anhydrous sodium carbonate) at a pH of 11.2 using a current density of 0.5 ampert per square decimeter (about 5 amperes per square foot). When using this procedure, platinum anodes should be placed relatively close to the cathode in order to maintain a high level of dissolved oxygen in the nearby electrolyte. After the proper current density level is attained, the object should be withdrawn, with the current still switched on, and rinsed in distilled water, then in ethanol.[2] Alternatively, the object can be passivated anodically by immersing it for five seconds in a solution composed of 0.5 gram of NaOH (sodium hydroxide) and 100 milliliters of water and applying a current of 0.5 ampere per square decimeter (5 amperes per square foot). This forms a porefree film about 0.03 micrometer thick.[3]

Neither ammonia vapor nor hydrogen sulfide attacks tin at room temperature, and the metal is virtually unaffected by acid vapors from wood. Carbonated water does not corrode tin faster than pure water. Hard water does not tarnish the metal, but soft water does, although the tarnishing occurs rather slowly.[4]

Lightly encrusted tin can be cleaned by gentle abrasion with rottenstone in mineral light oil. Heavily corroded tin usually requires treatment in solution, with the objective of dissolving the crust or removing it cathodically (the latter procedure is usually performed with an alkaline solution). Tin is, however, corroded by either strongly acidic or strongly alkaline solutions. The rate of attack is increased if traces of such metals as antimony, copper or bismuth are present in the liquid, but is dramatically minimized if the access of oxygen to the tin in the solution is prevented.

Of dilute acids in contact with air, the most corrosive to tin are hydrochloric, sulfuric, formic and acetic, in that order.[5] By far the least corrosive is phosphoric acid, probably because it is a poor solvent for the oxides that form on tin in the presence of air. Therefore, it is also a poor cleaner.

A common cleaner for corroded pewter is lye, that is, 5 grams of sodium hydroxide dissolved in 100 milliliters of water. It has been shown that a one–molar solution of sodium hydroxide (4 grams in 100 milliliters of water) dissolves pure tin at about the same rate as a one–molar solution of the less hazardous sodium carbonate (12.4 grams washing soda, sodium carbonate monohydrate, in 100 milliliters of water).[6] This rate is less than half that of sulfuric and previously mentioned organic acids. At low concentrations, sodium carbonate is less corrosive than acids that might be used for cleaning. Although scarcely practicable, these corrosion rates can be further diminished during treatment by eliminating oxygen, but in a deliberate passivation after cleaning has been completed, some oxidation to form a protective stannous oxide film is inevitable. If, instead, natural oxidation is allowed, the film will be less protective.

COPPER AND COPPER ALLOYS

The substantially pure, red metal copper was used in houses for roofing, gutters (eaves troughs) and downspouts. Bronzes, which are usually alloys of copper, tin and sometimes lead, were cast into hardware and ornamental items. Copper alloys that include zinc (i.e., brasses of various colors) served similar purposes and are called such names as ormolu (when gilt), architectural bronze, etc.

These alloys are relatively resistant to corrosion. However, if unprotected by varnishes, they discolor from their initial bright condition by the formation of an extremely thin invisible skin of oxide which turns brown and later black by an optical effect as a film of blue green copper sulfate develops. It blackens further into an overgrowth of dirt, soot and dust, a process that occurs especially rapidly in inhabited areas.

If regularly washed with water, some of the blue–green copper sulfate, which is water soluble, can become visible as a green stain in the area of runoff beneath bronze statuary unless the artist or founder has provided proper drainage. Subsequently, the surviving sulfate becomes more basic by further reactions and loses its solubility. After 10 to 25 years of exposure, depending on the site, an unstable green mineral will appear. In rural areas, the end product of corroding copper after a period of about 70 years is the completely stable green mineral brochantite.[7] In nonindustrial areas, the green mineral may consist of basic nitrate (usually found in mountains) or basic chloride (usually found along the seacoast), but that found on the Statue of Liberty is sulfate.

Other corrosion processes occur in other environments. In most cases, the factor controlling the corrosion rate is the access of oxygen to the copper, provided that sufficient moisture (80 percent relative humidity or higher) is present. One other notable corrosion process is *dezincification*, which results in the appearance of unsightly areas of pink pure copper on alloys of some other color. Dezincification is caused by local shielding of a surface in the presence of even mildly corrosive liquid. It has been observed on slightly sooty bronze objects taken from Indian temples and, more commonly, occurs inside brass plumbing fixtures.

The environment of an object made of a copper alloy and used in a building is seldom uniform around all of its surfaces. For example, a piece of hardware made of a copper alloy is usually attached to and in contact with an area of wood or stone. The consequences of this contact for conservation are manifold. First, different areas have different degrees of access to oxygen, resulting in differential aeration, which is one cause of corrosion. Second, some areas that are in close contact with supporting material trap air in pockets, which remain filled with the stagnant air and acquire a high moisture content. If the supporting material is wood, organic vapors are also trapped. Under these conditions, it is not uncommon for a white crust to form on some leaded copper alloys.

The alteration of copper alloys by corrosion processes can result in many different colors and surface textures, ranging from thin pink or brown films to thick gray, green or blue warty crusts. The growth of thin layers need not result in appreciable loss of mechanical strength to the whole copper or copper–alloy component or object, but the development of a thick crust inevitably results in a loss of strength, even though the component or object becomes thicker. This happens because the incrustation derives its metallic content from within the component, and the crust possesses mechanical moduli (strengths) quite different from those of the metal that it both penetrates and overlies.

The conditions favoring the corrosion of copper alloys in air include: moisture; acidity, caused by polluted air or water or by the presence of newly cut wood, which evolves organic acids for many years; salts, such as chlorides, which are most corrosive in acid, or acetates, which are most corrosive when neutral (that is, at a pH of 7); and ammonia that evolves from decaying organic matter.[8] Unfortunately, chlorides and acetates become trapped in the crust and continually stimulate change without themselves becoming fixed or lost.

The first few moments of exposure of a freshly cleaned surface determine its future. During this period, a protective film of pure cuprous oxide forms in the presence of unpolluted air. This film serves as protection even if the air subsequently becomes polluted with hydrogen sulfide. On the other hand, if a freshly cleaned surface is exposed to air containing sulfide, a much less protective film of mixed oxides and sulfides forms. Tarnishing thereafter is rapid and accelerating. This tarnishing may be visually acceptable or even desirable as an indication of age, but the appearance of nonuniform crusts usually is not.

A number of techniques, some of them laborious, are available for removing thin tarnish or heavy incrustation from objects made of copper alloys. The objective of treatment should be decided in advance. For example, it is often possible to clean and polish an object until it gleams as brightly as it did when first used, but it may become thinner as a result of the abrasion. Such verisimilitude may not be desirable because the new surface is modern, and the loss of metal needed to achieve the brightness shortens the life of the artifact. Such an extreme cleaning may be called "overcleaning" by those who prefer objects to retain the surface left by the last user, subsequently subdued by age. Only the person responsible for the restoration of an object is in a position to balance the gain in appearance against the cost of achieving it, as measured in terms of the manpower required for the treatment plus the partial destruction or loss of authenticity of the object.

Mechanical methods of cleaning make use of comparatively gentle abrasives such as pumice powder in mineral oil or bronze wool.[9] Steel wool should never be used for cleaning copper alloys because a corrosion inhibitor likely to stain copper is applied during the manufacturing process and also because the resulting abrasion transfers some steel to the copper alloy, which then becomes stained as the baser steel rusts.

Thin crusts can also be removed by chemical means. Suitable reagents include:

1. Silver Dip, choosing a formula of 8 milliliters of 85 percent so-called concentrated orthophosphoric acid, 7 grams of thiourea, 0.2 milliliter of a wetting agent (e.g., Kodak Photoflo) and enough water to make up to 100 milliliters. This solution must be fresh (i.e., unused on silver) before application to copper–alloy objects.

2. A reagent of 5 grams of citric acid, 1 gram of gum arabic, made up to 100 milliliters with distilled water. This solution is best used as a dip, swabbing at encrusted areas while the object is immersed in the liquid. The object should be carefully observed during treatment to forestall etching of the bare metal by removal and immediate rinsing.

3. A reagent of 6 milliliters of 85 percent orthophosphoric acid, 2 grams of sodium nitrite, made up to 100 milliliters with distilled water. This reagent cleans without brightening.

Thicker crusts require other reagents, for example:

1. A reagent of 5 to 15 grams of Calgon (the earlier unimproved variety, so-called sodium hexametaphosphate) made up to 100 milliliters with distilled water. This solution may be used hot, if necessary, to hasten the action.[10]

2. A reagent of 10 milliliters of concentrated sulfuric acid added slowly, while stirring, to 100 milliliters of water. Never add water

to acid: It may spatter the worker with oil of vitriol.[11] This reagent will "rot" large volumes of unwanted crust, which can then be brushed away.

In some circumstances, after this acid treatment, exposed metal is found to have become plated with pink copper. This can be removed by applying, to the pink areas only, a solution of 10 grams of silver nitrate made up to 100 milliliters with distilled water. A gray powder of silver will replace the pink copper areas; this powder can be brushed away (but retained for recycling!).

Freshly cleaned objects made entirely of copper alloys can be corrosion-inhibited by hard swabbing with a solution of 3 grams of benzotriazole (available from Fisher Scientific) or Cobratec 99 (available from Sherwin Williams or Maumee Chemical) dissolved in 100 milliliters of ethanol. When the object is dry, a thin coat of transparent Incralac, an acrylic resin containing benzotriazole, should be applied or the object should be waxed with Renaissance Wax (available through Smithsonian Museum shops and the Centuria Corporation, 1447 Peachtree St., N.E., Atlanta, Ga. 30309) if a less glossy appearance is desired.

Large objects can be repatinated black by all-over preparation with fine pumice in water, followed by swabbing with yellow ammonium polysulfide. Small objects can be repatinated black by brushing the objects with a thin paste made of barium sulfide powder and distilled water. Other colors of patina can be created, but the method must be varied to suit the size of the object and the nature of the alloy. Deliberately patinated objects usually require an application of paste wax—after cleaning with a hydrocarbon solvent—at intervals of six months in order to prevent changes in appearance through the previously discussed corrosion mechanisms.

IRON AND STEEL

Ferrous metals occur in several forms: as wrought iron, which is substantially chemically pure except for stringers of slag incompletely worked out during hammering and smithing; as mild steel, which has a relatively low carbon content; and as cast iron, which is a heterogeneous material containing several percent of carbon, most of it in a free condition, along with manganese, silicon and other elements.

As is commonly known, iron rusts. The change from strong metal to weak oxide may begin as disfiguring minute spots that penetrate into the metal, but eventually, the whole of an unprotected surface changes because the rust possesses negligible protective qualities.

Rusting occurs in the presence of oxygen and water vapor. The minimum relative humidity necessary to allow rusting has been stated to be 65 percent.[12] In practice, even 58 percent may allow rusting if the iron has been predisposed to rust by brief exposure to sulfur dioxide, deposition of dust containing ammonium sulfate or the presence of fingerprints. Once a rust film forms, its porosity serves as a reservoir for any liquid water, such as rain or condensation. Other corrosion-promoting ions such as chloride and acetate can then accumulate in the layer.

To conserve rusted iron or steel, the rust must be removed first. Then a resistant surface should be induced, followed by whatever kind of protection is aesthetically acceptable. If the iron has served as a structural member, its strength may have been reduced so greatly that it must be replaced. Door latches and other hardware may have been penetrated and replaced over much of their area by rust. An X-radiograph can usually establish this condition before cleaning is begun. If shape is retained as a mass of rust, then it is helpful to use electrolytic or other cleaning methods that do not remove all of the rust, but rather convert it from oxide back to iron and leave some material filling the cavities. These procedures preserve the shape of the damaged object.

As mentioned previously, tinplate consists of a sheet of iron thinly plated with tin. The tin provides extremely effective protection against rusting, but once any area of the film of tin has oxidized sufficiently to expose the iron, the presence of unchanged tin actually accelerates rusting because tin is the nobler metal. Then the growth of rust along the iron plate usually lifts overlying residues of tin and its oxides, and these residues vanish with the removal of their rust support during a cleaning process.

Mechanical methods available for removing rust include sandblasting, for large-scale work, and airbrasive, using a dolomite grit, for smaller objects.[13] Both of these methods leave a pitted surface, caused partly by the effects of the rusting and partly by the impingement of the abrasive particles. Such a pitted surface provides an excellent key for a protective lacquer or paint, and although such coatings may be objectionable on decorative objects, they may be desirable on structural ones.

Rust may be softened by saturation with penetrating oil, then freed by the judicious use of steel wool, taking care to remove the debris frequently to avoid abrasion of the exposed iron or steel.[14] Sometimes, usually on heavily corroded archaeological material, experienced workers grind away heavy crusts with a high-speed rotary tool in search of an original surface, perhaps marked by inlays or other decorations.[15]

Rust can be dissolved by many solutions, most of which have some disadvantage. Commercial rust removers intended for home application often consist of strong hydrochloric acid and a corrosion inhibitor. They can be identified by their choking odor and the fumes they form near an open ammonia bottle. Although immediately effective, these commercial solutions should be avoided because the chloride in them can cause conservation troubles in the future. Other types of remover based on phosphoric acid are slower in action but are generally more satisfactory. A typical formula is 10 milliliters of 85 percent orthophosphoric acid, 0.5 milliliter of a wetting agent (e.g., Kodak Photoflo), 1 gram of thiourea and enough water to make a solution of 100 milliliters. This remover can be applied by swabbing. A readily made formula contains 3.7 grams of ammonium citrate and 0.5 gram of gum arabic in 100 milliliters of water. This solution, with a pH of 5, becomes yellow when it contains dissolved rust, indicating the need for replacement. When swabbed on an object, it does cause slow growth of black oxide on bare steel. Treatment by immersion, rather than by swabbing, minimizes this oxidation.

A traditional method of removing the rust from small objects is to boil them in a sodium hydroxide solution. Caustic industrial formulas for sodium hydroxide solutions are fortified by sequestrants and surfactants to aid penetration and to keep insoluble material in suspension in the bath. One of these, Magnus 61 DRX, operates at a pH of 13.4 and strips rusted machinery in about 90 minutes at 60°C.[16] It is especially useful on cast iron which, as a result of corrosion processes, becomes veined with hairline cracks in which corrosive ions may lodge. Any type of solution cleaning process will be incomplete unless followed by the use of a dewatering fluid, preferably fortified with corrosion inhibitors, to eliminate moisture and residual solubles from crevices. Subsequently, a protective paint or lacquer should be applied.

The choice of protective coatings for iron and steel presents some difficulty. Cleaned tinplate is apt to be so pitted in the areas where tin has been lost that some form of reconstitution to approximate the original appearance is desirable. At present, this seems to be impracticable in an ethical manner,[17] but rerusting can be delayed by coating the object with an inhibitor and storing it in an area where relative humidity is controlled to about 50 percent.

Surfaces intended to appear clean can be lacquered. Protective transparent coatings can be found among the many varieties of alkyd. Because it is glossy, this type of coating is often unsatisfactory in appearance when sufficiently thick to afford good protection. Coatings with matt finishes may be preferable. Once alkyd coatings have cured fully, they also tend to be difficult to remove. Fortunately, iron is little affected by even the most powerful of paint removers. Thick coatings, which are less permeable and more protective, are easier to accept when pigmented (i.e., as paint). When painting is adopted, an approved paint system should be used, the metal should be thoroughly dry and a rust-inhibitive paint (red lead, zinc chromate or iron oxide) should be used as the primer.

Archaeologists are often satisfied with a two-coat finish—the first, a matt transparent lacquer; the second, a black matt paint that can be relieved at high spots to allow sight of the natural iron color.

Alternatively, most of the rust can be removed by a double application of 15 milliliters of 85 percent orthophosphoric acid in 100 milliliters of water followed by drying and steel brushing. The residue (especially that left to fill cavities) can then be converted into a less porous inhibitive tannate by wetting the object with acetone, then immediately with water, then many times with a solution of 20 grams of tannin in 100 milliliters of water and 15 milliliters of ethanol. Several days should be allowed for the initial brown surface to oxidize into a blue-black one.[18]

The restoration of physical strength to corroded iron may be possible to a limited degree if rusted-out spaces can be filled with a metal powder consolidated by a cold-setting synthetic resin. Measurements of physical strengths of representative composites of this kind are desirable.

LEAD

Lead is a blue-gray, soft ductile metal used in thick sheets for waterproofing and in pipes for plumbing. Apparently durable— lead objects have survived for millennia—the metal is seldom seen without its enveloping gray skin of mixed oxides, which appears to protect the lead object, although in fact the metal often continues to oxidize.

Freshly cleaned lead oxidizes immediately in air. If hydrogen sulfide is present (this gas is released by living bodies), the film will contain sulfide. The film is usually not protective; it is certainly not if formed in the presence of organic acid vapors, either acetic or formic, emanating from vinegar, wood, decomposing cellulose, etc. If such vapors are present, the lead will change slowly into either lead formate or the loose white powder of basic lead carbonate (i.e., hydrocerusite, white lead). This carbonate conversion usually happens when a lead object is stored in a wood cabinet.

The clean lead is attacked by both acid and alkali in solution. It briefly resists attack by cold dilute hydrochloric acid (pure, not commercial) because the chloride which forms immediately is insoluble in cold water. In the presence of oxygen, however, chloride trapped in a surface film stimulates corrosion. Lead turns white in dilute sulfuric acid, but the lead sulfate that forms is insoluble and partially protective. Even extremely dilute solutions of organic acids, such as are present in some soils, cause corrosion of lead into basic lead carbonate in the presence of atmospheric carbon dioxide. Once such a reaction has started, it appears to continue even after the object has been washed to remove any free acid.

Pure water (distilled, deionized and even some rainwater) corrodes lead, especially in the presence of carbon dioxide. Hard water, containing calcium and magnesium sulfates and bicarbonates, creates a protective film. A mild soap solution may also do so.

Sodium hydroxide and carbonate solutions, even if extremely dilute, form insoluble lead hydroxide that flakes off and exposes more metal to attack. Calcium hydroxide (e.g., the slaked lime of fresh mortar) attacks lead. Calcium bicarbonate (found in groundwater in limestone areas) deposits on lead are protective under mildly alkaline conditions (pH about 9).

The treatment of lead objects is directed toward (1) improving their appearance by the removal of unsightly or obscuring crusts, (2) improving their stability by the removal of crusts containing corrosion accelerators and (3) if they have become wholly mineralized, recovering their solidity by converting them back into metal. Although a corrosive ion held for decades in a film in constant contact with lead can cause immense damage, the same harmful ion may be used safely for a brief time in treatment, provided that it is removed completely after treatment.

A simple, often successful, method of removing a crust involves soaking the object, cold, in a solution of 56.5 grams of the tetrasodium salt of ethylenediaminetetra-acetic acid—Versene Powder (Dow) or Sequestrene NA4 (Geigy), 43.5 grams of ethylenediaminetetra-acetic acid—Versene Acid (Dow) or Sequestrene (Geigy)—and 1 liter of water. Alternatively, use 50 grams of disodium salt of ethylenediaminetetra-acetic acid (Fisher Scientific) in 1 liter of water. Soak for many hours until the object is clean; then wash it in several changes of tap water.[19] In this procedure, the reagent fixes the converted metal present in the crust and holds it in the solution together with the various corrosive ions. All are discarded with the solution. The method, therefore, cleans and stabilizes the object, provided that all of the crust is removed.

An object that has been completely changed into nonmetal by corrosion can be converted back to metal without a change in shape by a process known as *consolidative reduction*. In this process, the surface area of the object is estimated; then, the object is suspended on a lead strip that is connected as a cathode to a regulatable source of direct current, either 6 or 12 volts that can provide a current of more than 6 but less than 12 milliamperes per square inch of object surface. An anode made of sheet lead must be provided; it should be shaped and located so that, when placed in a glass or plastic tank, it is roughly equidistant from all surfaces of the object. With the current switched on, the electrolyte (10 percent sulfuric acid with a specific gravity of 1.066 at 20°C) should be poured into the tank and the current adjusted to more than 6 but less than 12 milliamperes per square inch. After 14 days of uninterrupted reduction, the object should be removed and the surface brushed. It is advisable to jettison the electrolyte, which contains the corrosive ions, at this stage and reelectrolyze for 24 hours in a fresh solution. While still wet, the object should be washed several times in an amount of distilled water that will just cover it in the narrowest vessel that will contain it, changing the water with each washing, until the pH of the water remains unchanged by contact with the lead for 30 minutes. The object should then be dried rapidly in hot air and impregnated with microcrystalline wax.

NOTES

1. W. E. Boggs, P. S. Trozzo and G. E. Pellisier "The Oxidation of Tin: II. The Morphology and Mode of Growth of Oxide Films on Pure Tin," *Journal of the Electrochemical Society* 108 (1961): 13–24.

2. S. N. Shah and D. Eurof Davies, "The Influence of Cathodic Treatment on the Subsequent Oxidation of Tin," in *First International Congress on Metallic Corrosion* (London: Butterworths, 1961), pp. 232-35.

3. A. I. Levin, M. E. Prostakov and V. P. Kochargin, "Thickness and Protective Action of Passive Films on Tin," *Journal of Applied Chemistry of the USSR* 33, no. 9 (1960): 2069–74; also reported by Henry J. Leidheiser, Jr., in *The Corrosion of Copper, Tin, and Their Alloys* (New York: John Wiley and Sons, Inc., 1971), pp. 300, 302.

4. T. P. Hoar, "The Corrosion of Tin and its Alloys: Part I—The Tin-Rich Tin-Antimony-Copper Alloys," *Journal of the Institute of Metals* 55 (1934): 135–47.

5. S. C. Britton, *Anti-Corrosion Manual* (London: Science Surveys, Ltd., 1958).

6. I. A. Ammar and S. Reed, "Effect of Sodium Pyrophosphate on Polarization and Corrosion of Tin," *Journal of the Electrochemical Society* 106 (1959): 926-29.

7. W. H. J. Vernon and L. Whitby, "The Open-air Corrosion of Copper. Part II—

the Mineralogical Relationships of Corrosion Products," *Journal of the Institute of Metals* 44 (1930): 389–96.

8. For a discussion of salts, see W. D. Robertson et al., "An Investigation of Chemical Variables Affecting the Corrosion of Copper," *Journal of the Electrochemical Society* 105 (1958): 569-73.

9. Joseph Ternbach, "Restoration of Bronzes, Ancient and Modern," *Bulletin of the American Group-IIC* 12, no. 2 (1972): 110–16.

10. Marie Farnsworth, "The Use of Sodium Metaphosphate in Cleaning Bronzes," *Technical Studies in the Field of Fine Arts* 9 (1940): 21–24.

11. Harold J. Plenderleith and A. E. A. Werner, *The Conservation of Antiquities and Works of Art,* 2d ed. (London, New York: Oxford University Press, 1971), pp. 250–51.

12. W. H. J. Vernon, "The Role of the Corrosion Product in the Atmospheric Corrosion of Iron," *Transactions of the Electrochemical Society* 64 (1933): 31–41.

13. B. M. Gibson, "The Use of the Airbrasive Process for Cleaning Ethnological Materials," *Studies in Conservation* 14, no. 4 (1969): 155–64.

14. Plenderleith and Werner, *Conservation of Antiquities,* pp. 291–95.

15. Robert M. Organ, *Design for Scientific Conservation of Antiquities* (Washington, D.C.: Smithsonian Institution Press, 1968), pp. 258–61.

16. William Henson, "Restoration of Modern Machinery," *Museum News* 49, no. 10 (June 1971): 13–17.

17. *The Murray Pease Report; Code of Ethics for Art Conservators; Articles of Association of IIC; Bylaws of the American Group* (New York: IIC-American Group, May 1968), pp. 63–64.

18. J. B. Pelikan, "Conservation of Iron with Tannin," *Studies in Conservation* 11, no. 3 (1966): 109–15.

19. Hermann Kühn, "Neue Reinigungsmethode für Korrodierte Bleigegenstände," *Museumskunde* 29, no. 3 (1960): 156–61.

COMMENTARY

ALBERT FRANCE-LANORD

Physical phenomena observed in the corrosion of metals are well defined, and methods for the treatment of corroded metals have been extensively studied experimentally for many years. Other methods, other products and other ways of providing protection against corrosion will certainly be developed in years to come. However, a major difficulty lies in the choice of the method used, and in a large measure, this choice is a function of what I call the *message* of the object.

I wish to emphasize this point: The treatment of deteriorated objects has become more scientific in nature, entrusted to specialists trained as physicists and chemists but with insufficient knowledge of problems involved in dealing with historic and artistic objects. Their colleagues trained only in the more traditional disciplines have a tendency to withdraw when confronted with the advice and activity of scientists. The result is that it is difficult to know what decision is best in a specific case. I have often observed this problem in France. This is why I believe that an effort should be made to coordinate scientific and traditional efforts and that it is necessary from the beginning to define terms completely and to gain a thorough understanding of relevant problems.

Consideration of the corrosion of metals only in its scientific aspect or in the manner in which industrialists view the problem

---

Albert France-Lanord is director of the Centre de Recherches de L'Histoire de la Siderugie, Jarville, Meurthe et Moselle, France.

is erroneous in the treatment of art objects or historic monuments. I suggest that specialized organizations, like the Rome Centre, take the responsibility to define conservation policies for different types of objects and monuments. Codes should be established to guide museum conservators and restoration architects in their attempts to halt deterioration. These codes should be developed by experienced conservators and restoration architects, in collaboration with scientists who understand the nature of deterioration and ways in which to remedy it. The papers presented at this conference give information that could perhaps be useful in developing such codes.

For example, the paper by John G. Waite, devoted to problems posed by metals used in architecture, is quite clear. The general survey on various mechanisms of corrosion affecting the metals he discusses and on methods generally used to remedy problems caused by these mechanisms make the paper a most useful document, whose circulation seems eminently desirable.

It would not be inappropriate, however, to point out that metals used in architecture require different kinds of treatment, that is, treatment that will be in keeping with what might be called the metal's function. One does not necessarily treat all of a metal architectural monument in the same manner, no matter whether the monument has only a technical or functional significance or whether it also has a historical or aesthetic value.

Effects of corrosion on old metal objects are often quite different from those one notices on modern metals. The urban atmosphere has certainly changed much throughout the centuries—first, because coal heating replaced wood heating; then, because fuels containing hydrocarbons began to be used extensively. This change in the atmosphere is why a metal that has undergone corrosion through several centuries of exposure does not behave the way a modern version of the same metal would when exposed to contemporary atmospheric pollution. As this contemporary pollution threatens human health, protective measures, which will ultimately be beneficial to monuments as well as to humans, have gradually been taken in all countries. One may even claim that in many cases the problem of protecting monuments will be solved when human protection is assured, whether the threat be that of atmospheric pollution or the danger of war.

The following comments were inspired by Mr. Waite's review of the problem, and the discussions on the corrosion of specific metals follows the same order in which metals are discussed in his paper.

258

ALUMINUM. The most ancient aluminum monument seems to be the famous statute of *Eros* in Piccadilly Circus in London, England. This work, by Sir Alfred Gilbert, was placed there in 1893 and it has dominated the city ever since. I do not know whether the conservation of the statue has given birth to problems in 80 years, but it would be interesting to find out what changes have been noticed as a result of corrosion and if any special protective measures have been taken. The question could be discussed with the Aluminum Development Association. I do not know of any example in France of such early use of aluminum, either in architecture or in decoration.

COPPER AND BRONZE. An interesting use of copper in the decoration of monuments has been the creation of large statues by the process of electrotyping. This process was used on a large scale in France at the end of the 19th century for the decoration of several palaces, e.g., the Grand Palais and the Opera in Paris. The purity of the metal obtained through this process has contributed to a large extent to the excellent condition of such statues and decorations today.

To the contrary, the conservation of bronze statues in large cities causes recurrent trouble to the authorities responsible for their maintenance. In Paris, several 20th-century statues, which are not old enough to have acquired protective layers of carbonates and sulfates, have been treated with different materials in attempts to prevent or limit corrosion, but no satisfactory method of preventing corrosion has yet been found. Whether conservators are confronted with problems involving the 17th-century bronze groups at Versailles or with Aristide Maillol's statues in the gardens of the Louvre, I consider that the best procedure for protecting monuments against corrosion, given the present condition of city air, is steady and frequent maintenance, including regular washing and treatment with protective substances.

Of course, all those who have dealt, or are dealing, with the conservation of famous bronze monuments know quite well that the difficulties presented are not always of a scientific nature, but too often are of a political or moral character. Harold J. Plenderleith mentions one of the best examples of this situation in his commentary—the horses over the main entrance doors of the Basilica of San Marco in Venice. In this case, too, it is evident that human factors play an important role.

LEAD. As Mr. Waite correctly mentions, mechanical effects are most prejudicial to lead roofs and monuments. There is no French word for *creep*, but it has been found that lead coverings must be completely renewed after 100 to 150 years, depending on the thickness of the metal. (As an aside, perhaps it should be noted that old lead is especially valuable to nuclear physics centers since the old lead, when fashioned into radiation shields, provides better protection against radiation than recently produced lead.)

The problem of 18th-century lead statues is of a more complex nature. For example, Stanislas Square in Nancy is decorated with monumental fountains ornamented with lead statues. Because of dilations, important deformations have occurred, creating fissures. Freezing has increased the damage and, at the moment, there are cracks as large as 1 to 2 centimeters wide. Welding cannot be used for repairs because of the deep corrosion of the metal; a number of experiments designed to achieve consolidation by means of epoxy resins are planned, however. Another more recent example is the monumental fountain that decorates the Place des Terraux in Lyon; it was made by a sculptor well known to Americans, Frédéric Auguste Bartholdi, sculptor of the Statue of Liberty in the New York City harbor. The monument in Lyon is particularly complicated: It includes rocks, cascades, horses, nymphs and all sorts of water gods. The monument is hollow and is set on an iron frame. Because of humidity, the iron frame has corroded and has gradually collapsed under the considerable weight of the lead, which is also deformed. During restoration, it was necessary to remove the iron frame, to set the statue upright again and to fit a new frame in place. This work, directed by the Department of Historical Monuments, is an excellent example of restoration.

I would add that in Venice most of the beddings of window shutters and balconies are made of lead. Because of the great amount of noxious substances in the atmosphere there, the lead has rapidly corroded during the past few years, and, in many cases, shutters and balconies are about to collapse and fall from building facades.

TIN (OR SHEET IRON). I am not aware of any case where galvanized metal has been used in French monuments. In certain mountain regions, however, such as Vosges, Savoy and the Alps, galvanized plates of sheet iron have been used to protect walls. I have been informed that such small plates were even used to cover a church tower. In general, these protective devices do not last long (about 50 years) and they have to be replaced. I know of one church where the galvanized plates were finally replaced by thin rustless steel plates which looked similar to, but were more lasting than, the sheet-iron plates.

IRON AND STEEL. If I am not mistaken, the amount of steel

destroyed every year because of corrosion represents about 20 percent of the annual production. Consequently, protection against corrosion is a major concern of those who produce and work with steel. However, the aim of this conference is to consider the conservation and preservation of metal elements of historical interest, and for such objects, the question of how preservation should be accomplished is even more complicated than it is for modern-day iron or steel objects. In fact (I hope my engineer and scientist colleagues will foregive me for saying this), the question of how much or what kind of scientific intervention will be allowed in dealing with major conservation problems involving historic metal monuments is often only of secondary importance; there are other considerations that take precedence.

A recent example was provided by the razing of the famous Central Market *(Les Halles)* in Paris, also known as the Baltard pavilions. This architectural complex, made primarily of cast iron, was erected in 1854 to shelter the market. The market recently moved to the suburbs, and the normal evolution of the city required the razing of the old buildings, which were no longer of any use. A great number of people belonging to different social categories protested this destruction for many different reasons. Many of them defended the complex simply because it was old. Finally, it was admitted that the buildings could not be adapted to new uses on their present sites and that they were not of major importance either from a technological or a historical viewpoint. Victor Baltard's *Halles* were, therefore, razed and one pavilion has been offered to anyone who will agree to reerect it somewhere else, but so far there has been no taker. This shows the complexity of the nature of choices that will undoubtedly appear in all countries in the coming years.

CAST IRON. One of the first major structures made of cast iron is the famous bridge of Coalbrookdale over the Severn River in England. Built in 1779, it still exists and has been classified as an "ancient monument" by the English Ministry of Works. I believe that it is in excellent condition and its conservation has involved no particular problems; only normal maintenance has been required. However, not everyone believed the bridge would survive. I recently acquired a wood engraving showing the bridge. At the bottom of the print, a French traveler had added his own observations, which included the following: "I have noticed that the iron has already been marked by weather (October 25, 1785), which makes us fear that the bridge might not last as long as one could think: the iron is not painted."

If it can be said in general that the conservation of cast-iron elements exposed to the atmosphere is not particularly difficult, the same cannot be said about cast-iron objects found on the bottom of the sea. Cannon and bullets from 17th and 18th-century ships have been altered so greatly that their conservation is particularly difficult. Iron dissolves in seawater and remains there as a mass of low-density graphite that retains the object's shape. (Despite this fact, foundaries recently actually suggested using cast iron to manufacture containers meant to stock radioactive residues to be discarded and left on the bottom of the sea!)

WROUGHT IRON. The composition of old wrought iron is rather variable and, hence, its resistance to corrosion varies. However, as pure iron resists chemical change better than carburized iron, wrought iron, when exposed to air, is reasonably well preserved. Nevertheless, normal maintenance is necessary. The door fittings of Notre Dame Cathedral in Paris, which date from the 13th century, are an example of well-preserved wrought iron. More recent works, from the middle of the 18th century, use decorative elements made of thin sheet iron shaped while hot and attached to strong iron frames. The bars of Stanislas Square in Nancy are a case in point. Their maintenance requires delicate procedures, and frequent restorations are necessary. For instance, the parts made of sheet iron are generally leaf gilded and have to be completely and systematically checked every 15 years.

At present, a difficult conservation problem has arisen, connected with the corrosion of the iron in the Paris Pantheon. For this building, erected at the end of the 18th century, architect Jacques Soufflot made ample use of iron tie rods in the masonry for traction. In a way, this type of construction prefigured the use of reinforced concrete. Humid air has now penetrated into the brickwork and corroded the iron, which swells and sometimes causes the masonry to burst into pieces, representing a real danger to visitors. A few days ago, public access to the structure was forbidden. Architects are now faced with a most difficult restoration problem.

The Eiffel Tower in Paris is one of the most important iron monuments in the world. Although it is 82 years old, its maintenance does not pose any particular problems. It was built of wrought iron rather than steel for economic reasons, since in 1889, steel was even more expensive in France than wrought iron. Because of this fact and the fact that iron is more resistant to corrosion and aging than steel, the famous tower is still in good shape. It is regularly repainted with paints containing iron oxide pigments, because such pigments have been found to have excellent resistance to erosion caused by dust brought by the wind, which, it seems, is the main destructive agent in this instance.

STEEL. This metal is still quite young. Nevertheless, after the lapse of 100 years, it must be admitted that most of man's steel monuments have disappeared. Among these are the ships that were the first large steel structures built. The famous cruiser *Aurora*, still at anchor in Leningrad, comes to mind, as one such example that has been remarkably well preserved. Its cannon, whose symbolic firing heralded a new era to the world, are still in good condition. It would be interesting to know what conservation methods have been used for the preservation of this ship, which is more than 60 years old, a great age for steel.

Among steel works conserved for historical reasons are heavy weapons and cannon of different calibres. In the yards of the Palais des Invalides in Paris, which shelter the Military Museum, are a great number of artillery pieces of the 19th and 20th centuries. These interesting weapons are more or less ruined because of the absence of any system of protection.

Corrosion is not the only factor in the destruction of steel; one must also take into account the phenomena of fatigue. One wonders what the life-span will be for certain reinforced concrete works whose steel armatures are submitted to prestressing. Finally, one must not overlook the phenomena of corrosion caused by electric currents resulting from defective insulation.

I would conclude my remarks on Mr. Waite's paper by noting that the paper's bibliography is quite extensive. For those who are familiar with French, I would add that the publications of the Centre d'Enseignement de la lutte contre la Corrosion (CELCC), Rueil–Malmaison, France, are also worthwhile reading.

Robert M. Organ's paper is complementary to Mr. Waite's. The author is conversant with problems of conserving antiques and metal objects. We have often had the opportunity to compare experiences, and I have always agreed with him in the application of the methods he has devised and practiced so successfully through the years. Therefore, I shall confine myself to remarks of a general nature.

First, old metals are seldom pure, and this makes corrosion particularly complex, so that there is a discrepancy between the theoretical reactions that conservation scientists can define and reality. This is the reason one has to be especially careful when using treatment methods and materials. Restorers must always conduct tests before carrying out any treatment, and the establishment of controls in the course of operations is essential to success.

There is a term that should no longer appear in any serious work on corrosion, because it is devoid of meaning: The word is *patina*. Patina is too often used simply to designate an artificial coloring applied to the surface of a new metal to change its appearance. One can give a patina to a bronze, just as one can give it to a piece of furniture or a stone statue in order to make the object appear different than it would normally or to give it an appearance of antiquity. Like *patina*, the term *rust* should be used sparingly in the conservator's vocabulary. It should simply designate the superficial accumulation of oxides that appears on corroded iron surfaces and that may be easily removed by abrasion or some solution without damaging the object.

Therefore, in discussing metals, one should use only the term *corrosion products*, which takes into consideration the notion of the object's primitive surface, which I call the *skin*. Corrosion products are either outside or under the skin, or both. Generally, corrosion products outside the skin are removed—this is cleaning; those under the skin are preserved, as they are part of the object. All the theory of restoration is summed up in the foregoing sentence. The terminology about conserving or removing patina is vague, ambiguous and dangerous.

In Mr. Organ's paper, there is a short sentence, apparently of little consequence, that I believe is extremely important: "The objective of treatment should be decided in advance." This decision represents the greatest difficulty in the conservation of metal objects. Mr. Organ makes another important point later in the paper: Who should be the person responsible for the restoration? I have practiced the restoration of metal objects for 25 years, and this point has given me much trouble. Should decisions on restoration be made by the museum curator or the head of the treatment laboratory? An ancient object is endowed with a double personality. In the first place, it is an object made of *matter*, the present matter sometimes being different from the original one. For instance, iron can be completely transformed into magnetite. At the same time, an object has a *message*. It is because of this message that man is anxious to conserve the object, not because of its matter. Therefore, the conservation of matter is essentially conditioned by the nature of the message. It must be admitted that the scientist in the laboratory can recognize matter and its alterations; however, he often does not have the training to identify the message. Sometimes the significance of an object lies in the fact that it is broken and to restore it would be an error. Therefore, the closest cooperation should be encouraged among curators, art historians or experts and chemists and physicists. One must admit that today, due to a lack of adequate understanding on all sides, cooperation does not exist.

In conclusion, I would mention that, according to my experience, the best means to conserve an old metal object is the impregnation of the object with wax that has been heated to about 110°C, a temperature higher than the boiling point of water. This operation will remove any trace of humidity. One must not forget to mention, however, that all means of protection and treatment of old metal objects must be rigorously reversible. In other words, conservators must be able to remove easily, at any point in the future, any product used to protect an object, without damaging the object.

COMMENTARY

CYRIL STANLEY SMITH

In a letter transmitting his commentary on the papers by John G. Waite and Robert M. Organ, Albert France-Lanord, who was unable to attend this conference, asked me particularly to emphasize his concern that scientists working as conservators should have an understanding of the history of art and be always aware of an object's message. Qualifications for a scientist specializing in corrosion to work in this field are quite different from those required for a corrosion specialist working in a university laboratory or in industry. Only if real communication exists between scientists and conservators can the proper course of action for the conservation of an object be determined so that the object and its message can be preserved to be seen and studied now and in the future. To this, I would add that museum personnel must know enough science to be able to evaluate scientific reports. Too many curators and art historians are overly impressed with mathematical analyses and tend to accept scientific reports uncritically, without studying their limitations and their meanings.

As a part-time historian of technology, I have come to feel, with Richard M. Candee, that the role of objects as records of human history has not been sufficiently recognized. Written documents require a great deal of interpretation, since everything that is written has passed through a fallible mind—and certainly everything

Cyril Stanley Smith is institute professor, emeritus, Massachusetts Institute of Technology, Cambridge, Mass.

that is made as a record for future scrutiny is a more or less conscious distortion. Understanding and documenting the history of technology, this major part of mankind's experience that has practically been ignored, can be done only through the study of objects, and the process begins in the conservator's laboratory. The conservator's primary obligation is to preserve, but his intimate knowledge of the ways in which things have been made can help historians to appreciate and understand man's history as a creator.

Mr. Organ mentions different forms of corrosion products and discusses the chemical compositions of these products and their reactions with other materials. Mr. France-Lanord points out that an original surface can be preserved under corrosion products. This, as conservators know, happens frequently with copper and bronze. On the other hand, it never occurs with iron except when a thick layer of hammer scale remained on the surface after the smith's work was completed.

One other point on corrosion should be mentioned. Although the initial rate of corrosion is soon diminished by the formation of a layer of protective products of the action, corrosion does not entirely cease thereafter, but continues by intergranular capillary penetration and diffusion of electrolytes. For this reason, corrosion produces effects in objects from archaeological times that are quite different from what would be expected on the basis of short-range tests.

As a metallurgist, I wish that Messrs. Waite and Organ had given more detail in their papers. Both authors pay far too little attention to the differences between alloys. The mechanical and chemical properties of two alloys of the same metal can differ much more than the mechanical and chemical properties of two different elements. There is also too little said about ways in which metals are shaped before architects and builders begin to use them in designing and building structures. Rolled or extruded rods and beams have a one-dimensional quality that precludes "organic" design, however skillfully they may be cut and joined. There are great differences between cast and wrought metal and between rolled and forged metal, in respect to both shapes that are formed naturally and properties of the material. Welding has greatly affected building construction. When metals had to be joined mechanically, by hammer-welding or by rivetting and could not easily be cut with the oxygen torch, the architect approached problems of design and construction in a manner quite different from today. Even the change from oxyacetylene to electric welding caused differences.

Practically every major change in human society (e.g., the rise and fall of various cultures and kings) followed some technological change that helped to make the old system less stable and opened new possibilities of human interaction. Fire-hardened ceramics and the development of copper alloys both marked a new level of man's understanding of his relationship to nature and to himself.

It is interesting to note that most important industrial developments, at least those in the field of materials, originated as discoveries in the field of decorative art. Discovery is an aesthetic process, and only development is purposeful.

One small, but important, example of this comes in building, starting in the 16th century when the rolling of H-shaped lead strips began to replace cast lead cames in stained glass windows. The first mill had grooved rolls, and a larger one of the same type was established in 1753 to hot-roll profiled iron bars for decorative balcony rails and window frames. Twenty years later, such a rolling mill was central to Henry Cort's revolutionary plant for producing merchant bars of wrought iron, and, today, it is used in modern giant mills producing structural steel and railroad rails.

Although the survival of most objects from the past depends on aesthetic considerations, these objects have an added value as records of technology. They were made by people who were not kings, councillors or connoisseurs. For the future, we should try more consciously to preserve a sampling of the things that make up the environment of the common man, of everyday objects as well as those that are considered by today's standards to be beautiful or important.

DISCUSSION

Comments made by the panelists and audience during the discussion on metals are summarized in the following paragraphs.

As is true for other materials of art and architecture, the preservation of metals raises not only technical problems but also philosophical questions. Perhaps the most difficult of these questions is "What should be preserved?"

In the art conservation field, this question is generally answered not by conservators but by curators. Normally, curators are responsible for the collections under their care, including any decisions about additions or restoration work. If a conservator disagrees with a curator over work requested, the matter may be debated, but the final decision rests with the curator.

Of course, the conservator, with a technical knowledge of materials, is in an excellent position to assist the curator in making decisions related to an object's aesthetics, since the scientific characteristics of the materials used undoubtedly affected the original aesthetic decisions made by the artist or craftsman. Unfortunately, some art historians and preservationists do not pay sufficient attention to the characteristics of materials and how these characteristics affect the interaction of the artist with the materials. One example may illustrate this point: Several years ago, the Dome of the Rock in Jerusalem was stripped of its gilt metal and gold anodized aluminum was applied in its place. Upon inquiry, it was revealed that no tests had been made to ascertain if all the different pieces of aluminum being used were of the same quality. No consideration had been given to the strain that would be caused by seasonal temperature changes and the resulting movement of the metal or to the question of how the different pieces of aluminum should be joined. Apparently, there was also little thought given to how thick the material should be to withstand natural or artificial sandblasting. These questions certainly should have been investigated thoroughly, because they have a significant impact on life expectancy. There are often great variations in the kinds of aluminum anodized; some are brittle, while others are flexible and bend easily. Then, too, if the corner of a piece is broken during shipment or installation, the anodized covering may separate from the aluminum underneath; water can then get between the aluminum and the coating and eventually do a great amount of damage. The only way to deal with such a problem is to have the aluminum reanodized at a mill under strict conditions. There are also many problems in fastening metals, as Mr. Waite's paper revealed.

Nontechnical problems are, however, perhaps the most difficult to overcome. For example, underlying Mr. France-Lanord's comments about the demolition of *Les Halles* in Paris is the basic assumption that there is no overriding reason to save this central produce market. He seems to accept the opinion that the buildings have outlived their usefulness. Should this assumption and this opinion go unquestioned? Why should there be protest from many citizens about demolition if the buildings have no significance?

Naturally, those who decide what should be saved attempt to be objective, but it is difficult to be free from personal prejudices and the tastes and politics of the times. Many decisions are reputedly based on "importance," but it should be recognized that everything had some importance in its own day. Perhaps, as Mr. Smith commented, greater efforts should be made to preserve ordinary objects and structures for future generations, even though it may be more difficult to convince people that the preservation of functional objects or structures associated with lower economic classes is warranted. Too often, the emphasis is on "tea party" preservation, that is, the preservation of only those objects and structures that are associated with the upper classes of society.

In addition to overcoming technical problems, suppressing personal prejudices and convincing the public that preservation is warranted, conservators and preservationists who are also responsible for restoration work must recognize why an object or building should be saved. Often, historical considerations must be taken into account. For example, as Mr. Organ pointed out, the significance of a broken object or a disfigured building may lie in the damage it has suffered.

The maintenance of such damaged or deteriorated cultural

remnants is usually easier for conservators, who can place an object in the stabilized environment of a museum. All preservationists can usually do is to save as much original fabric as possible. For example, a badly deteriorated tinplate roof may not be able to withstand such strong, but necessary, cleaning methods as sandblasting. The sheet iron underneath the tin plate or terneplate may be thin as a result of rusting from the bottom. Such rusting is common; vapor frequently condenses on the underside of roofs. Sandblasting in such a case may remove all or part of the protective covering, and once the tin or terneplate is pierced, it no longer protects the iron but rather hastens the iron's corrosion because tin is nobler than iron. To save a structure with a deteriorated tin roof from possible water damage, the only course available to the restoration architect may be the replacement of the roof.

Wear, not corrosion, is generally the major problem encountered in preserving old machinery, such as steam engines or mining equipment, because often the real educational value of the machine lies in showing how it actually operated. Demonstration does cause wear, though, which is, of course, to the detriment of the next generation. Fortunately, however, most wear occurs in localized places, and replacement was generally provided for in well-designed machinery. If replacement is not possible or is undesirable, it may be helpful to add modern materials, such as Teflon, to help bearing surfaces of old machines being demonstrated to better tolerate wear. Of course, if a machine is of great importance, it should not be operated at all. A reproduction may be made and demonstrated in place of the historic machine.

Paints and Varnishes

PROBLEMS IN THE RESTORATION AND PRESERVATION OF OLD HOUSE PAINTS

MORGAN W. PHILLIPS

This paper discusses problems in the preservation and restoration (meaning reproduction) of early American oil-based house paints and is presented with the hope that it will prompt basic technical study of the varied kinds of paint that were commonly used in early American buildings and that are well outlined in histories of early American house painting by Richard M. Candee and Theodore Z. Penn.[1] The suggestions offered here are based on informal observations of old paints in a number of buildings in New England and on somewhat more controlled studies of paints in the First Harrison Gray Otis House (1795–96), Boston, Mass., now headquarters of the Society for the Preservation of New England Antiquities (SPNEA). In attempting to restore original paint colors of the Otis House, I have had the invaluable help and guidance of Robert L. Feller of the Mellon Institute, who analyzed selected paint samples by emission spectrography and X-ray diffraction to supplement my own much less elaborate chemical and microscopic identifications. I also wish to thank Ruth M. Johnston of the Kollmorgen Corporation, Attleboro, Mass., for her help and suggestions about the use of spectrophotometry in the study of old house paints. I am further indebted to the Edward K. Perry Company, Boston, Mass., and the Cadilac Paint and Varnish Company, Allston, Mass., for their advice in matters of paint technology and craft.

Morgan W. Phillips is supervisor of properties of the Society for the Preservation of New England Antiquities, Boston, Mass.

PROBLEMS IN PAINT RESTORATION

Discoloration

The traditional method of reproducing the color of old house paints is simply to scrape clean a sample of the old paint and to match its color. However, it is suggested here that many samples which have been found and carefully matched in this way may be badly discolored and have led some restorers to believe incorrectly that interiors of Georgian houses were usually painted muddy colors.[2]

Original finish paints used in the Otis House appear to consist primarily of the following pigments: white lead, Prussian blue, yellow ochre, lampblack, chalk and perhaps also verdigris or copper resinate. The medium of the paints appears to be a drying oil, probably linseed oil. The paints were made glossy and resistant to dirt by means of thin oil-based glazes applied over them, as was common in the 18th century.[3] Most of the discoloration found at the Otis House is the result of two actions: (1) the fading of the Prussian blue and (2) the extreme yellowing of the oil. The original brightness of the Prussian blue appears to have been preserved only in areas where the pigment was always in darkness, as in the centers of thick lumps of paint in cracks and corners of the woodwork.[4]

It has been observed that the yellowing of drying oils is greatly accelerated by darkness and can often be partially reversed by exposure to light.[5] Original paint layers in the Otis House were put into darkness by the application of later paints in the early 19th century. When early paint samples were first uncovered about two years ago, the colors found were mostly yellowish pea-greens and brownish buffs. Since then, these uncovered areas have been exposed to diffuse interior light or to more intense light coming from nearby windows; during this time of exposure to light, the greens have become lighter and more blue and the buffs have lightened toward a cream color. Shocked by this change, we attempted to discover the original colors by finding lumps of the original paint inside of which the Prussian blue was preserved and then intentionally bleaching the oil inside the lumps through exposure to light for periods of days or weeks. Long-wave ultraviolet light appeared to bleach the oil fairly effectively and probably offers a rapid way of bleaching the oil in paints that contain only light-stable pigments. It is not known what type of illumination will cause the least damage to fugitive pigments, while still bleaching the oil. In the case of paints containing Prussian blue, for example, visible blue or violet light might be better for bleaching

274

than ultraviolet light. Visible light might affect the pigment less, since Prussian blue particles would probably reflect much of the visible blue light, whereas they would absorb much of the ultraviolet light.[6]

At the Otis House, both window light and fluorescent lamp light appeared to bleach the oil in the original paints faster than they faded the Prussian blue, thereby making yellowish green paints lighter and much more blue. Still better results could possibly be achieved by exposing the paint to fluorescent lamp light that has had the ultraviolet rays filtered out. An important advantage of using thick lumps of paint is that the paint inside them contains only its own oil; where a paint was spread thin, the oil of glazes, and perhaps of later paint coats, may have penetrated deeply into the original paint layer, greatly increasing the yellowing (fig. 1).

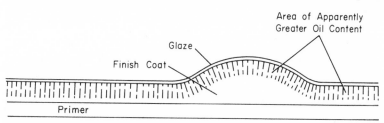

FIGURE 1. *Typical cross-section of original paint layers in the Otis House, Boston, Mass., showing a small lump, which might occur in a crevice of the woodwork, at the edge of a piece of hardware, etc.*

Also, there is evidence to suggest that the migration of oil toward the paint surface, or possibly into the substrate, during drying may sometimes have decreased the oil content of paint near the bottom of the layer. A low-power binocular microscope is necessary to find well-preserved lumps. One unknown factor is the relationship between the length of time that a paint was originally exposed to light and the rate of its yellowing after being covered.

Another form of discoloration in old paint, caused by oxidation and exposure to light, is *blanching* or *chalking*. Blanching fades the apparent color of a paint not by a photochemical change in one of the pigments but by degrading the oil, thus, reducing the paint's glossiness and causing diffuse reflections of incident white light.[7] It is unlikely that oils in old discolored house paints can be bleached to their original clarity without severely fading light-sensitive pigments or blanching the paint. Only the collective experience of future investigators will tell what early colors were really like. Much could be learned from more extensive study of written documents and of such graphic records as the many original drawings produced in the late 18th century by the architectural firm of Robert and James Adam, showing their brightly colored interior designs for great English houses.

LIMITATIONS OF QUANTITATIVE ANALYSIS. A thorough quantitative analysis of an old paint does not by itself produce a formula for a new paint that will match the original color of the old, since two paints of precisely the same chemical composition can have considerably different colors. There are a number of reasons for this: An important one is that a pigment's tinctorial strength (that is, its coloring power) varies in direct proportion to the exposed surface area of the pigment particles, which, in a given quantity of pigment, varies inversely with the size of the particles or of agglomerates of those particles. If the particles or agglomerates in a given quantity of pigment are large, much pigment material is contained within them and is thus concealed; if finely divided, more material is exposed and the pigment has much more effect on the paint color. Thus, for example, equal quantities of Prussian blue, when mixed with a given quantity of white lead, can produce either light grayish blues or darker bright blues according to the thoroughness with which the Prussian blue particles have been separated and intermixed with the white lead. This breaking apart and intermixing is called *dispersion*. Old paints were usually dispersed by hand, and most unevenly, so that each pigment exists in the paint in many different degrees of dispersion. Similarly, some pigments, such as most natural earths, are made up of particles of many different sizes. Thus, the original color of an old paint containing several pigments cannot be determined by a quantitative analysis solely, unless some method is developed to account for complex considerations of dispersion and particle size.

Another difficulty in attempting to duplicate an old paint on the basis of a quantitative analysis is that many impure pigments, such as natural earths, consist of particles of many varied colors, the combined effect of which may be hard to estimate.

USE OF SPECTROPHOTOMETRIC CURVE ANALYSES. One of the most promising methods for estimating the original color of yellowed and faded paint is through a comparative spectrophotometric curve analysis of different samples of the paint. The spectrophotometic curve of a paint may be obtained by illuminating paint samples with light of a number of different wavelengths, in succession, from violet through all the colors of the spectrum to red. At each wavelength, the percentage of reflectance is measured, as compared to the reflectance of a standard white, and these values, when plotted on a graph, form the curve. Colors appear in the curve as patterns of selective reflectance and absorption (the opposite of reflectance); thus, a yellow registers as the absorption of violet and blue light and the reflectance of all other light. A paint's spectrophotometric curve is related to the sum of the contributions of all the paint's ingredients, and these ingredients can often be distinguished by the way they affect the curve's shape.[8]

The following is but one example of the way in which comparative spectrophotometric measurements can often be used to estimate the degree of fading, yellowing or other discoloration in old paints: Measurements of two areas of an original green paint were made at the Otis House by Ruth M. Johnston; they helped confirm suspicions that the oil in the paint may have yellowed severely when covered by later paint layers and then may have been partially clarified by exposure to light. The spectrophotometric curve of a freshly exposed sample of the original paint had a shape showing certain characteristics that are often associated with a yellowed medium (fig. 2). A paint having a curve of this

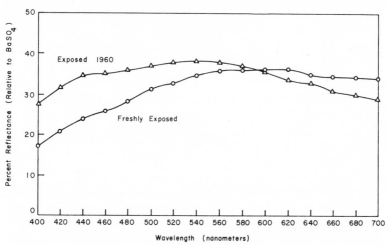

FIGURE 2. *Comparison of spectrophotometric curves of freshly exposed green paint in the Otis House and the same paint after 11 years of exposure to window light. Notice that in the curve of the freshly exposed paint, the low reflectance (that is, the high absorption) of blue and green light is shown by the depression of the left-hand portion of the curve, which slopes upward gradually from 400 to 580 nanometers. In the curve of the paint exposed since 1960, the left-hand portion of the curve has moved up, signifying more reflectance (that is, less absorption) of blue and green light and, therefore, suggesting a loss of yellowness during bleaching.*

shape probably could not have been made by any combination, in fresh oil, of the pigments found in the paint (that is, white lead, Prussian blue, yellow ochre, lampblack and chalk). An adjacent sample of the paint had been exposed since 1960 to the light of a south-facing window; this light had apparently bleached the oil more nearly to its original clarity, making the paint significantly more blue and less yellow. This bleached sample's spectrophotometric curve exhibited much less of that shape which is associated with a yellowed medium; this second curve more nearly resembles that of a paint that could normally be made by a combination of the previously mentioned pigments dispersed in fresh oil. Further evidence of the crucial role played by the yellowed oil in this comparison is that none of the known pigments in the original paint commonly exhibit the property of losing yellowness upon exposure to light.

It should also be remembered that some of the oil of the next later paint coat may have partially penetrated the original layer, thus drying in darkness and yellowing rapidly. In any event, the fact that daylight reduced the yellowness suggests that some of the yellowing occurred in the absence of daylight—in other words, after the paint had been covered. Thus, if one were to restore the severely yellowed color of a freshly exposed paint sample, the result would probably be a color never seen before in the room's history. I have observed similar evidence of yellowing and bleaching of interior paints in many buildings: Where later paint layers have peeled away from an early layer at some time in the past, the exposed early layer is often much less yellowed than it is in adjacent areas where it is freshly exposed by scraping.

CHOICE OF PIGMENTS IN PAINT RESTORATION. The fact that every pigment has its own spectrophotometric "fingerprint" points to the advantage of using the closest possible duplicates of original pigments in paint restoration projects. Because of the phenomenon called *metamerism*, two different pigments may match under one light and differ noticeably in another; another effect of metamerism is that two different observers may perceive a color match differently when comparing paints made with different pigments. Since rooms in museum houses are illuminated by daylight, which continually changes color, it may be impossible to match exactly, under all conditions and for all observers, the color produced by the original pigments unless those same pigments are used. If nontraditional pigments are selected to give greater permanence, they must be carefully chosen and combined so as to minimize this problem of metamerism.[9] It should be remembered that many pigments have different colors by reflected and transmitted light, and pigments that appear to be the same color when used singly (that is, their mass tone) often have different effects when used in mixtures with white pigments or when the paint containing them ages.[10] Architectural historians need guidance from conservators in the more precise analysis of early pigments, since individual pigment names, such as Spanish brown and vermilion, may embrace a number of materials not absolutely identical.[11]

Texture

Another problem in paint restoration is that of reproducing the original texture. Old paints generally display brush marks more noticeably than modern paints, partly because paints based on natural-oil mediums do not flow brush marks together as well as do most modern paints formulated with alkyd resin mediums. If alkyd-based paints are used in restoration, they should be formulated so as not to flow too well. In most old work, brush marks are carefully aligned with the design of the object being painted.

Other Appearance Aspects

In addition to color and texture, other aspects of appearance must be considered in an attempt at correct restoration. Among these is the degree of transparency. Some old oil-based house paints tend to be slightly transparent not only because of *pentimento* (that is, the increase in transparency resulting from a rise in the refractive index of the aging oil) but also because of the use of chalk as an extender, as was done in the original paints of the Otis House. Having an index of refraction close to that of oil, chalk admits light deeply into a paint film, so that when the light is reflected from within the paint it gives the impression that the paint is a material, having thickness, rather than simply being a color.

One pleasing appearance aspect of most old house paints is a certain liveliness imparted by particles or agglomerates of pigment large enough to be seen without magnification. While large particle size and imperfect dispersion of particles drastically reduce tinctorial strength, these factors are said to make a pigment more light stable, perhaps because the material in the interior of a large particle or agglomerate is partially protected from light or from chemical interaction with surrounding materials.[12]

Poor dispersion of pigments, which was common in many old paints, can cause a pleasing variation in color. The action of brushing often increases the dispersion and, thus, changes the color, according to the amount of brushing done in each location. Streaks caused by the initial brushing can be partially blended together by a final "cross-brushing" at right angles to the first brushing. The use of poorly dispersed pigments in restoration reduces the control over color reproduction but probably increases the accuracy of the overall effect.

Glazes and Verdigris

As important as paints themselves are glazes. A glaze may be simply a thin coat of oil or resin, or both, applied over an interior paint with a brush or rag after the paint has dried; it may be clear or it may contain a low pigment-volume concentration of colorant. (The pigment-volume concentration is the percentage of pigment, by volume, in the paint, excluding volatile thinners or solvents.) Glazing was popular in New England during the 18th and early 19th centuries. Glazes give paints some protection from light, air, dirt, smoke and abrasion; they greatly retard blanching. They impart glossiness and deepen the color by reducing diffuse reflections of incident white light from the paint surface. In addition to documentary study, the scientific examination of glazes and the determination of typical pigment-volume concentrations of old paints would help answer questions concerning the degree and types of gloss common in different periods. The pigment-volume concentration of an old paint may possibly be determined by a carbon and hydrogen analysis or by centrifuging solids out of dissolved paint samples. Personal, informal observations of old paints in New England buildings suggest that after about 1820, the oil content in most interior paints was reduced, glazes were not used as frequently and, as a result, there was less yellowing of interior paints.

One aspect of glazing that should be extensively studied is the use in glazes of transparent pigments, some of which may not be particularly light fast.[13] One of the most popular pigments, used in both paints and glazes, was verdigris. Some old formulas call for the use of balsam or rosin mediums to preserve verdigris.[14] Balsams are soft oleoresins and are said to be more impermeable to air and moisture than are oils or hard resins; thus, they are reputed to give special protection to unstable pigments.[15] Verdigris can react with resin, oil or protein mediums to produce transparent green resinates, oleates or proteinates. Any of these may be applied as a continuous film, and the resinates can be dried, broken up and used as granular pigment.[16] Although many paints and glazes containing verdigris have turned almost brown, I have seen three examples that have been protected from light and still exhibit the brilliant, lucid quality for which this pigment was noted. A transparent verdigris glaze over a reflecting light blue or green ground could have produced a striking interaction of ground and glaze colors, a perceptible depth of color and an appearance of light coming from within.

It is even more difficult to determine the original appearance of old glazes than of old paints, since the proportion of medium to pigment is much higher in glazes. Oil and resin mediums are complex organic substances and deteriorate in elaborate ways. While oils sometimes bleach in the light, resins more often yellow, confounding one's attempt to bleach a resinous glaze with light. There is no reason why the advanced technology of fine arts conservation could not be applied to the examination of old house paints and glazes, if only for the purposes of scholarship and quite apart from restorationists' needs. If further study leads to the discovery of many bright colors and rich visual effects, we may perceive a closer relationship between early American decorations and the opulent styles of England.

PROBLEMS IN THE PRESERVATION OF OLD PAINTS

The SPNEA is more concerned with the preservation of old paints than with their reproduction, since it has recently adopted a policy of leaving unchanged its newly acquired buildings. Of the utmost value are those few rooms that have not been repainted since the original date of construction or a later date still far removed into the past. But even in recently painted rooms, all the successive hidden paint layers form an irreplaceable record of changing color tastes.

Paint samples can be removed from a building and either stored at low temperature in the dark or sealed in glass tubes filled with prepurified nitrogen or an inert gas.[17] Nonetheless, the removal and storage of samples does not obviate the need to preserve a paint in situ. Many characteristics of an old paint layer, such as its brush marks, its varied discolorations and any decorative designs, must be studied by looking at many samples, large and small, in places that have been subject to different conditions.

Adhesion

The preservation of exterior paints presents massive problems. Fine arts conservators might help preservationists determine whether there is any more that can be done beyond obvious conservation measures. Clearly, water must not be allowed to penetrate into exterior woodwork, since it will swell the wood and break the bond between the wood and the paint. In general, a new exterior paint should be of a type that weathers away with time, so that a building does not accumulate thick, inflexible scales of paint that crack and peel off easily, taking all early layers with them.

The stabilization of temperature and humidity may benefit interior paints immensely by preventing the wood and plaster from alternately expanding and contracting, but the problem seems imperfectly solved with respect to interior surfaces of exterior walls.

Behind these surfaces are brick walls or stud spaces that defy easy climatic control. The introduction of any vapor barriers or insulation in these walls so disrupts the early construction and presents such hazards of moisture accumulation that it is not looked upon favorably by many preservationists and should be done only after scientific study searching far beyond the requirements of ordinary good building practice indicates such action is advisable.

Reattachment and Inpainting

In the hall of the Otis House, the SPNEA was able to preserve an original plaster skim coat that was peeling off of the rough plaster, along with all successive paint layers. This was accomplished by drilling small holes and injecting glue behind the skim coat. The method appears to have worked, but difficulties were lessened by the fact that the intention had been from the outset to repaint the surface after reattaching the plaster. In several buildings, the SPNEA is now confronted with the peeling of painted decorative patterns too valuable to be overpainted or defaced by the method of reattachment.

In cases where thick paint accumulations are peeling off, reattachment is only part of the problem: It must be determined what compounds are best for filling and smoothing rough holes left where paint has peeled off and has been lost. Where areas are to be inpainted selectively, the new paint must blend well with the old, while remaining distinguishable from it to some degree. The inpainting of decorative designs requires skills now quite rare.

New laws complicate the problem by requiring the removal or overpainting of lead paints and by forbidding their use in dwellings. Perhaps preservationists can secure legal exceptions where there is no danger to children and elsewhere can use a mixture of other pigments and extenders simulating white lead.

Protection from Light

Where valuable interior paints are still exposed to view, they may be severely threatened by light. Shutters or blinds can be closed when a building is not on display, and windows can be coated or double-glazed with ultraviolet-absorbing material. Light is probably more damaging to old paints than the darkness that results from keeping shutters closed.

Isolating Varnish

One major problem in preserving paints is minimizing bad effects of overpainting. In many cases, buildings that still exhibit interesting old interior paints are owned by people who refuse to live with the old colors and insist on repainting. Even when the top paint coat does not have great value, repeated overpainting obscures architectural detail; this hastens the day when someone may want to remove the paint and, in doing so, may destroy even the earliest layers.

Clearly, a practical isolating varnish would be of great value for protecting old paint from contamination by new paint and to permit the future removal of accumulated new paint without disturbing the old. Ideally, this varnish should be insoluble in the solvent used to remove the layers over it but easily soluble in water or some other solvent to which the old layers beneath are immune. A variety of materials suggest themselves, such as hide glue, some methacrylates or perhaps two-coat combinations of such materials. A varnish that serves this purpose well in the case of pictures (that is, easel paintings) must be tested for its practicality in buildings and in the hands of amateurs. To these ends, several special features are desirable in an isolating varnish:

1. Since it will be applied to large, poorly ventilated areas, the varnish and its solvents must not give off highly toxic vapors.
2. If water soluble, the varnish should not be so much so as to lose adhesion because of water vapor migration in the walls of old houses.
3. The varnish's solubility must be so firmly defined as to permit safe, selective paint removal by unskilled workmen.
4. The varnish's solubility must not decrease significantly with time.

Varnish for General Protection

All the previously outlined features needed in an isolating varnish are also required in a varnish to protect old paints from abrasion and pollution and to retard oxidative deterioration caused by light and air. Good protective varnishes have been developed for pictures, but they do not necessarily meet the foregoing requirements for use over valuable early house paints. Most particularly, they may tend gradually to become less soluble in the presence of light and air, through oxidation if not through the cross-linking of polymeric chains.[18] While the aging varnish on a valuable picture can be removed and renewed by a skilled conservator before it becomes too resistant to removal, removal is less likely to be practical with buildings, where painted areas are much larger and budgets proportionally smaller. Perhaps a safe varnish for this purpose does not yet exist.

Because of these problems in paint restoration and preservation, architectural historians desperately need more training in conservation science and more communication with fine arts conservators.

NOTES

1. Richard M. Candee, "Materials Toward a History of Housepaints: Materials and Crafts of the Housepainter in Eighteenth Century America" (M.A. thesis, Cooperstown Graduate Programs, State University of New York, 1965). Theodore Z. Penn, "Decorative and Protective Finishes, 1750–1850: Materials, Process and Craft" (M.A. thesis, University of Delaware, 1966). These two theses are excellent documentary histories of early American house painting.

2. Robert L. Feller, "Color Change in Oil Paintings," *Carnegie Magazine* 28, no. 8 (October 1954): 276–85. Dr. Feller outlines the most important reasons for color changes in paintings.

3. Nina Fletcher Little, *American Decorative Wall Painting* (New York: E. P. Dutton, 1972), pp. 5–6.

4. The best general guide for the preliminary examination of old house paints is Penelope Hartshorne Batcheler, "Paint Color Research and Restoration," *History News* 23, no. 10 (October 1968): 183–86. Also available as American Association for State and Local History Technical Leaflet 15.

5. Rutherford J. Gettens and George L. Stout, *Painting Materials: A Short Encyclopedia* (1942; reprint ed., New York: Dover Publications, Inc., 1966), p. 46.

6. H. C. A. van Beek and P. M. Heertjes, "Fading by Light of Organic Dyes on Textiles and Other Materials," *Studies in Conservation* 11, no. 3 (August 1966): 123–31. This article includes a brief discussion of relationships between absorption spectra of organic dyes and photochemical fading.

7. Ruth M. Johnston and Robert L. Feller, "Optics of Paint Films: Glazes and Chalking," *Application of Science in Examination of Works of Art, Proceedings of a Seminar: September 7–16, 1965* (Boston: Museum of Fine Arts, n.d.), pp. 86–95.

8. Ruth M. Johnston and Robert L. Feller, "The Use of Differential Spectral Curve Analysis in the Study of Museum Objects," *Dyestuffs* 44, no. 9 (December 1963): 277–86.

9. Norman Brommelle, "Colour and Conservation," *Studies in Conservation* 2, no. 2 (October 1955): 76–85. Mr. Brommelle discusses the perception, measurement and matching of colors. Eugene Allen, "Analytical Color Matching," *Journal of Paint Technology* 39, no. 509 (June 1967): 368–76. Dr. Allen explains instrumental methods for color matching both when the original pigments can be duplicated and when they cannot.

10. Ruth M. Johnston, "Spectrophotometry for the Analysis and Description of Color," *Journal of Paint Technology* 39, no. 509 (June 1967): 346–54. Miss Johnston mentions various conditions that affect color matches.

11. Candee, "History of Housepaints," pp. 42–43.

12. The state of aggregation of organic dyes is known to have an appreciable effect on their fastness to light. See van Beek and Heertjes, "Fading of Organic Dyes," p. 130.

13. Little, *Decorative Wall Painting*. pp. 5–6.

14. P. F. Tingry, *The Painter's and Colourman's Complete Guide*, 1st American edition from the 3rd London edition (Philadelphia: E. L. Carey and A. Hart, 1831), p. 73.

15. Arthur P. Laurie, *The Painter's Methods and Materials* (1926; reprint ed., New York: Dover Publications, Inc., 1967), pp. 45–46, 165.

16. Hermann Kühn, "Verdigris and Copper Resinate," Identification of the Materials of Painting Series, monograph no. 6, *Studies in Conservation* 15, no. 1 (February 1970): 12–36.

17. Sam J. Huey, "Low Temperature Storage of Color Standards Panels," *Color Engineering* 3, no. 5 (September–October 1965): 24–27. Mr. Huey favors storage of samples at low temperatures rather than in inert gas atmospheres.

18. Robert L. Feller, Nathan Stolow and Elizabeth H. Jones, *On Picture Varnishes and Their Solvents*, rev. ed. (Cleveland, Ohio: Press of Case Western Reserve University, 1971), pp. 154–64.

THE DETERIORATION OF ORGANIC SUBSTANCES AND THE ANALYSIS OF PAINTS AND VARNISHES

ROBERT L. FELLER

The deterioration and preservation of inorganic substances and metals have been primary topics of discussion in many of the papers given at this conference. Perhaps it is not without significance that wood, an organic substance, was the first material discussed. Composed principally of carbon, hydrogen and oxygen, organic construction materials tend to deteriorate more readily than inorganic ones through biological attack, fire or slow oxidation at room temperature. The deterioration of organic substances through their reaction with the practically unlimited supply of oxygen in the atmosphere is a fundamental consideration of preservation science. For this reason, a few words should be devoted to the general character of oxidative deterioration.

FUNDAMENTALS OF OXIDATIVE DETERIORATION

It has often been said that paints and varnishes begin to deteriorate from the day they are applied. The reaction of such organic substances with oxygen generally takes place through the formation of hydroperoxides. Thanks to the pioneering work of J. L. Bolland in the late 1940s and to the work of numerous organic and polymer chemists in more recent years, a great deal is known about the formation, reaction and decomposition of organic peroxides and hydroperoxides.[1] When the formation of hydroperoxides is involved, one of the chief characteristics of the oxidation

Robert L. Feller is a senior fellow of the National Gallery of Art Research Project at Carnegie-Mellon University, Pittsburgh, Pa.

of organic substances is that the rate of oxygen consumption is generally observed to increase with time. So striking is this behavior that it has been given the name *autoxidation*. Typical curves for the consumption of oxygen during autoxidation are shown in figure 1.

Autoxidation characteristically takes place in the absence of light; it is the result of (1) the general thermal agitation of atoms and molecules in organic compounds and (2) the fundamental chemical potential of these atoms and molecules to combine with oxygen, leading chiefly to the formation of organic hydroperoxides. Light can serve as an initiator or activator of the chain of chemical events that leads to hydroperoxide formation; ions of such metals as cobalt and iron (known as *transition elements* or *transition metals*) can act as catalysts to increase the rate of the initiation reaction. Thus, exposure to light and to transition-metal ions tends to shorten the time required to reach the maximum, or so-called steady-state, rate of oxygen consumption. In most cases, light and such metal-ion catalysts do not alter the fundamental

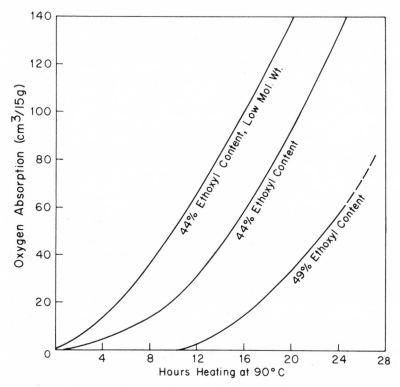

FIGURE 1. *Absorption of oxygen by ethyl cellulose at 90°C. Data source: L. F. McBurney, "Oxidative Stability of Cellulose Derivatives,"* Industrial and Engineering Chemistry *41, no. 6 (June 1949): 1251-56.*

288

propagation reactions in deterioration, only the rate of their initiation.

As already mentioned, one of the principal features of autoxidation is that the reaction of an organic substance with oxygen usually begins very slowly at first, increasing in rate until a maximum rate is achieved, then generally decreasing as readily oxidizable sites within molecules are depleted. The rise in the oxidation rate is frequently so pronounced that investigators speak of an *induction time* to designate the initial period in which little seems to be occurring. Data on the weight gain (oxidation) of dammar varnish prepared with xylene illustrate the principal stages described: induction time, rapid rise to a maximum rate and tapering off (fig. 2).

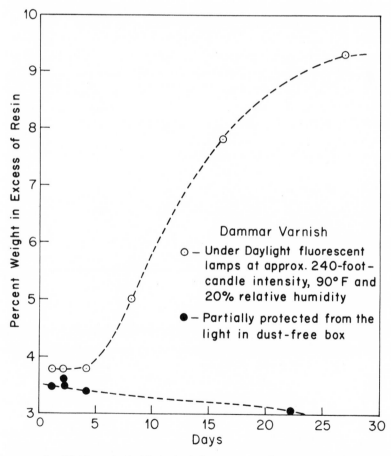

FIGURE 2. *Weight gain (oxidation) of dammar varnish prepared with xylene. Data source: Robert L. Feller, "A Note on the Exposure of Dammar and Mastic Varnishes to Fluorescent Lamps,"* Bulletin of the American Group—IIC 4, no. 2 *(April 1964): 12-14.*

Is there indeed an induction time to be observed in the deterioration of paints, varnishes and textiles? Consider the common phenomenon of fading: S. M. Jaeckel, C. D. Ward and D. M. Hutchings investigated the color change of British blue-wool fading standards up to Standard No. 6; their data indicate that an induction time definitely occurs, after which the rate of fading becomes appreciable (fig. 3). My own observations following the exposure of these standards on the wall of a daylighted gallery suggest that Standard No. 3 experienced an induction time of two to four years before it began to fade significantly, whereas the more fugitive dye in Standard No. 2 began to fade significantly after only six to nine months.[2]

An induction time is often observed in the discoloration of protective coatings; one author has even given this phenomenon the formal name used by photographic chemists, *inertia*.[3] Figure 4 shows a dramatic rise in the embrittlement of polyethylene exposed outdoors. Figure 5 reveals that there was an induction time of 11 to 12 years before the formation of insoluble matter (due to cross-linking) in certain types of acrylic varnishes exposed on the wall of the Fogg Art Museum laboratory, Cambridge, Mass. These examples demonstrate that the phenomenon of induction time can frequently be observed in a variety of materials and in measurements of a variety of properties.

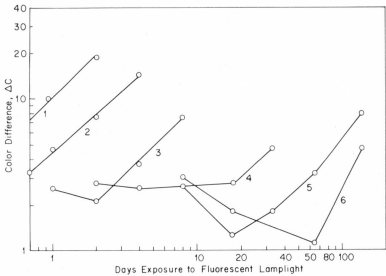

FIGURE 3. *Color change of BS1006: 1971 blue-wool fading standards vs. time of exposure to warm-white fluorescent lamps. Data source: S. M. Jaeckel, C. D. Ward and D. M. Hutchings, "Variation in Assessment of Light Fastness and on Rates of Fading and Spacing of the Blue Standards,"* Journal of the Society of Dyers and Colourists *79, no. 12 (December 1963): 702-22.*

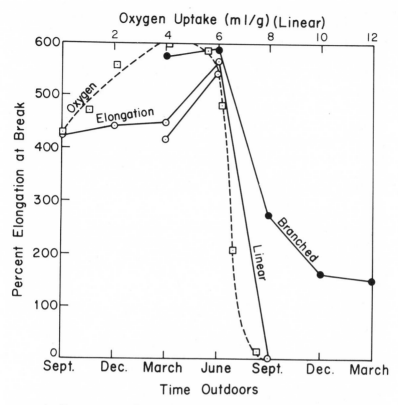

FIGURE 4. *Deterioration of polyethylene exposed outdoors compared with oxygen consumption. Data source: F. H. Winslow and W. L. Hawkins, "Some Weathering Characteristics of Plastics," in* Weatherability of Plastic Materials, *ed. M. R. Kamal (New York: Interscience, 1967), pp. 32-33. These authors cite R. A. Kinmouth's data of oxygen uptake and G. R. Cotton and W. Sacks' data on the elongation of the break.*

Not all oxidation or deterioration processes proceed by the mechanism of autoxidation. Nevertheless, it is profitable to look for evidence of an induction time or for possible reasons for its absence or negligible contribution in the life history of any particular material. For example, according to Milton Harris' and D. A. Jessup's data on the photochemical deterioration of silk, there is a definite induction time associated with the loss of tensile strength in silk cloth under alkaline conditions, but this induction period apparently disappears when silk cloth is exposed under acidic conditions (fig. 6). In laboratory tests, an induction time often becomes appreciable when the temperature of the experiment is lowered (although it may not be noticeable at higher temperatures).

Certain aspects of deterioration may be better understood if an effort is made first to determine whether a particular material

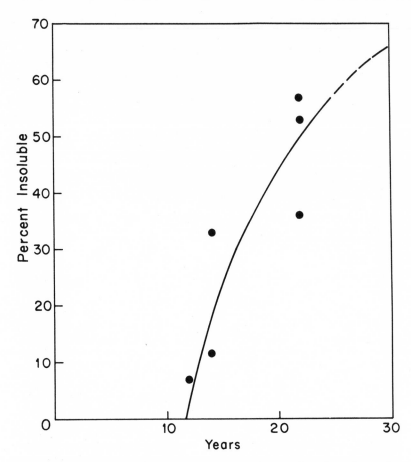

FIGURE 5. *Insoluble matter found in n-butyl and isoamyl methacrylate polymers exposed on a well-illuminated wall of the Fogg Art Museum laboratory. Data source: Robert L. Feller, Nathan Stolow and Elizabeth H. Jones, On Picture Varnishes and Their Solvents, rev. ed. (Cleveland, Ohio: Press of Case Western Reserve University, 1971), p. 159.*

tends to undergo autoxidation. Should it be found that autoxidation occurs, it may be possible to determine at any given point in a material's life history whether it is in the induction, the steady-state or the declining-rate state with respect to its reaction with oxygen. Better preventive methods may be developed if investigators can determine whether they are attempting to influence chemical reactions associated with the initiation, propagation or termination phases of hydroperoxide formation or the induction, steady-state or declining-rate stages of oxidation.

The loss of solubility in certain types of acrylic thermoplastic resins has been considered in these particular terms. The National Gallery of Art Research Project has investigated factors that influence the initiation of the cross-linking phenomenon and has re-

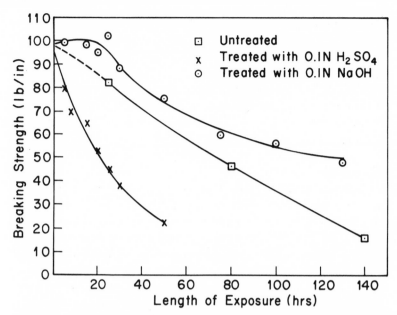

FIGURE 6. *Effect of light on the breaking strength of silk cloth. Data source: Milton Harris and D. A. Jessup, "The Effect of pH on the Photochemical Decomposition of Silk,"* Journal of Research, National Bureau of Standards 7, no. 6 *(December 1931): 1179-84.*

cently succeeded in increasing the induction time from 15 to 20 times the normal amount. In view of the normal, or uninhibited, induction time shown in figure 5 (11 years), this development, still in the experimental state, promises to be of considerable significance.

The foregoing remarks refer primarily to basic principles and suggest practical methods of preserving paints and varnishes only in the most general terms, such as keeping temperature and illumination at low levels in order to prolong the induction time and to retard the overall rate of deterioration as much as possible. I have reviewed characteristics of autoxidation in this paper for the same reason that I discussed principles of photochemical deterioration and heating effects of incandescent lamps in earlier papers: Significant developments in the future will depend upon a firm understanding of such basic principles of chemistry and physics.[4]

While investigations of basic reasons for deterioration are in progress, it is also profitable to consider the present internal evidence: What can the analysis of aged coatings reveal about their original character and the changes that they have undergone?

ANALYSIS OF PAINTS AND VARNISHES

Old paints and varnishes are analyzed in the course of historic preservation projects for two principal reasons: first, to help reproduce the original appearance of a room or building as accurately as possible and, second, to establish historical facts concerning materials and painting techniques of another day. It is of primary importance to learn what original materials were; otherwise, there is little hope for understanding or recreating the original appearance.

Analytical data can be used to reproduce original materials, but the exact replacement of materials may not always be the best or necessary course of action. For example, barytes (pigment based on natural barium sulfate) was widely used in house paints in the latter half of the 19th century, although there seems to be no compelling reason to employ it in paint today. Undoubtedly, many instances must occur in historic buildings where the use of durable modern vehicles and pigments is appropriate and desirable.

Research is needed to establish historical facts concerning decorative and protective coatings, both by analyzing the materials themselves and by studying the literature of the period. The foundation of an adequate bibliography has been made by Richard M. Candee, Teresa O. Green and Theodore Z. Penn.[5] Architectural historians will do well to acquire some of the neglected paint and varnish textbooks of the period from about 1868 to World War I while they are still available in the used-book market.[6]

Although historical research is needed, there is an even greater need for investigation of old paint specimens. The architectural historian is more fortunate than the analyst who must investigate pigments in fine paintings, for the former usually has the opportunity to obtain much larger samples. In view of the fact that fairly large samples can be removed from structures for leisurely study, it is an act of considerable negligence if those who have this opportunity to obtain much larger samples. In view of the fact that fairly that can be done is to set aside samples for later investigation.

Pigments

How does one learn about pigments? Rutherford J. Gettens' and George L. Stout's 32–year–old handbook on painting materials, now available in paperback, is a *must* on every preservationist's bookshelf.[7] Rosamund D. Harley's book on artists' pigments used from 1600 to 1835 is also recommended; this book gives a detailed description of materials used in that period in England.[8] Another valuable publication is George H. Hurst's book, which, beginning in 1892, went through many editions until World War I.[9] Candee's review, mentioned previously, is readily available as a reprint. These four publications give the basic information regarding the kinds of pigment one may expect to find in historic buildings.

To analyze a paint, it is recommended that a cross–section be examined, that pigments in the specific layer (or layers) of interest be isolated and examined with a microscope capable of from 100 to 1,000 times magnification and that an emission spectrographic analysis be made. An X–ray diffraction analysis can also be useful, particularly if one or two pigments predominate. If lead white and chalk are detected, they may be dissolved with mild acids and remaining acid–insoluble pigments identified.

The job of characterizing pigments in a paint is not always an easy matter, although it seems to be popular to give the impression that it is. It is perhaps simple enough to identify major pigments present, but pigments of subtle composition, such as copper resinate, sienna or Van Dyke brown, can easily be overlooked or incompletely identified. General methods of analysis and some possible pitfalls have been outlined elsewhere.[10]

Samples can be sent to commercial laboratories for X–ray diffraction and emission spectrographic analyses. However, commercial laboratories are not always fully aware of the historian's special problems. For this reason, it is imperative to have every sample examined under a microscope and to have the report from the analytical laboratory evaluated by someone experienced in the analysis of paints. Otherwise, important glazes and traces of pigmentation may be overlooked.

The cost of analysis, both in terms of man–hours and technical services, is significant and should be fully recognized.[11] Inspection, sampling and proper documentation of a paint specimen can take many hours. An analysis is a highly specialized professional service, the cost of which is always borne by someone even though the historian or preservationist may have the service donated by a generous and enthusiastic scientist colleague. Interpretation of results also requires time, additional study and, frequently, further sampling and analyses.

Color

To record the color of an old paint, it is desirable to ascertain the spectrophotometric curve of the reflectance at individual wavelengths of light, rather than simply to obtain a colorimetric measurement in terms of tristimulus values.[12] An abridged spectrophotometric curve, as well as a colorimetric measurement, may be obtained with a Color Eye, a portable instrument designed to be placed flush against a large flat surface such as a wall.[13] Older instruments can be modified to measure the spectrophotometric reflectance curve for an area of paint no greater than 3/16 inch in diameter by means of the Small Area View (popularly known as SAV) modification.

The investigator must be aware of what it means to seek an exact spectrophotometric match of a particular paint (which can be made only if identical pigments are used) and what it means to be satisfied with a reasonably close (or even perfect) colorimetric match using different pigments, that is, a *metameric match*.[14]

The objective of matching the original color appears to be limited and straightforward, yet it poses a number of problems that perhaps are only now being somewhat better appreciated. How does one decide what was the true color of a paint that has been affected by the discoloration of the original vehicle and pigments (e.g., indigo tends to fade to a shade that is not exactly the same as fresh indigo)?

A color-measuring instrument does not yield much information about the appearance that a paint may have had when originally applied, because color is only one aspect of appearance. In addition to the problems already mentioned, such as the yellowing of the vehicle or the fading of organic pigments, there may also be subtle changes in translucency with time, such as that associated with the phenomenon called *pentimento* in the study of easel painting. There is also the question of gloss and the use of glazes. Old painted surfaces are likely to be considerably altered from their original appearance. How much is known about the degree of mattness sought in historic finishes or about the use of glazes (that is, how frequently were transparent or translucent colored coatings employed)?

Vehicles

Vehicles tend to be highly complex. Partially because of this fact, analyses of old drying–oil and heat–processed resin–oil vehicles have revealed less information to researchers than the technical examination of pigments. Spirit varnishes can be identified reasonably well by infrared analysis, although one must be alert to changes in their spectra caused by age.

A simple technique to use in the study of the vehicle in a particular paint is to make a cross-section of the paint, perhaps merely by slicing diagonally through it in situ.[15] If this section is then examined for fluorescence under long–wave ultraviolet radiation, it can sometimes quickly be determined whether there are marked differences in the character of various layers. If the cross–section is embedded (and perhaps even if the exposed paint layers are examined in situ), the staining technique described by Meryl Johnson and Elisabeth Packard can be used to determine whether layers are oil or proteinaceous.[16]

As already mentioned, infrared spectrophotometry is useful for analyzing soluble resins found in spirit varnishes. (It is also useful in identifying pigments, although it was not widely employed for this purpose until recent years.)[17] However, infrared spectrophotometry is not particularly helpful in the characterization of oil varnishes or proteinaceous materials, except to identify them as falling into one or the other class. On the other hand, constituents of oils, tempera, glue, casein, water–soluble gums and organic-soluble resins can be characterized with considerable success by means of thin-layer chromatography. This method is not expensive, but it does require training and experience.[18]

Perhaps the most promising way to characterize a vehicle is by gas chromatography. Nathan Stolow employed this method in the identification of drying–oil vehicles with considerable success.[19] However, if the coating is old, it may be difficult to identify exactly what kind of oil is involved. John S. Mills has described the use of gas chromatography to identify proteinaceous vehicles as well as drying–oil types.[20] Ion–exchange chromatography has been applied as a means of identifying proteinaceous vehicles by Sheldon Keck and Theodore Peters, Jr.[21] *Pyrolysis* (that is, the destructive vaporization of the sample) can also be used in conjunction with gas chromatography to provide characteristic "fingerprints" of organic coatings. These advanced analytical methods are expensive, requiring highly specialized training and equipment.

CONCLUSION

The gross (or more obvious) effects of light and heat and of changes in temperature and humidity on the deterioration of organic materials are well known. As a consequence, certain general precautions can be suggested in order to prolong the useful life of paints, varnishes, paper and textiles. However, further investigation into fundamental chemical processes of deterioration is needed. Significant progress can be made in understanding causes of deterioration and in developing new means of retardation if problems are analyzed in terms of the initiation, propagation and termination phases of hydroperoxide formation or other chain processes of deterioration and also in terms of the induction time, steady-state or declining-rate stages of oxidation.

The conservation scientist has at his disposal sophisticated analytical tools through which much can be learned about paints and varnishes used in the past. The comparatively generous samples that can be obtained from historic structures present an unusual opportunity that should not be lost through neglect or indifference.

The least that can be done is to document and set aside samples for future study.

There is, at the present time, no simple handbook that tells one how to analyze small specimens of paint and varnish other than the four-page pamphlet by Penelope Hartshorne Batcheler.[22] With the aid of a grant from the National Foundation on the Arts, the National Gallery of Art Research Project is planning to cooperate with Rutherford J. Gettens in completing a model handbook on the analysis of pigments that will include monographs on about 10 principal pigments.[23] The publication is intended to evolve from seven monographs published under the general editorship of Gettens and the auspices of the International Institute for Conservation of Historic and Artistic Works, London.[24] It is hoped that this three-year project will produce the first of a series of handbooks, for there are about 60 pigments that eventually should be covered.

The technical analysis of paints and varnishes on historic architecture is practically an untouched field of investigation. There is perhaps no better way to learn than simply to begin.

NOTES

1. Gerald Scott, *Atmospheric Oxidation and Antioxidants* (New York: Elsevier Publishing Co., 1965).

2. Robert L. Feller, "Problems in Reflectance Spectrophotometry," in *1967 London Conference on Museum Climatology*, ed. G. Thomson (London: International Institute for Conservation of Artistic and Historic Works, 1968), pp. 257–69.

3. R. C. Hirt, R. G. Schmidt and W. L. Dutton, "Solarization Studies on Polyester Films Using a Heliostat-Spectrometer," *Solar Energy* 3 (April 1959): 19–22.

4. Robert L. Feller, "The Deteriorating Effect of Light on Museum Objects: Principles of Photochemistry, The Effect on Varnishes and Paint Vehicles and on Paper," Technical Supplement, *Museum News* 42, no. 3 (June 1964): i-viii; id., "Control of Deteriorating Effects of Light on Museum Objects: Heating Effects of Illumination by Incandescent Lamps," Technical Supplement, *Museum News* 46, no. 9 (May 1968): 39–47.

5. Richard M. Candee, *House Paints in Colonial America* (New York: Chromatic Publishing Co., 1967). Also see Teresa O. Green, "The Birth of the American Paint Industry" (M.A. thesis, University of Delaware, 1965) and Theodore Z. Penn, "Decorative and Protective Finishes, 1750–1850: Materials, Process and Craft" (M.A. thesis, University of Delaware, 1966).

6. Robert L. Feller, "Scientific Examination of Artistic and Decorative Colorants," *Journal of Paint Technology* 44, no. 566 (March 1972): 51–58.

7. Rutherford J. Gettens and George L. Stout, *Painting Materials: A Short Encyclopedia* (1942; reprint ed., New York: Dover Publications, Inc., 1966).

8. Rosamund D. Harley, *Artists' Pigments c. 1600–1835* (London: Butterworths, 1970).

9. George H. Hurst, *Painters' Colours, Oils and Varnishes*, 2d ed. (London: C. Griffin and Co., 1896); later editions coauthored with Noel Heaton.

10. Robert L. Feller, "Analysis of Pigments," in *American Painting to 1776: A Reappraisal*, ed. Ian M. Quimby (Charlottesville: University Press of Virginia, 1971), pp. 327–49.

11. Feller, "Analysis of Pigments," p. 341.

12. Feller, "Reflectance Spectrophotometry," p. 257.

13. Color Eye is a product of the Kollmorgen Corporation, Attleboro, Mass.

14. Feller, "Reflectance Spectrophotometry," p. 257. Also see Ruth M. Johnston, "Spectrophotometry for the Analysis and Description of Color," *Journal of Paint Technology* 39, no. 509 (June 1967): 346–54.

15. Joyce Plesters, "Cross-sections and Chemical Analysis of Paint Samples," *Studies in Conservation* 2, no. 3 (April 1956): 110–57. Also see Penelope Hartshorne Batcheler, "Paint Color Research and Restoration," *History News* 23, no. 10 (October 1968): 183–86. Also available as American Association for State and Local History Technical Leaflet 15.

16. Meryl Johnson and Elisabeth Packard, "Methods Used for the Identification of Binding Media in Italian Paintings of the Fifteenth and Sixteenth Centuries," *Studies in Conservation* 16, no. 4 (November 1971): 145–64.

17. Infrared Spectroscopy Committee of the Chicago Society for Paint Technology, *Infrared Spectroscopy; Its Use in the Coatings Industry* (Philadelphia: Federation of Societies for Paint Technology, 1969).

18. Françoise Flieder, "Mise au point des techniques d'identification des pigments et des liants inclus dans la couche picturale des enluminures de manuscrits," *Studies in Conservation* 13, no. 2 (May 1968): 49–86.

19. Robert L. Feller, Nathan Stolow and Elizabeth H. Jones, *On Picture Varnishes and Their Solvents*, rev. ed. (Cleveland, Ohio: Press of Case Western Reserve University, 1971), pp. 73–88.

20. John S. Mills, "The Gas Chromatographic Examination of Paint Media: Part I—Fatty Acid Composition and Identification of Dried Oil Films," *Studies in Conservation* 11, no. 2 (May 1966): 92–107.

21. Sheldon Keck and Theodore Peters, Jr., "Identification of Protein-Containing Paint Media by Quantitative Amino Acid Analysis," *Studies in Conservation* 14, no. 2 (May 1969): 75–82. Useful references to prior publications may be found here.

22. Batcheler, *Paint Color Research*.

23. Rutherford J. Gettens, "Proposal for a Handbook on the Analysis of Material of Paintings," in *Recent Advances in Conservation*, ed. G. Thomson (London: Butterworths, 1963), pp. 26–28.

24. Rutherford J. Gettens, Robert L. Feller and W. T. Chase, "Vermilion and Cinnabar," *Studies in Conservation* 17, no. 2 (May 1972): 45–69. References to the previous six monographs of the pigment series appear at the end of this publication.

COMMENTARY

PENELOPE HARTSHORNE BATCHELER

I must preface my comments on the papers about paints and varnishes by Morgan W. Phillips and Robert L. Feller by describing my relationship to this subject. As one of the restoration architects faced with having to understand the rather complex buildings at Independence National Historical Park in Philadelphia, Pa., I found that the study of paints in the buildings was not only a necessary research task, but also a valuable approach to comprehending the evolution of the buildings' structural changes.

In 1959, I called for help with my paint research from the then resident conservator of Independence National Historical Park, Anne F. Clapp, who is now at the Henry Francis du Pont Winterthur Museum laboratory. From Ms. Clapp's counsel and my instinct, we developed a few paint research procedures. In 1961, I wrote down these procedures for the benefit of architects and preservationists who participated in a conference on restoration techniques conducted by Charles E. Peterson. This do-it-yourself guide to paint research was later published by the American Association for State and Local History in its technical leaflet series. The fact that there has been some demand for the leaflet illustrates the need for such information.

If the purpose of this conference is to improve the quality of preservation and restoration of buildings and monuments, then in effect its purpose is to help architects and preservationists do

---

Penelope Hartshorne Batcheler is a restoration architect with the National Park Service, working at Independence National Historical Park, Philadelphia, Pa.

their jobs. My comments on the papers about paints and varnishes are aimed in this direction also.

Like Lee H. Nelson, George L. Wrenn and others, I have some concern for the busy architect who consults with a mechanical engineer one minute, talks with a client or administrator about budget estimates the next minute and then turns to discuss details of a ramp and twist stairway with a draftsman. This harried soul needs a complete, technically sound handbook for the restoration and preservation of old architectural paints.

Mr. Phillips' and Dr. Feller's papers discuss effects of paint deterioration, difficulties of color interpretation and the use of scientific paint analysis processes, which have been developed primarily for the field of fine arts conservation. I am not qualified to comment on these papers' technical contents, but I can comment on the implications for architects involved in preservation projects. It is clear to me that architects do not have the training, equipment or time to use the analytical processes described in these papers for the interpretation of old house paints. I was pleased to learn of the forthcoming pigment analysis handbook to be edited by Rutherford J. Gettens, but the handbook will be principally of value to conservation scientists.

What restoration architects need most are guidelines that will define logical and economical limits of the paint research an architect should attempt to conduct and that will establish the point at which a conservation scientist should be consulted. Architects need to know what conservation scientists can do, what results to expect, how valuable these results will be and how much such services will cost. An architect's main concern is how much paint analysis (at what cost) is justified for a particular building, considering the building's intended function and the quality of the maintenance it will receive.

The real achievement of this conference is in bringing together conservation scientists and practicing preservationists. As a restoration architect, I am pleased to know that conservation scientists are interested in the subject of old paints in historic architecture. Mr. Phillips and I agree that conservation scientists should be given an opportunity to study the behavior and components of old house paints in order to provide restoration architects with needed shortcuts for the restoration and reproduction of old paint colors.

It is to be hoped that this conference also will lead to the establishment of better lines of communication between these two disciplines. I propose that one of the results of this improved communication between conservation scientists and practicing preservationists be a handbook on historical paints. Dr. Feller writes, to my delight, that there is no better way to learn about paints and varnishes in historic buildings than simply to begin investigating the subject. Perhaps a team representing several disciplines could be organized for the purpose of developing the proposed handbook.

The handbook, in addition to serving as a guide to methods of research and color interpretation, should discuss methods of mixing and matching paint, using materials manufactured today, and procedures for maintaining paint in historic buildings. Therefore, the handbook team should probably include not only conservation scientists and restoration architects but also representatives of paint manufacturers' research departments and maintenance specialists from such institutions as Colonial Williamsburg.

The proposed handbook could include discussion on the following points:

1. What the study of paint layers can contribute to the understanding of a building's structural history.

2. Where architects should look for paint evidence.

3. How samples should be taken, identified, stored and used for reference or, as Dr. Feller emphasizes, stored for future research. (I have three museum cabinets full of identified samples that I have collected over 15 years; I was, therefore, more than pleased to read Dr. Feller's plea for the collection of such raw material.)

4. Basic components of old paints—what they are and how they react to light, temperature changes and time, that is, how oxidative deterioration causes fading, discoloration and embrittlement, as described by both Dr. Feller and Mr. Phillips.

5. Basic observations that architects can make concerning paint evidence and the equipment needed to make these observations: recording such surface characteristics as ropiness, glossiness and the use of glazes; determining the color sequence and which layers served as prime coats and which were finish coats; determining whether pigments were ground by hand or by machine; and determining whether the paint is oil or water based.

6. Additional analyses that can be performed by conservation scientists, the cost of such analyses and the ways in which results can be used.

7. Advantages and disadvantages of paint removal in preparation for restoration and methods to preserve original paint layers, such as by using isolating varnishes that Mr. Phillips hopes will be developed.

8. Recommended paint compositions for various needs, based on the degree of restoration accuracy wished, amount of expected

wear, quality of future maintenance and materials available from manufacturers. (Enough advice should be included to help restoration architects and other preservationists know, especially when confronted by paint salesmen, what type of reproduction paint is required.)

9. Methods to match, mix and record reproduction paint colors and formulas used; and methods of bleaching oil vehicles that have yellowed, as Mr. Phillips suggests. A discussion should be included on advantages and disadvantages of equipment, such as the Color Eye (Dr. Feller suggests this would enable architects to record old paint colors on graphs and then, for matching purposes, compare these graphs with the graphs of reproduction paints); systems such as the Munsell Color System; and techniques such as the freezing of paint samples at 0°F currently employed by Colonial Williamsburg for matching, mixing and/or recording.

10. Techniques of paint maintenance, such as washing, touch-up, the treatment of alligatored surfaces, etc.

11. A glossary and bibliography.

By making the retrieval of paint evidence an easy and familiar task for restoration architects, I am sure that the number of old paint specimens available for basic research will increase.

Arbiters of taste have always tried to prescribe colors; with proper research, we will be able to determine how quickly builders and homeowners followed these leaders of fashion.

People often telephone me saying that their houses were built in a certain year, and then ask me what colors to paint them. I respond by telling them to "ask" their houses—after all, the houses have the answers!

COMMENTARY

JAMES K. BARR

The papers of Morgan W. Phillips, Robert L. Feller and others have clearly shown how fugitive or short lived paint color is. One important reason for this is that paint vehicles and resins used in earlier times often yellowed severely; another is the rapid degradation of unstable pigments used then. Vehicles, resins and most of the unstable pigments used in the past are not used in modern architectural paints because their rather rapid reactions to light, oxygen and other substances make them undesirable for use today. Such reactions, of course, lead to changes in color, glossiness and texture, and they can even cause loss of adhesion.

Like Mr. Phillips, I do not believe that painted surfaces in many restored buildings represent the colors or glossiness of the surfaces' original paints. For example, I believe that many of the so-called Williamsburg colors do not even closely approximate the original colors used in colonial times; I am almost certain that the original colors were much brighter, less yellow and glossier.

In my judgment, it is not proper to simply obtain a direct color match between the paint used for restoration and a hidden paint layer discovered in a crevice or elsewhere in a building and determined to be the first layer. The original first layer can be expected to change color over the years even when it has been hidden from direct sunlight. An old paint's original color and glossiness can be re-created in a more scientific way, with results that more accurately represent the original finish.

James K. Barr is director of research of Pfizer, Inc., Easton, Pa.

To arrive at the actual original color, I suggest the following scheme, which, although it is somewhat technical, is well within the capabilities of modern science. This scheme is neither fool-proof nor particularly easy to use, but it can be applied success-fully to obtain more accurate results than are achieved simply by color matching.

First, determine what pigments were used in the paint whose original color and finish are to be reproduced. This can be done by subjecting a sample of the original paint to one or a combination of the following scientific analyses: X-ray diffraction, emission spectroscopy, electron or light microscope analysis and neutron activation analysis. The latter has not been used much recently, but it is quite economical, contrary to popular belief. Results of these analyses must be interpreted by a chemist familiar with pig-ments used in old paints.

Second, based on data from these analyses and the pigment-volume concentration and pigment ratios of the original paint (as determined from the sample), reconstruct a small amount of paint, using the vehicle and techniques that most likely would have been used to make the original paint. The choice of the vehicle is not particularly critical. However, it will be necessary to enlist the help of historians to make sure that pigments chosen are logical choices and that they are representative of the fashion of the period involved.

Third, apply a small amount of the reconstructed paint to a test panel that simulates the surface to be restored; then obtain a spec-trophotometric reflectance curve from the painted surface. This curve and a verbal description of the test panel's appearance, both obtained using the reconstructed paint, and data from chemical analyses of the original paint sample will be the only permanent record of what the original paint was like. The test panel itself will begin to undergo the expected color changes and will be useless as a reference in a few years. During this third part of the process, the color of the fresh, reconstructed paint should be compared with the color of the original paint sample. Obviously, if the reconstructed paint color differs greatly from the original paint sample color, analyses should be repeated to reverify the chemical composition of the reconstructed paint.

The fourth and final step is to send the reflectance curve ob-tained from the reconstructed paint to a paint manufacturer who will then match the color, using a modern paint vehicle and mod-ern stable pigments. It is often not necessary, or even desirable, to use original pigments to match the color of an old paint. There are many modern pigments that will achieve any color match desired.

Use of this four-step process will justify the choice of the color used in a restoration project, and, more important, the final color will be much closer to the original color.

DISCUSSION

Comments made by the panelists and audience during the discussion on paints and varnishes are summarized in the following paragraphs.

Reproducing old paint colors is often a major stumbling block for preservationists who are endeavoring to restore a past appearance of a house or room. The determination and reproduction of such colors are difficult for several reasons: fading; effects of pollution; the time, expense and complexity of a scientific analysis; and the general lack of knowledge about what vehicles and pigments were used and how paints were manufactured and applied.

Interwoven with the problem's practical and technical aspects are thorny philosophical questions. For example, if the goal of a restoration is to show a house or room as it was over a period of years rather than on a particular date in the past, are extensive research and expensive analyses aimed at discovering the precise original color really necessary? Would not a close match be just as satisfactory, both in terms of authenticity and economics? There is evidence that unstable elements in old paints often faded and yellowed, even when the paint was not covered in later years by other materials. Residents probably lived with the fading color for several years before repainting or otherwise covering the old paint. Therefore, the paint may have retained its original brightness for only a short time. Then, too, fading and yellowing are probably not the only sources of change in old paint. Preservationists should also consider the effects of pollution. Pollutants have almost certainly caused changes in paints, although little is now known about this matter. A real need exists for the measurement of the effects of pollutants and moisture on both old and new paints.

There are doubtless a few restorations that, because of the goals preservationists wish to achieve, should look "new," that should be painted in their original bright colors. But how should this be done? In view of the current shortage of materials that were used in old paints, should modern vehicles and pigments be used instead of traditional ones in reproduction paints? A paint that consists of a modern vehicle and pigments would be more lasting because modern ingredients are relatively stable. Such paint would, of course, require less maintenance and, therefore, be more economical than one reproduced with original materials. Also, the high standards for color matching of modern paints virtually eliminate the problem of matching color in various batches of paint. One system for measuring color differences is the McAdam units, one unit being the slightest color difference that is perceptible to the human eye. Modern paints are made to match to less than one McAdam unit. On the other hand, the use of paints formulated with original, often unstable ingredients would be more authentic. As Mr. Phillips pointed out in his paper, paints formulated with hand-ground pigments create a ropiness when applied; modern paints made with machine-ground pigments do not produce this effect. Why not paint a house or room with paint made of original materials to obtain a more correct surface effect and color, and then let it fade to show the effects of time?

If, after deciding which philosophical approach to take, a scientific analysis is deemed necessary, most preservationists face the question of cost. A thorough analysis of the paint involved in a major restoration project and the reproduction of it with original materials (either to use in repainting or to determine the correct spectrographic curve from which a modern reproduction paint may be formulated) may take two or three months. If the paint contains many pigments, the analysis may take longer. This work is neither simple nor inexpensive. A two or three-month job may cost several thousands of dollars. Such analyses require the skill of a trained technician and the use of sophisticated equipment. Necessary instruments are found in most modern laboratories, but technicians with a knowledge of old paint chemistry are difficult to find.

The expertise of a skilled, knowledgeable technician is essential because of the task's complexity. Not only does the technician have to identify the vehicle and pigments in the paint but also any impurities it contains. In addition, to reproduce an old paint color as accurately as possible, information is needed on the distribution (that is, dispersion) and size of pigments. All of these elements —the vehicle, pigments, impurities and degree of dispersion—

combine to give a paint its individual characteristics, including color.

Although the sophisticated laboratory instruments are useful, the identification of these elements can be complicated. First, a sample of the paint must be available for analysis, and it must be large enough or results may be compromised. For example, a fairly large area must be exposed to determine the pattern in a grained or marbleized paint. Such effects were often made by applying a thin coat of pigmented varnish over a light ground. Obtaining a large enough sample can be a problem if only limited areas of the original paint remain.

Also, there is now no known way of determining the original color of a vehicle. Thousands of different vehicles were used in old paints. Today, an experienced paint chemist can look at the infrared spectrum of a paint sample and make a good guess as to what vehicle was used, but this procedure is far from infallible. However, most restorers do not consider this problem to be a major one, because it is generally assumed that color is primarily a function of the pigments present. The only exception to this assumption is white paint, which is probably the most difficult kind of paint to analyze and reproduce.

Problems in identifying pigments are usually due to two facts: (1) they were often unstable and (2) they came from a number of sources and, therefore, varied greatly. This variety makes it difficult to date a paint layer by determining what pigments are in the paint. Some textbooks give dates of the first use of so-called common pigments, but these dates do not apply to all areas of the country. Thus, the compilation of a catalogue of frequently used pigments and their dates of first use would take a great deal of effort, although the information would be valuable, perhaps in authenticating museum pieces.

Hand grinding and other dispersion techniques used in the past generally resulted in a most uneven dispersion, which is difficult, if not impossible, to analyze accurately. Experienced paint chemists can, however, use an electron micrograph or light micrograph to make an estimated guess at the dispersion technique that was used and that will have to be repeated in reproducing the paint if a "perfect" match is desired.

When the initial research is completed, it should be possible to reconstruct a small amount of the original paint. This paint must, as Mr. Barr said in his commentary, be applied on the exact same materials as it is to eventually be used on, as the color and effect of a paint vary on different materials.

Detailed paint research such as that described is probably not necessary for every restoration. Intelligent guesses as to the color and type of paint used during various time periods in particular types of houses in certain areas may be based on extensive paint studies made in similar houses. A handbook, such as that suggested by Ms. Batcheler, would perhaps be useful for this purpose.

There are not only philosophical questions and difficulties in analyzing and reproducing an old paint color, but also problems in applying the reproduction paint, no matter whether it is formulated with original or modern materials. Cleaning the area to be painted is usually required, but such cleaning can leave residual oil, which can affect the color of the reproduction paint. Also, old paints did not hide the surface they covered very well. There was usually a bleeding through of the surface that produced a kind of luminous effect. If reproduction paint must be applied over later paint layers, this effect cannot be achieved.

Maintenance: The Life Expectancy of Materials and Problems of Increasing Visitor Use

ON FORMULATING NEW PARAMETERS FOR PRESERVATION POLICY

JAMES MARSTON FITCH

The international acceleration of interest in the preservation of the artistic and historic patrimony; the understanding that this patrimony must now be defined as including all sorts of sites, monuments, artifacts and landscapes—urban and rural, high–style and vernacular, historic, primitive and prehistoric; the enormous complexity of the technical problems thus raised; all of these developments require a much broader and more precise definition of both the scope and the levels of intervention that will be required for protection of this patrimony.

THE SCALE AND PROFUNDITY OF INTERVENTION

The Venice Charter of 1964, which attempted to identify the parameters of historic preservation, needs to be greatly amplified and much more precisely developed, since it is apparent that a whole spectrum of possibilities, and not merely a few simplistic alternatives, must constitute the core of a viable policy of protection of the artistic and historic patrimony of any country. Table 1 is a suggested classification of such possibilities.

It is apparent that in the modern world any of the levels of intervention listed in table 1 (or any combination of them) may be mandatory in a given situation. Of course, from a philosophical point of view, the upper parts of both scales are probably the most

James Marston Fitch is professor of architecture and director of the Restoration and Preservation of Historic Architecture Graduate Program at Columbia University, New York, N.Y.

Table 1 POSSIBILITIES FOR PROTECTING THE ARTISTIC AND HISTORIC PATRIMONY

Scale of Intervention[a]	*Profundity of Intervention*[b]
1. *Entire historic towns* Telc, Czechoslovakia Venice, Italy Williamsburg, Virginia	1. *Conservation* a. Natural features: California redwoods Rare birds and animals
2. *Historic districts* Vieux Carré, New Orleans Mala Strana, Prague Stare Miasto, Warsaw	b. Works of art: Sculpture, painting, frescoes, mosaics
3. *Historic building complexes* Regent's Park, London Lafayette Square, Washington, D.C. Kremlin Palace, Moscow	2. *Preservation* Hyde Park, New York Brighton Royal Pavilion, England Wavel Palace, Warsaw
4. *Individual historic buildings* a. In situ: Versailles, France Hampton Court, London Mount Vernon, Virginia	3. *Restoration* Independence Hall, Philadelphia Hradcany Castle, Prague Monticello, Virginia
b. Relocated on new sites: Boscobel Garrison, New York Abu Simbel, Egypt	4. *Adaptive modification* Castello Sforszeca, Milan Casa Rosa, Genoa Opera House, Warsaw Ford's Theatre, Washington, D.C.
c. Relocated in groups: Skansen, Stockholm Cooperstown Farm Museum, New York Freiland-museet, Copenhagen	5. *Structural consolidation* White House, Washington, D.C. York Minster, England Norwich Cathedral, England

5. *Building fragments—decorative arts museums*
Victoria and Albert Museum,
  London
Metropolitan Museum of Art,
  New York City
National Museum of
  Anthropology and Ethnography,
  Mexico City
	6. *Reconstitution*
	a. In situ:
	Santa Trinita Bridge, Florence
	Iwo Treasure Houses, Japan
	Illinois State Capitol, Springfield

	b. On new sites: Skansen, Stockholm Abu Simbel, Egypt London Bridge, Arizona
	7. *Reconstruction* Governor's Palace, Williamsburg Church of Jan Hus, Prague Fort Louisbourg, Canada Stoa of Attalus, Athens

	8. *Replication*
	Full-scale replica of the Parthenon,
	  Nashville, Tenn.
	Use of sculptural replicas
	  outdoors, Pisa and Florence

[a] In descending order of physical magnitude.
[b] In ascending order of severity or radicalness.

desirable. That is, since most historic architecture is in an urban setting, optimal protection is necessarily environmental or ambiental in nature. Moreover, a century's experience in both archaeology and architectural preservation indicates that the most conservative intervention is usually the wiser policy, if for no other reason than that it can be most easily rectified subsequently, if that proves necessary.

The question of the *scale* of intervention requires no extended theoretical discussion here, since what is possible in any given case will be largely determined by local exigencies. For example, it was possible to preserve the whole historic core of Williamsburg, Va., intact, whereas none of the approximately 30 buildings now at Old Bethpage Village on Long Island, N.Y., could have been saved except by moving them from their original sites to the architectural museum in Nassau County.

But the problem of the *profundity* of intervention required to save any artifact raises a host of intricate questions, ranging from the philosophical (ethical and aesthetic) to the practical (scientific and technological). All of these questions demand a great deal more theoretical attention than they have hitherto been given.

The recent policy change of the Society for the Preservation of New England Antiquities is highly significant in this respect. The curator of some 60 properties of varying dates, types and conditions, the society has until recently followed a conventional policy, varying between preservation and restoration. But under the new policy, the society will maintain all new accessions in exactly the condition in which they are received. No later and putatively less important elements will be removed; no earlier and putatively more significant elements will be restored or reconstructed. The only form of intervention will be that maintenance required to guarantee the physical integrity of the property in the exact state in which it was acquired.

OBJECTIVES OF PROTECTION, PRESERVATION

The protection of the artistic and historic patrimony may be said to have two broad objectives: (1) to preserve the cosmetic and structural integrity of the artifact against the attrition caused by environmental forces and (2) to display the artifact to the public in such a way as to minimize a second form of attrition, simple wear and tear.

The ultimate cultural objective of all preservation activities may be said to be didactic: to teach the citizen to better understand "where he came from" as a means of helping him to decide "where he ought to go." Preservation is thus fundamentally an

313

orientational device—conceptually, intellectually and even psychologically (as in the case of the consolidated ruins of Coventry Cathedral in England or the reconstructed Stare Miasto in Warsaw).

THE IMPORTANCE OF COSMETIC CONDITION

Under these circumstances, the cosmetic condition of the building to be preserved and exhibited is of critical importance. For though it is true that one experiences buildings with all one's senses, the sense of sight is of primordial significance in visiting a historic building. For preservationists, there are two aspects to this question of the cosmetic condition of a building: (1) diagnostic (i.e., as an index of its structural integrity) and (2) aesthetic and associative, as represented by "moss-covered walls," "weathered beams" or "mellowed colors." Although every element of the building will have cosmetic (external appearance) and structural (internal integrity) aspects, the two should not be confused, especially when diagnosis is concerned. For example, many baroque buildings exhibit stained and cracked stucco suggesting walls weakened by years of neglect and decay, even though they may have been carefully restored within the past year or two. This is typically the case in such cities as Prague or Cracow, where the burning of brown coal for heating produces smoke that quickly discolors stuccoed surfaces. For all their unfortunate visual consequences, such practices may continue for decades without serious damage to the stucco. On the other hand, in the case of marble and limestone, the combination of gases resulting from the burning of brown coal sets into motion a complex chemico-physical process, producing serious decay that is concealed by a surface coat of grime. This is typically the case in many Gothic structures in northern Europe. Surface cleaning may be the first stage of therapy in both cases, for aesthetic reasons in the first case and for diagnostic purposes in the latter. But the removal of the discolored surface crust on fine-scale sculpture can result in the permanent loss of irreplaceable detail, since the crust often conceals an underlayer of desiccated stone.

On the other hand, serious structural defects may display few cosmetic consequences. Wooden beams may be riddled with termites or dry rot without any external evidence. The White House, whose outdoor and indoor surfaces had always been carefully maintained, turned out to be on the verge of collapse when its structure was carefully examined in 1948. Similarly, cracks in the walls of Norwich Cathedral and York Minster were alarming only to specialists, who could tell from the location and direction of the cracks that they indicated grave structural weaknesses requiring immediate attention. Subsequent work revealed that the rubble interiors of these masonry elements (walls, buttresses, vaults) were riddled with voids caused by the desiccation and migration of the Norman cement: Thousands of gallons of cement grout had to be injected into the voids to consolidate them.

PHILOSOPHICAL ASPECTS OF COSMETIC INTERVENTION

Aside from the physical condition of the exposed surface (or of the structural member behind it), there are thorny and complex philosophical aspects of preservation-related cosmetic intervention. They deserve far more attention than they have received to date. One pivotal question is this: When the intervention (whether preservation, restoration, consolidation or reconstruction) is complete, should the building "look old" or "look new"? Should replaced elements be left to weather naturally or should they be antiqued to meld into the older tissue around them? There are competent experts on both sides of this argument. For example, in the restoration of the Collegium Maius in Cracow by the eminent Polish art historian, Carol Estreicher, all the new material was antiqued to match the original. On the other hand, when the curators of the Folkmuseet in Copenhagen must repair one of their old wooden farmhouses, they use new unpainted wood, allowing it to weather just as a peasant who lived in the house would have done.

The same problem is raised to even more critical levels by such activities as the cleaning of entire historic districts, such as the Marais district and the boulevards of Paris, or the restoration of the polychromy in many English churches. The results of such interventions are often startling, compelling many people to readjust radically their ideas of how Paris "ought" to look (i.e., blue gray, the way the Impressionists saw it) or of Westminster "the way it always was" (i.e., before it was cleansed of centuries of soot, smoke and dust).

CRITERIA FOR INTERVENTION

While the individual, layman or expert, is entitled to his preferences regarding cosmetic matters, the preservation community must develop broader, more objective and more comprehensive criteria for evaluating decisions about such matters. Certain parameters can be established for different types of preservation project. For example, the preservationist should consider the aesthetic ambitions of the original designers or owners of the structure or site. Most monumental architecture is urbane and upper class, the expression of a life-style that employed precise standards of display, etiquette and propriety, implemented by definite regimes of maintenance, housekeeping and repair. In the Western world, a cosmetic effect of wealth, affluence and good repair, if not shiny newness, was the criterion of owners. And, however fond one may have been of the Louvre when it was still sooty blue gray, one can rest assured that neither the French kings nor their architects conceived of the palace in such colors. Not only was the Louvre, like much of Paris, built largely of tawny pink stone, but much of its architectural ornamentation was conceived in that value and chroma, as is apparent now that the stone has been cleaned. Thus, when the surfaces of monumental upper-class architecture must for one reason or another be disturbed, the cosmetic criteria of restoration should be those of the creators, i.e., newness, brightness (of polychromy and gilt) and good housekeeping.

The reverse probably applies to most vernacular, peasant or primitive architecture. Although all buildings were at one time new and bright, and the builders were probably proud of them in that state, it is doubtful that there were any concious standards for keeping them that way. Until recent decades, painted woodwork, for example, would have been an unheard-of luxury even for prosperous farmers. Weathered shingles, mossy stones, patched fences and sagging gates would have been standard cosmetic conditions; only the village church may have been painted or whitewashed periodically and its cross or weathervane gilded. The landscape included none of the barbered lawns, clipped hedges or pleached allées associated with urbane upper–class architecture and townscapes. The aesthetic criteria of the restorationist of folk and vernacular buildings should reflect this condition. (Contrast, for example, the laissez-faire maintenance standards adopted by the young archaeologist-anthropologist James Deetz at Plimoth Plantation with the immaculate housekeeping in force at Colonial Williamsburg.)

For ruins (abandoned forts, castles, prehistoric sites, etc.), entirely different aesthetic criteria should apply. The stabilization of above-grade remnants and their maintenance should determine basic policy. In cold, wet climates, protective measures against moisture and freeze-thaw cycles are mandatory (e.g., at Fountains Abbey in England). In hot, humid climates, radical control of vegetation is mandatory, regardless of what the original landscape design may have been (e.g., in Mayan ruins of Yucutan and Guatemala).

For archaeological sites, a certain minimum of restoration is often essential to make the complex more intelligible to the visitor (e.g., at Delphi, Ephesus and Uxmal). Experience with such sites as Knossos suggests that such restorations should be extremely conservative. In certain special circumstances, where the artifacts or structures are both rare and fragile, it may be necessary to build completely new shelters over them (e.g., the glass–and–aluminum canopies over the great mosaics of Piazza Armerina in Sicily or the shelters over some of the rare prehistoric adobe structures in the American Southwest). The design of such devices requires good taste and great discretion on the part of the designer; certainly, all such shelters should be completely contemporary in both design and construction, so that no confusion between the original and the new is possible.

THE QUESTION OF CLEANING

Since cleaning is a necessary first step in the preservation of most types of structure, the cosmetic state is certain to be affected. Such cleaning, especially of stone and brick masonry and to a somewhat lesser extent of wood and metal, is necessary for two reasons, according to Bernard Feilden, restoration architect for Norwich, York Minster and St. Paul's cathedrals. It is a necessary prerequisite for an inch-by-inch examination of the fabric. It is often an essential step in halting various types of chemical action, such as rust, rot and efflorescence as well as the growth of moss and lichens. In many types of structural consolidation (e.g., injection of liquid grout into masonary structures as was done at York Minster and in many masonry structures in Tuscany), it is also necessary to clean exposed surfaces after the operation.

Often there are unanticipated results of complete cleaning: Many forgotten or unknown features of a structure may be revealed, e.g., the vaulted ceiling of the tower at York Minster or the marble polychromy of Garnier's Paris Opera.

There are specialized cases of preservation in the fields of science and technology where immaculate cleanliness and/or perfect maintenance are a sine qua non of the curatorial function. Under such a heading would fall scientific exhibits such as the observatory at Greenwich in England, recently reconstructed and re-equipped with great care to re-create 17th-century conditions. To replicate such an atmosphere effectively, equipment is carefully maintained, lenses are polished, metal parts are kept rust free and shining and all moving parts are kept oiled. An example of what happens if such curatorial standards are not observed is the Edison Laboratories in East Orange, N.J. This complex, now under the care of the National Park Service, purports to maintain Thomas A.

317

Edison's personal laboratory exactly as it was on the last day that Edison used it in 1932. Unfortunately, today it falls far short of this goal. Not only is the housekeeping routine, but even more important, the scientific equipment used by Edison is dusty and tarnished. Rectorts and beakers are full of anonymous desiccated materials, which contradict the image of Edison's carefully controlled scientific experiments. (He was actually working on the development of new sources of rubber at the time of his death.) In its present state, the laboratory fails in its central purpose—that of giving a vivid picture of this careful and methodical researcher at work. In preserving a record of this sort of activity for posterity, it is obvious that a new level of curatorial expertise is required.

Of course, the cleaning of any artifact or structure is a hazardous activity, as has been learned at great cost. Here again, a conservative policy is wise, and the rarer the artifact or structure, the more conservative the cleaning methods should be.

There is available now a whole spectrum of cleaning methods that can be arranged in increasing order of radicalness. For the cleaning of masonry buildings, for example, the following choices are available:

1. Continuous film of clean running water (1) without brushing, (2) with brushing and/or (3) with detergent or other chemical cleanser added to the water.

2. Jet of water, with or without brushing or detergent.

3. Steam cleaning.

4. Blasting with abrasives under pressure, using (1) wet or dry sand or (2) softer abrasives (crushed nut shells, buckwheat hulls, etc.).

Sandblasting is too severe for brick constructions and for almost all stone masonry. (It has been employed recently in Paris on the granite revetments of some of the quais without apparent damage, but many experts would argue against even this use.) For buildings of prime importance, pure running water (perhaps even distilled) is recommended, as in the recent cleaning of Notre Dame in Paris. Bernard Feilden used a continuous film of water with brushing at Norwich Cathedral and York Minster.

The cleaning of wood and metal structures requires other methods. Most types of paint are not water soluble; hence, chemical or mechanical means are usually employed to remove them. Sometimes burning off the paint with a small torch is necessary, but this method requires extremely careful workmanship because of the danger of scorching the surface or setting fire to the structure. The cleaning of plaster surfaces, especially if they are decorated, papered or frescoed, lies wholly in the field of the conservator of art and should be entrusted to him.

CORRECTION OF STRUCTURAL FLAWS

The correction of purely structural flaws in old buildings poses many complex technical and aesthetic problems, including the following:

1. Substitution of new materials and techniques. Because of the scarcity of traditional craftsmen and the expensiveness of their work, there is growing interest in the use of new materials and fabrication methods. Fiber-glass facsimiles are increasingly used as a substitute for hand-carved ornament in wood and stone (e.g., exterior balustrades, cornices or columns). These facsimiles are described as being cheaper, lighter, more durable and more maintenance free. (Thus, the reconstructed cupola of the Merchant's Exchange in Philadelphia is surfaced in a molded fiber-glass facsimile of the wooden original.) Other, more familiar substitutions are asbestos shingles, molded and colored to resemble weathered wood (used at Colonial Williamsburg), and cast-aluminum lampposts substituted for lampposts of cast iron (used at Historic Sacramento).

2. Correction of previous repairs. In historic complexes that have been continuously maintained (e.g., Oxford and Cambridge), ashlar stone walls have been cautiously patched for centuries. Since the size, scale and jointing of this masonry was an integral part of the original design and since the stone patches never match exactly in grain or color, the cumulative result of this patchwork is aesthetically disastrous. The new policy is to replace completely any single stone that is deteriorating.

3. Aesthetic hazards of inserting new tissue into old complexes. As long as structural intervention is completely concealed, the use of modern materials (e.g., steel or concrete members, modern fireproofing and flashing) is not only justified, it may even be preferable to the use of traditional materials, in that it simplifies future curatorial problems of dating, identification, etc.

When, for adaptive purposes, it becomes necessary to make alterations of any size or of visual importance to a structure, no attempt should be made to replicate the old elements. The only exception to this rule would be a situation in which some kind of serial or repetitive pattern, such as a row of columns or a series of uniform brackets in a cornice, has been disrupted and must be reconstructed to make clear the relationship of the whole composition to its original form. The hazards of not following this rule are painfully evident at Ephesus, where archaeologists have re-erected some colonnades to compensate for the missing elements. To dramatize the insertion of new tissue, drums of a different size and cross section from the original columns were used. The result is extremely unsatisfactory, making it actually more difficult to visualize the original building.

ADAPTIVE USE OF OLD BUILDINGS

There is a growing recognition that the preservation of old buildings as more or less inert museum houses or historic house museums has limits of both practicality and social utility. This is especially true if the buildings in question are a part of living urban tissue. Naturally, there are some buildings of such historical significance (Mount Vernon or Monticello) or of unique artistic merit (the Arena Chapel in Padua with Giotto's frescoes) that they should be restored only as museums. But increasingly, the only way to guarantee the existence of old buildings is to find new, and often unanticipated, uses for them. Architect Giorgio Cavaglieri's conversion of New York City's old Astor Library into a complex of of five theaters and his conversion of the old Jefferson Market Court House, also in New York City, into a library are two notable examples of the hundreds of such projects around the world.

Such adaptive uses often result in substantial structural and/or volumetric changes in the building itself and, hence, changes to its visual appearance (e.g., old City Hall, Boston, and New York Bar Association, Albany). Often, adaptive use involves new and unprecedented juxtapositions of small old buildings and large new ones (e.g., the 25-story addition to the original single story banking room of the Bank of California, San Francisco, and South Street Seaport, New York City). Such problems require new aesthetic perspectives on the part of the architect and urban designer and rejection of the misconception that there is something "unnatural" or "artificial" in these new relationships. The very process of urbanization makes such relationships inevitable, and urban planners and architects will have to develop the theoretical capacity to cope with them. Certainly, such new tissue cannot be disguised by draping it in a two-dimensional facsimile of older buildings, as is even now being proposed for new state office buildings in Annapolis. The aesthetic problem is one of real congruency, not mere superficial historicity.

RECONSTRUCTION

The reconstruction of vanished buildings, erected on the basis of archaeological and documentary evidence alone, has had a long

320

and distressing history in the past century and a quarter. Examples of reconstruction from the work of Viollet-le-Duc at Pierrefonds to that at Williamsburg and the Stoa of Attalus in Athens makes it difficult not to conclude that reconstruction is a radical and dangerous form of intervention. The many reasons for this opinion need no repetition here, but it should be observed that the reconstruction of a vanished building alongside the restoration of an extant one is tantamount to a museum curator's hanging known replicas alongside authenticated originals, a situation more apt to confuse the spectator than to raise his aesthetic standards or illuminate his understanding of history.

Nevertheless, there are probably cases in which the reconstruction of vanished buildings or complexes of buildings is ideologically justified and psychologically necessary. One such instance is the restoration-cum-reconstruction of medieval Warsaw. Two famous telegrams from Hitler and his general staff (now displayed in the city's Municipal Museum) ordered the absolute destruction of Warsaw. After the defeat of the Nazi regime, the Poles felt that they had no choice but to reconstruct their capital in its entirety, as symbolic evidence of victory. The policy concerning reconstruction might be generalized thus: The reconstruction of a vanished structure is justified if it is of absolutely prime importance to the society involved and if it is reconstructed during the lifetimes of the people who knew and valued it.

RECONSTITUTION IN SITU AND ON NEW SITES

Modern technology makes possible the complete reconstitution of old buildings, and modern conditions often make it mandatory. The reasons may be purely structural (e.g., the reconstitution of historically important but structurally unsound log cabins in Bethlehem, Pa.) or related to adaptive use of the building in situ (e.g., the dismantling and reerection of the old Illinois State House in Springfield to make possible the installation of an underground garage and the restoration of the mutilated interiors to their condition when the body of President Abraham Lincoln lay in state there in April 1865).

Much more common is the moving of old buildings to new sites. In this process, smaller buildings may be moved intact on trailers or disassembled and trucked to a new site for reassembly. An interesting instance of this latter technique was the disassembly in 1971 of the Edgar Laing Stores building in Manhattan. The disassembly of this 1845 cast-iron facade by James Bogardus was completely documented—all the elements were catalogued and marked, and complete drawings were prepared for its reconstitution as a part of the new campus for Manhattan Community College.

FACSIMILES AND REPLICAS

Largely because of the alarming increase in physical attrition of old structures as a consequence of environmental pollution, there is a new interest in the substitution of facsimiles in situ to permit the original object to be transferred to the controlled environment of a museum. Obviously, this technique is limited by the size of the artifact. Replicas of Michaelangelo's *David* in Florence or the sculptured figures on the Baptistry of Pisa have long acted as surrogates for the originals, which have been moved into museums. There is serious talk of doing the same thing with the portal of St. Trophime in Arles and the metopes on the Parthenon in Athens. The rate of attrition of the limestone masonry of the Spanish Chapel at the Cloisters of the Metropolitan Museum of Art in New York City has proved to be so rapid, and the use of chemical preservatives apparently so ineffective, that there are now plans to encase it completely in an air-conditioned glass-and-metal case. The design of such a protective device will require both taste and discretion on the part of the architect selected for the project, if the role of the Cloisters in the New Cork skyline is not to be seriously affected.

A new and surprising rationale for the use of facsimiles and reproductions has recently been advanced by James Deetz, the curator of Plimoth Plantation. This entire project has always been a reproduction of the original settlement, not even occupying the original site. Deetz feels that, in the past, this fact was not made sufficiently clear to visitors, who too often left with the impression that they had "seen the real thing." He has reorganized the entire interpretation program to shift the emphasis from the artifacts and structures to the processes that they supported. The visitor is now made to understand that nothing in the entire project is original or antique. This makes the policing problems much simpler and, incidentally, has reduced thefts to almost zero at a time when they are an increasingly serious problem at most historic restorations. On the other hand, Deetz does everything possible to guarantee that all the activities carried on, tools used and life-styles acted out are as accurate as modern research can make them.

RESTORATION: AN ON-GOING PROCESS

The restoration of a building does not end when the desired physical state has been attained; on the contrary, although it is seldom

322

anticipated, restoration has only begun. The maintenance of this physical state has been dubbed by Feilden as "four-dimensional preservation." Since no material can be expected to last forever, rational parameters for such maintenance need to be established.

Extrapolating from his experience in restoring three of England's great cathedrals, Feilden has attempted to establish optimal cycles for a continuing preservation program. At York Minster, he has set this cycle at 35 years. In other words, a continuing program of housekeeping and checkups will be phased so that every square foot of the structure's fabric will be examined, cleaned and, if necessary, repaired in not more than 35 years. Emergencies will, of course, be handled as such. However, with continuous inspection, emergency repairs should be held to a minimum. Only basic structural repairs to foundations and towers are exempt from this inspection cycle, because during the restoration, when new reinforced concrete members were introduced at the cathedral, all metal reinforcing rods were executed in stainless steel to assure as long a life as is currently attainable.

DEALING WITH ENVIRONMENTAL AND MECHANICAL FORCES

Today, normal attrition caused by exposure to environmental forces is aggravated by the fact that modern life has radically altered the nature of these forces. Industries are adding all sorts of new and complex pollutants to the air, earth and water that surround, support or underlie all buildings. Even in "sunny" Athens, the rate of deterioration of the Parthenon is severe and accelerating, as can be easily determined by comparing modern measurements with those made by the French in the 1820s or by comparing the in situ sculptures with the Elgin Marbles, which have been in the controlled environment of the British Museum in London for a similar period.

Modern transportation adds a whole new range of mechanical forces to threaten the integrity of old buildings. Structures in the approach lanes of modern airports are subject to serious airborne vibrations from jet aircrafts; the Coliseum in Rome has been seriously damaged by the motor traffic that swirls around it; and the wooden piling that supports Venice is being eroded by the wave action of propeller-driven boats on the canals.

All of these facts indicate that the preservation of historic architecture is an integral part of the larger problem of the protection of the environment as a whole. The pathologies of the first are causally related to the pathogens of the latter: Therapy requires the control of both.

MAN AS A DESTRUCTIVE FORCE

Superimposed upon the attrition caused by environmental exposure is the sheer physical degradation caused by tourist traffic. Ironically, the laudable growth of popular interest in the artistic and historic patrimony is becoming an increasingly grave threat to its survival. From a curatorial point of view, this degradation takes several forms: theft, vandalism and simple wear and tear. These are not new phenomena, since they are inherent in the process of exposing any work of art to public view. But under conditions of mass tourism, they are becoming increasingly acute. Thefts of artistic properties are the most newsworthy, the more so because they are frequently directed or inspired by well-informed experts and connoisseurs. However, mindless vandalism (slashing of paintings, hammering the nose off the Vatican madonna, spray-can graffiti and broken windows) constitutes a more serious threat. But beyond any doubt, the most severe attrition of historic sites and monuments comes from the orderly movements of law–abiding citizens.

The sheer impact and abrasion of thousands of feet constitute the gravest threat of all. For example, the wholly unanticipated volume of pedestrians passing through the stabilized ruins of Coventry Cathedral has forced the paving over of the roofless nave that had originally been landscaped as a quiet garden for contemplation. In essence, this situation is a problem of traffic management, that is, establishing the physical capacity of the monument and then setting up controls to keep the volume of tourists at that level or lower. This is not as simple as it sounds. It is easy enough to calculate the number of pounds that the reinforced stairs at Mount Vernon can safely support. It is much more difficult to decide how much space, time and leisure each visitor is entitled to if he is to absorb the lessons which the mansion can teach. And, once having established such a norm, how is it to be enforced? Through an arbitrary daily or hourly quota, as at the Winterthur Museum? Or by an increase in admission fees, as most American museums are doing anyway? Such measures are not apt to prove popular, especially if the monument is publicly owned (e.g., the White House or Independence Hall) or privately owned, but publicly significant (e.g., Mount Vernon or Monticello).

In the last analysis, the simplest way to reduce the traffic load on sites and monuments is simply to increase the number of them open to the public. Many more of them should be developed, and, when considered as a system, they should be open year round and not only during the constricted, overcrowded summer vacation period, as many are at present. As the 1969 conference of the

International Council of Monuments and Sites, held at Oxford, pointed out, this is a perfectly feasible possibility, since every country has perhaps 100 neglected or undeveloped sites of natural, historic or artistic interest for each one that it has developed. In addition, modern work patterns make midwinter vacations as easy as midsummer ones for most people. On a national scale, Bulgaria has already adopted such a policy of vastly increasing the number of developed sites of historic or scenic interest. Unlike neighboring Romania and Yugoslavia, where uncontrolled exploitation of the seashore rivals that in Miami, Bulgaria has stopped all development of additional tourist facilities along the Black Sea. Instead, the Bulgarians have adopted a program for developing sites of natural beauty and folkloristic interest throughout the country and are channeling tourist traffic to them. Such a policy could be applied productively even in such heavily developed countries as Italy, Greece or Portugal, where some sites and monuments are overcrowded while many others are still underused.

Of course, control of the tourist flow is not entirely a quantitative problem, as the current controversy over the future of national parks in the United States reveals. There are qualitative aspects as well. Instead of merely making it possible for every one with the means and leisure at his disposal to penetrate every square foot of every natural site or historic monument, development programs must incorporate qualitative controls. As is true of some natural sites, man-made artifacts of great significance are often too rare, too fragile and, hence, too valuable to survive public exposure. The Etruscan tombs around Tarquinia, the tomb of the Thracian warrior in Bulgaria and the painted caves at Lascaux are three classic examples. In such instances, visitors must often be limited to scholars and specialists (as done at the tomb of the Thracian warrior) or excluded altogether (at the caves at Lascaux). Whatever the controls and whatever the means taken to enforce them, it is clear that we shall require more of them in the future.

In any case, preservationists must recognize that mass tourism has raised the problem of preservation of the artistic and historic patrimony to an entirely new level of complexity. The rising volume of tourism cannot be reversed; indeed, it must not be, since in many countries (e.g., Greece, Italy, Egypt), tourism is the economic basis of institutionalized preservation. New philosophies, legislation and institutions must be perfected to cope with this situation.

THE LIFE EXPECTANCY OF MATERIALS AND PROBLEMS OF INCREASING VISITOR USE

SHELDON KECK

One purpose of this conference of architectural preservationists and art conservators is the examination of problems common to both and of criteria governing methods employed in their solutions. Perhaps there is no better way to begin a discussion of the life expectancy of materials than by presenting two of the few documented cases of deterioration that could involve both the preservationist and the conservator. A rather dramatic example described some years ago by Harold J. Plenderleith is the comparison between a photograph made in 1938 of a marble relief sculpture on the west frieze of the Parthenon and a photograph of a plaster of paris cast of the same sculpture made by Thomas Bruce, 7th earl of Elgin (1766–1841), in 1802 (figs. 1–2).[1] The marble remains an architectural element in its original setting on the Parthenon, exposed to weathering and the atmospheric pollutants of this industrial age. The cast of plaster, a material notably less durable than marble, is a museum piece, housed and protected at the British Museum in London. The difference in appearance between them is a measure of the erosion and deterioration of the marble during a 136–year period. Although the exact appearance of the marble sculpture upon its completion more than 2,300 years ago cannot be described with certainty, examination of the plaster

Sheldon Keck is a professor in the Conservation of Historic and Artistic Works Program, Cooperstown Graduate Programs (a joint project of the State University College at Oneonta and the New York State Historical Association), Cooperstown, N.Y.

FIGURE 1. *1938 photograph of marble relief on the west frieze of the Parthenon.* (*British Museum*)

cast reveals that surface pitting and spalling of the original marble had occurred by 1802. Also by that time, deterioration and loss were extensive in the lower half of the figure at the right side of the relief, but much of the sculpture remained crisply delineated. Many forms and surfaces elsewhere in the cast appear smooth, with little sign of wear. By comparing the condition of the fragile plaster with that of the rugged marble, it can be concluded that the permanence of materials is not simply a matter of physical properties and chemical stability. Longevity is also governed by the kind of environment to which materials are exposed. This first example speaks well for protecting a historic and artistic heritage from hostile surroundings by placing it in a buffered and less fluctuating climate, removed from exposure to the weather.

A second example involving both architecture and art occurs in the walls decorated more than 600 years ago by Giotto inside the Scrovegni Chapel in Padua, Italy (figs. 3–4). Only 12 to 15 years ago, parts of this magnificent cycle of fresco art were threatened with destruction by a mysterious exfoliation of the plaster and paint. Among the questions were: What is causing this deterioration? Will it spread to other parts of the building? Can the alteration be stopped or reversed? A conservator, Lawrence J. Majewski, and a chemist, Edward V. Sayre, from the United States, collaborating with Leonetto Tintori, the Italian conservator charged with the conservation treatment of the frescoes, studied the ambience

328

FIGURE 2. *Photograph of a plaster of paris cast of the same relief shown in figure 1. The cast was made in 1802 by Lord Elgin and has been housed since 1816 in the British Museum, London. Comparison of figures 1 and 2 clearly shows the extent of deterioration of the unprotected marble over a 136-year period. (British Museum)*

and investigated the materials of the chapel.[2] Their analyses showed that the surrounding air, polluted with sulfur oxides, together with airborne moisture and water seepage within the walls was more than sufficient to account for the conversion of the calcium carbonate in the plaster to the calcium sulfate dihydrate present in abundance only in the deteriorated areas. The plaster layer, expanded and powdery as a result of the conversion to calcium sulfate, could no longer either bind or support the paint on its surface.

When other monuments and works of art—for example, the cave paintings of Altamira, temples and tombs of Egypt, the Pantheon in Rome or sculptures from Greece and Rome—are examined, it may be observed that some have endured. If one were to judge from these examples alone, it could be concluded that the materials of art and architecture have life expectancies to be measured in millennia. At the same time, one must also be aware that not a single easel painting nor mural by an ancient Greek painter survived. Gone are the great paintings of Greece and Rome that were already of considerable age when they were seen and described by Pliny during the first century of the Christian era.[3] Fortunately, a few Roman decorative murals remain, preserved by

FIGURE 3. *Interior of the Scrovegni Chapel in Padua, Italy, showing the deterioration of the plaster and Giotto's fresco at the middle left of the rear wall. (Lawrence J. Majewski)*

burial in volcanic ash. In Egyptian tombs, however, numerous wall paintings and art objects 4,000 to 5,000 years of age, often of delicate organic materials, still exist, apparently only slightly altered by time.

CAUSES OF DETERIORATION

Students of the deterioration of materials and conservators trying to preserve works of art have long been aware of the anomalies mentioned. Scientists explain that matter always seeks a lower energy state and will undergo chemical and physical changes to achieve it. Almost any change in the form or materials of a work of art renders it less functional and constitutes deterioration. Sometimes the deterioration is explosively rapid; at other times,

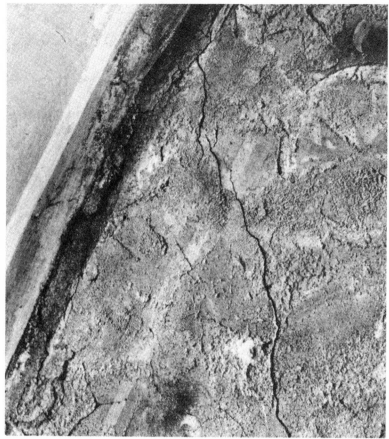

FIGURE 4. *Detail of the Giotto fresco in the Scrovegni Chapel showing damage to the plaster and paint due to the efflorescence of calcium sulfate dihydrate. (Lawrence J. Majewski)*

it is inexorably slow—so slow that alteration goes unrecognized and unrecorded.

In their daily work, art conservators observe that under normal indoor surroundings, the life expectancy of a work of art appears to be governed by two main factors: (1) the inherent stability or reactivity of materials comprising the work and (2) the character of the environment in which it exists. The former, when an object is constructed of interacting or unstable materials, is known in the vernacular of the insurance world as "inherent vice." The latter, the environment, consists of a blend of chemical, physical and biological agents that can act separately or in concert to alter, age and degrade materials. They are known as environmental agents of deterioration. Table 1 lists major environmental agents of deterioration and indicates their mutual action or influ-

Table 1 MAJOR ENVIRONMENTAL AGENTS OF DETERIORATION

Chemical ⟷	*Physical* ⟷	*Biological*
Oxygen	*Radiant energy*	*Vegetation*
Ozone	Sunlight	Algae
	Ultraviolet	Bacteria
Carbon dioxide	Infrared	Fungi
Sulfur dioxide	*Heat (high)*	Lichens
		Plant roots
Hydrogen sulfide	*Cold (frost)*	
Acids, alakalies, salts	Cycles of heat and cold	*Insects*
(airborne or in solution)		Ants
	Abrasives	Moths
Water	Dirt, soil particles	Silverfish
Ground water	Airborne dust and smoke	Termites
Cleaning solutions		Wood beetles
	Water	
Organic solvents	Liquid	*Rodents*
	Vapor	
	Cycles of relative humidity	*Man*
	Matter in motion	
	Mechanical stress	
	Impact shock	
	Wave or mechanical vibrations	

NOTE: Arrows indicate collaborative and simultaneous roles of various agents. Photochemical and electrochemical actions result from the collaboration of physical and chemical agents. Biological agents use physical-chemical means to ingest and digest matter. Natural aging (promoted by the joint action of many, though not necessarily all, of the environmental agents) is a gradual alteration involving changes in the properties and chemical state of materials. It is characterized by color and volumetric changes, loss of cohesive and adhesive strength and embrittlement.

ence. The action of environmental agents and mechanisms involved in deterioration are fortunately not the worry of conservators alone, but constitute a subject for continuing research by scientists and engineers in numerous professions and industries.

In categorizing causes of deterioration as chemical, physical or biological in origin, Glenn A. Greathouse and Carl J. Wessel remark that this kind of classification is arbitrary and artificial, particularly in regard to chemical and physical agents, which are collaborative, interdependent and in some cases interchangeable.[4] Water, for instance, can act as a physical or chemical agent. It may physically wash away particles or it may dissolve or chemically hydrolyze a substance. Greathouse and Wessel suggest, therefore, that perhaps a single classification encompassing both types of agent could be called "physical-chemical agents." As a temporary expedient, however, classification that separates specific contributors to deterioration is useful in studying them, understanding their actions and eventually controlling their activities. An example is fungi (a biological agent), some species of which attack and degrade paper, textiles, wood, leather and paint media. If the physical agent water, in the form of moisture contained in the ambient air, is reduced to 50 percent relative humidity or less, spores of most fungi normally remain dormant and, consequently, mold will not grow.[5]

"So infinite and complex are the possible interrelationships," write Greathouse and Wessel of the agents of deterioration, "that ultimately one must evolve, from a knowledge of the effects of individual agents and of the influence of each agent upon that of all the others, a sort of considered judgment as to what might be expected in a given complicated chemical-physical state of affairs. At our present level of knowledge, the judgment is often not much more than an educated guess."[6]

Under environmental conditions made favorable by nature and by man, sheets of paper made less than a century after the invention of papermaking in the year 105 in China have survived.[7] Fayum portraits painted in wax on thin panels of cypress during the first and second centuries of Christianity appear to be still pristine, and Egyptian paintings in a water-soluble medium on wood primed with gypsum and glue have endured for 4,000 years.[8] Finely woven linen textiles from ancient Egypt are still intact and pliant, as are more recent fabrics of pre-Columbian date made of cotton and wool and excavated from the rainless deserts of Peru.

MATERIALS OF ART AND ARCHITECTURE
The conservator's experience is usually in the preservation of relatively small, portable works of art normally sheltered in museums, churches, palaces or homes. Occasionally, the conservator is faced with preserving large paintings or sculptures fixed into architecture or with treating free-standing metal or stone sculptures exhibited outdoors. In any event, the works of art under the conservator's care are composed of diverse kinds of matter with a wide range of properties, including wood, stone, plaster, metal, glass, ceramics, textiles, paper, leather, parchment, paint, ink, dye, ivory, bone and even feathers. Of these materials, many are also within the province of the architectural preservationist. In fact, the conservator and the architectural preservationist share the care and treatment of composite structures containing in a single construction a number of the materials just mentioned. Differences between their operations appear in general to be in the physical scale of the constructions each must treat and in the ambience that can finally be provided for the treated work. A rela-

tively small scale permits the conservator to shelter works of art from extremes of climate, while the architectural preservationist has the task of protecting massive monuments and edifices directly exposed to the vicissitudes of weather.

Materials most commonly used in architecture which are also found in artifacts that may come under the care of a conservator are wood, plaster, stone and metal. For the conservator, wood is found in panel supports for easel paintings, in furniture and in polychromed or unpainted sculpture; plaster as a ground in mural paintings; stone in sculpture; bronze in sculpture and decorative vessels; iron and steel in weapons, armor, machinery, implements and instruments.

Wood

Because of its hygroscopic response to changes in environmental humidity, wood is one of the most intractable substances encountered in conservation. Richard D. Buck has found that with fluctuations in relative humidity, wood in Egyptian artifacts 3,700 years old continues to shrink and swell as extensively as do modern counterpart species.[9] Under conditions of extremely low humidity, wood can warp, check and split, as well as shrink. As paint on wood ages and becomes brittle, it can no longer expand and contract with the wood during cycles of relative humidity. As a result, the paint cracks, then loses adhesion, eventually buckles under compression and flakes away from the wood. The wood in the Fifth Dynasty sculpture of Ka-aper (The Sheikh el-Beled) in the Cairo Museum well illustrates these circumstances. Although well preserved after 4,000 years, the wood is checked and split. The stucco and polychrome that originally coated it have totally disappeared.[10] No treatment for completely stabilizing wood so that it will not shrink and swell has yet been found acceptable for use on art objects. The constant control of relative humidity currently appears to be the best solution to the problem. There is no doubt that such control is capable of prolonging the life expectancy of wood and of protecting composite artifacts containing wood from damage and loss.

Plaster

Lime plaster usually appears as an ingredient in a work of art; in frescoes, it is an important ingredient, serving as both the ground and binding medium for the pigment. In nonfresco murals, it often constitutes the ground. Murals on lime plaster survive from Minoan times (1500 B.C.), and although fragmentation has been caused by war, weathering and probably earthquake, the plaster itself is chemically sound.[11] More recent frescoes from medieval and Renaissance Italy show an apparent acceleration of deterioration due to industrial air pollution, no doubt enhanced by insufficient protective maintenance of buildings against moisture, rain and frost.[12] Recently in Italy, many murals were removed from the walls on which they had been painted; transferred to new, more inert supports; and, although now portable, installed against the walls of which they were formerly an integral part.

Stone

Stone sculptures inside a museum seldom present a conservation problem. There are exceptions. Porous limestone and marble absorb grease and grime from visitors' hands, as well as airborne particles such as smoke. Ancient limestone and marble sculptures excavated from saline soils begin to spall on the surface due to the efflorescence of water-soluble salts that recrystallize as moisture evaporates from the object's outer surface. Sometimes a visitor may accidentally overturn a sculpture and its pedestal, smashing them into fragments. As this paper was being written, the world-renowned *Pieta* by Michelangelo was disfigured and partially shattered by a madman with a sledge hammer. When stone sculpture is exposed outdoors, deterioration is considerably more rapid. The problem of preserving exposed stone has for many years been studied and investigated both in Europe and in the United States.[13]

In general, the life expectancy of stone preserved indoors is extremely long, perhaps longer than that of any other material. For example, the portrait of the Egyptian king Chephren in the Cairo Museum, skillfully carved in diorite about four and a half millennia ago, appears to have suffered loss only from what was presumably avoidable mechanical damage.[14] Alabaster vases and gypsum jars fashioned in predynastic Egypt have survived intact with no visible sign of aging.[15]

Metals

Bronze is considered an enduring material and, in confirmation, well-preserved examples have been excavated at Ur in Mesopotamia dating from 3500–3200 B.C.[16] Bronze sculptures and vessels from ancient Greece and the East have survived altered only by a chemical change in the surface, a corrosion that is highly admired and known as "noble" patina. Noble patina is compact, uniform in thickness and, in general, chemically benign or stable. Occasionally, salts of chlorine in solution or suspended in airborne moisture penetrate to the metallic surface to generate a kind of self-perpetuating powdery corrosion called "bronze disease."[17] Egyptian bronzes, with their usually unattractive, warty corrosion surfaces are particularly subject to bronze disease, although finer bronzes from Greece, China, India and the Near East are not immune. Bronzes that are situated outdoors and exposed to polluted air, moisture and sunlight deteriorate slowly, but much more rapidly than do those indoors in normal museum conditions, especially if a low relative humidity is maintained.

Iron and steel are definitely susceptible to deterioration by the joint action of moisture and oxygen, an action accelerated by wetting and drying, as well as by exposure to sulfur dioxide and hydrogen sulfide. When iron or steel items are housed in a museum, deterioration is retarded, and if they are further protected by thin films of colorless, transparent hydrophobic substances, suits of armor, weapons and vessels of iron or steel appear to show no change over periods of years. However, it is necessary periodically to replace the protective film. Although most iron implements from antiquity reveal themselves to archaeologists only as stains of iron oxide in the place where they were buried, the tomb of King Tutankhamen in the Valley of the Kings in Egypt contained several intact minature iron implements that have existed for more than 3,000 years.[18]

It is evident from the examples cited in this paper that objects made of many kinds of materials have survived for thousands of years and that, under favorable conditions, many more could have survived. That such a small percentage did can largely be attributed to unfavorable exposure of the remainder to environmental agents of deterioration.

INCREASING VISITOR USE

Increasing visitor use in museums does pose problems. Witness the wearing away with kisses of the sculptured toe of St. Peter at the Vatican and the closing of the caves of Lascaux following the degradation of the wall paintings there, a condition apparently caused by bacteria introduced into the caves on visitors' bodies or breath.[19] Increased crowds in museums make the protection of collections against handling, vandalism, accident and theft a more difficult task. But for the architectural preservationist, the problem of increasing visitor use is even more serious. For example, the Parthenon, in addition to having suffered from exposure to climatic cycles and from the ravages of a war in 1687, is now periled by an enormous number of visitors. In 1968, Georges Dontas, director of the Acropolis and Acropolis Museum, suggested that for the preservation of the Parthenon all tourists be excluded from the interior of the structure. He wrote, "One of the most serious dangers now threatening the Parthenon is the alarming amount of wear and tear to the horizontal flagstones caused each year by the thousands upon thousands of shuffling feet. This is a problem that of course affects not only the Parthenon itself but all other sites on the Acropolis as well as the rock platform itself."[20] Like the Parthenon, innumerable other outdoor and indoor "walk-in" exhibits are imperiled by increasing visitor use.

For museums, however, the problem of the life expectancy of materials in works of art is not so much a problem of visitor use, but one relating to that biological agent known as man. Until its acquisition by a museum or other institution where art is publicly displayed, a work of art from the past has had little or no visitor use. Of all the art created in the past, a small fraction remains, not by any grand selective design of man, but apparently because it was, for the most part, hidden from him. Perhaps the larger portion of what has been lost was destroyed through the action or attitudes of people: wars, iconoclasm, vandalism, neglect, ignorance, insanity and destruction in the name of progress. The remainder has been the victim of unavoidable natural cataclysms—fires, floods, tornadoes—that inflict rapid mechanical or chemical damage and of the slower relentless action of other environmental agents. If everything from the past had been permitted to survive, what other problems might humanity have today? The real problem, though, is that even the little that has survived may be degraded or wiped out by these same agents and processes. Although he has lost neither the inherent urge nor the capacity to destroy, man has retained the desire to immortalize himself by leaving his mark for posterity, by creating and preserving artifacts symbolic of his spirit and his time.

Accidents of history have made it impossible for man to select his cultural heritage, but he can, through understanding mechanisms of deterioration, increase his skills in preserving it intact for future generations. In this age of advancement in environmental studies, environmental controls, space research and the technology of space travel, the relatively simple problem of preserving indefinitely both great architecture and fine art from the past should not be far from man's capacity to solve.

I hope it is germane to the subject for me as a conservator to suggest to preservationists that the regulation and control of the environment surrounding structures, as well as of that within them, is a proper aspect of preservation. Archaeologists raise shelters over excavations to protect them from the weather; buildings are moved from their original locations to sites offering better protection. As Dontas suggests, the process of preservation may require some sacrifice in visitor use and, it may be added, some sacrifice in the aesthetics of display in order to achieve its goal of halting the attrition that comes with time. What about an air-conditioned geodesic dome for the Acropolis?

NOTES

1. Harold J. Plenderleith, *The Conservation of Antiquities and Works of Art* (London: Oxford University Press, 1956), pp. 316, 337.

2. Leonetto Tintori, Edward V. Sayre and Lawrence J. Majewski, "Studies for the Restoration of the Frescoes by Giotto in the Scrovegni Chapel at Padua," *Studies in Conservation* 8, no. 3 (August 1963): 37–54.

3. C. Plinius Secundus, *The Elder Pliny's Chapters on the History of Art*, trans. K. Jex-Blake, with commentary and historical introduction by E. Sellers [Strong] and additional notes by H. L. Urlichs (Chicago: Argonaut, Inc., 1968), pp. 87–173 passim.

4. Glenn A. Greathouse and Carl J. Wessel, eds., *Deterioration of Materials: Causes and Preventive Techniques* (New York: Reinhold Publishing Corp., 1954), pp. 71–233.

5. Rutherford J. Gettens, Murray Pease and George L. Stout, "The Problem of Mold Growth in Paintings," *Technical Studies in the Field of the Fine Arts* 9 (1941): 127. The authors of this article state that conditions necessary for mold growth are a temperature of roughly 70°–90°F, a relative humidity of more than 65 percent, moderate darkness and a moderate supply of oxygen. Also see A. Noblecourt, *Protection of Cultural Property in the Event of Armed Conflict*, Museums and Monuments Series, no. 8 (Paris: UNESCO, 1958), p. 93. This brochure advises that mold growth is inhibited at a relative humidity between 40 and 60 percent, 50 percent being very suitable, while less than 40 percent may be harmful to certain materials (e.g., parchment).

6. Greathouse and Wessel, *Deterioration of Materials*, p. 75.

7. Dard Hunter, *Papermaking: The History and Technique of an Ancient Craft*, 2d ed. (New York: Alfred A. Knopf, 1947), pp. 80–81.

8. Prentice Duell, "Evidence for Easel Painting in Ancient Egypt," *Technical Studies in the Field of the Fine Arts* 8 (1940): 184–86.

9. Richard D. Buck, "A Note on the Effect of Age on the Hygroscopic Behaviour of Wood," *Studies in Conservation* 1 (1952): 39–44.

10. David M. Robb and J. J. Garrison, *Art in the Western World*, 2d ed. rev. (New York: Harper & Brothers Publishers, 1942), p. 382.

11. Prentice Duell and Rutherford J. Gettens, "A Review of the Problem of Aegean Wall Painting," *Technical Studies in the Field of the Fine Arts* 10 (1942): 179–223.

12. Millard Meiss, *The Great Age of Fresco: Discoveries, Recoveries and Survivals* (New York: George Braziller, 1970), p. 8.

13. Seymour Z. Lewin, "The Preservation of Natural Stone, 1839–1965: An Annotated Bibliography," *Art and Archaeology Technical Abstracts* 6, no. 1 (1966): 185–272.

14. A. Lucas, *Ancient Egyptian Materials and Industries*, 4th ed. rev., ed. J. R. Harris (London: Edward Arnold, Ltd., 1962), p. 409.

15. Ibid., p. 407.

16. Ibid., p. 218.

17. Rutherford J. Gettens, "Patina: Noble and Vile," in *Art and Technology: A Symposium on Classical Bronzes*, ed. Suzannah Doeringer, David Gordon Mitten and Arthur Steinberg (Cambridge, Mass.: M.I.T. Press, 1970), p. 61; and Robert M. Organ, "The Conservation of Bronze Objects," ibid., p. 77.

18. A. Lucas, *Egyptian Materials*, p. 239.

19. "Lascaux under Treatment," *UNESCO Courier*, January 1965, p. 27.

20. Georges Dontas, "The Parthenon in Peril," *UNESCO Courier*, June 1968, pp. 16–18, 34.

COMMENTARY

ERNEST ALLEN CONNALLY

As an administrator with the National Park Service, I am concerned with administrative problems encountered in all types of preservation activity, including, but not limited to, those associated with the maintenance of and increasing visitation at cultural properties.

Although maintenance and visitation problems are discussed in both general and technical terms by James Marston Fitch and Sheldon Keck, I believe both authors avoid practical aspects of these problems. I am hesitant to comment on what roles conservators and scientists should play in solving these problems, so my remarks will be restricted to some pertinent administrative policies adopted by the National Park Service, its current attitudes toward various maintenance problems and increasing visitation and some experiments that the Park Service plans to conduct to investigate these problems. My remarks relate primarily to the kind of cultural resource that I am directly concerned with, that is, historic buildings, sites and monuments.

I should explain that the National Park Service is a public agency, charged by statute to preserve certain cultural resources in the United States that are important to the entire nation. At the same time, the Park Service must provide for public access to these buildings. According to the agency's legislative mandate, it is the Park Service's responsibility to maintain these buildings "for the

Ernest Allen Connally is associate director for professional services, National Park Service, U.S. Department of the Interior, Washington, D.C.

enjoyment and benefit of the people." Thus, the agency faces the problem of solving conflicts between its policies governing the use of facilities and its policies dealing with maintenance and preservation of the facilities. Attaining a balance between protective preservation policies and public use (or visitation) policies is not easy, especially since visitation, which is obviously increasing, threatens a building's structure.

In addition to the normal wear and tear caused by the weight of human bodies and the pressure of human feet, there are specific threats resulting from visitation. These specific dangers are often related to the times. For example, fashions of a period may bring about serious threats. Spike heels, which were fashionable on women's shoes a few years ago, are a recent, memorable example. These heels were only about ⅓ inch in diameter, which meant that, with each step, approximately half of the wearer's weight was concentrated in a fraction of a square inch. Anyone acquainted with the fragile nature of historic buildings will recognize the great strain that such a concentration of weight puts on parquetry floors, for example. Certainly the danger was recognized at Versailles and elsewhere, where shoes with this type of heel were not allowed to be worn in certain buildings. Even airlines were affected by this fashion, finding it necessary to increase the strength of materials used for fuselage cabin floors. Ideally, visitors ought to walk barefoot on delicate floors in historic buildings, but that presents practical problems too.

Of course, normal wear and tear cannot be avoided in historic structures that are open to the public, unlike museum objects that are usually handled carefully and infrequently. Because of this fact and the charge to preserve structures "forever," the National Park Service does not hesitate to use new materials to strengthen structural systems of historic buildings. For example, to preserve Independence Hall in Philadelphia, it was necessary to insert new structural steel members to support the second floor. This action was necessary not only for the preservation of the buildings but also to make it safe for visitors.

Experience has shown that structural reinforcement can be most effectively accomplished when done as a part of the restoration process. Inserting new materials that are structurally superior to original ones in places where the new structural members will not be seen often entails the removal of original materials, a process that requires a great deal of skill. However, when structural reinforcement is done properly, the building should be stronger than it was when first built, and its correct appearance in detail should not be visibly altered.

341

Another policy of the National Park Service is to control the environment of the furnishings and other contents of historic buildings through atmospheric control, that is, year-round control of the movement, temperature, humidity and purity of the air. Atmospheric control also makes visitors more comfortable, although that is incidental. In addition, it improves the quality of the visitor's experience in historic buildings in urban settings by reducing noise levels in the buildings' interiors. No doubt the sounds surrounding buildings of the 18th century were less intense and incessant than they are today.

In buildings maintained by the Park Service, fire and theft are controlled by installing alarm systems in the most inconspicuous way possible. The Park Service does not normally use sprinklers or similar devices for fire suppression that cannot be concealed. Administrative policies of the agency call for the use of highly sensitive detection systems connected directly to the nearest fire stations, so that when a certain temperature is reached, the alarm sounds and fire engines leave immediately. This makes it unnecessary to install fire suppression systems that might damage the building and its contents by drenching them with foam or water. Similar to the fire alarm systems, alarms that protect National Park Service properties against theft are wired into nearby police stations and are installed to be as unobtrusive as possible, even if they have to be installed behind an authentic surface of a building.

It is perhaps appropriate at this point to mention that truly successful preservation requires not only specific actions to control and monitor conditions within a building (that is, maintenance) but also actions to control the building's external environment. The general historical process, after all, is to use buildings until they wear out and to replace them. Historic preservation requires an interference with this process. Therefore, governments and private organizations concerned with preservation must adopt policies that will insure the permanence of historic objects. Such policies should, of course, include some control over threats that originate externally in the environment surrounding a historic object.

The problem of environmental control can be seen most clearly in a comparison between the fate of historic objects in environmentally controlled museums and that of historic structures. For example, as Mr. Keck mentions, the plaster of paris cast made in 1802 of a marble relief on the west frieze of the Parthenon in Athens has been protected in the controlled environment of the British Museum in London, thus preserving details that the original no longer has. But what can be done for a marble sculpture that remains at the Parthenon, exposed to weathering and atmospheric pollution? I am not prepared to take seriously Mr. Keck's suggestion that a plastic geodesic dome be placed over the Acropolis. However, preservationists do face problems regarding external surfaces of historic monuments.

One of the greatest external threats to historic monuments is the vibration of heavy traffic over the rough pavement of nearby streets. With smooth pavement and control of traffic, damage caused by vibration can be limited. This has been attempted in the area surrounding the Lincoln Memorial in Washington, D.C. The pavement is kept smooth and no heavy trucks are allowed on the roads circling the monument. A more elaborate solution to control vibrations was tried near the Villa Farnesina in Rome, where large shock absorbers were placed in the ground underneath the pavement to absorb shock at the point of impact, and thereby eliminate the radiating vibration that was fracturing the fragile villa. Where road conditions can be controlled, effects of vibration can be reduced, because even very heavy traffic on smooth pavement is less destructive than light traffic on rough pavement. Small 19th-century brick houses are especially vulnerable to damage caused by vibration from traffic, particularly where the widening of roads has brought traffic literally to their doorsteps. Some of these houses are being shaken to pieces. Thus, in addition to providing proper maintenance to keep historic buildings from falling apart, preservationists need to work on external environmental matters in cooperation with agencies that have the authority to control traffic and roads.

Another threat to historic buildings from the external environment is air pollution. Solutions to this problem also require cooperation between preservationists and agencies engaged in pollution control. In addition, preservationists must learn how to treat building surfaces that have been damaged by pollution. The National Park Service is currently working with the National Bureau of Standards on this problem, examining effects of pollution on some of the monuments in Washington, D.C.

Finally, visits to historic buildings, monuments and sites are bound to increase. The National Park Service has started to control visitation to some of the national parks in the West on an experimental basis. It is hoped that the knowledge gained from this experiment can be applied, in principle at least, to historic sites, which will probably soon be subjected to the same pressures that parks are experiencing now. Mr. Fitch said that the American people will never accept restricted access to these places. However, the Park Service has received complaints from some irate visitors who have been caught up in traffic congestion in places where they were expecting a satisfying, relaxing experience.

In addition to controlling the number of visitors to certain national parks in the West, the Park Service has stopped building campgrounds. Also, to prevent people from making futile trips to existing campgrounds that are already full, a reservation system has been established. The system is now being refined to permit anyone in the United States to telephone, direct and without charge, a proposed reservation bank, which will answer questions on the availability of accommodations in particular parks, make reservations for visitors, etc.

The Park Service believes that the quality of a visitor's experience at a national park or historic site, building or monument is just as important as the fact that the visitor was actually there. This experience cannot be appreciated unless the individual is accorded the dignity of a certain amount of privacy. Can a visitor to Independence Hall, for example, appreciate the building and its history when it is so crowded that he cannot see or hear anything? All the visitor may remember afterward is how uncomfortable he was.

I believe that the visitation situation at Mount Vernon, the Virginia home of President George Washington, is already critical. Going through the house can be a ghastly experience. The only thing a visitor can do is get in line and keep moving. One cannot take time to really see—and appreciate—anything. To assure people a thoughtful opportunity when they are visiting a historic house such as this, the number of visitors admitted at any one time must be controlled on a systematic and intelligible basis.

In addition to its current experiment in controlling the number of visitors in Western parks, the National Park Service is undertaking carrying capacity studies at historic sites. These studies should eventually enable planners to estimate not only development costs projected at historic sites but also optimal daily and annual visitation numbers. Plans are also being made to develop more visitor centers at historic sites. At these centers, visitors are exposed, in advance of their visit to the actual site, to films explaining the site and its history; other interpretive aids, such as exhibits and maps, are also available. It is anticipated that visitor centers can be useful not only in orienting visitors to sites but also in controlling visitation. It is contemplated that a center will issue each visitor a ticket, entitling him to spend a specified amount of time at the site, unhampered by talks, etc., and with enough privacy to make his experience meaningful.

Beyond these measures, our best hope is that the American people will change their habits. There is no reason why everyone should take a vacation in the summer. It would be better for both visitors and those in charge of historic sites if vacations were spread throughout the year. This is already happening in national parks in the West that used to be closed in the winter, but winter visits are becoming increasingly popular because the parks are less crowded then. Maybe someday the American educational system will adopt a sensible arrangement whereby schools will operate on an annual basis and students will take their vacations throughout the year. This arrangement will, no doubt, prompt corporations, travel agents and others to make similar adjustments. Perhaps more historic sites will be developed, as Mr. Fitch suggests, but in the meantime, if some traditional summer tourists can be encouraged to take their vacations at other times of the year, the approaches that are being developed to deal with maintenance and visitation problems at historic sites may function more effectively and also result in more meaningful experiences for visitors.

COMMENTARY

HAROLD J. PLENDERLEITH

The subjects of maintenance and the life expectancy of materials have come up repeatedly during these deliberations. Related as they are, these subjects form a major study of great complexity, but of supreme importance to architect-preservationists. For this reason, it is interesting to compare the lines of approach taken by the architects' representative on the one hand and by the scientists' spokesman on the other. These are illustrated in the papers presented by James Marston Fitch and Sheldon Keck, respectively. Mr. Fitch's scheme of classification of preservation problems according to the magnitude and the extent of intervention required for solutions may awe conservators by the variety of issues that architect–preservationists must face. Many of these problems are quite specialized and relate to individual projects; many are also outside the sphere of the conservator's work. On the other hand, Mr. Keck's table of the environmental agents of deterioration, which gives due importance to the ways chemical, physical and biological agents of deterioration work together against preservation, shows that conservators are entitled to a measure of sympathy, too. Preservationists are, no doubt, glad to leave much of this particular field of study to conservators.

The aim of the two groups must be to discover what problems are common to both, so that conservators and preservationists can determine the areas in which they can be of most help to one another.

Harold J. Plenderleith is director emeritus of the International Centre for the Study of the Preservation and the Restoration of Cultural Property, Rome, Italy.

346

It is noteworthy that conservators' services have been requested in all five of the types of intervention that are listed in Mr. Fitch's table under the heading "Scale of Intervention"—from the conservation of entire historic towns (e.g., Venice) to the conservation of building fragments. It seems entirely natural that conservators in museum laboratories have participated in such undertakings, either by performing actual treatment, providing research facilities or serving as consultants.

Consider the historic towns of Venice and Florence, each the victim of a catastrophe. These town were able to call on the Italian National Laboratories for assistance and to enlist the aid of the Italian National Council of Research. In each case, it was found to be necessary to establish a local conservation laboratory to provide day-to-day facilities for chemical testing and consultation. How this was accomplished is a matter of history, and these ad hoc facilities have proved to be of such value to preservationists and conservators faced with maintenance problems that they have now been established on a quasi-permanent basis.

Conservators have also provided services in the preservation of individual historic buildings and structures, for example, in the case of Abu Simbel in Egyptian Nubia. Mr. Fitch's table lists this great temple as one of several examples; it was, like many others, in the Nile Valley, sectioned and relocated on a new site. The operation could not have been accomplished without interdisciplinary cooperation on a wide scale. Suitable maintenance is, of course, still required and will have to be continued, because all problems relating to the stability of materials at Abu Simbel are exacerbated by the environment. At present, many of the temple's stability problems are basically of a chemical nature, although even here Mr. Keck's table, with its implication of joint action by chemical, physical and biological agents of deterioration, holds true. At Abu Simbel, preservationists now face, or will face, problems caused by chemical changes in materials that have been used to strengthen the sandstone and color changes in cements that may be weakened mechanically by the great summer heat and disintegrated not only by wind-blown sand but also by the exposure of the structure to unaccustomed humidity from the new Nasser Lake located nearby. The effect of sunlight on the organic synthetic impregnants and adhesive materials has yet to be seen and, overall, there are indeterminate forces that obviously will assert themselves while this great monument is slowly coming into equilibrium with its new environment. Clearly, there remain many opportunities for conservationists to help in solving a variety of maintenance problems.

While the Abu Simbel project provides a perfect example of the value of collaboration in the preservation of stone structures, other materials and structures have their problems too, and these may be no less urgent and exacting. John G. Waite and Robert M. Organ discuss the importance of maintenance to the longevity of metals and show that maintenance is as much of a necessity in preserving metals as it is in insuring the integrity of masonry. Too often one discovers cases of serious metal corrosion that could have been avoided by timely identification of the threat to the metal's stability and by the initiation of necessary prophylactic treatment. Sometimes, hollow metal castings crack and water gains access to the interior of statues. Mr. Waite gives an alarming but authoritative description of what may be expected to result when this situation occurs.

A recent example of the metallic corrosion of a famous monument concerns the four gilt-bronze horses that are positioned over the main entrance doors of the Basilica of San Marco in Venice. The horses are thought to have been cast some 2,000 years ago. Since being placed at the basilica, they have shown no signs of serious corrosion, until quite recently when green streaking was noticed. The streaking occurred in vestiges of the gilding, and it ran vertically down the statue toward the horses' bellies.

On examination, this phenomenon was found to be due to an electrolytic action between the gold used for gilding and the copper in the bronze, the horses being made of a bronze containing more than 97 percent copper. The electrolytic action resulted in the formation of copper sulfate, traceable to the presence of sulfur dioxide in the atmosphere, a consequence of recent intensified industrial pollution. To chemists, the presence of copper sulfate, which is soluble in water, is a clear signal of danger. What is happening is that the nightly condensation of dew on the cold metal provides a continuous supply of sulfurous acid to act as an electrolyte, and the copper in contact with the gold becomes a sacrificial anode and is dissolved as sulfate.

The options in the case are simple, namely, to dismantle the monument and reerect it in a museum or to plan and enforce a regular maintenance system that will protect the metal from the pollutant. A government commission is currently considering the problem and, while the commission's findings cannot be anticipated, the choice is most likely to be the initiation of a maintenance system that will allow the horses, so much admired by all who love Venice, to remain where they are. This example serves to illustrate the fact that the life expectancy of materials is closely related to regular inspection and maintenance.

Often, however, regular maintenance is neglected. How does one cope with the problems that result? First of all, preservationists who find it necessary or desirable to consult with conservators on such problems should realize that scientists think in terms of chemical substances, not trade names. The conservator's usual reply when asked if this or that proprietary product can be used for repair or consolidation purposes is "What is it?" The conservator must first know what the product consists of before saying whether it is safe to use or likely to be effective. No conservators carry in their minds an unlimited number of scientific facts. Their aim is to know where to find information when required, and they contribute to the corpus of information by experimental testing. Conservators have their own personal files that comprise their documentation. Architect–preservationists, I am sure, work similarly; they probably have on hand publications of the U.S. Forest Products Laboratory and various building research stations, as well as technical abstracts relating to their specialties. Among the most valuable and comprehensive abstracts for preservationists and conservators are those of *Art and Archaeological Technical Abstracts* (commonly referred to as *AATA* and formerly *The IIC Abstracts* issued by the International Institute of Conservation), which is published at the Institute of Fine Arts, New York University.

In order to keep fully abreast of preservation techniques, a central preservation exchange would be of the greatest value, as has been suggested several times during this conference. Nothing, however, can take the place of field work and laboratory testing, and the information available from such activities should be collected and made easily available to all interested parties.

Giorgio Torraca suggests an interesting idea in his paper on problems of stone preservation. He advocates that architects design for a certain type of maintenance, and this, I believe, is an intelligent and worthwhile approach to preservation. The formulation of a maintenance system should be regarded as the normal, definitive, last and essential act in the preservation–conservation operation. Restoration architect Bernard Feilden has provided admirable leadership for this idea. His phased checkup of the fabric in the English cathedrals that he has restored guarantees the complete and systematic coverage that is desired. Of course, such a checkup must be carried out under the control of those having both knowledge and authority.

Materials simply do not last forever, and that is why preservationists and conservators are particularly interested in substances that are chemically inert and therefore are unlikely to behave er-

349

ratically. Waxes are a case in point. The chemical characteristics of beeswax taken from King Tutankhamen's tomb have been found to be essentially the same as those of modern beeswax. Today, waxes with varying properties can be formulated by adding polyethylene wax or silicone to beeswax. Conservators sometimes look wistfully at the high-grade, lasting wax polishes used on luxury motorcars and learn from other technical specialists of facts that may be useful in their own fields.

Finally, a word must be said on the important bearing that the human factor has on the life expectancy of materials. As has been emphasized by others at this conference, man, the heir and lover of art, is accountable for much unnecessary damage. Thanks to today's enlightened educational systems, more people than ever before have an appreciation of the value of cultural property; unfortunately, this fact has to be offset by the "couldn't-care-less" attitude of many members of the public, by the fact that devastating wars continue to occur and by the admission that this era faces two additional, seemingly incurable scourges, namely, vandalism and pollution.

Vandalism, being unpredictable, is probably beyond control. As can be seen all over the world, it is but the work of a moment for some thoughtless person to spray paint on an architectural gem and leave behind an indelible disfigurement. Let us hope that this is just a craze that will soon pass. As for pollution, the only hope seems to be that this also may be given such a bad name that there will be a mass uprising against it before damage is irretrievable.

The best that conservators and preservationists can do is to speak with one voice against all evils that threaten man's patrimony and to work together to form or reform public and political opinion, in the hope that a time will come when there will be instinctive action to protect and save, at least, the best that remains.

To conclude on a more cheerful note, I feel that the increasing threats to man's artistic heritage have at last prompted preservationists and conservators to organize. There are now several professional associations devoted to the cause, many of them with a large and influential membership. It would certainly be worthwhile for preservationists and conservators to obtain a list of the official publications of these organizations. There are not only national governmental bodies concerned with these problems, but also international organizations and notably those sponsored by the United Nations. The list includes those with special concerns: the International Centre for the Study of the Preservation and the Restoration of Cultural Property, International Council of

Monuments and Sites, International Council of Museums, national museums associations and specialized research laboratories working for the preservation of cultural property throughout the world. All this activity is encouraging and every activity, such as this meeting, adds force to the movement.

Permanence is seen not only to be dependent upon the selection of materials and how they are used by artists and architects, but also on the varied life expectancies of these same materials in different environments. Regular inspection, early diagnosis to detect potential threats to stability and timely treatment are agreed to be the essence of successful conservation. An Italian proverb states, in effect, "If you do not sew up a small hole, you may later have to sew up a larger hole." Perhaps it is significant that this truism is reflected in aphorisms of many languages.

DISCUSSION

Comments made during the discussion on maintenance are summarized in the following paragraphs.

Maintenance of historic buildings is a multifaceted subject. It consists of all activities carried out to maintain a building's structural integrity and appearance after acquisition or after restoration has been completed. It ranges from the installation of fire-detection devices and other safety features to the control of tourism.

Restoration architects often find compliance with modern building and safety codes an especially difficult matter. While historic buildings open to the public as museums and those currently in use obviously must be safe for visitors and occupants, the fabric of most early structures usually cannot meet contemporary code requirements. Each building must be analyzed on an individual basis and reasonable arrangements for safety worked out with local building departments. Because buildings maintained by the federal government are exempt from certain local building codes, architects working on federal preservation projects are not constrained by the many stringent code requirements that architects working on private projects face, although certainly historic buildings under federal control must be safe.

Problems related to modern technological considerations are not, however, the biggest ones faced by those responsible for maintaining historic buildings and sites. Man is the greatest threat. As a tourist, man inflicts a great amount of wear and tear on historic buildings which require considerable maintenance work. Potentially damaging vibrations can come not only from the movement of tourists through a structure, but also from interpretive sound-and-light displays set up for their benefit. "Captive" tourists, such as schoolchildren and participants in prearranged tours, are another aspect of the problem of increasing visitation. Some may not be interested in the building or what it contains, and such groups are often herded through without having the time to really learn or experience anything. These "captives" do, however, contribute to the wear and tear the building must sustain. Imaginative ideas are needed to control visitation in historic buildings or sites. In some cases, entrance fees have helped, but charges of commercialism and elitism are often raised, especially when fees are suggested for significant monuments. Perhaps preservationists can learn something from the Japanese, whose temples attract an enormous number of visitors but are protected by certain customary practices, such as visitors' removing their shoes before entering the temple. The Japanese are also more amenable than some other peoples to the discipline of staying in line and not handling objects they are asked not to touch. A much greater understanding of man in the role of chief predator of historic buildings and sites is desperately needed. Preservationists should perhaps enlist the expertise of sociologists and psychologists in this search for a greater understanding.

Historic buildings maintained by organizations with limited resources are particularly susceptible to maintenance problems. There are so many of these buildings and so much work to be done that architects and others responsible for maintenance are kept busy with emergencies and have little time to study new conservation techniques that are discussed in professional journals, at conferences and elsewhere. Conservators should be aware of this problem, lest they become irritated at preservationists for not attempting to stay abreast of developments in the field on their own. In addition, many organizations simply cannot afford both professional consultation and corrective action. This is where dedication is needed; preservation professionals have a responsibility to encourage and assist these organizations in any way possible. More cooperative action between preservation organizations and the establishment of a central information clearinghouse would be positive steps toward solving the problem.

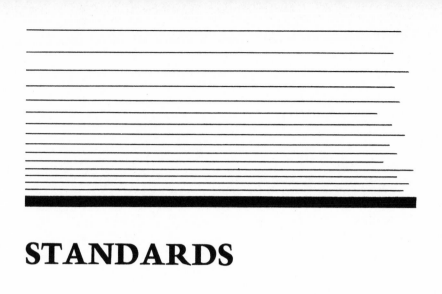

STANDARDS

Philosophy/Criteria

PRESERVATION AT THE CUTTING EDGE OF PUBLIC APPRECIATION

GEORGE McCUE

Among the most familiar and vexatious problems of conserving historic districts is that of designating which buildings and which parts of buildings speak for the synthesis that pronounces a district to be "historic." Just as familiar a problem and sometimes even more discomposing is the difficulty of identifying to the community the significance of its artifacts as life-enhancing materials when experts disagree over many of the crucial issues in evaluation.

What in our cities represents a priceless heritage and what simply the debris of past civilizations? We have no certain knowledge and little enlightened opinion.[1]

URBANITY AS A LIFE PROCESS
Harmony by Constraint
Remnants of vintage districts that are found in central-city areas rarely represent a unity of period or architectural style. Districts that were rebuilt following clean-sweep disasters—San Francisco after its earthquake; Atlanta after General Sherman's march; Chicago, Baltimore and Saint Louis, among others, after great fires— were homogeneous for a while because each was the product of a vast and almost simultaneous reconstruction effort. These efforts were not embodied in urban renewal plans such as those of today with their compositions of building masses, the introduction

---

George McCue is editor of the music and arts page of the *St. Louis Post-Dispatch*, Saint Louis, Mo.

of new circulation patterns, provisions for open space and landscaping and an architectural concept to which all construction is more or less committed. During the reconstruction of such districts, high land costs and the need to resume business dictated that rebuilding be generally on the same property, within the same street grid and according to owners' needs and preferences. A further requirement was that the reconstruction be done quickly.

Nevertheless, each rebuilt district represented the construction technology and fashion of one period. Two catastrophic fires in New York City destroyed 700 buildings in 1835 and 300 buildings in 1845 in the area bounded by Wall and Broad streets and the East River. Since iron structural elements and prefabricated fronts had just become available around that time, these construction techniques were seized upon "as matter of desperate necessity."[2] Iron construction was widely used in Saint Louis after the riverfront fire of 1849 destroyed more than 400 commercial buildings and houses in 15 blocks. (Most of this area was demolished in clearance for the Jefferson National Expansion Memorial, site of the Eero Saarinen Gateway Arch.)

Even with differences in style, the rebuilt districts maintained a high degree of harmony in finish and scale. The latter was due to a number of common constraints, among them the confines of old lot boundaries and, in the case of commercial buildings, height limits imposed by masonry and early iron structures, by stairway access and by the short range of rope-operated, steam-driven and hydraulic elevators.

Harmony by Happy Circumstance

In these rebuilt districts as well as in those untouched by act-of-God land clearance, additions, modifications and replacements were part of the continuous process of urban life. Greenwich Village in New York City, for example,

is the only surviving section of Manhattan where one can see the major architectural styles of the early City displayed, side by side, ranging from the most naive to the most sophisticated versions. ... The principal architectural styles ... are the Federal, Greek Revival, Italianate, French Second Empire, Neo-Grec and Queen Anne. The streets offer a delightful mixture of these styles. ... For every recognizable architectural style there are other transitional buildings which bridged the gaps between styles, borrowing a little from both the preceding and the new.[3]

The Vieux Carré of New Orleans, which tourists are likely to see as old buildings of a general similarity romantically garnished with lacy ironwork, includes the considerable stylistic range of

French and Spanish Colonial, Federal, Creole, Greek Revival, Victorian and various transitional and modern styles.[4] Lately it has acquired, on several central blocks, some conspicuous examples of "Motel Neo-Throwback." Then there are the shotgun and the camelback houses. The Vieux Carré existed for a long time before the ironwork that is now so indelibly impressed on visitors' perceptions made its appearance—after 1850.[5] As long ago as the turn of the century, "Northern building ideas and inappropriate suburban types began to change the character in the French Quarter."[6]

Broad Street in Charleston, S.C., which was included in that city's historic district in 1966, is described by Mrs. S. Henry Edmunds as "an amazing conglomeration of America's architectural fads from 1712 through the Victorian Age. Here on this one street is the history of the developing America in her buildings."[7]

The 24 town squares of Savannah, Ga., were laid out over a period of 120 years, with each new square respecting the character and scale of those already developed. "New squares were not extremely different from the old ones; yet each square reflected its own time."[8]

Attrition

Exposure to the elements and to vicissitudes of human use makes a city's structures subject to erosion, modification, breakdown, disaster and mutilation, but it also imparts a patina. Time adds the factor of association to those of aesthetics, appropriateness, feasibility for continued use and whatever others are weighed in the landmark judgment scale. Time is one of the dynamics of urban life. When a neighborhood is being assessed for its historical worthiness, time works against buildings that are in the gray zone between elderly and venerable, but it bestows a degree of authority on those that have broken the century barrier. There may be a psychological parallel in the tendency of the young generation to reject its parents and to regard its grandparents as senile, but to be interested in ancestral ties with its great-grandparents. The last 100 years encompasses most of, if not all, the history of many an American community, and the celebration of centennials, sesquicentennials and bicentennials brings architectural artifacts of a city's early days, such as they may be, into a new focus of public attention.

Greenwich Village included more than 1,000 buildings predating the Civil War when it was designated a historic district in April 1969, and the official description of attrition there is applicable to almost any historic district:

The defacing of fine old facades with materials which are out of character, the removal of ornamental features, such as lintels, cornices and ironwork, the destruction of doorways and other forms of damage threaten the aesthetic and historical continuity and value of the community. Such piecemeal changes threaten these values almost as much as the construction of new apartment houses and other buildings, many of which are visually inappropriate to their surroundings.[9]

PRESERVATION AS A PEOPLE PROCESS

The Williamsburg–Disneyland Syndrome

Cities over the country are becoming increasingly aware of the need to do something about their historic districts. This may mean accelerating programs for getting rid of them because of a concern that they will be formally identified as historic, with the consequent inconvenience to a redevelopment project or an expressway. Other communities, surprised and impressed by the financial showing of such enterprises as San Francisco's Ghirardelli Square and the Cannery and by the profitable magnetism of the Vieux Carré; Larimer Square in Denver, Colo.; Underground Atlanta, Ga.; and Old Town in Chicago, Ill., are reacting to that new dimension of aesthetics that is called "feasibility."

The decision to restore and preserve an old district is likely to amount to deciding whether to arrest the life process, to reverse it or to cultivate it under conditions that encourage ongoing contributions of worthy character.

Any of these decisions involves evaluations that may seem to the layman to be laboring over the most rarefied subtleties. The architect who undertakes to spell out fine distinctions at a public hearing can expect to see aldermanic eyes becoming glazed. The preservationist speaking out at a public hearing should not be demoralized if, after devoting most of his time allotment to what he believes to be explicitly the "meat and bones" of the issues, he is asked to come to the point. The public official operates in the pragmatic political frame of reference, which has its own subtleties. Somewhere in the history of an old part of town that has become an urban historic district there was a moment when the pragmatic subtleties and the rarefied subtleties coalesced.

Experienced public officials are more knowledgeable and sophisticated about rarefied subtleties than might be suspected—after all, they sit through many hours of hearings and public meetings at which professional and man-on-the-street viewpoints are argued. What public officials ask of a presentation, especially if it is before a committee that has to report, make recommendations to its parent body and argue for its position, is that the proposal offer them a few handholds on the kind of semantics and values that are in the public domain.

The role of a newspaper writer interested in preservation is to help maintain a courier service, bringing criteria of authorities in the field to the attention of the general public, which is so often subjected to efforts at instant education regarding preservation opportunities and responsibilities under suddenly desperate circumstances.

When the public is uncertain about something, it looks for a categorical answer, and the press—meaning all the communications media—has a tendency to polarize every issue. Almost every preservation issue involves fine distinctions and highly developed attitudes, which the specialist can bring into focus out of his background of study and experience. Lacking this background, the layman, whose concern may be offhanded in the first place, draws on superficial impressions of historic places, remembered vaguely from walk-through or drive-through visits, to jump to firm, impulsive conclusions.

The term *historic district* means, to an incalculable number of people, something like Colonial Williamsburg, even though there is nothing like Williamsburg. The details of how Williamsburg came into being in its present condition by means of archaeological research and other authentic evidence are of minor concern to many of its visitors. They see a charming colonial town in practically a new state of maintenance. What else have they seen? Sturbridge Village? Plimoth Plantation? Mystic Seaport? Perhaps the words *historic district* bring to their mind a Victorian stage set in Disneyland, reduced somewhat in scale to make it more approachable, bright with color and saturated with nostalgia and euphoria. Maybe *historic district* makes them think of Front Street in Dodge City, Kan., or of one of the "Pioneer Village" claptraps thrown together along some highway.

As self-evident as the various criteria involved in these different projects may seem to be, preservationists will be better prepared for some situations if they are haunted by the likelihood that all these kinds of reincarnated environmental experience are blurred in visitors' minds into a confused notion of what is intended by historic preservation.

The uncertainty gained from a kaleidoscopic exposure to casually observed images comes home to roost when the tourist is back home considering the merits of preserving a block of slumbering warehouses on the riverfront or near the old railroad station, when they appear to him to be merely old buildings with dirty windows standing in the way of progress. What makes them historic and worth preserving when there is no association with George Washington, Wyatt Earp, O. Henry, the Overland Trail or the flying cannonballs of a Civil War engagement? Are they worth preserving when there is no local legend associated with them and they are simply in the old part of town?

Preservation enterprises that are privately and securely funded can afford to be unconcerned about whether the public really understands what they are all about. However, most preservation issues sooner or later become public issues, usually overnight in an urgent need for moral support or perhaps in a situation that calls for well-informed letters to legislators.

Attrition by Renovation

The public enjoyment of an American historic architectural ambience seems to be related to the degree to which two main conditions are satisfied: (1) The building needs to be at least 100 years old (200 years is more than twice as good) and (2) it needs to look new.

The question of whether to stop the clock, turn the clock back or let time go on becomes crucial in decisions about:

1. Removing accretions in order to achieve an appearance from some past date or period
2. Replacing original elements that have been eroded or damaged with duplicate new materials
3. Adding new construction to fill gaps or to replace inappropriate structures

Since the Historic District Ordinance was enacted by New Orleans in 1937 to protect the Vieux Carré, the preservation effort there has meandered toward conflicting goals.[10] A problem of particular urgency is that of the appropriate design of new buildings to fill in gaps and to replace structures.

It is difficult to assemble large parcels of land in the Vieux Carré, but several new hotels and parking structures have found locations. Considerable capacity has been added to a 1965 room count of 1,550 units. "It is expected that by 1985 there will be a demand for over 3,300 hotel and motel rooms in the Vieux Carre. . . . By the year 2000, conservative forecasts indicate the demand will reach 4,900 rooms."[11] The report on the preservation program within the Vieux Carré mentions nine existing multilevel garages with capacity for 2,550 cars, in addition to 1,500 curb parking spaces and 4,500 off-street spaces.[12] Traffic in the area is expected to increase by 65 percent by 1980. A survey of attitudes held by local leaders disclosed a high, though somewhat divergent, sensitivity to the unique character of the Vieux Carré, but there was also unanimous concern about its deficiencies in tourist facilities and services.[13] The Vieux Carré could become a victim of its own popularity.

Much of the new hotel architecture in the area expresses a clearcut value judgment: Nothing succeeds like excess. Several hotels in the central blocks are composites of historic styles, with iron-fringed galleries, segmental arched openings and mansard roofs, and they are out of scale with their older neighbors. Le Downtowner du Vieux Carre, a new five-story, 186-room motor hotel, advertises "balcony and grillwork in keeping with old architecture but completely modern otherwise."[14]

The late John W. Lawrence, dean of the School of Architecture at Tulane University in New Orleans, identified the weakness of this thinking:

New structures in any style, built on the aborted bones of the authentic old, cannot enhance the cause of preservation. In the case of buildings destroyed in the Vieux Carré, it was said, as the wrecking ball tore at the *tout ensemble*, that the replacements would be more in keeping with the character of the area. What, however, can be more in keeping with the Vieux Carré than the Vieux Carré itself?[15]

A design problem assigned to a group of Dean Lawrence's students was that of relating contemporary structures to the *tout ensemble*. The results, juried in 1971, exhibited a promising understanding of the possibilities of modern design in expressing its own vitality but not being boorish, and certainly not being subservient to older designs.

Widely published reports on three contemporary buildings in historic settings make strong cases for letting time go on; these buildings are not only excellent independent architecture but they also maintain a gentlemanly demeanor in the presence of their senior neighbors. Each new building contributes to the individuality of the surrounding older structures, and the design relationship takes on the nature of good conversation.

In the Georgetown area of Washington, D.C., the Trentman House designed by Hugh N. Jacobsen, Architects, at 1348 27th Street, N.W., is situated between two period structures and harmonizes with them in color and mass and picks up the alignments of horizontal bands. It is fully a 20th-century house in its bold window designs, its functionally large social rooms downstairs and its rhythmic arrangement of small openings in the private second floor.

The New York State Bar Center at Albany by James Stewart Polshek incorporates the brick facades of three 19th-century row houses with a limestone headquarters building in a gracious synthesis of old and new.

The headquarters of the Jehovah's Witnesses by Ulrich Franzen and Associates emerged from a painful ordeal of trying to reconcile large space needs with the small scale of a mellow Brooklyn Heights neighborhood in Brooklyn, N.Y. Five predecessor design studies, by another firm, were rejected because these timid proposals failed to grasp the extent to which new architecture can maintain a robust sovereignty while also minding its manners.

These three completed projects make their points with the positiveness and clarity that help the public to cultivate a constructive point of view about urban experience. It is during the discussion about concepts that issues are hard to spell out.

The restoration of the Faneuil Hall–Quincy Market area of Boston, Mass., in its setting of the 18th-century buildings and the last vestiges of the city's 17th-century street pattern, is pending the solution to a difficult problem. The problem seems to some of those involved to be a troublesome abstraction—the question of whether this famous historic district should retain some of the marks of the vicissitudes of its long existence.

The vicissitudes include worn granite stones in building walls and steps and, more prominently, roofline extensions that converted some attics under the gabled roofs into two additional stories with 19th-century ironwork of neo-Georgian style. The Boston Redevelopment Authority adopted a proposal "using [architect Alexander] Parris's original plans and modern rehabilitation methods [that] will return to their original appearance and prepare the interiors for further adaptation to modern commercial needs." [16]

The Faneuil Hall Markets, with their 45 joined buildings in two rows flanking the 535-foot-long Quincy Market building, are historic in their modifications. The present rooflines, with some original gables and some extensions, comprise the look of mixed eras with which several generations of Bostonians feel an intimate identification. The attic extensions have the further historical virtue of representing the building techniques used in past times for gaining interior space within an augmented facade. To remove all traces of this would be to take away features with their own claim to historical significance; when combined with the new stonework, proposed multipaned windows, new slate roofs and interior gutting for modernization, the redevelopment would seem to present Boston with a new 1835 phenomenon, with all subsequent associations peeled away or sterilized and the dignity of wrinkles emphatically denied.

It is unfortunate that preservation has generally followed the American pattern of attempting to maintain an illusory air of eternal youth. Too often the interesting and informative accretions to buildings are removed in order to make them "authentic." . . . From a cityscape point of view—that is in terms of real life—it is deplorable to find a rigid and doctrinaire approach to the visual properties of buildings, no matter what era's aesthetic may be the viewer's ideal.[17]

The final resolution of the question raised in the restoration of the flanking buildings hinges on the acceptance of a redeveloper and possibly of plans that would keep at least some of the accretions. The issues of this restoration problem may in time take on a classic import.

NOTES

1. Stephen W. Jacobs and Barclay G. Jones, "City Design Through Conservation: Methods for the Evaluation and Utilization of Aesthetic and Cultural Resources," 2 vols. mimeographed (Berkeley: University of California, 1960), vol. 1, chap. 3, p. 7.

2. Carl W. Condit, *American Building Art: The Nineteenth Century* (New York: Oxford University Press, 1960), p. 28.

3. *Greenwich Village Historic District Designation Report*, 2 vols. (New York: Landmarks Preservation Commission, 1969), 1:15.

4. Samuel Wilson, Jr., "Analysis of Styles" in "Part II—History and Architecture of the Vieux Carre," *Plan and Program for the Preservation of the Vieux Carre* (New Orleans: Bureau of Governmental Research, 1968), pp. 19–35.

5. Ibid., p. 31.

6. Buford L. Pickens, Introduction to *A Guide to Architecture of New Orleans 1699–1959* by Samuel Wilson, Jr. (New York: Reinhold Publishing Corp., 1959), p. 8.

7. Mrs. S. Henry Edmunds, "The Charleston Story, Preservation in Charleston," *Historic Preservation* 23, no. 1 (January–March 1971): 7.

8. Paul Muldawer, "Criteria of Urban Design Relatedness," ibid., p. 30.

9. *Greenwich Village Designation Report*, 1: 14.

10. *Plan and Program of the Vieux Carre*, p. vii.

11. Ibid., p. 67.

12. Ibid., p. 70.

13. Ibid., p. 74.

14. George McCue, "New Orleans' Vieux Carre," *Art in America* 59, no. 3 (May–June 1971): 97.

15. John W. Lawrence, "Contemporary Design in a Historic Context," *Historic Preservation* 23, no. 1 (January–March 1971): 27–28.

16. Press release from the Office of Mayor Kevin H. White, May 6, 1970.

17. Jacobs and Jones, "City Design Through Conservation," vol. 1, chap. 3, p. 31.

HISTORIC PRESERVATION:
PHILOSOPHY, CRITERIA, GUIDELINES

PAUL PHILIPPOT

The origins of historic preservation are linked with those of the modern historical consciousness, which matured toward the end of the 18th century.[1] The word *preservation*—in the broadest sense, being equivalent in some cultures to *conservation* or *restoration*—can be considered, from this point of view, as expressing the modern way of maintaining living contact with cultural works of the past. This way of maintaining contact evolved after the outburst of the Industrial Revolution and the development of a historical conscience brought an end to the traditional link with the past, which may be said to have lasted, in various forms, from the origin of civilization to the end of the 18th century.

Indeed, since this rupture, the past has been considered by Western man as a completed development, which he now looks at from a distance, much as one looks at a panorama. On one hand, this new historical distance has produced the conditions necessary for a more objective, scientific approach to the past in the form of historical knowledge. But purely scientific knowledge cannot in itself insure the continuity that was guaranteed by tradition. To bridge the gap that the historical conscience opened between the past and the present, a new kind of contact developed, based on the feeling that the past has indeed been lost, but continues to live through nostalgia. This romantic nostalgia of the past, which replaced the traditional continuity between the past and the present,

Paul Philippot is director of the International Centre for the Study of the Preservation and the Restoration of Cultural Property, Rome, Italy.

combines historicism and nationalism and has led, since the end of the 18th century, not only to various revivals of past styles of art and architecture but also to an unfortunate confusion of preservation and reconstruction.

A scientific archaeological approach to the past and nationalistic revival are closely interwoven in Eugène Viollet-le-Duc's theory[2] and in all 19th-century restoration work in Europe, where these ideas have not yet died out completely. Modern nationalism also seems to foster revivals and reconstructions in most young countries that have recently become independent.

In the meantime, however, the scientific approach to the past has surpassed national borders and now considers products of all cultures as part of one cultural patrimony of mankind. Living contact with this patrimony can no longer be achieved in revivals— nor, consequently, in reconstructions based on the symbolic value given to a style of the past by romantic nationalism. It can be achieved only through a new approach that will acknowledge simultaneously the uniqueness of every creation of the past and the distance from which it is appreciated in the present.

John Ruskin was the first to express a full awareness of the consequences of this break in the continuity of tradition introduced by the development of the modern historical consciousness:

Neither by the public, nor by those who have the care of public monuments, is the true meaning of the word restoration [meaning the reconstruction, whether total or partial, suggested by revivalism] understood. It means the most total destruction which a building can suffer: a destruction out of which no remnants can be gathered: a destruction accompanied with false description of the thing destroyed. Do not let us deceive ourselves in this important matter; it is impossible, as impossible as to raise the dead, to restore [meaning reconstruct] anything that has ever been great or beautiful in architecture. That which I have above insisted upon as the life of the whole, that spirit which is given only by the hand and eye of the workman, can never be recalled. Another spirit may be given by another time, and it is then a new building; but the spirit of the dead workman cannot be summoned up, and commanded to direct other hands, and other thoughts.[3]

Modern developments of aesthetics and principles of historical criticism and philology can only confirm the truth expressed by Ruskin.[4] Each work of art, each piece of decoration, each historic document is unique and cannot be repeated without faking. It is like a dead language: One can know and understand Latin or Sanskrit, but one cannot speak these languages anymore because such speech could not be genuine expression. The genuine voice of the past is exactly what must be safeguarded by preservation/

conservation. The survival of traditional crafts should not mislead one here. What survives of the craftsman's tradition in the new industrial world is its practical skill, and while this skill can certainly be of great use in conservation, it is no longer a genuine expression either of the past or of the present. To ignore this would mean to close one's eyes to the fact that the modern historical consciousness has irreversibly broken the traditional continuity and, therefore, would lead to a faked expression. If the conservation of an object or building requires an intervention or substitution, the intervention should be recognized as a modern, critical action. How to integrate the modern intervention without faking the original object is an essential question of conservation, and the way in which the modern intervention is handled makes the difference between the restorer or conservator and the traditional craftsman.

WHAT TO PRESERVE AND INVENTORY: CRITERIA

Every object (or complex of objects) that is recognized to be of artistic or historical significance is entitled to be safeguarded as an item of cultural value and as a legacy of the past to the present and the future. The recognition of such significance, however, does not depend upon the fulfillment of preestablished criteria, but rather upon the progress of the development of the historical consciousness and the culture of the people involved. This progress is expressed by the work of historians and the sensitiveness of cultivated people.[5] As a matter of fact, the range of interest in this connection has been continuously expanding since the beginning of the 19th century, progressively including all cultures of the world and all kinds of folklore and reaching up to the threshold of the present, which in turn will deserve protection whenever its objects qualify as items with artistic or social value. The universality of this modern viewpoint, as compared to the classicistic or nationalistic one, does not prevent some fluctuation of values from one nation to the other. In fact, this fluctuation is quite justified inasmuch as the significance of the past is indeed relative to the peoples who recognize it as their past. Any other view of universal values would be a purely abstract one.

Since the first step toward conservation is to establish an inventory of what should be conserved, criteria that recognize the creative quality, documentary significance and impact of the object on human consciousness must be established. Such criteria will, of course, never crystallize in fixed rules but will reflect the development of each country's culture.

METHODOLOGY

The Approach to the Object

The first operation in any conservation process is to assess accurately the substance of the object to be safeguarded. This may seem obvious but, alas, is not, and ignoring this operation by considering it to be obvious may result in irreparable mistakes. The problem's main aspects may be summarized in three questions: (1) What is to be considered the whole of the object, to which all operations must be referred? (2) What is the context of the object? and (3) What has been the history of the object?

THE WHOLE OF THE OBJECT. The importance of the whole must be stressed because positivistic habits of classification have accustomed us to divide various arts according to technique and to split the whole of a monument into various pieces scattered throughout various sections of museums and galleries. What was once a Gothic altarpiece may be dismantled into isolated sculptures, easel paintings and decorative carvings, the result being that the experience of the altarpiece as a whole has to be rediscovered. This rediscovery includes, for example, defining the artistic relationships that existed among sculptures, reliefs and paintings.

The same situation applies to architecture, which today is often reduced to that part of the building that can be expressed in architectural drawings, thereby arbitrarily separating structure and decoration. One especially vivid example of this kind of separation concerns the plasterwork within a structure and its color. The result of this separation is that today original plasterwork is becoming so rare that it is difficult to know its genuine character in various periods and styles.

Germans have a convenient word to stress this importance of the whole of the monument. By *Gesamtkunstwerk*, they mean the unity resulting from the cooperation of the various arts and crafts that combine to make a monument and cannot be divided from it.

It is obvious that what is a whole must be treated consistently as a whole, and this implies that close cooperation among various specialists in preservation—architects, conservators, artisans—under one consistent policy is necessary. On the other hand, each fragment will have to be treated as such, keeping in mind the whole to which it once belonged.

CONTEXT. Context refers to an object's immediate surroundings, inasmuch as these determine the approach and, thus, the correct interpretation of the object; that is, the frame of a picture, traditional surroundings of a monument that are essential to its scale and significance and social circumstances in which the object is or was used, this consideration being especially important for liturgic or ethnographic objects.

In some cases, the context may be an object, as is the case, for instance, of minor architecture in historic centers, when no individual building is a work of art but the whole becomes a monument in itself (e.g., the Campo dei Fiori in Rome). An object should never be deprived of its context, if the object is to avoid becoming isolated and "museumized," that is, segregated from life.

The recognition of the value of the whole and the object's context leads logically to the principle that every object should, whenever possible, be conserved in situ if one wants to save the full value of the whole and of the parts. This applies to wallpaintings, altarpieces and sculptured decoration. It also applies to architecture and to its architectural or natural surroundings. Exceptions to this principle must be made, however (e.g., in situations where a fresco or building can be preserved only by disassembling and moving it, even though the movement will produce unavoidable and irreparable damage). The open-air museum is an emergency solution and is almost a contradition in itself, since vernacular architecture is existentially linked to its surroundings, even more so than major monuments that can impose themselves on their surroundings. Hence, there is the almost inherent tendency of the open-air museum to evolve into a Disneyland: No longer is it a preservation of history in the present, but rather a projection of fantasy into objects of the past, which is a special variety of faking.

THE OBJECT'S HISTORY. A monument of the past, be it architecture, sculpture, painting or any combination of these forms of art, has come to man through time and history. During this period, it usually undergoes changes of various kinds—additions, reductions or modifications in shape, use or sense due to man's interventions and material alterations due to physical and chemical processes.[6] Furthermore, the way the object is perceived is continuously evolving as the result of the historic development of a culture, especially aesthetic sensitiveness. Each new experience in art changes one's view of the history of all art in the way that one's vision of colors is no longer the same after experiencing Impressionism.

All this history must be taken into consideration when establishing what is the whole to be safeguarded. Indeed, history and time cannot be undone; they are irreversible. However, those additions that are recognized to be of no historical or artistic significance and that distort or obliterate the object can rightly be re-

FIGURE 1. The Laokoon *in the Vatican Museum as restored by Montorsoli in the 16th century. (Vatican Museum)*

moved. But removal always requires a justified decision, thus showing the inescapable freedom and cultural responsibility of the restorer in making history.

It is an illusion to believe that an object can be brought back to its original state by stripping it of all later additions. The original state is a mythical, unhistorical idea, apt to sacrifice works of art to an abstract concept and present them in a state that never existed. Tendencies, much supported by archaeologists, to strip medieval churches of their baroque or even 19th-century decora-

372

FIGURE 2. The Laokoon *after recent restoration work, which destroyed the work of Montorsoli, showing only the original pieces, including the newly rediscovered right arm. (Vatican Museum)*

tion in order to discover naked walls without their original plaster or furnishing and to undo old restorations of classical sculpture have led to a great deal of destruction without ever succeeding in reestablishing the appearance of the work at a real historic moment (figs. 1–2).[7]

The patina resulting from material alterations of an object has been the subject of much controversy, especially in the field of easel paintings.[8] This, however, should be considered as only a particular case of a more general problem. Physical and/or chemical alterations of original materials are unavoidable and usually irreversible. They may, however, up to a point, be anticipated by the artist or accepted as an additional aesthetic value, like the traditional acceptance of the patina of bronzes, sometimes called "noble" patina. The point when such alterations are felt to be distortions of the object's value and not enhancements of its aesthetic quality cannot be defined objectively and is, therefore, a matter of critical interpretation and cultural responsibility. It should be clear, in any case, that simple removal of the patina on a bronze or a painting will not recover the object's original appearance, but only uncover the present state of the original material. Furthermore, what is the original appearance? At what moment can it be fixed? Obviously, the original state is an abstract idea and not a historical reality. Bear in mind also that any attempt at removing a patina, which is, of course, a modification of the original material, will necessarily result in a further alteration of the material. It should be admitted, therefore, that the patina is a part of the object's original substance as transmitted to man through history and that any attempt to eliminate it will damage the original substance and introduce a historical contradition, inasmuch as removal will show an old object in fresh, or new-looking, material. For example, the drastic cleaning of pictures or bronzes is in no way an objective approach to the object, and it would be easy to show that the decision in recent times to so treat an object being "restored" has been greatly determined by a definite aesthetic approach, influenced by the new sensitivity to materials developed by Expressionism and the Bauhaus.

The cleaning of facades, inaugurated in Paris as a matter of political prestige, brings to the fore the complicated nature of this problem. Assuming that cleaning will not harm the original material, it remains that the appearance of each building will look "correct" only when all the surrounding buildings are equally clean, but the patina, or dirt, forms again so quickly on the freshly cleaned facades that such a general unity is never reached. What results is that cleaned buildings look like white ghosts in their darkened context. Even regular maintenance is hardly a solution as long as the causes of pollution are not eliminated.

The Fragmented Object; Lacunae and Their Integration; Archaeology and Museum Objects

The problem of lacunae (i.e., missing parts of objects) and the object in fragments may best be approached from the viewpoint used in dealing with museum objects and archaeological remains which, being free from the requirements of practical functions, allow for the strictest interpretation of basic principles.

The lacuna, be it in a picture, sculpture or monument of architecture, appears to be an interruption of the continuity of the object's artistic form and its rhythm. Since the object's completeness is no longer a necessity (and often, the fragmented object has acquired a value in its fragmented state, as is the case for a ruin or a torso), the only aim of restoration should be to reduce or eliminate the disturbance caused by lacunae in such a way that the intervention can be unmistakably identified as such (i.e., as a critical interpretation).

Philology has shown the way to achieve that aim in a long tradition of the editing of old manuscripts. In the editing, the missing word or words are never added by the editor unless they can be safely reconstructed, and this interpretation is then clearly indicated as a reconstruction by the use of special printing devices and footnotes. Missing words are never written on the original manuscript. Since in the case of a work of art the editing has to be done on the object itself, the same principles require that special practical devices be applied to a painting, sculpture or monument of architecture, while the basic philosophy is fundamentally the same as that applied in philology. Therefore, in each case, it is necessary to make a distinction between lacunae that may and lacunae that should not be reintegrated.

Reintegration will be justified only when lacunae are relatively small and so situated that there can be no doubt about what was lost and when the new work is sufficiently limited so as to avoid the reconstruction's appearing to quantitatively overwhelm the original parts and making the whole seem to be a fake or a copy. The reintegration (used in preference to the terms "retouching" and "inpainting") should then aim to reestablish the continuity under normal conditions, while being easily identified on closer inspection. There are various technical solutions to this problem, and the restorer will have to use his artistic feeling, as well as his knowledge of materials, to find the best answer, one essential point being the consistency of the reintegration system. Hatchings in paintings and changes of material or of surface treatment (akin to but different from the original) in sculpture and architecture have given satisfactory results (figs. 3–7).

When lacunae cannot be reintegrated because this process would be too hypothetical or because there would be more lacunae reintegrated than there would be remains of the original, restoration should consist of treating lacunae in such a way that their disturbance is reduced to a minimum. As Cesare Brandi has shown

FIGURE 3. *Detail of the Arch of Titus in the Roman Forum as restored by Valladier, using travertine instead of marble and leaving the modern parts unfinished. (F. Rigamonti)*

in a penetrating study where he refers to the structures of perception according to Gestalt psychology,[9] the treatment should consist of preventing lacunae from becoming so patterned over the work that the original image recedes into the background. Lacunae. should, on the contrary, be made to appear as the background before which the work is perceived. The disturbance due to lacunae will then be reduced to a minimum. Here again, the technical

376

FIGURE 4. *West sidewall of the Arch of Constantine. Lacunae in the middle show more respect for the original and are better integrated than those at the base of the wall, where white patches are disturbing. (F. Rigamonti)*

devices may be many, but consistency in approach is essential. As a rule, the object's technical construction, especially that of a painting, will suggest solutions, such as lacunae being treated as the receding surface of the ground or the support or arriccio in wallpaintings, with a conveniently adjusted texture and color if necessary.

A special problem arises in the archaeological field. A ruin is

FIGURE 5. *Wall of the Curia in the Roman Forum showing good restoration technique. Restoration was completed with bricks placed slightly below the level of old bricks and a hammered surface to allow easy distinction of old and new. (F. Rigamonti)*

normally considered the object to be preserved, not as a fragment of the object, since ruins themselves are cultural objects with their own specific emotional values and appeals to the imagination, which would be completely destroyed by an attempt to restore the ruin to its original state.

There is one case, however, where such an intervention may be contemplated. When all fragments of a part or the whole of a building have been preserved and can be reassembled with the certainty that in so doing the original shape is restored, then one may be justified in performing an *anastylosis* (i.e., the reconstruction of the object from its scattered fragments), with modern additions being strictly limited to what is required for static safety and justified as reintegration. Obviously, anastylosis can be contemplated only when the building is of dry masonry (i.e., joints allow for an exact restitution of the original shape) and pieces have not suffered deformation by erosion.

378

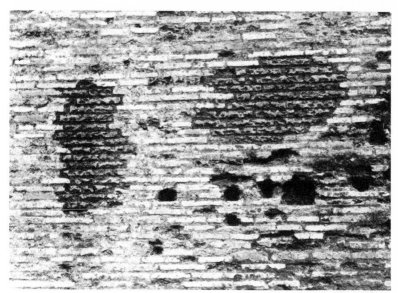

FIGURE 6. *Detail of the Curia wall, showing the surface treatment of bricks used for filling holes. (F. Rigamonti)*

When joints are made with mortar, as in brick structures, disassembling and reassembling even a complete building will result in faking, as the old mason's peculiar rhythm in laying the bricks is replaced by a mechanical dryness and hardness of line due to the modern way of working.

As is stated in the Venice Charter of 1964, anastylosis is the only justified form of archaeological reconstruction, because it is the only one that can reestablish the genuine object. Any other kind of reconstruction that the archaeologist may be able to achieve on the basis of fragments, iconographic documents or descriptions can refer only to a knowledge of the lost object. Such a knowledge cannot be identified with the real object without faking; it should, therefore, be materialized in drawings or models, but never in actual reconstruction of the object.

The Object Still in Use and Its Context

Once the guidelines for safeguarding an object's value have been defined in the "pure" situation of archaeological and museum objects, one may consider what special adjustments may be necessary for objects that have retained a practical social function; this refers in particular to architecture and to ethnographic objects in traditional societies.

As regards architecture, it is obvious that lacunae may have to be supplied to a much larger extent than may be justified on aesthetic grounds for archaeological remains. However, the two

FIGURE 7. The Flagellation *by Piero della Francesca in the Ducal Palace, Urbino, Italy. Detail with retouching in hatching technique* (tratteggio). *(F. Rigamonti)*

basic requirements for reintegration and easy identification of the intervention are still valid in this instance, their validity extending up to the point where the intervention would become hypothetical or so extended that only a modern creation would avoid faking. When an entirely contemporary intervention is called for, original parts of the structure (or group of structures) will constitute the basic elements of the design problem, the aim being to achieve a harmony within the larger unity of a contemporary environment.

Such creative integration requires a study of the old building, its context and perhaps the whole historic center where it is located in order to establish the peculiar rhythm of the old complex and to adjust the scheme of the modern creation to the basic modules and materials that already exist. Since control of social and economic factors will also be essential in achieving a harmonious development, a new, dynamic and multisided systematic study of historic complexes in the larger, town-planning frame of reference will have to be developed in order to bridge the gap between the classical conservation approach to the structure and the need to maintain a living, human environment.[10] One point ought to be stressed in this regard: A detailed evaluation, through a thorough study of the structure or complex of buildings, must always precede any study of adaption to new functions. Otherwise, restoration will unavoidably give way to exercises in modern architecture made at the expense of old buildings.

Ethnographic objects, although when taken individually do not differ from other museum objects, present a number of special problems when they are considered in their contemporary contexts. For instance, an object may lose all its sense once separated from its original function. Hence the question: What is to be preserved? Should interest be limited to the object and not to its social environment? It is clear that conservation activity cannot be separated from information gained in the collection of materials and documentation in the field. This is all the more true when the material of the object may make conservation almost impossible: Shall the symbolic wedding cake be conserved or the ceremony carefully documented? The tendency of modern art to overemphasize the event (or happening) and to despise the resulting object might lead to similar considerations.

The deeper problem of the conservation of the ethnographic patrimony of traditional cultures is that of a "museumization" of a culture through an anthropological approach. But is this situation not in a way parallel to that of functioning buildings in a historic center? Here again, a creative integration is needed. This, however, is threatened by two terrible forces: the tourist coming from the industrialized world who, in the same manner as King Midas who changed into gold everything he touched, (1) changes tradition into an empty show and (2) fosters the illusion that traditional crafts can remain genuine when kept unchanged in a changing society, which in fact results only in encouraging new varieties of cultural kitsch.

FIGHTING THE CAUSES

Any long-term conservation policy must be concerned more with fighting causes of deterioration than with repairing its effects. It should be realized, therefore, as Max Dvorak has,[11] that the main causes of the deterioration of cultural property are human ones, which may be identified and classified as follows:

1. Neglect due to ignorance or lack of cultural interest.
2. Purposeful disrepair or destruction for ideological reasons.
3. Destruction due to priorities being given to economic considerations and traffic.

381

4. Fake reconstruction due to various factors:

a. The romantic confusion of a revival versus a genuine historical experience.

b. The illusion that the survival of traditional craftsmanship can express traditional values in a world where values have changed.

c. The confusion of archaeological knowledge and the actual monument or structure.

d. The exploitation of monuments or structures of the past for symbolic-ideological purposes.

No philosophy of restoration based on safeguarding the authentic witness of the past will ever be successfully carried out unless these adverse forces are fought and defeated.

NOTES

1. On the history of restoration, see Carlo Ceschi, *Teoria e Storia del Restauro* (Rome: Mario Bulzoni, 1970).

2. Eugène Viollet-le-Duc, *Dictionnaire raisonné d'Architecture* (Paris: F. de Nobele, 1967), s. v. "Restauration."

3. John Ruskin, *The Seven Lamps of Architecture* (London: George Allen and Unwin, Ltd., 1925), chap. VI, aphorism 31, pp. 353–54.

4. See Cesare Brandi, *Teoria del Restauro* (Rome: Edizioni di Storia e Letteratura, 1963).

5. See Giulio Carlo Argan, "La Storia dell'Arte," *Storia dell'Arte* nos. 1–2 (1969): 5–36. See also Roland Günter, "Glanz und Elend der Inventarisation," *Deutsche Kunst und Denkmalpflege* 28, nos. 1–2 (1970): 109–17.

6. Brandi, *Teoria del Restauro*, pp. 99–103.

7. On the unjustified removal of baroque decoration in medieval churches, see Benedikt Nicolson, "Restoration of Monuments in Tuscany," *Burlington Magazine* 113, no. 813 (December 1970): 789–92; on the equally unjustified removal of Renaissance, baroque and classicistic restoration of antique sculptures, see Jürgen Paul, "Antikenergänzung und Ent-Restaurierung," *Kunst-Chronik* no. 4 (April 1972): 85–112.

8. See Paul Philippot, "Le notion de patine et le nettoyage des peintures," *Bulletin de l'Institut Royal du Patrimoine Artistique* 1, no. 9 (1966): 138–43.

9. Cesare Brandi, "Il trattamento delle lacune e la Gestalt-psychologie," in *Studies in Western Art: Acts of the XX International Congress of History of Art.* ed. Millard Meiss et al. (Princeton, N.J.: Princeton University Press, 1963), vol. 4, *Problems of the 19th and 20th Centuries*, pp. 146–51.

10. Compare, in this regard, Ingrid Brock, Roberto Giuliani and Christian Moisescu, *Il Centro antico di Capua: Metodi di analisi per la pianificazione architectonico-urbanistica* (Padua, Italy: Marsilio Editori, 1972) and D. Stephen Pepper, "Conservation and Its Social Context," *Paragone* 22, no. 257 (July 1971): 77–85.

11. Max Dvorak, *Katechismus der Denkmalpflege* (Vienna: Julius Bard, 1918).

COMMENTARY

WILLIAM J. MURTAGH

I was so stimulated by the remarks of Paul Philippot and George McCue that I drafted two sets of criteria, one concerning districts and the other related to individual elements within districts (see the sections following, "Proposed District Criteria" and "Proposed Criteria for Elements Within Districts"). I hope these criteria will prove to be as enlightening as the papers that prompted me to draft them.

Mr. Philippot, I believe, lists all of the abstracts necessary to evaluate the worth of a thing, whether it be a building, an object, an open space or whatever. These abstracts may be useful in helping to solve a problem that preservationists in the United States face, that is, in answering the question "What qualities and values must be considered when one is evaluating the linkages of buildings in an area (or what is in the United States called a historic district)?" Mr. McCue, on the other hand, attacks the subject of preservation philosophy and criteria from the same viewpoint that I would have chosen, as we both have been exposed many times to actual situations and programs in local communities throughout the United States. We also share the experience of believing we have been addressing the crux of a preservation issue before a city council only to have an alderman say, "Come to the point. What are you talking about?"

At this juncture, I would like to share with you a recent an-

William J. Murtagh is keeper of the National Register of Historic Places, National Park Service, U.S. Department of the Interior, Washington, D.C.

nouncement made by the Secretary of the Interior. He announced the approval of an apportionment of almost $7 million to assist in the acquisition and restoration of historic resources in the United States. For the benefit of those from other countries, I should explain that these funds are administered through the grant-in-aid program of the National Register of Historic Places, a branch of the National Park Service, U.S. Department of the Interior. This is a 50 percent matching program, so there will be approximately $14 million available in the next year for surveys to find out what historic resources exist in the country, for the development of statewide plans in each state to determine what should be done with these resources and for the actual development of these resources. Forty-seven states, the District of Columbia, American Samoa and the National Trust for Historic Preservation will share in this almost $7 million grant.

These funds reassert this country's national commitment to historic preservation, which was originally set forth in the National Historic Preservation Act of 1966. As keeper of the National Register and, therefore, an administrator of the act, I consider it to be a piece of environmental legislation concerned with man-made America. It charges us with the responsibility to keep the cultural ecology of our country in balance. My remarks here are not directed toward economic or sociological aspects of that responsibility; they are instead made in terms of aesthetics and visual impact.

However, before commenting specifically on points raised in the authors' papers, I would say that, by and large, restorationists in the United States are aware that fine arts conservators generally have a greater degree of laboratory expertise than do restorationists, who deal with the same materials as conservators but in an uncontrolled atmosphere. In fact, to my mind, the *raison d'être* of this conference is to discover the differences and similarities between the two fields and to ascertain how each can help the other. I have decided to approach this commentary on a district basis because the question that I am asked constantly all over the country is "How does one know when a district exists?" This is also the reason I drafted the criteria mentioned previously.

There are four points in Mr. Philippot's paper that piqued my interest: his concepts of the whole of an object, its context and its impact on human consciousness and his statement that removal of any fabric will always require a justified decision and, thus, show "the inescapable freedom and cultural responsibility of the restorer in making history."

Additions, deletions and modifications are generally made to an object (or building) on the basis of historical associations and/or the artistic quality reflective of the period when it was created. Consideration should also be given to whether such changes will distort, obliterate or enhance the intangible values that are associated with the object, building or collection. Of course, changes may affect these intangible values in either a positive or negative manner. Problems that result from such changes are encountered more frequently and are of a more difficult nature when a collection of buildings, rather than a single building, is involved. This is so because a collection is relatively immobile, whereas a small, single building can be moved easily to another site. The same is true for objects that are in the care of conservators. No matter what decision is made—that is, whether changes are allowed or not—it will always, as Mr. Philippot points out, require a justified decision by the restorer.

There has been an increasing interest in public and private sectors of this country in the development of criteria to evaluate sites, structures, buildings, objects and districts. Criteria promulgated by such organizations as the National Park Service and the National Trust have been published and used as guidelines by other groups. For instance, a criterion of the National Historic Landmarks Program states, "When preserved or restored as integral parts of the environment, historic buildings not sufficiently significant individually, by reason of historical association or architectural merit, to warrant recognition may collectively compose a historic district that is of historical significance to the nation in commemorating or illustrating a way of life in its developing culture." Essentially, this program, which is under the supervision of the Park Service, allows the Secretary of the Interior to designate districts, sites or buildings as landmarks of national significance. In May 1971, President Richard M. Nixon issued an executive order directing all federal agencies to nominate their historic resources to the National Register. The definition of a district developed by the Park Service as a result of that order says, "A geographically definable area, urban or rural, possessing a significant concentration or linkage of sites, buildings, structures or objects unified by past events or aesthetically by plan or physical development."

I believe neither of these definitions spells out in sufficient detail criteria for a district. Also lacking are guidelines relating to the preservation of individual significant structures within a district. I call such structures *pivotal buildings*. Every district has a "bone structure" of pivotal buildings; these are usually public buildings that are surrounded by vernacular structures, which together give a sense of time and place. Pivotal buildings may be defined as those significant structures in an environment that receive their scale and emphasis from their relationships with anonymous buildings that surround them and link the area into a cohesive whole. Therefore, it follows that if the linkage of anonymous structures surrounding pivotal buildings is changed by destruction, which introduces missing parts into the fabric, or by replacement, which may change the nature of the fabric, the district's bone structure of pivotal buildings may be improved or destroyed, according to the quality and degree of change. *Gesamtkunstwerk*, that catch-all German word mentioned by Mr. Philippot which means a sense of unity, is, therefore, either improved or impoverished by changes. To be insensitive to this *Gesamtkunstwerk*, to not understand its importance or to ignore it lays the basis for the destruction of a district. Gradual incursions on this sense of the whole will eventually result in a changed environment or context. The previous urban fabric disappears, and all that is left are pivotal buildings, which remain because of their scale, happenstance of placement, historical associations or aesthetic quality. Such pivotal buildings thus become isolated structures out of context and out of sympathy in scale, touch, texture, color, mass and materials with other structures in the redeveloped area. They then function only as isolated visual reminders of what once was there.

This situation can easily be seen in the redevelopment areas of downtown Saint Louis, Mo.; southwest Washington, D.C.; and in many other neighborhoods in this country where the drastic surgery of government-supported urban renewal has leveled vast areas or where private development, unfettered by sufficient control through master planning at municipal, county or state levels, has allowed democratic enterprise to run amuck. This is not to imply that change should not take place in "living" districts, as Mr. Philippot calls them, but it does imply that a district's intangible qualities can be destroyed suddenly by the total or near-total clearance of an area or gradually by attrition, as Mr. McCue points out. In any case, any substantial amount of change produces changed relationships and results in a new and different ambience.

The Trentman House in the Georgetown section of Washington, D.C., mentioned by Mr. McCue as a contemporary building that has through its scale, design, etc., retained the particular sense of the whole of Georgetown, is an excellent example of the problem that faces architect-preservationists and planners when the introduction of a new element in the linkage is proposed. No informed individual would deny that this house is an excellent contemporary design and that it exists in harmony with its older neighbors by virtue of its material, height, proportion, color, mass, rhythm of solids and voids, etc. However, it replaced an early 19th-century, one and a half story structure that was on a raised basement and had a gable roof with two dormers. It was an average house, set slightly back on its lot and with clapboarded sides painted white, but it was a decent expression of its age. The immediate area is a melange of one and a half, two and three story brick and wooden structures of the 18th, 19th and 20th centuries. Questions then arise: Was the destruction of the earlier house a loss of the sense of the whole? If so, why? If no, why not? The earlier structure was wood and created a break in the street wall by its setback; the facade of the new house lines up with those of its neighbors and is brick as they are. Is the replacement better than the earlier structure or should the early 19th-century house have been retained? Why? I leave you with these questions.

Mr. McCue outlines another problem, which Mr. Philippot calls the history of the object, namely, the restoration of the Faneuil Hall–Quincy Market area in Boston. Mr. McCue points out that in deciding how the restoration of the area should be approached, there is a troublesome question of "whether this famous historic district should retain some of the marks of the vicissitudes of its long existence." The Quincy Market buildings were enlarged over the years, as was Faneuil Hall. The difference lies in the visual result of the enlargements. Faneuil Hall retains the same general shape, silhouette and scale as it did originally; only its size has changed. However, the shape and silhouette of the buildings that comprise Quincy Market have changed greatly. Many of those buildings' gable roofs were changed into flat roofs. The problem restorers face seems to be one of aesthetics, but it also involves the history of the area. Therefore, while recognizing the fallacies of the philosophy that assumes the validity of restoration to a particular point in time, the "let-it-alone" philosophy appears to have a point of diminishing returns in allowing any accretion to remain on the basis of its sheer existence. A value judgment must be made. The problem, it seems, harks back to that "inescapable freedom and cultural responsibility of the restorer in making history."

Although the discussion thus far has dealt primarily with problems of districts, single buildings in districts and relationships of pivotal buildings to each other and to the anonymous structures that surround them, all of these entities function in relation to spaces between, around and among them to form the context of the whole. Thus, changes in street or sidewalk width and in surface material, height, proportion, scale, color, etc., of street facades results in open spaces assuming new relationships to the whole.

The quality of such abstracts as continuity, relatedness and rhythm among all elements in a district—buildings, open spaces, street furniture, etc.—produces a positive or negative effect on the environment.

One purpose of this commentary is to suggest criteria for the preservation of individual elements within a district in ways that will maintain the collective impact of the district. One assumes that this impact on human consciousness comes mainly from visual aspects, or creative qualities, of elements that compose the district and that, therefore, aesthetics should be the primary basis for preservation decisions, with other aspects of significance secondary. This is not true in the United States. In reading preservation literature from abroad, one finds that aesthetics, or visual impact, is given first priority and history second. In the United States, however, historical significance has traditionally been the primary justification for preservation, followed by cultural value. I believe this emphasis on history has caused many of those local preservation battles Mr. McCue mentions to be lost.

I present the following lists of criteria for facilitating not only the recognition of a historic district but also the recognition of preservable elements within a district, whether they be buildings, objects, sites or streets. These criteria are based on criteria set forth in the College Hill Study, a report concerned with an area in Providence, R.I.; the report on Savannah, Ga., prepared by Eric Hill Associates, Planning Consultants, and Muldawer and Patterson, AIA, Architects and Urban Designers; the papers presented at this conference by Mr. McCue and Mr. Philippot; and other sources. They are offered in hopes that further discussion will refine them to the point where they can be applied to our efforts to better the environment.

PROPOSED DISTRICT CRITERIA*

The quality of a district's significance can be ascribed to a collection of buildings, structures, sites, objects and spaces that possess integrity of location, design, setting, materials, workmanship, feeling and association such as:

Location: Areas that consist of a linkage of buildings, sites, objects and spaces, a majority of which continue to exist within the area

---

* These criteria have been further developed since this conference was held. The refined criteria have been published by the National Trust for Historic Preservation for the Rome Centre Committee of the Advisory Council on Historic Preservation under the title Historic Districts: Identification, Social Aspects and Preservation.

where they were first created in a mutual relationship of traditional acceptability.

Design: Areas that have a sense of cohesiveness expressed through a similarity and/or dissimilarity of detail, architectural or otherwise, based upon the abstracts of aesthetic quality. (These include scale, height, proportion, materials, colors, textures, rhythm, silhouette, siting, etc.)

Setting: Areas that are readily definable by man-made and/or natural boundaries and/or areas that have a major focal point or points within them.

Materials: Areas that have a sense of cohesiveness expressed through a similarity and/or dissimilarity of materials, based upon traditional use, which contribute to a sense of locality.

Workmanship: Areas that have a sense of homogeneity reflecting quality aesthetic effort of those periods in which the majority of the units that compose the district were constructed.

Feeling: Areas that impact human consciousness with a sense of time and place.

Association: Areas that relate on national, state or local levels to the lives of individuals, to events created by these individuals and/or to those visual aesthetic qualities that reflect the feeling of time and place.

PROPOSED CRITERIA FOR ELEMENTS WITHIN DISTRICTS

The quality of significance in any element of a linkage of buildings, structures, sites, objects or spaces is found in those refinements of visual relatedness that impact human consciousness with a sense of time and place to collectively create a sense of district through:

Scale: Based on local traditional relationships between spaces and facades defining scale and the component parts within a facade that relate to man.

Proportion: Based on local traditional height–width relationships of facades and the component parts within a facade that reflect the visual elements in the area that contribute to a district feeling.

Rhythm: Based on local traditional solid–void relationships of facades and the component parts within a facade that reflect the visual elements in the area that contribute to a district feeling.

Silhouette: Based on local traditional methods of handling the component elements that dictate the visual impact of mass on human consciousness and that reflect the visual elements in the area that contribute to a district feeling.

Height: Based on a mean derived from local traditional existing maximum–minimum heights within the area and within 10 percent of the height of existing adjacent elements.

Materials, Colors and Textures: Based on local traditional materials, colors and textures that reflect the visual elements in the area that contribute to a district feeling.

Design: Based on an element's reflection of local traditional design characteristics of a type, period or method of construction that embodies quality aesthetic effort representative of the time, place and period of construction of other elements or elements that represent the work of a known artisan, craftsman or architect, local or otherwise.

Association: Based on significant national, state or local events or individuals whose activities are linked with the building, structure, site or object.

COMMENTARY

DONALD W. INSALL, FRIBA

The papers presented by Paul Philippot and George McCue contrast with and illuminate each other. Mr. Philippot's paper deals with the philosophy of restoration and suggests some criteria and guidelines. Mr. McCue's paper discusses a different area, preservation, and he focuses on the question of public appreciation. I find myself magnetized by his unspecified, but quite clear question: What does one do when experts disagree?

I have many friends who are experts in different ways. In Britain, we define an expert as "a man who knows more and more about less and less." For this reason, is it not actually the function of experts to differ? The expert is a partisan. He is partial in more ways than one, for he is, perhaps, less than complete in the sense of the Renaissance man. Let us look at some of these experts who are my friends.

One kind of expert is the *historian:* He is interested in time—that is, in continuity and change. The historian accepts not only past change but present change, and every evidence of change is most precious to him. Architecturally, he enjoys walls with bits of the plaster peeled off to exhibit the layers of historical evidence beneath. He laments the loss of historical data that results when a tidy-minded parish council decides to remove or regroup the headstones in a churchyard to make a place for children to play.

Donald W. Insall, FRIBA, is a restoration architect and planner in private practice in London, England.

We can well understand how the historian feels, but would we not occasionally differ with him? Would some experts not feel that a building's architectural integrity might be impaired by stripping it to show its history?

Another expert is the *nostalgist,* who is interested in the memory of emotions and in architecture that evokes recollections. He is a poet, too. Like the historian, he is mainly interested in things that are changing, especially things that are changing for the worse. And he would say, "What is not changing for the worse?" This nostalgia, which we all share in varying degrees, is associated with the slightly vulturelike sense of impending destruction that is evoked by the smell of steam evaporating from tractors or by the sight of a windmill without sails, like a fly without its wings. The nostalgist may not be very sympathetic toward town planning; might you sometimes be unsympathetic, too? Or, if you are a planner, would some of the ideas of the nostalgist seem to you to be perhaps impractical or uncomplete?

The *archaeologist* lives for the pleasure and the zest of discovery, which for him is its own reward. It must be a rewarding experience, for there is little money in the field. Like the reader of a detective story or the solver of a "who-done-it," the archaeologist revels in revelation. He is sometimes curiously unsympathetic to the public's desire to enjoy his revelations too. Like the writer of mystery plays, he would almost like to ask his audience not to divulge the plot and would prefer deliberately to disguise the plot with decoy characters. It does not bother him to record a discovery and then cover it up again. Of course, it is true that this is usually done to prevent the discovery from being destroyed. As far as this archaeologist is concerned, when the primary pleasure of discovery is past, nothing further remains to be done. Therefore, he is suspicious of educators, exhibitors and display experts. Sometimes I agree with him; would not you?

The *town planner* is an environmental expert. He is not so much concerned about the past as about today and tomorrow and about cultivating surroundings fit for our children to live in. (Actually, his touch is surer in dealing with today's challenges than in planning for tomorrow's, although he does not always realize this.) The planner sees clearly that a town must be viable and successful if it is to continue and to live. He is a bit of an opportunist. Often, he has been trained as an architect and, as such, seeks to conserve any felicitous grouping of buildings that presents an enjoyable experience, such as the experience afforded by just about every square foot of Venice, with its countless vistas and architectural contrasts. At times, the planner becomes desperately upset by archaeologists, whom he feels show little concern for the physical appearance of things and even less for their survival. Having been trained as an architect myself, I sympathize with this expert. At times, when I disagree with him, I have an awkward feeling like the feeling I have when I get cross with my son, who has his father's faults.

The *medical doctor* is another friend who is an expert. His life is dedicated to maintaining his patients' lives, health and vitality. He takes a unique interest in each of them and finds remarkably few of them unworthy of this interest. Sometimes, he may agree that additional advice might be sought from a specialist, but in doing so he is always a little skeptical, feeling that a surgeon will suggest the knife instead of medication and pills, which his own training suggests is the right treatment.

There are, of course, many other specialists. There is the *antique dealer* who delights in the best work of distinguished furniture manufacturers. He looks for the maker's name on every piece of furniture and insists on good workmanship. He does not hold at all with the *aristocrat*, who has a seedy, stately home full of bits of furniture that his grandfather liked but that is not at all "correct" in period. I also have a *philatelist* friend, who is mainly interested in defects or irregularities in stamps, such as an upside-down picture. Fortunately, he does not like architecture. There is also the *zoologist*, who is concerned with animals and animal behavior as it relates to the environment. He is fascinated by family likenesses and by vernacular and everyday things. He cannot stand the antique dealer.

Then there is the *museum curator*. The objects he collects are not allowed to undergo further change; they are displayed in a cabinet alongside similar artifacts from different periods selected as evidence to support the art theories of the day. The curator appreciates such open-air museums as Pueblo Español at Barcelona and Spon Street in Coventry, where a variety of objects are displayed side by side and can be easily studied and compared just as one does with a collection of butterflies pinned on a tray for display. The curator has an excellent staff of *conservators,* whose main concern is in determining and restoring the original identity of artifacts and relating other data to this original aspect. They give high marks only to what is original, and they are suspicious of the *architect* because he makes value judgments and feels he may reasonably make choices about what he likes.

I have two more specialist friends: One of them is a *commentator,* a diarist, a guide. He collects, rearranges and describes impressions. He aims to share with others his own highly developed power of observation and his travel experiences, as did his fore-bears.

I have many other friends who are simply *preservation minded*. They do not very much like change; they like the status quo. They point out, as Mr. McCue does in his discussion of the Fanueil Hall Markets, that generations have liked a particular thing the way it is, so why change it? Actually, sometimes I believe I hate change too. Certainly I hate the roads that border my garden and the cars that travel the road and disturb me. On the other hand, I get quite cross when I go places and cannot park my car simply because other selfish people did not want parking lots bordering their gardens.

Lastly, there is the *restorer*, who sometimes calls himself a "restorationist." He seeks the most precise information possible concerning the original structure and appearance of an object and then refines any conjectures about what is missing. He delights in making scholarly reconstructions. He likes to re-create actual ways of life and to revive crafts. He trains craftsmen to copy original products. (Unfortunately, he has no control over the marketing of these products, and the uses to which they are put are not always authentic. For example, a Norfolk latch may be inappropriate on a flush door.) The restorer specializes in restoring things to a specific date, that is, to a specific point in history. This sometimes leads him to undo the work done in previous restoration attempts. He hates "patina" and does not much rejoice in the wrinkles on a face. He prefers to see things as they were at what he believes to have been their best moments.

Because I like all these experts in their different ways (each, of course, seeming to me so inferior to my own field of expertise!), I would not even wish to see them always agree. Should not special-ists agree to differ?

To summarize, I enjoyed enormously Mr. Philippot's thought-provoking, penetrating and true analysis of philosophies. I believe his analysis derives from the expert thinking with which I have the most sympathy—that of the conservator. The terms *restoration* and *preservation* might provoke some disagreement among us, but the message of his paper rings true. These philosophical ideas offer a delicate contrast to Mr. McCue's penetratingly observed carica-tures of the public attitude. And we must admit that we all are the "public," just as we are all at times "tourists." We all possess both these depths and these trivialities of observation in varying degrees, depending on our trades.

This recognition of the frailties of various experts strengthens my belief that conservation, whether it is the conservation of towns, buildings, gardens, decorations or furnishings, succeeds best as a team activity. This is true despite the fact that every member of the team may be a specialist, that all are experts and that, therefore, they all will differ and disagree. I suspect that only by agreeing to differ can experts learn from one another and learn to collaborate. I suspect, too, that only if experts work as a team can there be real success in recognizing and coordinating such a variety of approaches. Is this because conservation and preservation are essentially subjective and personal, even when they aim to be objective and universal? Does not conservation require a recognition of the past and a projection of it as a part of someone else's future?

My real uneasiness as a specialist derives from the fact that when, with the best will in the world, we experts try to assess the impact of an object on human consciousness, that is, when we try to project not only the shape or identity of a building but also its context into a different world—for instance, into the roaring traffic of Rome or the screaming motor horns of Naples—all decisions must be based on personal choice. For all choice is personal, and all experience is merely an experience of today. All judgment is subjective, and its wise employment calls for humility, adaptability, sometimes compromise and always love.

If this conference has taught us anything, surely it is this: As specialists, we will always differ, but in working together as a team lies our greatest hope of success in preserving the past for the future.

Procedures and Performance Standards

HISTORIC BUILDINGS: PROCEDURES FOR RESTORATION

W. EUGENE GEORGE, JR., AIA

This paper concerns procedures reasonable for the restoration of historic buildings. The procedures that follow are discussed individually in a sequential order. The order will be appropriate to many restoration projects but not necessarily to all. Each historic building will require an individual approach to its restoration, and each project will have its own particular set of problems to solve using its available resources. In each building to be restored, a sequence of procedures most applicable to the project should be identified.

Procedures to be discussed, in sequential order, are (1) the selection of personnel, (2) stabilization of the building, (3) initiation of a research program, (4) preparation of an architectural program, (5) development of design studies, (6) development of construction drawings and specifications, (7) reconstruction and restoration and (8) project follow-up.

PERSONNEL

A key individual in the restoration effort is the restoration architect, who must possess a spectrum of talents ranging from a knowledge of period architecture to a thorough understanding of modern building practice. He must prepare an architectural program satisfactory for established modern requirements, while at the same time preserving the historic nature of the structure. He must be able to adjust an old structure to new requirements of govern-

W. Eugene George, Jr., AIA, is resident architect at Colonial Williamsburg, Va.

ing codes and ordinances and to secure the inevitable variances. He needs to have not only a knowledge of building technology from several considerations but also an understanding of problems created by sinking foundations, crumbling walls and rotten timber.

In addition to these skills, the restoration architect must have site planning ability. He must be able to solve problems of providing parking and service elements and of installing and screening utilities and other technical necessities and human conveniences.

Most of all, the restoration architect must be a good designer, who is sensitive to and knowledgeable of the nature of historic aesthetics—qualities in space, geometry and proportion that constitute the essence of the architectural art. The architect particularly must have the ability to handle problems of architectural scale, because it is probable that the scale proper to the historic structure will be different from that of its younger neighbors. This difference, if well handled by the architect, can contribute to viewers' understanding of earlier life-styles.

Working with the architect should be an apprentice architect-draftsman, or several, and an architectural historian. All should collaborate as an inquisitive, imaginative and productive team. Their collaborative functions will be outlined in detail later.

Equally important is the client, generally an organization, which in this paper will be called the "committee." The committee's function is to define the particular historical value to be emphasized, to decide the function desired of the building, to measure the progress of the effort and to provide funds to accomplish the task.

Other necessary personnel will be discussed later.

With the committee appointed and the restoration team selected, three things should take place: stabilization of the building, initiation of a research program and preparation of an architectural program.

STABILIZATION OF THE BUILDING

Immediate action should be taken to stabilize the building temporarily, to negate effects of damaging insects and to arrest decay. Alarm systems may be installed on a temporary basis; the building may be secured and access to it controlled by responsible individuals. If, at this time, it is determined that certain materials known to be scarce will be required for the project, the materials should be identified, acquired and stored.

RESEARCH

Documentary research is a desirable first step in the restoration process, since it may reveal information pertinent to the direction of archaeological and physical research. A chronology of the life of the building should be the first effort. Although there will be interim reports concluded to satisfy certain questions, it is possible that the research task will never be totally finished. Thus, a reasonable part of the initial research effort should be the establishment of a system for filing future materials.

Physical research conducted at the building should commence with its careful measurement and be followed with the recording of these measurements through drawings accompanied by photographs. An engineering analysis of structural components, including foundations, should be made. There should also be a careful analysis of the site, indicating the position and size of all utilities, special drainage requirements and the possibility of foundation problems. Archaeological research should occur simultaneously with, if not before, the physical research.

The physical analysis and archaeological research should be reviewed continually with respect to the chronology defined during the documentary research stage. The chronology will determine what happened and when it occurred. The site work will reveal how and where it happened, as well as characteristics unique to the building's occupancy.

PROGRAMMING

Early discussions between the architect and committee should define the historical value to be emphasized and the period to which the building is to be restored. In addition, there should be a serious economic assessment of the building in its new role, attempting to measure personnel, physical restoration, operational and maintenance costs and comparing these costs with the building's potential income.

With the building chronology understood, a set of architectural measurements and photographs completed and archaeological and site analyses accomplished, the architectural program can be written.

The architect, having affirmation of the building's historical value, should at this point reassess the feasibility of using the building for the function proposed by the committee. A program will then be written to define each space required to satisfy the proposed function. Structural and mechanical requirements should be defined and specialists from these fields retained. Governing codes, ordinances and regulations should be assembled. When the program is approved by the committee, design studies may begin.

DESIGN

After approval of the architectural program, the architect is ready to make design studies to satisfy the program by the best use of the historic structure within the concept of the proposed function. It is probable that the original design was based on an established spatial concept. A spatial concept is the organizational arrangement of rooms (or spaces) in a building and their mutual relationship to each other, to outdoor spaces (courts, gardens, etc.) and to circulation elements (corridors, vestibules, doorways, etc.) that connect them. A related term is *plan type,* although in the minds of many, this term neglects the essential ingredient of architecture —space. Spatial concepts, although they may take several different forms during a historical period, are usually consistent within that period. Subsequent alterations and additions often distort the original concept. The architect's ability as a designer will be tested by how well he can reestablish, preserve and perhaps extend this concept to serve the building's new functional requirements.

The architect will also, during the initial design studies, be faced with two realities: One is that functional requirements will change in future utilizations of the building, and the other is that any program developed within the building is subject to expansion. Thus, the design should consider how best to maintain the building's historical value through many generations of use but to permit that use to expand and even to change while retaining the historical value.

The introduction of mechanical and electrical systems should in particular be studied carefully during the development of the design. Not only are these systems expensive to install, but they should be installed so that their replacement may be accomplished with ease. Site planning and landscaping are also important design elements and must be considered.

The research conducted during design studies should include additional detailed physical analyses—particularly to verify craft techniques, to establish original paint colors, to analyze plaster or mortar ingredients, etc.—and a determination of how items might be most readily procured or reproduced. Craftsmen in the restoration field should be consulted and arrangements made for their employment. Variances from governing codes and ordinances may need to be procured at this stage. Also, the acquirement of difficult-to-obtain materials should commence at the end of this stage.

Design drawings, research documents and a preliminary budget should be presented to the committee for its approval prior to the development of construction drawings.

CONSTRUCTION DRAWINGS AND SPECIFICATIONS

Following approval of the design by the committee, construction drawings may be prepared. Input from consultants and the continued evaluation of the existing building should be included as part of this preparation. The process of preparing drawings and specifications is a lengthy one, often requiring hundreds of man-hours. Alterations of the design after drawings are in process waste many hours, introduce more delays and mistakes and result in the added expense caused by such delays and mistakes. Costs skyrocket when the design is changed, especially during construction.

It is desirable to select a building contractor on a cost-plus or salary basis while drawings are in the final stages of development. A construction crew should be assembled to commence work when the drawings are completed. Restoration craftsmen are less numerous than mechanics serving the present building industry, and there should be adequate time allowed to acquire their services.

RECONSTRUCTION AND RESTORATION

On completion of drawings and specifications, contracts may be let, a building permit acquired and the physical reconstruction begun. An estimate of costs should be submitted, and a budget should be allocated in response to this estimate. The actual cost of work as it progresses must be measured continuously against the budget and adjustments made when necessary.

During construction, the primary role of the architect is one of supervision and assistance to the construction team, especially checking surfaces that have been removed, revealing any old work. New understanding may be gained when such old work is exposed, and readjustment of plans may be necessary because of such new evidence. In collaboration with craftsmen, the architect should conduct additional experiments to establish that the new work is accurately reproducing the old work. Drawings and photographs should be made to document all phases of the work as it progresses.

During reconstruction, an inspection and maintenance program should be established to guarantee longevity of the restored structure. Critical materials important for future repairs and replacement should be acquired. It is probable that maintenance will begin before the restored structure is ready for occupancy.

PROJECT FOLLOW-UP

Ultimately, the construction work will end, the committee will be dissolved and the restoration team will move to other commissions. Prior to this cessation of activities, the responsibility for perpetuating the goals that have been realized by the project should be established. The historical integrity of the building should be maintained even though changes will occur, and the building's particular historical values should be fixed in the minds of those who are to be responsible for maintaining its integrity. Future repairs and minor alterations should be accomplished only after a review of the previous effort, and this work must use similar materials with the same standards of craftsmanship.

Research discoveries and all the documentation accumulated during the course of the work should be organized, duplicated and housed with responsible agencies.

Properly restored and maintained, historic buildings are landmarks of cultural accomplishments—accomplishments that will have meaning and inspiration for those generations who are to come.

FORMAL PROCEDURES:
THEIR EFFECT ON PERFORMANCE
STANDARDS IN CONSERVATION

RICHARD D. BUCK

At the first meeting of the American Group of the International Institute for Conservation of Historic and Artistic Works (IIC-AG) in 1960, Murray Pease, conservator at the Metropolitan Museum of Art in New York City, proposed that a statement be drawn up outlining suggested standards of practice and professional relationships for conservators. A committee was appointed and in due time offered its report, now known as the Murray Pease Report, which IIC-AG adopted at its meeting in June 1963. On August 7, 1963, the report was approved for legal sufficiency.

The purpose of the report was to state certain general policies and procedures considered necessary as a basis for responsible professional behavior. By its existence alone, this report established standards that might be evoked for reference in the case of a controversy or legal action.

The Murray Pease Report was circulated in the United States and abroad.[1] The report, therefore, was made general and flexible enough to have application to persons whose training and operating habits differed widely. All members of the IIC, in the United States and abroad, are influenced in their professional procedures and behavior by this report.

Performance standards, of course, involve the competence of personnel. Any general discussion of this subject can only enumerate elements to be judged and circumstances of judgment. The

Richard D. Buck is director of the Intermuseum Laboratory, Intermuseum Conservation Association, Oberlin, Ohio.

final judgment on performance standards can be made only with reference to results. A judgment on results of a treatment becomes in a large degree subjective, governed by the sensitivity of the conservator or his critic to the aesthetic gestalt inherent in the object. This is a matter beyond this paper's scope.

I propose to describe practices and procedures used by the laboratory of the Intermuseum Conservation Association (ICA) in Oberlin, Ohio. Because of geography, the ICA has, from its beginning, communicated chiefly in writing with its member museums. To anticipate questions and avoid the misinterpretation of data, clarity and explicit detail have been mandatory in these communications. The ICA has, therefore, given much thought to the formalizing of procedures, to the organization of reports and to the precise meaning of words.

It is appropriate, in this connection, to pose some questions raised by some words used in the preliminary outline of this conference. The words *conservation, preservation* and *restoration* seem to be used more or less as synonyms but with application to different classes of objects. For instance, I am concerned with the maintenance of the structural and aesthetic integrity of museum objects. I call myself a *conservator* and my vocation *conservation*. I would willingly use these same words with reference to architecture. However, it appears that the maintenance of the structural and aesthetic integrity of a building is called *preservation*. Is there a defense for this apparently duplicating terminology? Does *conservation* signify taking steps to protect something from harm or deterioration, whereas *preservation* implies the rescue of a structure from threatened demolition? For instance, is Carpenters' Hall in Philadelphia preserved by establishing, through legal processes, its immunity from urban encroachment? Does *conservation* refer to the replacement of rotted sills and a leaky roof? Finally, does *restoration* cover studies carried out to determine an original paint color or the original design and subsequent changes made to the present structure? These are shades of meaning that are not clearly distinguished in the dictionary, but if vagueness and confusion are to be avoided, it would be wise to agree upon any special connotations.

A description of the formal procedures and specialized terminology used at the Intermuseum Laboratory, both of which have a bearing on standards of procedure and performance, may demonstrate the usefulness of such agreement.

INTERMUSEUM LABORATORY PROCEDURES

Inspections

The initiative procedure in the conservation of a collection is the inspection.[2] Periodic inspection is a condition of membership in the ICA. Inspections are carried out in the gallery. Observations are noted on permanent record cards and are updated through periodic rechecks, usually made annually. In the past two decades, several thousand cards have been accumulated, providing a valuable body of technical history. Recommendations for special care or treatment are indicated by colored signals attached to the cards. Each member museum keeps the inspection records on its own collection; thus, the museum administration has at hand the basic information on which to assess needs of the collection, to schedule necessary examinations or treatments and to make reasonably precise estimates of annual budgetary needs. In short, long-range conservation can become a responsible and administratively sound operation, alive to needs of the collection, with costs anticipated and budgeted.

Examination

Requests to the ICA for laboratory services are initiated by member museums (fig. 1). As a matter of policy, the Intermuseum Laboratory initially accepts objects only for examination. A uniform examination procedure is followed. A standard form, which serves as a kind of checklist of detail and a repository of data, is used (fig. 2). This examination record has three parts. The first identifies the object, its owner and its size, shape and accessory parts; it also lists and dates all photographs and radiographs available. The second part details the type of materials and construction methods composing the object, based on results of examinations performed at the Intermuseum Laboratory or, if necessary, at specialized analytical laboratories. The last part provides for a description of any deterioration or defects. Some IIC-AG members are evolving a standard terminology to describe defects and to simplify communication. Brief glossaries of this terminology have been published.[3]

Reporting on Condition

The examination record does not leave the laboratory. The data on the record, however, are used to prepare the ICA Report on Condition, which is sent to the object's owner. This report is an essay of a varying amount of detail that follows a rigid outline. In the first part, the data describing materials and constructions are assembled. All of these data have historical significance. They may have a bearing on the date, provenance or authenticity of an

INTERMUSEUM LABORATORY
ALLEN ART BUILDING   OBERLIN OHIO 44074

Request For Laboratory Report

Identification of Object

_____
I.C.A. Reg. No.

Type (painting, sculpture, etc.)_____

Artist or School_____

Subject _____

Approximate dimensions (H)_____ (W)_____ ( )_____

Accompanying accessories (frame, base, etc.) _____

This object is registered at _____ as No._____

Reports Requested *(one or more of the following must be checked at the left, below). See Notes 1 and 2 on the reverse.*

_____ A report summarizing the condition of the object described above.

_____ A proposal for treatment.

_____ A report of laboratory examination describing significant materials and constructions.

Authorization

The undersigned requests and authorizes the Intermuseum Laboratory to receive, examine, photograph, make x-radiographs, and to take specimens for analysis from the object described above insofar as the Intermuseum Laboratory finds necessary in order to supply the information requested, ALL SUBJECT TO THE TERMS AND CONDITIONS APPEARING ON THE REVERSE SIDE HEREOF.

The undersigned represents, certifies and warrants that it is the sole owner of the object described above or that it has been duly authorized by the owner to make this *Request for Laboratory Report* subject to all the terms and conditions appearing on the reverse side hereof. The undersigned further agrees to indemnify and hold harmless the Intermuseum Conservation Association and Oberlin College from all claims and demands of any such owner for loss or damage to such objects however occasioned and whether or not due to the negligence or default of the Intermuseum Conservation Association or Oberlin College.

_____
DEPOSITING INSTITUTION

_____
RESPONSIBLE OFFICER AND TITLE

Date_____   _____
OWNER AND ADDRESS

FIGURE 1.   *Request for Laboratory Report used by the ICA.*

NOTES

1. Beyond the examination here authorized no treatment of an object will be undertaken until the Laboratory's *Proposal For Treatment* has been approved in writing by the owner.

2. Facts produced by technical examination may have a bearing on the date or provenance of an object, but the Laboratory *cannot and does not* give opinions or issue statements on questions of style, authorship or monetary value of an object.

3. Laboratory records of examinations and treatment of objects are kept on file in the Laboratory and are treated as confidential. Transcripts of such records will be furnished at cost but only on written order of the owner of those objects. In the event that ownership of such objects has been transferred since their release from the Laboratory, the Laboratory may ask for proof of ownership before supplying such transcripts.

CONDITIONS

Intermuseum Conservation Association hereinafter called 'the Association' is a charitable organization formed for the purpose of furthering conservation in relation to works of art and objects of cultural interest, and for the purpose of assisting and rendering conservation services to charitable and educational institutions. The Association carries no insurance on the property of depositing institutions. Its acceptance of objects for examination or treatment is therefore subject to the following express terms and conditions.

1. Objects forwarded to the Association are at the sole risk of the depositing institution at all times. The depositing institution hereby waives and releases any and all claims which may hereafter arise against the Association or Oberlin College for loss or damage to objects however occasioned and whether or not due to the negligence or default of the Association or Oberlin College or their trustees, agents, officers, or employees.

2. In consideration of the giving of requested transcripts of records of examination and treatment, reports or opinions concerning objects, the owner agrees to indemnify the Association, the Laboratory, Member Museums, Oberlin College, their trustees, agents, officers and employees from any and all liability in the event of any claim by any other persons based in any way upon the rendition of such records, reports or opinions, and agree that such transcripts, reports or opinions shall not be used for any but scientific and educational purposes.

3. Objects will be released by the Laboratory only to the depositing institution. Release to any other institution or to any person will be made only upon written authorization of the depositing institution. In the event that such objects are on loan to the institution depositing them, such an authorization must be countersigned by the owner of the object.

4. In the event of danger arising from an Act of God, or as a result of prevailing international conditions including a threat of military violence, the Association and the Laboratory, with respect to the objects listed on the face of this form, will be free to determine the course to be followed with respect to removing these objects and storing them, and any such determination shall be final and shall not subject the Association, the Laboratory, Member Museums, Oberlin College, their trustees, officers, agents and employees to any liability whatever.

5. The provisions hereof shall be binding upon the depositing institution or other owner, his or its heirs, legal representatives, successors and assigns.

407

NO.
KIND

OWNER
ADDRESS

ARTIST
SUBJECT

1 SHAPE

2 SIZE

height a) b) c)

width a) b) c)

thickness a) b) c)

description of measure

3 FRAME

4 MOUNTING

5 DISTINGUISHING MARKS

6 TECHNICAL HISTORY

7 PHOTOGRAPHS

8 NOTES: X-RADIOGRAPHS

9 NOTES: INFRA-RED PHOTOGRAPHS

10 NOTES: ULTRA-VIOLET FLUORESCENCE

EXAMINER

DATE

FIGURE 2. *Laboratory Examination Record form.*

DESCRIPTION OF MATERIALS AND CONSTRUCTION

SUPPORT
11 material

12 fabrication

13 no. members
14 joins
15 color   16 surface character
17 auxiliaries

18 former treatment

GROUND
21 layers (lowest first)
22 materials
23 structure
24 thickness
25 fibrous binder
26 color
27 conformation
28 former treatment

PAINT OR DESIGN LAYERS — typical areas a)   b)   c)
31 layers (lowest first)

32 medium

33 pigments

34 structure

35 thickness

36 handling

37 transparency

38 solubility

39 former treatment

SURFACE COATING
41 materials
42 layers
43 solubility

44 thickness
45 original color
46 former treatment

DESCRIPTION OF CONDITION

50 weakness of materials

51 defects in construction

52 crack-tear

53 disjoin

54 cleavage

55 crackle

56 missing part

57 hole
58 flaking-chipping

59 abrasion

60 bulge-warp
61 wrinkle-draw
62 crease-groove
63 scar-dent

64 mold damage
65 insect damage
66 corrosion

67 darkening
68 yellowing
69 fading
70 blanching
71 crazing
72 accretions
73 dullness
74 opacity
75 scratches

80 GENERAL

81 SUMMARY OF CONDITION

82 Structural insecurity

83   estimated extent of treatment

84   urgency of treatment

85 Permanent damage to design

86 Temporary disfigurement

87   estimated extent of treatment

88 BRIEF NOTES ON TREATMENT OR CARE

411

object. In the case of much-restored objects, it is necessary to identify for the owner the chronology of layers and characteristics of the added materials, as well as the evidence on which conclusions are based.

The second part of the report is a description of the object's condition. Condition is a word so loosely used in the art world that a digression is justified to explore the concept.[4] Bitter controversies over the cleaning of paintings flourish because the term *condition* is misunderstood. Damage occurs to art objects because their condition is misunderstood. Many owners of works of art are disappointed to learn, after purchase, the true condition of their prizes.

It is understandable, if an object is marred by layers of soil and accretions, that its condition may be considered poor. Yet cleaning might show that it has suffered little. The condition of another object harmed by scars and abrasions may also be called poor. In the first case, the reference is to design, and in the second, the reference is to material components. In the first instance, the defect can be corrected; in the second, the defect can only be softened or masked by restoration.

There are, obviously, at least two different aspects of condition. One aspect may be called *damage*, that is, the permanent alteration of any materials or constructions composing an object. The other may be referred to as *disfigurement*, that is, the alteration of any aesthetic elements of the design. There is, in fact, another aspect of condition, one of basic importance in conservation: *Insecurity* is any inherent weakness or threat to the object's physical integrity. Insecurity may not be easily recognized. The cause may be the embrittlement of organic materials, weakening of adhesives, dangerous stresses induced by the reaction of hygroscopic materials to environmental conditions, susceptibility of materials to chemical or biological attack or loosening of joins or cleavage between layers. If insecurity is recognized or diagnosed, corrective treatment can be instituted, with the hope of preventing damage before it occurs. Unheeded, insecurity matures into damage.

Damage may also be the immediate consequence of a catastrophe (such as fire, flood or mechanical violence) or the result of misguided or incompetent care or treatment. Both insecurity and damage are tangible aspects of an object's state of preservation and may be determined by an objective examination.

Disfigurement, referring to defects in design, is an almost inevitable corollary of damage. Some success in reducing incoherences and distortions caused by damage may be achieved by those procedures called *restoration*. Incrustations, accretions, stains and

412

darkened coatings obscure and falsify an object's design without inherently damaging it. Disfigurement from these causes is temporary, subject to remedy by various abstergent processes.

The relationship between disfigurement and damage is a peculiarly confusing one. It is unlikely that an object can be damaged without producing some alteration of the design, that is, some disfigurement. For some kinds of disfigurement, however, there exists a surprising tolerance. For example, the green gray enamel-like mineralization of a metal—undoubtedly damage—is accepted as an enhancement of ancient Chinese bronze pieces. Also, there are those who hesitate to accept the evidence that Greek architecture and marble sculpture were highly colored and that the loss of the ancient paint is damage, because this fact is not easily reconciled with the established concepts of classical restraint in design. The romanticist admires the new and strange design of time; he does not see a work of art disfigured. The weather-beaten, vine-covered structure, the fallen column and the dingy dirt-encrusted painting are things that "moulder into worth," as Hogarth ironically alleged in his engraving of *Time Smoking a Picture*. Because of these inconsistencies, disfigurement alone is an unreliable basis for a judgment of the object's condition.

To return to a discussion of the second part of the Report on Condition, there are three subsections headed "insecurity," "damage" and "disfigurement," each accompanied by a modifier. Since there is no standard scale to measure these defects, the Intermuseum Laboratory uses an arbitrary scale of five degrees—negligible, slight, moderate, marked and extreme. Thus, in object A, it may be found that insecurity is extreme, damage slight and disfigurement slight. Without stating the precise nature of the insecurity, the description of the object's condition indicates the urgency of treatment. In the case of object B, the report may state that insecurity is slight, damage moderate and disfigurement marked. It is evident from this assessment that treatment may be expected to clarify one's perception of the design, but that such treatment is not urgent and could safely be postponed in favor of treatment for object A. Object C may be found to be structurally sound and visually acceptable but its apparently coherent design to be due to a restoration hiding extreme damage. Hardly more than the skeleton of the original pictorial statement remains. In this case, an estimate of disfigurement is little more than an academic exercise. The report on the extent of damage should be conclusive to a purchase committee or an art historian. These examples show that condition can be described with a practical accuracy that can be useful to an art owner, scholar or conservator.

413

INTERMUSEUM CONSERVATION ASSOCIATION

INTERMUSEUM LABORATORY

ALLEN ART BUILDING OBERLIN OHIO 44074

Proposal For Treatment

Identification of Object I.C.A. Reg. No.

Type

Artist or School

Subject

Object registered at as No.

The above proposal is accepted and the Intermuseum Laboratory is hereby authorized to carry out the above proposed treatment, SUBJECT TO ALL THE TERMS AND CONDITIONS APPEARING ON THE REVERSE SIDE HEREOF.

The undersigned represents, certifies and warrants that it is the sole owner of the object described above or that it has been duly authorized by the owner to instruct the Intermuseum Laboratory to carry out the above proposed treatment subject to all the terms and conditions appearing on the reverse side hereof. The undersigned further agrees to indemnify and hold harmless the Intermuseum Conservation Association and Oberlin College from all claims and demands of any such owner for loss or damage to such object however occasioned and whether or not due to the negligence or default of the Intermuseum Conservation Association or Oberlin College.

____
DEPOSITING INSTITUTION

____
RESPONSIBLE OFFICER AND TITLE

Date _______________

____
OWNER AND ADDRESS

FIGURE 3. *Proposal for Treatment form.*

NOTE

Laboratory records of examinations and treatment of objects are kept on file in the Laboratory and are treated as confidential. Transcripts of such records will be furnished at cost but only on written order of the owner of those objects. In the event that ownership of such objects has been transferred since their release from the Laboratory, the Laboratory may ask for proof of ownership before supplying such transcripts.

CONDITIONS

Intermuseum Conservation Association hereinafter called 'the Association' is a charitable organization formed for the purpose of furthering conservation in relation to works of art and objects of cultural interest, and for the purpose of assisting and rendering conservation services to charitable and educational institutions. It does not engage in any commercial activity and is not in competition with commercial organizations. The Association carries no insurance on the property of depositing institutions. Its acceptance of objects for examination or treatment is therefore subject to the following express terms and conditions.

1. Objects forwarded to the Association are at the sole risk of the depositing institution at all times. The depositing institution hereby waives and releases any and all claims which may hereafter arise against the Association or Oberlin College for loss or damage to objects however occasioned and whether or not due to the negligence or default of the Association or Oberlin College or their trustees, agents, officers, or employees.

2. In consideration of the giving of requested transcripts of records of examination and treatment, reports or opinions concerning objects, the owner agrees to indemnify the Association, the Laboratory, Member Museums, Oberlin College, their trustees, agents, officers and employees from any and all liability in the event of any claim by any other persons based in any way upon the rendition of such records, reports or opinions, and agree that such transcripts, reports or opinions shall not be used for any but scientific and educational purposes.

3. Objects will be released by the Laboratory only to the depositing institution. Release to any other institution or to any person will be made only upon written authorization of the depositing institution. In the event that such objects are on loan to the institution depositing them, such an authorization must be countersigned by the owner of the object.

4. In the event of danger arising from an Act of God, or as a result of prevailing international conditions including a threat of military violence, the Association and the Laboratory, with respect to the objects listed on the face of this form, will be free to determine the course to be followed with respect to removing these objects and storing them, and any such determination shall be final and shall not subject the Association, the Laboratory, Member Museums, Oberlin College, their trustees, officers, agents and employees to any liability whatever.

5. The provisions hereof shall be binding upon the depositing institution or other owner, his or its heirs, legal representatives, successors and assigns.

INTERMUSEUM LABORATORY
WORK SHEET

I. C. A. Reg. No. _____   Owner's Reg. No. _____

Object: Kind _____   Owner _____

   Artist _____   _____

   Subject _____   _____

Instructions

Date received _____

Date authorized _____

Date wanted _____

Estimated cost:

Photography	Negs.	Prints			Professional Services				
					Hours	Operator	Rate		
X-radiography									
Packing					Summary				
					Accounting—				
					Services				
Shipping					Expense recovered				
					Total				
Special materials or supplies					Invoicing—				
					Examination				
					Treatment				
Services purchased					Photography				
					Shipping				
					Other expense				
		Total			Total				
Entered					Invoiced				

FIGURE 4. *Work Sheet used to record time spent on the examination and treatment of an object, operations performed and materials used.*

Month	Day	Operator	Time		Treatment

ICA No. _____ Artist_____ Subject _____

Owner _____

417

The Proposal for Treatment

A step-by-step proposal of measures to be taken to correct insecurity or to reduce disfigurement follows logically from the Report on Condition. The Proposal for Treatment (fig. 3) is, in a sense, a contract between the laboratory and the object's owner. At the Intermuseum Laboratory, estimates of the time required for each step are made, and the total time requirement is used as a factor in establishing the cost of treatment.

The Report on Condition, accompanied by documenting photographs and X-radiographs, and the Proposal for Treatment, prepared in duplicate, are submitted to the owner. One copy of the Proposal for Treatment is signed and returned by the owner to ICA, authorizing the laboratory to begin the designated treatment.

A Work Sheet (fig. 4) is issued when an object comes to the laboratory to record the time spent on examination and treatment and to provide a daily log of operations carried out and materials used. When the work is complete, notes from the Work Sheet are transcribed on a formal Treatment Record, which is returned to the owner to become a part of the object's technical history. The lack of such records creates that enigmatic complexity of condition so frequently encountered in the examination of an object.

PURPOSE AND VALUE OF DOCUMENTATION

Lest it seem that there is unnecessary duplication in this series of procedures—the laboratory examination repeating the inspection and the report on condition repeating the laboratory examination—it should be stressed that the purpose of each procedure is different. The inspection is an assessment of a collection's condition, and inspection records become the basic reference source for the administration and financing of conservation. The form used by the ICA for the laboratory examination is simply an in-house convenience that organizes and disciplines the examining procedure. The Report on Condition is the principal communication between the laboratory and the object's owner, organizing diffuse data into useful conclusions with a minimum of technical pedantry. The Proposal for Treatment is in the nature of a contract with the owner. The Treatment Record completes the documentation to be preserved by the owner.

One may ask if this documentation is practical or economically possible. I do not believe these questions are valid. This system of documentation has been used at the Intermuseum Laboratory since its inception 20 years ago. There are more than 1,500 sets of records in ICA files dealing with objects sent to the laboratory. The laboratory's use of inflexible procedures and specialized terminology, as outlined in this paper, has insured a high degree of competence in examination, clarity of communication with owners and the integrity of objects.

Performance standards are, of course, related to communication standards. There is wide scope for further improvement in communication. The next challenge is to use records designed so that data are retrievable; experiments of this sort are under way.[5] Computers can collate and analyze these data. Such a source of information on the nature and history of objects can lead to further advances in performance standards in conservation.

SUMMARY

Although professional members of the iic follow the standards set forth in the Murray Pease Report, the nature of the records and reports prepared is extremely varied. If records and reports are incomplete or confused, some important phase of treatment may be overlooked, some facts of the object's technical history may go unobserved and some of the internal evidence, accessible only when an object is in a laboratory, may be lost.

NOTES

1. "The Murray Pease Report," *Studies in Conservation* 9, no. 3 (August 1964): 116–21. Also *The Murray Pease Report; Code of Ethics for Art Conservators; Articles of Association of IIC; Bylaws of the American Group* (New York: IIC-American Group, May 1968), pp. 55–61.

2. Richard D. Buck, "The Inspection of Art Collections," *Museum News* 29, no. 7 (October 1, 1951).

3. See Dorothy H. Dudley, Irma B. Wilkinson et al., *Museum Registration Methods* (Washington, D.C.: American Association of Museums, 1968) and Caroline K. Keck, *A Handbook on the Care of Paintings* (New York: Watson-Guptill Publications, 1965).

4. Richard D. Buck, "What Is Condition in a Work of Art," *Bulletin of the American Group-IIC* 12, no. 1 (October 1971): 63–67.

5. Hermann Kühn and Christel Zocher, "Feature Cards for the Storing of Technical Data Which Result from the Scientific Examination of Works of Art," *Studies in Conservation* 15, no. 2 (May 1970): 102–21 and W. A. Oddy and H. Barker, "A Feature Card Information-Retrieval System for the General Museum Laboratory," *Studies in Conservation* 16, no. 3 (August 1971): 89–94.

COMMENTARY

ABBOTT L. CUMMINGS

As a commentator on the papers by W. Eugene George, Jr., and Richard D. Buck, I am impressed, first of all, with the concern expressed by Mr. Buck for the establishment of criteria to elucidate the semantics applied to all the different types of activity within the fields of preservation and conservation. He identifies a looseness in both fields toward this problem of semantics, which has had no little effect upon the establishment of performance standards and the development of preservation philosophy. If one accepts his interpretation of the word *conservation* as meaning steps to protect something from harm or deterioration, the word *preservation* as having the implication of the rescue of a structure from threatened demolition and the word *restoration* as an activity aimed at the recovery of an object's original or earlier aspect, then one may readily define areas for further consideration.

Mr. Buck, a conservator whose primary concern is with the maintenance of the structural and aesthetic integrity of museum objects, describes two aspects of condition, *damage* and *disfigurement*. His remarks make perfectly clear how these two terms are defined in relationship to a painting. Damage, he explains, is "the permanent alteration of any materials or constructions composing an object." Disfigurement is "the alteration of any aesthetic elements of the design." These terms, I believe, have relevance for the preservationist and restorationist of historic buildings.

Abbott L. Cummings is director of the Society for the Preservation of New England Antiquities, Boston, Mass.

Before proceeding, I should, for the purpose of clarity, state that in using the term *preservation*, I invest it with a shade of meaning beyond Mr. Buck's definition. This added meaning is simply that of preserving intact all of a building's elements, both original and later ones, as opposed to the restoration of the fabric to an arbitrary moment in time. The latter course of action presupposes the attitude that physical additions to the structure made subsequent to its original construction may be removed, though some preservationists qualify this statement by saying that removal of any existing fabric should be subject to a cautious review.

Mr. George notes that the client, sponsor or organization responsible for and underwriting a restoration project is generally represented by an individual, a board or, most often, a committee. "The committee's function," he writes, "is to define the particular historical value to be emphasized, to decide the function desired of the building. . . ." Without naming any specific individual, board or committee, it can be argued that much of the irreparable damage done to historic buildings, singly or in the aggregate, over the past 75 years can be laid to imprecise, uniformed or capricious, not to add quixotic, thinking on the part of such individuals or committees. Often, the only requirement for fulfilling so sensitive a role is based on an individual's civic record, wealth, availability or amateur enthusiasm—anything but a hard, cold, measurable knowledge of the values involved, as well as of clearly defined specifics in the field of American architectural history. There seem to be no guidelines for determining what qualifications are necessary for serving as a committee member. This problem is perhaps the thorniest one preservationists face in their efforts to establish standards and criteria.

As an illustration, I recall one restoration crisis in New England in which a board of arbitration had to be convened. In this case, a professional restoration contractor who was experienced and had a crew of well-trained craftsmen, but who lacked knowledge of period detail and was thoroughly opinionated as well, was yoked with a committee, the most important member of which was a dedicated old-house enthusiast. This antiquarian was a local amateur, but modest, self-effacing and quite willing to accept what the evidence indicated. He was not, however, socially prominent, and when a disagreement arose between the contractor and this committeeman, the establishment-oriented board of arbitration had little trouble in coming to a decision, especially since the contractor had already made a sizable financial commitment to the project. In this case, the local antiquarian was dismissed, with disastrous results. The restoration of the building thereafter took

421

several notable "wrong turns," due to the uninformed evaluation of structural evidence. On the other hand, of course, it is often the dedicated amateur with more enthusiasm than learning who creates problems. I do not wish to belabor the point. The issue was raised, however, and one can only suggest that established criteria and high-quality performance standards may easily be circumvented by a lack of professionalism among trustees of a project.

Both Mr. George and Mr. Buck, quite naturally, confine their papers to the artifacts peculiar to their professions, and it should perhaps be noted that the one element that buildings and paintings have in common is their painted surfaces, whether on wood, canvas or plaster. In building interiors, of course, decorated surfaces can include paintings of landscapes or other embellishments upon woodwork or plaster walls. A recent experience of the Society for the Preservation of New England Antiquities, of which I am the director, illustrates this point well. The society maintains almost 60 historic properties, and recently there has been some concern with the conservation of painted surfaces within the buildings. Our first exploratory contacts with professionals in the identification of early paint colors and conditions and in the technology of paint conservation have been not only with scientific laboratories but also with conservators who normally devote their talents to the study of paintings. A building certainly may be said to possess a considerably larger range of conservation problems than that associated with paint conservation, and as Mr. George wisely points out, those responsible for the sympathetic rehabilitation of an early structure must be prepared to draw upon widely diversified skills of many different types of technologist in deciding which materials to use, how engineering problems should be handled and what kind of environmental system should be installed.

There are also noticeable differences in the approaches of these two authors to their subject. In seeking to define these differences, I may reveal a personal bias, but it is my intention as a commentator to point out many contemporary currents of thought in the fields that may or may not be reflected in the papers. For example, the procedures set forth by Mr. George for attaining high-quality restoration work seem admirable, with one or two reservations based on alternative approaches that he does not mention. I refer, for example, to Mr. George's discussion of personnel and his consideration that the key individual in a preservation project is the restoration architect. Inasmuch as architecture is a creative discipline and the restoration field has become increasingly archaeologically oriented, there are many professionals today who would argue that the key individual, the person with whom final responsibility rests, is the architectural historian and not the restoration architect, although, as Mr. George points out, the quality of any restoration project will depend on the range and variety of skills that are brought to bear. Nevertheless, in light of the increased emphasis upon archaeology in restoration projects and, more important, in light of increasing demands for honesty in restoration, it is not entirely clear, to me at least, why "the restoration architect must be a good designer." If he is indeed, as Mr. George writes, "sensitive to and knowledgeable of the nature of historic aesthetics —qualities in space, geometry and proportion that constitute the essence of the architectural art," then what may be expected when the restoration architect is asked to exercise his talents upon a building from the past that is mediocre in both design and construction?

Of greater interest and importance than this difference of approach to the subject, however, are the differing philosophies that seem to emerge from the two papers. The philosophic concept of architectural restoration in America, with well-discerned roots in the 19th century, has become a clearly recognized profession in the 20th century, with well-defined axioms and a fast-growing body of performance standards. As an example, preservationists have advanced in the 1970s to a point in the analytic identification and reproduction of early paint colors far beyond that even contemplated by earlier generations of restorationists. However, contemporary preservationists have recognized the validity of the antirestoration philosophy advocated during the 19th century by William Morris and his followers in the Society for the Protection of Ancient Buildings in England, a group whose philosophy has cut at the very root of restoration. Preservationists who only recently labored to save a building from demolition and then turned without much inner questioning to its restoration to an earlier point in time are now increasingly searching their consciences, and many are adopting the philosophy of conservators, who seek to maintain the structure of an object as it has evolved, to keep it in good condition and to regard recent changes within the fabric as being of equal significance to the earliest changes. So much has this become the case that one is becoming accustomed to hearing nowadays, as a variation on the familiar alarm "threatened with demolition," that a certain building is "threatened with restoration."

If, for well-considered philosophic reasons, didactic or otherwise, it seems wise to restore a structure to a particular moment in its history and thus deny the concept of the building representing an architectural continuum, the performance standards outlined by Mr. George are representative of modern professionalism in the highest degree. However, preservationists should be aware that an unexamined assumption of the appropriateness of restoration for all buildings can have a tremendous effect on many architectural features that have been added to early structures, the result being that such features may be subject to damage or disfigurement as defined by Mr. Buck.

Of course, in the conservation of buildings or paintings, there may well be a loss of some original material. Both Mr. George and Mr. Buck stress the importance of technology and craftsmanship in the justifiable replacement of original material that is so deteriorated it cannot be stabilized, resuscitated or retained through the impregnation of supportive elements.

The authors also stress the need for technical and proficient record keeping of both photographic and written records, stored under ideal conditions for permanence and retrievability. It is clear that preservationists' record keeping has not equaled that of fine arts conservators. The emphasis upon this necessity represents an ideal for preservationists to keep in mind if performance standards and procedures are to meet the test of highest qualification.

In scientific areas of building conservation, preservationists have some catching up to do. However, recent successful scientific experiments, for example, an X-ray analysis of walls and frame joints, and the current effort to perfect an electronic device for measuring the moisture content in building frame timbers are representative of developments that may add an important new dimension to the potential for improved performance standards.

Perfection is, as always, unattainable. To underscore the conservator's philosophic approach once again, there is food for thought in Mr. Buck's comments on disfigurement, for some kinds of which he points out we humans have a surprising tolerance.

Accreditation/Licensing

ACADEMIC ACCREDITATION AND PROFESSIONAL LICENSURE OF ARCHITECTS IN THE UNITED STATES

RUSSELL V. KEUNE, AIA

Two of the 12 occupations discussed in the opening session of this conference, architecture and law, require individuals to have professional licenses before they may legally practice their chosen occupation in the individual states. Some of the other occupations, such as landscape architecture, are in the process of establishing academic accreditation and licensing requirements. Planners wishing to become full members of the American Institute of Planners must take an examination administered by the institute. Historic site archaeologists have in the past considered the compilation of listings reflecting professional qualifications. The two national organizations representing interior designers are debating the pros and cons of registration laws. The American Association of Museums recently embarked on an official museum accreditation program.[1] The focus of this paper is on the accreditation and licensing process as it relates to architects and to preservation and conservation, the subjects of this conference. In the United States, there are approximately 37,000 licensed architects.[2]

HISTORICAL PERSPECTIVES

Needs of society have resulted in the public control of the use of professional titles and offering of professional services. What are now viewed as accepted controls are results of attainments achieved over a long period of time.

Russell V. Keune, AIA, is vice president for Preservation Services, National Trust for Historic Preservation, Washington, D. C.

In the Middle Ages, architects were trained and qualified for practice through practical tests administered by the craft guilds. During the 17th and 18th centuries, royal academies were established, in which membership was determined by royal appointment of established practitioners and not by official examinations. Prussia developed a system in the early 19th century to officially establish the competence of architects. In France, the Ecole des Beaux-Arts administered the first diploma examination for architects in 1862. By 1882, examinations became compulsory for attaining membership in the Royal Institute of British Architects.[3]

The U.S. Constitution left the regulation of professional licensure to the individual states. Under the Constitution, the police power (i.e., the inherent power of government to exercise control over persons and property in order to guard the health, safety and welfare of the people) is reserved to the individual states.[4] The state, therefore, is the public authority that issues such licenses, while a privately incorporated professional society, such as the American Institute of Architects (AIA), can only restrict its membership to those individuals of proved competence—such as those holding a license to practice architecture.

The states' precedent-setting procedures for the regulation of public health services during the last quarter of the 19th century interested a number of individuals practicing architecture. In 1882, the Architects Association of Minnesota was the first of a new group of professional architectural societies dedicated to the improvement of architectural services. The Western Association of Architects, formed in 1884 under the leadership of Dankmar Adler, proposed a fully developed licensing and registration act. The first such act was passed by the state of Illinois in 1896; it was not until 1951 that all states had enacted similar legislation.[5]

In 1895, there were nine schools of architecture in the United States; by 1911, there were 20. This rapid growth led to the formation in 1912 of the Association of Collegiate Schools of Architecture (ACSA) with 10 schools as charter members. The organization's primary objective was the improvement of architectural education. The admission of additional schools to membership in the association was based on quantitative written reports that were measured by existing members against a set of minimum standards. Membership in the ACSA was then the only form of national recognition. By 1925, many of the administering boards for the 28 state registration acts recognized training obtained in approved schools as an element in evaluating a candidate's credentials for licensure.[6]

The National Architectural Accrediting Board (NAAB) was created in 1940 by the joint action of the ACSA, AIA and National Council of Architectural Registration Boards (NCARB), a council consisting of representatives from each state registration board. The NAAB charter directed it to publish a list of accredited schools of architecture based on minimum adequacy and to compile such lists by gathering factual data and conducting firsthand inspections. World War II interrupted the board's work, and the first list was not published until 1945. By 1953, 45 of the 56 schools in existence were accredited.[7]

ACCREDITATION

To a student wishing to pursue a career in architecture, it is all but mandatory, if he wishes to eventually be licensed, to enroll in a university with a school of architecture that is accredited by the NAAB. At present, the student has a choice of 67 accredited schools in the United States.[8]

After initial approval, all schools normally are visited at five-year intervals; each school is required to submit an annual report. Some 50 elements within the following broad categories of interest are examined: parent institution relationships, school characteristics, budget, facilities and quarters, library, students, curriculum and faculty. Factual data supplied by the school are evaluated and compared through on-site inspections, which average three days in duration. An evaluation team is generally made up of an educator, a practitioner and a member of a state registration board. The factual report submitted by the school and the interpreter's report, submitted by the evaluation team, are used by the national board in making annual evaluations.[9]

The NAAB has striven to avoid creating conditions that will tend to standardize educational philosophies or practices. It has encouraged the development of practices suited to the special conditions of each school.

The NAAB accredits schools only on the basis of their granting of the first professional degree. Thus, the several graduate-level programs developing in areas related to historic preservation are not presently subject to the NAAB review process.

The NAAB's high standards and achievements are reflected in the acceptance of the board's list by all state registration boards.

As related to the specific interests of this conference, some elements used in accrediting schools have come under question by members of the AIA's Committee on Historic Resources, particularly standards for the teaching of architectural history and design as it concerns the placement of a new building in existing environments of major architectural significance.

427

APPRENTICESHIP

Any person who wishes to be licensed to practice architecture must present evidence of participation in the field for a period of at least eight years. Such participation may consist of actual work experience or work experience in combination with educational pursuits leading to a first professional degree from an accredited school of architecture. Each applicant for licensure must serve a minimum of three years in the employment of a practicing licensed architect. During this period, he is expected to gain a diversified background of actual work experience.

Qualifying summer employment performed while in school may be counted as actual work experience, in addition to that following receipt of the degree. With the accumulation of three years' work experience, the apprentice may apply for the licensing examination.

As an example, all of my experience during this apprenticeship period was directly associated with historic preservation projects and was under the supervision of licensed architects, beginning with summers spent with field teams of the Historic American Buildings Survey (HABS) and continuing, after having received my Bachelor of Architecture degree, with the Historic Structures Branch of the National Park Service.

LICENSURE

The first step in pursuit of a license comes in the submission of an application to the appropriate state registration board. The application includes a comprehensive description of the applicant's educational achievements, related work experience and character references.[10] Often, while awaiting review of the application and granting of approval from the state board to take the licensing examination, the applicant enrolls in a refresher cram course. The selection of available short courses may include those offered by commercial enterprises, those of local university extension programs or those of local AIA chapters.[11]

The state board's review procedure usually includes not only a check with the applicant's listed character references, but also a review of forms submitted by former employers that include descriptions of the nature and caliber of the applicant's work. This information serves as a check against what is stated on the individual's pending application form. An affirmative response from the state board to the application serves as the applicant's admission ticket to the examination room. The examination is held twice a year in most states.

After passing the examination, the applicant is issued a license to practice in that state by the state board. The license is usually renewable each year by payment of the license fee.

Registration of architects is thus a function of the officially constituted boards of registration within the 50 states, District of Columbia, Canal Zone, Guam, Puerto Rico and the Virgin Islands.

Each of the registration boards is a member of the NCARB, which maintains professional records of architects and issues certificates that enable architects to acquire reciprocal registration.

Since its founding in 1920, the NCARB has sponsored registration laws in all states, formulated and edited an examination syllabus, established basic requirements in education and training for the issuance of its certificate and maintained individual records of its candidates for certificates.[12]

The NCARB has reciprocal agreements with some foreign countries and is involved in negotiating agreements with other nations in an attempt to enable architects to expand their practice to include projects in countries other than the United States.[13]

It has also achieved licensing reciprocity among states and has developed a uniform examination that may be used by all constituent boards. One four-hour part of the current examination is entitled "History and Theory of Architecture"; other parts are on site planning (five hours), architectural design (twelve hours), building construction (three hours), structural design (five hours), professional administration (three hours) and building equipment (three hours).[14]

In June 1972, the NCARB approved new licensing examination procedures. An equivalency examination for candidates without a degree from an accredited school but with adequate experience or a combination of education and experience will go into effect in December 1972, while the NCARB licensing examination for candidates holding professional architectural degrees from accredited schools will be first used in the summer of 1973.

POST-REGISTRATION RECOGNITION

The official processes described thus far encourage the recognition of a generalist in the practice of architecture. However, there are several avenues open to the practitioner who wishes to achieve recognition for a specialization in historic preservation work after having achieved licensure. The most obvious is the actual practice of restoring, rehabilitating or otherwise conserving existing buildings. In addition, there are other methods for focusing public attention on this specialization. The following serve as examples of such methods.

American Institute of Architects

Membership in the AIA affords the practitioner an opportunity to hold various offices that tend to identify him, both within the profession and to the general public, as a specialist in one area of the practice of architecture, including historic preservation. At the local chapter level, there may exist the position of chapter preservation officer; an architect interested in historic preservation might also serve as chairman or as a member of the chapter's historic buildings committee.

At the state level, a member may be invited by the AIA's president to serve as the state preservation coordinator.[15] With the ever-growing role of the state government in supporting statewide surveys, planning and preservation grants, this office can afford a unique opportunity for professional identification in historic preservation.

At the national level, membership on the AIA's Committee on Historic Resources provides a potential for influencing national policy of the AIA with respect to preservation. Four avenues exist for national recognition within the profession—the AIA National Gold Medal, annual National Honors Award Program, election to the AIA College of Fellows and recognition as an honorary member of the AIA. While the Gold Medal has never been awarded to an individual solely on the basis of achievements in historic preservation, the annual Award Program has in recent years included several awards presented for preservation-related projects.[16] The College of Fellows has numerous members honored principally for their contributions in historic preservation; many of them are participating in this conference.

Government Employment

Within the federal government, the largest contingent of architects hired for preservation work is found in the National Park Service. While listing on the U.S. Civil Service Commission's register for architects is a standardized procedure for qualified individuals, job descriptions for preservation architects can be so written as to insure that only those architects possessing special training or experience in preservation are eligible for a position that must be filled by drawing from the open register. An architect holding such a position in the National Park Service is almost automatically assured of some degree of public identification as a specialist in preservation. The undergraduate architectural students hired for the summer programs of the HABS are now exempted, because of the specialized nature of their work, from taking the regular civil service summer employment examinations.

One especially interesting title given to a federal civil service position was "building restoration specialist." This category was necessitated by the need to hire construction specialists—carpenters, stonemasons, etc.—during the Mission 66 program era in the National Park Service. That program was in operation from 1956 to 1966 and included various projects designed to ready national parks for the 50th anniversary of the park system.

The experience of state or local civil service employment is generally similar to that of the federal government.

Government Programs

The National Register of Historic Places requires that prior to any state's participation in the survey, planning and grant-in-aid aspects of this national program, the state must present evidence of having staff competency in architectural history and have a qualified architect on the state's review committee, which oversees nominations to the National Register. As for the latter requirement, the keeper of the National Register has to concur with the selection of professional members of the review committee and thus passes on the professional resume of the architect.[17]

While the National Register exercises no control over individual architects retained for projects receiving National Register matching grants-in-aid, the Register's professional staff does review all plans and specifications for architectural projects. The preservation-related matching grant programs of the U.S. Department of Housing and Urban Development currently do not exercise any review over the selection of architects retained by grant recipients.

The appointment of an architect to one of the four federal advisory bodies concerned with historic preservation carries with it a public identification of specialized skill and knowledge in preservation. In its six-year existence, the Advisory Council on Historic Preservation has never had an architect appointed as a member. The Secretary of the Interior's Advisory Board on National Parks, Monuments and Sites has one architect serving on it at present. The HABS Advisory Board has five licensed architects as members. The American Revolution Bicentennial Commission has no architects serving as full commission members.

CONCLUSION

Both the accreditation of architecture schools and the licensure of architects are established facts, and procedures for achieving both have been well coordinated on a national basis. The end result is a recognition of professional competency as a generalist. New licensing examinations will even further broaden the generalist approach. The recognition of a specialization, if desired, comes with graduate studies and through specific employment or research opportunities, particularly after licensure. While the majority of small architectural practices exist on a diversity of commission types, it appears that the larger firms are, more and more, assuming identities in specialized areas of practice—office buildings, schools, hospitals, etc.

From my position in the preservation movement, I hear a growing number of voices asking for someone, somewhere, to provide some standard and means of identifying and recognizing professional competence in the practice of architecture as it relates to historic preservation, particularly in those cases where the historic properties in question are of recognized national significance, either historically or architecturally, and where the properties are being subjected to a museum-quality preservation treatment.

I see the expressed need coming from all levels of government—national, state and local—that are committing public funds to preservation activities, from private organizations and individuals investing funds in such projects and from spokesmen within established preservation organizations and professional organizations.

In a recent preliminary report of the AIA Department of Education and Research to the AIA Planning Committee, one objective listed under the section dealing with registration was to "develop mechanisms for post-registration recognition of architectural specializations."[18] The Association for Preservation Technology (APT), when it was formed in 1969, conceived of its membership being drawn by invitation from the ranks of active professional practitioners. Membership in the APT would thus constitute a recognition of professional status in preservation. This course of action was not followed (membership is open to all) and it is perhaps noteworthy that in 1971, it was proposed that a special title or class of membership be established within the APT, which would render a valuable public service by identifying specially qualified individuals.[19]

As an outgrowth of the 1968 report of the Whitehill Committee,* the National Trust for Historic Preservation has proposed the establishment of a preservation institute that would include some means of recognizing special professional attainment in preservation.[20]

The Alabama Council of the AIA recently cooperated with the Alabama Historical Commission, the designated state liaison office for purposes of the National Historic Preservation Act of 1966, in

---

* For more information on responsibilities and findings of the Whitehill Committee, see "The Education of Architectural Preservation Specialists in the United States" by Stephen W. Jacobs, AIA, pp. 457–479.

conducting a survey of architectural firms in Alabama that have experience and an interest in historic preservation work. The list was published in the council's April 1972 newsletter.

The AIA has published two items that contribute to needs of clients in understanding the architect's role in preservation—a 1970 brochure on preservation, entitled *Window, Anchor, Catalyst, Root,* and chapter 21 of the 1971 official handbook, entitled "The Architect as a Preservationist."

At its May 1972 meeting, the AIA Board of Directors adopted a position approving the compilation and maintenance of specialized listings of architects in "circumstances in which the interest of the profession, the public, and the Institute are fully protected."[21]

Theoretically, the opportunity now exists for a preservation-related organization (for example, the National Trust or the APT) to enlist the cooperation of the AIA and its membership in compiling a list of architects with expertise in historic preservation activities.

NOTES

1. *Museum Accreditation: A Report to the Profession* (Washington, D. C.: American Association of Museums, 1970).

2. *American Architects Directory, 1970,* 3d ed. (New York: R. R. Bowker Co., 1970).

3. Turpin C. Bannister, ed., *Evolution and Achievement,* vol. 1 of *The Architect at Mid-Century* (New York: Reinhold Publishing Corp., 1954), pp. 353–54.

4. U.S. *Constitution,* Amend. 10.

5. Bannister, *Evolution and Achievement,* pp. 356–57.

6. Ibid., pp. 283–84.

7. Ibid., p. 287.

8. *1971–72 List of Accredited Schools of Architecture* (Washington, D.C.: National Architectural Accrediting Board, 1971).

9. Bannister, *Evolution and Achievement,* pp. 285–86.

10. See, for example, *Rules and Regulations: Architectural Section* (Richmond: Virginia Department of Professional and Occupation Registration, 1955).

11. See, for example, the brochures "Architect's Review" (Arlington: Northern Virginia Center of the University of Virginia, 1971) or "Architectural License Seminars" (Los Angeles: Architectural License Seminars, 1972).

12. *Regarding NCARB Organization, Services and Procedures, Records, Certifications, and Examinations,* NCARB Circular of Information 3-71 (Washington, D.C.: National Council of Architectural Registration Boards, 1971).

13. *Regarding NCARB Services for Architects from Foreign Countries*, NCARB Circular of Information 400–71 (Washington, D.C.: National Council of Architectural Registration Boards, 1971).

14. *Subject Matter Outlines for Uniform Examinations*, NCARB Circular of Information 9–66 (Washington, D.C.: National Council of Architectural Registration Boards, 1966).

15. "Mailing Lists and Other Information for AIA's Preservation Organization," mimeographed (Washington, D.C.: AIA Committee on Historic Resources, 1970).

16. See, for example, "1972 Honor Awards," *AIA Journal* 57, no. 5 (May 1972): 31 or "1971 Honor Awards," *AIA Journal* 55, no. 6 (June 1971): 45.

17. *Historic Preservation Grants-in-Aid Policies and Procedures: National Register of Historic Places* (Washington, D.C.: National Park Service, 1972).

18. J. E. Ellison, "Looking Ahead in Education and Research," *AIA Journal* 57, no. 5 (May 1972): 41–44.

19. Harley J. McKee, president of APT, letter to APT members, September 8, 1971.

20. "Proposal for the Creation and Funding of an Institute for Historic Preservation and Restoration and Related University Programs," mimeographed (Washington, D.C.: National Trust for Historic Preservation, 1970).

21. "Policy Statement 207, Lists, Special," mimeographed (Washington, D.C.: American Institute of Architects, 1972).

ACCREDITATION, CERTIFICATION AND LICENSING OF ART CONSERVATORS

PETER E. MICHAELS

The practice of art conservation encompasses numerous areas of concentration, including the treatment of paintings, decorative arts, metals, sculptures, jewelry, paper, books, textiles and archaeological materials and the scientific study of art materials utilizing chemical and physical sciences. The high levels of skill required in these areas demand long periods of training. Nevertheless, little definition has appeared detailing the prerequisite academic study or means by which proficiency may be judged. Confusion arises as to whether art conservation is indeed a professional activity or rather a highly skilled artistic craft. The nature of professionalism has recently received attention, but adherence to professional procedures and codes of ethics remains an imperfectly realized hope.

There are approximately 440 members of the American Group of art conservators, while the International Institute for Conservation of Historic and Artistic Works (IIC), located in London, has about 1,500 members (including American Group members) throughout the world. Many others who are not members of either organization practice art conservation both in the United States and abroad, but the field as a whole is still quite limited in size. Practical problems deriving from the diversity of skills and the limited number of IIC members make the establishment and administration of criteria for certification difficult. The enforcement of certification programs may prove futile under the free enterprise

Peter E. Michaels is president of the Twelve Oaks Regional Fine Arts Conservation Center, Baltimore, Md.

system unless state legislation requiring the licensing of practitioners can be effected.

A recently organized profession, art conservation is beginning to formulate standards that in time may result in the establishment of some form of certification. The following discussion outlines the situation concerning certification and licensing in its historical and ideological perspectives and as it relates to current training and practice conditions.

HISTORICAL BACKGROUND

Arising from the highly skilled, but somewhat secretive, art restoration practices of the early 20th century, art conservation, as it is known today, began to emerge around 1930. At that time, a new attitude was infused into the field; this attitude was characterized by scientific objectivity and the utilization of scientific instruments, particularly X-ray machines and microscopes, for the examination of works of art. Within a decade, several museums established conservation departments that undertook the treatment of works of art and conducted research into the nature of art materials. Within two decades, considerable publication of research appeared in print.[1]

In 1950, the IIC was founded by a group of eminent conservators, museum administrators and scientists to "provide a permanent organization to co-ordinate and improve the knowledge, methods, and working standards needed to protect and preserve precious materials of all kinds."[2] This international organization continues today as a central office through which much important information passes and under whose direction five international conferences have been organized. The IIC's quarterly periodical, *Studies in Conservation*, provides a forum through which conservators and other interested persons may exchange research and data. Perhaps it is this open exchange of information, more than any other characteristic, that distinguishes art conservation today from practices of 50 years ago.

Membership in the IIC is open to any interested person. Associate members receive the organization's periodical publications and announcements, but have no voting privileges. Fellows, whose membership applications must include written recommendations from five current fellows, are considered professional conservators and are the only members eligible to vote. However, there has been no definition of the requirements for qualification as a fellow, leaving the decision up to those recommending and approving each new applicant. Although a certificate is issued to each new fellow at the time his application is approved and a card is issued annually upon payment of dues, neither document certifies the competence of the person either as to his training or special field of practice. Currently, there are about 1,350 associate members and 165 fellows throughout the world. In addition, there are two honorary fellows and numerous institutional members. Because of the variations in ethnic origin, cultural heritage, language, weather conditions, economic structure and history, several regional groups have been established, drawing members into closer contact within their geographical areas through regular regional meetings.

THE IIC-AMERICAN GROUP

During 1958–59, a local group of conservators formed the regional American Group under IIC (IIC-AG). The IIC-AG held its first annual meeting in Boston in May 1960. Membership in the organization was open to all IIC members on the American continents; its purposes were similar to those of the parent body. From its original group of 25 members, the organization gradually increased to its present size of approximately 440 active members. Annual meetings have occurred regularly since its founding. The *Bulletin of the American Group-IIC* is published twice yearly; it includes articles, papers, notes and announcements. At present, legal actions are under way to incorporate the IIC-AG as a separate entity, with the name American Institute for Conservation of Historic and Artistic Works, Inc. (AIC).

Under the IIC-AG's impetus have appeared two reports of great significance to the certification of art conservators. In 1963, *The Murray Pease Report: Standards of Practice and Professional Relationships for Conservators* stated fundamental concerns relating to the examination of art objects, reports to owners, contractual arrangements and safety precautions.[3] In 1967, a *Code of Ethics for Art Conservators* was adopted and further defined responsibilities of the conservator in specific matters relative to works of art, the owner, colleagues and the general public.[4] These two reports were adopted by a majority vote of the IIC-AG. In principle, they form a fundamental condition for membership and practice. However, neither report contains any provision for the enforcement of the standards and procedures recommended. Adherence to the principles set forth in these reports has been incorporated as a condition for membership in the proposed AIC.

Since my experience is directly related to the activities of the IIC-AG, I shall not attempt to outline similar efforts that have occurred in other parts of the world. In some countries where cultural properties are predominantly under the care of the central government's museum system, questions of competency and certification may be of little meaning, because conservation activities are fully controlled by a cultural ministry that (it is hoped) maintains a consistent standard in such matters.

CONSERVATION IN THE UNITED STATES

In the United States, the IIC-AG mainly represents conservators employed by museums or publicly owned collections at the federal, state, county and municipal levels. The number of members who do not work with museum conservation departments is relatively few. This situation presents a distorted picture of art conservation activity in the United States. It is estimated that more than twice as many persons are engaged in treating works of art outside museums as those who work within them. Furthermore, the number of objects treated annually by independent conservators and conservators employed by commercial art dealers may range from 5 to 10 times the number treated by conservators working in museums. In order to ascertain more accurately the overall activity in conservation, it would be enlightening to survey several main urban centers on the number of active full-time and part-time conservators in the area, their training, workshops, assistants, number of works treated, charges, extent of technical records and range of clientele.

In the United States, any person, regardless of background or skill, may undertake the conservation of works of art without satisfying formal requirements, obtaining a license, registering or fulfilling any legal formalities. It is common for practicing artists to supplement their income by doing various kinds of "restoration." Indeed, the public generally considers art conservation an adjunct of creative art, and conservators of paintings in particular find themselves approached as artists first, conservators second. To change this attitude will require long-term public relations work, not only to inform the art-collecting public about the principles of professional art conservation but also to educate museum curators.

As efforts to achieve these goals proceed through publications, lectures, exhibitions, films and personal discussions, a simultaneous frustration occurs, resulting from the rapid increase in the number of museums throughout the country and from the growth of the public's interest in collecting art. During the affluent decade of the 1960s, art prices increased at an astonishing rate; individuals suddenly began to appreciate the monetary value of their artistic properties and sought the services of conservators. This demand drew many artists who had no formal preparation or training in conservation into the field, mostly as part-time practitioners.

438

The many new museums, needing staff to manage their activities, hired persons with little or no knowledge of art conservation to oversee conservation services. Wielding the authority to authorize the needed conservation work, such persons, acting without sufficient consultation, sometimes unwisely undertook conservation as a "do-it-yourself" project or handed over valuable objects to local artists untrained in conservation. This situation was particularly evident in historic house museums, small historical societies and university museums, all of which made use of poorly trained part-time volunteer staff. These conditions continue today.

TRAINING FOR CONSERVATORS

Another element directly related to certification concerns the training of the conservator. At present, there are three academic programs in the United States that offer conservation training. Programs are under way at the Conservation Center of the Institute of Fine Arts, New York University, New York City; the Cooperstown Graduate Programs, Cooperstown, N.Y.; and the Intermuseum Laboratory of the Intermuseum Conservation Association, Oberlin, Ohio. Other programs are in the planning stages. As yet, the IIC-AG has made no formal attempt to coordinate the curricula of these various academic centers nor to establish standards for the accreditation of training centers. Since the latter two institutions have not yet graduated their first class of students who have completed the entire conservation program, it may be too early to expect standardization.

A far larger number of conservators continue to be trained by the time-honored apprenticeship method, both in museums and with private conservators. Here, too, the IIC-AG has not attempted to establish standards or procedures by which training programs could be accredited and individuals licensed. This year, however, efforts have been made to codify certain standards for training conservators of works of art on paper by the apprenticeship method. A draft proposal is to be circulated to the membership of the IIC-AG for comment and approval.

DE FACTO CERTIFICATION IN THE UNITED STATES

The field is not entirely chaotic. There are several functional forms of certification of competency that have evolved or that appear to be emerging.

Personal Recommendations

Major museums across the country, especially those with art conservation departments, find the poorly informed public turning more and more to museum staff members for advice and recommendations. Many museums do not undertake the treatment of art works owned by the public, but since the total number of reliable art conservators is relatively small, museum staff members usually do recommend individual conservators within their geographic areas. These recommendations from museum staff members, made on the basis of their personal acquaintanceship with the work of individual conservators, act as a kind of informal certification.

Commercial Art Dealers' Recommendations

Of much less gravity, but representing a huge bulk of work, are recommendations made by commercial art dealers, who employ conservators directly and who also direct clients to independent conservators whose work is known to them. Conservators working through dealers are poorly represented in the IIC-AG, leaving a large segment of the field without an adequate voice. Although business relationships between conservators and art dealers encompass a wide range, many craftsmen spend a major part of their careers working in this way. An ongoing professional relationship between a conservator and one or more commercial dealers may represent another type of informal certification (which should be studied more closely) that is related to the informal certification provided by recommendations from museum staff members.

Academic Training Programs

Graduates of some training programs receive academic degrees and certificates of advanced study in the conservation of historic and artistic works. It is not known to what extent this kind of certification specifies professional competency, but it may be observed that graduates who have entered professional practice as art conservators seem to present to prospective employers an aura of competency seldom shared by persons who were trained through nonacademic channels. Such academic certification appears to be a potent force in the development of professional standards for art conservators.

Certification by Professional Societies

As has been stated, neither the IIC nor the IIC-AG has defined procedures for the certification of members. In theory, certification by the IIC-AG could be established as a primary function of the organization. Alternately, accreditation of training programs might produce similar results at less cost. Since the total membership of the IIC-AG is only about 440, it is difficult to imagine how the complex procedures needed for certification in the many fields of concentration could be achieved without extensive changes in the organization's administrative offices, including a substantial increase in funds. If established, certification by the IIC-AG might eventually achieve its purpose by the gradual widening of its high reputation, but the organization would need to encourage membership among the large number of independent conservators and conservators employed by commercial art dealers who are not presently represented and whose needs differ from those of museum employees. The amalgamation of this large group of conservators into the IIC-AG would make the organization far more representative and at the same time increase the organization's resources.

LICENSING

Little discussion of licensing is heard within the IIC-AG. To pursue the legal framework to establish licensing and to publicize the need for licensing art conservators to legislators in all 50 states presents enormous obstacles. However, licensing is the strongest possible means to enforce standards of practice. It is the step dividing the unregulated craftsmanlike attitude of art restorers of the past and a true professional outlook for the future. When the extremely mobile character of present-day life in the United States is considered, it may prove to be essential to seek some form of licensing. Only through legal restrictions can uniformity of practice be achieved. Art conservation, however, lacks two primary elements upon which licensing for other professions is based: (1) the protection of personal health and (2) the protection of public safety. For these reasons, it seems unlikely that licensing could be easily achieved.

SUMMARY

After a brief examination of the history of art conservation as a professional activity, it may be observed that there is now a trend in this country toward the formulation of procedures and codes of ethics by the IIC-AG and the establishment of centers for academic training. Several forms of informal certification are in existence already, in particular: (1) personal recommendation from museum staff members; (2) recommendation through commercial art dealers; and (3) certification to graduates of academic training programs.

Additionally, formal certification through a professional organization is sought by some members of the profession as a means of improving and regulating standards of practice.

Artists and craftsmen have repeatedly rejected restraints imposed by tradition or law. Today's young art conservators, clothed in the black robes of academia, remain as independent in thought and temperament as their predecessors, making agreement on matters of principle and details of practice difficult. Perhaps one fruitful path through this maze of conflicting opinions consists of a multipurpose program combining the following as its main features:

1. Standardization and accreditation of training programs, specifically for the basic corpus of information prerequisite for all fields of concentration.

2. Expanded membership in professional organizations to include virtually all practicing conservators so as to represent all views and needs.

3. Improved communication among conservators, curators, collectors and dealers to acquaint all parties with each other's opinions and their common concern for the preservation of cultural properties.

NOTES

1. For further references regarding the history of art conservation, consult the superb bibliography compiled by Joyce Plesters in *The Cleaning of Paintings* by Helmuth Ruhemann (London: Faber and Faber, 1968), pp. 363–481.

2. *The Murray Pease Report; Code of Ethics for Art Conservators; Articles of Association of IIC; Bylaws of the American Group* (New York: IIC-American Group, May 1968), p. 3.

3. Ibid., p. 55.

4. Ibid., p. 63.

COMMENTARY

DONALD W. INSALL, FRIBA

The demand and market for architects who wish to devote their time to conserving old buildings is already great, and it grows every day. This demand raises several questions about the training, licensure and accreditation of architectural specialists in this field. For example, what is the scope of this work?

In Britain, the job includes supervising grant-aided repairs made possible by the British system of historic buildings grants. This grant program is administered with the advice of the Historic Buildings Council for England. The council advises the government on the allocation of grants from funds that are increasing, even if in an undramatic fashion. At present, the program's annual budget is £1 million per year. These funds have been wisely administered for some years, and during this time they have attracted a remarkable matching response from private owners, who otherwise might be much more reluctant to repair the historic buildings they own. All this grant-aided work requires architectural supervision. So far, no specific qualification requirements have been set forth for architects who are in charge of this work; there are suggestions that it is time this was changed. However, the work must be open to inspection and approval by specialist architects from the British Department of the Environment, themselves a band of devoted and remarkably knowledgeable conservators.

A second and endless job is that of giving advice on the survey

Donald W. Insall, FRIBA, is a restoration architect and planner in private practice in London, England.

and repair of Britain's churches. Survey and repair work must now, by law, be carried out at least once every five years by a qualified architect. Of 17,717 parish churches in Britain, as many as 11,000 are of architectural and historical importance. In addition, there are 56 cathedrals in Britain, many of which go back to Norman times. From these figures, it is evident that this is no small task, nor is the job of advising owners of historic properties, whether they are private individuals (who are hagridden by the crippling estate taxes) or organizations like Britain's National Trust for Places of Historic Interest or Natural Beauty, which now looks after more than 1,000 historic buildings. All the large preservation societies like the Society for the Protection of Ancient Buildings (SPAB), the Georgian Group and the Victorian Society, as well as countless national, regional and local pressure groups and technical societies interested in everything from windmills to vernacular architecture need professional advice and service—so, too, does the nation itself, which has taken into guardianship many ruined castles and derelict abbeys.

A third field of work is town planning. All development in Britain, including the altering of an old building, requires specific town-planning consent. Central departments advise on applications affecting buildings listed nationally as of architectural or historical importance. In London, the Greater London Council has a special Historic Buildings Division. More recently, special *conservation areas*, perhaps somewhat akin to America's *historic districts*, have been designated under Britain's town and country planning legislation. Beginning in September 1972, the study and enhancement of these areas will receive a considerable "shot in the arm" in the form of an additional allocation of £500,000 on the advice of the Historic Buildings Council.

All of this work requires architects who specialize in the conservation of old buildings, but I wonder whether other countries find it any easier than we in Britain do to assess the number of architects required for this work and how many should be trained in the field. Twelve years ago, recognizing this need for education, a Conference on Training Architects in Conservation was set up. This conference is a voluntary body with representatives of virtually all the principal preservation concerns: consumers and all the major professional institutes. With the aid of a generous grant from the Calouste Gulbenkian Foundation, the conference was able to promote a two-year postgraduate architectural conservation training course at the School of Archaeology at the University of London. This ran most successfully for five years before it ran aground on the financial rocks of national economic strin-

444

gency. Perhaps the idea was premature?

I know from the experience of our own team, which includes four graduates of the University of London course, that the benefits of such an education are real and practical. Two others of the team were trained under a different system—the time-honored Lethaby Scholarship of the SPAB. This latter system offers a less academic, more practical and intensely valuable six months of training acquired while traveling throughout Great Britain.

This year, a new conservation course has been established at the Institute of Advanced Architectural Studies in the University of York. This course is envisaged as one that will be of most benefit when taken immediately after graduation rather than as a mid-career course.

To give some facts for comparative purposes, Britain has approximately 20,000 architects, serving a total population of 55.5 million. Fifty percent of these architects are in private practice; 40 percent, in public service (in local authorities, public boards and the central government); 10 percent, in industrial posts and teaching. The title *architect* is registered by law, and the Architects' Registration Council of the United Kingdom can accept only those applicants who have passed approved professional examinations. These are the final examination of the Royal Institute of British Architects (RIBA) or the examinations of one of some 30 recognized architecture schools in the United Kingdom, the one recognized school in Dublin or one of the almost 20 recognized schools overseas. The RIBA strongly recommends that those who wish to become registered architects obtain their educations by attending a full-time five-year course at one of the recognized schools.

Visiting boards responsible for recognizing these schools consist of 14 architects, 7 of whom are in private practice and 7 in teaching positions. A board's function is to examine courses and examinations quinquennially to determine whether a school is in compliance with standards. If suitable standards are being maintained, recognition is recommended. Graduates of recognized schools are exempt from taking the RIBA examination.

Several "sandwich" and other part-time educational arrangements are also possible, but are officially discouraged. In any event, a student must have at least two years' practical experience in an architect's office, or possibly in part with a contractor, before taking an examination in professional practice. At least one of these two years of experience must be gained after passing the main part of the RIBA or equivalent approved examination. Thus, the average full-time student takes seven years to qualify for registration as an architect; those who succeed in doing so on a part-

445

time basis may take eight or nine years, or considerably longer. Similar professional organizations are in charge of the training and examination systems for surveyors.

Unhappily, it seems at present that the RIBA does not yet appreciate the strength of this need for specialized education in architectural conservation. It is, however, hoped that a RIBA working group will be established to study the feasibility of a centralized, recognized diploma in conservation. Perhaps this recognition will have to come from another body. It seems hopeful that such recognition may come as a result of preparations for the European Architectural Heritage Year, 1975.

Other questions are raised by this matter: What should be the aim of such an education? What should its syllabus include? The indispensable basis of an education in architectural conservation is simply a deep and understanding knowledge of straightforward traditional building techniques. Once, this knowledge was every architect's birthright; now, it is the almost private joy of a very few. The next aim is also simple: to inculcate in the would-be architect an awareness, an openness of approach, a sensitivity, a receptiveness that will prepare him to "listen" to each historic building and a proud humility that will allow the restoration architect to receive graciously the greatest of accolades, that is, for others to say "I did not know you had been there and repaired that building, but I thought it looked quite well!" The third basic requirement is sound ability and experience in job management and cost control. Is this ability an art, a science, or is it both? Certainly, the management of a job or the control of costs cannot be achieved without experience. This is where the old system of apprenticeship scored. There is no better teacher than an experienced one.

When this corps of restoration architects has been fully trained, how shall they be recognized? This varies with the size of the nation. In a small land like Malta, I believe virtually all conservation work is in the hands of the same team. In Britain even, most of us who specialize in conservation work at least know of one another, and there is a close comradeship in sharing problems and experiences. Bodies like the Conference on Training Architects in Conservation have tried to pioneer the way by establishing a list or register of those known to be interested in this kind of work. However, this type of approach, based upon people's own evaluations of themselves, is not sufficient, but at least it is a start.

Many in Britain would like to see the establishment there of a real corps of specialists like the French *Architectes-en-Chef des Monuments Historiques,* which are limited by number and by strict examination, or like Britain's own Royal Designers for In-

446

dustry, in which membership is by jealously guarded invitation. In this way, we may be able to establish and build up a central team of teachers, who are so essential to the success of any specialist course; examiners; and experienced practitioners. Otherwise, *Quis custodiet custodiens!*

Surely, what is really needed to serve this body of trained architects and teachers is a network of lively, thriving and devoted conservation centers, with adequate facilities for specialized study, research and documentation. These might even in addition undertake the actual training, licensure and accreditation of specialists as part of their function of focusing, consolidating and sharing the knowledge and experience of this art—the conservation of man's building heritage. Furthermore, when effective conservation centers have been established, locally and also in each country where their knowledge is most relevant, should they not also be tied together into an international network? In this way, we all might share, as we have done at this conference, the work of our colleagues in this great and common task.

COMMENTARY

PETER JOHN STOKES, MRAIC

The suggestion that professionals who wish to practice in the preservation field be accredited and/or licensed worries me, because accreditation and licensing has the connotation of a closed circle, a professional elite, a jealous pack, witch doctors and even a new breed of bureaucrats! It should be remembered that the preservation field includes a number of people who came in by the back door, so to speak. Architects engaged in preservation work seem sometimes to suffer the "master art" syndrome. Perhaps the source of this problem is the national professional societies of architects, such as the American Institute of Architects (AIA) and the Royal Architectural Institute of Canada (RAIC), which some years ago began the process of building an image of architecture as the "master art." This view is, to say the least, most presumptuous.

The Association for Preservation Technology, organized in 1968 as an interdisciplinary group of practitioners and those interested in the field, has been rather reserved in its attitude toward accreditation and licensure of preservation professionals. The association's hesitancy to approve this method of setting and enforcing standards may be due, in part, to the fact that one reason the organization was established was to attempt to define terms used in the field and also to encourage the free exchange of information for better understanding by all concerned. As we have seen at this conference, definitions of terms can vary greatly from speaker to

Peter John Stokes, MRAIC, is a restoration architect in private practice in Niagara-on-the-Lake, Ontario, Canada.

speaker. This problem of varying definitions highlights the difficulty in setting standards. Standards of training often do not continue beyond on-site work. Such standards developed from practical experience may not become part of the practitioner's background or contribute to his education, and they may vary from project to project and create further confusion. Where working methods or procedures are woefully deficient on a project, standards deteriorate. A code of performance standards is just now beginning to be developed. Standards of communication are almost totally lacking, as we have noted, and problems will no doubt arise even after terms are fully defined. For example, I wonder how Abbott L. Cummings, with his definition of *preservation*, would approach the difficult problem of preserving "pleasing decay."

Determining the qualifications for being a preservationist also presents problems. Several of the papers presented at this conference list desirable characteristics and mention the mechanics of establishing a set of qualifications for accreditation purposes. However, few speakers have discussed the attitude a preservationist should have, which I believe is most important. By attitude, I mean the breadth of interest of all those who are involved in preservation efforts—conservators, architects and others. Can an indication of good character, such as membership in the AIA or the RAIC (both of which require references to verify an applicant's good character) define a person's breadth of interest? The definition of "good character" is itself subjective and does not indicate anything about an individual's competence. Sometimes, incompetent government employees are "kicked upstairs" to seemingly more important positions than they currently hold; this is a useful method of getting them out of the way. However, as has been discovered far too often, difficulty, if not disaster, is the likely result when a person temperamentally unsuited is recommended for a preservation project.

By attitude, I also mean the rapport of a preservationist with other people, with both those who are experienced in dealing with preservation problems and those who are not as well qualified for preservation work as may be desirable or who have little practical experience in the field. For example, restoration architects must work not only with conservators and archaeologists but also with workmen on the job and enthusiastic laymen in the preservation movement who are often unaware of the complexity of problems that may arise.

Although adequate training is necessary for preservation work, it disturbs me when training is emphasized as a guide to an indi-

449

vidual's ability to fulfill a particular role in a preservation project. There are pitfalls in this approach. For instance, the Canadian Museums Association sponsors a sort of short-course training program. Students earn credits until they finally reach a certain level of proficiency. I believe such short-course training programs have disadvantages. Graduates of these programs may be able to parrot all the things they have learned, but they may not be whole persons, that is, they may not consider all the relevant factors before making a decision.

To be fully qualified for work in the preservation field, an individual should have not only a good attitude and adequate training but also experience. Many types of experience are valuable; on-site work is, of course, invaluable, and it is useful to have experience in dealing with preservation organizations and groups sponsoring specific restoration projects.

I believe the useful preservationist has the following qualities:

1. *Broad human interest.* The restoration architect who has a limited view of the total environment is far less useful in preservation efforts than one who has an interest in landscape design, horticulture, planning, urban affairs and ecology. Hopefully, the well-rounded architect, who is interested in the total environment, will be among the leaders of the preservation movement.

2. *Critical observation.* Preservationists should constantly question the validity of decisions. I do not mean they should be cynical, but they should not necessarily accept the first solution that comes to mind. Unlike computers, which provide consistent answers to questions, human beings can either say "I do not know what to do" when confronted with a problem, or they can devise many different ways to approach the problem. The North American edition of *Building,* which I am most familiar with, reflects this diversity of approaches only too well: The architectural solution is, in fact, seldom the builder's solution.

3. *Sensibility.* Sensibility is a lovely word that was used often in the late 18th and early 19th centuries. It is generally associated with the short-lived picturesque movement. To me, it means common sense combined with sensitivity, imagination and, to a certain extent, discipline.

4. *Application.* Caroline K. Keck explains this term well. She indicates in her paper that there is a certain dedication involved in preservation work. Dedication is rather an overused word nowadays, but it does apply in this situation.

5. *Optimism.* It is important for preservationists to be optimistic and to have enthusiasm and a sense of humor.

6. *Humility.* Good rapport is a reward of humility. A preservationist who tries his best to make correct decisions should always be open to the ideas of others who believe those decisions are wrong.

7. *Integrity.* Integrity is unassailable no matter what efforts are made to break it down.

Another of my concerns is judging preservationists' activities. Such judgment is complicated and makes accreditation extremely difficult. All aspects of a project must be considered in such an evaluation. The interpretation policy adopted must be kept in mind. Remember, there are many ways a project can be approached. Another aspect to be evaluated is the effort expended; this includes how much cooperation there is among all the professionals involved. Finally, consideration must also be given to the means adopted to achieve the goals established, the result and the project record, which is important because it may become the basis for future interpretation. There are also continuing problems in judging preservation activities—for instance, the maintenance problem. Buildings are made of expendable materials; they do disappear. But physical condition is not the only continuing problem: What about a preservationist's reputation? What happens to an individual's reputation when uninformed changes are authorized after the consultant has completed his work for the organization responsible for the restoration? These changes should be discouraged, but often the consultant has no time to return and make sure his suggestions are followed.

I have grave doubts about the feasibility and practicality of accreditation and licensing because of the scope of interest required of full-fledged preservationists. How would the judgment, which is necessary, be made? Would a guild of one's peers decide? There is a danger in this approach because peer groups sometimes judge individuals on the basis of who they are rather than on what they know and can accomplish. If accreditation and licensing procedures are ever adopted, a probationary period should be provided to allow new preservationists to practice in the field but not to be judged until they have gained experience and handled enough problems to be judged fairly.

In conclusion, I believe that a real horror not only for preservationists who face many frustrations, but for everyone in difficult situations is to lose these three essential attributes: one's sangfroid, one's sense of humor and one's genius for compromise.

DISCUSSION

Comments made by the panelists and audience during the discussion on standards are summarized in the following paragraphs.

The lack of standards in the historic preservation field affects not only significant cultural property but also those who are involved in preservation efforts. Preservation professionals are often too readily identified with volunteers. Both groups are, of course, important in the preservation movement, but professionals must endeavor to establish and continue their identity in order to maintain their status as full-fledged professionals and to be adequately compensated for their services.

Considerable progress has been made in establishing standards for the preservation of historic property owned by the federal government, and several states and major cities are now beginning to develop similar standards to protect and preserve their publicly owned property. However, much remains to be done to develop standards that will protect significant property in private ownership. Preservation techniques involving less-than-fee interests hold great potential in providing protection for such property and may aid in reducing the high values now assessed on historic property and upon which local taxes are based. More study and investigation, as well as the development of prototype programs, are needed to make techniques involving less-than-fee interests easy to understand and to use. Private owners must be made aware of their tremendous responsibility as trustees of the nation's architectural and cultural heritage and its future.

Perhaps the time has come for the United States to study and evaluate, for potential application here, the incentives that other countries provide for saving significant cultural property. Attention should be given to how such countries aid private owners in the preservation of the historic property they own. Great Britain, for example, has a quite advanced program of incentives and aid for the preservation of private property; in fact, it was expanded recently with the authorization of additional funds for the program.

In contrast, in the United States, national public policy, particularly as expressed through the Internal Revenue Code, provides incentives for the demolition of buildings. Incentives for preservation, rather than demolition, are urgently needed on all levels—national, state and local. Several states have taken steps to encourage the preservation of historic property. The New Mexico legislature, for example, enacted a bill that provides some relief from the heavy property tax burden that falls on historic structures. Perhaps such tax programs and other incentives to encourage preservation should be preservationists' next major area of national attention in the battle to save the country's architectural heritage.

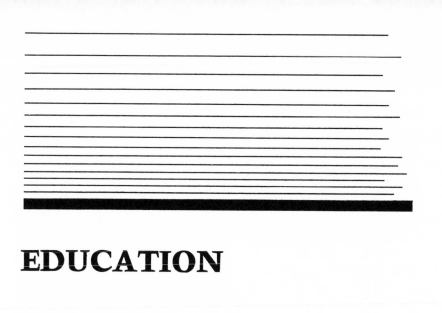

EDUCATION

University/Apprenticeship/ Continuing Education

THE EDUCATION OF ARCHITECTURAL PRESERVATION SPECIALISTS IN THE UNITED STATES

STEPHEN W. JACOBS, AIA

Today architectural preservation offers significant opportunities for professional specialization in the United States. New educational programs and scholarly enterprises are beginning to reflect the opportunities, needs and increasing sophistication of the field. In many areas, architects able and willing to cope with the complications of historic site work are finding sufficient demand for their services to justify the development of a preservation practice. They must be ready to make archaeological and adaptive use studies, to provide working drawings and specifications and to administer contracts (including consultation with clients and agencies, the letting of bids and the supervision of construction, specialists and suppliers). Architectural historians able to search out, document, evaluate, interpret and publish information about preservable buildings and areas are now finding new opportunities outside the traditional academic setting for their endeavors, working with private organizations and public agencies dedicated to preservation. University programs, especially those of professional schools of architecture, are beginning to display interest in problems associated with the local heritage. There has even been some revival of concern for everyday relics of the technologically obsolete past that created our monuments. An interest in the archaeological relics of the Industrial Revolution has been added to an

Stephen W. Jacobs, AIA, is professor of architecture at the College of Architecture, Art and Planning, Cornell University, Ithaca, N.Y.

earlier concern for fabrics produced by a vanished age of handicraft.

RECENT HISTORICAL DEVELOPMENTS

Several national scholarly organizations have recently been formed, attesting to an upsurge of interest in the architectural and engineering achievements of postcolonial America. These new organizations include the Society for the History of Technology, founded in 1958; Victorian Society in America, 1966; Society for Historical Archaeology, 1967; Association for Preservation Technology, 1968; and Society for Industrial Archeology, 1972.

Many more societies with regional or typological interests (such as the Friends of Cast-Iron Architecture or the Cobblestone Society) devote themselves to publicizing and rescuing relatively little known portions of America's building heritage. Of course, there are also a growing number of international organizations giving part or all of their attention to preservation problems, ranging from those with a general, global concern for preservation —for example, the International Council of Monuments and Sites (ICOMOS) and the Committee on Historic Urban Areas of the International Federation for Housing and Planning—to newly formed and highly specialized groups, such as the International Committee for Architectural Photogrammetry. All contribute to our knowledge, understanding and enthusiasm for preservable parts of the man-made environment. They broaden our range of interests and activities, disseminate technical information and make possible a higher level of expertise and professionalism in the preservation field.

The last generation of architects to be trained in the traditional way established in schools of architecture a century ago is now dying out. These practitioners were exposed to historical archetypes as models and were expected to be able to produce reasonable imitations of the more admired features of archaic structures. Many of these practitioners were sufficiently scholarly and sympathetic to original materials, or sufficiently imbued with ingenuity and a flair for the picturesque, to make memorable contributions to preservation. Others had a limited repertoire and little sympathy for the offbeat or atypical relic, replacing or "colonializing" buildings of all eras. In any event, they have few direct heirs, although some will be succeeded by younger men trained in their offices.

Until recently, architecture schools provided relatively little help. Since 1945, training available in the regular professional curricula has been inadequate to qualify architects for historical work.

458

From 1945 to 1960, the emphasis was on "modernity" and "progress," with little sympathy displayed by most practitioners or educators for evidences of the past that might inhibit new schemes. Historic structures were thought to be technically and socially obsolete; they were considered to be planning obstacles and to represent losses of financial opportunity rather than important environmental resources. The design religion of the "Old Masters" from Europe—Le Corbusier, Gropius, Miës van der Rohe—even though clearly based on a knowledge and an analysis of achievements of the past, required a rejection of all existing values and forms in order to avoid the hazard of imitation or the conventionality of quotation. Cubist aesthetic and machine-age dynamism, new building technologies and new transport patterns seemed to put a brave new world within reach, but one that had no desire to appear rooted. Even today an expendable, unstable environment is regarded by some as a desirable design objective.[1]

A reaction to this rejection of the past, however, has been under way for some time. There is now a growing appreciation for irreplaceable elements of the man-made environment. In addition to those enthusiasts and aesthetes who have all along taken an interest in architectural relics for personal reasons—artistic, social or philosophical—relatively unsophisticated citizens who find themselves with the leisure and the inclination to travel or who look for an alternative to the stereotyped and sterile settings offered to them by most developers today are encouraging owners and authorities to reconsider their attitudes about amortized or "obsolete" facilities. Social scientists are discovering the value of landmarks for humanizing man-made environments.

Conservationists have shown that concerted efforts to protect basic ecosystems can and must be made if the planet is to remain viable, and they have done much to demonstrate how destructive exploitation of outstanding natural features and areas can be limited through community action. In the last decade, conservation of key features and areas of the man-made environment has been added to the picture, and consequently, the limitation of development rights, even in congested urban areas, is now regarded as a sound practice.

The preservation legislation enacted by the United States Congress in 1966 enlarged the scope of government-supported preservation activities enormously. Traditional preservation activities of the National Park Service were given additional encouragement, and the groundwork was laid for a nationwide inventory of historic places. More comprehensive preservation planning by the states was sought. A review of federally funded projects, including transportation plans and building proposals, was mandated to determine whether they might adversely affect properties of historical or architectural value. The various acts passed that year provided new tools and resources needed to reinforce the efforts of those fighting destructive changes in the environment. They also opened a vast field to professionally trained preservationists interested in working with agencies and commissions.

Few students, however, have access to training or scholarly programs adequate to prepare them to take advantage of the present and emerging opportunities for careers in historic preservation.

A major effort to analyze preservation education deficiencies and to make constructive recommendations was made in the report submitted to the trustees of the National Trust for Historic Preservation in 1968 by a special study committee chaired by Walter Muir Whitehill. The committee's statement is often referred to as the Whitehill Report.[2]

The report discussed two major topics: professional and public education for preservation. It also made interim suggestions about publications of value to professional preservationists. Architectural curricula were reviewed to discover programs that would encourage professionalism in historic preservation. The graduate programs at the schools of architecture at Virginia, Columbia and Cornell universities were found to offer worthwhile preservation training. The report urged immediate support of university programs through substantial, specially solicited foundation grants.[3] The committee recognized the urgency of increasing the number of professional restorationists not fully engaged by large organizations in the field, such as Colonial Williamsburg or the National Park Service, and concluded that efforts to improve professional education in historic preservation should be "rigidly limited to architecture and the building crafts."[4] The relatively undeveloped character of preservation curricula was recognized.

The conditions prevailing in the education of restoration architects and restoration planners can be characterized as elementary. . . . there appears to be relatively small awareness within the architectural and planning professions of the importance of restoration and preservation techniques. There is, consequently, an even smaller level of awareness among laymen who own or control historic properties of the need for professional guidance, to the detriment of the nation's historic sites. . . . the type of leadership needed is one that encourages, coaxes, inspires, nourishes and nutures growth of the professional spirit in preservation.[5]

The committee determined that specialization in restoration and preservation was most effective on the graduate level and recommended that National Trust support of graduate programs

460

should look to the geographic spread of available programs to provide each region of the country with a center.

The study committee's Subcommittee on Conservation of the Traditional Building Crafts recognized the marginal nature of employment opportunities for restoration craftsmen and recommended that skilled preservationists among active masons, plasterers, wood-carvers and painters be sought out and assured of regular and suitable employment before additional trainees were enlisted. On–the–job training for qualified journeymen under expert supervision was recommended as the best method of training restoration craftsmen. It was suggested that a successful program would require the collection of documentary material in a special archive (a function now in part fulfilled by publications of the Association for Preservation Technology) and the provision of a clearinghouse to put craftsmen or restoration teams in touch with clients rehabilitating historic properties.[6]

PRESENT RESOURCES

Most professional education programs have been slow to investigate or cope with planning and technical issues now faced as a consequence of the preservation field's new maturity, resources, demands, legislation and sophistication. A few enterprising urban professional schools have managed some contact with adaptive use problems and rehabilitation of historic structures as a by-product of efforts to put students in touch with community issues and programs.[7] However, most of those involved have been more interested in a contemporary solution than in one that profited from available architectural resources on the site.

On behalf of the Committee on Historic Resources of the American Institute of Architects (AIA), F. Blair Reeves, professor of architecture at the University of Florida at Gainesville, prepared a questionnaire in March 1971 on current architecture school curricula in architectural history and preservation. Computer tabulation and analysis and preliminary findings suggest that these subjects do not have sufficiently high priority among architectural educators. The response to the questionnaire was representative, since it reported on more than half of the members of the Association of Collegiate Schools of Architecture and more than half of the 20,000 students thought to be enrolled in architectural curricula throughout the United States. (The current membership of the AIA is 23,000.) Fifty-one schools training approximately 13,000 architecture students responded; all but seven are accredited.

Relatively few programs attempt to provide leadership in the use of the local architectural heritage. Ninety percent of the replies indicated that the area where the school is located is not history oriented and does not support preservation programs, even though nearly one-third have surroundings rich in historic architectural resources and nearly half have an "adequate supply." Almost one-third of the schools offer opportunities for specialization in architectural history at the graduate level, but only 20 percent offer such opportunities to undergraduates. On the other hand, the questionnaire findings indicate that two-thirds of the faculty in the schools participate in preservation as consultants or practitioners and as advisers to state and local preservation groups. Although 40 percent of the schools of architecture responding to the survey offer separate history courses on American architecture, they are a required part of the curriculum in less than 10 percent. Few schools offer historical course work on interiors, American archaeology or regional or local architecture. Less than one-fifth of the schools provide technical courses of value for preservation work. Although the opportunities for historical study and preservation training are improving in most professional architectural curricula, they are still far from adequate and are often poorly organized.

Graduate Programs

Of the 93 members of the Association of Collegiate Schools of Architecture in the United States and Canada, four have established programs in preservation at the graduate level. These are Columbia University, New Cork City; Cornell University, Ithaca, N.Y.; the University of Florida at Gainesville; and the University of Virginia at Charlottesville. The program offered by the University of Florida Department of Architecture is the newest of the four and the most clearly oriented toward the training of architects. Begun in the fall of 1970, it is designed for students with professional degrees in architecture and offers specialization in architectural history or architectural preservation to students seeking a Master of Arts degree in architecture. The program was developed by F. Blair Reeves with assistance from Carl Feiss, professor of architecture and urban studies at the University of Florida. Some of the historic preservation and restoration courses offered by the University of Florida's College of Fine Arts and Architecture are regarded as "core courses in which the primary focus is on one or more aspects of urbanism"[8] and are accredited for the university's certificate program in urban studies, which was begun in the fall of 1971.

At the University of Virginia, a commitment to architectural history goes back to 1919 and the establishment of the School of

FIGURE 1. *"Design and Conservation" seminar, one of the introductory courses in the Preservation Planning Program at the College of Architecture, Art and Planning, Cornell University. (Cornell University)*

Architecture when Fiske Kimball developed a strong history program. In 1958, Virginia offered the first undergraduate degree in architectural history available in the United States, and in 1964, a graduate program leading to the degree of Master of Architectural History was inaugurated. The curriculum attempts

to answer the needs for training architectural historians in three fields: (1) architectural survey, preservation, and restoration of historic buildings in conjunction with the many urban renewal programs coming into being; (2) new and expanding educational programs conducted by colleges, universities, and museums; and (3) news media and journals coverage of our generally expanding society, with particular emphasis on editorial positions.[9] Special attention is paid to the use of original sources, both textual and architectural, and the methodology of restoration is thoroughly explored. The student is expected to investigate the broad culture base in the fields of his chosen projects as well as their architectural manifestations.[10]

The program was developed by William B. O'Neal, chairman of the Division of Architectural History, and Frederick D. Nichols, Cary D. Langhorne professor of architecture.

Since 1964, Columbia University's School of Architecture has offered a two–year curriculum in historic architecture as one of three programs leading to the Master of Science in Architecture degree.

463

The aim of the program in Restoration and Preservation of Historic Buildings is to train professional preservationists. . . . The program provides . . . an understanding of the philosophical and theoretical problems in the field, the techniques of surveying actual buildings and the knowledge of materials and construction techniques.[11]

Students admitted to the program need not have architectural training, but all are expected to develop competence in recording historic buildings during the two semesters of course work required. The program is directed by James Marston Fitch, professor of architecture and director of the graduate program, in association with Charles E. Peterson, adjunct professor of architecture. Students may elect a joint program with the Department of Art History and Archaeology and benefit from the availability of one of the "world's leading architectural libraries, the Avery Memorial Library."[12]

Cornell University's College of Architecture, Art and Planning has offered graduate work in architectural history since 1963. In 1971, this course work was combined with offerings in the history of city planning and preservation to form a new graduate field, the history of architecture and urban development, offering programs leading to scholarly rather than professional degrees. Candidates for master's or doctoral degrees can select the history of architecture or the history of urban development as major or minor subjects. At present, preservation planning is offered only as a minor subject. The master's degree program is intended to qualify students for research, teaching, specialized practice or government service. The doctoral program is intended to prepare students to make creative contributions to the field. Barclay G. Jones, chairman of the Department of Policy Planning and Regional Analysis and acting director of the Center for Urban Development Research, and I collaborated on the development of the program.[13]

In 1972, Cornell's Department of Architecture instituted a four-year undergraduate major in the history of architecture. Students enrolled in this program receive a Bachelor of Fine Arts degree. They take the first two years of the professional undergraduate architectural curriculum, obtaining the basic skills and sensitivities needed for preservation work, including the recording, interpreting, restoring or adapting of historic structures.

A number of other architectural schools offer some course work in preservation or related subjects, but to date, none of them have developed widely publicized specialized degree programs. An example is the School of Architecture of the University of Maryland at College Park, which benefits from the collaboration of restoration architect Orin M. Bullock, Jr.[14] There, Anatole Senkevitch, Jr., teaches courses in preservation.[15]

Both graduate and undergraduate work in historic preservation is offered by the Department of Environmental Design of the University of Georgia at Athens, while one of the programs offered by the Cooperstown (N.Y.) Graduate Programs, which lead to a Master of Arts degree in historic museum training, offers some architectural preservation studies. (The other two programs offer master's degrees in American folk culture and the conservation of historic and artistic works.) A cooperative venture of the New York State Historical Association and the New York State University College at Oneonta, the Cooperstown Graduate Programs was begun in 1964, largely as a result of the efforts of Louis C. Jones, the director emeritus, and Frederick L. Rath, Jr.

In the past, Rath has conducted a seminar on historic preservation planning at Cooperstown. Today, other preservation courses are offered as well. According to the most recent catalogue, a course on problems in history museums permits "concentrated in–depth study in a specific aspect of the history museum field such as historic house restoration, historical archaeology, or museum education."[16]

Several universities, including the University of Michigan at Ann Arbor, the University of Pennsylvania at Philadelphia and Boston (Mass.) University, offer graduate American studies programs that permit specialization in architectural history, historical archaeology or other preservation-related areas.

Summer Courses

Three pioneer ventures in preservation education were undertaken in the summer of 1972: (1) the European Traveling Summer School for Restorationists sponsored by the Rome Centre Committee of the U.S. Advisory Council on Historic Preservation, (2) a lecture course on architectural conservation at the New School for Social Research in New York City and (3) a ten-week course on Nantucket Island, cosponsored by the University of Florida at Gainesville and the Nantucket Institute.

In a one-month period, the traveling school, directed by Charles E. Peterson of Columbia University, visited London and sites in the south of England, then moved to Paris and northwestern France. After stopovers in Louvain, Ghent, Utrecht and Amsterdam, the tour concluded with visits to Manchester and York. Participation was limited to 25, with 17 places reserved for students and practicing professionals in architecture, restoration and preservation from the United States.

The architectural conservation course offered during the summer term of the New School for Social Research was organized by William C. Shopsin, chairman of the Historic Buildings Committee of the New York Chapter of the AIA. The class met for two hours on Monday and Wednesday evenings to consider historic New York architecture, recognition of stylistic elements and rescue of landmarks. Walking tours supplemented the lectures, which included talks by architects, planners and landmarks experts.[17]

The Nantucket Institute, with the cooperation of the National Trust and the National Park Service, offered preservation courses for "preprofessionals" and a workshop for professionals. The new program was organized by F. Blair Reeves of the University of Florida at Gainesville, who has directed Historic American Buildings Survey recording teams on Nantucket for several summers. Fifteen architecture students were admitted to take five of the preservation courses regularly offered at Gainesville.

Less structured summer programs can be arranged for outstanding students. For example, some of the participants in the Columbia and Cornell University programs have occasionally been invited to work with the New York City Landmarks Preservation Commission or with similar local agencies, while architecture students from the University of Virginia have obtained on-the-job experience through summer internships provided by Colonial Williamsburg.

Historic Buildings Surveys
The Historic American Buildings Survey (HABS), under the Office of Archeology and Historic Preservation of the National Park Service, a part of the U.S. Department of the Interior, conducts summer field projects as part of its continuing program of recording outstanding examples of American architecture. For many years, teams of architectural students (mainly undergraduates, but often including graduate students of architecture or architectural history) have worked in small groups supervised by teachers of architecture or architectural history to prepare records of historic structures for deposit at the Library of Congress in Washington, D.C. In addition to measured drawings (which, if complete, make possible the reconstruction of damaged or destroyed monuments), photographs and written histories of buildings or areas studied are prepared. Students generally find the process of making detailed measured drawings under supervision a rewarding experience; however, only a few architecture school curricula require the measurement of a historic building to HABS standards. An effort is made by the HABS office to enlist students and conduct summer

projects in all parts of the country. Generally, teams are located in centers where there is sufficient local interest to provide some support for the work.[18]

Occasionally, state preservation agencies, such as the New York Preservation Board, have sponsored summer student recording teams on the model of HABS project groups. To date, the most extensive use of student talent for recording historic architecture has been in Canada, where information on a vast number of buildings has been gathered for the Canadian Inventory of Historic Buildings. Because of the careful organization of this computerized survey and the training program provided, students engaged in this activity need not have previous experience or indoctrination. Training of professionals who may become preservation specialists is not an objective, as it is for the Park Service's HABS program. Rather, the Canadian inventory, as conducted by the National Historic Sites Services of the Canadian Department of Indian Affairs and Northern Development, through summer employment, and recording projects has created considerable enthusiasm for the nation's architectural heritage in a significant portion of the university population. This should increase public awareness of the potentials of preservation and, perhaps, induce a few summer surveyors to take up related professional careers.[19]

CONTINUING EDUCATION

Short Courses

Two universities offer intensive one-week courses in preservation planning. At Cornell, the course on historic preservation programs has been a mainstay of the institute held each June since 1966 to further continuing education in planning. Given in cooperation with the National Trust, the institute attracts a variety of participants from locations throughout the United States and Canada. The majority are professionals active in preservation. Presentations are made by experienced practitioners of preservation specialties, including survey, restoration, law, design, government and development.[20]

At Chapel Hill, N.C., the Institute of Government of the University of North Carolina and the North Carolina Department of Archives and History have cooperated in staging a one-week course, entitled "Planning for the Preservation of Historic Buildings, Sites, Districts and Areas," every other year, beginning in March 1968. Robert E. Stipe, assistant director of the Institute of Government, took the initiative in developing the program, which includes sessions on "A Planning Setting for Historic Preservation," "Historic Buildings, Sites and Areas: Identification and

Evaluation," "Developing Plans for the Historic Area" and "Preservation Action: Legal, Administrative, Financial and Political Aspects."[21]

Seminars

Some annual programs are sponsored by agencies engaged in encouraging appreciation of folklore, local history or antiques. Occasionally, as part of their commitment to adult education in the museum field, they schedule seminars relating to architectural preservation. An example is provided by the Pennsylvania Historical and Museum Commission, which sponsors such seminars as the Institute of Pennsylvania Rural Life and Culture at the Pennsylvania Farm Museum in the Landis Valley north of Lancaster and the four-day Pennsbury Manor Americana Forum held near Morrisville on the Delaware River. In June 1972, the 16th Institute of Pennsylvania Rural Life and Culture included a course on farmhouse architecture, a subject relatively unfamiliar to younger preservation specialists.[22] The first day of the fourth annual Americana Forum, held in 1968, was devoted to a preservation session and was cosponsored by the National Trust. It was followed by informative discussions of the role of archaeology in preservation. The fifth Americana Forum, held in September 1969, devoted one day to preservation reports and two days to discussions of restoration technology.

Other state historical commissions have sponsored regional preservation conferences, often with the cooperation of the National Trust. Lately, the Trust has also organized its own regional preservation workshops, with varying degrees of response.

Perhaps the best known seminars on American culture have been presented by the New York State Historical Association at Cooperstown. The seminars consist of two sets of courses that are offered in consecutive midsummer weeks. In 1964, one of the three morning courses offered in the first week discussed "Saving the Past: Historic Preservation and City Planning." It was paired with an afternoon seminar entitled "Architecture Worth Saving." The following year, courses on restoration architecture and restoration archaeology (with case studies) were offered. More recently, the 1970 program included the courses "American Architecture to 1915" and "State and Local Architecture in Historic Site Surveys." In 1971, a week of afternoon sessions on "Looking Forward to the Past" considered the past, present and future of the preservation movement. In 1972, further introspection was provided by the course "A Historian Looks at Historic Preservation," a report on the history of key preservation agencies and organizations in the United States.

Programs of the AIA

For more than a century, the AIA has been in the forefront of efforts to educate architects and the public in preservation matters. At the 1869 national convention of the AIA, Richard Upjohn gave a paper on colonial architecture that mentioned the need to preserve and record historic American buildings.[23] For many years, a number of devoted practitioners have made valiant efforts to upgrade the AIA's preservation activities.[24] The AIA has supported a number of educational ventures of value for preservation, including lectures, symposia and student chapter presentations, preservation sessions, architectural tours and awards. Publication and research projects have been sponsored, and considerable attention has been given to the problem of the development of the AIA headquarters on the grounds of the Octagon House, the mansion in Washington, D.C., first occupied by the AIA in 1898 and recently restored. The AIA cooperates closely with other organizations active in preservation, especially in matters of national policy and legislation, and was one of the original sponsors of the HABS.

The Committee on Historic Resources is one of the more active components of the AIA's Commission on Building Design; the committee holds three meetings a year, responds to "brush fire" emergencies when historic structures are threatened and issues a newsletter shared with the AIA's State Preservation Coordinators Council.[25]

Since 1968, the Committee on Historic Resources has sponsored and provided funds for a series of workshops on architectural preservation. These are one or two–day programs given at architecture schools to stir up interest in preservation among students, faculty, administrators, professionals and local citizens and to develop better understanding of educational programs, opportunities and needs in the field of architectural preservation. Generally, experts and administrators of preservation agencies describe important facets of ongoing preservation efforts and discuss possibilities of additional local input and achievement.

Society of Architectural Historians

The Society of Architectural Historians (SAH) has become more active in preservation matters, to some degree compromising its traditional pose of scholarly detachment. In the past, historians kept aloof from the preservation alarms and battles that preoccupy those architects who feel some responsibility for the fate of the outstanding works of their forebears. With increasing frequency,

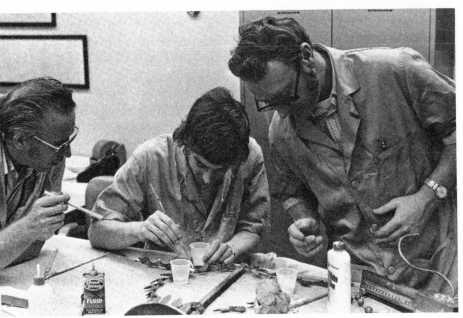

FIGURE 2. *Apprentice Nicholas Quinn (center) is instructed in the restoration of gilt gesso by John Melody (left), conservator of furniture, and his assistant, Mervin Martin (right), at the Henry Francis du Pont Winterthur Museum. (Winterthur Museum)*

opinions, testimonials and suggestions are solicited from the SAH's Committee on Architectural Preservation by those attempting to cope with preservation problems both in the United States and abroad. The committee has been greatly enlarged and offers a forum for the airing of current problems at the SAH annual meeting. In addition to scholarly lecture sessions, which include one devoted to preservation and open to the public, the annual meetings provide for tours in the vicinity. Longer tours of significant educational value are arranged by the SAH main office for members and friends. Generally, there is at least one tour abroad each year and one in the United States for which student scholarships are offered through cooperating schools. Tours are usually organized by local specialists and, often, significant historical documentation is developed for them. The society's *Newsletter*, which grew to a six-page publication issued six times a year while James C. Massey was editor, provides excellent coverage of preservation activities, including reviews of the work of other organizations, books and articles, exhibits and courses and conferences.

National Trust for Historic Preservation

The National Trust's annual meetings and associated tours concentrate on preservation to a much greater degree and attract a

470

greater proportion of laymen than do those of the SAH (which holds joint sessions with the College Art Association every other year). Because of the greater popular interest and the appearance of more socially prominent participants, Trust meetings tend to have a greater impact on the localities where meetings are held than do comparable meetings of professional organizations.

Many of the National Trust's activities serve to further education in the preservation field. The Trust Department of Publications, directed by Terry B. Morton, and with pioneer preservationist Helen D. Bullock as a consultant, centers an excellent publications program on *Preservation News*, a tabloid reporting monthly on current issues, and the quarterly magazine, *Historic Preservation*, which contains articles of lasting interest. In 1972, *Historic Preservation* was redesigned to provide a more attractive format and greater visual appeal.[26] For those interested in preservation careers, the Trust Department of Education organizes conferences and seminars, often in cooperation with other preservation organizations, such as Colonial Williamsburg.

METHODS OF TRAINING

Apprenticeship

It is significant that a socially obsolete term, *apprenticeship*, is still in use to describe the kind of training program considered best by experienced practitioners to assure an adequate supply of skilled people to carry out architectural restoration projects. A close working relationship with experienced craftsmen or architects is regarded as the most valuable kind of education for those who do the work and are responsible for its quality, that is, its authenticity, its appropriateness, its durability and its aesthetic appeal.[27] However, the organization of the building industry and the building trades, as well as the unfamiliarity of most building craftsmen and architects with traditional materials and methods, have made ordinary on–the–job training difficult or impractical. Now vocational training in special centers is proposed for craftsmen, and certification has been suggested for architects wishing to be restoration specialists.

Craft Training Centers

The uncertainty of supply and demand, as well as the complications of working closely with a skilled craftsman on the job, have made traditional apprenticeship, which involved indenture for a term of years to a master and generally living in his establishment, unacceptable today. Since vocational schools have replaced indentures, it seems logical to encourage those schools providing training in construction techniques, which have knowledgeable craftsmen on their staffs, to undertake limited training programs for young people interested in developing skills and expertise in traditional building methods. A pioneering effort has been made in Massachusetts, where the Groton Area Technical High School District is training apprentice restoration carpenters, offering them opportunities for field work at Plimoth Plantation.[28]

Despite the efforts of the National Trust to serve as a clearinghouse and promotional agency, there is at present little information available about career opportunities and specialized training for restoration craftsmen in the United States. Agencies whose properties require large ongoing restoration programs may have in-house capacity for limited traditional apprentice training programs. State historical commissions, the National Park Service and some of the more active museum villages are in a position to maintain a staff of restoration craftsmen on a continuing basis, as is done by many government-supported national monuments organizations abroad. They should be encouraged to provide for the training of additional specialists as a desirable by-product of their own housekeeping activities.

Occasionally, association with traditional craftsmen is regarded as a worthwhile experience for college students. A group of 10 students from Williams College in Williamstown, Mass., spent a month at Mystic (Conn.) Seaport Museum working with the assistant curator of small craft studies, John Gardner, a boatbuilder from Maine. In the museum's ship restoration shed, they put together a traditional 13½-foot wooden fishing boat and received "a lesson in what craftsmanship is all about."[29]

In 1968, the Office of Archeology and Historic Preservation of the National Park Service drafted a proposal for the William Strickland Preservation Center with a three-year pilot program to be funded by the National Parks Foundation. The ultimate objective was "a fully implemented branch of historic building technology, within the budgeted programs of the National Park Service." Three programs were envisaged: a building crafts programs to develop proficiency in traditional skills and to recruit craftsmen for Park Service restoration projects; a professional field program to provide on-the-job experience in historic preservation for graduate students and to assist Park Service staff recruitment; and a technical studies program to provide an architectural study collection emphasizing building technology and craft techniques. A Philadephia location was suggested, and the creation of two additional regional centers was proposed.[30]

Although the Strickland Center proposal proved premature, the need for training programs for restoration craftsmen continues to be urgent. In November 1971, the National Trust conducted a conference on preservation technology that considered the problem and elicited support from representatives of the AIA, among other groups. New proposals for craft training programs, perhaps with the support of the building trade unions as well as restoration architects, can be anticipated.

Certification

The AIA has not yet agreed to support postlicensing accreditation of preservation architects, suggested as a possibility by the National Trust. It is assumed that accreditation would lead to higher standards in the work accomplished and that educational and training opportunities for preservation architects would be better coordinated, publicized and supported. If a certification procedure for preservation specialists were instituted, methods of specialized technical investigation and on-the-job training for architects would be emphasized, perhaps with the aid of new craft centers. Although it would simplify the job of selecting restoration architects for specific projects and would to some degree protect the public from the misguided enthusiasm or shoddy performance of a few professionals, there is considerable resistance to the accreditation proposal. In part, this resistance stems from the wide variety of demands and judgments faced by the restoration architect in practice. Since divergent criteria may apply to museum reconstructions and to adaptive use projects and since technical methodology for building preservation is evolving rapidly, specialists with considerable experience in the field question whether satisfactory tests can be devised for those seeking accreditation as preservation architects. One solution might be the development of a certificate program in a center supported by national organizations interested in preservation. Knowledge of the latest preservation techniques, as well as of traditional crafts and experience with analysis and design of historic forms, could be required. Ideally, workshop training would be provided, using the case-study method to develop programs and design solutions for historic structures or areas, supplemented by supervised field experience.

FUTURE DIRECTIONS IN PRESERVATION EDUCATION

There is a great and growing need for preservation professionals. Public agencies at all levels of government—federal, state, county and municipal—must meet new demands and legal requirements for preservation planning and administration. Volunteer groups and regional preservation agencies are developing resources and programs that will require a great increase in preservation and rehabilitation work, demanding services of restoration architects and craftsmen, as well as specialist consultants. The success of historic districts as upper middle-class residential areas has created a knowledgeable clientele of activist citizens, many of whom will support preservation ventures for themselves and others. In addition, the economic impacts of new preservation planning techniques, such as the transfer of unused development rights and of traditional tourism, with preserved properties serving as destinations or distractions for our aging but mobile population, will make preservation attractive to businessmen and economists.

Preservation education must be more forward-looking than it has been in the past. Its repertory cannot be limited to 18th-century apprenticeships for craftsmen or 19th-century studio and office operations for architects. Many more disciplines beyond those of design and construction are required to successfully meet preservation needs in the 20th century. Scientific laboratory methods are now being applied to preservation problems with great success, particularly in such matters as the analysis of paint colors or the stabilization of wooden trim elements with epoxy.[31] New and complex technology is now being used, involving chemistry, spectrographic analysis, carbon dating, resistivity testing and many other arcane procedures.

New tools of enormous importance are available to preservationists, who will need scientific training to use them effectively. Among these are two key items for surveys and records: computer technology, essential for adequate retrieval of recorded information; and photogrammetry, which solves many difficult problems of search and makes the production of accurately dimensioned visual records relatively easy and inexpensive. New archaeological techniques make possible a better analysis of site evidence and, ultimately, more complete, understandable and satisfactory preservation projects. Theodore A. Sande, president of the Society for Industrial Archeology, recently pointed out that:

for those who intend to become industrial archaeologists, regardless of their particular college major, two skills stand out as having obvious importance. . . . The first is a solid background in the history of the country and a comprehensive understanding in the history of technology. Secondly, a competence in the methodology of industrial archaeology. This would include mastery of methods of research, field surveying and recording techniques, and a knowledge of historic preservation procedures. Both of these capabilities should be developed through interdisciplinary courses of study that force crossing of traditional departmental lines within the university in order to achieve the best possible cultivation of the student's talents with respect to the several possible roles that he or she might select.[32]

FIGURE 3. *Craftsman prepares woodwork in the dining room of* Woodlawn
*Plantation, a property of the National Trust for Historic Preservation, for repaint-
ing during restoration work in 1951. (National Trust for Historic Preservation)*

We need only substitute *architectural preservationists* for *industrial archaeologists* in Sande's statement to see its applicability.
He goes on to recommend that students consider combining studies in a variety of departments and in more than one branch of
learning to prepare themselves for the varied opportunities and
responsibilities of this new discipline.

Because of the increasing complexity of both problems and solutions for preservation projects, university and other research facilities will be involved in preservation more and more. It is hearten-
ing to learn that the Rome Centre has not only inaugurated a new
architectural preservation curriculum to which students from the
United States have access but also has established a well–equipped
laboratory. This will enable the architectural preservationist to
have the benefit of some of the experiences, resources and vital
information available to fine arts conservators.

The growing body of specialized literature about early building
technology will also tend to make preservation practice less the

exercise of a limited number of traditional skills and more a responsible procedure in which library study and comparative analysis will enable structures of all vintages and techniques to be properly maintained or restored. The practice (established by Charles E. Peterson) of recording notes on early building methods is now blossoming into informative monographs about methods and materials employed in key historic structures.[33]

The last point to be made about the future of preservation education is that it will need, and probably get, much greater support, particularly from the public sector. Despite the current disenchantment with the attitudes of some relatively conspicuous students and teachers, the American tradition of sacrificial piety toward education and appreciation for its role in increasing opportunities for individuals and analyzing (if not solving) social and technical problems will probably continue. It is to be hoped that foundations will come to understand the importance of supporting the training of preservation professionals to maintain the quality of the environment and everyday life and will make contributions to the appreciation and proper exploitation of our architectural heritage. Even more is to be hoped for from government, since recent legislation and executive orders have mandated many procedures and judgments requiring the input of trained preservation specialists. Both agencies and educators should be interested in supporting the work of the comprehensive programs that develop. It is to be hoped that professional and scholarly leadership will be forthcoming to lead us into the "promised land" where all our earthly goods will be responsibly sorted, maintained and enjoyed.

NOTES

1. The English "Archigram" group is an extreme case.

2. "Report of Committee on Professional and Public Education for Historic Preservation to the Trustees of the National Trust for Historic Preservation," mimeographed (Washington, D.C.: National Trust, 1968). In addition to Dr. Whitehill, who is director and librarian of the Boston Athenaeum, three other National Trust trustees served on the committee: Leonard Carmichael, vice president for research and exploration of the National Geographic Society; Ronald F. Lee, former special assistant to the director of the National Park Service; and Charles van Ravenswaay, director of the Henry Francis du Pont Winterthur Museum. The other members of the committee were Francis L. Berkeley, Jr., assistant to the president of the University of Virginia and vice chairman of the committee; J. O. Brew, director of the Peabody Museum of Archaeology and Ethnology at Harvard University; John Peterson Elder, dean of the Graduate School of Arts and Sciences at Harvard University; and Ralph G.

Schwarz, director of operations, Ford Foundation. A grant from the Ford Foundation made it possible to employ William G. Wing, a journalist interested in conservation, to do the committee's staff work.

3. As early as 1963, the College of Architecture, Art and Planning at Cornell University made a proposal to the National Trust for assistance in funding and enlarging its educational and research program in preservation. An ambitious document, the proposal stated, "In order to be comprehensive the program should include studies in the documentation, evaluation, interpretation, preservation, restoration, renewal, planning and administration of artifacts, documents, buildings, sites, and areas of historic, artistic or social significance. It should be concerned with archaeological investigation, and artifact and archive collection as a basis for research. Research must be conceived as a necessary part of the training program and as fundamental to the continual enrichment of its teaching aspects." "Proposal to the National Trust for Historic Preservation for an Educational and Research Program for the Conservation of the National Heritage of Buildings, Sites, and Artifacts," mimeographed (Ithaca, N.Y.: Cornell University, May 1, 1963), p. 3. By October 1967, Cornell had joined with Columbia and Virginia universities in submitting (at the Trust's request) proposals for funding graduate preservation programs. Further efforts were made to coordinate the proposals of the three schools and to arrange for authorization of a preservation institute at the National Trust to administer grants-in-aid to educational institutions. These negotiations were successfully concluded in 1971. However, the National Trust's solicitation of funds to support these programs has been unsuccessful thus far.

4. Ibid., p. 5.

5. Ibid., p. 7.

6. Ibid., pp. 11–26.

7. An example is given in "The New Look of Cincinnati's Old Mt. Auburn," *Historic Preservation* 24, no. 2 (April-June 1972): 31–37. Bruce Goetzman, an instructor in the University of Cincinnati School of Architecture, served as liaison with the Mt. Auburn Community Council for groups of architecture students interested in assisting the community with the development and drawing up of remodeling and rehabilitation plans. Similar efforts to assist low-income groups have been made by staff and students of most major architecture schools.

8. Elizabeth M. Eddy, *Urban Studies at the University of Florida* (n.p., n.d.), p. 2.

9. "Proposal to the National Trust for Historic Preservation for a Graduate Educational and Research Program in Architectural History and Preservation," mimeographed (Charlottesville: Division of Architectural History, University of Virginia School of Architecture, October 1, 1967), pp. 6–7. The degree in architectural history is offered by the School of Architecture in collaboration with the university's Corcoran Department of History. The graduate curriculum in the Division of Architectural History emphasizes documentation and the development of individual projects.

10. Ibid., appendix B, p. 42.

11. *School of Architecture 1970–1971* (New York: Columbia University School of Architecture), p. 22.

12. Ibid., p. 4.

13. I am field representative for the graduate field of history of architecture and urban development. Nine colleagues who are members of the Cornell graduate faculty help direct the work of students majoring or minoring in the subjects offered. Approximately half the students enrolled in the program have had professional architectural training. They benefit from the availability at Cornell

of outstanding archival collections on the history of American city and regional planning.

14. Mr. Bullock is author of *The Restoration Manual* (Norwalk, Conn.: Silvermine Publishers, Inc., 1966).

15. Associate Professor Dora L. Wiebenson helped develop the program at the University of Maryland, convening a group of consultants at College Park on May 15, 1971, to discuss the establishment of a graduate program in history and preservation at the School of Architecture. This was followed by a workshop on architectural preservation on December 4, 1971.

16. *1972–1973 General Catalog* (Cooperstown, N.Y.: Cooperstown Graduate Programs), p. 11. Mr. Rath was formerly director of the National Trust and senior research associate of the New York State Historical Association. He is now deputy commissioner for historic preservation in the New York State Parks and Recreation Department.

17. "New Life for Landmarks" (New York: New School for Social Research, 1972). Mr. Shopsin is a member of the AIA's Committee on Historic Resources.

18. HABS projects are scheduled for 13 weeks, with students on duty for 90 days. Summer team applicants are expected to have at least two years of undergraduate training in architecture. The pay is good, and teams are usually located in attractive areas. Among the projects carried out in the summer of 1972 were the following: Cliveden (a National Trust property), Germantown, Pa.; central business district, Kansas City, Mo.; Stockade area, Kingston, N.Y.; Tennessee Historical Commission, Memphis, Tenn.; reorganization of survey records, Mobile, Ala.; Fort Adams, Newport, R.I.; Naval Air Station, Pensacola, Fla.; historic district, Ponce, P.R.; and Shenandoah Valley stone buildings, Winchester, Va.

19. See Meredith Sykes and Ann Falkner, *Canadian Inventory of Building Manual* (Ottawa: National Historic Sites Service, 1970) and "A Canadian Inventory of Historic Building," *National Historic Park News*, no. 4 (autumn 1970). The Canadian national survey is the first computerized comprehensive architectural inventory. It was begun in the summer of 1970 in 24 cities ranging from Dawson in the Yukon to St. John's on Newfoundland.

20. With the assistance of Barclay G. Jones, I have been responsible for this offering since its inception.

21. "Planning for Historic Preservation" (Chapel Hill: Institute of Government, University of North Carolina, 1968 and 1970).

22. Topics covered by the instructors of the farmhouse architecture course, Arthur J. Lawton and Beauveau Borie, IV, (principals of B. & L. Associates, Folklife Consultants of Ambler, Pa.), included "Techniques of Construction," "Use in Daily Life" and "Research and Restoration."

23. George E. Pettengill, "AIA in the Preservation Movement," *AIA Journal* 19, no. 6 (June 1953) pp. 271–73.

24. Among the most energetic chairmen of the AIA's Committee on Historic Buildings, predecessor of the present Committee on Historic Resources, was Earl H. Reed.

25. In addition to 41 architect members, the Committee on Historic Resources has 12 consulting members representing agencies and organizations in the preservation field. There is a subcommittee on education.

26. A useful brochure published by the National Trust is *Historic Preservation: Careers for Archaeologists, Architects, Curators, Historians, Landscape Architects, Lawyers, Planners* (Washington, D.C., n.d.).

27. "Report of the Committee on Professional and Public Education," p. 14.

28. "S.L.O.'s Liaison With CHR," *Committee on Historic Resources/State Preservation Coordinators Newsletter* 3, no. 1.5 (June 1972), p. 4.

29. "Experimental Course at College Has 10 Students Building Boat," *New York Times*, July 29, 1972, p. 26. During the month set aside for experimental courses emphasizing self-expression, these students lived on one of the museum's sailing ships.

30. "A Proposal to Establish the William Strickland Preservation Center," mimeographed (Washington, D.C.: Office of Archeology and Historic Preservation, National Park Service, October 23, 1968). This proposal was made in response to the Whitehill Report. The three-year pilot program was to be carried out by a nonprofit corporation in Philadelphia at a total cost estimated at $309,000.

31. See the *Bulletin of the Association for Preservation Technology.*

32. Theodore A. Sande, "Some Thoughts on Industrial Archeology, Preservation and Training," *Newsletter, Society for Industrial Archeology*, supplementary issue no. 1 (March 1972): 2.

33. Mr. Peterson inaugurated the American Notes section of the *Journal of the Society of Architectural Historians* many years ago. Two recent examples of publications on methods and materials include Diana S. Waite, *Nineteenth Century Tin Roofing and Its Use at Hyde Hall* (Albany: New York State Historic Trust, 1972) and John G. Waite, "The Edgar Laing Stores (1849)," in *Iron Architecture in New York City: Two Studies in Industrial Archeology*, ed. John G. Waite (Albany: New York State Historic Trust, 1972), which includes a discussion on construction details of James Bogardus' Laing Stores building.

THE EDUCATION OF ART CONSERVATORS

LAWRENCE J. MAJEWSKI

It is generally recognized that one of the most important duties of an enlightened society is the care and conservation of products of human genius. Objects of historic and artistic merit belong to all mankind and need to be preserved and cherished by means of the most advanced methods of care and handling, exhibition or storage and scientific conservation. The task of extending the life-span of such objects lies in the hands of collectors, museum personnel, art historians, scientists and professional art conservators. Of these custodians of objects, the conservator is the "art doctor" who examines, diagnoses, prescribes and treats, in consultation with curators, historians and scientists.

In order for an art conservator to properly practice his profession, he must be prepared through sound educational training. Ideally, the conservator should have the combined skills of the art historian, artist and scientist, and each of these disciplines should be so thoroughly a part of the conservator that he thinks and speaks naturally of the object in historic, aesthetic and scientific terms. The conservator should also be something of a linguist to enable him to consult the technical literature in languages other than his own, as well as to confer with colleagues in other countries.

The professional conservator must be able to examine an object, determine its materials and methods of manufacture, estimate

Lawrence J. Majewski is chairman of the Conservation Center of the Institute of Fine Arts at New York University, New York, N.Y.

with accuracy its appearance when it was created and then indicate how and why changes have occurred through time and from what elements of deterioration. Having recorded the results of this examination, he may then prescribe a procedure for preservation and treatment and finally employ such measures and treatments as are necessary to consolidate, preserve and present the object. To carry out such an examination and treatment, the conservator must have intelligence, manual dexterity and skills that are obtained through carefully planned periods of training and supervised practice.

In the not-too-distant past, the conservator was usually the product of an apprenticeship—learning his "secrets" from the master and then in turn passing on the trade to his offspring or apprentices. However, in recent years, structured training programs on a university level have become a means for preparing students for professional competence as conservators. University programs combine studies of conservation theory and techniques; the history of art, connoisseurship and museology; physical and chemical properties of materials; and various types of construction used in creating works of art.

At this writing, three university programs in the United States offer courses of study in the conservation of art objects. These are the Conservation Center of the Institute of Fine Arts, New York University, New York, N.Y.; the Cooperstown Graduate Programs, Cooperstown, N.Y.; and the Intermuseum Conservation Association Laboratory, Oberlin, Ohio. As chairman of the Conservation Center of the Institute of Fine Arts, I should like to describe the program of study there.

THE CONSERVATION CENTER

The Conservation Center was established in July 1959 through a grant from the Rockefeller Foundation and is housed in the Institute of Fine Arts at 1 East 78th Street in New York City. Space, but no financial backing, is provided by New York University. All financial support has come from grants from foundations, government agencies and individuals. As stated in the summary of the proposal presented to the Rockefeller Foundation in 1958, the purpose of the center is to fulfill "the need for a program in the United States to teach, conduct research and set standards in conservation of works of art, not only paintings, but objects of all kinds." The training was to provide instruction in the theory of conservation and practice in conservation techniques, as well as a background in scientific problems of conservation and the history of art, connoisseurship and museology on which the conservator would base his decisions and procedures. Studies were to include the materials of art and archaeology, construction and character of art objects, deterioration of materials and structures, control of damaging agents and materials and methods of repair. This training was to be carried out within a university art history department in close contact with museums and museum personnel, but it was not to be subject to existing museum practices or policies. The number of students to be admitted to the program was to be small to assure adequate personal supervision of conservation activities. The Conservation Center admits only four or five students per year.

The first students were admitted to the program in September 1960. To qualify for the program, students must meet requirements for admission to New York University's Graduate School of Arts and Science, the Institute of Fine Arts and the Conservation Center. These requirements are a bachelor's degree from an accredited college; sufficient knowledge of art history to enable the student to do graduate work in the field; the equivalent of 12 credit hours of laboratory science at a college level, 6 of which must be in chemistry; and demonstration of manual dexterity as shown in drawings, paintings or other products of studio activities of the applicant.

The graduate program is for four years, including an internship of at least seven months, and leads to a master's degree in the history of art and a diploma in conservation. Qualified students who have a master's degree in the history of art may complete the program for a diploma in conservation in three years, including internship.

Staff

At this writing, the staff of the center consists of the following: Lawrence J. Majewski, chairman and associate professor of conservation; Edward V. Sayre, adjunct professor of fine arts (also senior scientist, Brookhaven National Laboratory); Norbert S. Baer, assistant professor of conservation; Norman Indictor, research associate (also associate professor of chemistry, Brooklyn College of the City University of New York); Noel Kunz, research associate; Kathryn Scott, consultant on textile conservation; Violet P. Bourgeois, administrative assistant; and Joyce H. Stoner, managing editor, *Art and Archaeology Technical Abstracts.*

The center's first director was Sheldon Keck who served from 1961 through 1964. I have been chairman of the center since 1964. In addition to the staff, a board of consulting fellows provides consultation and criticism. The board consists of 11 well-known conservators, scientists, museum curators and art historians from the United States and abroad. From time to time, the board meets at the Institute of Fine Arts to review the Conservation Center's program and to advise on research and teaching procedures.

Program

The four-year program is arranged as follows: First-year students enroll in the regular first-year program courses of the Institute of Fine Arts. They take classes in the history of art and introductory courses in conservation. The first of two foreign language examinations, one in French and the other in German, is taken during this year. In the first term at the institute, a written paper is submitted in connection with one art history course. The first qualifying paper for the master's degree is completed during the second term.

Second-year students complete any outstanding requirements for a master's degree in the history of art, including taking the second foreign language examination, preparing the second qualifying paper and completing basic introductory courses in conservation.

These basic introductory courses in conservation are taught by materials. For convenience in surveying most of the materials of art and archaeology, the studies are divided into two categories, organic and inorganic materials, which are taught in alternate years. All first and second-year students are given lecture and laboratory assignments in the same material. This means that second-year students are working with new students and to some extent, the second-year students help with instruction, as they already know laboratory procedures and examination techniques and thus can aid first-year students in adapting to course methods.

During the year in which organic materials are studied, students investigate fibers and textile materials; paper and papyrus; parchment and leather; bone and ivory; wood; polychromy of objects with organic supports; and polymeric materials, both ancient and modern.

During alternate years, inorganic materials are discussed. These are lime, plaster and related materials, including frescoes and mosaics; stone and minerals; ceramics and glazes; glass; metals, by type of metal (for example, gold and electrum; silver and silver alloys; copper and copper alloys; lead, tin and pewter; and iron and steel); and pigments, media and paintings.

Each material is considered from several aspects, including the raw material and its sources, history of its use, methods of manufacture of objects from the material, nature and causes of its deterioration and procedures for examining, recording, preserving, handling, storing, exhibiting and repairing objects made of the material. Each student is required to work with the raw material and create a simple artifact from it. The student must also examine and give both oral and written reports on an object made from the material. For example, when studying ceramics, the student makes a few pots from clays following ancient techniques and then fires the pots in a kiln. He is also assigned a piece of broken pottery to examine in detail and treat according to prescribed methods (fig. 1). Students work with objects covering a variety of historical periods. After completion of the study of one material, reports on results of the examinations are given to the class in a seminar; thus, all students benefit from the activities of their colleagues.

Examination techniques are taught with objects in hand (fig. 2). These include visual examination for gross characteristics, microscopic examination, techniques for measuring physical properties, photography with varied illumination (including ultraviolet and infrared light), radiography, microchemistry and a variety of techniques for instrumental analysis (fig. 3). A detailed record is kept of the examination.

Scientists teach chemical and physical properties of materials and analytical procedures for examination and treatment, as well as a limited amount of pure science. Specialists in the conservation of specific materials are invited to the Conservation Center for periods of a few days to several weeks to lecture and demonstrate their treatment procedures.

On completion of this two-year survey of materials and the other requirements listed previously, the student is awarded a master's degree in the history of art. At this point, he decides on the conservation area in which he wishes to specialize and chooses a subject for a research project. During the last two years, a variety of objects are assigned to the student for examination and treatment and at least one research project is advanced or completed.

Research projects at the center have been carried out on a variety of materials, construction methods and treatment procedures (fig. 4), and a number of papers have been published on the results.[1] A few of the research projects are analyses of fresco materials and techniques, causes of fresco decay and treatment procedures; causes and mechanisms of stone deterioration and treatments for hardening calcareous stones; an evaluation of materials used in paper conservation, including adhesives and consolidating materials; techniques of carving and coloring and problems of deterioration and authentication of ancient and medieval ivories; mate-

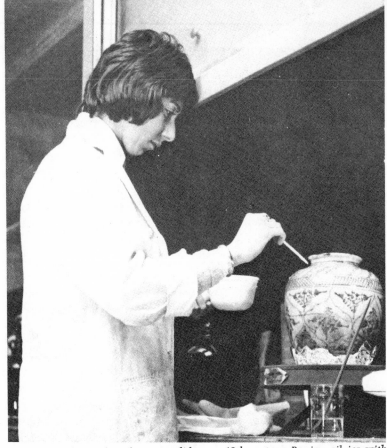

FIGURE 1. *Advanced student consolidates a 19th-century Persian oil jar with synthetic resins. (Conservation Center, Institute of Fine Arts, New York University)*

rials used in the preservation and treatment of museum textiles; the technology and fabrication of ancient Near Eastern pottery from Al Hiba, Iraq; and materials and types of construction of Indian miniatures from medieval and modern times. These and other research projects have thrown new light on the technology of structures, as well as on deterioration processes and methods for treatment.

On completion of the third year, the student is assigned to a conservation laboratory in the United States or abroad where he spends at least seven months (one term and a summer) as an intern under the supervision of the staff of the assigned laboratory. In the United States, students have interned at the Metropolitan Museum of Art, Museum of Modern Art, Brooklyn Museum and Pierpont Morgan Library, all in New York City; Library of Congress, Textile Museum, Smithsonian Institution's Conservation-Analytical Laboratory, United States National Museum (now the Museum of History and Technology and the Museum of Natural

FIGURE 2. *Chairman of the center, Lawrence J. Majewski, supervises students in the examination of objects. (Conservation Center, Institute of Fine Arts, New York University)*

FIGURE 3. *Microchemical techniques aid students in identifying pigments and other materials. (Conservation Center, Institute of Fine Arts, New York University)*

FIGURE 4. *Author and a student discuss research on the behavior of drying oils. (Conservation Center, Institute of Fine Arts, New York University)*

History), National Portrait Gallery and Freer Gallery of Art, all in Washington, D.C.; Intermuseum Conservation Association Laboratory, Oberlin, Ohio; Mellon Institute, Carnegie-Mellon University, Pittsburgh, Pa.; Walters Art Gallery, Baltimore, Md.; and Los Angeles County Museum of Art, Los Angeles, Calif. Conservation laboratories abroad where interns have been assigned include the British Museum, Victoria and Albert Museum, London University School of Archaeology and Courtauld Institute, all in London; Institut Royal de Patrimoine Artistique, Brussels; Istituto Centrale del Restauro, Rome; and the laboratory of Leonetto Tintori, Florence. During summer vacations, students generally are involved in some conservation activity, such as field work at archaeological sites in Greece, Turkey, Egypt and Iraq or service as assistants in museums or laboratories.

After the intership, the student returns to the center for the second term of the fourth year for conservation practice and research under the supervision of the center's staff and with outside consultations when needed. The diploma in conservation is awarded after completion of the fourth year and a review of the student's achievements in both research and treatment.

488

The center has completed 12 years of training, and at this time, there are 22 graduates, 2 advanced students, 3 fourth-year students, 3 in the third year, 4 in the second year and 4 in the first year. All 22 graduates are employed in conservation activities—16 in museums, 3 in universities and 3 in private practice. A number of foreign students have studied for short periods at the center to gain experience in various techniques. They have come from Japan, Korea, Taiwan, Turkey, Mexico and Austria.

Facilities

The center has an excellent library (fig. 5) of more than 3,000 volumes and 2,000 offprints on conservation subjects, including the history of technology, materials science, analysis techniques, ancient and modern technology, deterioration, examination and treatment. The center also subscribes to several conservation and materials science journals.

The conservation laboratory has nine rooms and is well equipped. Among the major pieces of equipment used in the program are six binocular microscopes (fig. 6), a research polarizing microscope, nine polarizing microscopes for student use, two research metallographic microscopes, equipment for sectioning and polishing stone (including a Hipa cutter), a Buehler polishing apparatus, a thin-section grinder, an environmental test chamber, five ovens, three kilns, a high-temperature box furnace, an ultrasonic cleaner, X-ray diffraction equipment, spectrographic equipment with a comparator, infrared and ultraviolet spectrophotometers, a colorimeter, two large vacuum hot tables, a Coulter counter, a folding tester, distillation apparatus, complete photographic and laboratory facilities, two X-ray machines for radiography, a viscometer, a Polarograph, an Instron tensile-strength tester and S.S. White airbrasive equipment.

Cooperation with Other Institutions

While the center owns many objects received as gifts for experimental, examination and treatment purposes, most paintings and artifacts are supplied by museums and other institutions on a loan basis for treatment. No charge is made to the museum or institution for such examination and treatment, and no object is accepted for such purpose unless it aids the training program. Paintings are not usually accepted if they need only cleaning. Each object is evaluated as to the contribution it will make to the learning process.

The Conservation Center has continued its close association with the Metropolitan Museum of Art, New York City, in the examination and treatment of objects, as well as in research on a

FIGURE 5. *Students in the conservation library. Approximately one-fourth of a student's scheduled time is spent here. (Conservation Center, Institute of Fine Arts, New York University)*

FIGURE 6. *Research associate and students use a binocular microscope to examine fake paintings. (Conservation Center, Institute of Fine Arts, New York University)*

number of projects. Among other museums, historical societies, universities and collections that have provided materials for study and treatment are the Newark Museum, Newark, N.J.; John and Mabel Ringling Museum of Art, Sarasota, Fla.; Museum of Primitive Art, American Museum of Natural History, Finch College and

490

New York University, all in New York City; Knox College, Gales-
burg, Ill.; University of Notre Dame, Notre Dame, Ind.; Duke
University, Durham, N.C.; Franklin D. Roosevelt Library, Hyde
Park, N.Y.; Lyndhurst (a property of the National Trust for Historic Preservation), Tarrytown, N.Y.; Smithsonian Institution,
Washington, D.C.; and the collection of Nelson A. Rockefeller,
former New York governor.

Publications

Articles written by staff and students are published in various
technical journals. In addition, the journal *Art and Archaeology
Technical Abstracts* is published at the center for the International
Institute for Conservation of Historic and Artistic Works (IIC)
in London. Manuscripts are prepared and edited at the center, with
an advanced student, Joyce H. Stoner, serving as managing editor,
and Edward V. Sayre of the center; Robert L. Feller of the Carnegie-
Mellon University, Pittsburgh, Pa.; Curt W. Beck of Vassar College, Poughkeepsie, N.Y.; and myself serving as editors.

Assistant Professor of Conservation Norbert S. Baer is the American editor of the conservation journal *Studies in Conservation*,
published quarterly by the IIC. He receives all articles from American authors and sees that each is properly refereed, edited and
checked for accuracy.

Summary

This paper has described how art conservation is taught at the
Conservation Center. The graduates are a credit to the center, as
is evident from the positions they hold and their contributions
through publications, as well as their examination and treatment
of many objects of great aesthetic and historical significance.

Other centers mentioned and a few new training centers about
to be formed will continue to help fill the need for "engineers in
conservation" as described by Sheldon Keck in his paper for the
1961 conference of the IIC, held in Rome.[2]

THE ART CONSERVATOR AND THE ARCHITECTURAL
PRESERVATIONIST

It should be self-evident that architectural preservationists and
art conservators can be of great assistance to each other. The Conservation Center, for example, has made a number of analyses to
assist architectural preservationists in determining causes of deterioration, materials of construction and procedures for preserving artifacts, wall paintings and mosaic floors that are integral
parts of buildings. Likewise, preservationists have developed techniques for treating on a grand scale—techniques that are of value

491

to the art conservator undertaking the treatment of large art objects such as sculptures or paintings.

On archaeological excavations, the architectural preservationist and art conservator often work together alongside the archaeologist in examining finds, recording condition, analyzing structures and carrying out restorations. At the archaeological exploration of Sardis, the preservationist on this panel, Stephen W. Jacobs, and I often called on each other for assistance while studying the condition of walls, foundations, plasters, wall paintings and mosaics.[3] Art conservators and preservationists look at problems with somewhat different approaches, and their combined efforts have resulted in documentation and restoration procedures that they could not have produced separately.

It might be well for the future of man's dwindling patrimony if preservationists and conservators combined their talents more often. The scientific approach to treatment of stone, metal, wood and other materials certainly applies to both the preservation of buildings and the conservation of historic and artistic objects.

NOTES

1. A few of the papers on the center's research include the following: Edward V. Sayre and Lawrence J. Majewski, "Technical Investigation of the Deterioration of the Paintings," Studies for the Preservation of the Frescoes by Giotto in the Scrovegni Chapel at Padua Series, *Studies in Conservation* 8, no. 2 (May 1963): 42–54; Edward V. Sayre and Heather N. Lechtman, "Neutron Activation Autoradiography of Oil Paintings," *Studies in Conservation* 13, no. 4 (November 1968): 161–85; and Norbert S. Baer, Barbara Appelbaum and Norman Indictor, "The Effects of Long-Term Heating on Ivory," *Bulletin of the American Group-IIC* 12, no. 1 (October 1971): 55–59.

2. Sheldon Keck, "Training for Engineers in Conservation," in *Recent Advances in Conservation*, ed. G. Thomson (London: Butterworths, 1963), pp. 199–201.

3. For preliminary reports on excavations and restorations of Sardis, see *Bulletin of the American Schools of Oriental Research*, no. 166 (April 1962), no. 170 (April 1963), no. 174 (April 1964), no. 187 (October 1968) and no. 199 (October 1970).

COMMENTARY

F. BLAIR REEVES, AIA

The papers by Stephen W. Jacobs and Lawrence J. Majewski are clearly the work of two fine minds totally in command of their subjects and confident of the facts they present to describe the education available to preservationists and conservators. However, what really should demand our attention, comment and discussion are not the details of these papers but the obvious differences they reflect between the two professions and in educational programs that are available to students wishing to become either conservators or preservationists.

The conservator, whom Mr. Majewski defines as an "art doctor," is a precise professional who, like the medical doctor, benefits from a four-year general undergraduate education; profits further from four years of graduate work, which includes an internship; studies in a controlled scientific laboratory situation; and enjoys the authority of scientific procedures and absolutes. Graduates of this educational system are, predictably, precise professionals who are ready to offer their services to clients who willingly seek and respect their advice. From the preservationist's viewpoint, the conservator is in an enviable position. The conservator is thoroughly trained in a precise science and fills a well-defined and comprehendible role; his services are obviously necessary to insure the accuracy of a restoration project.

Compare the role of the conservator with that of the architect-

F. Blair Reeves, AIA, is professor of architecture at the University of Florida, Gainesville, Fla.

preservationist. Mr. Jacobs, Charles E. Peterson and Eugene George consider in their papers the role of the general practitioner of architecture who accepts contracts to handle preservation projects. They discuss the confusion general practitioners may face with regard to professional expectations, their educational inadequacies for preservation work, their failures in handling such projects and potential conflicts that may arise with other professionals involved in preservation projects. Mr. Jacobs also reports on preliminary results of surveys that analyze preservation education; considers the status of programs suggested in the Whitehill Report, issued by the National Trust for Historic Preservation; reviews existing preservation-oriented programs of architecture schools and those sponsored by public and private agencies; and directs attention to some future directions in preservation education.

Neither Mr. Peterson nor Mr. Jacobs elects to concentrate on problems resulting from the internal disagreement within architectural philosophy, education and practice, that is, the basic conflict between the traditional and innovative aspects of the profession. Mr. Peterson's testimonial of "taking the veil" of the preservationist in lieu of specializing in contemporary design comes close to the mark. Conservators do not face such a problem. Their position is firm, without conflict.

I came to this conference from Nantucket, Mass., where I have been teaching design and preservation to 14 undergraduate and graduate students in architecture and interior design. These students were participating in the academic program of the Preservation Institute: Nantucket, a summer course of study sponsored by the Nantucket Historical Trust, Colonial Williamsburg, the National Park Service, the National Trust and the University of Florida, which administers programs offered by the institute.

Being unusually close to these students was a stirring experience for me, even though I have been involved in ordinary classroom and laboratory routine for some years. It was both a painful and a pleasant privilege to be in direct proximity to struggling participants in a learning and creative process. Proximity, involvement, conflict, frustration, revelation, wonder and pride are all proper words to use to describe this recent experience.

The greatest revelation of my summer work in Nantucket was to find that architecture students have an unusual ability to keep preservation in a logical perspective (even in Nantucket!) and to see potential preservation opportunities and obligations as determinants in the design process for which they are educated. While these students may not intend to "take the veil" of a preservationist, they will never forget problems of designing within the historic fabric of Nantucket, the "fun in the sun" of documentation and battles with a historic districts commission retarded by an unfortunate set of codes. Perhaps with luck and a proper apprenticeship, these students will become professional architects who can exploit (in the positive sense of the word) preservation opportunities, convince clients that in preservation projects additional expertise is essential and yet continue as practical participants in their diversified, innovative profession.

The after-school dilemma of an uncertain future is not unique to these 14 students of the Preservation Institute: Nantucket. Every student and faculty member from any educational program in preservation must honestly consider what happens to the neophyte preservationist between the academic experience and the achievement of professional expertise. As Mr. Jacobs indicates, Columbia, Virginia, Cornell and, most recently, Florida universities are the only educational institutions offering specialization in preservation at the graduate level. I believe that we all would agree, if experts can agree on anything, that additional professional schools in universities throughout the nation should begin to develop similar programs, especially programs that offer preservation education to student architects, planners, landscape architects and interior designers. As new programs develop, however, the problem of providing sufficient postgraduate experiences becomes further intensified.

While on the subject of preservation education at undergraduate and graduate levels, some thought should be given to the need for the participation of students from disciplines other than architecture, planning and interior design. Preservationists, all of like mind, like to talk to themselves. They usually do a great deal of wailing and breast-thumping at symposia or conferences like this one, crying about the poor quality of preservation work and the lack of public concern or extolling the great, but as yet unappreciated, benefits of educational processes that emphasize the value of preservation or professional participation in worthy preservation projects.

Preservationists, particularly those specializing in education, need to consider techniques of how to reach students before they graduate from college and are often no longer receptive to learning anything that is not directly tangible to their specialization or livelihood. The new two-year preservation program at the University of Florida at Gainesville is intended to instruct graduate architecture students in documentation, traditional materials and methods of construction, preservation technology and further studies in architectural history, which are considered to be essential to their professional well-being. What is more important is that several of these preservation courses are available to graduate and to undergraduate students studying landscape architecture, interior design and other subjects. Already, students specializing in social history, building construction, archaeology, real estate and pre-law studies have participated in courses, and it is anticipated that economics, education, engineering and geography students will register for courses in the future. I might add that two undergraduate students, one majoring in architecture and the other a pre-law student, combined forces on a recent project to teach architectural preservation to junior high and high school students.

It is becoming clear that the typical professional school of architecture within a university will do well to inform the general student population, not only architecture students, about historic preservation; to offer special instructions to those students who show interest, knowledge and skill in preservation; and to provide some preservation experiences for the university community. It is equally obvious that today's students who wish to specialize in preservation must develop their proficiency through postgraduate learning experiences. Schools should promptly pursue every opportunity to insure that a student's formal education will be enriched through postgraduate learning experiences that expand upon the basic knowledge gained from formal course work. Students should be encouraged to participate in summer field projects of the Historic American Buildings Survey (HABS) or to work with agencies responsible for local or state preservation planning or those responsible for making nominations to the National Register of Historic Places. They should be encouraged to become involved in the European Traveling Summer School for Restorationists, sponsored by the Rome Centre, and in the programs of Historic Deerfield, Cooperstown, the National Trust and Colonial Williamsburg. Most of all, young architects interested in preservation must be given an opportunity to work in offices where significant preservation work is done, but also where experiences are offered that will satisfy the creative impulses that motivate all young architects.

I believe it is appropriate to conclude these comments with a few recommendations based on ideas presented by Mr. Majewski, Mr. Jacobs and other participants in this conference. Differences between the education of the conservator and that available to the architect-preservationist are derived from the basic differences between the professions. While a conservator's practice is clearly specialized, an architect usually has a general, diversified practice, at least until graduate study, an internship and/or early practice experiences identify him with a specialty. The conservator learns in the laboratory what the architect must discover through actual practice. This difference suggests that architect-preservationists must have access to laboratory facilities and to continuing sources of reliable information. Because the United States is so diversified in geography, social structure, cultural achievements, politics and the like, it is obvious that these proposed laboratories should be regional in location, information and facilities. They may be sponsored by public or private agencies. The new regional field offices of the National Trust may be a logical beginning for such a program. Perhaps these regional field offices should be established in locations where they could most effectively serve as liaisons between professional schools of architecture and existing conservation centers. (Parenthetically, I believe that those of us who live and work along the Atlantic seaboard sometimes forget that most of the nation's architectural heritage is of the mid-19th and early 20th centuries. We also fail to recognize the finite problems of distance, time and accessibility faced by preservationists in other parts of the country.) At such regional centers, archives with computer recall systems could be maintained and perhaps keyed to the system developed by the Library of Congress for the HABS archive and to additional resources at other national and international preservation centers. Testing and analysis equipment would also be available, along with conservators who would provide immediate and tangible assistance to laymen, students and professional preservationists. While national and international centers will obviously be of great value, preservation battles will always be fought on the local level.

Every effort should be made to record what the few competent preservationists of today have learned. These "masters" of preservation have performed their tasks admirably, but they have not recorded their experiences to share with future preservationists. By this, I do not mean studies of preservation materials and methods, of which there is some good work including the papers presented at this conference, but rather published accounts of specific preservation projects. Mr. George's paper, which gives a general outline of the responsibilities of an architect working on a preservation project, and chapter 21 of the AIA handbook, entitled "The Architect as a Preservationist," represent a step toward recording this information, but much more is needed. How many published office diaries of both great and humble preservation projects have found their way to practitioners' desks or to library shelves? Do these records indicate that decisions were a result of the collaboration of a number of experts or that they were made primarily by one "big-name" professional? When should a depository for such documents be formed? Where should it be located?

Perhaps it is time for a team of experienced preservationists and conservators to start working with schools and universities that are beginning to indicate an interest in preservation education. The ongoing program of preservation workshops sponsored by the American Institute of Architects at accredited schools of architecture could provide the organizational tool for such a campaign. As a recent editorial from the *New York Times* said, "We have chronically expected too much from our schools and the schools have suffered much from exaggerated expectations; the antidote is not to declare schools inefficient, but to help improve them."

COMMENTARY

SHELDON KECK

Before commenting on either Stephen W. Jacobs or Lawrence J. Majewski's paper, I would like to refer to the printed program for this North American International Regional Conference on Preservation and Conservation. On the last pages are a number of basic presuppositions that demonstrate the need for closer relations between restoration architects and art conservators. At least two of these presuppositions, which were made by members of the Rome Centre Committee of the U.S. Advisory Council on Historic Preservation, have a direct bearing on the subject of education, especially in the field of architectural restoration:

(a) that many architects are called upon to perform restoration work, although few possess competency in this particular specialty;
(b) that in order to be a competent restorationist, the practitioner should have special knowledge beyond that normally required of an architect: an intimate knowledge of the history of architecture and a knowledge of the history of building technology, of research techniques and of the composition, deteriorating factors and treatment of historic building materials.

From my scanty knowledge of the curricula of architecture schools, from what I have gathered from the papers prepared for this conference and from what I have occasionally seen perpetrated in the name of architectural restoration, I am inclined to

Sheldon Keck is a professor in the Conservation of Historic and Artistic Works Program, Cooperstown Graduate Programs (a joint project of the State University College at Oneonta and the New York State Historical Association), Cooperstown, N.Y.

accept the validity of these presumptions. There are, of course, some restoration architects who represent notable exceptions to this supposed deficiency in the education of architects who perform restorations. I presume that some, if not all, are participants in this conference. It also has been made clear that there are a fair number of nonarchitects who participate in architectural restorations; their qualifications to do so would not be acceptable to the American Institute of Architects. Nevertheless, they influence much of what is done in the name of architectural restoration, often for the better, sometimes for the worse.

In his paper on the education of art conservators, my colleague Mr. Majewski defines the properly educated conservator as one who combines the "skills of the art historian, artist and scientist." Actually, these disciplines are considered prerequisites (to be acquired by a student while an undergraduate) for admission to a graduate training program in art conservation, where the student acquires special knowledge and skills beyond that normally required of an artist, scientist or art historian. Also, it is important to note that Mr. Majewski employs the word *skills* in reference to artistic ability and that the word *creativity*, a prime requisite of any artist who is to find a place in the history of art, has been, I hope, purposely omitted. Too often in the past, and even today, masterpieces of art have been "restored" by creative artists who had the arrogance and audacity to think that they could improve or update inept passages in works by such masters as Dürer, Holbein, Titian, Rubens, Bronzino or almost any other old master one wishes to name. The conservator who is creative in the artistic sense can seldom resist being too creative on someone else's work.

I believe there is a parallel between the presumptions made concerning the competency of architects performing architectural restorations and experiences with artists in preserving and restoring works of art. Since each is competent to perform creatively in his own field, the general public, including educated people who should know better, take for granted that the architect or the artist is equally well qualified to repair the ravages, deterioration and physical damage an architectural masterpiece or work of art has undergone. It may be that the good architect's urge to create is as detrimental in the architectural restoration field as is the artist's creativity in the art conservation field. Perhaps the architect, like the artist, must be taught to subdue his creativity in order not to falsify the style, documentary significance and organic structure of something that was created at a much earlier period. If the public could be informed of the fallacy of their present assumption and both architects and artists made to realize that specialization in preservation and restoration requires additional training, possibly more universities would consider establishing and supporting the necessary educational facilities.

In the field of art conservation, there is another problem: Not only do artists assume the responsibility for restorations, so do picture framers, who are constantly encouraged to "clean up" or "fix up" paintings they are about to reframe. As much butchery has been done to works of art by framers as has been done by artists. Even though art conservators have begun, as Peter Michaels points out in his paper "Accreditation, Certification and Licensing of Art Conservators," to formulate standards of practice, there are as yet no controls, no machinery for accreditation and no licensure of practitioners. Artists and framers have as much legal right to establish a practice in art conservation as one who has spent three or four years in specialized graduate training.

As Mr. Majewski mentions, in addition to expanding his artistic and scientific skills and his knowledge of art history, the art conservation student must master several disciplines to attain competency. These include studies and practice in the materials and technologies of past arts, an understanding of the causes and chemical and physical mechanisms of deterioration and alteration and a knowledge of conservation theory and methodology. Implicit in this training, and an important part of it, is the continuing development of manipulative craft skills, coordinating the eye and the hand in the performance of various operative procedures, often of a very delicate nature, employed in the conservation treatment of works of art. Also implied is training in methods of examining the artifact, recording its condition and documenting its treatment. Furthermore, it is equally important that a professional attitude be instilled in the student—an approach that involves responsibility to and humility before a work of art; a regard for the creativity, as well as for the limitations, of the artist who created the work; and a deep respect for the work's aesthetic, historical and structural integrity. The Cooperstown Graduate Programs offer a course under the tutelage of Caroline K. Keck entitled "Responsibilities of the Conservator," which delves deeply into ethical and practical aspects of those responsibilities. Theoretical studies include discussions of philosophical overtones present in every problem of preservation and restoration. Why is man motivated to conserve? What is meant by preservation and restoration? What distinguishes a restoration from a replica, a reproduction, an imitation and a forgery? Can a valid restoration be produced on a 17th-century cellar hole? How little of an original construction can we begin with and morally call what we have done a preservation? Can a breadth of standards that ranges from a New Castle, Del., to a Disneyland be tolerated?

One would think that the architect is much better prepared for further specialization in one of the four graduate programs in architectural restoration described by Mr. Jacobs than is the artist who wishes to obtain training in art conservation, particularly since the architect's previous schooling must include the subject of specifications, properties and aging characteristics of materials employed in the construction of a building. Students in art schools are usually taught nothing about materials they use, since for several generations, art schools have been almost totally unconcerned about the technology and materials of painting.

Mr. Majewski also touches on the former use of apprenticeships for learning the practice of art conservation, as has Mr. Jacobs concerning the acquisition of craft skills in preservation. To depend on an apprenticeship alone to provide a complete education in art conservation is often disastrous, since modern apprenticeships, unlike those controlled by the ancient guilds, are usually completely unregulated and quite unsystematized. No formal obligation exists on the part of either the apprentice or the master. After six months or less, an apprentice can leave the master's shop and begin his own practice. A master can, if so inclined, exploit his apprentice as cheap labor, giving minimal instruction to his charge. Therefore, as Mr. Majewski has said, the apprenticeship has been replaced with structured university programs, which surely can be much more comprehensive.

In each of the university programs in art conservation in the United States, the internship concept, like that followed in medical training, has been accepted and incorporated as a necessary part of the student's educational development. "Real-life," but supervised, experience under nonacademic conditions appears to be an excellent way of preparing for professional practice the student who has mastered conservation theory and methodology. Whether it is called an apprenticeship or an internship the learning process involved has not been discarded, but has been absorbed and, we hope, regularized as an inherent part of structured training programs.

A recent report made after a careful and lengthy study of existing training programs in painting conservation in Western Europe and the United States recommended to the British Standing Commission on Museums and Galleries and to the Calouste Gulbenkian Foundation that an apprenticeship be a large part, but not all, of the education of a painting conservator.

In other basic presuppositions in the conference program, the

Rome Centre Committee hints that conservators may be especially well equipped to provide useful information to restoration architects, particularly after they become acquainted with problems confronting architects. As a conservator, I welcome the opportunity for continuing my own education through the exchange of ideas and experiences and discussions of problems and methods for solving them with architect colleagues who are endeavoring to preserve and restore remnants of our architectural past. Mr. Majewski also calls attention to the frequent collaboration between conservators and architects in archaeological procedures, as have other speakers at this conference. He mentions as well the admirable work of the Conservation Center of the Institute of Fine Arts, New York University, in assisting preservationists in determining causes of deterioration, identifying materials used in constructing old buildings and developing methods to preserve wall paintings, mosaics and stone elements that are integral parts of buildings. All of us in art conservation are flattered and pleased to contribute in whatever way we can to the solution of the enormous and varied problems facing architectural restorationists. Their problems appear to be much more complicated than those encountered by art conservators, which are difficult and complicated enough.

Formal university training in art conservation has been offered in the United States for only about 12 years. In Europe, there were academies and institutions teaching conservation as much as 30 to 40 years ago. Art conservation as a professional activity has been gradually developing over a period of perhaps 50 years, although in Europe, there have been both sporadic bloomings and recessions in the field from about 1800. In comparison, architecture has been an established profession for a much longer time. However, architectural restoration as an organized discipline with established standards appears to be even newer than art conservation. Both disciplines have a common goal. Each has something to learn from the other and will continue to as each develops new methods and research. I hope restoration architects and art conservators continue to cooperate and collaborate so that this common goal can be achieved more speedily.

DISCUSSION

Comments made by the panelists and audience during the discussion on education are summarized in the following paragraphs.

Job opportunities in both the art conservation field and the architectural preservation field are growing, but there definitely is a shortage of qualified applicants for positions. Directors of training programs in conservation and preservation report a continuing demand for program graduates, but there sometimes seems to be a reluctance to expand current programs or to begin new ones. Perhaps this reluctance exists because exact needs in the two fields are not known. Needless to say, a determination of how many conservators and preservation professionals will be required in the future would be of great assistance to educators, administrators and others who are attempting to plan educational programs to meet the fields' future needs.

At present, the preservation field is especially confused for several reasons, some of which have been mentioned at this conference (e.g., the lack of standards and inconsistent terminology). The result is that few agencies or organizations can write a totally clear job description for a position in preservation. Actually, this situation may be healthy for the field, because it affords talented, ambitious people an exceptional amount of choice and opportunity. Over the next 10 to 20 years, the field undoubtedly will become more structured and such opportunities will become rare.

The confusion in the field not only is evident in the job market but also is reflected in the different approaches adopted by the established postgraduate preservation programs at the University of Florida, University of Virginia, Cornell University and Columbia University. The University of Florida program is, as Mr. Jacobs said in his paper, decidedly oriented toward the training of architects. The program at the University of Virginia tends to focus on documentation and its importance in the preservation process. At Cornell, the emphasis is on planning and integrating historic buildings into the ongoing life of the community. Columbia's program takes a general approach, incorporating many disciplines. Graduates of each of these programs have much to offer the preservation community.

It is regrettable, however, that specialized education in preservation is available almost exclusively on the postgraduate level. The undergraduate curriculum in most of today's architecture schools tends to ignore preservation needs while emphasizing modern design and techniques. A few schools are becoming interested in preservation, often as a result of encouragement by students who have worked for the Historic American Buildings Survey (HABS). This dynamic group of HABS alumni is, in large part responsible for whatever movement there is in schools toward the establishment of courses with a focus on preservation.

One particular problem faced by professionally trained architects who have become involved in preservation is the control of their creativity. As Mr. Keck said in his commentary, creativity in either the conservation field or the preservation field can be destructive. Much good architecture has been destroyed in the name of preservation by "creative" architects. However, it must be recognized that the practice of architecture does involve some degree of creativity; the problem in preservation work lies in deciding when it is appropriate to adopt a creative approach. Successful restoration architects must, first of all, understand the scope of the problem they face. Certainly, they must recognize that old buildings within a city are valuable pieces of real estate and often must remain productive elements within the community in order to survive. In such cases, restoration architects frequently must use their creativity to adapt these buildings to new uses without destroying original fabric. They must also employ their creativity to solve the problem of providing modern human necessities (e.g., rest rooms and parking areas) in buildings that, because of their original function, were constructed without much thought to these amenities. However, restoration architects must also exercise self-discipline with regard to their creativity. They should view the structures they preserve as artifacts that should be approached with humility as an inheritance from the past.

The control of creativity may depend partly on the architect's personality. According to a long-time architectural faculty member, architects may be divided into two categories; this division is in no way based on intelligence or ability. One type of architect is an expert at visualization. This type of individual is a good designer in the three-dimensional development of concepts, but is generally impatient with architectural theory and abstract conceptualization. The second type of architect has a different interest and personality. This architect is fascinated by the conceptual, abstract aspects of a problem and generally adopts a more modest approach to a design problem than the designer-architect. The second type of architect is also more interested in the social and cultural aspects of the solutions suggested. This architect is basically an environmentalist, not an antiquarian, but is frequently attracted to the historic preservation field. Unfortunately, the emphasis on design in undergraduate architecture schools and the fact that specialized preservation programs are currently offered only at postgraduate levels sometimes keeps this second type of individual from becoming a restoration architect.

As for the education of other preservation professionals, several universities have recently established programs in historical archaeology, and that field is beginning to grow significantly.

After graduation, trained conservators and restoration architects both face competition from untrained practitioners in their fields. There are a tremendous number of "commercial restorers" in the conservation field, that is, artists with little or no formal training in restoration who accept assignments to restore paintings and other works of art. Some architects likewise accept restoration projects, claiming some degree of expertise in preservation. Often, the client finds out too late that the "restoration specialist" has an interest in preservation but is not really qualified for the task at hand. There is a great need to educate the public to these practices.

Despite the shortage of qualified practitioners, owners of priceless works of art and historic buildings, including organizations and governments, must continue to be encouraged to seek quality work. They can become discouraged when they discover that it may be difficult to find the right person for their project not only because of the shortage of personnel but also because the kind of specialist they need is not located in, or even near, their area. In fact, in many parts of the country, there are no or few professionals with an understanding of the special problems involved in preservation projects. Owners who wish to engage the services of a professional with an expertise in preservation may find it useful to check first with local, state or national preservation organizations. The National Trust for Historic Preservation, for example, maintains a reference file, as a service for its membership, that contains data on architects, landscape architects, planners, contractors, lawyers and other professionals knowledgeable about preservation techniques. Experienced professionals are provided a standardized data card to complete for placement in the file.

Continuing efforts must also be made to make owners realize that quality conservation or preservation work cannot be obtained at bargain counter prices. Materials can be expensive, and good work requires sufficient time. Owners should also realize that competitive bidding is not usually the best way to select a conservator or restoration architect. The price may be lower but so too may be the quality of the work.

There are, of course, differences between the preservation and conservation fields that relate to education. First, the preservation of a building generally is more complicated than the restoration of a work of art, simply because buildings are so diverse and, thus, the problems of preserving them vary greatly in complexity. A restoration architect may be working on a small, simple stone house one minute and the next minute be involved in restoring or adapting a large, elaborate state capitol. Second, the architect requires the services of a whole crew of craftsmen; the conservator generally does not. This point is important because it is difficult, if not impossible, to restore a building properly without well-trained craftsmen and a foreman who understands project needs. Slipshod work is often the result when workers do not understand what is required.

The lack of craftsmen trained for preservation work has been a problem for some time, and although it has been discussed often and several studies made on the subject, no strong positive actions have been taken to correct the situation. In 1955, the National Park Service initiated a successful program for training craftsmen for preservation work. However, after the mid-1960s, one by one, these craftsmen became discouraged and left the program, primarily because of bureaucratic disinterest in their work and administrative problems. The Whitehill Report, issued by the National Trust in 1968, discussed this problem well but not in sufficient depth. For example, it contained no positive suggestions for the implementation of training programs. Of course, there are some craftsmen who are qualified for such work. Generally, they are overburdened, but their pride in their work is almost always evident. This kind of pride and individualism often stirs the interest of others. The idea of historic preservation is being accepted by more and more people, but unfortunately, it has not been accepted fully by one important sector—the building industry. Perhaps the only way to get more qualified craftsmen is for the restoration architect to personally teach workers. This, of course, means that the architect will have to become experienced in many crafts.

In discussing education, one should not forget the need to introduce young people to conservation and preservation concepts. It is important for conservators and preservationists to extend their concern for the objects they care for beyond their own professions and the adult community. They should attempt to instill in children a sense of respect and responsibility for works of art and historic buildings; otherwise, these same children may grow up to obliterate the work of this generation of conservators and preservationists.

The subject of education in the conservation and preservation fields covers such a wide range of topics and problems that it might be appropriate to consider conducting another professional meeting to further explore this area.

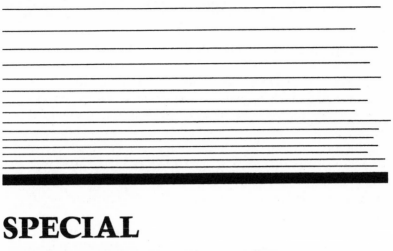

SPECIAL
PRESENTATIONS

THE EARLY RESTORATIONISTS OF COLONIAL WILLIAMSBURG

CHARLES B. HOSMER, JR.

First, let us pose a rhetorical question: Why memorialize the early restorationists of Williamsburg, Va., four of whom are present at this conference? They were, and I am sure they are aware of it, members of the first real school of restoration in the United States. Probably after phase one of the restoration of Williamsburg ended in 1934, a little more than 30 people had real training in certain aspects of what it meant to carry out a scholarly restoration. They can be called the first group of architects who steeped themselves in a knowledge of one particular period and building tradition, and they gained their knowledge from studying actual sites, from on-the-job experiences.

Colonial Williamsburg, in phase one at least, was an architectural enterprise, as I mentioned in my commentary on the professions involved in preservation. The reason for this is twofold. First, John D. Rockefeller, Jr., the patron of the project, gradually became intensely interested in the architectural aspects of the restoration, almost to the exclusion of the other aspects, in fact. That alone would be a good reason, but there is another. Of the four major professions that ultimately contributed to this restoration—history, architecture, landscape architecture and archaeology—I submit that when the restoration really got under way (in 1928), architecture had by far the best qualified practitioners for

---

Charles B. Hosmer, Jr., is an associate professor of history at Principia College, Elsah, Ill. He is author of *Presence of the Past: A History of the Preservation Movement in the United States Before Williamsburg* (New York: G. P. Putnam's Sons, 1965).

this type of work. I also submit (since I am a member of that profession) that historians were the least qualified to contribute. As Charles E. Peterson said in his paper, "The Role of the Architect in Historical Restorations," there were many architects in the late 1920s who could easily draw up plans for a Georgian building. They could not necessarily restore one, but they had the feel for such buildings. They had studied architecture from a historical point of view, and they were good draftsmen.

Some may not be familiar with the chronology of the Williamsburg restoration, so I will review the steps that led to it. I will mainly deal with the period from 1924 to 1934. The reason for the 1934 cutoff is that in that year Mr. Rockefeller concluded that for the time being the restoration was finished. Mr. Rockefeller had, I gathered from several people I talked to, a very categorical mind. He saw things one step at a time, and he wanted to study carefully what was being done in Williamsburg. When the Raleigh Tavern, Travis House, Capitol and Governor's Palace were completed, Mr. Rockefeller decided it was time to stop, do some studying and find out what was going to happen. I believe from the beginning there were two questions that he hoped would be answered by 1934.

One concerned the ultimate governing body of the restoration, how it would be handled. He and Kenneth Chorley, who by that time was primarily in charge of the restoration, concluded that there were at least three alternatives. Mr. Rockefeller's original intent was that the project would be a joint enterprise with the College of William and Mary. In fact, it was seriously proposed that the Ludwell-Paradise House, the first house involved in the restoration, be owned by the college. But Mr. Rockefeller became troubled when he saw the problems that, because of the college's relationship with the state of Virginia, might arise if William and Mary administered the restoration. He then thought about the National Park Service as a final answer, but again he was worried about politics. In 1933, his close confidant and friend, Horace M. Albright, left the directorship of the National Park Service. Mr. Rockefeller realized that successive secretaries of the Interior and National Park Service directors would have duties and interests that would not always center on Williamsburg. So it seemed the restoration was heading toward some kind of private organization to administer it.

The second question for which Mr. Rockefeller needed an answer was "How will the public treat it?" Would people come and what would be their response? He also chose 1934 as the time to sever officially the project's connection with the architectural firm of Perry, Shaw and Hepburn and to thereafter retain them only as consultants to the restoration. For a few years after that, the architectural department of Colonial Williamsburg was two people, one of whom (A. Edwin Kendrew) is present at this conference. He was one of the two survivors (the other being Singleton P. Moorehead) who had been in the Perry, Shaw and Hepburn drafting room and who remained with Colonial Williamsburg throughout successive phases of the restoration.

The story of the Williamsburg restoration might be said to have begun in 1923 when the Reverend William Archer Rutherfoord Goodwin returned to Williamsburg. He had been in the town early in the 20th century and had restored Bruton Parish Church and written about it. In 1923, he came back to Williamsburg to the College of William and Mary, primarily to raise funds for the college, as what would be known today as a director of development.

The following year, Dr. Goodwin approached Henry Ford, who had just purchased the Wayside Inn in South Sudbury, Mass., and was collecting antiques on a scale hitherto unknown to man. In the warehouses of his River Rouge plant in Dearborn, Mich., pianos were stacked on pianos, Chippendale couches on Chippendale couches, etc. Dr. Goodwin wrote Mr. Ford a letter proposing that he buy Williamsburg and restore it. Mr. Ford never saw the letter; it came back with the kind of polite decline that Mr. Ford's secretary, Harold Cordell, sent to so many in those days. But Dr. Goodwin was not the kind to be discouraged by one letter. He approached Mr. Ford's brother, William, with another letter the same year. I do not believe William Ford ever saw that letter, but somehow it fell into the hands of the *Baltimore Sun*, which published it with a rather raucous editorial about this insane Episcopal minister in Williamsburg, Va., who wanted Henry Ford to buy the town and restore it. Dr. Goodwin wrote the paper a six-page letter explaining that he was serious about the idea.

Meanwhile, Dr. Goodwin persuaded the Colonial Dames to help him buy the Wythe House for Bruton Parish Church, and during its restoration in 1926, fate intervened. Boston architect William Graves Perry was motoring through Williamsburg that year for the first time in his life. He was with a friend who had an attack of appendicitis and had to stay there for about a week. So Mr. Perry went around Williamsburg looking, sketching and generally enjoying the town. He walked by the Wythe House, and he could hear noises of hammering and so forth. He walked in and discovered Dr. Goodwin busy with his restoration work. Mr. Perry sketched a molding for him, which Dr. Goodwin thought was a miracle, so beautifully turned out on a sheet of paper. The architect also noticed that there were some locks missing, and he said he had a whole box of old locks in Boston and that he would send some to Dr. Goodwin to see if they would fit any of the doors in the Wythe House. I do not believe Mr. Perry had any idea that he was going to turn the whole field of restoration upside down by sending Dr. Goodwin a box of old locks, but that is ultimately what happened.

Dr. Goodwin first met Mr. Rockefeller at a meeting of the Phi Beta Kappa Society in New York City in February 1924. He had been designated to attend the meeting by the president of the College of William and Mary, J. A. C. Chandler, in order to solicit funds for a building on the campus to be finished in 1926 in time to commemorate the 150th anniversary of the founding of the society. In the spring of 1926, Mr. Rockefeller visited Hampton Institute in Hampton, Va., and at the invitation of Dr. Goodwin and the president of the institute, he drove to Williamsburg where Dr. Goodwin met him. Dr. Goodwin showed Mr. Rockefeller around and did something very uncharacteristic, but very smart: He put on a soft sell. He did not tell Mr. Rockefeller what he had in mind; he just wanted him to enjoy Williamsburg.

Dr. Goodwin then went to New York City in November 1926 and approached Arthur Woods, an associate of Mr. Rockefeller, for an interview that was cordial but noncommittal. That same month, Mr. Rockefeller came to Williamsburg to attend the banquet held when the Phi Beta Kappa Hall at William and Mary was dedicated. During the banquet, he sat next to Dr. Goodwin and said he would make available to him a sum not exceeding $10,000 for the preparation of a plan showing what Williamsburg would look like if it were restored. There was no commitment to anything further, no use of Mr. Rockefeller's name, and—this, I believe, was very uncharacteristic of Mr. Rockefeller—he gave Dr. Goodwin the job of picking the architect.

Dr. Goodwin's heart was pounding, and I am sure he was not listening to the speeches at the Phi Beta Kappa banquet. The first architect that came to his mind was a man who was an expert on colonial architecture, Thomas E. Tallmadge of Chicago. He wrote to Mr. Tallmadge right away and asked if he would be willing to prepare the plan. Mr. Tallmadge replied no, he was busy writing a book and did not have the time. Dr. Goodwin wrote back, "I was giving you a chance for immortality," which he meant. Then he wrote the Boston architect who had sketched a molding in the Wythe House for him earlier in the year. Mr. Perry immediately telegraphed Dr. Goodwin that his firm would be delighted to accept the project and that he would be happy to come to Williamsburg, which he did in January 1927. He then measured the town and began to formulate plans. (Mr. Kendrew was in the office when the drawings were being made to show what Williamsburg would look like if restored.)

Perry, Shaw and Hepburn was an ideal architectural firm to have been chosen for the purpose. It was a balanced firm in the sense that the three men each brought something particular in his character to the task; also, it was a reasonably new firm and had not formed an image like some of the more prosperous New York and Boston firms at the time. A fair portion of their work had been college buildings and that sort of thing.

In the spring of 1927, the architects were told to prepare drawings and study in detail what they were going to propose. Dr. Goodwin was then given the go-ahead to start acquiring land. He began buying $2 million worth of property up and down Duke of Gloucester Street, along the Palace Green and elsewhere. What rumors that produced! Word of what was going on finally got into the local papers, although the mysterious patron was unknown. Henry Ford generally ended up being chosen as the most likely one to be financing this operation.

In 1928, when Walter Macomber arrived in Williamsburg to be the resident architect and a staff began to come into his office to begin preparing the drawings, an advisory committee of architects was appointed, an important step in the restoration process. The advisory committee had several purposes, all of which were fulfilled. One of them was to involve Virginians in the Williamsburg restoration, because Perry, Shaw and Hepburn had brought down a whole busload of Bostonians, New Yorkers, Californians, people from everywhere but Virginia. So Richmond, Fredericksburg and Norfolk architects could be involved through this advisory committee of architects. Also, convincing proof of the legitimacy for what was being done was necessary. Major decisions had to be debated, and they were. Minutes were taken, and every step of the way, one can find the advisory committee approving things that were done or debating them. These decisions of the advisory committee had an effect not only on the Williamsburg restoration but also on other restoration projects, because some of the committee members were highly respected and active in their various fields.

The dominating figure of that committee was Fiske Kimball, the director of the Philadelphia Museum, who was also a great Thomas Jefferson scholar and was the restorer of Monticello and Stratford Hall. A. Lawrence Kocher, the editor of *Architectural Record*, was also on the board, as was architect Milton Medary from Philadelphia who had a high standing in his field and Robert Bellows from Boston. All of these people "spread the word" wherever they went.

Allow me to mention a few of the issues debated at the first meeting of the committee of advisory architects in the fall of 1928 to show some of the problems that were encountered. For instance, Mr. Kimball asked, "Do we intend to restore or do we intend to reconstruct? What is the purpose of this thing? Are we going to hire an archaeologist?" (He had an archaeologist in mind, Prentis Duell, an Egyptologist from the University of Pennsylvania, who did come to help excavate around the Wren Building.) "Are we going to allow reconstruction to dominate the restoration?" Mr. Kimball brought up this latter question in every advisory committee meeting he attended, and he kept the issue alive in the preservation movement for the rest of his life. He also argued passionately in favor of putting signs on reconstructed buildings until finally signs were put on the clapboards, or wherever they could be put, to note whether buildings were reconstructed or not. He insisted that the restoration staff keep a record of all decisions made, photograph copiously what was done and—this was a hot issue—keep all good pre-1840 houses. One story will illustrate the problems that arose with regard to this latter point.

The Maupin House had been build just a little before 1840 on Duke of Gloucester Street across from Bruton Parish Church. It was sort of a countryfied Greek Revival-style building with a porch, quite similar to what the center part of the Coke-Garrett House used to look like before its porch was removed. From the beginning, the house posed a problem, primarily because in the minds of Mr. Rockefeller, Mr. Perry and some others, the phrase "painting the picture" had begun to creep into the restoration idea. Now when one begins to view the restoration as "painting the picture," there are, of course, going to be difficulties in keeping pre-1840 but postcolonial houses if they are in prominent locations, such as across from Bruton Parish Church on Duke of Gloucester Street! Should the house be moved or left alone? Should it be torn down or colonialized? All of these points were debated and the committee, on almost all of them, divided 50-50 on what to do with the Maupin House. Resident architect Macomber, who was quite a purist, insisted that it not be colonialized, which is to his everlasting credit. This was not the big issue of the day, but it illustrates the kinds of problems the architects debated in 1928, 1929 and 1930. The house finally was razed, by the way, in 1931. The final decision to tear it down was based partly on the idea of "painting the picture." Also, the foundation of an older house was subsequently discovered in front of the Maupin House on the setback line where the rest of the houses are as one moves along Duke of Gloucester Street. I believe that if the Maupin House had been in any other location in Colonial Williamsburg, it would still be there today. The survival of the Coke-Garrett House proves this point. So much of the Coke-Garrett House is of the 19th century, yet it still stands because it is in a secluded location, away from the Capitol, surrounded by trees. But because the "picture" was involved, the Maupin House had to go. When saying that Colonial Williamsburg destroyed X number of 19th-century buildings in the process of restoration, remember this destruction was not done lightly. There was a lot of debate, a lot of soul-searching and probably a good deal of sorrow over what was done.

I want to summarize the pluses and minuses about the Williamsburg restoration and mention a few of the people involved.

Let us review the minuses first, because I would like to end on the pluses. There were some tragedies in the first stage of the Williamsburg restoration. One that came up incessantly in the meetings of the architects, and a few meetings of the historians, was that almost nothing was published about what was going on. The only architectural book that came out of the Williamsburg restoration immediately was the one that Thomas T. Waterman and John Barrows brought out on their own about the domestic architecture of colonial Virginia. If there had been some publications, the public might have been given a better idea of how decisions were arrived at, how restoration techniques were worked out. Who is to blame for this? I am afraid in this case the blame ultimately has to rest with Mr. Rockefeller. The question of publication repeatedly came up through Mr. Chorley to Mr. Rockefeller, and he consistently said, quite characteristically for his categorical mind, "We are restoring Williamsburg. We are not going to publish something now. We do not have time to think about that now."

A second tragedy was that of letting go so many of the knowledgeable young architects in 1933. Many of them joined the staffs of the National Park Service or the Historic American Buildings Survey. Some ultimately returned to Williamsburg for phase two of the restoration.

The third tragedy is the one most often pointed out and the one for which I believe the restoration was in no way responsible, that is, the slavish and not-so-slavish copies of Williamsburg houses that sprang up in suburbs and in ladies magazines all over the country. I have researched a lot of materials in Mr. Chorley's files, some of Mr. Rockefeller's files, Dr. Goodwin's files and Perry,

Shaw and Hepburn's files, but I found no instance where the architectural staff ever sent out a plan of a Williamsburg house to anyone who wanted to build a copy elsewhere. I found evidence that the staff tried to dissuade people from building copies of the houses, for example, the copy of the Wythe House in Scarsdale, N.Y., which was done anyway. I can blame Williamsburg for what happened in one sense: What was done there was so well done and so beautiful that it flip-flopped the whole practice of architecture. But I do not believe Mr. Rockefeller or the staff had such a thing in mind; it just happened.

I believe there were victories, too. For instance, this was the first school of architectural restoration, people who had worked on the project were trained in a way that architects had never been trained before—with a real historical sense. Every weekend, the staff in the drafting room at Colonial Williamsburg went out to measure and photograph buildings along the rivers of Tidewater Virginia; then they pooled information, studying precedents, photographs, insurance policies, drawings, any kind of document that they discovered. Ultimately, they had a great effect on other restorations. Just to cite two examples: Perry, Shaw and Hepburn's staff restored the Moore House in Yorktown, Va., for the National Park Service; Mr. Kimball, in restoring Stratford Hall, the birthplace of Confederate Gen. Robert E. Lee, near Lorton, Va., used ideas from the Williamsburg restoration; Harold (Paul) Shurtleff in the research office in Williamsburg helped the Stratford Hall restorationists in their research on the Lee family. Later, the staff helped others who were restoring the Woodrow Wilson birthplace in Staunton, Va., and letters asking for advice began to pour in from everywhere.

There are a few people that should be included in the list of early restorationists. Dr. Goodwin certainly was the father of the idea. He was a driving force, often driving too hard and too fast for Mr. Rockefeller and for some others, too. He had some excellent ideas and some odd ideas. For example, it was Dr. Goodwin who dreamed up the tunnel that runs under Colonial Williamsburg as the solution to the problem like that Mr. Peterson encountered when he tried to route the Colonial Parkway through Bassett Hall woods on the south side of Williamsburg and discovered that it was Mr. Rockefeller's backyard. No highway was going through there, and no highway was going through the campus of William and Mary or the middle of Williamsburg. Dr. Goodwin kept saying, "Dig a tunnel, dig a tunnel." The tunnel there today works quite well.

He had some other unusual ideas, too. He hated the Geddy

House on the corner of the Palace Green. He would have given anything in the world to have torn it down. I interviewed Mr. Macomber this summer, and he said that Dr. Goodwin came to him one day and asked, "Mr. Macomber, have you really excavated the Neale House yard?" (They called it the Neale House then.)

"Oh, yes we have."

"Did you find the foundation of an earlier building? A brick building?"

"No, the Neale House is it. It's 18th century and it stays."

So Dr. Goodwin could not get rid of the house.

Mr. Rockefeller is extremely important, not only because he paid attention to many details, put up the money, had the interest, wanted professional help and was willing to make expensive changes when research showed they needed to be made. Mr. Rockefeller also unwittingly helped to give Williamsburg one of its "bad names." He had a passion for neatness. He could not stand peeling paint, crabgrass and all of the other things that might have aged the restoration, so every year the buildings and grounds had to look as if they had just been finished. If one must lay blame for this inaccurate representation of the colonial environment, it would have to be Mr. Rockefeller's fault.

Mr. Perry was crucial to the restoration because he was the one person who seemed to get along with everybody. He was the diplomat who worked with all of the crew that restored Williamsburg, and that is quite a statement! Andrew Hepburn was the great delineator, the artist, the purist. Thomas Mott Shaw was the great problem solver. He worked on problems like the shopping district. The partners studiously avoided living in Williamsburg, however, which they considered a form of exile. (Mr. Macomber told me that the first day he saw Mr. Chorley, after the new director had come down from Mr. Rockefeller's New York office to assume his position, Mr. Chorley was acting as if he had been sent to Siberia!)

Mr. Macomber, the resident architect, was a purist who had a passion for moldings; he collected and studied moldings and old woodwork, some of which is in the Ludwell-Paradise House. Mr. Kendrew was hired to organize the office, which had fallen into a state of disorganization by early 1930 because of battles between the contractors and the architects, and he did succeed in organizing it. Mr. Shurtleff was an architect who was brought in to manage the department of research and records, and he did a magnificent job. He was a brilliant man who drove himself into going back to Harvard for a Ph.D. in history because he thought he needed that degree, in addition to his architectural training, to effectively direct the department. Another unsung hero of the Williamsburg restoration was Rutherfoord Goodwin, son of the minister. He wrote the history of Williamsburg, which is still being sold. He trained the first guides, ran the archaeological museum and wrote magnificent statements on the purposes and goals of the Williamsburg restoration.

The first president of Colonial Williamsburg, Arthur Woods, made a great contribution also in harmonizing, like Perry, various interests. Mr. Woods and Mr. Chorley, as administrators, show in their reports and in the way they worked with the architects a tremendous capacity for learning what was going on and understanding it. Of course, the architects were learning too. Mr. Perry said to me that he really did not understand the term *restoration* when he came to Williamsburg. They all had to learn what restoration was on the job, both the architects and the administrators. But Mr. Woods and Mr. Chorley had to be expeditors, to keep the work moving, because the contractors were always trying to save Mr. Rockefeller money and the architects were always trying to go slow and do the job properly.

Susan Higginson Nash should be mentioned as the decorator who checked on paint colors. She studied the available documents and scraped down and got the paint colors. The archaeologists I have already mentioned. Then there is an elusive figure that I am glad I do not have much time to talk about, because the temptation to expound on him would be too great. His name was Arthur A. Shurcliff; he did the landscape work at Williamsburg. He studied a great deal of landscaping in England and collected a lot of documents on southern gardens, because frankly there was not much to go on, archaeologically, for colonial and later garden designs. So a great deal more imagination went into the Williamsburg gardens than into some of the architectural projects where 18th-century precedents were available.

Finally, I must mention the real heroes of the restoration in my mind, and probably the most important people of all, the men in the Perry, Shaw and Hepburn drafting room, sweating in the old wooden parish house of Bruton Parish Church that stood next to the Armistead House on Duke of Gloucester Street, who went out on weekends to collect drawings and photographs, studied and worked and really took this project seriously.

I might add that because there has never been a publication about the restoration that emphasizes it, I believe the uniqueness of the project needs to be brought out and fully understood. Another project like Williamsburg probably cannot and should not be done. It was a staggering idea from the standpoint of expense, scale, number of people involved, amount of research and so forth. It was a valuable experiment, but imitations of it have often been tried by others who did not see the uniqueness of what these restorationists were doing. I regret that there have not been more publications, so that instead of being impressed with the sheer beauty of Williamsburg, visitors could understand the amount of archaeological, documentary and photographic research that went into the project. If they could read the minutes of those meetings of the advisory committee of architects, they would see the many issues that were debated seriously and could come to understand how the decisions were made. I will say that the Rockefellers are God's gift to historians: Mr. Rockefeller insisted on having minutes of every discussion, verbatim minutes in some cases, so that readers of such documents can really see how a decision was made, a project accomplished.

This overview of the Williamsburg restoration is only the beginning of the story. More fascinating aspects lie behind the guidebook, in the history of the town prior to 1927 and in the people who actually were involved in the restoration. I believe the highest tribute for the Williamsburg restoration is a statement that I have heard Mr. Peterson make several times—that he learned a great deal of what he knows about architecture, architectural restoration and professionalism from his association with the staff of Perry, Shaw and Hepburn during those first years of the development of Colonial Williamsburg.

RESTORATIONS OF INDEPENDENCE
NATIONAL HISTORICAL PARK

ERNEST ALLEN CONNALLY

National parks in the United States include not only the scenic and scientific wonders of the land but also some of the country's important historic sites. Independence National Historical Park in Philadelphia, Pa., falls into the latter category, of course.

It has been pointed out at this conference that unique circumstances produced the restoration at Colonial Williamsburg. In many ways, Independence National Historical Park is a unique place, too. Situated in the heart of the old city, the park is an area of about four large blocks. The open, parklike character here has been recaptured, and studded among the green spaces are a number of 18th and early 19th-century historic buildings. Most of the urban fabric and patterns that once complimented the buildings are, of course, gone, so they now stand almost alone, like gems on a jeweler's cloth. A sense of spatial order is being restored slowly as surrounding trees grow, making the buildings appear not quite as isolated as they once did.

How did this kind of historic preservation, which some now frown upon because of its incomplete approach to preservation, come to be practiced in a national park in the heart of a city as large and as important as Philadelphia? To answer the question, it is necessary to understand when and how Independence National Historical Park developed.

Consider what Philadelphia was like at the beginning of World

Ernest Allen Connally is associate director for professional services, National Park Service, U.S. Department of the Interior, Washington, D.C.

War II. At that time, it was the third largest city in the United States, with a population of about 2½ million. Its density was high and its streets congested. Air pollution in the city was probably at its worst then, because coal was burned as fuel. Soot filled the air and covered practically everything in some areas. In one such area were a dozen or so historic buildings that almost miraculously had been spared from the destructive ways of progress, but they were surrounded by modern, large-scale buildings that overpowered them. These 18th and early 19th-century buildings still housed some of the businesses that had grown up in this old financial quarter, and on the nearby waterfront there were industrial buildings, docks and markets. The whole area was congested and dirty. Remember, too, that in 1939 there were no conscious federal efforts to introduce open spaces into cities and no urban renewal programs.

Public interest in preserving these important buildings had been expressed for some time by city and state residents. In 1939, the area was designated a National Historic Site in nonfederal ownership; this designation was at that time given for properties of the highest historical importance that were not owned by the federal government. The action prompted a private group of citizens to come forward with a preservation proposal, which was unveiled in 1942 and became the basis for planning of the park. The advisory commission that was formed as a result of that proposal has actively participated in the park's development since the commission was established. In 1948, the public law establishing Independence National Historical Park was approved by Congress. An agreement in 1950 between the city of Philadelphia and the U.S. Department of the Interior gave the National Park Service responsibility for administering the Independence Hall group of buildings and Independence Square, but the city retained ownership of the property.

Ever since the concept for the park was proposed, there has been a great deal of discussion about how the park could best serve that part of Philadelphia in which it is located. The initial idea was to provide a parklike setting for these important buildings and to introduce green open spaces into this dense, built-up area. The goal was not only to commemorate the significant events that happened in some of the buildings, but also to preserve those buildings that did not have historical associations but were of architectural merit. This concept principally included buildings of the colonial period and the early days of the republic. There were other, later buildings in the area that were, individually, important in the history of architecture. One might wish they had been

FIGURE 1. *View of Independence National Historical Park from Chestnut Street, showing Old City Hall in the background, Congress Hall at right and Independence Hall with its wing buildings between the two. (Jack E. Boucher, Historic American Buildings Survey)*

allowed to remain. However, they inevitably would have been divorced from their previous environment, left to stand in a starker isolation than that experienced by earlier buildings in the area. It was believed also that the park would be a place for people to escape the many streetcars and trucks on the congested Philadelphia streets. It should be recognized that there was a natural tendency on the part of the Park Service planners to think in terms of green open spaces, because the open space concept was very much in their own tradition, as this professional corps was dominated by landscape architects. At that time, however, the removal of several blocks of buildings on the waterfront was not foreseen, nor was the construction of the mall that lies north of Independence Hall.

The development of the park is only now reaching its final

FIGURE 2. *Facade of Independence Hall with its familiar, "restored" steeple. (Ralph H. Anderson, National Park Service)*

stages, just as Americans prepare to celebrate the 200th anniversary of the country's establishment. The development has taken a long time, required enormous expenditures of money and benefitted from the ideas and efforts of many talented people. To date, work on the park has included more than two decades of painstaking historical and curatorial research, archaeological investigation and architectural research and restoration. Yet philosophical questions regarding principles and practices used in the preservation of this historic area continue to be raised. It must be remembered that a whole generation has passed since the concept for the park was first proposed; ideas about preservation have changed. If the legislation that created the park were passed today, I believe the approach to the park's development would be quite different. This is inevitable, since 30 years have passed since the project was formally launched.

Today, visitors to the park view a number of buildings that are associated with some of the events that brought this nation into being. The primary attraction, of course, is the building known as Independence Hall. In its Assembly Room, the Continental Congress of 1775 met and united the colonies in common action. On July 4, 1776, in the same Assembly Room, the Continental Congress adopted the Declaration of Independence, and work on the Constitution was completed there on September 17, 1787. There is hardly a building anywhere in this country more revered as a patriotic shrine than Independence Hall.

Actually, the building, known since its construction as the "State-House," first served as the province house and later as the statehouse of Pennsylvania. Construction began in 1732, about 50 years after the establishment of the colony and the city. The area known as Independence Square comprised several orchards. Independence Hall is not monumental architecture; it is, by any standards, a simple provincial building. However, it should be remembered that at the time it was built, Philadelphia was still a young, growing town, albeit one of the most important ones in the colonies. The construction of the building was then a monumental undertaking; it took 15 years to complete the work.

Two wings were added to the statehouse and were ready for occupancy in 1736. One was used for public records and the other as accommodations for Indian delegations. The wings have been subjected to many changes. The building was finally completed in the mid-1750s with the construction of a bell tower and steeple. The steeple was, of course, there when the Declaration of Independence was signed, but it had not been maintained well. As a result, all the wooden steeple had to be removed, and only the brick part of the tower remained by the time the Constitution was adopted. The steeple that is there today is an early attempt at historical reconstruction; it was built in 1828 after initial interest in preserving the building had been aroused. The restored steeple has been so identified with Independence Hall that there was never any question about its being retained. However, it is not exactly like the one that stood there in the 18th century. When the wooden steeple came down, so did the bell, which has become imbedded in the patriotic mythology of the country as the "Liberty Bell."

Downstairs in Independence Hall are the Assembly Room and the provincial Supreme Court Room. The restoration of the latter room has just been completed. Much of the wainscotting on three of the room's four walls had survived, but some of the furnishings and fixtures are conjectures of what might have been there. For example, behind the judge's bench, there is a framed oil painting of the arms of the commonwealth of Pennsylvania. A wooden, gilded

FIGURE 3. *Assembly Room in Independence Hall before restoration. (Jack E. Boucher, Historic American Buildings Survey)*

FIGURE 4. *Park Service workmen install a panel in the Assembly Room during 1964 restoration effort. (George Eisenman, National Park Service)*

FIGURE 5. *Assembly Room after restoration (Jack E. Boucher, Historic American Buildings Survey)*

carving of the British royal arms was once there, but when independence was declared, that rich baroque carving was riped down and thrown into a bonfire. Instead of trying to reproduce the carving, about which little is known, an original 1785 painting of the state arms was acquired for the room. It had been painted on commission for the state by George Rutter, who repeatedly sent bills to the government but never was paid. Finally, his heirs repossessed the painting, and it was in their possession when the Park Service discovered it. Upstairs in the building are the Governor's Council Chamber, the Assembly's Committee Room and the Long Gallery, which was used for banquets and other public functions.

The initial concept of the early builders of the statehouse was to have a civic center on the square. It was to include three government buildings: the statehouse in the center, country courthouse on one side and city hall on the other. The latter two buildings were built in the 1780s and 1790s. The two buildings were first modified after the adoption of the Constitution when the federal government moved to Philadelphia, pending the design and construction of the new federal city of Washington. When the federal government arrived, the United States Congress was allowed to adapt the county courthouse for its use. The Hall of Representatives was downstairs; upstairs was the Senate chamber.

FIGURE 6. *South wall of the Supreme Court Room before restoration. Paint on the walls was removed so that original panels could be studied. (Jack E. Boucher, Historic American Buildings Survey)*

The building is now called Congress Hall. The city hall was adapted for use by the United States Supreme Court.

After 1800, when the federal government moved to Washington, Congress Hall was subjected to numerous changes, but the restoration of the building is now finished. The furnishings are complete: In fact, a number of original pieces that were in the building have been returned. Some served as models for the reproduction of others to complete the setting. The main problem in the restoration of Old City Hall was a bit different. There was little satisfactory descriptive historical evidence on what the building was like when it was used by the Supreme Court. Like Congress Hall, it also underwent a number of changes, and about the time of World War I, it was subjected to a "restoration." That restoration remains intact today, primarily because the Park Service does not know exactly how the building was modified for the Supreme Court's

FIGURE 7. *Carpenters at work during the recently completed restoration of the* Supreme Court Room *(George Eisenman, National Park Service).*

FIGURE 8. *Supreme Court Room after restoration. (Jack E. Boucher,* Historic American Buildings Survey*)*

use nor how it was furnished.

After 1800, the state government also left Philadelphia, and the statehouse stood empty for a while but remained in state ownership. There were threats that the property would be sold and developed as building lots. Finally, in 1815 the city of Philadelphia bought the statehouse.

The first impetus for preservation of the buildings came when the Marquis de Lafayette made his return visit to the United States in 1824. A great temporary triumphal arch was set up on the square, and Lafayette was received in the "Hall of Independence," as the statehouse's Assembly Room was called on that occasion. Thus began the use of the name "Independence Hall," which later was applied to the whole building. This revived interest in the building led to the reconstruction of the steeple in 1828 and the "restoration" of the Assembly Room in 1831. The building was used for various public and private purposes. There was an attempt at further restoration for the centennial of 1876 and another at the end of the 19th century. For the Park Service to restore the building to its original character of the Georgian period required exhaustive detailed studies.

There are other buildings in the park that are not owned by the city or the federal government. Philosophical Hall, which stands just behind Old City Hall, was built in the 1780s. It is the headquarters of the American Philosophical Society, the country's premier learned society, founded by Benjamin Franklin and others in 1743. Directly across the street from it is a reconstructed building that now serves as the society's library. The front portion of the building is a reconstruction of Library Hall, a public library that was built on the site in 1789-90. Farther east is Carpenters' Hall, which remains in the private ownership of the Carpenters' Company of Phildelphia, but through a cooperative agreement is included in the park. It is a small Georgian building of quite handsome proportions with a small cupola, dating from the 1770s. It served as the guild hall of the Carpenters' Company, which was established in 1724, and is important historically because the Continental Congress of 1774 met there. There are two reconstructed buildings in front of Carpenters' Hall, New Hall and the Pemberton House. New Hall is a replica of a building that was used as headquarters of the War Department when the federal government was in Philadelphia. Pemberton House is a reconstruction of a house that was located on the other side of the alley leading to it. These buildings now serve as museums of the armed services. The reconstructions form something of a stage set, and

FIGURE 9. *First Bank of the United States, which will be restored for use as a center where the executive branch of government, as constituted during the Washington and Adams administrations, will be interpreted. (Jack E. Boucher, Historic American Buildings Survey)*

I believe the decision to reconstruct those buildings would be considered a bit more carefully today.

There are also two former bank buildings in the park, the First Bank of the United States and Second Bank of the United States. The First Bank was built between 1795 and 1797. It has a marble front and portico, which have badly deteriorated because of air pollution. In 1812, a private bank purchased the building and subsequently modified the interior, later inserting a rotunda and making several other changes. The Park Service's policy is to leave the additions. The bank building will be used to interpret the executive branch of government during the Washington and Adams administrations.

Restoration work is still in progress on the Second Bank of the United States, which was this country's first great marble temple in the Greek Revival style. Designed by William Strickland, it was the finest public building in the United States when it was built (1819-24). The building became a customs house after the bank lost its charter in the 1830s, but later, a larger customs house

FIGURE 10. *Second Bank of the United States, now under restoration. When the work is completed, portraits of historical figures associated with the Revolution and the establishment of the republic will be hung in the building. (Jack E. Boucher, Historic American Buildings Survey)*

was built down the street. The bank building was then used for a variety of purposes. Why did the Park Service decide to include it in the park? What should its use be? Actually, the building was saved because it is a significant work of architecture. The Park Service's general approach to buildings of this kind is to use them for an appropriate adaptive purpose. In Independence National Historical Park, the Second Bank building will be a portrait gallery of historical persons who figured in the Revolution and the establishment of the republic. About 180 portraits will be hung there; the collection includes works by James Peale, Charles Willson

Peale, Rembrandt Peale and other artists.

The Philadelphia Exchange, which housed the Philadelphia Stock Exchange for many years, is another one of Strickland's marble temples. Located on Walnut Street, it has been adapted for use as headquarters of the Northeast Region of the Park Service. Several rowhouses on Walnut Street have also been preserved. One of the most complete and best architectural specimens there is the Bishop White House, built in 1786-87. It was the home of Bishop William White, rector of Christ Church and an organizer and one of the first bishops of the Protestant Episcopal Church in this country. At the end of the block is the Todd House (1775), which is open to the public as a museum. The buildings between the Todd House and the Bishop White House are of less historic interest. Their exteriors have been restored and their interiors adapted for modern purposes.

Another important area of the park is Franklin Court. In front of the court, on Market Street, are several houses, some of which were rental properties owned by Benjamin Franklin and one of which served as his printing shop. Behind the houses through a passageway was Franklin's own house, which stood in a secluded courtyard. After Franklin's death in 1790, the house was used for various purposes; it was destroyed early in the 19th century. It was a great temptation to reconstruct Franklin's house. He is the only important figure in the formation of this nation for whom no house associated with him survives. However, current Park Service policies permit reconstruction only under rather stringent conditions: Reconstructions are permitted where a historic scene would be incomplete unless the reconstruction were allowed. Also, the reconstruction must be built on the original site, and there must be sufficient historical, archaeological and architectural data to insure that the reconstruction is, in fact, a reproduction of what stood there. That assurance simply could not be given in the case of the Franklin house. The ruins there will be interpreted, however, and in new construction on that site, guides and exhibits will explain Franklin's role in the events that led to the establishment of the republic. The exteriors of the other houses on Franklin Court will be restored and their interiors adapted for other uses.

There are a number of other interesting buildings that are not actually part of the park. Several churches are nearby—St. Joseph's Roman Catholic Church, Arch Street Meeting House, St. George's Methodist Church and Christ Church, which is only about three blocks from the park. Christ Church was closely associated with figures of the Revolutionary period. The Park Service has made an agreement with the governing body of the church that no actions affecting the integrity of the church's fabric will be carried out without prior consultation.

I hope this sketch of the park's development and the buildings that compose it helps convey the message of Independence National Historical Park.

ICOMOS: ITS ROLE IN INTERNATIONAL PRESERVATION ORGANIZATIONS

RAYMOND M. LEMAIRE

I have been asked to speak about the International Council of Monuments and Sites (ICOMOS), an international body which, although still relatively new, already has a number of achievements to its credit in the field of historic preservation. ICOMOS was founded in Warsaw, Poland, in June 1965. Its sponsors—the United Nations Educational, Scientific and Cultural Organization (UNESCO), International Centre for the Study of the Preservation and the Restoration of Cultural Property (Rome Centre) and International Council of Museums (ICOM)—have greatly assisted in the development of ICOMOS and now look upon the council as a mature, functioning organization with fully developed goals and programs. The statutes of ICOMOS and the council's aims and activities are similar to those of ICOM, which, by sharing its considerable experience with ICOMOS, has helped ICOMOS grow rapidly into a leader in the international preservation field.

Let us consider more closely what ICOMOS is and examine its statutes, aims, membership, past and current activities and program for the future.

The council's aims are clearly stated in its statutes. ICOMOS, they say, shall be "the international organization to link public authorities, departments, institutions and individuals interested in the preservation and study of monuments and sites." It has two aims: "to promote the study and preservation of monuments and sites"

Raymond M. Lemaire is secretary general of the International Council of Monuments and Sites, Paris, France.

and "to arouse and cultivate the interest of the authorities, and people of every country in their monuments and sites and in their cultural heritage." The statutes also define the major activities that ICOMOS may undertake to reach these objectives. Those activities are:

1. Encourage the preparation and adoption of international recommendations applicable to the study, preservation and restoration of monuments, sites and works of art.
2. Cooperate at national and international levels in the creation and development of documentation centers.
3. Cooperate at national and international levels in the preparation of inventories, directories, topographical maps, photographic and photogrammetric archives, etc., relating to monuments and sites.
4. Study and disseminate information on all techniques, including the most up-to-date ones, for the preservation, restoration and enhancement of monuments and sites.
5. Establish within the framework of the activities previously mentioned permanent working parties, study commissions and special committees of experts.
6. Cooperate with existing commissions and committees that are concerned with the preservation of monuments and sites, as well as with those that might be created in the future.
7. Produce and sponsor specialized publications on the aforementioned subjects.
8. Establish and maintain close cooperation with UNESCO, the Rome Centre, ICOM and other international or regional organizations pursuing common goals.

Thus, broad international cooperation constitutes one of the foundations of the ICOMOS program of activities. At the same time, ICOMOS activities are designed to benefit those countries that need them most, and one of the council's major concerns is to give assistance to developing countries in the protection of their architectural heritage.

Who is responsible for achieving these aims and for carrying out such activities? In other words, who is entitled to become a member of the council? Like many organizations, ICOMOS has two main categories of membership, active and associate. This certainly does not mean that active members do all the work, while the others do nothing! The distinction is less simple than that. In fact, any person competent in a scientific field related to the protection of the architectural heritage or any qualified person who shows an interest in the council's aims may apply for membership. However, the status of active member may be granted only to individuals who are actually engaged in the conservation of monuments and sites. This includes specialists in private practice and those on the staffs of national organizations responsible for the preservation and protection of monuments, sites, fine arts or antiquities.

Members of ICOMOS are formed into national committees, which are limited to a maximum of 15 active members. All other members are associates. At present, 46 countries are represented on the council. Only active members have the right to vote at the ICOMOS general assembly. The restriction in the size of national committees exists in order to insure equal representation of all countries at the general assembly. In fact, many national committees provide for one-third of their active membership to be replaced every third year. In this way, all members have an opportunity to participate in the organization's international activities and in activities of their national committees.

Although my purpose is not to discuss in detail the organizational structure of ICOMOS, I should outline the major features. The structure is quite similar to that adopted by other international organizations. The ICOMOS general assembly, which is convened every three years, is the organization's governing body. The assembly is held in a different country each time at the invitation of the national committee of that country. What is the task of the general assembly? First of all, it elects officials: president, vice presidents, secretary general, treasurer and members of the executive committee, which constitutes the governing board of the council. The daily conduct of the organization is assumed by the president, treasurer and secretary general. (At present, Piero Gazzola of Italy is president and Maurice Berry of France is treasurer; I serve as secretary general.) At first glance, the organization may seem to have a rather cumbersome structure since there are many committees and, therefore, a lot of meetings. In fact, this system works quite well because of the devotion, breadth of mind and constant cooperation of all members.

But what about the council's activities? What has ICOMOS achieved over a seven-year period? First, ICOMOS has cooperated in numerous ways with international organizations and national committees dealing with the protection of the architectural heritage. The ICOMOS staff works on an almost daily basis with UNESCO, taking an active part in the elaboration of international safeguard instruments, such as the criteria for the legal protection of cultural heritage, recommendations concerning the preservation of cultural property endangered by public or private actions and the international regulation for the protection inter alia of monuments, groups of buildings and sites, which is to be submitted to the UNESCO general assembly in a few weeks. General or specific reports dealing with the protection of monuments are submitted regularly to UNESCO, and advice is offered when experts must be recommended or selected for specific projects. The same friendly understanding and cooperation exists between ICOMOS and the Rome Centre, ICOM, the Council of Europe, the Organization of American States and any government and nongovernment organizations that may find the scientific knowledge or experience of ICOMOS members to be useful.

The most important activity of ICOMOS has been the promotion and coordination of studies necessary for the protection of monuments and sites. For this purpose, panels of experts have been created and technical symposia organized. To insure continuity in this work and to make sure that concrete, usable results are obtained, a number of well-defined fields of study have been chosen. Starting with the most immediate problems, ICOMOS has devoted several symposia to the preservation of old towns and cities, which has become a matter of the greatest urgency. General aspects of the preservation of old cities were discussed in 1966 in Cáceres, Spain. In 1967, specific problems of Muslim towns in North Africa were discussed at Tunis, Tunisia. Problems posed by traffic in historic cities were reviewed at the ICOMOS symposium held in Graz, Austria, in 1969. In 1973, there will be a symposium to study the problem of the "streetscrape" in Lausanne, Switzerland, and another meeting, to focus on the problems encountered in the preservation of wooden structures and objects, is planned to be held in Sweden. Another field of study is the preservation of building materials. ICOMOS has attacked this problem by organizing, in collaboration with the Rome Centre, symposia devoted to the weathering of stone. Such symposia are held every year, usually in Brussels. Another problem about which ICOMOS is concerned is the question of moisture in old buildings. A meeting on this matter took place in Rome in 1967. The preservation of historic gardens was dealt with for the first time in Fontainebleau, France, in 1971, and it will be studied further next year in Granada, Spain, and in 1975 in Czechoslovakia. I do not want to lengthen this presentation, but I should mention that many other questions—the general philosophy of preservation, the use of photogrammetry in the preservation of monuments, the preservation of unburnt brick structure and so forth—have been studied in ICOMOS meetings and that work on these will continue.

Publications are yet another of the council's activities. ICOMOS uses three channels to inform the public about its activities and philosophy. The first is a series of specialized volumes containing reports or minutes of symposia sponsored by ICOMOS. The second is the magazine *Monumentum;* many of you know of it already. It is an international journal devoted to the expression of new ideas, techniques and recent achievements in the protection of the architectural heritage. The third channel of communication to the public is the *ICOMOS Bulletin,* which is distributed free of charge to members. Generally, each issue reviews the specific problems of one country in the preservation of its various monuments. A newsletter also allows the secretariat to inform all members about global activities of the council.

Needless to say, all these activities cost money. Who pays for them? Let me say first that ICOMOS is not rich and, like a majority of international organizations, is seriously handicapped by this lack of funds. Nevertheless, I can tell you that the council has succeeded in accomplishing all its activities without going into debt. There are two direct funding sources. First, there are members' dues, but since ICOMOS has relatively small membership, the total amount from this source is not large. The council is, however, making a great effort to recruit new members. The council also receives an annual grant from UNESCO, which, at present, amounts to $12,500 a year. The remaining funds necessary to sponsor ICOMOS activities come from various national committees, who are asked to help finance international activities that take place in their own countries. Let me give some examples of the support given by countries. André Malraux of France, when minister of culture, invited the council to settle in Paris, promising ICOMOS suitable premises and an annual grant for the operation of the secretariat. These promises have been kept: The French government restored a part of a historic hotel in the famous Marais district of Paris to serve as ICOMOS headquarters, an investment equivalent to approximately $300,000, and the French provide an annual grant equivalent to $17,000 to finance the secretariat. As a second example, the publication of *Monumentum* is paid for by the Belgian government, which spends for this purpose approximately $10,000 a year. All ICOMOS symposia and general assemblies are financed by the host countries, and anyone who attended the last general assembly in Budapest and enjoyed the outstanding hospitality of the Hungarian people will know the scale of financial effort involved.

All this belongs to the past, to yesterday, but the council is interested in the present and, above all, the future. What important projects does it hope to realize in the years to come? My purpose is not to enumerate all the projects adopted by the last general assembly in Budapest. Let me stress only the most important element of the ICOMOS program. The council will continue, of course, to organize symposia, publish symposia proceedings, etc. It will also continue to cooperate with national and international organizations. The council's major project is however, to a large extent, due to the initiative and devotion of the United States National Committee. I refer to the creation of an international documentation center for the protection of the architectural heritage. The idea of setting up such a center was first expressed during a symposium on documentation that took place in Brussels in 1966. Stephen W. Jacobs, professor of architecture at Cornell University, Ithaca, N.Y., represented the United States National Committee at this symposium. The committee generously offered to finance a feasibility study on the center, and I wish to express the deepest gratitude of ICOMOS to the members of that committee for taking an initiative that will have a considerable impact on the future of ICOMOS. Milton E. Lord, former librarian and director emeritus of the Boston Public Library, kindly agreed to oversee the study. The proposal submitted to the council was extremely ambitious but seemed so excellent that it was adopted by the ICOMOS executive committee in December 1971. Moreover, René Maheu, director general of UNESCO, has since approved the project and informed all member states of the creation of this new channel of information and international cooperation.

It would take too long to describe in detail the structure and function of the center. I should mention, however, that the center is not to be for on-the-spot consultation, but will essentially collect and disseminate information. Its main objective is to place the experience of certain people at the disposal of others without delay and, more particularly, to make that of highly developed countries readily available to less developed ones.

The center will be expanded progressively, according to the council's financial means, since a great deal of money will be needed for this project. The daily operation of the center will require $50,000 the first year, $80,000 the second year and $100,000 a year for following years. Necessary technical equipment will cost approximately $150,000 in addition to some $45,000 already spent by UNESCO. Although the economic situation is bleak, the council, nevertheless, hopes to raise the necessary funds with the help of all those who are convinced that the protection of masterpieces of the past is essential to the development of tomorrow's culture.

I hope I have presented ICOMOS as it really is, stating the facts without sentimentality or exaggerated enthusiasm, so that you can judge with objectivity what ICOMOS stands for and decide if it is worthy of your support.

LIST OF CONTRIBUTORS

Titles listed for conference participants are those that were in effect at the time the conference was held. Any subsequent change in title is not reflected in this publication.

JAMES K. BARR
Director of Research
Pfizer, Inc.
640 North 13th Street
Easton, Pa. 18042

PENELOPE HARTSHORNE BATCHELER
Restoration Architect, National Park Service
Independence National Historical Park
313 Walnut Street
Philadelphia, Pa. 19106

RICHARD D. BUCK
Director, Intermuseum Laboratory, Intermuseum Conservation Association
Allen Art Building
Oberlin, Ohio 44074

ORIN M. BULLOCK, JR., FAIA
Restoration Architect
1432 John Street
Baltimore, Md. 21217

RICHARD M. CANDEE
Researcher in Architecture
Old Sturbridge Village
Sturbridge, Mass. 01566

ERNEST ALLEN CONNALLY
Associate Director, Professional Services, National Park Service
U.S. Department of the Interior
Washington, D.C. 20240

ABBOTT L. CUMMINGS
Director, Society for the Preservation of New England Antiquities
141 Cambridge Street
Boston, Mass. 02114

ROBERT L. FELLER
Senior Fellow, National Gallery of Art Research Project
Carnegie-Mellon University
Mellon Institute Building
4400 Fifth Avenue
Pittsburgh, Pa. 15213

JAMES MARSTON FITCH
Professor of Architecture and *Director*
Restoration and Preservation of Historic Architecture Graduate Program
Columbia University
New York, N.Y. 10027

ALBERT FRANCE-LANORD
Director, Centre de Recherches de L'Histoire de la Siderugie
Route de Fleville
Jarville, Meurthe et Moselle, France 54, 140

W. EUGENE GEORGE, JR., AIA
Resident Architect, Colonial Williamsburg
Williamsburg, Va. 23185

HARMON H. GOLDSTONE, FAIA
Chairman, New York City Landmarks Preservation Commission
305 Broadway
New York, N.Y. 10007

CHARLES B. HOSMER, JR.
Associate Professor of History
Principia College
Elsah, Ill. 62028

DONALD W. INSALL, FRIBA
Restoration Architect and Planner
Donald W. Insall & Associates
19 West Eaton Place, Eaton Square
London S.W. 1, England

STEPHEN W. JACOBS, AIA
Professor of Architecture, College of Architecture, Art and Planning
Cornell University
Ithaca, N.Y. 14850

CAROLINE K. KECK
Professor, Conservation of Historic and Artistic Works Program
Cooperstown Graduate Programs
Cooperstown, N.Y. 13326

SHELDON KECK
Professor, Conservation of Historic and Artistic Works Program
Cooperstown Graduate Programs
Cooperstown, N.Y. 13326

RUSSELL V. KEUNE, AIA
Vice President for Preservation Services
National Trust for Historic
Preservation
740–748 Jackson Place, N.W.
Washington, D.C. 20006

RAYMOND M. LEMAIRE
Secretary General, International
Council of Monuments and Sites
Hôtel Saint Aignan
75, rue du Temple
75003 Paris, France

SEYMOUR Z. LEWIN
Professor of Chemistry
New York University
4 Washington Place, Room 514
New York, N.Y. 10003

LAWRENCE J. MAJEWSKI
Chairman, Conservation Center of the
Institute of Fine Arts
New York University
1 East 78th Street
New York, N.Y. 10021

GEORGE MC CUE
Editor, Music and Arts Page
St. Louis Post-Dispatch
910 North 12th Boulevard
St. Louis, Mo. 63101

HARLEY J. MC KEE, FAIA
Professor Emeritus of Architecture
Syracuse University
701 Crawford Avenue
Syracuse, N.Y. 13224

PETER E. MICHAELS
President, Twelve Oaks Regional Fine
Arts Conservation Center, Inc.
1922 South Road
Baltimore, Md. 21209

JOHN D. MILNER, AIA
President, National Heritage Corporation
309 North Matlock Street
West Chester, Pa. 19380

BRUNO MUHLETHALER
Chief, Research Laboratory
Landesmuseum
Fabrikstrasse 46
8005 Zurich, Switzerland

WILLIAM J. MURTAGH
Keeper, National Register of Historic
Places
National Park Service,
U.S. Department of the Interior
18th and C Streets, N.W.
Washington, D.C. 20240

LEE H. NELSON
Restoration Architect, National Park
Service
Independence National Historical Park
313 Walnut Street
Philadelphia, Pa. 19106

ROBERT M. ORGAN
Chief, Conservation–Analytical
Laboratory
Smithsonian Institution
Washington, D.C. 20560

CHARLES E. PETERSON, FAIA
*Architectural Historian, Restorationist
and Planner*
332 Spruce Street
Society Hill
Philadelphia, Pa. 19106

PAUL PHILIPPOT
Director, International Centre for the
Study of the Preservation and the
Restoration of Cultural Property
Via di San Michele, 13
00153 Rome, Italy

MORGAN W. PHILLIPS
Supervisor of Properties, Society for the
Preservation of New England
Antiquities
141 Cambridge Street
Boston, Mass. 02114

HAROLD J. PLENDERLEITH
Director Emeritus, International
Centre for the Study of the
Preservation and the Restoration of
Cultural Property
Via di San Michele, 13
00153 Rome, Italy

F. BLAIR REEVES, AIA
Professor of Architecture
University of Florida
Gainesville, Fla. 32601

JOHN I. REMPEL, MRAIC
Restoration Architect
140 Bessboro Drive
Toronto, Ontario, Canada M4G 3J6

EDWARD V. SAYRE
Senior Chemist, Brookhaven National
Laboratory, and *Adjunct Professor of
Fine Arts*
Conservation Center of the Institute of
Fine Arts
New York University
1 East 78th Street
New York, N.Y. 10021

CYRIL STANLEY SMITH
Institute Professor, Emeritus
Massachusetts Institute of Technology
Cambridge, Mass. 02139

STANLEY SOUTH
Archaeologist, Division of Advanced
Studies and Research, Institute of
Archeology and Anthropology
University of South Carolina
Columbia, S.C. 29208

ROBERT E. STIPE
Professor of Public Law and
Government and *Assistant Director*
Institute of Government
P.O. Box 990
University of North Carolina
Chapel Hill, N.C. 27514

PETER JOHN STOKES, MRAIC
Consulting Restoration Architect
P.O. Box 170
244 King Street
Niagara-on-the-Lake, Ontario, Canada
L0S 1J0

HAROLD TARKOW
Assistant Director, Chemical
Utilization and Protection Research
U.S. Forest Products Laboratory
Forest Service,
U.S. Department of Agriculture
P.O. Box 5130
Madison, Wis. 53705

GIORGIO TORRACA
Deputy Director, International Centre
for the Study of the Preservation and
the Restoration of Cultural Property
Via di San Michele, 13
00153 Rome, Italy

JOHN G. WAITE
Senior Historical Architect, Division
for Historic Preservation
New York State Office of Parks and
Recreation
South Swan Street Bldg., South Mall
Albany, N.Y. 12223

GEORGE L. WRENN III
Associate Director, Society for the
Preservation of New England
Antiquities
141 Cambridge Street
Boston, Mass. 02114